D0621193

Joseph Goebbels

Also by Toby Thacker:

THE END OF THE THIRD REICH: DEFEAT, DENAZIFICATION, AND NUREMBERG, JANUARY 1944–NOVEMBER 1946

MUSIC AFTER HITLER, 1945–1955

Joseph Goebbels

Life and Death

Toby Thacker
Lecturer in Modern European History, Cardiff University

© Toby Thacker 2009

All rights reserved. No reproduction, copy or transmission of this
publication may be made without written permission.

No portion of this publication may be reproduced, copied or transmitted
save with written permission or in accordance with the provisions of the
Copyright, Designs and Patents Act 1988, or under the terms of any licence
permitting limited copying issued by the Copyright Licensing Agency,
Saffron House, 6–10 Kirby Street, London EC1N 8TS.

Any person who does any unauthorized act in relation to this publication
may be liable to criminal prosecution and civil claims for damages.

The author has asserted his right to be identified as the author of this
work in accordance with the Copyright, Designs and Patents Act 1988.

First published 2009 by
PALGRAVE MACMILLAN

Palgrave Macmillan in the UK is an imprint of Macmillan Publishers Limited,
registered in England, company number 785998, of Houndmills, Basingstoke,
Hampshire RG21 6XS.

Palgrave Macmillan in the US is a division of St Martin's Press LLC,
175 Fifth Avenue, New York, NY 10010.

Palgrave Macmillan is the global academic imprint of the above companies
and has companies and representatives throughout the world.

Palgrave® and Macmillan® are registered trademarks in the United States,
the United Kingdom, Europe and other countries.

ISBN-13:   978–0–230–22889–4   hardback

This book is printed on paper suitable for recycling and made from fully
managed and sustained forest sources. Logging, pulping and manufacturing
processes are expected to conform to the environmental regulations of the
country of origin.

A catalogue record for this book is available from the British Library.

A catalog record for this book is available from the Library of Congress.

10   9   8   7   6   5   4   3   2   1
18   17   16   15   14   13   12   11   10   09

Printed and bound in Great Britain by
CPI Antony Rowe, Chippenham and Eastbourne

You fear the dismemberment of your being in all the piecework of human wishing and knowing, and fail to notice that you yourselves cannot achieve wholeness if you reject such large and essential parts of that which 'has been allotted to all mankind'. You seek the indivisibility of man's being, and yet assent to its being torn apart ...

The philosopher Paul Natorp, in a warning to German youth in 1920*

* Paul Natorp, 'Hoffnungen und Gefahren unserer Jugendbewegung', Werner Kindt (ed.), *Grundschriften der Deutschen Jugendbewegung* (Düsseldorf and Cologne: Eugen Diederich, 1963), pp. 129–47, pp. 144–5.

Contents

List of Illustrations

Unless otherwise acknowledged, the illustrations here are taken from Nazi Party publications, or are my own photographs. I am grateful to Heidelberg University Library for permission to use the images from the *Völkischer Beobachter* and from *Das Reich* (illustrations 5, 7, 38, and 46). Thanks to Howard Mason for drawing the maps in illustrations 4 and 35, and to Ian Dennis for drawing the maps in illustrations 3, 9, and 45.

Acknowledgements

Many people and institutions have been involved in the preparation of this book. I am particularly grateful to the staff at the Bundesarchiv Koblenz, and at the Bundesarchiv, Außenstelle Berlin, for their help in finding a way through the complexities of their cataloguing systems, and with the practical difficulties of using and copying documents on microfilm and microfiche. Similarly, I would like to take this opportunity to thank the staff at the Zeitungsabteilung of the Staatsbibliothek zu Berlin, who enabled me to see copies of *Der Angriff* from 1927 through to 1934, and of Heidelberg University Library who helped me to see copies of the *Völkischer Beobachter* and *Das Reich*, and kindly gave permission to reproduce images from both newspapers for this book. In Britain I am grateful to the staff of Cardiff University Library, of the Bodleian Library and the Taylorian Institute in Oxford, and of Gloucester City Library.

I would like also to record my thanks to Frau Cordula Schacht for her permission to cite from the unpublished papers in the Nachlass Joseph Goebbels in the Bundesarchiv Koblenz, and to the Bildarchiv Preussischer Kulturbesitz for permission to use the photograph reproduced on the front cover of this book. Historians generally owe a debt of gratitude to often unsung colleagues who transcribe and edit published collections of documents, and I wish to acknowledge here my reliance on the sustained scholarship of Elke Fröhlich and her team who have produced the complete edition of Goebbels' diary from 1923 to 1945, and to the earlier work of Helmut Heiber, who transcribed many of Goebbels' speeches from 1932 to 1945 from sound recordings to make them more widely accessible to historians.

Many individuals have helped me with advice, constructive comments, and in general conversation about Goebbels and his place in history. I am grateful to current and former colleagues at Cardiff University, including Jessica Horsley, Neil Fleming, Gerwin Strobl, and Gregor Benton; special thanks to Jonathan Osmond and Kevin Passmore who both took time to read and comment upon earlier drafts; to Howard Mason and Ian Dennis who drew the maps, and to John Morgan who helped with the preparation of the illustrations. As with my previous books I owe a special debt to my friend and colleague Dirk Deissler of Heidelberg University for his generous help in tracking down obscure publications in Germany, and to him and his wife Chrystelle for their hospitality on research visits there. This is the place to record my thanks to Simon Curle, Lee Russell, and James Reeley, who accompanied me on research visits to Poland, and to John Forster, Clinton Wood, and Roger Headland for their support throughout the writing of this book. I wish also to thank my fellow singers Paul Foster, Jen Madden,

David Thompson, and Anna Simon for their help with issues of translation, and insights into Goebbels' personal relationships. Others like my brother Bevis and my long-standing friend Chris Mitchell have contributed their thoughts and ideas, and I thank them. I am particularly grateful to the anonymous reader for Palgrave who responded with wise and constructive comments to an earlier draft of this book. I hope that reader will feel that I have gone some way to meeting the perceptive criticisms made at that stage. Thanks also to my editors Michael Strang and Ruth Ireland at Palgrave, and the team there which has been so helpful in the production of this book.

Finally I wish to record again my thanks to Susan, Amy, and Phoebe, who have had to live with me while I have been working on this book. They make everything possible.

Toby Thacker, 2009

A Note on Translation

Unless otherwise stated, all translations in this book from German and from French are my own. German does not translate exactly into English, and I have sought, particularly when translating from Goebbels' writings and speeches, to render as closely as possible the sense of his words rather than to try to produce some kind of idiomatic or contemporary English equivalent. In addition to words like *Reich*, *Reichstag*, and *Wehrmacht* which are now widely understood in English, there are a number of key terms in the vocabulary of German right-wing ideology of the 1920s and in Nazi discourse, such as *Volk* and *Führer*, which I have retained in the German original after providing an explanation of them. Similarly, I have kept the original titles of German newspapers for which there is no straightforward or meaningful English equivalent, after providing an initial translation.

Introduction

Do we need a new biography of the most notorious demagogue of the twentieth century? Joseph Goebbels was a man who lived most of his adult life in the full glare of publicity, much of it self-created. When, in 1926, he arrived to take charge of the Nazi Party in Berlin, he quickly became a controversial public figure, delighting in the title of 'super bandit' which was bestowed on him by his opponents. From 1932 until shortly before his death in 1945 Goebbels was seen regularly by German cinema audiences in newsreel film, and his speeches were heard by millions of radio listeners. After the Nazi accession to power in 1933 Goebbels and his growing family were frequently photographed for the German press. Internationally Goebbels was indissolubly linked with the mass hysteria of Nazi rallies, and with the persecution of the Jews. Well before the collapse of the 'Third Reich' in 1945, Goebbels' name and public image had become synonymous with the most paradoxical aspects of Nazism, its doctrine of racial superiority, its unconcealed aggression towards the outside world, and its huge popularity inside Germany. The uniquely shocking circumstances of Goebbels' death, and the decision he took with his wife Magda to kill themselves and all six of their children in Hitler's bunker as the Soviet forces closed in around them, have served only to heighten the repugnance he evokes.

The first biographical study of Goebbels was published in 1933 by a subordinate in his own Propaganda Ministry; others who worked under him between 1933 and 1945 have since produced other accounts of varying quality and reliability.[1] The émigré journalist Curt Riess wrote the first post-war biography of Goebbels in 1948, and he was followed in 1960 by Roger Manvell and Heinrich Fraenkel, who similarly drew extensively on the oral testimony of people who had known Goebbels.[2] The German historian Helmut Heiber, who later performed such valuable work in transcribing and publishing Goebbels' speeches, published a more scholarly biography of Goebbels in 1962.[3] Viktor Reimann's 1971 biography also used many of Goebbels' published works between 1925 and 1945 to explore his ideas in greater detail.[4] In the meantime ideas about Goebbels and images of him have become commonplace. There is hardly a book or documentary film about Hitler and the 'Third Reich' in which Goebbels does not make a cameo appearance. His distinctive appearance, and clichés related both to his diminutive stature and to his physical disability, are universally known. He is one of those historical figures whom even reputable historians quote without providing a reference, as though statements or actions attributed to him are self-evidently accurate.[5]

Our knowledge of Goebbels has been substantially altered though by the rediscovery and publication of the diary he kept between 1923 and 1945. Fragments of these were published in English translation as early as 1948, and other small sections appeared at intervals after this.[6] It was not until the 1980s that much larger sections from the original handwritten and dictated diary entries were made accessible to scholars, and published.[7] A huge project, to transcribe, edit, and publish as much as possible of Goebbels' diary, was started then by the Institute for Contemporary History in Munich and the Federal German Archive; it was given extra impetus in the early 1990s by the release of microfilmed sections of the diary from the Russian State Archive in Moscow, and was completed only in 2006. A scholarly edition of 29 volumes, covering the period from October 1923 to April 1945, is now available.[8] Much new material has thus come to light only very recently, and it is clear that the image of Goebbels which has been disseminated since the 1930s, and is now deeply embedded in wider public consciousness, is in many respects seriously flawed. Numerous books and articles about Goebbels have been published at the same time as more and more of his diary has become available – notably the biography by Ralf Georg Reuth – but inevitably they have failed to keep pace with the new material.[9]

This extraordinary personal record does not stand in isolation. Goebbels was a prolific writer and journalist, and from 1925 onwards he published a stream of pamphlets, books, and articles.[10] Dozens of his speeches were transcribed and published before 1945, and others have been published since then.[11] We can now compare, literally day by day, what he was saying and writing in public, with the amazingly frank record of his personal and inner life.

When he started to write his diary, in October 1923, Goebbels was an unemployed ex-student, and lived almost as a recluse in his parents' house. He had unfulfilled literary and theatrical ambitions, and imagined himself as a cultural critic.[12] He had no interest or involvement in party politics, nor could he imagine any of the public roles he would assume in the future. His diary was first and foremost a record of his inner emotions, his relationship with his girlfriend Else Janke, and his relationship with the arts. This included his love of and involvement with music, something overlooked by all previous writers on Goebbels. Casting himself as the melodramatic personification of a larger cultural and spiritual crisis, Goebbels as a young diarist reflected upon his inner self in a way which, as a recent historian has noted, is typically only brought about by the sustained intervention of a therapist.[13] In later years, as Goebbels moved into public prominence, he used his diary also as a documentary record of larger events. The hugely successful publication of an edited section of his diary in 1934, and of an earlier account of the 'struggle for Berlin' which drew heavily on his diary,[14] encouraged Goebbels to develop this side of his writing further, and, particularly in the war years, he spent hours every day dictating what he thought were events and details of historical note. With his close access to Hitler, and to the apparatus of the German state and the Nazi Party, as well as to international news media, he was uniquely well-informed. He never lost the habit of recording his emotions alongside public and political developments. Wherever he went, on business or pleasure – and Goebbels was an exceptionally active individual – he still found time to keep his diary. In over twenty years, the longest gap in his diary is of twelve days around Christmas 1938, when he was physically ill and at a psychological low point.

How far should we trust the diary of one of the great liars of history? Even as a young man, in his autobiographical fiction and in the written 'memories' of his youth, Goebbels made conscious efforts to mythologize his own life. In 1936 he concluded a lucrative deal with the Nazi Party publishing house Franz Eher for future publication of his diary, and this project was undoubtedly in his mind in the years after this. As Propaganda Minister of the 'Third Reich' after March 1933 Goebbels often displayed a brazen contempt for the truth which appalled contemporary observers and became the subject of jokes amongst the German public. His distortions and misrepresentations became one of the distinguishing features of Hitler's Germany.

Ironically, Goebbels' diary is remarkably trustworthy. We should bear in mind that the only section published in his lifetime was carefully edited, and that he intended to do the same with future publications which in fact never materialized. Goebbels actually took great care to record accurately places he went to, with times, and details of who was present. When cross-referenced with published and unpublished archival material, with newspapers and magazines from inside and outside Germany (both supportive of and hostile to the Nazis), with the mass of surviving photographs and films, and with the testimony of other witnesses, the accuracy of his diary as a factual record is invariably confirmed. It can indeed be used to highlight inaccuracies and vagueness in many other contemporary accounts, or in memoirs which were compiled years after the event. The diary contains many subjective expressions of Goebbels' judgement on matters large and small, and on people and affairs he was involved with, and he is remarkably free with his criticisms of others, not just his opponents, but his Nazi colleagues, up to and including Hitler. He felt no compulsion to replicate in his diary the unqualified faith in 'final victory' which he publicly proclaimed up to the last days of the Second World War. Indeed, Goebbels' apprehension about the possibility of war is apparent from 1935, and an underlying sense of pessimism is present from the moment Germany found itself in a wider conflict with Britain and France in September 1939. After the invasion of the Soviet Union in 1941 it is not difficult to detect in Goebbels' diary, under the celebration of successes and the pride in German achievements, a growing sense of despair.

Goebbels also wrote with extraordinary candour about some of the most gruesome Nazi crimes, not least because he did not think of them as crimes, but as great or necessary achievements. It is difficult to imagine any future histories of the Holocaust which will not rely heavily, as the best recent treatments of this subject already do, on key passages from Goebbels' diary. One example, drawn from another area of Nazi racial and economic policy, serves to illustrate his alarming frankness. During the trial of surviving Nazi 'major war criminals' before the International Military Tribunal at Nuremberg, the Assistant French Prosecutor introduced a document relating to a meeting between Goebbels and the then Minister for Justice, Otto Thierack, held in Berlin at 1.00 p.m. on 14 September 1942, to discuss the treatment of foreign labourers. The document presented this summary of part of their discussion:

> Concerning the extermination of asocial elements, Doctor Goebbels is of the opinion that the following groups must be exterminated: All Jews and gypsies; Poles who have to serve 3 or 4 years penal servitude; Czechoslovakians and Germans who have been condemned to death or hard labor for life or placed in protective custody. The idea of extermination by work is best.[15]

One might expect that Goebbels, if he did refer to this meeting in his diary, might have been deliberately obscure about the proceedings. This is the relevant part of his diary record for that day:

> Thierack wants to resolve the question of asocial elements by putting the habitual criminals with the longest penal sentences in punishment companies and packing them off to the East. There they will carry out work under the harshest conditions. Those who succumb to this work are no great loss. At any rate I advise him urgently not to judge simply mechanically and schematically by the length of the prison sentence, but to leave room for individual judgements here. There are many cases, in which very hard punishments must be pronounced, but where we are not however dealing with elements that are completely unusable for the life of the state. Thierack represents here a very ambitious, also a national socialist viewpoint. I think I will be able to work well with him.[16]

Goebbels' diary is clearly less detailed than the official minutes of the meeting. From the position of the passage above in a long entry we can confirm the time of the meeting in the middle of the day. Goebbels does not refer to the different racial or national groupings mentioned in the minutes, or to the differing scales of punishment suggested for them, but he does not conceal the topic of discussion – 'asocial elements' – or his callous endorsement of the idea of 'extermination by work'. If on this occasion he suggested that the proposal for 'extermination' came from Thierack, rather than from him as the minutes of the meeting suggest, he was often – as we shall see – happy to identify himself as the proponent of the most shocking ideas.

Goebbels was of course selective in his diary. Frequently he referred to events and people in a terse and abbreviated form. Although he wrote in some detail about his personal relationships with his girlfriends before 1931, and after that about his relationship with his wife Magda, he was reticent about his extra-marital affairs. Although these have undoubtedly been exaggerated by almost all commentators, we know that in the mid-1930s he had a passionate and sustained affair with the actress Lida Baarova. There are only cryptic references to this in his diary. Although Goebbels recorded that he quarrelled frequently with his wife, he rarely indicates what the subject of these disputes were. Another lacuna is Hitler's relationship with Eva Braun, which Goebbels strangely did not mention until 1943.[17] Goebbels also did not report uncomplimentary views of himself, unless it was to mock them. He was an enormously self-assured man, and although as an adolescent and in early adulthood he experienced a prolonged period of existential uncertainty, he did not expose his own ideas to critical examination. This lack of self-reflection sets his diary as a literary creation entirely apart from that of someone like his near contemporary Victor Klemperer. Nonetheless, critically interpreted, it is a unique twentieth-century record of public events and a private life.

We know now, for example, that while Goebbels posed for the cameras during the huge propaganda spectacle of the Olympic Games in Berlin in 1936, he was actually tortured by the discovery that his wife was having an affair with another man. We know similarly that while Goebbels publicly celebrated the 'union' with Austria in 1938 as a consummation of German national destiny, he privately despised most Austrians, and particularly the Viennese. Although these examples suggest that Goebbels was able and willing to manipulate a public image as he deemed necessary, the fuller knowledge which we now possess confirms that he was not the pure opportunist stereotyped in the academic and popular literature on Nazi Germany, but a man of deeply held convictions. After years of preoccupation with structural factors, historians of Nazi Germany have arrived at a recognition of the importance of individual agency and of ideology. Belatedly, some are beginning to realize that leading ideologists, like Goebbels – and Hitler himself – may have meant what they said and wrote. The fact that so many of their ideas may be fantastic and morally repellent does not absolve the historian from the obligation to try to understand them, and the contexts in which they arose.

The diary compels us also to reassess Goebbels' wider role and significance in the history of Nazism and the 'Third Reich', above all his relationship with

Hitler. Indeed, they provide so much intimate detail of the conversations between these two men that Ian Kershaw, writing before the full Goebbels' diaries were available, felt that they – in large part – justified a new biography of Hitler.[18] How much more do they justify a new biography of their author! It is clear now that Goebbels had a uniquely close relationship with Hitler, one based not only on their shared experience of what they called the *Kampfzeit* or 'time of struggle' in the later years of the Weimar Republic. On the personal level, both men competed for the affections of Magda Quandt in 1931, and when she decided to marry Goebbels, the union had Hitler's blessing. He retained a particular affection for her, and the strength of this triangular relationship played no small part in the decision of all three to kill themselves in 1945 rather than to face retribution at the hands of the Allies. Goebbels and Hitler also shared a pathological hatred of the Jews, and their shared discussions of this subject on almost every occasion they met have a direct bearing on that most vexed and controversial issue, the decision to murder the Jews of Europe. Goebbels must now be placed much closer to the heart of this process than was previously thought.

Goebbels occupies a unique position in the larger history of Nazism. Alone amongst the circle of senior Nazis close to Hitler from the 1920s, Goebbels became more and more important both to Hitler and to the German public as the Second World War changed from a succession of German victories into a long attritional struggle, and ended in the trauma of invasion and defeat in 1945. Several of the 'old fighters' close to Hitler, like Röhm and Gregor Strasser, died (or were murdered) earlier; others, like Otto Strasser and later Rudolf Hess, left Germany. Some, like Göring, Rosenberg, and Ribbentrop, lost their influence and retreated into luxury or private fantasy. Heinrich Himmler is one other 'old fighter' who steadily extended his influence and power, but even after he was appointed Minister of the Interior in 1943 his activities were confined to specific areas, and he was relatively little known to the German public. Martin Bormann, a relative latecomer, also extended his power, but he was never more than a gatekeeper, and had little influence over decision making. In contrast, Goebbels, whose official responsibility from March 1933 as 'Minister for People's Enlightenment and Propaganda' suggests no more than a public relations brief, constantly sought to enlarge his role, and maintained the close contact with ordinary people which had been the hallmark of his style as a politician from 1924. He saw his own role as Propaganda Minister as one which extended into education, the media, and the arts. He meddled constantly with the operation of justice and the law inside Germany, and from 1939, across occupied Europe. Once the war started he saw himself as the guardian of morale on the German home front, and involved himself tirelessly with issues which Hitler neglected, such as the provision of housing, food rationing, the regulation of labour, and, increasingly, the whole complex of problems which arose from the British (and later American) bombing of German cities. Hitler himself became increasingly distant from the German people, living in the isolation of his field headquarters in East Prussia, and appeared in public ever more infrequently. By 1943 Goebbels had difficulty even getting Hitler to agree to broadcast to the German people. In contrast, Goebbels stepped up his popular journalism, his broadcasting, and his public speaking. After 1943, as the aerial offensive against Germany intensified, he supervised the provision of relief for bombed cities, and made it a point of honour to visit them, and to speak in public, often in ruined buildings. He did not rely on the comfort of selected audiences and prepared venues, and was always willing to improvise speeches, in front of factory workers, or in the street or marketplace. He – and his wife Magda – were the recipients of a flood of letters from ordinary German people, on subjects large and small, complimentary and critical.

In December 1944, with his field headquarters in East Prussia threatened by Soviet troops, Hitler returned to Berlin. From then on, he saw more and more of Goebbels, and the two of them retreated further into their self-created world. The report prepared for Stalin in 1948 from interrogations of two of Hitler's closest adjutants, and only recently made accessible, is absolutely clear about this final period, stating: 'Hitler received him [Goebbels] daily and discussed every question with him for hours on end.' In a subsequent passage, the report continues: 'He [Goebbels] had enormous influence over Hitler, and in the last weeks of the war enjoyed his unlimited trust.'[19] At the very end, when all the other senior Nazis around Hitler fled, Goebbels alone chose suicide with him, and – again with his wife – took the decision to kill their children as well, all of them too young to have had any responsibility for the crimes their parents were implicated in.

Goebbels was not (and we shall see that this was a problem for him) one of Hitler's earliest supporters. He played no part in the early development of the Nazi Party in Munich before 1924. From shortly after his first involvement with the Party, in 1924, until his suicide in 1945, Goebbels was at the heart of its affairs. He probably knew more about domestic and international developments between 1933 and 1945 than anyone else in Germany. Thanks to his diary, we can now trace Goebbels' involvement in and his view of these developments, and see how they related to his personal life.

Most biographies follow a roughly chronological path, but separate areas of their subject's life for convenience. Frequently they look ahead and judge events in the light of later developments. This makes it easier to structure a narrative, but presents a false view. All men and women, and Goebbels was no exception, actually experience their lives as a continuously unfolding whole. They conduct their working lives at the same time as their personal and family relationships; they cannot choose when to experience illness or good health, and even politicians in positions of power find that they are all too frequently at the mercy of events rather than in control of them. They can try to judge the potential effects of their actions, but they cannot be sure of them. The salient events in the rise of Nazism, the years of relative peace in Germany from 1933 to 1939, and the subsequent course of the Second World War, are so well known to us that it is difficult to avoid imposing elements of hindsight when constructing a narrative of events around Goebbels' life. I have tried nonetheless to follow, as far as possible, a strictly chronological path in this biography, blending what we can discern of his inner life, his relationships with literature, music, and nature, with women and male associates, with his outer life, from his schooldays, through a difficult and prolonged adolescence, to his emergence as a radical political speaker in 1924 and his subsequent engagement with the Nazi Party. Given the layers of mystification and deliberate deceit which have been embedded in the secondary literature on Goebbels from the 1920s onwards, I have sought at all times to base this account on reliable primary sources. Although reference is made to Goebbels' work as a propagandist, and to his involvement as Propaganda Minister with the control of the arts in Nazi Germany, these aspects of his working life are not my central focus.[20] Inevitably, given the vast range of domestic and international affairs with which Goebbels was involved, I have had to be selective, and readers will find specialist literatures on many of the separate incidents and themes touched upon here. Nor is this intended as a definitive study. Given the vast amounts of available material, published and unpublished, relating to Goebbels, it would be straightforwardly possible to conduct more detailed studies of any number of topics concerning him. Many aspects of his life will become clearer with future work.

Joseph Goebbels is presented here as a human being, albeit one who moved from provincial obscurity to public fame and notoriety. The reader will find here no attempt to 'rehabilitate' him, nor to relativize the nature or extent of his misdeeds. Goebbels was a man who preached hatred of his enemies, and took pleasure in dealing harshly with individuals who crossed him, whether, early in his career, in the rowdy milieu of a crowded and smoky meeting, in a street brawl, or later in his position as a government minister. He openly advocated the extermination of the Jews, and felt no shame or embarrassment in arguing that others should be literally worked to death. He tirelessly advocated the harshest punishments for those in occupied Europe who resisted Nazi authority, and for those German citizens who broke the law, often in seemingly trivial ways. A mordant sarcasm was the hallmark of his public speaking throughout his career. But Goebbels was also a devoted father, a lover of literature, poetry, music, and landscape. He was a very competent administrator, and a talented writer. Although we may be horrified by the content of his speeches, and by the ideas he propagated with such vigour, there is no doubt that he was one of the most gifted public speakers of the twentieth century. Until the last days of the war he was – if by no means universally popular – one Nazi leader with whom many soldiers, workers, and housewives felt a genuine bond. By any standards his life was an extraordinary one. Now that we are in a position to dispel many of the myths and misunderstandings which surround Goebbels, it is time to try to understand him better. In doing so we may also gain new insights into the short-lived 'Third Reich'.

1
'This Awful Waiting'

A wild yearning for strong feelings burns inside me, for sensations, a fury against this faded, flat, normal, and sterile life. I have a mad impulse to smash something, a department store perhaps, or a cathedral, or myself, to commit outrages, to pull off the wigs of a few revered idols, to provide a few rebellious schoolboys with the longed-for tickets to Hamburg, to seduce a little girl, or to stand one or two representatives of the bourgeois order on their heads. For what I always hated and detested and cursed most inwardly was this contentment, this healthiness and cosiness, this carefully preserved optimism of the middle classes, this fat and prosperous brood of the mediocre, the normal, the average.

Hermann Hesse, *The Steppenwolf*, 1927[1]

There was little in the outward childhood of Paul Joseph Goebbels to suggest the huge influence he would subsequently exert on twentieth-century history. He was born on 29 October 1897 in the small manufacturing town of Rheydt, which lies some 25 kilometres west of Düsseldorf, and 35 kilometres east of the Dutch frontier. Rheydt adjoins the larger town of Mönchen-Gladbach, and both are close to the industrial area of the Ruhr, which lies on the eastern side of the River Rhine. In the late nineteenth century, fuelled by the rapid expansion of German industry, Rheydt's population was increasing rapidly, and a new town hall, completed in 1896, symbolized local pride and economic achievement. Goebbels' father, Friedrich, or 'Fritz', was a clerk in a small firm; his mother Katherina, was, according to Goebbels' early biographers, 'a simple woman of little education'.[2] Both parents were devout Roman Catholics, and models of respectability. Goebbels had two older brothers, Konrad and Hans, and two younger sisters, Elisabeth and Maria. When Joseph was still an infant, his parents were able to move to their own terraced house close to the centre of Rheydt, within walking distance of its railway station and the red-brick Church of St Mary. The most remarkable thing most can find to say of Goebbels' childhood is to repeat anecdotes about his disability, and how resentment about this fed into his adult development.

1. The house in Dahlemer Strasse, Rheydt, where Goebbels was brought up as a child and lived with his parents until 1924. Goebbels wrote that 'as if by a miracle' it survived the British bombing of the city on 1 September 1943; the houses originally to either side of it were destroyed. (*TBJG*, 1 September 1943, TII, 9, p. 399.)

Our knowledge of this German childhood is though very speculative, and much of it has an anecdotal quality, inevitably, since it has been passed down orally.[3] We know that the young Joseph Goebbels suffered from an infantile paralysis of the right foot, and that after years of difficulty, his foot was operated on, unsuccessfully, in 1907. After this, he walked with a noticeable limp. It is reasonable to assume that he suffered insults from other children, and, in a society which exalted strong military virtues, that this might have caused particular anxiety. At any rate, Goebbels from a very young age was solitary and reclusive, keeping his own company, and becoming an intensive reader. In an account of his childhood and youth written in the summer of 1924, Goebbels himself described his life after the operation on his foot: 'Childhood from then on pretty joyless. I could no longer join in the games of others. Became a solitary, lone wolf.'[4]

This was an extraordinarily austere childhood, stamped by Roman Catholic piety and a rigorous adherence to Prussian values of thrift, discipline, and hard work.[5] Literally every pfennig was counted in the household accounting, and from an early age Joseph was chosen as the child most likely to fulfil his parents' dreams of upward social mobility. This parental favour derived partly from his disability, but was also due to the academic and artistic potential he displayed from an early age. As he neared adolescence, his parents took two notable steps: after scrimping and saving, they bought a piano for him to learn on, and in 1908 they entered him for the local *Gymnasium*, or grammar school. Goebbels later recounted how the neighbours all came out to watch as the piano was brought into the house, wondering where the Goebbels family had found the money for this 'symbol of education and prosperity'. The piano was installed in the parlour – which was otherwise reserved for important occasions or for respectable visitors – and young Joseph was now allowed to enter the room every day. In the winter months, if we are to believe his later reminiscence, he sat there playing the piano in a coat, hat, and scarf, only able to read the music if there was sufficient moonlight.[6]

At the *Gymnasium*, Goebbels was an unusually intense student, and he did exceptionally well, particularly in languages, the arts, and in history, where he was brought up on the nationalistic narratives consolidated since 1871 in the German educational system. His school reports, uncluttered with today's educational jargon, consistently described his progress in most subjects as 'good' or 'very good'.[7] From childhood Goebbels was a voracious reader, and from a young age he became also a writer. Significantly, his earliest surviving poem, written in 1912 when he was 15, is about 'the dead friend' who has departed life too early, leaving the author alone and without hope:

> Here I stand by the funeral bier
> And look upon your cold limbs.
> You were my friend, yes, the true friend
> Whom I held dearest in my life.
>
> You had to take your leave from me so early
> Leave life, which waved to you,
> Leave the world with its joys,
> Leave hope, which signalled to you.[8]

Goebbels' schooldays were interrupted by the outbreak of war in 1914. Unlike other young men and schoolboys of his age, including his two older brothers, Goebbels was not able to serve in the ranks; he had to stay at home while they experienced the growing horror of the fighting on different fronts. According to his early biographers, after being rejected by the army on account of his disability, Goebbels withdrew into his room for several days, unable to bear the rejection and humiliation.[9] Whether this is true or not, over the next few years, his lack of what became known in Germany as the *Fronterlebnis* (front experience), the shared experience of war, marked him out from many of his gender and generation. His family shared the intense anxiety common over all Europe in the first years of war. Both older sons served on the Western Front, and Hans was captured by the French in 1916; it was five years before he returned to Rheydt. More tragically, Goebbels' sister Elisabeth died from tuberculosis at the age of twelve in 1915. The already austere tone of the Goebbels household was intensified by personal tragedy and material hardship.

As he grew up, Goebbels was intellectually conservative: he drank in ideas, lapping up the commonplace assumptions and prejudices of Wilhelmine Germany, steeped in the inflated, melodramatic language of Romanticism, and, after 1914, laced with platitudes about war, heroism, and final victory. He developed an intense nationalism, and words like *Volk*, *Vaterland*, and *Deutschland*, began to take on in his mind the elevated, mystical qualities they later assumed in Nazi discourse. He accepted without reserve that Germany was fighting a justified, defensive struggle for survival against remorseless enemies on all sides. Like many, he developed a faith in the idea of a 'people's community' or *Volksgemeinschaft*, which would emerge from the crucible of war, uniting different social classes in a common national purpose. For many young German men, the *Volksgemeinschaft* was an ideal briefly realized in the trenches, where class, regional, and confessional differences were renounced and replaced by bonds of manly comradeship. Goebbels obviously did not experience this but he did share in the other great, albeit temporary realization of the *Volksgemeinschaft*, the (subsequently mythologized) passion of August 1914 when Germans of all parties and all areas of society stood united against their enemies in a spirit of patriotic dedication and sacrifice.

From his early teens, Goebbels was a prolific writer. He wrote stories, verse plays, and poetry; his early personal letters had a self-consciously literary quality, which was heightened by the circumstances of war. He wrote to the family of his friend Fritz Prang in 1918 on hearing of the death of Fritz's brother:

> Hans was a true and loyal comrade. What drew me to him particularly and will always make me proud to have known him, was his pure and unspotted character, his truly noble attitude, and his unspoiled way of life, even though in a restrained and yet virile way he was not the type to conquer hearts in a flash. He certainly did something more precious: he knew how to win the hearts of his friends for ever in hours of quiet communion …[10]

In March 1917, Goebbels was chosen to give the valedictory address to his class before leaving the *Gymnasium*. He spoke of 'that great Germany upon which the entire world gazes with fear and admiration', and concluded with a peroration which displays some of the hallmarks of his later style:

> And Thou, Germany, mighty Fatherland, Thou sacred land of our fathers, stand fast, stand fast in Thy hour of need and death. Thou has shown Thy heroic strength and shalt go forth victorious from the final struggle ... We do not fear for thee. We trust in the everlasting God, Whose will it is that Right shall prevail, and in Whose hand the future lies ... God bless our Fatherland.[11]

Goebbels went almost immediately to university, enrolling as a student in Bonn in April 1917. Over the next few years, he studied briefly there, in Freiburg, Würzburg, Munich, and in Heidelberg, taking courses in history, literature, philology, and art. (Later he wrote of Freiburg: 'Here I lived, loved, and suffered.'[12]) His family could not afford to support him away from home, and he relied heavily on loans from a Catholic charitable society to pay for his board and lodgings. This was an unusual time for a young man to be at university, as the war intensified. To the shock of most people at home, the German effort collapsed in October and November 1918. When the armistice was agreed, by which time the Kaiser had abdicated, and a Republic had been proclaimed, Goebbels was in the small Baroque town of Würzburg, from where he wrote to his schoolfriend Fritz Prang:

> Don't you feel that the time will come again when people will yearn for intellectual and spiritual values rather than brutal mass appeal? Let us also wait for that moment, and meanwhile persevere in steeling our brains for the tasks then awaiting us. It is bitter enough to have lived through those dark hours of our Fatherland, but who knows if one day it might not profit us after all. The way I see it, Germany has certainly lost the war, but our Fatherland may well turn out the winner.[13]

Already, several enduring characteristics of Goebbels' thought, speaking, and writing, are clear: an emotional, fervent style, at once seemingly open, revealing, and appelatory; a bombastic use of language; a passionate nationalism, confused with religious sentiment; and an alarming lack of any sense of critical doubt. Even at this early stage, Goebbels, and many like him, had identified 'the Jews' as the enemies of Germany. Writing later of a meeting of staff and students in the university in Würzburg at the end of the war, Goebbels stressed that Jews were excluded from the proceedings.[14]

The immediate post-war years were formative in Goebbels' life. This was the time in which his view of the world, his philosophy, his religion (or lack of it), his understanding of history and the arts, his relationship with nature and with society, what he would have called his *Weltanschauung* (or 'world-view'), was crystallizing. It was for him an intensely paradoxical period, in which he was often depressed, alone, and in poverty. It was a particularly difficult time for young men, when prospects of employment were poor. Many were in any case already dislocated by the experience of war, and when demobilized they were thrown on a labour market disrupted by growing inflation. Just before Christmas 1918 Goebbels' father wrote anxiously to his son about developments in Rheydt, where a curfew had been imposed by occupying Belgian soldiers: 'Here a bitter, evil time is starting.' He urged his son to come home if necessary.[15] Allied troops were to remain in parts of the west bank of the Rhine until 1930. All over Germany there were strikes, riots, and social disturbances. Communist risings in several cities were suppressed by armed, uniformed bands of former soldiers, the *Freikorps*. Individual leaders were murdered. From the right, a military coup in 1920, the Kapp *Putsch*, initiated a period in which many nationalistic and militaristic groups formed in German cities, notably in Munich, where Goebbels spent the winter of 1920/21. Strikingly, Goebbels at this stage of his life was not involved with politics. He had no connection with the Nazi Party while in Munich. Despite this detachment, he could not help but see changes and disturbances all around him. When he went home for the first time after the war in January 1919, he had to travel through a British checkpoint at Cologne; trying to get back to Freiburg a few weeks later, he was allowed through a control point at Ludwigshafen by a black French soldier. He stood aloof from all political movements, adopting the pose of an observer. Significantly, even though he had no interest in any party politics, or in the proceedings of political groups, he did develop a growing, unfocused anti-capitalism.

For several years after leaving school in 1917, Goebbels went through a prolonged crisis of identity. The psychoanalyst and historian Erik Erikson, analysing a very different young man in an earlier period of German history, wrote a passage which is highly relevant:

> In some young people, in some classes, at some periods in history, this crisis will be minimal; in other people, classes, and periods, the crisis will be clearly marked off as a critical period, a kind of 'second birth', apt to be aggravated either by widespread neuroticisms or by pervasive ideological unrest. Some young individuals will succumb to this crisis in all manner of neurotic, psychotic, or delinquent behaviour; others will resolve it through participation in ideological movements passionately concerned with religion or politics, nature or art. Still others, although suffering and deviating dangerously through what appears to be a prolonged adolescence, eventually come to contribute an original bit to an emerging style of life: the very danger which they have sensed has forced

them to mobilize capacities to see and say, to dream and plan, to design and construct, in new ways.[16]

It was to be several years before the young Joseph Goebbels was to complete his 'second birth', and to find 'an emerging style of life' to which he could contribute his own remarkable energies. In the meantime, both his sense of personal suffering and his intellectual understanding of the troubled world around him were heightened by his friendship with Richard Flisges, a former schoolmate from the Rhineland. Flisges was from a farming family, had served at the front, been decorated, and returned wounded in mind and body. After failing his university exams, Flisges was forced to work as a labourer. Goebbels idealized Flisges, coming to see him as a heroic representative of three creative German archetypes, the soldier, the artist, and the worker. He even copied the way Flisges dressed, adopting the trench coat which later became almost a signature garment. Flisges and Goebbels had a shared literary outlook, nursing ambitions to write, and a common nationalism, passionate and increasingly angry. Both saw themselves as outcasts, unable to conform to the demands of a corrupt modern society. Flisges, who has been described as 'an anarchist', introduced Goebbels to the literature of Marxism, and more importantly to the Russian novelist Dostoyevsky. Together, Goebbels and Flisges worked up a passionate hatred for the state of contemporary Germany, riven by internal strife, and oppressed by its enemies, which they identified as 'international Jewry'. They linked this perception of German suffering with their own failure to find appropriate work or recognition, and cast themselves in their imagination as heroic fighters against a cruel destiny.[17]

Goebbels had two clear centres to his otherwise vague beliefs, a passionate sense of nationalism, and a developing concern with class divisions, with what would now be called social justice. In the autumn of 1918, he had written a verse drama, *Judas Iscariot*, in which he sought to cast the traitor Judas as a heroic figure. This had led to a difficult confrontation with his parish priest, Johannes Mollen, who asked him to destroy the manuscript. Over the next year, influenced by Flisges and the literature he was being introduced to, Goebbels lost any Roman Catholic faith that he might earlier have had, a cause of great concern to his father.[18] In a letter written in November 1919, Fritz Goebbels anxiously posed two questions to his son: 'Have you written, or do you intend to write books which do not accord with the Catholic religion? Do you intend to take up a profession, in which Catholics do not participate?' In the same letter, Fritz Goebbels tried to reassure his son that all young people experienced doubt, and wrote about this in language uncannily reminiscent of that which his son would use in later years: 'Here also one comes only to victory through struggle.'[19] We do not know how Goebbels answered his father's questions, but he never returned to the Catholic faith.

The young Goebbels was still a voracious reader and lover of music, and through his university years and afterwards, he steeped himself in German culture. He was a huge admirer of Goethe, and of the nineteenth-century novelist Wilhelm Raabe, from whose work he took his pen-name of 'Ulex'. His doctoral dissertation, written for Heidelberg University in 1921, was on a little-known nineteenth-century writer, Wilhelm von Schütz.[20] All writers on Goebbels have picked up on his vanity in using his doctoral title in later years – although he would indeed have been unusual in Germany in the 1920s and 1930s if he had *not* insisted on this – but what is more striking today is how little influence his disjointed formal studies appear to have had on his intellectual development. He appears to have been far more influenced by his private reading, and by the views of his closest friends.

Alongside this developing artistic and intellectual consciousness, there were significant developments in Goebbels' emotional and sexual life. Most importantly, in May 1918, at Freiburg University he met and fell in love with fellow student Anka Stalherm. She was not his first girlfriend, but this was his first important relationship with women. For all that biographers and historians have pictured Goebbels as a young man filled with repressed hatred because of his disability, he was clearly very able to attract women of his own age. From the age of 15 (when he retrospectively recorded his 'first love with Maria Liffers'[21]), he was more or less continuously involved with one or more women in intimate relationships. His whole mood and outlook fluctuated in sympathy with the changing fortunes of these relationships, which were invariably stormy, interrupted by difficulties with money, and beset with jealousy and misunderstandings. Goebbels' relationship with Anka Stalherm was characterized, like those that followed, by alternating periods of blissful happiness and bitter reproach. Most commentators on Goebbels single out his fascination for beautiful women, and typically highlight how, in his later life, he would abuse his position of power to gain their sexual favour, but this is to simplify hopelessly. As a young man his relationships with women also had other dimensions. His girlfriends, as well as being objects of unfulfilled sexual longing, were sounding boards for his passionate, strongly articulated but incoherent views on life and art. The women he was most closely involved with as a young man, that is to say Anka Stalherm and Else Janke, were, fortunately for them, strong-minded and capable, and both succeeded in keeping him at arm's length.

If the young Goebbels could be charming and captivating, there was a less attractive side to his character which became evident during these years, and which he inflicted upon all around him. Goebbels came to maturity in a disjointed time, and he found himself entirely lacking in purpose. He had a strongly developed sense of his own intelligence and insight, but was painfully aware after finishing his university studies in 1921 that he did not know what to do with himself. He developed a huge sense of frustration, and of resentment, seeing himself as a personification of the larger suffering inflicted on the German people. At its worst this resentment shaded into hatred, a hatred which was, like Goebbels' passionate longings, incredibly unfocused. Like many others in Germany at this time, he was coming to see 'the Jews' as the source of all evil. Most writers on Goebbels have highlighted his resentment against individual Jews, like the publisher Rudolf Mosse in Cologne, who rejected his application for employment in 1923, or his doctoral sponsor in Heidelberg, Professor Gundolf, but in his actual writing Goebbels rarely mentioned individual Jews. Typically, he wrote impersonally about 'the Jews', or 'international Jewry', or 'the Jewish spirit'.

Anka Stalherm came from a well-off family in Recklinghausen in the Ruhr, and it appears that they disapproved of her relationship with this penniless student. Nonetheless, for two years Goebbels and Anka continued their love affair. In the summer of 1920, while both were studying in Heidelberg, Anka, perhaps repelled by Goebbels' increasingly strident anti-capitalism, left him for another man, Georg Mumme. Typically, Goebbels believed that the collapse of their affair was a consequence of international capitalism's exploitation of Germany, which highlighted their different class backgrounds, writing to her: 'Don't you see that our love has become a victim of this rotten state of affairs?'[22] When Goebbels, accompanied by his friend Flisges, pursued Anka, she and Mumme engaged a lawyer to tell him to desist, and to return all her gifts and letters.[23] Goebbels was left in suicidal despair. He had to return home to Rheydt, where his gloom was consolidated by reading Oswald Spengler. Later he wrote of this time, calling Anka a 'murderer': 'Pessimism. Doubt. I no longer believe in anything.'[24] The time spent with Anka left Goebbels with indelible, frequently bitter, feelings. For years afterwards, he wrote poems about her, and referred to her in his diary, his memory triggered by places they had been in together, by experiences they had shared, or by other women who reminded him of her. Often he dreamed about her at night. In 1928 he wrote: 'A person has one great love in a life. Everything else is an illusion or an affair. Mine is called Anka.'[25]

After successfully completing his doctorate in Heidelberg in November 1921, Goebbels had to live in the family home in Rheydt for the next few years. He had no regular income, and could not afford to live elsewhere. His sense of personal failure was compounded by sexual frustration, and an acute consciousness of what a disappointment he was to his parents. Goebbels earned a few marks here and there for occasional private tutoring, and in 1923 he worked for some months at the Dresdner Bank in nearby Cologne. After initially commuting to and from Rheydt, he briefly stayed in digs in Cologne. He could not submit to the demands of a full-time but unfulfilling job, and was unsuited temperamentally to the tedium of routine administrative work. His observation of the workings of a large bank as inflation soared out of control in Germany fuelled his growing anti-Semitism and anti-capitalism. In many respects Goebbels seems an archetypal representative of what Detlev Peukert, in his analysis of Weimar

Germany, called the 'superfluous generation', born too late or otherwise unable to fight in the war, and psychologically unfitted for life in peacetime.[26] This was an intensely difficult time for a German nationalist in his mid-twenties. Goebbels lacked a clear direction, but knew that he was energetic and talented. He felt keenly the stigma of poverty as well as its practical consequences. In addition to the humiliating confinement to his family home, with all its restrictions, he was unable to keep up with the social life of his women friends. His hatred for capitalism had been one cause of his break-up with Anka Stalherm, and financial difficulties played a part in his next important relationship.

In 1922 Goebbels began an intimate friendship with Else Janke, a young schoolteacher in Rheydt who had known the Goebbels family for some time. Just as with Anka, Goebbels fell passionately in love with Else Janke, and her companionship was one of the few bright stars in a dismal firmament as he sat unemployed at home. Early in 1923, Goebbels learnt that Else had a Jewish mother, and this soured his earlier feelings for her. He was reading the work of Houston Stewart Chamberlain, which posed an opposition between a creative, Aryan (or German) race, and a destructive Jewish race. Wherever Goebbels looked, at the economy, at the arts, or international relations, he saw evidence of this antagonism. Nonetheless, he could not but respond to Else's concern for him, and her many small acts of kindness in a time when he was frequently depressed.

Goebbels had by this time developed a sense of himself as an artist. In addition to many poems, he had now written three completed plays, as well as an autobiographical novel with the title *Michael Voorman's Youth*. None of his plays had been produced on the stage and neither his novel nor his poetry had been published. He was allowed in October 1922 to give a talk on German literature at a technical school in Rheydt,[27] and he had a few small articles published in local newspapers, but got no further than that. Already Goebbels had developed a characteristic pattern of hectic creativity alternating with sluggish passivity. While creative he wrote for hours on end, and the positive, life-affirming, idealistic side of his nature came to the fore. Once he had finished a particular writing project, he lapsed into inactivity and depression, consoled in his melancholy only by the thought of Anka, or Else, and by the arts. His deepening sense of tragedy was quickened by the increasingly desperate state of Germany in 1923, and the obvious failure of his own efforts as a writer. In January 1923 the whole of the Ruhr was occupied by the French and the Belgians in an effort to extract reparations payments in kind from the Germans, and the passive resistance mounted by the population there added to the already great economic hardship.

In July 1923 came the news that Richard Flisges had been killed in a mining accident in Bavaria, an incident construed by Goebbels as both conspiratorial and symbolic. As the inflation in Germany came to a head, Goebbels decided to leave his menial job at the Dresdner Bank. Later he wrote that after Flisges' death he was 'alone in the world'. There was 'chaos in Germany'. Cruelly, he wrote that 'Else doesn't understand me', even though he spent a happy time on holiday with her on the island of Baltrum in August 1923.[28] On his return, he was dismissed from the bank and, with no money, had no choice but to return to Rheydt.

Confined again to the family home, with long hours to fill, and keenly aware of his parents' anxiety, Goebbels began to keep a diary, using a notebook which Else had given him. He had as a teenager sometimes kept a diary, but had not maintained this systematically. In the summer of 1924, by which time he had been conscientiously writing his diary for almost a year, he wrote a long reminiscence of his childhood and youth, and he described how he came to start his diary in the difficult circumstances of October 1923: 'I can't bear the agony any longer. I have to write the bitterness out of my heart. Else gives me a book for daily use.'[29] This retrospective use of the present tense was artificial, but his determination to write was real, and with his first entry, on 17 October 1923, Goebbels began a habit which he maintained until his death in 1945. In his first entry, he put his feelings for Else at the centre of his emotional life, already cast in a heroic mode, and juxtaposed this with an observation on Germany:

> Yesterday Else gave me this book, and therefore I want to start it right away with her name. What else could I begin today without her?
>
> You Beloved, you Goodness! You pick me up and always give me new courage, when I doubt myself. I can not express what gratitude I owe to you.
>
> How miserable it is today to take a walk through the streets of the town. Groups of the unemployed stand on all corners, debating and speculating. It is a time to laugh and to cry.[30]

The diaries are such an important source for our knowledge of Goebbels that their construction merits some analysis. When he started keeping a diary in 1923, Goebbels was totally obscure. He could have had no idea of how this record would later be seen and used. He was nonetheless aware of the diary as a literary form, and wrote his with considerable artifice. His day-to-day entries have a clear narrative form, with himself cast as a romantic hero at the centre of an epic struggle. He reflects on his own emotional and artistic development, and expresses this largely through world-historical observations, combined with artistic criticism. At times in the first few months of the diaries he breaks off from his carefully ordered prose, and includes a poem. These poems are cast in the characteristic mode of Romanticism, mixing yearning, suffering, and pathos with nature worship and a diffused religious sense.

Writing a diary quickly became a kind of therapy for this troubled young man, and several historians have commented on how extraordinarily candid and revealing Goebbels was, particularly in his early years as a diarist. The editor of the now complete edition of his diaries has argued that Goebbels used his diary as a 'substitute confessional', supporting this with reference to entries in which he himself used this kind of language, and to his expressed wish to render account of himself in his diary, but this must be qualified.[31] Goebbels did frequently, in his early years as a diarist, include himself in excoriating general condemnations of mankind, and he did recognize that he was frequently unkind and unfair to Else, but he did not subject his own intellectual views, or his rancorous prejudices, to any sustained critical analysis.

Notably, in the first few months of the diary, Goebbels displays very little interest in day-to-day politics. He writes at length and in the most general way about the state of Germany, of Europe, and of the world; he anxiously notes the depths Germany is cast into, and sometimes, in a strikingly detached way, refers to specific disturbances, but he has virtually no interest in the details of party politics or of elections. He comments, but only in the broadest way, on great social questions like the relationship between the sexes, or between capital and labour. Not surprisingly, given that he was more or less stuck in Rheydt, travelling no further than to nearby towns, the doings of the German government in Berlin appear remote, and are almost never alluded to. More surprisingly, given Goebbels' later involvement with the mass media, he displays no interest in newspapers or journalistic discourse. There was at this time no radio, and Goebbels went only rarely to the cinema.[32] He lived largely in his own imagination. His first diary entry combines the different strands which clearly dominated his imagination, and set a pattern which he followed for the next two years. After writing about Else, he mused about the parlous state of contemporary poetry, unable – in his view – to voice the cry of the German people in their suffering, and continued:

> Europe is a great spiritual problem. The economic only swims on the surface. Otherwise all would have been sorted out long ago. However, under the surface, the great spiritual powers are in a struggle with one another. That which is younger, and stronger and more certain of victory will triumph, even if at the moment it succumbs.
>
> In this problem of Europe lies the old, holy, Russia. A land which I have the deepest honour for without actually knowing it first-hand. Russia is past and future, only no present. The Russian present is only a soapy lather, the heavy lye is underneath. The solution to the great Russian enigma is incubating in the Russian earth. The spirit of a great man, Dostoyevsky, hovers over the still, dreaming land of Russia. If Russia awakes, then the world will see a wonder. *Ex oriente lux*.[33]

The shift to Latin for an aphoristic conclusion was a device frequently used by Goebbels. At this stage of his life he was preoccupied with this idea that Russia represented the future, that a mystical folk community embodying the qualities Goebbels derived from his reading of Dostoyevsky would 'awaken' there. He also read Tolstoy and Gogol, and they buttressed this fervour without supplanting Dostoyevsky in his pantheon of artistic greatness. This involvement with Russian literature was one of few significant excursions Goebbels made outside traditional 'German' culture. Another was Shakespeare: like most educated Germans, Goebbels knew several Shakespeare plays in translation, and he frequently referred to him in the same breath as his other favourites, Goethe and Dostoyevsky.

A second strand of Goebbels' artistic outlook, displayed in his first diary entry, was his discontent with the state of contemporary German culture. He wrote that the last giants of German literature, Gerhard Hauptmann and Thomas Mann, had lost any relevance to German youth. Oswald Spengler, whose *Decline of the West* had greatly impressed Goebbels, he thought was Thomas Mann's brother in spirit, and Goebbels linked his own situation with this larger cultural pessimism: 'It is a terrible agony', he wrote, 'to stand on the grave of his [Spengler's] culture.' In a self-pitying and self-dramatizing vein which was a constant feature of the early diaries, he lamented that there was no place in this degraded world for someone like him: 'The deepest cause of my agony is that I have no home [*Heimat*].'

In this mood, he then turned to the dead Richard Flisges, addressing him as if he were present:

> How often already have I yearned for you since you went away, dear friend Richard? You were so much to me. You were happier than me, because you were more carefree. I had only one friend, and that was you. You understood me, without my having to say anything. You had a connection with the old Mother Earth. From this you drew your lordly powers. It was so beautiful to see the powers of nature playing in you. I believe it was good for you, that you went on ahead.
>
> What a good Fate it was that bestowed death upon you as you were working, while working amongst the people of the *Volk*. That is surely a sign.[34]

Since Goebbels used the word '*Volk*' from the first entry in his diary, frequently in other compound nouns, or in its adjectival and adverbial forms, it is worth exploring what he meant by it. Even at this early stage, before he had attached himself to an interest group or party, he clearly subscribed to the beliefs of the *völkisch* philosophy in Germany. The concept of the *Volk*, and the central ideas of *völkisch* thought have been subjected to minute analysis by historians and linguists. The most convincing understandings are those which recognize the *Volk* as an idealized construction, an example of one of Benedict Anderson's 'imagined communities', or, as George Mosse put it, 'a metaphysical entity, an eternal and unchanging ideal'.[35] Kurt Sontheimer describes the *Volksgemeinschaft*, the community of the *Volk*, as 'something organic, something mystical'.[36]

In this construction, the German *Volk* was a community linked by shared inheritance and physical characteristics. Given that Goebbels himself was not tall, blond-haired, or blue-eyed, it is unsurprising that he tended to stress more the imagined mental characteristics of the *Volk*, thus a nobility of character, a deep spiritual capacity for artistic experience and expression, and a heroic bearing in the face of adversity. For someone like Goebbels, who had no direct experience of many parts of Germany, let alone of foreign countries, any conception of 'the German people' was necessarily vague, and in the early years of his diary he never went beyond the most loose, dithyrambic descriptions of the *Volk*. Critical to this understanding of the *Volk* is some kind of binary opposite, another group against which the *Volk* can be defined, and here we encounter an increasingly vicious side of the young Goebbels. He had since his teenage years identified the Jews as the enemy of the German *Volk*, and by 1923 this had become an obsession. Intriguingly, Goebbels rarely singled out in his diary as enemies, or oppositions to the German people, the victors of the First World War, the British, the French, or the Americans. He appears to have been equally uninterested in the daily confrontations between Germans in the Rhineland and the Ruhr and their French and Belgian occupiers, even though this situation had become much more tense after January 1923.[37] Instead, he transferred the blame for all Germany's misfortunes onto 'the Jews', a group he defined as vaguely as 'the *Volk*'. The third entry in his diary, dated 22 October 1923, is the first in which he refers explicitly to the Jews. After musing about a novel by Jakob Wassermann, *Christian Wahnschaffe*, which he described as 'A typically Jewish book',[38] Goebbels wrote:

> I think so often about the Jewish question. The problem of race is indeed the deepest, and most secretive which must be grasped in public life today. Is there an opposition: Race – Intellect; Creativity – Reproduction; Art – Science; Industrial capitalism – Stock Exchange capitalism? How far these different orders appear to lie from one another.

As with his wider view of culture, Goebbels linked his view of race with his own personal life, bluntly raising his perception of Else as partly Jewish, and contrasting her with Anka:

> E. can also not disavow her Jewish blood. There is something strikingly destructive in her character, above all mentally; but this is less obvious because her mind is not fully developed. She is the directly opposite pole to An., who had a racial nature of first-class quality. How to love both? How to hate both? How to give myself to both?[39]

Although Goebbels only periodically highlighted this issue quite so explicitly in his diary, over the next few years it was a gnawing presence in his fluctuating relationship with Else. His *völkisch* understanding that racial characteristics were inherited meant that he could not, however strong his feelings, deny to himself that to marry her, or to have children by her, would be a racial sin.

In the autumn of 1923, the early problems of the Weimar Republic came to a head. Goebbels, while noting some political and economic developments, remained largely detached from them. On 23 October he wrote with contempt that 'Riff-raff drive through the streets in stolen cars, and proclaim the free Rhenish Republic. In Gladbach there were many dead and wounded.'[40] On 10 November he wrote:

> A nationalists' *Putsch* in Bavaria. Ludendorff has once again gone walking. In the Ruhr area, the coal mines have laid off the workers. Riots of the unemployed here in Rheydt and in most of the Rhineland towns ... Murder and killing. Desperation and hunger.

Typically, Goebbels dedicated more of his diary entry that day to the arts than to politics. He had been to a concert of contemporary music in nearby Mönchen-Gladbach the previous evening, and he wrote about each of the pieces he had heard:

> H. Wetzler, previously director of opera in Cologne, an Overture to 'As You Like It', brave, healthy, but not overdone. P. Hindemith, *Nuschi-Nuschi Dances*. Marvellous, spiritually rich instrumentation, with an equal fullness of sound and beauty of tone. The opposite of the Wetzler, spirited, a foxtrot, but always interesting and original. Hindemith will be of significance in the future.

Goebbels commented approvingly on *Til Eugenspiegel* by Richard Strauss, and more dismissively on a Max Reger violin sonata which had also been performed. Later that day he spent time at the piano with a book of Schumann pieces which Else had given him for his 26th birthday on 29 October, and read some Hermann Hesse.[41] He did not refer to the failed Nazi *Putsch* in Munich over the next few days or weeks.

Since 1918, a huge body of literature has sought to analyse the pervasive sense of disillusionment and unease which affected young Germans in the early years of the twentieth century and was hugely intensified after 1918. Contemporary novelists like Thomas Mann and Hermann Hesse addressed this theme in their work. Hesse, who before 1914 had written romantic novels of disillusioned youth and frustrated artistic spirits, turned in the 1920s to more critical portrayals of alienated intellectuals, producing in the character of Harry Haller – the 'Steppenwolf' – one with some uncanny similarities to the young Goebbels.[42] Philosophers and historians – of whom Oswald Spengler undoubtedly influenced Goebbels most strongly – wrote about the 'decline of the West'.[43] The revolutionary journalist Victor Serge, portraying the situation in Germany for a French journal in 1923, wrote:

> Above all [thinkers] were discussing a great pessimistic book, steeped on every page with reactionary assertions, by Oswald Spengler, called *The Decline of the West* ... Those for whom culture is the most precious result of societies' efforts were living under the influence of a heartbreaking influence with decadence ...[44]

Musicians and composers, threatened by modernist atonality, the commercialization of popular music, and new forms of mechanical reproduction, added to the chorus of voices announcing a crisis of German culture. The elderly representative of German late Romanticism, Hans Pfitzner, wrote in 1920 about the 'new aesthetic of musical impotence', blaming this on 'the Jewish-international spirit which has placed the alien madness of destruction and demolition in the German mind'.[45]

Victor Serge asked: 'what is happening to intellectuals amid this collapse of culture?', and answered by stating: 'The majority vegetate, embittered.'[46] Later historians, seeking to understand the fragility of the Weimar Republic, have written about 'the politics of cultural despair',[47] of a 'hunger for wholeness', and of a collective 'love affair with unreason and death'. Peter Gay notes how this 'complex of feelings and responses' was 'awash with hate'.[48] The political scientist Kurt Sontheimer has surveyed this whole literature using the analytical category of 'anti-democratic thinking'.[49] Klaus Theweleit has used techniques drawn from psychoanalysis and Marxism to focus on the relationships between *Freikorps* veterans and women.[50] Where did the young Goebbels fit into this picture? In many ways, as we have seen, he was a typical example of a young man particularly susceptible to this intellectual climate. He was steeped in the literature of cultural pessimism, and articulated his own thoughts in the language of writers who had influenced him. Like many young Germans, Goebbels had been captured by reading Herman Hesse's first novel, the autobiographical *Peter Camenzind*, published in 1904. This portrayed the prolonged adolescence of a young poet, and, in the words of Hans Mayer, expressed 'disenchantment with the people and circumstances of late bourgeois society'. It was 'a lament over the terminal state of the spirit, of true poetry'.[51] We can see why Goebbels identified so strongly with it. In *Peter Camenzind* Hesse wrote: 'I had to spend the years of my adolescence without a friend', and that he 'derived pleasure from melancholy fancies, thoughts of death and pessimistic reflections'. Like Goebbels, Hesse's Peter Camenzind spent hours reading in an attic, and had an unrequited love for a beautiful young woman. Hesse might have been describing Goebbels when he wrote: 'So this first love affair of mine never came to a conclusion; instead it echoed enigmatically all through my youthful years and accompanied my later love affairs like a quiet elder sister.'[52]

In Theweleit's analysis of *Freikorps* veterans, these are portrayed – through the lens of their own autobiographical writing – as having a deep fear and hatred of women. They divide women in their imagination into polarized categories: 'Red women' – their class enemies – and 'white nurses' – chaste, racially pure German women of good social background. Brutalized by their war experience and accustomed to the all-male comradeship of the trenches, they want to rape 'red women' and to beat them into bloody, shapeless masses. Unable to relate to 'white nurses' as real people, or even to refer to them by their individual names, they elevate their mothers, wives, and sweethearts to a position of sanitized, godlike virtue. Even then, Theweleit suggests, this worship may typically conceal deep-seated hatred and dread. Intriguingly, Theweleit uses extracts from Goebbels' own 1928 novel *Michael* to support his analysis, although Goebbels was not a war veteran or *Freikorps* volunteer, and had not been socialized in the trenches. In some respects the passages by Goebbels which Theweleit selects do support his broader thesis. Goebbels did idealize women, particularly those with suitable racial characteristics and appearance, like Anka Stalherm, but he did not display the hatred and the almost uncontrollable urge towards violence against women of the actual *Freikorps* men Theweleit examines. Although the heroine of Goebbels' novel *Michael*, Hertha Holk, is a superficial and idealized stereotype of 'Aryan' femininity, in his diary Goebbels wrote about real women as larger characters, and as individuals. He always used their names. Although he shared most of the prejudices of his time about the role of women and their place in the public sphere, he wanted his own girlfriends to be present in his life, not to be, as in Theweleit's analysis of the 'best category' of women, absent.[53]

In addition to these more personal affinities, Goebbels shared several of the broader social experiences in Germany which were shaping this mood of cultural pessimism after 1918. He had not served in the First World War, but close relatives of his had, and he had suffered some of its consequences. Goebbels' home town, Rheydt, was in the area of the Rhineland occupied by Belgian troops after the war, and subsequently declared a 'demilitarized' zone. Goebbels had studied at several universities, amongst student fraternities universally agreed to be hotbeds of 'anti-democratic thinking'. He and his family experienced poverty and the inflation which came to a head in 1923. The notebook Else had given Goebbels to use as a diary had cost the fantastic sum of one thousand million Marks.[54] In other ways though, Goebbels was not typical, and at this stage of his young adulthood he did not join the most popular movements which attracted disillusioned young men of his social class. It is unsurprising, given his disability and his consequent lack of military experience, that Goebbels had no involvement with the *Freikorps* movement nor with any of the other paramilitary bands which exerted such a formative influence on many future Nazis. Goebbels never displayed any interest in the idealized agrarian schemes which appealed to many critics of capitalist industrialization and urbanization; nor was he attracted, as many were, to esoteric forms of occult thinking and practice. Perhaps more surprisingly, given that Goebbels was a lover of nature and landscape, and – despite his disability – enjoyed walking, he took no part in any of the autonomous youth movements which flourished in Germany after 1918.

Jeffrey Herf has introduced the ideal typical concept of 'reactionary modernism' to the analysis of right-wing intellectualism in the Weimar Republic, seeking thereby to extend our understanding of those who, while hostile to central currents of Enlightenment thought, embraced the use of modern technology, and sought to integrate this with anti-democratic and illiberal doctrines. He frequently uses Goebbels as an important representative and spokesperson of 'reactionary modernism', drawing on speeches he made after 1930.[55] We should be clear that the young Goebbels was in no meaningful sense a 'reactionary modernist'. It is striking how little interest he took in anything technical or technological. He did not, for example, share the widespread passion in Germany for aviation, a key marker of technological modernity; he was not interested in weapons, or in any branch of military technology. Even in the arts, he had no apparent interest in the fields of culture and media most affected by technology, that is to say cinema and photography. His own creative energies were expressed with the most traditional tools: pen, ink, and paper.

Having been brought up in a small town of around 45,000 inhabitants, Goebbels actually had a limited experience of modernity. He had briefly lived as a student in Munich, and worked in Cologne, both much larger cities, but his overwhelming experience was decidedly provincial. Goebbels had chiefly experienced modernity in two ways. Rheydt was part of a much larger industrial area and he had grown up alongside factory workers, alternating between shifts. In his early writings Goebbels had engaged with some of the social problems thrown up by industrialization. He was also aware of certain incursions of modernism in culture and the arts. It is clear that he had seen a number of plays which he himself described as 'Expressionist', and had adopted certain aspects of their style in his own play *Die Saat: ein Geschehen in drei Akten* (*Sowing Seeds: An Occurrence in Three Acts*), written in 1920. He was similarly aware of some of the developments in music which were alarming conservatives like Hans Pfitzner, and here it appears that his own attitude was entirely reactionary.[56] Towards both industrialization and artistic modernism Goebbels had very equivocal attitudes. To understand these we need to look very closely at the words he used when referring to them. Goebbels in 1923 did not write down in extended form what he believed in, nor did he develop sophisticated critiques of social, cultural, or political currents around himself. He wrote allusively and aphoristically, often structuring his most important ideas around pairs of words, or oppositions. This use of key antagonisms – that between Western 'civilization' and German *Kultur* is one example – was characteristic of much *völkisch* and 'anti-democratic thought'.[57] We should be aware that typically the individual words meant much more than might initially appear from their translation into English. Kurt Sontheimer notes:

> In the centre of anti-democratic thought there is a series of concepts, which serve as *topoi* through the whole anti-democratic literature. They are more than descriptions of a thing, they are verbal symbols for political myths, they are leading ideas [*Leitideen*] which were to become a vision, and to inspire political action.[58]

With this in mind we can better understand the series of oppositions Goebbels had presented in his diary: 'Race – Intellect; Creativity – Reproduction; Art – Science; Industrial capitalism – Stock Exchange capitalism'. The first pairing in particular appears strange in English, as the two nouns are not straightforwardly related or opposed. By 'race' Goebbels meant everything genuine, pure, spontaneous, organic, natural, inspired, and authentic. He meant the 'German race', a vital wellspring from which all else flowed. In contrast, by 'intellect' Goebbels meant everything contrived, overwrought, artificial, shallow, imitative, devious, and manipulative. Here he saw all the qualities of the Jewish mind, and it was from this initial polarity that his other three oppositions took meaning. Thus the German race alone – he thought – could be genuinely creative. This was its great enduring quality. The Jewish race, in opposition, could only reproduce, or produce pale and distorted imitations. The opposition between art and science is at first sight puzzling, and might be misinterpreted to cast Goebbels as a romantic and a Luddite. 'Art' is clearly associated here with the German race, and is its great creation and treasure. 'Science', by contrast, is understood as a Jewish manipulation, a particular mode of thinking, and is not intended to include the insights of German physics, mathematics, chemistry, or the products of German industry. This is reflected in the final opposition, a commonly voiced polarity in *völkisch* circles between the idea of productive labour, identified as a German virtue, associated with genuine need and use, and Jewish 'stock exchange capitalism', or 'finance capitalism', perceived as entirely unproductive, again manipulative, exploitative, and destructive. This is why Goebbels preceded his four pairings with the declaration that 'The problem of race is indeed the deepest, and most secretive which must be grasped in public life today.' He saw all aspects of human behaviour as derivations from and reflections of race.

This also helps us to understand the young Goebbels' attitude towards party politics. Spengler had written: 'But to-day Parliamentarism is in full decay ... Every modern election, in fact, is a civil war carried on by ballot-box and every sort of written and spoken stimulus.'[59] Following this view, Goebbels detested the idea of multi-party democracy, seeing it not as a system allowing a robust contestation of plural viewpoints, but as a dishonest and commercialized arena for haggling and trading. Thus he saw it as dominated by 'the Jewish spirit'. He mistrusted the idea of any party which openly represented a sectional interest, like the Social Democrats, the Communists, or the Catholic Centre, and at this stage of his life he wished a plague on all their houses. This is why he stood aloof from the disturbances in Rheydt and Mönchen-Gladbach which surrounded him in October 1923, and commented with equal scepticism on all the parties involved.

He adopted instead an attitude of waiting in supplication, in hope for some kind of solution which he could as yet only dimly discern. This was a politics of deep pessimism, but not of despair. In another passage from Hesse's *Peter Camenzind*, which had impressed Goebbels so much, the novel's young hero articulates a strikingly similar attitude: 'Despite my cynicism and mild sophistication, I still kept an aim in my thoughts, a target of happiness and self-fulfilment. I had no idea what form it would take. All I felt was that life was bound to spill some wonderful piece of luck at my feet, fame of some kind, love perhaps, a satisfaction of my longing and a heightening of my being.'[60]

It was in this mood of deferred hope that Goebbels wrote in his diary a sentence which he later used in a fictional work, one which has frequently been quoted out of context and typically misunderstood: 'What we believe in is indeed also immaterial, if we only believe. The *Volk* which loses its belief loses itself.'[61] The first of these two propositions (which is usually quoted in isolation) has typically been understood as an expression of boundless cynicism and opportunism.[62] Goebbels did not mean that all systems of thought were equally valid, or that one could simply pick and choose amongst them as appeared tactically useful. It was an expression of a hope still inchoate, a belief in the *Volk* as yet unaccompanied by any clear sense of how the *Volk* would escape from decline and chaos.

Goebbels' mood fluctuated violently at this time. In quick succession he produced three literary works, and while he was writing there were moments when he was intoxicated with creative spirit. On 2 November he started a drama called *Prometheus*, which he dedicated to Richard Flisges. Over the next few days he worked obsessively, completing *Prometheus* in a fortnight. At the same time, after lying awake all one night, he worked out the idea for a second play, *The Wanderer*, in which the figure of Christ returned to the earth and visited suffering mankind.[63] This too was soon finished, and on 12 December he sent *Prometheus* to the City Theatre in Düsseldorf, and *The Wanderer* to a theatre in Cologne, with high hopes that they would be accepted for performance.[64]

At the same time, Goebbels was still reading voraciously: he wrote at some length about his reading of Dostoyevsky – of course – Strindberg, Hesse, Gogol, and the Swedish female writer Selma Lagerlöf. Although living in straitened circumstances, he was still able to attend public lectures, plays, concerts, and recitals. On 23 November he wrote:

E. Potz (from Rheydt) played Bach on the organ. (Obviously, Bach belongs to the organ.) Bach, a towering edifice of sound, harmony, and counterpoint. A good, German soul, restorative for us modern men.[65]

On 13 December he attended a talk on Vincent van Gogh which impressed him hugely. Van Gogh, he wrote, was 'A seeker after God, a Christ figure.'[66]

Just as Goebbels' mood alternated with his bouts of creativity, so it oscillated with his feelings for Else Janke. She was often away from Rheydt at this time, leaving Goebbels to reflect on her, and on their feelings for one another. On 27 October he noted that they had arrived at a new compromise, writing: 'I believe that she loves me very much.' However, later in the same entry he wrote: 'She is of the wrong race.'[67] On 14 November 1923 Else was back in Rheydt:

Yesterday evening walked with E. after the theatre through the clear, cold star-bright night. A mist was rising from the darkened meadows. Silence and stillness. Darkness and the light of the stars in constant struggle. Blessed wandering through the night. Mute, silent, close to the world-spirit [*Weltgeist*].

Earlier in the same entry, he had written:

Jewry is the poison which is bringing the body of the European *Volk* to death.[68]

As the nights grew longer and the winter set in, Goebbels was preoccupied with death. On 12 December he recorded the fate of an old woman living nearby who had died of hunger and cold in her room, without coal. Else was ill, and clearly things were very difficult with his own family.[69] On 23 December, thick flakes of snow began to fall, prompting the lonely writer to think of the dead Richard Flisges, and of 'a still, hero's grave at Schliersee in the deep, deep snow'.[70] The evening before, the local newspaper in Rheydt had published a small eulogy by Goebbels, 'To his dead friend Richard Flisges', in which he explored themes of redemption and resurrection which already preoccupied him. Goebbels concluded the article with a poem, writing: 'So I send this greeting to you, even in the empire of the dead.'[71] Despite this minor literary success, Christmas brought no joy. Rather the reverse: on 29 December Goebbels poured out his pent-up frustration in his diary:

Mother is ill in bed. Disorder upon disorder in the house. A terrible, desolate scene this morning. I've had enough of it here. I sense that I am too much here. I have to get out of this hole. I am on the verge of breaking out, maybe never to come back. If only I knew where! Here I have plenty to eat, elsewhere though nothing, absolutely nothing. Here in the house nobody knows anything about spiritual need. Here man lives from bread alone. It is dreadful, atrocious. I am the bad one here, the renegade, the apostate, the outlaw, the atheist, the revolutionary. I am the only one who can do nothing, whose advice is never sought, whose judgement is too unimportant to listen to. The others – particularly Conrad – they are the virtuous, the clever ones, the ones who understand business. People interfere with my private affairs, they want to know whether I go to church, tell me that I don't need a room to work in … O suffering upon suffering. And no way out. What shall I do?[72]

Without money, Goebbels was trapped in Rheydt, and he knew it. On New Year's Eve, he reflected further on his situation:

I love Else, and feel myself more deeply tied to her since she gave herself to me. But love for her is at the same time joy and agony. If we join together, we will have to fight always, infinitely for our love. It is said, a man can only experience one great, unconditional love in a lifetime. If that is true, then mine was my love for Anka. I did love her most deeply; I loved her as one loves in heaven. That is why I can never, never, forget her. I want, even today, to tell Else the truth about this. She must understand this. How often I long for you with all the heat of my yearning in the long, bitter, sleepless nights, Anka, my dear, my divine.[73]

Although there is a suggestion in the first line of this extract that Else had agreed to have sex with Goebbels, from all other evidence it seems that Goebbels was referring to a renewed mental commitment between the two of them. It was therefore in a state of turmoil that Goebbels started 1924. He was further cast down within a few days by news that his plays had been rejected in Cologne and in Düsseldorf. Undaunted, he sent the manuscripts to theatres in Frankfurt and Duisburg. As ever, he sought consolation in the arts. On 25 January he wrote in great anticipation about the impending visit of the Resi Quartet to Rheydt: 'The last Beethoven string quartets: only a god can speak like that. Beethoven writes his late music like the evangelist.'[74] The concert did not disappoint him, and he subsequently compared the Resi Quartet to other ensembles:

The Budapest: Quartet of precision. The Gewandhaus: Quartet of the sweets. Resi: Quartet of the four temperaments … Quartet op. 131. Beethoven's last offering. One thought the earth must have disappeared. One stands before the doors of eternity. Can one sense anything deeper?[75]

He turned also to Tolstoy over the next few days, and in February he again had the opportunity to hear some contemporary music. Walter Gieseking was playing Pfitzner's Piano Concerto in nearby Mönchen-Gladbach, conducted by Walter

Abendroth, and Goebbels' enthusiasm for this music, and what he thought it represented, spilt over into a vicious tirade. Pfitzner, he wrote, was a 'good, German, master'; his concerto was 'grand, gracious, light, sparkling, dreamily romantic, breathlessly growing to a brilliant conclusion'. It reminded him of other great German artists, of Dürer, Grünewald, Eichendorff, and Mörike, but it provoked him also to think of the contemporary modernist composer Franz Schreker, and he wrote: 'Pack up your music, Herr Franz Schreker. Go and play in Jerusalem, or in a café.'[76]

Still his relationship with Else alternately repelled and attracted him. They met up in nearby Remscheid, and Goebbels wrote: 'Else got on my nerves from time to time, and then she was good and loving again. I am not finding any clarity with her.'[77] Despite his failure to get *Prometheus* or *The Wanderer* accepted for performance, Goebbels was still writing, working now on an autobiographical novel, *Michael Voorman: The Destiny of a Man in Pages from his Diary*, and taking some pleasure in that. Goebbels had first written an autobiographical manuscript with this title in 1919. In 1924, he wrote a very different manuscript, dedicated to Richard Flisges, using the same title, in which the central character was, as he put it, 'a combination of two people, Richard and I'. 'Michael Voorman' in this version was a wounded war veteran who leaves student life to dedicate himself to work as a miner amongst the *Volk*. There he finds a new sense of belonging and faith, but meets a 'hero's death' in a mining accident.[78] In early March Goebbels finished *Michael Voorman*, and wrote:

Again, the well-known time of tiredness and apathy after intensive work. I have not the least inclination either to read or to write. The only thing which pleases me is the sunshine, which lies with youthful pleasure on streets and fields. God be thanked. That was a real winter inside and outside. And now the spring will come.

He finished his entry with these words:

With Else, agony and stress; it must come to an end soon. And then? Don't think about it! Wait, wait on all things, while one is so stretched and taut. The most terrible pain of youth: this awful waiting!!![79]

2
'Starting to Find Firm Ground'

In Munich, Nuremberg, and Bayreuth a boundless jubilation would have broken out, a huge enthusiasm through the German Reich, and when the first division of the German National Army had left the last square meter of Bavarian soil and for the first time stepped on Thuringian land, we would have seen that the *Volk* there would have rejoiced. The people would have recognized that German suffering has an end, but could only come through an uprising. The pacifist, defeatist, completely immoral government in Berlin would have had to bend before the storm.

> Adolf Hitler, speaking about the potential outcome
> of the failed Nazi *Putsch* in Munich during his trial
> for high treason, 28 February 1924.[1]

On 13 March 1924, Goebbels made a striking entry in his diary: 'I am busying myself with Hitler and the national socialist movement, and will indeed have to do this much more. Socialism and Christ. An ethical foundation. Away from ossified materialism. Back to dedication and to God!'[2] Over the next ten days, Goebbels commented several times more on Hitler. On 15 March he noted the range of issues that Hitler was addressing: 'Communism, the Jewish question, Christianity, the Germany of the future', and added, 'I will have to grapple seriously with them.'[3] On 17 March he wrote: 'Hitler touches on many questions. But he makes the solution very simple. Perhaps the end is right, but I am not convinced about the means. And the Christ-like nature of this man has indeed nothing any longer in common with Christ himself. What is liberating about Hitler is the involvement of a really upright and truthful personality. One finds that so rarely in our world of party interests.'[4] Three days later, his enthusiasm was growing: 'Hitler is an idealist, who has enthusiasm. A man who is bringing new belief to the German people. I am reading his speeches, I am allowing myself to be inspired by him and carried to the stars ... National and social consciousness. Down with materialism. New fervour, real dedication to greatness, to the Fatherland, to Germany. We are always seeking the way. But here is a will. He is already finding the way.'[5] On 22 March he wrote: 'Only Hitler continually concerns me. This man is indeed no intellectual. But his wonderful *élan*, his verve, his enthusiasm, his German feeling.' Later in the same entry, he added, sarcastically: 'In Munich the Hitler trial is coming to an end. The state prosecutor has demanded that Adolf Hitler should get eight years of fortress imprisonment. Perhaps the most ardent German will be locked up – to protect the Republic.'[6]

Like many Germans, and indeed many others outside Germany, Goebbels' first acquaintance with Hitler – or rather, with his ideas – came from newspaper reports of his trial for high treason in Munich, which followed the failed Nazi *Putsch* of 9 November 1918. As we have seen, the actual *Putsch* seems not to have greatly interested Goebbels, and nor had he previously taken any particular note of either Hitler or the Nazi Party in Munich. These must indeed have seemed very distant to the young writer hundreds of miles away in the Rhineland. At the trial, which lasted from 26 February to 27 March 1924, Hitler was allowed to deliver lengthy speeches, and these were widely reported in Germany and abroad.[7] Although Goebbels clearly had certain reservations about Hitler, he clearly sensed from this first engagement that he was in some ways a kindred spirit. Even though Goebbels was not actually to meet Hitler for many months, this was a turning point in his life, propelling him into an active engagement with politics. Within days of the conclusion of the Hitler trial, Goebbels was planning the publication of a newspaper with his old school friend, Fritz Prang, who had previously been involved with the Nazi Party in Munich. On 5 April 1924, Goebbels and Prang founded 'a regional national socialist group',[8] and over the next few weeks they, and a few others, threw themselves into campaigning for the *Reichstag* election which had been announced for 4 May.

Following the *Putsch* of November 1923, the Nazi Party had been banned, and when Hitler was sentenced to five years' imprisonment in March 1924, the party fell into some disarray. This suited Hitler, who did not wish to see anyone else usurp the leadership in his absence, and he was relatively content to let the party's affairs fall into disorganization, and for its senior figures to bicker amongst themselves. The NSDAP (*Nationalsozialistische Deutsche Arbeiterpartei* (National Socialist German Workers' Party)) had been largely a regionally based, Bavarian organization. Its headquarters was in Munich, and its popular base – such as it was – was also there, and in surrounding towns and villages. The party newspaper, the *Völkischer Beobachter* (*Racial Observer*), edited by one of Hitler's earliest comrades, Alfred Rosenberg, had been published in Munich; along with the party itself, it was proscribed after the November *Putsch*.[9] All around Germany there were hundreds of right-wing, nationalist, militarist, *völkisch* groups, and it was with one of these in the Rhineland, the *Deutschvölkische Freiheitspartei* (or German-*völkisch* Freedom Party), led by Friedrich Wiegershaus, that Goebbels had his first practical experience of politics.[10]

Significantly, at this early stage, Goebbels was concerned above all with cultural politics. He described how the newspaper he planned with Fritz Prang was to

2. Ludendorff and Hitler during their trial for high treason in March 1924. Hundreds of miles away, Goebbels – who had never met Hitler – wrote: 'I am reading his speeches, I am allowing myself to be inspired by him and carried to the stars.' (*TBJG*, 20 March 1924, TI, 1/I, pp. 108–9.)

be 'a monthly journal for German art and culture in the Rhineland, in a greater German, anti-internationalist spirit. Therefore to a degree national socialist, while avoiding anything demagogic or cheaply patriotic. Towards a national people's community (*Volksgemeinschaft*). Out of the morass of party politics.' Goebbels was now obsessed with what he called the 'Jewish question'. Echoing a central *völkisch* concern in the early Weimar Republic, he wrote that 'the Jewish spirit of decay is most terribly effective in German art and science, in theatre, music, literature, in schools, and in the press'.[11] At the foundation meeting of the 'national socialist group' in Rheydt, the perceived threat from the Jews was apparently the chief topic of conversation, and in Goebbels' summary of the meeting, combating this threat was identified as the group's priority: 'The political question is in this connection of secondary importance. The Jew poisons us with sweet, insinuating methods. The proclaimed Zionist is indeed the most respectable Jew. One knows then where one stands. The so-called national Jews are the most dangerous. They are the snakes which we are clasping to our own breast.'[12] Over the next few days, Goebbels came back and back to this, 'the most burning issue of the present'.[13]

Typically, he was reading about the 'Jewish question'. In early April 1924 he read Henry Ford's *The International Jew*, and although he was no natural friend of Ford, whom he identified as 'the richest man in the world', he was doubly impressed that Ford should see 'Jewish capitalism' as such a pernicious influence. Through Ford, Goebbels was introduced to the 'Protocols of the Elders of Zion'. This document purported to be the account of a conspiracy of Jewish 'Elders' with 'the single aim of achieving Jewish dominion over the entire world'. It was a forgery produced and first published in Tsarist Russia before 1914, and in numerous translations around the world after 1918. The first German edition appeared in 1920, and it rapidly became a best seller. Around Germany, numerous public meetings were devoted to discussion of the 'Protocols', and there was considerable debate about their authenticity.[14] Goebbels was intelligent enough to see that the 'Protocols' were not genuine, but his response to them was revealing: 'I believe that The Protocols of the Elders of Zion are a forgery; not because the world view or the Jewish aspirations outlined in them are too utopian or fantastical – one sees indeed how one demand from the Protocols is linked to another, how a systematic plan to destroy the world and leave it in ruins is laid out – but because I don't believe the Jews are so boundlessly stupid that they would not have kept such important protocols secret. Therefore: I believe in the inner truth, but not the factual truth of the protocols.' Musing further about the problem, he proclaimed his own, newly found standpoint: 'I stand on the *völkisch* side: I hate the Jew from instinct and from understanding. I hate him from the depths of my soul.'[15]

Goebbels' confusion about Else was never far from his feelings about the wider 'Jewish question', and typically, as on 31 March 1924, after raving in his diary about the destructive evil of the Jews, he turned to her:

Now I hope to become free of all racial ties. How often has the Jewish spirit in a part of Else's behaviour oppressed and anguished me. I have suffered infinitely in my soul from it. And indeed, I have not been able to free myself from it. Partly from old love, partly from pity, from consideration, from sentimentality. Else is so dear and good. But I don't love her any more. The occasional emotional outbursts I have for her are mostly whims, sap rising, and sensuality. But, damn it again, I have got to get away from this.

Her sister Trude is a typical Jewish girl, who unites in herself, in concentrated form, all of the physical and mental signs of her mother's race.

A bastardized race will be sterile, and must go under [*kaputt gehen*]. I cannot help them out!!![16]

Clearly, Goebbels did communicate his ambivalent feelings for Else to her, but he was unable to break away. On 3 April he wrote: 'Else cried the whole day.'[17] On 5 April, before he plunged into his reading of Henry Ford and the 'Protocols of the Elders of Zion', he saw her off at the station, when she went home to nearby Mörs: 'The poor, dear, good thing. Tears came into my eyes. With what anguish of soul she travels away. And she bears no atom of guilt. She is so good. She still wanted to make me joyful when we parted. And I was so full of doubt, and divided. Anguish upon anguish!'[18] On 15 April he met with Else in Krefeld, and his confusion was renewed: 'Else in despair. And I can't help her any more. We must get through this. No bastards as children. I love her more than ever. But the future. The responsibility. God, what should I do? Help her! I have to help myself ... Else, I love you more than I had ever thought.'[19]

In these first months of his political awakening, Goebbels was equally involved with literature and music. He still had time to read, and was again revising *Michael Voorman*. Laboriously, he typed several copies, and sent them hopefully to four publishers in early April. He sent another to Richard Flisges' fiancée Olgi Esenwein, who was then living in Switzerland.[20] On 28 March he went to a performance of Bach's *St Matthew Passion* in Mönchen-Gladbach, and, significantly, wrote more about this in his diary than any of his entries on Hitler at this time. The music impressed him deeply, particularly the chorales, but he was critical of the text, writing that several of the sentiments it expressed were 'tasteless'. He singled out the frequently repeated words from the closing chorus, 'rest peacefully' (*ruhe sanfte*), which he described as a 'banal conclusion'.[21] The *St Matthew Passion* is a setting of the story of Christ's crucifixion, using the text from the gospel according to Matthew, interspersed with a commentary written by Christian Friedrich Henrici. Goebbels' response to the work in early 1924 reveals much about his evolving relationship with Christianity. He had been brought up in an intensely devout, church-going family, and his parents had entertained hopes that he might become a priest. He had experienced a great deal of religious instruction in school, and was well versed in the Bible. He was fascinated by the figure of Christ, and undoubtedly identified himself, and others, like Richard Flisges, and now Adolf Hitler, with Christ. The semi-autobiographical hero of *Michael Voorman* was consciously modelled on Christ, and Goebbels thought it an astonishing coincidence, if not a sign from fate, that Hitler appeared to him to resemble his own fictional creation.[22] As we have also seen, Goebbels frequently called upon God in his diary, invoking his name in moods of desperation and self-pity.

By 1924, though, Goebbels had moved a long way from central aspects of the Christian religion, above all its messages of compassion, forgiveness, and recon-ciliation. As he became involved with practical *völkisch* politics, he celebrated the engagement, the struggle, and the hatred which characterized this fissiparous movement. Repeatedly, in the spring of 1924, he wrote about his new political faith in mystical tones, but he also celebrated a commitment to action, a credo he summed up in the formula 'Idealism and fanaticism'.[23] It was Bach's pietist message of renunciation which he found so unsatisfactory, even though he was moved by the music. Goebbels was in no mood to 'rest peacefully' in the weeks before the *Reichstag* election in May 1924. He was attending meetings, discussing issues, posting up placards, and getting involved in confrontations with Communists. Politics in Germany at this time were conducted in an atmosphere of violence, and Goebbels revelled in this. In May, as the voting was concluded, he wrote: 'He who has the stronger fist always has the final right.'[24] Some weeks later, he recorded that he had been attacked by six to eight men, an event arranged, he thought, by 'damned Semites'.[25] More significantly, it was in this election campaign that Goebbels gained his first experience as a political speaker. His first speeches were given to small groups of local activists, and appear to have been carefully written beforehand. On 3 May 1924 he wrote: 'Yesterday a talk on our goals and the Semitic danger before an invited circle. Spoke freely for the first time. Good success.'[26]

The *völkisch* 'block' for which Goebbels campaigned in Rheydt and surrounding towns had some success in the May elections, gaining 6.5 per cent of the vote nationally, or 32 *Reichstag* deputies under the Republic's proportional voting system. Ten of these deputies were from Hitler's still proscribed NSDAP. In the months after the election the *völkisch* alliance fell apart, riven by regional and ideological differences. Goebbels had been temporarily buoyed up by the campaigning, but found himself stagnating in the weeks after this. He and Prang discussed again their planned cultural-political journal, and he wrote that they intended to travel to Munich to talk to Hitler about it, but this was only a pipe-dream. There were occasional political meetings, but Goebbels saw all too clearly the limitations of many of the people who were attracted to the movement; and he was appalled by the triviality of local politics. He set out to draft a series of three talks to be delivered in the towns of the occupied Rhineland, starting with 'an introduction to the Jewish problem', but found it difficult to sustain his motivation. As the days lengthened, he had long hours to spend alone, at home, and he relapsed into depression.

None of Goebbels' literary offerings had been accepted for publication, and he was desperately short of money. He proclaimed in his diary his need to work, but in truth he was doing little but reading. In these weeks he got through Marx's *Das Kapital*, works by Hoffman, Daudet, d'Annunzio, Cervantes, and Herwig, as well as a number of *völkisch* texts. He also read books by political opponents, including Gustav Noske, Rosa Luxemburg, and August Bebel. He turned back to Dostoyevsky, rekindling his faith in the Russian people. He was still corresponding with Olgi Esenwein, and wrote about this to her. She replied, perhaps speaking for Richard Flisges as well: 'In a certain sense Russia really does remain our homeland [*Heimat*].'[27] Goebbels also read Richard Wagner's autobiography, and identified strongly with the young composer in his Paris years, when he felt himself unrecognized and oppressed by Jewish theatre directors. This prompted him to write: 'The eternal question of one's own significance! What am I, what am I for, what is my task, and what is my meaning? Should I believe in myself? Why do others not believe in me? Am I a layabout, or a genius, who is waiting on God's word?'[28] Goebbels stayed up late into the night to finish Wagner's autobiography, taking some consolation from learning that for five years, in the middle of his composing career, Wagner had not written a note of music. Interestingly, Goebbels did not share Hitler's unqualified admiration for Wagner. He admired the composer as a young man, but criticized his predilection in later life for luxury and splendour. He compared the master of Bayreuth unfavourably with Beethoven.[29] To compound Goebbels' misery, Else left in early August to holiday in Switzerland; he could not accompany her as he had no money.

There was one ray of hope on the horizon: the annual meeting of the *völkisch* groups was due to take place in Weimar in mid-August, and Goebbels planned to attend this with Fritz Prang, combining his interest in politics with a visit to a city linked with the giants of German literary culture, Goethe and Schiller. Prang had assured Goebbels that he could get the money to pay his railway fare. On 14 August Goebbels went to meet Prang at the station, only to be told that there was no money. Prang boarded the train, leaving Goebbels to walk home and reflect again on his apparently hopeless situation. The next day he was writing in his diary that a party conference like that in Weimar was in any case an awful idea. 'If only Else were here,' he added, but he then wrote: 'The money is there! Off to Weimar!'[30]

The Weimar meeting in 1924 has been written off as fairly insignificant, demonstrating only how impotent and divided the *völkisch* movement was without Hitler's leadership. Several standard histories of the Nazi movement do not even mention it.[31] Its importance in Goebbels' early political development should not be underrated. His visit to Weimar came at a vital point, when he was losing his faith with politics. This was the young activist's first real participation in a wider national movement. In Weimar he saw crowds of nationalists, walking in the streets, gathering in the National Theatre, and drinking in pubs. For the first time he was part of a Nazi festival, and he revelled in the sight of marching columns with flags and swastikas, of lorries full of uniformed SA men, in the sound of singing and of calls of '*Heil*'.[32] He observed the presence of men from different parts of Germany, notably from Bavaria, and he enjoyed the way that Rhinelanders like himself were celebrated as 'frontline' opponents of the hated French occupiers. In his diary he sketched impressions of the senior figures of the movement who were present: Ludendorff, the old war hero; von Graefe and Gregor Strasser, leaders of the *völkisch* groups in north-west Germany; Gottfried Feder, Hitler's economics adviser; and Julius Streicher from Nuremberg, the editor of the anti-Semitic magazine *Der Stürmer*. Goebbels was not so carried away as to overlook the obvious failings of some of these. Streicher, he noted, was a 'Berserker. Perhaps a bit pathological.' He was unimpressed by some of the speakers he heard, and we sense already his own feeling that given the chance, he could do better. Goebbels still felt he was something of an outsider in this gathering, but he plucked up the courage to speak to Ludendorff, and felt that he had been acknowledged. He also spoke for an hour with Theodor Fritsch, the editor of the *Handbook of the Jewish Question*, an anti-Semitic book first published in the 1880s, and still selling in revised editions. Fritsch, Goebbels wrote, was like 'a dear old uncle', one who nonetheless strengthened all Goebbels' anti-Semitic convictions.[33]

Goebbels' impressions of the Nazi movement in Weimar were deepened by his perception that this was the cradle of German culture. He felt that he, and the others there, were 'under the eyes of Goethe'. He found time to visit Goethe's house, and sat for an hour in Goethe's favourite spot, where he wrote a few lines to Else. He also visited Schiller's house, and was deeply moved by a sense of identification with the great writer. He visited the Liszt memorial, and reflected on how the young Richard Wagner, fleeing from the authorities in Dresden, had stopped in Weimar. Reflecting on the greatness of German culture, and on the readiness for suffering these artists had shown, he wrote: 'The strong fist alone will not suffice. Only the spirit lasts through the centuries.' He concluded his account of the weekend thus:

> The *völkisch* question is becoming mixed in my mind with all intellectual and religious questions. I am beginning to think in a *völkisch* way. That has nothing more to do with politics. That is a world view [*Weltanschauung*].
>
> I am starting to find firm ground. Ground that I can stand on. We are fighting for only one thing: for real German freedom. One should think of nothing else today, than that Germany must again be free.[34]

Given that *völkisch* nationalism and Nazism are not typically associated with 'freedom', it is worth considering what Goebbels meant by 'real German freedom'. He certainly did not mean anything like the typical liberal-democratic understandings of the word 'freedom', associated above all with respect for the individual and with constitutional protection for individual rights such as the freedom of conscience, of expression, of association, and from arbitrary arrest. Kurt Sontheimer has analysed how in *völkisch* ideology 'freedom' was conceived of as an organic moral connection to a hierarchically structured community. In this sense it meant acceptance of the precedence of the community over the individual, of the role of 'the leader', and an enjoyment of the order and discipline consequent upon the working of this hierarchy. It was 'the freedom of belonging'. In a collective sense the 'freedom' of the German *Volk* meant freedom from the shackles of the Treaty of Versailles, and from the imagined exploitation of international Jewish finance capital. Sontheimer concludes: 'The anti-democratic versions of the idea of freedom are fundamentally nothing other than seductive variations of un-freedom in the name of freedom.'[35]

Goebbels was not troubled by these liberal scruples. He did experience uncertainty after Weimar, but there was no doubt that his future now lay in the Nazi movement. In the next few months he threw himself into local politics, displaying the extraordinary energy which marked his rise to prominence. This was when he found his *métier*, when, significantly, his political engagement crystallized around two activities: writing and speaking. A day after returning from Weimar he had completed five articles intended for publication in the journal *Völkische Freiheit* (*Völkisch Freedom*), run by Friedrich Wiegershaus. That same evening, he met with a small group of supporters in Mönchen-Gladbach to found a regional group.[36] Significantly, rather than remaining on the edges of this meeting, Goebbels spoke for one and a half hours on 'the fundamental problems of the *völkisch* world-view', and wrote about this experience: 'A young man sat directly in front of me, and I noticed during the speech how his eyes started to glow. His inner passion came back to me and had the effect of creating a deep inner connection between us two unknown people, which appeared to leave him and me related, as if in our souls, at that moment.' Goebbels was beginning to realize the effect that he – as a speaker – could have on an audience.[37]

It is important to consider the time and place in which Goebbels created himself as a young politician. The Nazi Party itself was at this time fragmented, disorganized, and leaderless. Even in Bavaria it had broken up into different local groups, and separate organizations like the SA. Some of its earlier leading figures, like its figurehead, Ludendorff, were drifting away, in his case towards a patently absurd form of mysticism. Hitler himself, although initially receiving visitors in Landsberg prison, had withdrawn into work on his book, and did not concern himself with details of political circumstances outside. In large parts of Germany, the Nazi Party had only skeletal local organizations, and it appeared of little relevance on the national stage, where acceptance of the Dawes Plan, rescheduling Germany's reparations payments, had paved the way for a period of relative economic stability. Almost exclusively, the Nazi Party was still a presence in and around Munich; much of its support there was drawn from the lower middle class.

In the Ruhr and the Rhineland, conditions were in some senses particularly unfavourable for the Nazis.[38] This was a densely urbanized industrial area, one of the most concentrated in Europe. Large cities like Düsseldorf and Cologne acted as centres for finance and administration; others like Essen and Duisburg were centres of heavy industry. There were dozens of smaller towns, often very sizeable in their own right, typically devoted to one or two industries. Some were based on iron and steel, many on coal mining; others, like Rheydt and

Mönchen-Gladbach, on textiles. Many of the towns, their populations swollen during the rapid industrial growth of the nineteenth century, had swallowed up surrounding villages, and now almost joined up with one another. Only thin stretches of countryside separated the built-up areas. The population of the Rhineland-Ruhr was overwhelmingly involved with industry: hundreds of thousands of people worked in the traditional heavy industries, coal, iron, and steel. The Social Democrats and the Communists, with their trade unions and networks of affiliated social groups, all with their own journals, newspapers, and local organizations, were strong. It was in this harsh industrial landscape that Goebbels learnt his trade. Just as Hitler's individual strength of personality and influence as a public speaker had played a critical role in the development of the Nazi movement in Bavaria, Goebbels contributed single-handedly to the creation of a parallel phenomenon in the most industrialized region of Germany. One difference stands out: in Munich Hitler attracted the attention, and the lavish financial support, of wealthy individuals and families. He soon affected a rather grand lifestyle, travelling in a Mercedes, supported by a retinue of dedicated helpers. Goebbels detested wealthy people, and, whether from indifference, unwillingness, or idealism, did not court them as Hitler did. He was more at home with workers, and, perhaps because he lived like them, in real poverty, they responded to him.

Goebbels' political activity after Weimar started at home. The following week, Else returned from Switzerland, and Goebbels met her for three days in Cologne. Evidently, this time brought them closer together, and Goebbels was able to share his new commitment with her. He had been made 'editor' of Wiegershaus' journal, the *Völkische Freiheit*, to be published in nearby Elberfeld, and on 1 September 1924 he took delivery of a new typewriter. He had not previously done much typing, and his first priority was to become proficient at this. He was delighted when Else and her friend Alma showed enthusiasm for learning to type, and greatly enjoyed sharing his new work with them. On 5 September he wrote, with almost breathless excitement: 'Little Else is my good little imp. She wants to help me with my work. Wants to learn to type and to be my secretary. That will make for beautiful, working winter evenings. I am looking forward to them.'[39] Almost every entry in his diary during this period contains some expression of his love for Else and appreciation of how good she was to him.

For the actual newspaper, which had only a tiny local circulation, Goebbels had to write 'a cultural-political essay, a review of the week's politics, a glossary, and various other small things'.[40] Wiegershaus had arranged for ten daily newspapers to be delivered to his new editor, and Goebbels noted with some distaste how he had to spend time reading them. This was his first involvement with practical journalism, and he learnt quickly. A significant feature of his early writing was his 'political diary', a personal column which he used to gain experience in commenting on foreign affairs. He developed a working style which demanded manic energy, often returning from a meeting in the small hours and then staying up to work on the newspaper. Goebbels was now speaking frequently to small meetings in and around Rheydt, and at first he was embarrassed, and characteristically cynical. On 3 September he spoke to a group of 'good burgers' in Wickrath. 'I will be a demagogue of the worst sort', he wrote, 'A people's speaker. But, along with that, one must work on oneself.'[41] A few days later, Goebbels attended a commemoration in nearby Elberfeld of the battle of Tannenberg in 1914; this was the last time he went to one of these meetings as a spectator rather than a participant, and had to watch others perform. He noted with dismay that there were arguments between national socialists and *völkisch* speakers, and gave a clear indication of his own sympathies in his comments on the leading Nazi present: 'Strasser speaks. The Municher. Hitler's spirit in his heart. The national socialist. We need to get someone like that here in the industrial area.'

Gregor Strasser, a tall man with great physical presence, was a pharmacist by training, who had risen to the rank of First Lieutenant during the First World War. Much of his political appeal was based on his ability to communicate with ex-soldiers. He had been active in the NSDAP since 1921, and his talents as an organizer and a speaker were highly regarded by Hitler.[42] Evidently, Goebbels was now coming to the attention of more established figures in the movement. At this meeting in Elberfeld he managed to get himself presented to Ludendorff, and he spent some time talking with Gregor Strasser. He also met Ernst Röhm, one of Hitler's closest personal friends: 'His face knocked about. The field soldier.'

Goebbels' point of contact with these men was Wiegershaus, who unwittingly thereby wrote his name into history. Goebbels desperately needed the *entrée* to higher Nazi circles that Wiegershaus could give him, and the opportunity to write and produce a small newspaper, but he thought the man a fool, likening him to the Weimar Republic's elderly President: 'Fritz Wiegershaus is the Papa Ebert of the company. But harmless.' Goebbels, who was much preoccupied with the issue of leadership, did not think for a moment that any of those at this meeting in Elberfeld, or the rally in Weimar, had the potential for leadership. He put his faith in the absent Hitler, whom he thought might be freed from prison in October: 'The movement lacks the unifying thought. That is Hitler: the firm pole around which all national socialist thought circles.'[43]

On 17 September Goebbels gave his next speech, but it was to 'daft peasants' in the village of Wickrathberg, a few miles south of Rheydt, and he admitted that he had stirred up no great enthusiasm.[44] The next night he had more success before a group of workers in Mönchen-Gladbach: 'The people were restlessly excited. Now the fire is spreading.'[45] In the next few days a 'worker friend' invited him to address a meeting in the nearby town of Neuss, and he spoke again in Rheydt. After this Goebbels noted:

My reputation as a speaker and cultural-political writer is going through the ranks of the adherents of national socialist thinking in the whole Rhineland.

This evening I have to speak in Neuss. I am not preparing for it at all. I am finding it not half as difficult as I had thought to speak extempore. But one has, above all, to have practice for that. And I am getting that in these little meetings of supporters.[46]

Evidently, the speech in Neuss went well, and Goebbels appears to have succeeded in creating a genuine sense of communion between speaker and audience: 'Saturday in Neuss was a great success. The idea is marching. We need not doubt anything with human material like this in our ranks.'[47]

Goebbels had discovered that he could get along with ordinary people, and this sense of shared endeavour was intoxicating. His diary at this time is full of reference to late night talks with small groups of workers, and with individuals like 'locomotive driver Florack'. He stayed up one night at home with him and seven others: 'A policeman, officials, a writer, a secretary, a wonderful little people, these Germans. Yes, with this *Volk* we can really start something.'[48] A few weeks later, a member of the local group in Rheydt gave Goebbels a present, a pedigree Dobermann bitch. Again and again he wrote of his belief in the workers, and in German youth.[49] He balanced this dewy-eyed romanticism with a shrewd appraisal of individuals. Fritz Prang, who had introduced Goebbels to the Nazi movement, was a frequent visitor in Rheydt at this time, but Goebbels was leaving him behind: 'Fritz Prang is diligent in our affairs, but somewhat nervous and haphazard in his work. We will have to take him in hand.'[50]

Even as Goebbels gained confidence in his own abilities, he saw ever more clearly the limitations of those around him. In October he spent a few days in Elberfeld working with Wiegershaus, and started to build a power base there. In speeches there he built up an enthusiastic following, although he was ever more critical of Wiegershaus, whom he saw as an over-comfortable bourgeois. Elberfeld, part of a conurbation with the town of Barmen on the opposite bank of the Rhine from Rheydt, was to be a centre of intrigue for the next six months as Goebbels commenced his dramatic rise to prominence in the Nazi movement. He had also come to the attention of the occupation authorities. On 23 October, the Goebbels' house in Rheydt was searched by Belgian police, which upset Goebbels' mother 'terribly', and after this Goebbels had to report to the local German police. They clearly sided with him, though, and Goebbels noted that the inspector who interviewed him in the morning greeted him cheerfully in Elberfeld on the same evening![51]

Goebbels now had his eyes set on greater things. Wiegershaus had invited him to travel to Berlin to discuss personally with Ludendorff whether the Field Marshal should stand in a future election for the Presidency of the Republic. On 30

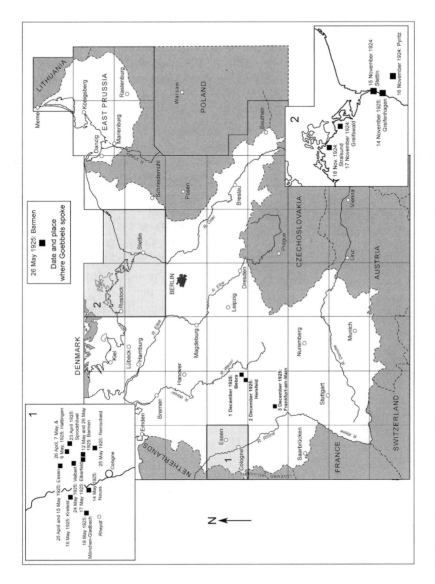

3. Map of Germany in the 1920s, showing some of Goebbels' first speaking tours.

October 1924 Goebbels took the train with Wiegershaus to the metropolis. Most writers on Goebbels have depicted romanticized versions of his first encounter with Berlin, placing it later in his career, and describing his shocked reaction to the fleshpots of the capital.[52] In fact, he recorded that on this first visit, he 'saw scarcely anything of the city'. His time was totally taken up with talks with various *völkisch* leaders, including Ludendorff, for whom Goebbels still had an unbounded admiration. He was less taken with the other *völkisch* deputies he met there: Graefe, Wulle, Reventlow, and Kube. Wiegershaus impressed him least of all.[53] Others, though, were impressed with Goebbels. He was invited to work in distant Pomerania by the leader of the Nazi and *völkisch* movement there, Theodor Vahlen, but he turned this down.[54] He did agree to travel to Pomerania for a series of speeches, and shortly after returning to Elberfeld he was back on the train.

On 13 November Goebbels travelled to Berlin, and from there to Greifenhagen on the Baltic coast, where he spoke, in his own words 'to an empty room'. Things were better in Stettin, where the hall was full, and in Pyritz, where he felt he had a great success. On 17 November he reached the university town of Greifswald, where he was hosted by a lawyer, Dr Jarmer.[55] Greifswald had recently been the scene of violent demonstrations after a planned visit there by the French anti-war writer Henri Barbusse. Vahlen, a professor of mathematics at the university, had stirred up controversy with outspoken speeches denouncing the French, and the German republican government which was prepared to allow people like Barbusse to speak in Greifswald. Nationalist and Nazi feeling was strong amongst the student body and some of the academic staff.[56] On the evening of 17 November Goebbels spoke in the town hall, 'in front of 1,000 people. I came right out of myself. People were raving with excitement. I was celebrated like a god. Much usable material. Oh, my Greifswald!'[57]

Goebbels was realizing that he possessed an extraordinary talent as a speaker. We may allow that he inflated the figures attending some of these early meetings, and that he idealized the enthusiasm of his audiences, but there is no doubt that he had an ability which put him head and shoulders above all other Nazi speakers, with the one exception of Hitler. Nor should we underestimate the difficulties facing him. Although he was often addressing a tiny audience of faithful supporters, he had always to face the possibility of the presence of opponents, mainly Communists, who would think nothing of disrupting proceedings. After his return from Greifswald, he spoke in Mönchen-Gladbach to an audience (by his reckoning) of '1,200 people, including 800 Jews.'[58] How he could identify these people as Jews is not clear. Most probably, he meant simply opponents. A few days later he spoke in Hamborn in the Ruhr 'in front of the Communists'.[59] These were not polite meetings, where a speaker might be listened to quietly, or with indifference. Indeed, Goebbels came to pride himself on his ability to win over a hostile audience.

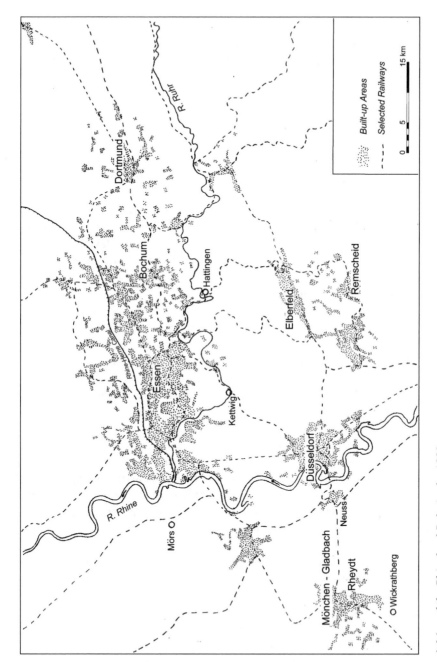

4. Map of the Rhineland-Ruhr in the 1920s.

We know little about Goebbels' early style as a public speaker; the first sound recordings of his speeches date from the early 1930s. He must have had a powerful voice, and been able to project this to crowds without amplification. Although he liked to prepare his speeches thoroughly beforehand, until the end of his life he could always improvise if called upon, and deliver an effective speech, even in the open air. After Victor Klemperer first heard Goebbels speaking, he wrote that he 'was doubly surprised at his bass and at the pastoral unctuousness and heartfelt tone of his delivery'.[60] This author would describe Goebbels' voice rather as a rich and sonorous baritone, unusually strong for a man with such a small frame. One thing should be absolutely clear: Goebbels did not copy Hitler. He had not heard Hitler speak when he took his first tentative steps as a public speaker, and he developed the techniques which were to serve him so well in the years ahead *before* he met him.[61] Goebbels combined an academic command of vocabulary and sentence structure with an ability to present ideas with great simplicity. He learnt to manipulate the emotions of an audience, using words, gestures, intonation, and tone. The pointing index finger, raised in admonition or warning next to his face, became a characteristic gesture, as did his more academic habit of striking the lectern or table in front of him to emphasize particular words.

Goebbels has often been described as an empty vessel, a man with no real feelings who mimicked a range of emotions as he felt necessary, and shamelessly manipulated the feelings of others. His detachment has often been cited as evidence of this, the way in which, after a speech, he would analyse his own performance and the reaction of the audience, looking to see which techniques had been most effective. There is abundant evidence to suggest that he did analyse his own performance after every speech – and indeed it would have been strange if he did not – but this does not mean that the emotions he projected during a speech were necessarily false or insincere. There is much more evidence to suggest that he was a passionate young man, who mingled his own personal discontents with wider public sentiments, and learnt how to articulate the feelings of larger groups. And although Goebbels used a self-consciously academic style, larding his speeches with literary quotes, and with historical examples, he could also make his audiences laugh. He developed a cruel and menacing style of sarcasm, in which he caricatured opponents, often with a deceptive flattery, and this was particularly savoured by his audiences. In an age before television, and in the last years before radios became household items in Germany, a working-class audience going to hear Goebbels speak was promised a heady mixture of confrontation, emotion, and entertainment. We will never now recapture the full flavour of these early speeches, because the first printed versions did not contain his extempore demolition of hecklers, and this was, by all accounts, what his audiences enjoyed most; this was why Goebbels particularly relished speaking to an audience which contained a fair leavening of opponents.

One early listener to Goebbels was Albert Krebs, who later served as *Gauleiter* (or area leader of the Nazi Party) in Hamburg between 1926 and 1928. He heard Goebbels speak in the winter of 1924, in Frankfurt-am-Main, and he later wrote that Goebbels, dressed in a green army shirt and the grey trousers of an infantry officer, started this speech with the words 'We who have been shot in the World War ...!' Krebs asserts that everyone in the audience presumed that the speaker had been wounded at the front; some thought Goebbels was an ex-fighter pilot. Apparently this later became something of a scandal in the movement, when Goebbels was accused in 1927 of pretending to be something he was not. Goebbels defended himself by arguing that in the winter of 1924–25 any speaker who wanted to challenge the politics of the establishment had to defend themselves against the charge of war-mongering, and that only war veterans could effectively do this; his adoption of the uniform was therefore no more than a harmless, and justified propaganda trick.[62] It is a bizarre story, and seems implausible. One would imagine that with audiences containing a high percentage of men who had been at the front, Goebbels would, pretending to be a wounded veteran, have run a grave risk of being exposed as a charlatan, with potentially fatal consequences for his credibility. If it is true, it certainly suggests a flexible approach to any idea of 'truth'.

In December 1924, as the *Reichstag* elections approached, Goebbels again had the opportunity to speak outside his home territory, and travelled to Hesse. A meeting in Frankfurt-am-Main went smoothly (this was presumably the one attended by Krebs), but others in Bebra and in Hersfeld were broken up by opponents. In the last days before the voting he spoke again locally in Velbert and in Kettwig, but the election results were disastrous for the *völkisch* block. It gained only 3 per cent of the votes, and its 32 deputies were reduced to 14, including only four Nazis. Goebbels was unimpressed by the electoral setback. He was by this time up to his neck in intrigues to replace Wiegershaus as *Gauleiter* of North Rhineland with one of two new colleagues, Axel Ripke and Karl Kaufmann. In January 1925, Wiegershaus dismissed Goebbels from the *Völkische Freiheit*, bringing to an end his first period of journalistic activity. Much has been written about the ensuing power struggle, and how over the next few months Goebbels adopted a socialist position, following Ripke, Kaufmann, and their superior, Gregor Strasser.[63] We should be cautious about this. Goebbels did frequently use the word '*Sozialismus*', and, as we have seen, he had an idealistic view of the German working class. He was repelled by the internationalism of Marxism (which he saw as a Jewish creed), and his brand of 'socialism', while rabidly anti-capitalistic, was always primarily nationalist in orientation. He had little interest in or knowledge of economics, and in his own understanding he inverted the Marxist idea of base and superstructure. For Marx, economic affairs took primacy, and determined the form of politics and of culture. Goebbels believed conversely that the 'idea' and the 'will' were formative, and that economics were secondary to them.

Goebbels had varying levels of admiration for Ripke, Kaufmann, and Strasser. Although he did in the winter of 1924–25 develop a genuine affection for Kaufmann, he was never close to Strasser. He admired Ripke, who was a writer, for his intellect, but in the final analysis, Goebbels thought he was a bourgeois, and not a revolutionary.[64] Curiously, Goebbels never thought of himself as the long-awaited leader of the *völkisch* movement. Even though he had not met Hitler, and learnt little more about him in these months, he anxiously awaited his release from Landsberg, and speculated about the direction he might then take. On 19 December he wrote: 'In the next few days it will be decided whether Hitler comes out. Lord God, give us this man back.' As ever, Goebbels mixed the personal with the political. On the same day he wrote: 'I have got to know a lovely woman. Elisabeth Gänsicke ... She reminds me greatly of Anka.'[65] Over the next few days this relationship strengthened, and Goebbels soon lost his head. Over Christmas and the New Year he was alternately seeing Else and Elisabeth, and conducting a similarly turbulent relationship with both. He quarrelled bitterly with Elisabeth in January, evidently over sex, and taxed himself in his diary with his unfairness to Else. Clearly his strong feelings for Elisabeth were, to an extent, reciprocated, and Goebbels continued seeing her for several weeks, but he was unable to commit to her. Else, perhaps suspecting something was afoot, was also demanding more from her penniless and often distracted suitor, and Goebbels noted sadly at this time that she still wanted to be 'a woman, and can not be a comrade'.[66] By the end of February, both women had broken off relations with him, leaving him sunk in self-pity.

For months Goebbels had been awaiting Hitler's release from prison, but this did not lead immediately to the resolution of his political problems. Interestingly it was only three days after Hitler's release from Landsberg on 20 December that he wrote in his diary: 'Adolf Hitler is free! Now we will separate ourselves from the reactionary *völkisch* people, and will be real national socialists again. *Heil, Adolf Hitler!*'[67] It was not until 27 February 1925 that Hitler spoke in public again, and announced the re-establishment of the Nazi Party; after this he was banned from further public speaking in Bavaria and in Prussia. For several months he effectively retired from public life to concentrate on preparing his prison writings for publication, leaving Goebbels and others to their own efforts.

Shortly before Hitler's formal announcement of the re-formation of the Nazi Party, changes were made to its organization in the Rhineland and Ruhr. Gregor Strasser was entrusted with the overall direction of the Party in northern Germany, and at a meeting in Hamm in February 1925, Goebbels was appointed as the business manager of his office in Elberfeld, with a small salary to commence in April.[68] Much has been written about this phase of the Nazi Party's history, and there has been considerable analysis of the development of Strasser's 'Westblock', the association of Nazi groups in north and western Germany.[69] In policy terms, Strasser's greater commitment to socialism has been stressed, and many writers have mistakenly portrayed Goebbels at this time almost as a frustrated Communist, moving into ideological opposition to Hitler.[70] In fact, there were in 1925 two developments which were of great significance in Goebbels' emergence as an important politician: first, his growing experience and reputation as a speaker, particularly before working-class audiences; and, second, his evolution as a political journalist. Both developments happened before Goebbels met or heard Hitler in person, at a time typically depicted as one of stagnation in the larger development of the Nazi Party.

After quarrelling with both Else Janke and with Elisabeth Gensicke, Goebbels again experienced a period of depression in the spring of 1925. He was still desperately poor, and experienced many indignities and frustrations because of this. Politically, Hitler's inaction was deeply disappointing to Goebbels, and he found fault in many of his colleagues. He took some consolation from reading and from music. On 27 March he heard a performance of Bach's *St Matthew Passion* and was again deeply impressed. In his diary he wrote that he yearned for his old life 'in the arts'. Again, he identified himself with Christ, and singled out Karl Erb, who had sung the part of Christ in the Passion: 'So beautiful, one thought the earth must sink.' Goebbels then quoted a number of the key lines about Christ in the text: 'I want to wait with my Jesus'; 'and he cried bitterly'; 'My God, why hast Thou forsaken me?' 'Then he cried out once more, and died.' After reflecting further on his own misery and confusion, Goebbels closed his diary entry by repeating 'My God, why hast Thou forsaken me?'[71]

Goebbels was characteristically roused from this slough of despond by renewed political activity and by a resumption of his relationship with Else. He had been speaking sporadically earlier in the year, and made a second tour to Pomerania in March, shortly before the first round of the Presidential election, in which Ludendorff, standing as the *völkisch* candidate, was soundly beaten by his old comrade in arms, Field Marshal Hindenburg. Before the second ballot, Goebbels gave several speeches in the Ruhr, to audiences of miners and steelworkers, and drew fresh energy from his success with them. Although he was still quarrelling with Else, he persuaded her to come to one of these meetings, in Hattingen: 'Into the hall. Absolutely full. I deliver a brilliant speech. Else is sitting in the front row. Everybody is restlessly stirred up.'[72] A few weeks later, an appearance in Remscheid was followed by a pitched battle in a railway tunnel between the Nazi supporters and hundreds of Communists. In situations like this, where many on both sides were hardened war veterans, it was particularly important for Goebbels to prove his physical courage, and he proudly noted how he had stood his ground in the middle of the fighting.[73] For men who had experienced actual warfare, the brawling which attended political meetings was an opportunity to relive these most intense moments of their former lives. We cannot underestimate the importance it had for Goebbels, seeking to share both the experience which he had previously missed, and its associated comradeship.[74] Although he was always closely guarded by 'party comrades' when speaking and going to meetings, there can be no doubting both the danger he exposed himself to, and his courage.

In June 1925, Goebbels moved into new offices in Elberfeld, which included a two-room flat for him, and, he noted, a piano. A police report compiled later stated that he had been forced by the occupation authorities to leave the Rhineland 'because of subversive political activities', so it would appear that the move was helpful to him for several reasons.[75] He escaped the confines of his parental home, and was able to expand his political activities without the supervision of foreign police. This was also when his first writings appeared in the main Nazi Party newspaper, the *Völkischer Beobachter*, which had resumed publication in February 1925. In May 1925 the *Völkischer Beobachter* carried an article on 'National Socialism on the Rhine and the Ruhr', which quoted a lengthy passage from an open letter from Goebbels to his erstwhile *völkisch* comrade Reventlow.[76] The prose in this 'letter' was stilted and tedious, but three weeks later the *Völkischer Beobachter* carried a whole article by Goebbels, entitled 'Idea and Sacrifice', in which we can read his distinctive voice. The article was again in the style of an open letter, a format he had used in the *Völkische Freiheit*, which allowed him to adopt a personal and intimate narrative tone. 'Idea and sacrifice' was addressed to an imaginary former Communist who had now joined the ranks of the Nazi Party, and Goebbels used it to advocate his belief that the Nazis should be 'a party of class struggle'.[77] The 'letter' took an embattled, but lyrical tone, and built towards a rapturous conclusion, tinged with a sense of menace: 'Thus we fight for our freedom, with an endless love for all like us who live in servitude, and with an endless hatred against all who are guilty of making us slaves.'[78] Both as an orator and as a political journalist, Goebbels was still learning

5. 'Idea and sacrifice', Goebbels' first published article in the Nazi Party newspaper, the *Völkischer Beobachter*, 14/15 June 1925. Here he explored some of the ideas which preoccupied him until his suicide in 1945.

his trade, but he was learning rapidly, and effectively. In quick succession he had two further articles published in the *Völkischer Beobachter*, and he proudly noted that he received letters expressing support for his ideas 'from all sides'.[79]

Goebbels' first articles in the *Völkischer Beobachter* stressed the 'socialist' side of the Nazi programme, and were directly addressed to the proletariat of the Ruhr. Goebbels was deeply troubled by the thought that others around him, like Ripke, and possibly even Hitler himself, were not sufficiently hostile to capitalism, but his fears were temporarily abated in August by his second visit to Weimar for what was now billed as a Nazi Party rally. Here Goebbels actually saw Hitler and heard him speak for the first time on Saturday 12 July 1925. In his diary, he described how Hitler's arrival in Weimar was delayed, and the Party faithful – as ever – were kept waiting for him:

> Then a call and a sign. He is there. Still a wait of half an hour. *Achtung!* Calls of *Heil*. There he is.
> Dinter [*Gauleiter* of Thuringia] greets him. And then Hitler begins to speak. What a voice. What gestures, what passion. Exactly what I had wanted from him. I can scarcely contain myself. My heart stands still. I hang on every word.

Goebbels managed to shake Hitler's hand after the speech, but he was clearly still some way from the centre of power in the Party. Writing up his impressions a couple of days later, Goebbels pledged himself to Hitler: 'Now I know that he, who leads, is born to be the *Führer*. I am ready to sacrifice everything for this man. History gives peoples the greatest men in the greatest times of need.'[80]

Goebbels' statement that he saw now that Hitler was 'born to be the *Führer*' is significant. One of the central themes of *völkisch* ideology was its rejection of the idea of an elected leader, and its concomitant call for a leader who would derive legitimacy from talent, instinct, and a willingness to take responsibility for all decisions. This was a concept with pronouncedly mystical dimensions. This imagined *Führer* would carry within him something divine, and would emerge from the *Volk* almost as a force of nature. Oswald Spengler had expressed this in typically obscure and metaphysical terms, writing: 'The genuine statesman is incarnate history, its directedness expressed as individual will and its organic logic as character.' The binary opposition to the *Führer* was the idea of his followers (*Gefolgschaft*), who in turn would owe him complete dedication, obedience, and loyalty. Spengler also explained this, in slightly clearer terms:

> The genuine statesman is distinguished from the 'mere politician' – the player who plays for the pleasure of the game, the *arriviste* on the heights of history, the seeker after wealth and rank – as also from the schoolmaster of an ideal, by the fact that he dares to demand sacrifices – *and* obtains them, because his

feeling that he is necessary to the time and nation is shared by thousands, transforms them to the core, and renders them capable of deeds to which otherwise they could never have risen.[81]

Numerous writers in the Weimar Republic picked up this theme, revelling in what Peter Gay calls 'the voluptuous passivity of total obedience'.[82] Hans Blüher wrote in 1924:

The leader [*Führer*] and the people differ in one important respect: the leader does not need the people to be a leader; but the people only becomes a people through its leader. In the absence of a leader it remains a milling crowd, a multiplicity of individuals ...[83]

An untrammelled veneration for 'the *Führer*' was the basis of Goebbels' subsequent relationship with Hitler, and it meant that from the outset Goebbels saw Hitler as much more than just an individual politician. He saw in him the force of 'History' and of 'Race', and abdicated all sense of his own individual responsibility before him.

As it had the year before, contact with the wider national socialist movement in Weimar gave Goebbels new inspiration. Over the next few weeks his faith in Hitler was strengthened by his reading of *Mein Kampf* (which was published in July 1925), and Goebbels was inspired to create one of the dramatic inversions he was fond of: 'Hitler is the idea, and the idea is Hitler.'[84] On 22 August, Goebbels attended a procession of the SA in Essen, in the heart of the industrial Ruhr, and his account of this is revealing. After watching a march of stormtroopers to the Bismarck memorial in the town centre, Goebbels went with others in a lorry to a packed hall, where (according to him) a noisy and excited crowd of 3,000 was waiting for Artur Dinter to speak. Dinter had not turned up though, and Goebbels takes up the story:

I therefore have to fill in for him. I am greeted with a storm of applause. And then I speak. For half an hour. And in front of these silent, still people my enthusiasm grows, and I enthuse them as well.

A storm of applause at the end. I am surrounded by people on all sides.

Back home in a lorry with the troop from the Falken [a youth movement]. These Falkeners are good fellows. I really like them. Through the black night, celebrating through the towns.[85]

It was this kind of comradeship which really inspired Goebbels. One can only try to imagine how intoxicating it must have been for a young man, hitherto reclusive and solitary, to find that he had the nerve to improvise a speech in front of a huge, turbulent audience, to be received like a hero, and hours later, to travel home through the darkened streets of the industrial towns with a gang of cheering lads. A few weeks after the Essen speech, Goebbels was carried through the hall by a crowd in nearby Düsseldorf.[86] His journalism was also beginning to attract attention. He noted in October that orders for the new newspaper he was editing, the *Nationalsozialistische Briefe* (*National Socialist Letters*), were coming in 'from all parts of the *Reich*'.[87] He had also been writing a small pamphlet, the *Das kleine abc des Nationalsozialisten* (*The Little ABC of the National Socialist*), intended as a catechism for the Nazi supporter. On 26 October 1925, Goebbels wrote that he had heard that Hitler wanted to offer him the editorship of the *Völkischer Beobachter*. He was on the threshold of great things. He concluded that day's entry:

> The ABC is ready. Good. I am pleased with it.
> I will travel through the whole world. I will speak everywhere.
> Else is coming tomorrow. Hurrah!
> I am happy.[88]

3
'The Coming Dictator'

> For we are here, and remain, mortal enemies: we reject international Russian communism exactly as we reject international Marxist Socialism, because both, according to our deep conviction, can not obtain or secure either German freedom in foreign policy, or the economic freedom of the German worker!
>
> Gregor Strasser, in the *Völkischer Beobachter*, 22 October 1925.[1]

On 10 September 1925, Goebbels attended a closed meeting of leading Nazi officials from north and west Germany in the town of Hagen, on the south of the Ruhr area. The meeting had been called by Gregor Strasser, and Goebbels had helped to prepare the plan carried through there, to form a 'North-west German Working Community' of the Nazi Party, with a distinctly anti-capitalist programme. Even though Strasser was not there in person, Goebbels wrote that his group got 'everything as we wanted it' from the meeting: Strasser was confirmed as leader of the Working Community, and its office was established in Elberfeld in the Ruhr, where Goebbels would be the 'manager'. The group would publish a fortnightly sheet, the *Nationalsozialistische Briefe*, to be edited by Goebbels.[2] Over the next six months this group was constantly active, not just in holding meetings and demonstrations, but to the extent of developing a 'programme' which it hoped to see promoted to the status of Party doctrine. Early historians of the Nazi movement even portrayed Strasser's Working Community as a 'separate party', or as a 'Strasser party in the Hitler party',[3] but this is mistaken. It was clearly established with Hitler's approval. Shortly before Christmas 1925, the 'Chancellery' of Adolf Hitler sent a circular to all regional branches of the Party commending the 'outstanding' pamphlet produced under the auspices of the Working Community and edited by one 'Dr Goebbels', *Das kleine abc des Nationalsozialisten*. The regional leaders were 'strongly recommended' to read the 'information sheet' produced by the Working Community, the *Nationalsozialistische Briefe*.[4] The police had also noted the activities of Goebbels and Strasser, in particular their joint production of *Nationalsozialistische Briefe*.[5]

In Hagen Goebbels had to negotiate with several future political companions. Some, like Helmuth Elbrechter, Theodor Vahlen, and Karl Kaufmann, he already knew well; others, like Hinrich Lohse, the *Gauleiter* of Schleswig-Holstein, Franz von Pfeffer, an ex-*Freikorps* commander, Ludolf Haase from Göttingen, and Robert Ley, the *Gauleiter* of Rhineland South, were newer to him. In some cases he would work with them for years to come. Goebbels was not a kind judge of other men, and he thought little of most of these. Vahlen, who was in his mid-fifties, he thought was too old, and too conservative. He wrote: 'For us in the West there can be no doubt. First the socialist redemption, then, like a hurricane, national liberation.' Goebbels thought Elbrechter too contented and bourgeois, and he was scathing about Robert Ley from Cologne, who had evidently dissented at the meeting: 'Dr Ley is a blockhead, perhaps an intriguer. He must get out of the Working Community.'⁶ Goebbels had mixed feelings about Gregor Strasser himself, whose patronage he depended upon as he made his way into the Nazi Party hierarchy. As one of the Party's four *Reichstag* deputies, Strasser was entitled to parliamentary immunity and also to free railway travel throughout Germany, and Goebbels actually saw far less of him than of others based in the north-west. Strasser travelled almost continuously at this time, moving between his power bases in the industrial areas of Germany, in the Rhineland-Ruhr, Berlin, and Saxony, speaking frequently. Goebbels often wrote quite warmly about Strasser in his diary, but he was never totally convinced by him. He had no great regard for his intellect, but was impressed by his concern for ordinary workers, which was based on an appeal to the comradeship of the trenches. He also admired Strasser's radicalism, and his ability as a speaker. After watching him in action in Hamm, Goebbels wrote: 'Strasser speaks. Brilliant. I have never heard him like this before. With earthiness, humour, sharpness, sarcasm, irony. All passions are let loose. An electric current of fury and indignation goes through the hall.'⁷

Karl Kaufmann was the other Nazi Goebbels was closest to at this time. Goebbels thought him 'a fanatic', and admired his impatience and resolution. There was an instability in Kaufmann which Goebbels perversely preferred to Strasser's more stable temperament. The two men often sat late into the night talking politics. Goebbels even thought Kaufmann might replace Richard Flisges as a friend. On some occasions when Goebbels met up with Else, Kaufmann socialized with them. Goebbels developed a real affection for Kaufmann, tinged with an indulgent tolerance, an attitude which was to become increasingly strained. Kaufmann also shared Goebbels' interest in the arts, and together they went to concerts, and occasionally to see a silent film.

Much has been made of the idea that Goebbels flirted with opposition to Hitler and the Nazi Party in the winter of 1925–26. Strikingly, the two men still had very little actual contact, and for Goebbels, Hitler remained an enigmatic and distant figure. There were certainly times when Goebbels felt frustration with his idealized leader, but this was confined by an almost unbounded admiration. Given how little he actually knew Hitler, it seems that Goebbels had a psychological need to attribute to him a Messianic status. On 14 October 1925 he made a famous entry in his diary: 'I am finishing Hitler's book. With raging excitement! Who is this man? Half plebeian, half God! Really Christ, or only John?'[8] A few weeks later, after several missed appointments, Hitler came to Braunschweig, one of the few places in Germany where he was still allowed to speak, and Goebbels was able to meet him again. It had been arranged for Hitler to speak in one hall, and for Goebbels to address an overspill meeting in another. For days beforehand Goebbels was anxious, wondering what impression he might make on Hitler, and hoping that he might get some time with him. Given what we know of Hitler's style as a speaker, his habit of arriving late, and of cloistering himself in a hotel room before and after a meeting, and that he and Goebbels would be addressing separate meetings at more or less the same time, Goebbels had reason to be nervous. He wrote: 'Perhaps I shall succeed in collaring Hitler for a while. I shall go straight to the point. I shall tell him everything which burns in my soul. Everything depends on it.'[9] Presumably Goebbels was referring here to the ideas of the Working Community.

On 5 November, Goebbels called on Hitler in Braunschweig. Hitler was captivating, but elusive: 'Half past seven. We go in the car to Hitler. He is having his meal. He jumps to his feet, there he is. Shakes my hand. Like an old friend. And those big blue eyes. Like stars. He is glad to see me. I am really happy.' For all that he seemed like an 'old friend', Hitler quickly dismissed Goebbels, and retired to prepare his speech. Goebbels went to his allotted meeting, where he claims to have spoken for two hours, 'to great applause'. Then Hitler arrived:

> And then shouts of *Heil* and clapping. There he is. He shakes my hand. His big speech has completely finished him. Then he makes another half-hour speech here. With wit, irony, humour, sarcasm, with seriousness, and glowing with passion. That man has got everything to be a king. A born people's tribune. The coming dictator.

Hitler evidently left immediately after this, and later Goebbels tried to see him again: 'Late at night I wait for him in front of his house. A handshake.' After that Goebbels was driven back to the home of Bernhard Rust, the local *Gauleiter*, and shortly after 2.00 a.m. he took a train back to Elberfeld.[10] Goebbels was left wondering quite what Hitler stood for, and how he viewed the Nazi Working Community in the north.

Goebbels applied himself with tremendous energy before and after the meeting in Braunschweig. His reputation was spreading to most corners of Germany, and Party branches in distant towns were now keen to host him as a speaker. When his diary for 1925–26 was first published, Goebbels was accused of inflating his own success as a speaker, exaggerating the numbers of those in the audience, and their reactions.[11] The evidence available today does not always support this. Travelling around Germany, spending nights and days on the train, often fantasizing about the women he shared compartments with, he obviously spoke to some meetings which were poorly attended, and to audiences which were not well-disposed towards him. He hated speaking to farmers and middle-class groups, preferring the outright hostility of Communists and Social Democrats to the domesticity and indifference of more prosperous audiences. He had to stay with local activists, and although he sometimes found them congenial company, he often had to put up with hours of stifling tedium. If on occasion he was too weary to inspire an audience in a cold hall, he was far more often obviously successful, and was compensated for his trials by the huge enthusiasm he generated, and by the adulation which he received. In many places he was welcomed and seen off by SA guards of honour, and his speeches often turned into turbulent demonstrations. Fighting and interventions by the local police were common. Increasingly, as Goebbels became more deeply involved in Party intrigues, he came to value this wider reception he met from ordinary 'Party comrades' around Germany.

On 11 November 1925, Goebbels set off for Osnabrück, 160 kilometres to the north-east; the next day he travelled 200 kilometres further, to Hamburg: 'Through this giant city. To the port. Out there in fog and smoke lie the ships. There is a feeling of the sea and of America.' He proceeded to Itzehoe in rural Schleswig, where he thought arrangements were 'primitive'. Then it was back to Altona, a Prussian port adjacent to Hamburg, where he was met by Hinrich Lohse. Goebbels' speech to dock workers there turned into a huge fight with chairs, and the hall was cleared by police.[12] The next morning he returned to Elberfeld, and after writing an article for the *Völkischer Beobachter* he left the next day for Plauen, 400 kilometres to the south, in industrial Saxony. After a big meeting there he travelled on to Chemnitz, where his 'quiet and factual' speech to 'two thousand Communists' again degenerated into a fight, with many injured, and according to Goebbels, two people killed. He then spoke in Zwickau, but his next meeting in Werdau was cancelled by the local police. Goebbels then returned to Plauen at the invitation of the local *Gauleiter*, Martin Mutschmann ('a decent, brutal leader'). To his 'great joy', Goebbels also met Hitler there. 'He greets me like an old friend. And looks after me. How I love him! He gives me his photograph.' Intriguingly, a 'small meeting' was held, and Hitler asked Goebbels to speak first. No doubt he wanted to test him out. Goebbels headed back north the next day, and met Gregor Strasser, Kaufmann, and Elbrechter in Hanover for discussions. They decided to prepare a 'programme' of the North-West Working Community, to be ready for January 1926.[13] After that Goebbels headed on to Bielefeld, where he spoke at a 'thundering meeting'. He spent a few days at home in Rheydt, where he briefly saw Else, before heading off again, this time to Berlin.

In Berlin, the 'Babel of sin', Goebbels spoke, he claimed, to 'thousands', including Gregor Strasser and his brother Otto, Gottfried Feder, Wilhelm Frick (another of the Nazi Party's *Reichstag* deputies), and the local Party leader, Ernst

Schlange.[14] Otto Strasser was five years younger than Gregor, but like him was strongly oriented towards socialism in his politics. He had indeed been a member of the Social Democratic Party before joining the NSDAP in 1925. At this first meeting, Goebbels was favourably impressed, noting: 'Strasser's brother as orderly as he is. I will be his friend.' The next day he was taken to the *Reichstag* itself by Gregor Strasser, and had a first glimpse of the corridors of power in the capital city. He was disgusted: 'Into the restaurant. There Locarno is the subject of chatter. All the great Excellencies stalk about. Horrible! Jews and their servants! I sit at the parliamentary group's table. Strasser makes sarcastic remarks.' Ludendorff arrived, and Goebbels was still so overawed that he could 'only gaze at him'. Then Goebbels was taken into the debating chamber and saw the Republic's political representatives conducting business. He was particularly struck by a speech by the Communist deputy Clara Zetkin: 'Trenchant, acute, clear, with grey hair, a pioneer of Bolshevism.' He was impressed by the *völkisch* deputy Graefe, whom he described as 'Dashing, sparkling and thoughtful', but not by the others: 'All the rest is shit. They walk about in the corridors. Political corpses. Parliamentary morass.' That evening Goebbels was taken out to the luxurious home of Hitler's supporters, the Bechstein family, where he was received 'like an old friend', but he was more refreshed by the subsequent Party meeting where he spoke again. In the early morning, as snow fell, he left Berlin and slept through the long journey back to Elberfeld.[15] What a contrast it must have been for him, from sweaty meetings in overcrowded halls, to the spectacle of the *Reichstag* in session. There is no doubt which he preferred.

After just one day in Elberfeld, where he briefly met Else, Goebbels took the overnight train to Dresden. He had the energy to give a successful speech here to a large audience, but was on his way back to Berlin in the morning. From there he journeyed on to the Baltic coast at Lübeck, where his talk was only a 'moderate' affair, in a hall 'half full'. The next day he managed a tour of the town, which provoked him to think of Thomas Mann (who had set his first novel *Buddenbrooks* there) and the 'stagnating spirit of the bourgeoisie', before moving on to Schwerin in Mecklenburg where, after a speech, he stayed up late into the night with the *Gauleiter*, Friedrich Hildebrandt. The next day he was put on the wrong train, and wasted many hours before starting the long journey back home. Eventually he travelled back through Hamburg, where he mused on 'the German spirit of enterprise, exploited by the Jews'. The train dawdled through the Ruhr; at Recklinghausen, Anka Stalherm's home town, he thought of her. Finally he got off in Elberfeld, and walked back to his office at two in the morning, through 'deep, soft snow' to find 'stacks of work' on his desk.[16]

After this intense activity, the next few weeks were more restful for Goebbels. On 15 December he went to a concert with Karl Kaufmann, at which they had heard Grieg's *Peer Gynt*. Goebbels was moved by the music to consider how much more expressive than poetry it could be. Music was, he wrote, 'chaste like the youngest child of nature'.[17] His relationship with Else was as difficult as ever. In mid-December she wrote him a 'farewell letter', which left him cast down, and contemptuous of himself and the world. After a long, intimate talk with Kaufmann, Goebbels in his diary posed some questions which revealed much about his attitude to women: 'Why can a woman not commit to us unreservedly? Is it possible to teach her? Or is she in the end of inferior worth? Women can only be heroines in exceptional circumstances! Else thinks so much about herself.'[18] On 21 December he was carried 'shoulder high' through the hall after a solstice festival speech in nearby Düsseldorf, and although he described this as 'embarrassing' in his diary, it must have been some consolation.[19] Christmas at home in Rheydt was difficult, and Goebbels again quarrelled with his father. Since taking up his activist career in *völkisch* and Nazi politics, relationships with his family had been far from easy. Their son had found himself paid employment, but it was far from secure, and involved him with many men of dubious repute. He had forsaken his religion, and become well-known, not to say notorious, for his demagogic speeches, which, as his parents must have known, were often attended by violence. After a painful family Christmas, a genuine consolation arrived in the form of a present from Hitler, a copy of his book *Mein Kampf*, bound in leather, with a dedication thanking Goebbels for the 'exemplary nature of your struggle'.[20]

Goebbels saw in the New Year of 1926 in bizarre circumstances. He was with Kaufmann, who, for reasons which are unclear, suffered 'one of his most appalling mental breakdowns', raved like 'one possessed' and tried to throw himself into the river as the clock struck twelve. Goebbels and a friend had to try to calm him, and get him to a bed.[21] The knowledge of Kaufmann's mental instability haunted Goebbels over the next few weeks, when, although Kaufmann recovered slightly, he remained in a very disturbed condition. On 4 January Goebbels recorded that Gregor Strasser was also very ill.[22] A few days later he and Else had a harmonious day together, walking along the banks of the Rhine.[23] Goebbels had the opportunity to read again, and was greatly struck by Ernst Jünger's *In Stahlgewittern*, a memoir of service in the trenches, known in the English-speaking world as *Storm of Steel*, which he described as 'the gospel of the war'. On finishing *In Stahlgewittern*, Goebbels excitedly wrote that this was 'the German war book'. Goebbels did note Jünger's 'passionate nationalism', but it is not clear how far he was impressed – at this stage – by Jünger's 'romanticism of steel', a celebration of the wartime synthesis of *völkisch* nationalism, violence, and new technology.[24] Goebbels was even more impressed by *Das Dritte Reich* (*The Third Reich*), written by Moeller van den Bruck, who had recently committed suicide. It is no coincidence that Bruck, as well as having an idealistic vision of a future German empire in which social differences were reconciled in a united *Volksgemeinschaft*, was an ardent fan of Dostoyevsky. One wonders whether Goebbels later remembered this passage from Bruck's work:

It is nowhere written that a people has a right to life eternal. For every people the hour at length strikes when they perish either by murder or by suicide. No more glorious end could be conceived for a great people than to perish in a world war where a world in arms overcame one single country.

Goebbels did wonder why Bruck had not seen the real consequences of his convictions, and committed himself to the struggle with the Nazis.[25] Perhaps the most important thing Goebbels took from Bruck was the title of his book. The idea of the 'Third Reich', an empire to follow the 'first' established in the Middle Ages and the 'second' founded after Bismarck's wars of unification in the nineteenth century, was not new in German right-wing circles, but Bruck's work gave it a much wider currency. Goebbels saw the propagandistic potential in the title, which combined a sense of organic German historical tradition with belief in a glorious future and the prospect of certain fulfilment. He quickly incorporated it into his own, and the Nazi Party's vocabulary.[26]

Goebbels was also applying himself to the Working Community's 'programme'. It is striking how difficult he found this. He struggled with practical social and political issues, and although he had developed his knowledge of current affairs through his journalism, he was still much more comfortable in cultural and racial affairs, where his talent for words and for drama could compensate for his lack of real knowledge. Ironically he received a letter from Hitler, which brought him 'great joy', on 20 January, even as he was grappling with the programme.[27] Four days later Goebbels was back in the fray, travelling to Hanover for a 'big meeting' of the leaders from the North and West. Ludendorff also attended, as did Franz von Pfeffer. Gottfried Feder had come up from Munich, and evidently had an uncomfortable time as Goebbels and Strasser presented the programme. Feder was not allowed to speak.[28] They carried the day, but Feder reported back to Hitler on the adoption of the programme, which clearly challenged his own 'Twenty-five Points', drawn up in February 1920, and declared immutable. This document, which presented a set of vague demands, had since served as the Party's manifesto.[29] Clearly in some turmoil, Goebbels travelled to Berlin on 4 February, having heard that Hitler was apparently 'furious about the programme'.[30]

What did Goebbels say in his speeches and articles at this time? And what did he believe? Most writers on Goebbels have asserted that he was a nihilist and an opportunist, and used any argument he thought might be persuasive without genuine adherence to any. The criticism that his early political views had little content is much more accurate. From what we can tell of what he said and wrote at this time his views were all very general, and very repetitive. Alfred Krebs, *Gauleiter* of Hamburg between 1926 and 1928, wrote:

The Hamburg people had an extraordinarily high estimation of him as a speaker, apparently, because his slick dialectic, his Romance diction and pose, his wit and his ice-cold irony were so completely alien to their own deliberate, coarse, or humorously crafty manner. Among the Hamburg Party comrades, the question of whether Hitler or Goebbels was the best speaker was frequently raised in these early years of struggle. Many thought Goebbels was, and this often led at the same time to the idea that he was better suited to be Party leader.

Krebs added, in a general observation:

As far as I can remember, he spoke with enthusiasm about cultural and artistic matters, he skirted around political matters, and, in contrast to Strasser, he avoided internal Party questions and problems with great care.[31]

There can be no doubt that Goebbels possessed an extraordinary, perhaps unique, talent for public speaking. Although it is difficult to reconstruct the precise conditions in which he spoke, it is clear from all the evidence that he had a remarkable capacity to compel his listeners, to use an elevated linguistic register to communicate with ordinary people, and to engage their emotions. Several of the testimonies of SA men from the 'years of struggle' collected in 1934 by the American sociologist Theodore Abel referred specifically to this. One steelworker from the Ruhr wrote about the experience of hearing Goebbels in 1924:

At the first meeting, comprised of about fifteen people, a Herr Fuchs spoke about the treason of Marxism. I listened in silence and digested everything he said. Inwardly, however, I was completely disturbed. When I compared the speaker's words with what had happened, I was forced again and again to conclude that what I heard was the truth. Two weeks later I went to another meeting. A Dr. Goebbels of Elberfeld spoke on the theme 'What does Adolf Hitler want?' The attendance was not much larger. I followed every word of the speaker. I felt as though he were addressing me personally. My heart grew light, something in my breast arose. I felt as if bit by bit something within me were being rebuilt. Dr. Goebbels did not complete his theme that evening. He promised to come back in two weeks and finish the lecture. I passed those fourteen days in delirium. I could hardly wait for the day of the meeting. I was there punctually and at the close of the meeting I silently went home ... I became a National Socialist.[32]

Although none of these early speeches was captured in a sound recording, Goebbels was beginning to get his work published. In 1926, one of his speeches, 'Lenin or Hitler' (first developed in late 1924, and delivered over a hundred times), was published in a small pamphlet. A series of his 'letters to contemporaries' from the *Nationalsozialistische Briefe* was also published as a small book with the title *Die zweite Revolution* (*The Second Revolution*) in 1926. These 'letters' were undoubtedly very similar in content and tone to his speeches; they use the same key words that appear in his diary, and frequently share its narrative style. Sometimes the same sentence appears verbatim in different 'letters'. We can identify several deeply felt convictions in his thought at this time.

First, Goebbels, speaking almost exclusively to working-class audiences, sought to convert workers from Marxism to his own belief in a German 'community of need, bread, and fate'. This community was defined not least by the exclusion of Jews from all Nazi Party meetings, and in his speeches Goebbels identified himself with his audience, using phrases such as 'the same spirit and the same blood as we'. He argued passionately that Bolshevism in Russia was a nationalist phenomenon, and that German Marxism was manipulated from Russia. Bizarrely, he combined this sense of a threat with his mystical veneration for the Russian people, and used both to suggest that there must be, in foreign policy, some accommodation with Russia.

Second, Goebbels offered workers not a detailed programme for their own social improvement, but a *völkisch* notion of 'German freedom'. He did not have to explain to his audience what this meant, but used the phrase rather as a *Leitmotif*. His audiences understood well that he meant freedom for the German *Volk* from foreign and Jewish subjugation, and a sense of ordered belonging within the *Volk* for its 'racial comrades'. Goebbels' use of the word 'freedom' enabled him to take up a heroic mode, as in an imaginary letter to a Communist worker, 'National Socialism or Bolshevism', published in the *Nationalsozialistische Briefe* in October 1925: 'For this freedom the people will have to fight, and will be impelled to fight when it has become a nation.' He liked phrases which inverted words in a seemingly portentous way: 'The path to freedom leads through the nation. The more united the nation, the stronger and more fervent the will for freedom.'[33] Goebbels also made a virtue of the idea of revolution, and was developing a notably violent language, here in an example from his 'Lenin or Hitler' speech: 'If we want the state of the future, then we are dealing with revolution, not reform. The system of liberal-capitalist democracy is already inwardly so rotten, so decayed, that there is nothing left to mend or reform. It must fundamentally be destroyed, spiritually and politically smashed.'[34]

He had a genuine aversion to capitalism, which he saw as an international Jewish conspiracy. Again addressing an imaginary Communist, he appealed to a shared hatred of the Jews: 'Yesterday you beat about the bush on the Jewish question. I know why. Please don't object. We don't want to deceive each other. You are an anti-Semite as I am.'[35] He made no bones about the place of anti-Semitism in his thinking. In another of his 'letters to contemporaries', he addressed former *völkisch* colleagues like Wiegershaus, and wrote: 'Yes, you are right, anti-Semitism is the starting point of our understanding.'[36] And lest there be any misunderstanding about how Goebbels thought the Jews should be treated, this is a passage from another 'letter': 'How will we come to the end of our struggle? We are infested with parasites, and we will not go along with our enemies. O God, a communist, a rogue, someone with no fatherland, a traitor, a fraudster – a Jew! Beat him to death! And that's the end of that!'[37]

These early journalistic writings display other hallmarks of Goebbels' style. He used a conversational tone which suggested a sense of empathy, for example, addressing an imaginary Communist: 'I liked you, you are a fine fellow!'[38] He was often sarcastic, posing questions which subtly distorted the viewpoints of others. Frequently he answered his rhetorical questions with a mock politeness, using courteous modes of address to conceal contempt or aggression. He expressed open disdain for 'bourgeois' values in debate and political life, as in this passage near the end of his 'letter' to former *völkisch* allies: 'Do not believe that our present silence means hesitation. We are working restlessly and unerringly; the day is no longer far away when we shall say everything, everything. Then even you will learn that we are anything but a black-white-red security police for middle class self-interest and petty-bourgeois peace and quiet.' When speaking of National Socialism, of Hitler, or of the coming revolution, Goebbels was lyrical, and struck a poetic note in his moments of exultation. Before threatening his own compatriots in the passage above, he described how he and other 'National Socialists' would turn to those they had left behind: 'When we stand on the highest peak we will signal to you and wave our hats and shout joyously "We made it. Long live the new, the Third Reich!"'[39]

The most successful of Goebbels' early writings was *The Little ABC of the National Socialist*, a 22-page pamphlet first published late in 1925 with money donated by a supporter from Hattingen. The first edition of 10,000 copies soon sold out, and by 1927, 75,000 had been printed. The pamphlet sold for only 15 pfennigs, or less if it was bought in bulk, and it was cleverly written in a question and answer style, to serve as a catechism, or guide to the essential beliefs of National Socialism. Goebbels drew freely, and shamelessly, on the tropes of the Catholic Church to infuse the whole pamphlet with a sense of fervour. Starting with the Party slogan 'Community need before individual need', Goebbels proclaimed that the 'first commandment' of every National Socialist was: 'Love Germany above everything and your people's comrades as yourself', and declared that the goal of National Socialism was 'the people's community [*Volksgemeinschaft*] of all honest working Germans'. He asked 'Who is our German people's comrade?' and answered: 'Every honest creative German, in so far as he is of German blood, German tradition and German culture, and speaks the German language.' Goebbels asked whether there was a contradiction between the words 'national' and 'socialist', replying: 'No, the opposite! The genuinely national man thinks in a social way and the true socialist is the best nationalist!' Goebbels explicitly rejected the idea of class struggle, stating that 'class war divides the German people in two parts and makes it incapable of becoming a nation'. There were frequent references to the Jews, and as in all early Nazi Party literature, they were placed at the centre of analysis. Goebbels asked 'How do we elevate and increase our German people, German culture and tradition?', and replied: 'By cutting everyone of foreign blood and from foreign lands out of the body of the German people'. Throughout the pamphlet, the Jews were identified as the controlling hand behind international stock exchange capitalism, behind the Communist and Social Democratic parties, and the democratic system of the Weimar Republic. Intriguingly, although Goebbels stated that the Nazi Party wanted to install a 'National Socialist dictatorship', headed by 'a strong German leader', he also declared that in the longer term the Nazis would establish an elected, corporatist parliament, 'divided not by party groups, but according to occupational groups'. Goebbels was absolutely clear about who the 'strong German leader' was, asking: 'Who will lead the German workers in the future?', and answering: 'Adolf Hitler!'[40]

Das kleine abc des Nationalsozialisten

Von Dr. Jof. Goebbels.

Freiheit und Brot!

6. *The Little ABC of the National Socialist*, a guide to the core beliefs of Nazism. This was the first and most widely distributed of a series of pamphlets published by Goebbels from 1925. The subtitle reads 'Freedom and Bread!'

The Working Community's programme which Goebbels developed with the Strasser brothers was very different from these speeches and publications, because in composing it, Goebbels and the Strassers had to try to formulate precise lines of policy. Goebbels, who had become used to writing quickly and fluently, turning out articles to a deadline, struggled terribly with the Working Community's programme. It finally proposed a corporatist state, based on a racial understanding of the 'nation'. Significantly it called for a 'national dictatorship', and for Jews to be 'declared foreigners'. Those who had arrived in Germany since August 1914 were 'to be expelled within six months'. Many clauses displayed considerable amateurishness, like that which called for a 'large proportion' of wages to be paid in kind. In the economy there was to be 'far-reaching transfer of the ownership of the means of production to the general public', but this was, in an unspecified way, to be balanced 'with maintenance of private enterprise and with regard for the sense of property'. In many ways, as Reinhard Kühnl points out, the programme largely added more detail and precision to Hitler's very vague 'Twenty-five Points'.[41]

Hitler had heard from Gottfried Feder a report on the Hanover meeting on 24 January, and he had received from Gregor Strasser a 'draft' of the Working Community's programme.[42] He now determined to assert his authority and call the dissidents to order. Even if on most policy details the programme did not differ significantly from his 'Twenty-five Points', Hitler was no longer prepared to tolerate the semi-autonomous way in which the Working Community was now operating. He arranged a meeting of selected officials on 14 February in the Bavarian town of Bamberg, where the local Nazi Party was strong. Anxiously, Goebbels and Strasser attended, hoping to persuade him to accept their programme. Hitler made a stage-managed late arrival in his motorcade, and spoke for several hours to the 60 or so senior Nazis present. He insisted on certain broad points of domestic and foreign policy, rejecting any accommodation with Russia. He demanded unconditional loyalty from all his supporters, and affirmed that his 'Twenty-five Points' of 1920 were inviolable. He declared that there was no place in the Party for separate working communities or any other groups. Strasser in reply spoke for half an hour, hesitantly and without conviction. Goebbels for once said nothing.[43] His diary conveys something of his reaction to the proceedings:

Hitler speaks. Two hours. I am almost beaten down. What kind of Hitler? A reactionary? Amazingly clumsy and uncertain. Russian question: Altogether beside the point. Italy and Britain the natural allies. Horrible! It is our job to smash Bolshevism. Bolshevism is a Jewish creation! ...

The programme [Hitler's Twenty-five Points] is good enough! Content with it. Feder nods. Ley nods. Streicher nods. Esser nods.

It hurts my soul to see you in this company!!![44]

Hitler, although decisively overruling the northern leaders at this meeting, was careful to preserve personal relations with Strasser and Goebbels. The *Völkischer Beobachter* stressed in its account of the Bamberg conference that 'complete unanimity' was reached on 'various programme issues'.[45] Hitler had recognized that Goebbels was potentially a formidable ally, and he did not want to alienate Strasser. Goebbels' reaction to the Bamberg meeting has often been quoted, and used to bolster the idea that he had lost faith with Hitler at this point. This should be treated with caution. He had earlier asked whether Hitler was really Christ, or only John, but he had never thought of any other leading Nazi in anything like similar terms. Gregor Strasser came out of the meeting more damaged than Hitler in Goebbels' eyes. Over the next few days, Goebbels recovered something of his fighting spirit. He again embarked on a round of travel, going to Göttingen and Berlin, where he met up again with Strasser and his brother Otto. They resolved to continue their work, but were already displacing their disappointment from Hitler to those around him in Munich, like Gottfried Feder and Hermann Esser.

Goebbels called in Berlin to meet with the Strasser brothers, and then set off on his longest journey yet, to Königsberg in East Prussia. This involved travelling through the 'Polish Corridor', territory taken from Germany and given to Poland at the Treaty of Versailles, and it prompted Goebbels to one of his diary entries which betray a growing coarseness of thought: 'What a shitty people we are!' In Königsberg, which Goebbels saw as a beleaguered island of German culture, he delivered his 'Lenin or Hitler' speech to a large meeting in the Opera House. For three hours, he claimed, he spoke in a breathless silence, before being acclaimed. He was escorted to the station by SA men, and stopped briefly at the restored Teutonic castle of Marienburg before re-crossing the 'corridor' and returning to Berlin. Goebbels then attended another Working Community meeting in Hanover before returning to Elberfeld.[46] On 5 March Gregor Strasser wrote to the members of the Working Community asking them to return all copies of the programme, which were subsequently destroyed.[47]

In the weeks after the Bamberg conference, Goebbels had no direct contact from Hitler, and only confused indications of his attitude reached Elberfeld. He used work to get through the crisis, and maintained his hectic level of activity. In early March he travelled to Saxony, speaking in Leipzig, Chemnitz, and in Annaberg, near the Czechoslovak frontier. The visit brought him little joy.[48] Goebbels had embroiled himself in increasingly vicious disputes with other Nazis, like Elbrechter locally, and with Julius Streicher in Nuremberg, and was much preoccupied with accusations and counter-accusations. On a brief visit home he met with Else, and felt himself 'somewhat ashamed' with her and his family. The tension now between this domesticity and his violent, confrontational, and exhausting working life was becoming hard to bear. To compound his tensions, news arrived that Gregor Strasser had been injured in a road accident.[49]

We can detect a sea-change in Goebbels' attitude in mid-March. Although certain entries in his diary suggest that the Working Community was still a going concern, he knew that it was falling apart. On 13 March he read a pamphlet by Hitler on the South Tyrol, and his faith was rekindled.[50] He spent a week travelling south, to Stuttgart, Mannheim, Neulussheim, and then to Nuremberg. The speech in Stuttgart was, he thought, one of his best yet, and he was moved by the strong reaction he evoked there. In Nuremberg, he and Streicher smoothed over their differences, and Goebbels spoke to a noisy meeting of 3,000 local Nazis. Implying that they were perhaps accustomed to Streicher's particularly crude brand of anti-Semitism, Goebbels cynically noted that it was 'difficult to teach them to think'.[51] After a couple of days at home, Goebbels then travelled to Essen, to Halle in Saxony, and to Weimar. He enjoyed speaking in Essen, and was more impressed by the industrial city of Halle than he had expected. In Weimar he again drank in the cultural atmosphere, and wondered whether he had lost something by going into politics. He heard here about further intrigues being conducted against him, and moved on to Erfurt, where he evidently took pleasure in dealing successfully with two Communist hecklers.[52] Back in Eberfeld, things seemed at last to be coming together. Goebbels had seen Else again, and they had patched things up. In an unusual arrangement, Goebbels was appointed at this time to a shared leadership of the Ruhr *Gau* with Kaufmann and Pfeffer.[53] On 29 March, he received a letter from Party Headquarters, inviting him to speak in Munich on 8 April, and to holiday in the Bavarian mountains afterwards.[54] Over the next few days, his plans for this visit were firmed up, and Goebbels also moved into new Party offices in Elberfeld. He noted with pleasure that he now had a room of his own, with a telephone.[55]

After a visit home at Easter, Goebbels took the train to Munich on 7 April. There he was subjected to a sustained charm offensive by Hitler, to which he succumbed totally. Hitler's car was waiting at the station to take Goebbels and his travelling companion, Pfeffer, to their hotel. On the way, Goebbels saw huge posters advertising his forthcoming speech at the 'historic' Bürgerbräukeller. Hitler called the next morning: 'Tall, healthy, full of life. I like him a lot. He is embarrassingly good to us.' Hitler then lent them his car and driver for the afternoon, and they were taken on a drive at high speed out to the Starnbergersee. Goebbels, who had always enjoyed travelling to and from Nazi meetings in lorries, or on motorbikes, thoroughly enjoyed this. When they returned to Munich, Goebbels was taken to the Bürgerbräukeller, where he was introduced by Streicher, and spoke for over two hours on 'National Socialism or Communism'. Hitler was in the audience, and Goebbels recorded that he embraced him afterwards, with tears in his eyes. Goebbels was taken back through the crowds to his hotel, where he dined alone with Hitler, before going to a concert together.[56]

The next morning, Goebbels was taken to the Party Headquarters, where he took a keen interest in the staff who worked so closely with Hitler. Goebbels, Kaufmann, and Pfeffer were taken into Hitler's room, and taken to task for their conduct over the past few months. The programme of the Working Community evidently also came up for scrutiny. Goebbels admitted that he and Strasser did not come well out of this. But Hitler rose above the personal and political differences of his squabbling lieutenants, and stressed the importance of unity. He concluded the session with handshakes all round. After this, Goebbels was taken to the office of the *Völkischer Beobachter*, where he met the editor Alfred Rosenberg, and saw with pleasure that his speech the previous evening was being favourably reviewed. He chatted briefly with Hitler's secretary Rudolf Hess, before a more serious, three-hour session with Hitler, where matters of foreign and

Nationalsozialistische Deutsche Arbeiterpartei

Nationalsozialisten!   Schaffende aller Stände!

Erscheint alle zu der am

Donnerstag, den 8. April 1926, abends 8 Uhr, im Bürgerbräukeller, Rosenheimer Straße, stattfindenden

Massen-Versammlung

Es wird sprechen:

Pg. Dr. Goebbels, Elberfeld

über:

Unsere zweite Antwort an die Börsen- u. Marxisteninternationale
Nationalsozialismus oder Kommunismus

Juden haben keinen Zutritt! Kassaeröffnung 6.30 Uhr, Beginn 8 Uhr.

Eintritt für Mitglieder gegen Ausweis 30 Pfennige, für Nichtmitglieder 50 Pfennige. Für erwerbslose und kriegsbeschädigte Parteigenossen gegen Ausweis 10 Pfennige.

Einberufer: Philipp Bouhler.

7. For the first time, the *Völkischer Beobachter* announces a speech at a 'mass meeting' in Munich by 'Party Comrade Dr Goebbels, from Elberfeld', 8 April 1926. After the speech Goebbels wrote: 'At the end Hitler embraces me. There are tears in his eyes.' (*TBJG*, TI, 1/II, 13 April 1926, p. 72.)

domestic policy were discussed.[57] Goebbels was fully under the sway of Hitler's oratory, and he recorded: 'We ask. He answers brilliantly. I love him.' Evidently they went over – with Hitler doing most of the talking – some of the principal areas which had previously divided Strasser and Goebbels from Hitler. Again Hitler stressed his hostility to Russia, and his leaning towards Italy and Britain; this obviously conflicted with Goebbels' idealized vision of the Russian people, and his low opinion of the Italians and the British. Hitler also stressed his belief in a mixture of collectivism and individualism as the guiding principle for the conduct of economic policy. His respect for private property again clashed with Goebbels' strongly-felt anti-capitalism. But Goebbels, whose own thinking on all these issues was vague, was easily won over by what he called Hitler's 'completely new insights', continuing: 'He has thought through everything ... I am pacified by him on all things.'

Intriguingly, Goebbels noted that when von Pfeffer and Kaufmann left the next day to return to the Ruhr, 'there was something between us'; perhaps they sensed that he was now completely in Hitler's palm. If they had, their suspicions were confirmed within a few weeks when the police recorded, without troubling to use the correct Party vocabulary, that Goebbels was 'Führer of the NSDAP in north-west Germany'.[58] Goebbels left his colleagues to travel to nearby Landshut, with another of Hitler's lieutenants, Heinrich Himmler: 'A good fellow, very intelligent. I like him.' Goebbels stayed at the Strasser family home in Landshut, and fitted in speeches there and in Dingolfing, before returning to Munich. Although Goebbels was charmed by the friendship and hospitality he experienced, his summary of this excursion was double-edged: 'That is Bavaria. Loyalty and beer.'[59] Back in Munich, he spent more time alone with Hitler, and was taken out by car, with Hitler 'laughing, singing, whistling', to the medieval town of Ulm, and on to Stuttgart. Here he and Hitler again spoke to separate audiences, but on this occasion it fell to Goebbels to catch the end of Hitler's speech, and then to follow him for another half hour. 'How hard that is', he wrote. Afterwards the two met for dinner: 'Hitler embraces me when he sees me. He praises me greatly. I believe he has taken me to his heart.' The two then parted, leaving Goebbels to travel overnight back to Elberfeld.[60]

This visit has been mythologized in accounts of the early development of the Nazi Party. Goebbels himself wrote a rapturous article about Hitler for the *Nationalsozialistische Briefe* shortly afterwards; this was quickly reprinted in a collection of Goebbels' early writings, *Wege ins Dritte Reich (Roads to the Third Reich)*, published in 1927.[61] It is a good example of the way in which central aspects of a narrative were established by Goebbels himself, and have subsequently been adopted by other writers. In a book purporting to portray Goebbels in 'sketches from those around him' published in Berlin in 1949, Goebbels was reported as quoting what Hitler had said to him after the meeting in the Bürgerbräukeller and the long conversations of that evening: 'Goebbels, you are the one of my colleagues who stands the closest to me as a human being.' Unfortunately the quotation is not referenced, and the whole anecdote is so vaguely presented that one suspects it was a later reminiscence of Goebbels.[62] If the precise date and accuracy of the quotation can not be established, it does express something which now became a determining factor in Goebbels' life, the uniquely close understanding established between him and Hitler in April 1925.

Although Goebbels came away from Munich thinking that there were still some policy differences between him and Hitler – notably over Russia – they were totally overshadowed by his admiration for the 'Führer'. He had seen Hitler now not only as the activist and speaker, but as the man of business, and importantly, as a man of status. Goebbels had for years lived in poverty; we have seen how he rejoiced in having a telephone in his office. He was undoubtedly impressed by Hitler's style, his car, and the atmosphere he cultivated around him in Munich. From this time forward Goebbels was committed unreservedly to him. Nor did he rest on his laurels after the Munich meeting. In the next few weeks he was again active, speaking in Hildesheim, Holzminden, Bochum, and Herne. He briefly met up with Else before making the long journey to Dresden, where he addressed a large meeting, from there to Berlin, on to Hamburg, and to Rendsburg in Schleswig-Holstein. Back home, he spoke again to meetings in Essen and in Hattingen, before travelling to Bavaria in May. Here he spoke in Bamberg and Nuremberg, and made a first visit to what was already established as a Nazi shrine, the Wagner family home at the Villa Wahnfried in Bayreuth. He was taken by Winifred Wagner, the wife of the composer's son Siegfried and 'a fanatical partisan of ours', to see the elderly Houston Stewart Chamberlain. The philosopher of nineteenth-century racism, whose ideas had so impressed Hitler, was barely able to speak, but Goebbels was touched by the old man's evident emotion at meeting him. After visiting Wagner's grave, Goebbels was taken to see the 'master's room', preserved intact since his death. Later he went backstage at the *Festspielhaus*, and reflected on the impression Wagner's *Tannhäuser* had made on him when he first heard it as a 13-year-old.[63]

On 10 May, Goebbels, again crossing from one end of Germany to another, made a 17-hour journey to Breslau, in Silesia; after speaking there, he travelled on to Gleiwitz on the Polish frontier to speak at a turbulent meeting. Back in Elberfeld, Goebbels met briefly with Else, whom he was seeing ever more infrequently, and also went with Kaufmann to see the 'Bolshevik film *Battleship Potemkin*'. Goebbels was not yet a close analyst of cinematic technique, and the film appears to have made little distinct impression on him.[64] He was preoccupied with plans for another visit to Bavaria, and to Munich. He had a crowded schedule, with meetings in Esslingen, Ulm, Feuerbach, and Stuttgart before he reached the Bavarian capital. As ever, these meetings were stormy. In Ulm, Goebbels was received with 'shouts and jubilation', but in Feuerbach there was fighting amongst 'lousy proletarians who don't want to be converted'. Any frustration Goebbels felt there was overcome by his second appearance in the Bürgerbräukeller in Munich, where he was welcomed 'with joy and enthusiasm'.[65] This was the Party's annual general meeting, all the senior figures were there, and Hitler spent two hours reviewing the activity of the past year. He singled out Goebbels in an important section of his speech, on the Party's speaking programme, declaring: 'I am happy that also in this year a number of first class speakers have emerged, at their head our friend from Elberfeld, Goebbels.'[66] He had indeed arrived.

These were defining weeks for the young Goebbels. Several regional branches of the Nazi Party, not least those in the Rhineland and the Ruhr, were dominated by acrimonious internal intrigues, and by financial difficulties. His relationship with Else, after five years, was approaching a final crisis. In June 1926 she wrote him 'a brief, matter-of-fact, farewell letter'.[67] It is not clear what the reasons for their final break were, but Goebbels' underlying awareness of her Jewish parentage conflicted ever more with his growing obsession with Nazi politics. He had been travelling constantly for the last year and more, and he had realized that to progress further in the Nazi Party he would have to move away from Elberfeld, perhaps to Munich, and that he would have to finish with Else.

The only constants in Goebbels' life at this time were his infatuation with Hitler, and his growing status in the Nazi Party. On 3 July, the day before the annual Party meeting in Weimar, an article by Goebbels, in which he surveyed the Party's 'first year' since Hitler's release, and looked towards the future dominated the front page of the *Völkischer Beobachter*. Here is the distinctive voice of the future Propaganda Minister, combining force, passion, and menace: 'The political gaze of Germany is notably directed more towards us. From sympathetic smiles comes mockery; from mockery comes slander; from slander comes terror; and when all that no longer avails, a fight for life and death. Today people are beginning to fear us again. One thing gives the movement its clearest stamp, ... the singular importance of the leadership principle.'[68]

In early July, Goebbels again attended the annual rally in Weimar. There was a significant difference between his experience in 1926 and in previous years, encapsulated in a frequently published photograph. It was taken on Sunday 4 July, during a march past of the SA held in Weimar's marketplace. On the right of the photograph, surrounded by a dense crowd, is Hitler's stationary car. On the left, the head of the SA column is shown giving the Fascist salute – what was to become known in Germany as the 'Hitler greeting'. Hitler himself stands in the car, replying to the salute with his hand outstretched. Behind him, still seated, is Rudolf Hess. In front of Hitler, standing on the running boards of the Mercedes, also saluting the marching column, and beaming with pleasure, is Goebbels, now centre stage.[69] Nor was this an isolated moment. Throughout a crowded weekend, Goebbels was at the centre of events, and often at Hitler's side. On the Saturday he was driven through the streets by Himmler on a motorcycle, before, significantly, taking part with Hitler in a 'Propaganda and Organization Committee' meeting. That evening, Goebbels spoke on 'Propaganda' in the National Theatre, and he recorded how his satirical style generated merriment as well as excitement. Hitler 'laughed himself half-dead'. On Sunday evening Goebbels was carried into the hall, before making another brief speech. In his diary he wrote: 'the Third Reich is appearing'.[70]

After Weimar, Goebbels went south, to Berchtesgaden in the Bavarian mountains, where he spent two weeks as Hitler's guest at the Hotel Krone. Hitler at this stage was not a property owner at Berchtesgaden, or on the Obersalzberg nearby. Berchtesgaden was a small village south-east of Munich, only a few kilometres from the frontier with Austria. The Obersalzberg is a foothill of the

Bavarian Alps outside Berchtesgaden, lying at an altitude between 900 and 1,000 metres under the nearby Kehlstein, which reaches 1,885 metres, and beyond that, the Hoher Göll, which towers at 2,523 metres on the actual frontier. Hitler had first come to the Obersalzberg in April 1923, and had fallen in love with its spectacular mountain landscape. The owners of a hotel there, the Pension Moritz, were amongst Hitler's earliest supporters, and they allowed him to stay in a small wood cabin they also owned. Subsequently, another ardent follower of Hitler's, Helene Bechstein – wife of the piano manufacturer – helped Hitler to rent out a holiday home on the Obersalzberg, the Haus Wachenfeld.[71]

This episode on the Obersalzberg in July 1926 has often been described as a blissful idyll in Goebbels' life, when he communed with Hitler, drinking in his words, feeling a mystical consummation, summarized by his description of how, as they chatted one evening, a cloud over the mountains formed the shape of a swastika. In fact Hitler only joined Goebbels for four days on the Obersalzberg, and as ever, he did most of the talking then. Goebbels was fascinated by what he perceived as Hitler's mastery of diverse subjects, from international affairs to architecture, and he was deeply flattered by what he took as Hitler's personal concern for him. For much of the rest of this fortnight, Goebbels was alternately bored and sexually frustrated. Unlike Hitler, he did not like the mountain air. He lusted after various women he saw, and suffered the tedious company of others around Hitler, like Bernhard Rust. He did enjoy being driven around in Hitler's car; he was even given some driving instruction by Hitler's chauffeur, Emil Maurice. Finally, Maurice drove Hitler, Goebbels, and Hess back to Augsburg, where they were welcomed at an enthusiastic meeting, before Goebbels made his way home on the train.[72]

In the weeks after his return from Bavaria, Goebbels' outer life resumed its earlier course. He addressed meeting after meeting around the Ruhr and the Rhineland, and was constantly embroiled in squabbles with the increasingly fractious local leaders. He wrote more articles for the *Nationalsozialistische Briefe*. His public profile had grown, and for the first time he was involved in court proceedings, as a witness. He was not intimidated, and wrote contemptuously about the court in his diary.[73] He found time to take walks with his dog, and even to go canoeing on the Ruhr on Red Front Day – the annual celebration of the paramilitary 'fighting league' of the Communist Party – at the end of August. In his inner life, Goebbels was confronted with two questions: Else and Berlin. A few days before the Weimar rally, Goebbels had noted that the party in Berlin wanted him there, 'as a rescuer'.[74] It appears that through the summer of 1926 pressure was put on Goebbels to take on the post of *Gauleiter* of Berlin, but that he was initially very reluctant to do so. A police report noted on 29 July that Goebbels had been offered the *Gau* leadership in Berlin but had turned it down.[75] On 27 August Goebbels himself wrote that he had been invited by the 'Party leadership' to 'take over the *Gau* Berlin for four months like a commissar', but he sent a 'semi-refusal' the next day, writing in his diary that he did 'not want to kneel in filth'.[76] Anecdotally, Goebbels is alleged to have said in September 1926 that 'Berlin can only be described as a self-important hydrocephalus, a repulsive accumulation of pirates, pederasts, gangsters and their like, a city which for the best must disappear from German soil.'[77]

Goebbels hardly knew Berlin. He had travelled through on the train, and visited the city briefly for meetings. In his diary, and later in his journalism, he portrayed Berlin as an 'asphalt desert', suggesting an opposition between the unhealthy capital city, and the more human provincial town or countryside. This usage also carries much more freight than the later English term 'concrete jungle'. Victor Klemperer, who subsequently analysed Goebbels' use of language, wrote:

Aspahlt is the man made surface which separates the city-dweller from the natural soil. It was first used metaphorically in Germany (around 1890) in the poetry of Naturalism. At that time, an 'asphalt flower' was a Berlin prostitute. It implied little or no censure because in these poems the prostitute was more or less a tragic figure. In the case of Goebbels, an entire asphalt flora blossoms, and every one of its flowers is poisonous and proud of the fact. Berlin is the asphalt monster, its Jewish newspapers, sorry efforts of the Jewish yellow press, are asphalt organs, the revolutionary flag of the NSDAP must be vigorously 'rammed into the asphalt', the path to ruin (Marxist attitudes and statelessness) is 'asphalted by the Jews with hollow phrases and hypocritical promises'. The breathless speed of this 'asphalt monster has made people heartless and unfeeling'; as a result, the inhabitants are a 'formless mass of anonymous, global proletarians', and the Berlin proletarian is 'a thing without a real home'.[78]

Goebbels knew some of the Party leaders in Berlin quite well, like the *Gauleiter* Ernst Schlange, and Erich Schmiedicke, who took over the leadership from Schlange in June 1926. He knew that the Party in Berlin was weak, disorganized, and divided, with only 2,000 or so members. The SA there, run by Kurt Daluege, had become alienated from the local leadership.[79] The city was dominated politically by the Social Democrats and the Communists, who were strongly entrenched in the working-class districts. Berlin was 450 kilometres from the Rhineland, and Goebbels knew that if he moved there he would become increasingly distant from his family, and from Else. Equally, he was thoroughly fed up with the quarrelling leadership in the Rhineland-Ruhr, and keenly aware that the centre of gravity in the Party lay elsewhere.

In the event, Goebbels' collapsing relationship with Else was one factor which finally pushed him to decide for Berlin. Despite the 'farewell' letters and tearful partings of preceding months, the couple had continued to meet into September 1926, and Goebbels still recorded good times together. But every meeting now was clouded by arguments and forebodings. In August Goebbels upset Else by not taking up an invitation to her sister Lotte's wedding. He wrote that this was because he was short of money, but Else was evidently deeply offended.[80] The relationship was now close to breaking point. On 3 September they 'spent a few hours together, beautiful but partly also sorrowful', before Goebbels left for Bayreuth, where he was to start yet another speaking tour, addressing a nationalist gathering at Wagner's grave.[81] After only a day at home he then travelled to Dresden for a round of speeches in Saxony. Before he left, he made a significant change of plan. Instead of going to 'Saxon Switzerland', after speeches in Meissen and Zittau, Goebbels arranged to travel instead to Berlin.[82]

He arrived there on Wednesday 16 September, and wrote cynically about what he found:

Reception by a body of the discontented. Stier also there. Miserable whinger. In the afternoon alone in a café. I cannot bear those querulous people. In the evening I receive Schlange and Schmiedicke. Both want me to come. Shall I or shall I not? A long time with friends in the Wilhelmina Café. Then we amble through the streets. Berlin at night! A cesspool of sin! And I am to throw myself into that?

Goebbels' mood changed next day, when he went out to Potsdam, where seeing the palace of Frederick the Great and his tomb inspired him to reflections on German genius and greatness.[83] Returning to Elberfeld for the weekend, Goebbels arranged to see Else. They met in Cologne on Sunday 23 September, and 'parted with a row'.[84] A few days later, Else called on Goebbels while he was in Rheydt. She evidently told him that the relationship was finished: 'She leaves and will not return.' The next day, the two met by accident, and Else was 'curt and clipped'. Goebbels' sister Maria convinced Else to see him again, but it was only to confirm that all was over. With more than a note of melodrama, Goebbels described their parting: 'We have to wait long for the train, which won't come. Autumn is upon us. The train roars in. A voice calls mercilessly, "Is the luggage van ready?" A signal! The train moves out. Else turns round and weeps. Then I close the window. The rain drums on the carriage roof! I have taken leave of life! Heartbreak!'[85]

The next day Goebbels wrote: 'I am dead and have long been buried. My heart is heavy. Tomorrow I go to Hanover and Brunswick. I am sick of it. So let's do some work. Work is the last consolation.'[86] He had decided to leave the area he had travelled through so often over the last two years, and, he now 'sadly said farewell' to some of his favourite audiences, like the 'splendid people' in Bochum.[87] On Saturday 10 October Goebbels called in Berlin for further negotiations, and had what he called a 'great day'. He was driven around the Avus, a racing track to the southwest of Berlin, and in the evening he took part in a torchlit procession celebrating the NSDAP's first 'Mark Brandenburg Day'.[88] The acting *Gauleiter* Schmiedicke wrote to Goebbels on 16 October requesting him formally to take on the leadership in Berlin; if he did not, Goebbels was told, the local party would disintegrate.[89] On 18 October he was back in Elberfeld, and wrote: 'On 1 November I finally go to Berlin. I am pleased. Berlin is really the centre. For us too. A world city.'

Even though he knew now that his future lay elsewhere, Goebbels was not finished with his home territory. He was planning the disruption of a Social Democrat meeting in Hattingen, an industrial town where he had enjoyed a long relationship with the strong local Nazi group.[90] Goebbels, Kaufmann, and the local SA men occupied many of the seats at the meeting before it began and successfully broke it up once it had started. Goebbels was still thinking of Else, but he recorded, there was 'no word' from her. It was on another strenuous round of speeches that Goebbels received, in Plauen, a letter from Hitler confirming his appointment as *Gauleiter* for Greater Berlin, with complete authority over the party there.[91] Early in November, Goebbels travelled again to Bavaria, and conferred with Hitler about Berlin. He gave an interesting insight into the Party leadership, writing: 'Afterwards I sit with the Chief, Himmler, Hess, and Maurice together. The Chief is marvellous, as ever. He likes me a lot. He explores big plans.' It was in this informal company that Goebbels' mission was sealed.[92] Symbolically, Goebbels finished a volume of his diary before he left Elberfeld a few days later: 'Off to battle! Berlin! Asphalt or Fulfilment?'[93]

4

'You Are the Nobility of the Third Reich'

When in the autumn of 1926, I sought out the office of the Nazi Party in Greater Berlin for the first time, I was genuinely dismayed. It was in a cellar, in a back courtyard on the Potsdamer Strasse, and was known by the Party comrades themselves, with biting self mockery, as the 'opium den' ... I was strengthened in my conviction that only an energetic, intelligent, and diligent man would suffice to raise up the Party in Berlin. This man arrived in the course of the winter.

> Julius Lippert, later the editor of Goebbels' newspaper *Der Angriff*.[1]

Joseph Goebbels was 29 years old when he arrived in Berlin on 9 November 1926 to take charge of the Nazi Party there. He was a small man, weighing only 50 kilogrammes, and slightly over 1.5 metres tall. His head, with its large brown eyes, seemed almost too large for his body. His dark hair was already receding at the temples. Although he walked with a limp, he was active and energetic. He was a man with a totally focused sense of purpose, single-mindedly dedicated to his leader and to advancing the Nazi Party. He had no fear of the Party's enemies, or of dissident elements within. He was contemptuous of other political groups and politicians, filled with a burning sense of hate and resentment, and he had an unqualified faith in the ultimate success of the Nazi cause.

On his arrival in Berlin, Goebbels was taken to his first lodgings in the city, in the apartment of Hans Steiger, editor of a local newspaper and a friend of the Strasser brothers. Goebbels' room here was 'right in the middle of the big city on the Potsdamer Strasse', not far from the Party Headquarters in Berlin, a dingy basement on the same street. Goebbels did not start his campaign for the city from these inauspicious premises. He spent much of his first full day in Berlin with Hitler, at the house of the Bechstein family. Although Hitler evidently spent some of the time on one of his favourite topics, reminiscing about the *Putsch* of 1923, their conference was significant. Goebbels took up his post as *Gauleiter* for Berlin-Brandenburg with Hitler's full confidence, and knew that Hitler would support whatever measures he took. On 11 November there was a general meeting of the Berlin Party in Spandau, and this was Goebbels' first appearance as the new leader.[2] In a three-hour speech he made it clear that he demanded unconditional loyalty, and was not sorry when one of the SA leaders, Hauenstein, walked out of the meeting with 50 of his supporters. At the end of his speech, given (he thought) with 'an angel's tongue', Goebbels was acclaimed by those who had stayed. The next day he dictated his first *Gau* circular.[3]

This document, backdated to 9 November 1926, is revealing.[4] In it Goebbels dissolved all existing local groups of the Party, and reformed them as 'sections', with leaders chosen by him. Party members were informed that the Party Headquarters were 'not to be confused with a place to get warm', and more significantly, that the Berlin SA would still be led by Kurt Daluege, but could only appear in public with Goebbels' agreement. The new leader also announced that he was instituting a 'school for speakers', which all 'Party comrades' were free to attend.[5] Here we see the three planks of Goebbels' strategy in Berlin: the assertion of his own leadership; control of the local SA, which alone could provide physical protection and intimidate opponents; and his emphasis on the use of propaganda.

For some time Goebbels had concerned himself with this theme. He had spoken about propaganda, and taken part in meetings on this subject with Hitler. In August 1926 he had composed a memorandum on 'New methods of propaganda', very probably the same as the essay with this title he published in 1927.[6] Given his future role as Propaganda Minister, and his place in history as the great manipulator of the twentieth-century mass media, it is worth considering what Goebbels understood by 'propaganda' at this early stage of his career. Essentially, he meant two things: the spoken and the written word. He had not had opportunities to use the technologies of film and radio, as neither he nor the Party yet had access to these media.[7] Public radio broadcasting had started in Germany only in October 1923, and was still in its infancy. Like Hitler, Goebbels believed that the power of the spoken word was his most important weapon. He devoted great attention to the preparations for his speeches, and as we have seen, critically observed those of other Party speakers. In his 1927 essay he argued that there must be a centralized, coordinated approach to all the Party's propaganda, and consideration of the atmosphere in which a speech was delivered, arguing that 'an overflowing guest room is better than a huge empty hall'.[8] In his 1931 account of the 'struggle for Berlin', he wrote: 'Propaganda in itself has no basic methods of its own. It has only one goal, and in politics this goal is always the conquest of the masses. Every means which serves this goal is good ... modern propaganda also depends essentially upon the spoken word. Revolutionary movements are not made by great writers, but by great speakers.'[9]

As a practising journalist, with unfulfilled literary ambitions and a studious nature, he also attributed great importance to political writing, and was beginning to appreciate the importance of all publicity, good or bad. He was delighted that the Berlin press took early note of his arrival there, even if only to complain about him. Strikingly, Goebbels at this stage had little sense of the importance of visual symbolism, unlike Hitler, who had written about the importance of colour and form in his *Mein Kampf*.[10] A surviving poster for one of Goebbels' speeches in May 1926 is revealing: it was produced by the Party in Breslau, and announces a 'protest meeting', at which the 'famous pioneer' of the Rhineland and the Ruhr will speak on 'the road to power for workers of the hand and brain'. Goebbels' name is incorrectly spelt as 'Göbbels'. At the top of the poster is a small picture of Hitler (which appeared in many Nazi publications), his mouth sealed, with slogans to either side contrasting the ban on Hitler speaking with the freedom given to 'racketeers and bosses'. The whole production is strikingly amateurish.[11] All this was to change. Goebbels had in October 1926 met a young Berlin caricaturist, Hans Schweitzer, who worked for the Strasser brothers, and was on good terms with Goebbels' host Hans Steiger. From their first meeting Goebbels was impressed with Schweitzer's artwork and, once established in Berlin, Schweitzer became his closest confidant. On 14 November, having asserted his control over the local party, Goebbels hosted a convivial gathering. Hitler was there, with his driver Maurice, Daluege, Gregor Strasser, and Hans Schweitzer. They sat up late, listening to Hitler.[12] Schweitzer had already developed a forceful individual style as a poster artist and cartoonist, using stark colours, and typically juxtaposing images of noble, heroic Aryan figures with seedy, obese, lecherous Jewish stereotypes. Schweitzer became Goebbels' chosen illustrator, producing dozens of posters and cartoons for him over the next few years, adding a powerful visual element to Goebbels' propaganda offensive in Berlin.[13]

If Schweitzer's style was crude and unsubtle, Goebbels' combination of elements of propaganda in the support of 'the cult of dead heroes' was more complex.[14] Goebbels came to adulthood in a society which had lost over 2 million dead and many more wounded in the First World War. He grew up in an area where mining accidents were not infrequent. His friend Richard Flisges combined these two misfortunes, and well before Goebbels met Hitler and became acquainted with his ritual celebration of Nazi 'martyrs' he had developed his own romanticized vision of the passage to death in which images of funerary ritual, graves, memorial architecture, and the surrounding landscape were invested with great significance. He had developed a powerful sense of redemption, believing that the influence of a dead comrade lived on to inspire the living. In one of his first published articles, in December 1923, Goebbels had written in this vein about the 'hero's death' of Richard Flisges, greeting him 'in the empire of the dead' with the words: 'Youth is not dead. It lives and believes.' In his as-yet-unpublished novel *Michael Voorman* Goebbels had used an imagined description of Flisges' funeral as the dramatic culmination of the whole book, writing with studied simplicity: 'miners carried him to his grave'.[15] As Goebbels helped to build up the Party in the Ruhr, funerals had been used as public demonstrations of the Nazi movement and its concern for its members. Where Hitler celebrated the marchers who had been shot by the police in Munich in November 1923, Goebbels elevated to the status of heroes those, like Flisges, who lived a simple life of work, duty, and honour amongst the *Volk*.

8a. *Paths to the Third Reich* (1927), a pamphlet in which Goebbels popularized a phrase taken from the title of a book by Moeller van den Bruck. The cover picture is by Hans Schweitzer.

8b. Goebbels' first and only published novel, *Michael: A German Destiny in Pages from a Diary* (1929). This was a revised version of a manuscript written in early 1924.

Goebbels brought to his exploitation of these dead heroes an individual dimension lacking in Hitler's steely, impersonal vision of the Nazi martyr. Given Goebbels' total lack of sympathy for his opponents, it is difficult to judge how genuine his sympathy was for the Nazis who were killed and injured in the political violence of what he and other Nazis called the *Kampfzeit*, or 'time of struggle'. His own words suggest that he was genuinely moved by the funerals of dead 'comrades'. In December 1925 he had recorded his attendance at a wintry funeral in the Ruhr: 'Yesterday a burial in Oberhausen. The Storm Detachment with flags. One of our best men a casualty in a mine. I spoke as the darkness fell.'[16] Earlier that month he described the commemoration festival held for Leo Schlageter, a young man executed by the French occupation forces in 1923, after being tried for sabotage: 'Yesterday and the day before in Düsseldorf. On

Sunday a big Schlageter Festival. In the morning at the Zoo. Beethoven and Grieg. Then my remembrance speech in front of 2,000 people. I spoke from a whole, full heart. And the people thanked me from full hearts ... And then out into the deep white snow. 1,200 SA men on the route to Schlageter's grave. A hollow. In the centre a cross and spade, on top a steel helmet. Our people have worked wonders. I had a comrade ... Kaufmann speaks. Going to the heart. Muffled drumbeats go by.'[17]

Goebbels had no sooner arrived in Berlin than he had to visit Party members in hospital, mainly SA men injured in fighting in the working-class district of Neukölln. He made this public attention to the wounded, and to the families of those SA men who were killed a central part of his propaganda over the next few years. In his diary he described Berlin as 'cruel asphalt', and rejoiced in the prospect of violence. On 20 November, he wrote, characteristically: 'Now we can get to the great work. Attack upon attack. Blood is flowing.'[18] In early January, a Party member from Unna in the Ruhr sent Goebbels a 'wonderful Browning pistol'. He added: 'It shall be my loyal accompaniment.'[19] In all his verbal imagery for the early Nazi Party, and in his private life, Goebbels used the theme of sacrifice. As soon as he had reorganized the Party in Berlin he set up what he called a 'Community of Sacrifice', an inner group of supporters giving 10 per cent of their incomes to the Party. From contemporary reports written by Reinhold Muchow, a committed young Nazi in Berlin, it is clear that in these first few weeks in Berlin, Goebbels succeeded not only in suppressing dissent within the Party there, but in generating a sense of inspiration and purpose, and in recruiting many new members.[20]

With Else no longer part of his life, Goebbels was longing for female company. His gaze lingered on women he met in Berlin, and he wrote repeatedly of his desire for a woman. He had a completely split view of women, and his longing for a sexual and emotional partner who would conform to an image of Germanic virtue was matched by his disdain for women in the Party. In Berlin he had no sooner arrived than he had to deal with Elsbeth Zander, the leader of the *Deutscher Frauenorden* (Order of German Women). In a Party that openly advocated that women should play an exclusively domestic role, she was an exception. Zander has the unique distinction of subsequently being the only female member of the 'Reich Organization Leadership'. She must have been a remarkable woman, by any measure, but Goebbels treated her with contempt. On 21 November 1926 he wrote:

Discussion today with Miss Zander. The affair of the *Deutscher Frauenorden* has now been ruled upon. One has to give the women something to do. Things to do with love are best.[21]

He was evidently more impressed with the new 'typing girl' he employed in the Party office. 'She brings a bit of sunshine into the everyday greyness. We can use that.'[22] A few days later he came back to her in his diary, describing her with a now dated German expression:

> Our typing girl, Ilse Bettge, is brave and good and virtuous and dependable. She can help me with everything. Right now she is registering my post and is happy in that, as only a teenage girl [*Backfisch*] can be.[23]

As Christmas approached, Goebbels spent a great deal of time with Hans Schweitzer and his wife Margarete, and through them he was introduced to 20-year-old Dora Henschel. On 17 December he had to attend the Christmas celebration of Zander's Order of German Women, but he was far more excited about the prospect of meeting Dora Henschel the next day.[24] When he went home to Rheydt for Christmas, Goebbels even met Else again. They spent an 'afternoon filled with happiness, alone' on Christmas Day at the house of Else's sister Lotte.[25] Despite this lyrical description, the time together seems only to have rekindled their confused feelings of previous years, and nothing further came of the reunion.

Back in Berlin, Goebbels threw himself into political struggle. As well as taking new inspiration for his visual propaganda from Schweitzer, Goebbels was elevating violence to key status in the public display of the Nazi Party. A meeting in Spandau in January 1927 developed into a brawl with Communists, and Goebbels recorded his satisfaction: 'In my wildest dreams I had not imagined anything like this! Where there is fighting, there is only victory and defeat. This was our victory! When I drove home, there were 2,000 fanatical fighters there to celebrate me. Now I really am the leader of these searching, yearning people. God protect the German *Volk*! ... Work! Struggle! Victory!!! That is where I am in my element!'[26] The Berlin Party now had enough money to buy a six-seater Benz, and a few days later Goebbels was driven out to the industrial town of Cottbus in the car. There he led an SA procession through the town, and spoke in the marketplace, he claimed, to 12,000 people. His speech was interrupted by 'bloody fights' with the police, and there were 'badly wounded on either side'. On arrival back in Berlin, Goebbels found that there had been a bomb attack on the new Party Headquarters in the Lützowstrasse, leaving 'many, many, wounded'.[27]

On 11 February Goebbels held his often-described meeting at the Pharus Hall in Wedding, a Communist stronghold, which again degenerated into a pitched battle. After visiting wounded SA men in hospital the next day, his car was showered with stones, and it was only 'as if by a miracle' that Goebbels was unscathed.[28] The 'Pharus Hall Fight' was quickly mythologized by Goebbels, and over the next few years he produced a number of heroic accounts of it, which have since served as fodder for later writers. According to this narrative, the

Nazis at the meeting were greatly outnumbered by the Communists, but once they were brutally attacked, they responded heroically to defend themselves, to clear the Communists from the hall and, after the arrival of the police, to allow Goebbels to continue his speech. Several of the SA men, wounded in the fight, were brought up onto the stage, bandaged, where as martyrs they heard the words of their new leader.[29]

By this time the authorities were well aware of the danger posed to public order by Goebbels' movement in the capital, and his meetings were attended by large numbers of police. On 15 February he spoke again in Spandau, his entourage travelling with him in two cars, 'armed to the teeth'.[30] In March there was another violent confrontation, which began when Nazis returning from a march outside the city attacked a group of Communist musicians coincidentally in the same train. The police report on the disturbances which followed at the Lichterfelde-Ost station suggests that Goebbels' claim to be 'armed to the teeth' was not mere bravado:

The national socialists attacked the communists under the onset of heavy revolver fire and with lance-like, iron flagpoles, after which something like nine lightly and five severely wounded were taken away from the battle field.[31]

After this the Nazis marched back into the city, and Goebbels recorded a disturbing incident: 'A procession through the town ... Our brave lads hauled a Jew out of a bus. How I love these lads! We are creating uproar all over Berlin.' Goebbels did not explain why it was courageous of his young thugs to single out a Jewish man for intimidation like this, nor did he record what happened to the victim.[32] Goebbels' enthusiastic follower Reinhold Muchow wrote a detailed account of the whole confrontation at Lichterfelde-Ost, alleging that the revolver fire came from the Communist musicians on the train, but describing how sustained attacks on them with stones eventually left their carriage totally wrecked, and all the Communists inside badly injured. He proudly noted how the face of the first man to be brought out afterwards was 'a shapeless bloody mass'. Muchow then recorded how, while a column of 800 uniformed SA men accompanied by 1,000 others marched through Steglitz and Friedenau, 'insolent Jews were beaten up without further ado'.[33] This was the first display in Berlin of this kind of Nazi behaviour, which was to become commonplace all over Germany after 1933, and of course over much of Europe after 1939, and it caused considerable outrage in the Berlin press, which demanded that further pogroms be prevented, and the perpetrators punished. Several SA men were in fact arrested and later sentenced to prison terms for their part in these brutal assaults. Goebbels himself was called as a witness in the case, but managed to frustrate the first efforts to interrogate him a few weeks later. He was on a brief speaking visit to the Ruhr when he was named by the police, and when they tried to speak to him on his return to Berlin Goebbels was surrounded by a crowd of his supporters on the platform at the Anhalter station, and was carried on their shoulders to his waiting car. Summoned to appear in court next day, he refused to give a statement.[34]

Conscious that he was gaining ever more publicity with his tactics of violence, and that he was physically overawing the Communist opposition, Goebbels now focused his attention on getting Hitler to speak in Berlin. He was now in much more frequent contact with his beloved leader, and on 1 May, Hitler arrived. After speaking to a large closed meeting, he addressed two smaller gatherings the next day, one of them on the theme of 'sacrifice'. Hitler had brought an old comrade with him, Captain Göring, and although Goebbels was in awe of the First World War pilot, he felt initially disappointed in him. His slightly touchy response to meeting Göring may also reflect some jealousy of another man so close to Hitler.[35] Days later, another of Goebbels' meetings closed with two companies of police searching all attending for weapons. After this, on 5 May, the Berlin-Brandenburg Nazi Party was formally dissolved by the Prussian police, and Goebbels himself was banned from speaking in Berlin. On 12 May a 'mass protest' against the ban was banned by the police, but Goebbels relished the confrontations that developed with the police when a crowd of his supporters hoping to hear him speak was locked outside a hall in Charlottenburg.[36]

Although horrified by the expense of employing lawyers, Goebbels was learning to exploit the strengths and weaknesses of the legal system in Weimar Germany. He was utterly unscrupulous in this, taking advantage of the slow communication between different regional courts, and of the tendency of many prosecutors and judges to sympathize with political activists on the right who appeared to be motivated by patriotic sentiment. While contemptuous of the respect for procedure displayed by the police and by court officials, Goebbels was quite prepared to take advantage of all possibilities the system offered for delaying, obstructing, or appealing against the same procedures. He immediately lodged an appeal against the ban on him speaking, and subsequently a formal complaint against the dissolution of the Nazi Party in Berlin.[37] He could afford to be fairly content in the meantime. In only six months, Goebbels had transformed the situation of the Nazi Party in Berlin. From an impotent, fractious group, it had become a tightly organized, disciplined, and violent movement with the potential to mobilize crowds several thousand strong. Its activities, and the 'riots' it was causing, were the subject of constant attention in the press.[38] Garish posters all over the city were bringing the Party, its imagery, and the names of its key figures to much wider notice. The ban on the Party lasted until 31 March 1928, but was constantly subverted in the meantime, for example by Party groups meeting under the guise of sporting or musical associations. Goebbels turned to other forms of propaganda, and devoted his energies largely to the production of his own newspaper.

During these early months in Berlin Goebbels spent much of his free time together with Schweitzer and his wife; often they sang and played music together. In December 1926 Goebbels sat for a portrait by Schweitzer. He wrote that he was developing a new style of speaking, in which he 'dematerialized' people and ideas, concentrating on types rather than individuals.[39] He might have been describing the stereotypes in Schweitzer's caricatures. It is no coincidence that Goebbels in early 1927 developed the theme of 'the unknown SA man' in his speeches and articles, celebrating an idealized but anonymous martyr to the movement. 'You are the nobility of the Third Reich' he declared in one article titled 'The unknown SA man'.[40] In a series of drawings Schweitzer developed a visual counterpart to Goebbels' spoken and written portrayal. The image of a brutish, square-jawed SA man with a bandaged head became a regular feature of Nazi posters. The two men also went to the cinema together, heightening further Goebbels' interest in the visual media. In January 1927 they saw one of the 'mountain films' of Otto Fanck, *Der Heilige Berg* (*The Holy Mountain*) and Goebbels was moved to write in his diary about the combination of natural scenery, human drama, and dance it presented, 'so much in our own spirit'. He was particularly struck by the dancing of one of the young actresses: 'A woman, no, an angel, Leni Riefenstahl. She danced in the open before the film showing. A delightful, delicate, creature ... I was blissfully happy.'[41] In March Goebbels went with the Schweitzers to see Fritz Lang's *Metropolis*, but although he was impressed by the production he thought the film's content too sentimental.[42] Films in 1927 were still silent, but Goebbels was alive to the power of music, and spent time recruiting a marching band, and getting the composer Hans Gansser to write songs for the Berlin SA choir.[43] He was enthusiastic about some of Gansser's songs, but still felt that the movement needed something better, a hymn to rival the Communist anthem, the *Internationale*, as a statement of belief and common purpose.[44]

If there is a moment in Goebbels' life when we can identify his emergence as – in Jeffrey Herf's terms – a 'reactionary modernist', it is this. Goebbels had overcome his earlier distaste for Berlin, and was replacing this with an idealized vision of 'the city of millions'. Although he still enjoyed using descriptions like 'the asphalt desert', this was now double-edged, tinged with veneration for the SA men who sought to dominate this alien, and modern, world. Goebbels had for the first time access to a car for his own personal use, and was developing a passion for motor vehicles. More importantly he was beginning to see the value of modern mass media as tools of communication. In the years to come he would increasingly seek to present technology and its fruits not as components 'of alien, Western *Zivilisation*', but as 'an organic part of German *Kultur*'.[45] The word 'modern' became a term of approbation in Goebbels' vocabulary.

In 1927, his focus was on popular journalism. Goebbels had previously worked on several newspapers, but they had been controlled by others. The *National-sozialistische Briefe*, which he had edited, was a sheet intended primarily for

Party officials, and was used by other senior Nazis as a forum for discussion. It had carried articles by others such as Rosenberg, disagreeing with Goebbels' own views on subjects like Russia. It was published by the *Kampfverlag* (The Fighting Press), a house owned by the Strasser brothers, which produced several newspapers, including the *Berliner Arbeiter Zeitung* (*Berlin Worker's Newspaper*). In March 1927 Goebbels was offered the editorship of the *Nationalsozialistische Monatshefte* (*National Socialist Monthly Journal*), which was produced by Franz Eher, the Party publisher in Munich, but this was not what he wanted. His violent tactics in Berlin had attracted much criticism, above all from the Strasser brothers, and he wanted a newspaper which he controlled, could aim at the ordinary party member, and by extension to the man in the street in Berlin. He also wanted an opportunity to develop his own style of journalism. As early as December 1926 Goebbels was writing privately about his erstwhile comrades in the damning, vitriolic way that he was using publicly for his opponents. After receiving a letter from Gregor Strasser warning him that his tactics would lead to catastrophe, Goebbels wrote: 'Strasser has written a stupid, illogical letter to me. They both remain what they are: an apothecary and a lawyer.'[46] Two months later Goebbels wrote his account of a defining moment during a conversation which took place in the Steiger household, where he was still staying, significantly on the subject of Jakob Goldschmidt, a director of the Dresdner Bank. Goldschmidt was Jewish, and Goebbels subsequently made him the target of many attacks:

> To the house. The Strassers are there. We fall into conversation. Frosty, cold. And suddenly they showed their true colours. 'Goldschmidt stands as close to God as Parsifal.' This is what Otto Strasser said, and Gregor nodded his assent. Conclusion! Full stop! The end of the Strasser chapter. It happened. One more disappointment. Now we are only Party comrades. Nothing more.[47]

After this Goebbels developed a particularly rancorous hatred for Otto Strasser. Two days later he wrote: 'Dr Otto Strasser is causing me concern. Until I have the dog exterminated.'[48] Goebbels never recovered confidence in the Strassers. In the manner that was endemic in the Nazi Party he became involved in the exchange of insults, slurs, and innuendos, both directly with them, and through others. It is deeply ironic, and somehow salutary that the worst accusation that could be made in this climate was of Jewishness, or of a hint of Jewish inheritance. An article was published in the Strasser newspapers on 23 April 1927, ostensibly by an old colleague from the Ruhr, Erich Koch, indirectly suggesting that Goebbels was congenitally disabled, and thus hinting at Jewish ancestry. Goebbels, who dismissed Koch as a 'proletarian',[49] was certain that the article had really been written by the Strassers, and took his complaint against them directly to Hitler, when the two met for a Nazi march in Essen on 27 April. After the ceremony he collared Hitler: 'Afternoon in the hotel. Hitler let me come up. I complained about Strasser. He was quite of my opinion. He hates Dr Strasser [Otto]. Now the matter in Berlin will come to a decision.'[50] In fact over the next few weeks Hitler did nothing, while the feud between his lieutenants deepened.

After the ban on the Berlin Party in May it came out into the open. 'Either they stay or I do', Goebbels wrote on 7 June 1927. Three days later he convened a meeting of his Berlin Party leadership at the offices of the German Women's Order in Steinmetz Strasse. There were 16 people present, including Goebbels, the SA boss Daluege, supporters like Hans Schweitzer, and Elsbeth Zander. A report of the meeting was sent to the Party Headquarters in Munich, describing how Goebbels called for a vote of confidence before reading out Koch's defamatory article from one of the Strasser newspapers. He alleged that 'Koch was not endowed with sufficient intellect to compose such an article', and that it had been planted by the Strassers. He had further been told by a third party that the article was a production of the *Kampfverlag* intended to undermine Goebbels' position in Berlin. Finally, Goebbels said that 'the article in question was all the more monstrous as his club-foot was not congenital, but the result of an accident in his youth'. Cleverly he left the room while the vote of confidence was debated. The Strassers were not present, and in Goebbels' absence, his friend Schweitzer spoke up. He said he

> had come to know Dr. Strasser [Otto]. From the beginning he had disliked Dr. Strasser's sugary and excessively friendly manner, and he had been unable to get used to it for a long while. He then criticized Dr. Strasser, and, quoting another Party comrade, said that Dr. Strasser had a shot of 'Jewish blood in his veins'. Visible evidence was his red crinkly hair, the hooked nose and his obese, fleshy face. He, too, expressed the opinion that Dr. Strasser was the author of the article in question and condemned the conduct of the Kampfverlag.

Goebbels got his vote of confidence, and he also crucially got a ruling from this meeting that his own newspaper *Der Angriff* (*The Attack*) would henceforth be the regular paper for the Party membership in Berlin.[51] A few days earlier, in Munich, Goebbels had sought and gained Hitler's approval for the newspaper.[52] Gregor Strasser immediately wrote to Hitler to defend himself against Goebbels' accusations, but Hitler met Goebbels on 20 and 21 June, and after long conversations agreed to publish a declaration of his confidence in Goebbels in the *Völkischer Beobachter*. He also agreed that *Der Angriff* would henceforth be published by the Party house in Munich.[53] At the same time he refused to endorse any of the allegations made against the Strassers, and over the next few months he studiously avoided being drawn further into this festering dispute.

Strikingly, while the conflict between Goebbels and the Strasser brothers became steadily more acrimonious, Goebbels took his case not only to Hitler and to the Party leadership in Berlin, but to ordinary members around Germany.

Aside from the personal slurs being traded, the principal charge of the Strassers against Goebbels was that his violent tactics in Berlin were counter-productive, as evidenced by the prohibition of the Party there. Although banned from speaking in Berlin, Goebbels still spoke in other parts of Germany in May and June 1927, and used these meetings to defend his tactics in Berlin, and to mythologize the actions of the SA there. While in Munich to press his case with Hitler, Goebbels also addressed a Party meeting on the evening of 20 June. At the time, Goebbels was so preoccupied that he devoted only one sentence to this meeting in his diary, but an anonymous police informant was also present, and sent in a summary of events to the Munich police. According to this source, there were some 450 Nazis present, only a few in uniform. Goebbels apparently spoke at length about the activities of the Party in Berlin, claiming that they had recruited 600 new members there in April alone. He contrasted its activist approach with what he saw as the supine conduct of the *Stahlhelm* (or Steel Helmets), a nationalist veterans' organization led by the ex-officer Franz Seldte. The *Stahlhelm*, although sharing many of the Nazis' nationalist, militarist, and anti-Semitic views, was committed to 'just and peaceful means'.[54] The police informant quoted Goebbels as declaring that if 120,000 SA men were to march in Berlin, they would not

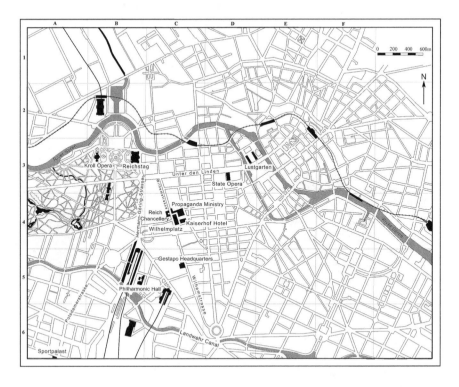

9. Map of Berlin, city centre, 1939.

leave the city as they found it, a sarcastic reference to the peaceful conduct of the *Stahlhelm*, which had recently mobilized 132,000 men for a memorial march in Berlin. Goebbels apparently continued by threatening the authorities in Berlin who attempted to repress the Nazi Party there, that the time would come 'when the National Socialists would pay them back in the same coin, with interest and with compound interest'.[55] This revolutionary rhetoric was standard fare for Goebbels at the time, but these words were to come back to trouble him later.

While the Party was banned in Berlin, Goebbels diverted much of his energy to the production of his newspaper. He had settled on the name *Der Angriff* in May 1927 and wrote a great deal in his diary about his hopes and fears for the newspaper. By pestering various supporters he scraped together the money, but his plan was almost undone at the last moment by the arrest and imprisonment of his editor, Julius Lippert, for unpaid fines.[56] Curiously Goebbels was briefly away from Berlin, speaking for the first time in a foreign country, in the Sudeten region of Czechoslovakia, when the first issue was published on 4 July 1927,[57] after a sustained and clever poster campaign, and he only saw the second issue a few days after its publication. He had travelled by train, hoping to speak in Vienna, but was turned back at Passau on the border after objections to his travelling were raised by the German government. He then went to Munich but found to his chagrin that Hitler was, paradoxically, in Berlin. While travelling back, he was given a copy of *Angriff*, which he thought was 'brilliant!'[58] The next issue, he wrote, was 'Masterly!'[59]

10. The masthead of *Der Angriff* (*The Attack*), the newspaper established by Goebbels in 1927. The newspaper pioneered a new style of popular journalism and this is reflected in its modern typography, unchanged here 16 years later in 1943.

Although there were considerable difficulties with the early issues of *Der Angriff*, it became a key weapon in Goebbels' struggle for influence in Berlin. At first the newspaper had only a print run of 2,000, and came out weekly, but over the next few years, its circulation grew, and from October 1929 it was issued twice weekly. After November 1930 it was published daily. By then it was the most widely read

Nazi newspaper in northern Germany, as well as in Berlin. Goebbels proudly described it as a 'revolutionary fighting newspaper', and in *Der Angriff* we can identify several distinctive features he contributed to Nazi journalism. The paper was written in an outspokenly aggressive manner, and although it was similar to existing Nazi papers in giving extensive coverage to Party activities and affairs, Goebbels, who wrote all the leading articles, also used a more direct, personal style to create a sense of embattled sympathy amongst Party 'fighters'. His most effective articles were written in the style of his diary, in a breathless first-person narrative. The front page of *Der Angriff* always carried a cartoon by Schweitzer, under the pseudonym 'Mjölnir' (a Norse word meaning 'Hammer of Thor' or 'Destroyer'), and these accentuated the ostentatiously anti-Semitic tone of the paper. The first issue had a caricature of the Jewish banker Jakob Goldschmidt on the front page, and in his first leader Goebbels declared: 'Germany is an exploitation colony of international Jewish finance capital.'[60] The second issue attacked several Jewish lawyers by name.[61] Many subsequent issues had front-page leaders devoted to the 'Jewish question'.[62] *Der Angriff* frequently carried hints of

11. 'The Future is Ours', a poster by Hans Schweitzer for the Nazi Party Rally in Nuremberg, September 1927. Schweitzer became Goebbels' closest confidant in Berlin between 1926 and 1930, and alerted him to the possibilities of the visual image in propaganda.

menace about how Jews and other opponents of Nazism might be treated in the future, not only in its leading articles. For example, the issue of 19 September 1927 carried a small piece describing how an SA man had been stabbed in Cottbus by a Jew. The article was sarcastically titled 'A Jewish knife hero', and ended with the words: 'Nothing will be forgotten. Come the day!'[63]

Der Angriff was aimed at the working man, and was in many respects similar in its style to the existing Communist newspaper *Die Rote Fahne* (*The Red Flag*). Communists themselves were always portrayed in *Der Angriff* as dupes of Moscow, cynically manipulated by their German leaders. In Schweitzer's cartoons, Communists, if portrayed with 'Aryan' features, were typically represented as slobbish and undisciplined, in stark contrast with the taut, controlled manliness of the SA. From the inception of the newspaper Goebbels included a column headed 'The fight for Berlin' which portrayed the Berlin SA as heroic, embattled fighters, and gave news and announcements about local Party events, and he soon added a regular column titled 'From the asphalt desert' which extended this theme with a focus on local confrontations. Goebbels also instituted a 'political diary' which he used to comment on wider affairs. At the back of the newspaper there was a bizarre mix of everyday advertisements for (non-Jewish) Berlin shops and for specialist suppliers of Nazi literature and clothing.

Der Angriff was outspokenly hostile to all republican politicians and institutions as well as to individual opponents. Goebbels created in *Der Angriff* an antithesis to his own leadership of the Nazis in his presentation of the Berlin Police Vice President, Bernhard Weiss, as the Jewish stereotype of 'Isidor'.[64] Over the next few years, Weiss – a decorated veteran of the First World War – was presented as a personal opponent, determined to use any means to suppress the Nazis, but at the same time viciously mocked for his Jewishness.[65] Goebbels became so obsessed, and self-satisfied, with his mockery of Bernhard Weiss that he went on to publish two books devoted to offensive jokes and cartoons by Schweitzer about him.[66] Although many were repelled by the 'harsh and uncouth' language of *Der Angriff*, others were not, and it evidently drew some people into the Nazi movement. One ex-soldier, who was not yet a Nazi Party member, wrote:

> One day early in 1927 I bought a copy of a weekly, *Der Angriff*. The name of the magazine attracted me. After a study of the first copy I could not wait to see the next, and I fervently read its attacks on the Republican regime. From then on I became a regular reader of *Der Angriff*, which brought me in close contact with the Party fighting for a new Germany.[67]

While the first issues of *Der Angriff* were circulating Goebbels was still preoccupied with his quarrel with the Strassers. He returned immediately to Berlin after his failed journey to Vienna, to try to speak to Hitler about this. He found that Hitler had not discussed the allegations traded between Goebbels

12. The second book, published by Goebbels in 1931, viciously attacking Berlin police chief Bernhard Weiss. Note the use of a Hebraic script for 'Isidor'. The book's title, *Knorke*, is a word from Berlin dialect, best translated as 'Brilliant' or 'Cracking', which Goebbels took to using after his arrival in Berlin in 1926.

and the Strassers with anyone, and now insisted on discussing preparations for the forthcoming annual Party rally, to be held for the first time at Nuremberg, rather than in Weimar. Schweitzer joined them, and impressed both Hitler and Goebbels with a poster he had drawn for the rally, with the legend 'The Future is Ours'.[68] A week later, Goebbels left Berlin for a short holiday in Bavaria. He went to visit the grave of Richard Flisges in Schliersee, and returned to Munich for the general meeting of the Party on 30 July. For all his adulation of Hitler, Goebbels was developing a strong aversion to Munich and the whole atmosphere around Hitler there. He wrote of the meeting: 'Boring reports. Finance, organization, and goodness knows what. Then Hitler speaks. Brilliant as ever. In front of this Munich crowd, pearls cast before swine.' The next day, Goebbels was thrilled when Hitler took him out to Schliersee in his car. The two went for a long walk, and settled that Goebbels would speak on propaganda at the Nuremberg Rally. Sitting by a mountain stream, it seems again that Hitler did most of the talking, and reminisced about his family. It became a conceit of Goebbels that his and Hitler's family backgrounds were remarkably similar, another proof of the common destiny which he felt bound them together. Hitler then returned to Munich, leaving Goebbels to stay in the village. He watched some folk dancing, and recorded an incident which suggests that he took his aggressive dislike of Jews into his private life: 'In the evening I watch the dancing. A row with a greasy Jew, who came too close to a German girl. And Israel took himself off.'[69]

The Nuremberg Rally, held over the weekend of 19–21 August, was the first which Goebbels had been involved in planning. It followed the pattern of earlier meetings in Weimar, with a succession of marches and speeches, and great celebration of contingents arriving from distant parts of the country. Nuremberg itself was a historic city in southern Germany where the Nazi Party was strong. The town's long-established associations with German culture, art, and singing were all grist to the Nazi mill. There was a torchlit night parade by the Party's uniformed organizations, the SA, the SS (a recently formed personal bodyguard for Hitler), and the Hitler Youth. The police took careful note of the proceedings, and a report to the government estimated that there were 8,500 uniformed men and 300 youths present. It put the overall turnout of supporters at 15–20,000, roughly twice as many as in Weimar the preceding year. The SA was most strongly represented by a contingent from the Ruhr, and the police noted the presence of a Berlin SA group which had walked all the way to Nuremberg, and carried a banner with Goebbels' slogan *Trotz Verbot – nicht tot!* ('Despite the ban, not dead!')[70] Goebbels made much in *Der Angriff* and in subsequent accounts of this first Nuremberg Rally of how the Berlin SA was particularly feted, and idealized the unemployed SA men who had walked all the way to Nuremberg for the rally. He described their joy as they were able to don their banned SA uniforms once they had left Berlin.[71] A constant theme of the speeches in Nuremberg was hatred for the Jews, both abroad and inside Germany. The rally passed off peacefully. Significantly, Hitler and Goebbels commissioned a film of the rally, further proof of a developing recognition of the potential this medium had for propaganda.[72]

Goebbels, for all the show of public unity at the Party rally, was by this time obsessed by his differences with the Strassers. Every meeting with Hitler appeared to him first and foremost as an opportunity to speak about this. But Hitler refused to be drawn onto the subject. When he called in Berlin in September, he cleverly used the presence of his sister and his niece Geli Raubal, and events like the showing of the film of the rally to avoid giving Goebbels the opportunity to speak about the Strassers. Even Goebbels' unconditional loyalty to Hitler was tested. In November Hitler demanded from Goebbels a truce with the Strassers, to which Goebbels assented, not for a moment in private renouncing his ill-feelings towards them.[73] Aware that the Communist press was writing about divisions in the Nazi Party, Hitler staged a 'United Front' meeting in Munich on 19 December 1927, appearing alongside Goebbels and Gregor Strasser. The *Völkischer Beobachter* carried a long article on the spectacle, ironically titled 'The "divided" NSDAP'. It displays in its bombastic and ponderous style a striking contrast with Goebbels' own more lively prose:

> The masses in the densely occupied hall of the *Hofbräuhaus* also showed their interest in the news of a division, in giving an enthusiastic, heartfelt ovation

13. Poster for a meeting in Berlin on 8 November 1927, at which 'Dr. Goebbels' will speak on 'The German *Volk*'s Dance of Death'. This was Goebbels' first public speech in Berlin after a long ban, and he attracted a large audience, writing: 'I have rarely seen such an overflowing hall.' (*TBJG*, 8 November 1927, TI, 1/II, p. 289.)

to the three 'disunited' leaders when they entered the hall together. They came, according to the understanding of our asphalt friends from Berlin, to see a party not only once, but in three ways divided, and they found a united front of 'disunited' directions of which any other party would be proud. They found a united Hitler, Strasser, Goebbels front, which means more than a comradely, coincidental coming together. Rather it is underpinned by the common belief in a high, holy, mission and from a feeling of loyalty, that they are bound in the same common idea, and also to the same leader in the person of Adolf Hitler.

That is why the succinct words of Gregor Strasser were so convincing in their precise formulation, as he put forward a confession of faith in the national socialist movement and its leader, fully in the spirit of the old front soldier, for whom the political struggle had also become a form of responsible service ...

That is why Dr Goebbels correctly remembered the spirit of every dead member of the movement, whose blood sacrifice imposed a similar responsibility on the living ...

Adolf Hitler however, the enthusiastically celebrated Party Leader, was able today to point to this united front in spirit and in deed, which had everywhere shown how national socialist men unfurled the swastika banner in the hard years of the fight.[74]

Not the least interesting aspect of this report is its use of one of Goebbels' own journalistic phrases, 'the asphalt press', for the Berlin newspapers, here sarcastically rendered as 'our asphalt friends'.

Although constrained publicly to go along with the spectacle of unity presented in the *Hofbräuhaus*, Goebbels still fulminated in private about the Strassers, particularly Otto. His record of the 19 December meeting contrasted sharply in its brevity with the tedious prose of the *Völkischer Beobachter*. It does not suggest that the 'united front' was genuine:

First Strasser speaks, then me, then the chief. An explosive mood. People virtually pull my hand off.

Finish at 11.00pm. Strasser takes his leave.[75]

Hitler and Goebbels had another matter to debate in these months, the issue of 'parliamentarianism'. Goebbels had fashioned himself as a revolutionary, and was totally scathing about parliamentary democracy. In June 1927, at the height of his dispute with the Strassers, he had gone to the *Reichstag* and seen Gregor Strasser speaking. This prompted him to write: 'The road to life for the German people goes over the corpse of this institution.'[76] After the ban on the Berlin party, Goebbels was forced to conform to Hitler's plan of pursuing a legal route to power. *Reichstag* elections were due in May 1928, and the Party had to devise a strategy. On 24 November 1927, Goebbels discussed this with Hitler:

> The Chief laid out the next election campaign. I will unconditionally get into the *Reichstag*. Albeit that may damage my reputation, but against that will be the immunity.[77]

Reichstag deputies were at this time elected by proportional voting, from a Party list. Those candidates placed highest on a party's list had the best chance of a seat in the *Reichstag*, with the free rail travel and immunity from prosecution which accompanied this. Having been promised a place at the top of the Nazi Party list by Hitler, Goebbels threw himself into the first of a series of nationwide electoral campaigns. Over several months he travelled intensively, speaking in dozens of towns all over Germany, taking advantage of the freedom given to him to speak again in Berlin after 30 October 1927.[78] A few days after this, he was charged in court for the first time, in Elberfeld, with incitement to resistance against state power. He was fined 100 marks, but proudly noted that in the judgement he had been credited with 'noble motives for the fatherland'. He celebrated with an old friend from the Ruhr, Viktor Lutze, and together they griped about the Strassers.[79] Goebbels affected a show of bravado in his diary when writing about his many court appearances (most of which arose from libellous articles in *Der Angriff* or from incitements to violence in his speeches), and at times even appeared to welcome the prospect of imprisonment, which would provide an opportunity for martyrdom, but in truth he did not want to be incarcerated. The closer the elections in May 1928 came, the more he looked forward to the prospect of parliamentary immunity.

As in his days in the Rhineland-Ruhr, Goebbels still loathed speaking to middle-class audiences; it was left to Hitler to court the captains of industry and reassure them that their property would be safe under a Nazi dispensation. Goebbels did enjoy speaking to students, and of course to workers. Nor could he resist the use of violence. In February, as the elections drew closer, and the Nazis sought to whip up frenzy, at least amongst their own hard core of supporters, Goebbels spoke to several meetings in Berlin. After he gave three speeches in one day on 24 February there were fights between Nazis and Communists; Goebbels' driver Tonak was stabbed three times, not fatally.[80] The next morning Goebbels was hauled out of bed at 6.00 a.m. by the police, taken to the station in Moabit, eventually charged on five counts, and released.[81] On 28 February Goebbels was sentenced to six weeks' imprisonment for incitement to violence. He cast himself as a Christ-like martyr, commenting that 'now Isidor will have his fun, as he has again put someone on the cross'.[82] Goebbels again managed by appealing to delay the imposition of this sentence.

As well as spending more and more time in court, either as the accused, or as a witness, Goebbels was now using his greater prominence to try to reassert himself as a writer. His 1923 play *The Wanderer* had been rewritten, and was premiered in Weimar's Wallner Theatre in November 1927.[83] The reviews were very mixed, but the production of *The Wanderer* brought about a personal meeting which was much more important than the play itself. On 6 March 1928 Goebbels was in Weimar to see the performance. Goebbels claims that it was followed by a huge ovation, but his pleasure at this was quite overtaken by a surprise when he returned to his hotel: 'Then the door opens, and before me stands – Anka Stalherm. I shake, I stutter, I quake with joy: Anka!' Briefly, Anka explained to Goebbels that she was now married, had a four-month-old child (by another man), was unloved, and joyless. He lay awake all night, and they met again in the morning before he had to return to Berlin, for yet another speech in Potsdam.[84] Goebbels' unexpected reunion with Anka threw him into turmoil. Since arriving in Berlin in November 1926, he had courted several young women, and eyed up many others. His acquaintance with Dora Henschel had come to nothing, but he had developed a closer relationship with Tamara von Heede, a Russian émigrée he met in December 1927. As they spent more time together, Goebbels had even wondered if he was in love with her. Seeing Anka again made him realize that he was not, and in the weeks leading up to the election in May 1928, Goebbels was constantly distracted by the possibility of renewing his relationship with Anka.

He was captivated by her, as he had been almost ten years previously, and they met several times. According to Goebbels, she told him of her current difficulties; their continued love for one another was felt but not spoken. In April he introduced her to some of his Berlin friends and colleagues, the Schweitzers, Tonak, and his secretary Ilse Bettge. He was doing a round of election speeches in Thuringia, and was able to call in Weimar to see Anka. She was, however, a respectably married woman, and it was clearly not easy for her to go out in public with Goebbels and his friends. When they called on her to go to the theatre, she made an embarrassing scene outside her house, and told Goebbels she could not go. Later, she turned up as he and his friends left the theatre, but although he tried to forgive her, he was wounded. The next day, in a long discussion, she confronted the prospect of separating from her husband to take up with Goebbels again, but stepped back from the brink. Goebbels was even introduced to her husband, and some of Anka's friends, and he was repelled. They were too bourgeois for his liking, and he wrote in his diary that Anka herself was, in the final analysis, a bourgeoise. He concluded that he could not help her.[85]

On 13 April 1928, Goebbels celebrated the formal re-establishment of the Nazi Party in Berlin. He described it as a 'historic hour', and incorporated the date into the mythological narrative of the Party in Berlin which he was assiduously constructing. The ban on the Party had been lifted after the announcement of the *Reichstag* elections, and the campaign now moved into a frenzied tempo. The election manifesto issued by Goebbels in *Der Angriff* shows how duplicitous his commitment to the path of legality advocated by Hitler was, and is striking for the crudity of its language. It presented 16 demands, some of which, like that for 'the restoration of German honour', or for 'apartments and bread', sounded reasonable, if very vague. One called unambiguously for 'an end to the parliamentary swindle'. Several were openly anti-Semitic, one demanding 'Jews out of German administration and economy', and another calling for 'the right of the front soldier above the Galician intruders'. The penultimate demand used one of Goebbels' favourite phrases at this time: 'To the gallows with profiteers and black-marketeers.'[86]

Goebbels was slightly shocked by the prison sentences given on 17 April to a number of his men involved in the gun fight at Lichterfelde-Ost back in March 1927, but he maintained a furious programme of public speaking. On 28 April, Goebbels and his office manager, Dagobert Dürr, were both sentenced in Berlin to three weeks' imprisonment for 'distortion of name and personal insult' in a case against Bernhard Weiss.[87] Goebbels appealed against the sentence, and hoped that forthcoming immunity as a *Reichstag* deputy would keep him out of prison. On 1 May he spoke to two meetings in Düsseldorf, and was delighted to see his mother and a number of close relatives there.[88] He alternated speeches in and around Berlin with others given as far away as Aschaffenburg, Schweinfurt, and Leipzig. Days before the election he travelled to Munich where he spoke to four meetings in quick succession, and fitted in a brief talk with Hitler before returning to Berlin. In the last few days before the voting he focused on Berlin. On 16 May he led his SA men on a provocative march through working-class districts of Berlin. They proceeded through Spandau, Neuendorf, Tegel, and into Wedding, through streets lined with Communist supporters, whistling and jeering. Remarkably, there was no violence. After two more meetings in Friedrichshain on 20 May Goebbels and his associates retired, with high hopes, to the Party Headquarters to await the results.

Not until the evening of 21 May were sufficient results announced to make the overall picture clear. The Nazis had made no breakthrough, gaining only 2.6 per cent of the vote, much less than in 1924. In Berlin itself, for all Goebbels' efforts, they received only 1.7 per cent of the vote.[89] The two parties of the left, the Communists and the Social Democrats, made considerable gains. Under the Republic's proportional voting system, the Nazis were entitled to only twelve *Reichstag* deputies, but these included Goebbels. This compensated significantly for his disappointment. His diary for 21 May reads: 'Inner depression. The necessary reaction to the last few weeks.'[90] The next day he wrote: 'I am therefore a member of the *Reichstag*. Immune, that is the main thing.'[91]

5
'We Will All Three Be Good to One Another'

One night in October 1930, about a month after the Elections, there was a big row on the Leipzigerstrasse. Gangs of Nazi roughs turned out to demonstrate against the Jews. They manhandled some dark-haired, large-nosed pedestrians, and smashed the windows of all the Jewish shops. The incident was not, in itself, very remarkable: there were no deaths, very little shooting, not more than a couple of dozen arrests. I remember it only because it was my first introduction to Berlin politics.

> Christopher Isherwood, in his 'Berlin Diary, Autumn 1930'.[1]

The *Reichstag* elections of May 1928 were a grave disappointment for the Nazi Party. For all the intensive campaigning – to which Goebbels had made a significant personal contribution – the Party had patently failed to attract mass support, or to detach voters from the Communists or Social Democrats. The disappointment inaugurated a period of reorganization which lasted for two years, and paradoxically saw a deeper commitment to the electoral process as the means of gaining power and installing a Nazi dictatorship. For Goebbels this was a profoundly painful period. He had styled himself as a revolutionary; he was most at home in the atmosphere of a public meeting conducted with opponents present, and followed by street fighting. He had developed a fascination with the themes of martyrdom and sacrifice, and with funeral rites. He exalted the figure of the 'unknown SA man', an anonymous working-class hero ready to sacrifice all for the cause, and he had utter contempt for the democratic process. He found himself profoundly out of sympathy with several of the directions taken by the Party after May 1928.

Membership of the *Reichstag* itself brought Goebbels little joy. The Nazi 'fraction' of twelve deputies had virtually no power, and direct involvement with parliamentary procedures only heightened Goebbels' contempt. After his first session on 13 June he described the *Reichstag* as a 'palaver'.[2] In *Der Angriff* he wrote that the Nazis came into the *Reichstag* 'like wolves amongst a flock of sheep', and contemptuously styled their deputies not as 'Members of the *Reichstag*', but as 'Holders of Immunity and a Free Travel Pass'.[3] Goebbels benefited directly from both of these; the prison sentence passed on him shortly before the election was not enforced, and several other cases against him were abandoned over the next few months. Goebbels determined not to be drawn into parliamentary activity, and carefully limited the time he spent there. He used his first *Reichstag* speech, on 10 July, to make a coarse attack on the institution.[4] Nor was he impressed by closer contact with Germany's leading politicians. In November 1928 he wrote: 'Yesterday Stresemann spoke. A terrible jellyfish. I was able to see him from quite close up. So that is the *Reich*'s Foreign Minister. Terrible! Poor Fatherland!'[5] As far as Goebbels was concerned, the real business of politics took place outside the *Reichstag*, and he was relieved that his fellow Nazi deputies were not seduced by being part of the institution.

Although Nazi electioneering had previously been concentrated on the cities, the Party's vote in May 1928 had gone up significantly in several rural areas, and Hitler now made for the first time a determined effort to appeal to small farmers and agricultural workers. This move was supported by a restructuring of the Party's *Gau* boundaries, to make them correspond with the electoral districts of Germany. Goebbels' *Gau* Berlin-Brandenburg was divided in September 1928, and the rural areas surrounding Berlin were detached from his control.[6] The Nazis had also at this time to clarify the position of women within the Party. Goebbels' view on this was clear. He shared Hitler's vision of clearly separated gender roles, with women restricted to the domestic sphere. Since arriving in Berlin in November 1926, he had had many dealings with Elsbeth Zander's Order of German Women, which was only later affiliated to the Nazi Party, and regarded this mainly as a tedious chore. In a speech to the Order in October 1927 he had said, echoing Hitler:

> Struggle is a matter for men, the woman's role is to be a mother. The mother is the symbol of the future and of fertility, she is the law of life and of the community of fate. Women must do auxiliary service and support the state through educating the young offspring. The future of the nation lies in the hands of the woman. She will, if she recognizes this duty, look down with contempt on modern emancipated females. She will recognize that war is the father of all things. She bears her child in battle and protects it. It remains in combat throughout its life until death.[7]

In his diary, Goebbels, put all of this more succinctly: 'Women should have nothing to say about politics.'[8]

After the elections of May 1928, it nonetheless became increasingly important for the Nazi Party to organize the many disparate women's groups which bizarrely supported it. Even Goebbels had noted, after telling the Women's Order that

14. 'Goebbels speaks', a poster for a meeting in Berlin in November 1928, showing a developing awareness of visual imagery. Like many of Goebbels' early speeches, this one is directed at Marxists, asking why they have murdered their fellow worker, the SA man Kütemeyer.

motherhood was their allotted role, that 'the women are the most fanatical'.[9] It is impossible to avoid the suspicion that his dislike of the 60-year-old Elsbeth Zander was founded largely on her appearance and age. A historian of women in Nazi Germany writes: 'Zander, wearing shapeless housedresses, with her hair carelessly arranged in a bun, projected a most ordinary image.'[10] The same writer notes Zander's ability as an orator, but Goebbels never remarked on this. More typical was his comment in March 1929, when he met her in Zweibrücken: '*Fräulein* Zander is also there. Awful!'[11] In 1928 and 1929 Goebbels had to put in many appearances with the Women's Order in Berlin, and to encourage them in their 'auxiliary work'. An important component of this which Goebbels did appreciate was the provision of nursing help for injured SA men. From January 1929 he acceded to the Order's request for its own newssheet, and this appeared as a fortnightly supplement in *Der Angriff*, entitled *Heim und Welt*, or *Home and*

World. The first issue's leading article proclaimed that *Home and World* would 'not speak of rights, but of duties'. This was followed by a piece addressing that burning question for Nazi women, 'Blonde or Dark?' Urging women not to be sidetracked into too much concern with this, the article stressed that 'the task of the woman' was to create the National Socialist family.[12] Goebbels, who certainly preferred blondes, took some pleasure from simply being amongst so many young women, and from the adulation of several. He developed closer relationships with a succession of young members of the Women's Order, including Hannah Schneider, Jutta Lehmann, and Xenia von Engelhardt, but none of these developed beyond a hopeless infatuation.

15. The leadership of the Nazi Party at a meeting in Weimar, 20 January 1929. Goebbels has made sure he is centrally positioned, next to Hitler. Second from right in the front row is Elsbeth Zander, the only woman in the group. Goebbels had only contempt for Zander, who was the leader of the Order of German Women, but on this day his attention was focused on Anka Stalherm, the first love of his life, who called on him during the meeting. He wrote: 'Anka comes in the break. She is really enthusiastic about all these people.' (*TBJG*, 20 January 1929, TI, 1/III, p. 168.)

Goebbels was still corresponding with Anka, and occasionally seeing her, and the contrast between this worldly, mature woman, and the girls of Zander's Order was obvious to him. Frequently he wrote that knowing Anka had made it impossible for him to get on with other women. At Easter 1929 Anka and her husband Georg Mumme joined Goebbels and the Schweitzers for a brief holiday in the Harz mountains, but the whole episode was painful, frustrating, and embarrassing for Goebbels.[13] In July 1929, Anka and her husband invited Goebbels to stay with them in Weimar. Goebbels recorded that one night during his brief stay Anka came to his bedroom at 2.00 a.m., and told him that her husband was not returning home that night. Unwilling to abuse his host's hospitality (according to his own account), Goebbels told Anka that she must return to her own room. The next morning, after bidding them farewell at the station, Goebbels wrote: 'Live well, both of you. I must leave you in all your tragedy and your nothingness. I have no time to give myself over to women.'[14]

Goebbels frequently used this rationalization, that he was too busy, as he wrestled with his continuing inability to form a lasting relationship with a woman. All around him, colleagues and contemporaries were getting married, some like Hans Schweitzer having children, while he remained single. Nor was it only female companionship which eluded him. Goebbels was at this time a profoundly lonely man. Although often in the company of others, at the centre of crowded events and gatherings, he had no real friends. He was still physically separate from the Party leadership in Munich, and from his hero Adolf Hitler. Indeed, he was contemptuous of those around Hitler, few of whom he thought rose above 'beer hall level'. In Berlin, the nearest he had to a friend was Hans Schweitzer, who at least shared his radicalism, and his interest in the arts and music. But Schweitzer was now a married man with the responsibilities of fatherhood, and, for all that he thought him an illustrator of genius, Goebbels did not consider him as an intellectual equal. Night after night, as he worked in his bachelor flat, or as he travelled from one speaking engagement to another in the train, Goebbels felt his isolation. His health was often poor, not least as a result of his strenuous lifestyle. He was often in pain from his foot. Frequently, after working in the Party office all day, he would visit several sections around Berlin in the evening to check on progress and to whip up morale. He wrote constantly, for *Der Angriff* and for other Party newspapers. When he was speaking in other cities, he typically sat up late with local Party supporters, and travelled on the next day after only a few hours' sleep. He was maintaining an extraordinarily demanding schedule. The *Völkischer Beobachter* produced a list of the Party's main speakers in 1928: Goebbels had addressed 188 meetings, a figure exceeded by only two others.[15]

If Goebbels found solace in his work, it was also a constant source of worry to him. Above all he was alarmed by Hitler's temporary rapprochement in the summer of 1929 with right-wing groups, like the veterans' organization the *Stahlhelm*, and the Nationalist Party, led by the press baron Alfred Hugenberg. This shaky alliance was formed to campaign against the Young Plan, which had rescheduled Germany's reparations payments. Goebbels gloried in the irresponsibility and clarity of pure opposition, and loathed the idea of any compromise, even with other nationalist groups. He was particularly sceptical about those he described as 'bourgeois', and was keenly aware that as Nazis became involved in

everyday politics, not only in the *Reichstag*, but in municipal and regional admin-
istrations around Germany, there was a real temptation for them to abandon
their revolutionary stance. He was fully aware of Hitler's public commitment to
legality, and he dutifully echoed this in the columns of *Der Angriff*, but actually
steered a difficult course between street violence and electoral participation. In
moments of solitude and doubt he even feared that Hitler was losing his way,
and would be seduced into compromise. He wrote long letters to him, some of
which went unanswered, and he fretted about the influence of the sycophants
around him in Munich. He even voiced criticism in his diary. In March 1929 he
wrote: 'The Chief, as ever, is not available, and avoids any decision.'[16] A few weeks
later he wrote: 'No word from Hitler, although I have questioned him urgently
about the matter of the *Stahlhelm*. That is somewhat lazy.'[17]

Even though Hitler was after September 1928 permitted to speak in public, he
still came only infrequently to Berlin, and Goebbels saw little of him. When he
did, all his doubts were overcome, and his veneration for 'the Chief' was renewed.

16. Goebbels speaking
in Bad Freienwalde,
13 October 1929. In
the 'time of struggle'
Goebbels frequently
gave speeches in the
open air, without
any amplification.
On this occasion
he wrote: 'I spoke
in the overflowing
marketplace. Speaking
out in the open always
makes one terribly
hoarse.' (*TBJG*, 14
October 1929, TI, 1/III,
p. 348.)

Goebbels' total dependence on the still distant figure of Hitler is illustrated by an incident in September 1929, when, just as he was about to address a packed hall in Breslau, he was handed a telegram, apparently signed by Rosenberg, stating baldly that Hitler had been fatally injured in an accident. Unable to proceed, Goebbels left the platform to telephone Munich. For half an hour he waited, 'the most terrible time that I have yet lived through', before being reassured that Hitler was alive and well. The telegram was a hoax. Although Goebbels returned to the meeting and spoke for two hours in an emotional atmosphere, he could not recover his equilibrium. 'I am unable to sleep the whole night. Now for the first time I realize what Hitler is to me and to the movement: Everything! Everything!'[18]

In fact, the Party's commitment to elections provided Goebbels with the perfect opportunity for the kind of political activity he excelled in, frequent public meetings, often with Communist opponents present. Communal elections for Berlin were held in November 1929, and Goebbels used these to stir up a violent and feverish atmosphere. His still small Nazi movement was not the most pressing public order issue confronting the Berlin police. They had been confronted in early May 1929 with several days' of street fighting, in which 33 people were killed and hundreds injured, in Communist districts of the city, and now had to protect Nazi meetings from violent disruption, an irony not lost on Goebbels.[19] In September 1929, he and his driver were set upon by an angry crowd of workers after an SA march in the working-class district of Neukölln, and only just managed to escape after Tonak was hit by a stone. Subsequent Nazi propaganda alleged, not implausibly, that shots were fired at them.[20]

In preparation for the communal elections, Berlin was saturated with Nazi posters, flyers, and announcements. Sales of *Der Angriff* were slowly rising, and dozens of meetings were held in a frenzy of propagandistic activity. Goebbels had no particular policy programme for Berlin, but made it abundantly plain that the Nazis viewed this, as other local elections, as just one step on the road to power. Once in power, beyond the establishment of a dictatorship and vague promises to rebuild a national community, or *Volksgemeinschaft*, there was again no specific programme. The results, announced on 18 November 1929, were hugely encouraging. The Nazis polled 132,000 votes in Berlin, compared to only 39,000 in May 1928. These regional elections are overlooked in many general histories, but this was a critical point in the Party's history. Dietrich Orlow notes that 'Almost overnight, the local elections of 1929 brought the NSDAP to national political prominence.'[21] Goebbels was one of 13 Nazis appointed to the Berlin municipal council, an activity he treated with the same calculated indifference that he displayed towards his *Reichstag* membership.

Although Goebbels did not comment in his diary on the Wall Street crash just before the November elections, its effects were quickly apparent in Berlin and in Germany. The numbers of unemployed rose rapidly, and government at all levels was forced to cut spending. Conditions for the poor, and above all for the unemployed, were desperate. Goebbels shared the sense of crisis, and it was heightened for him by the death of his father in Rheydt in December 1929. In his diary Goebbels sanctified this in the language he now habitually used for SA men killed or wounded by political opponents: 'He was a complete man. A good fellow! A man of duty. A fanatic for work. A berserker in the execution of his tasks, however small they were.' Goebbels wrote that at the funeral, while his sister Maria and his mother wept unrestrainedly, 'I hold myself strong.' Later, Goebbels revisited the grave with his mother: 'My father now sleeps a long sleep under flowers and wreaths after a life full of work and duty.' For all these sentimental outpourings, Goebbels' relationship with his father had long been difficult and distant, and Goebbels had frequently before described his father as a 'petty-bourgeois and a philistine'. Coincidentally, Goebbels met Else Janke after the funeral, and she asked him whether he often thought of her. He wrote: 'I lied and said yes. She has not changed at all. Still as dainty and tender as back then.'[22]

His father's death brought home to Goebbels a keen sense of his own isolation, and a personal dimension to his perception of the growing crisis engulfing the country. Even as the Party began to improve its electoral showing, he feared that it was losing its way internally. Throughout the winter of 1928–29 Goebbels was preoccupied by possible developments in the world of Nazi newspapers. He had plans for *Der Angriff* to appear as a daily paper in Berlin, but knew also of plans by his arch enemy, Otto Strasser, to issue his own daily, using the presses of the *Kampfverlag*. Again and again Goebbels pressed Hitler to sanction his scheme and to disavow Strasser's, but Hitler hesitated. He had as far back as March 1929 offered Goebbels the post of *Reich* Propaganda Leader,[23] but had not yet finalized this, or announced it to the Party. Goebbels had to try to plan for practical eventualities, such as whether he would need to take a flat in Munich and to spend time there regularly, without being absolutely certain that the job was his.[24]

After spending Christmas at home with his grieving family, Goebbels returned to isolation in wintry Berlin, and tried to deal with all these issues in an atmosphere of growing tension. His sense of the presence of death was heightened by further events. On 28 December 1929 he attended the funeral of Werner Wessel, a young SA man who had died in a skiing accident. Five hundred uniformed comrades marched past carrying torches. Goebbels 'could hardly speak'.[25] On 14 January Werner's elder brother Horst was shot in the face by Communists who entered his flat. Horst Wessel was a pastor's son and former student who had abandoned his studies to take up the Nazi cause, becoming an SA *Sturmführer* (the title given to the leader of an SA squad or 'storm'). Wessel had, rather in the manner of Goebbels himself, been particularly aggressive in leading incursions into Communist territory and giving inflammatory speeches in an atmosphere of confrontation. Wessel had impressed Goebbels with his 'fanatical idealism', and Goebbels felt a keen sense of personal involvement as soon as he heard of the shooting. On four occasions he visited the hospital where Wessel languished before dying on 23 February.[26] Goebbels had frequently to console Wessel's mother, distraught at the loss of a second son, and realized immediately that he had before him the prototypical martyr of the movement.

Goebbels directed all his propaganda methods onto the mythologization of Horst Wessel. He described him as a 'Christ-socialist' in *Der Angriff*, and presented there a narrative of Wessel's life which explicitly drew on the tropes of the Passion.[27] In one of several emotional articles, Goebbels wrote that Wessel was one who 'through his death, called out "Come to me and I will bring you redemption"'.[28] Shortly after Wessel's death Goebbels was given his 'political diary' by Wessel's mother, and this provided him with copy for further articles in *Der Angriff*. Wessel had left another testimony in the form of a song, *Die Fahne hoch* (*The Flag Held High*). This hymn-like march song, which became the anthem of Nazi Germany, the *Horst-Wessel-Lied*, had in fact been adopted by the Berlin SA months before Wessel's death. Like many Nazi songs, it was an existing tune with new words. Earlier in September 1929 Goebbels had been sufficiently struck by the song at a meeting to make a special note,[29] and he took to using its first line, '*Die Fahne hoch!*', as an expression of commitment in his diary, and at the end of articles in *Der Angriff*, rather as years before he had written '*Sieg und Heil!*'[30] The song was printed in *Der Angriff* in September 1929, and its popularity quickly spread outside Berlin. It was sung at the set-piece of Wessel's funeral on 1 March 1930, a turbulent ceremony conducted amongst large crowds of hostile Communists. On the same day, the words of the song were printed on the front page of the *Völkischer Beobachter*, under the title 'Horst Wessel's greeting to the coming Germany'.[31] This was the song Goebbels had been looking for which could act as an anthem for the movement. With its four-square tempo it worked as a marching song; emotionally it combined a degree of solemnity with triumphalism, which made it perfect for Nazi ceremonies. It could be performed effectively by voices alone, but gained in power if accompanied by a military band or a full orchestra. By May 1930 it had become part of Nazi ritual to close every meeting with a communal rendering of Wessel's song.

Goebbels saw in Wessel's funeral a huge opportunity for propaganda, and was genuinely dismayed by Hitler's decision not to come to Berlin to take part. He was further incensed by Communists who had daubed 'A last greeting to the pimp Horst Wessel' in large white letters on a wall of the cemetery, and tried to prevent the funeral cortège from reaching its destination. The graffiti referred to Wessel's girlfriend; according to the Communists a working prostitute, according to the Nazis a reformed woman. Hitler was meanwhile relaxing in the mountain air on the Obersalzberg, and Goebbels was forcibly struck by the contrast between this behaviour and the tense situation in Berlin. It came at a point of unprecedented disillusion. Despite all Goebbels' scheming, and a thinly veiled warning published in *Der Angriff*,[32] Otto Strasser had started to publish his new daily newspaper, the *National Socialist*, on the same day as Wessel's funeral, and used it to advocate a more left-wing course. Goebbels saw this as a direct threat to his own position and an open challenge to Hitler's leadership. He desperately urged Hitler to intervene and to forbid the paper or to expel Strasser from the Party. As Hitler temporized, Goebbels became more and more exasperated. Several entries in his diary catalogue his feelings. On 2 March 1920 he wrote: 'I am very sceptical whether [Hitler] will not, as ever, avoid the issue'.[33] Two weeks later he was more vehement: 'Munich, including the Chief, has lost all credit with me. I don't believe them any more. Hitler has – for whatever reasons, it doesn't matter – broken his word to me five times.' On 28 March he wrote: 'Hitler has in this matter alone [the Strasser newspaper] already broken his word on four occasions. I don't believe him at all any more.'[34]

Finally, on 27 April, Goebbels was invited to Munich with other leaders, and saw the issue resolved. Hitler had finally decided to force a breach with Otto Strasser and to communicate this to the Party leadership. His brother Gregor had opted to side with Hitler, and listened 'with a guilty conscience' while Hitler announced his decision. At the end of the meeting, Hitler announced Goebbels' appointment as *Reich* Propaganda Leader with immediate effect to 'a breathless silence'. Confident in his belief that Otto Strasser at least would be thrown out of the Party and his paper closed down, Goebbels returned to Berlin in an exultant mood. After the crisis of the past few months, he felt the intoxication of success.[35] He had, he recorded, pursued a four-year struggle against Otto Strasser.[36] In fact, Hitler still waited, and it was not until 30 June that he ordered Goebbels to carry out an 'unrestrained purification' of the Party, in other words to expel Strasser and his supporters.[37] Otto Strasser and a handful of his followers saved Goebbels the trouble by resigning on 4 July. Gregor Strasser distanced himself from his brother, who formed an organization called the 'Black Front', which attracted little support.[38]

Through the summer of 1930, Goebbels remained doubtful about Hitler, and privately criticized his leadership methods. The contrast between Hitler's leisurely and self-indulgent lifestyle in and around Munich contrasted too blatantly with the embattled mood in the Party's Berlin office, and on the city streets. Goebbels had during the months of crisis, found if not a friend, at least a companion. He had come to spend more time with fellow *Reichstag* member Hermann Göring and his Swedish wife Carin, and he warmed to both. After his election to the *Reichstag* in 1928, Göring, who had no official position within the Party, had taken on a renewed public role, and became a frequent speaker at Goebbels' meetings in Berlin. He consistently took Goebbels' side in the conflict with Otto Strasser, and Goebbels came to value Göring's companionship. Sometimes he met with Göring and other former flyers, and he was thrilled by their tales of First World War adventure. Through Göring, Goebbels was introduced to members of the aristocracy, and although he still felt a residual hostility to the rich, he was increasingly tempted by the pleasures of relaxation in comfortable surroundings. In April 1930, Goebbels travelled with the Görings to Sweden for a brief holiday. He thoroughly enjoyed this excursion but was unimpressed by the Swedish Nazis he was introduced to. He was fascinated by the 'divine blonde women', but less impressed by the Swedish men, whom he thought 'too blond to be clever'. Watching the changing of the guard outside the royal palace in Stockholm, he thought the Swedish cavalry lacked the precision of the Prussians. At a social gathering he had an argument with one officer, whom he felt had the characteristics of many Swedish men. Goebbels summarized this as 'German on the outside, half-Jewish inside.'[39]

Conversely, as Germany plunged into economic chaos, the lifestyle of the Nazi elite became strikingly more luxurious. The Party was beginning to attract substantial funds from businessmen, and on 2 May 1930, just after Hitler's purchase of the so-called 'Brown House' in Munich, Goebbels moved his Party office into substantial new premises in Berlin's Hedemannstrasse. The day before, he, Göring, and Tonak travelled to Leipzig to take possession of a new seven-seat Mercedes Kompressor, bought by the Party in Bamberg and sent to Leipzig on a railway flatcar. The car, wrote Goebbels, was 'like a poem', 'a sleek bitch'.[40] Over the next few months the 'glorious Kompressor'[41] was to transport Goebbels to dozens of election meetings, and to towns all over Germany. In 'a massive political blunder',[42] Heinrich Brüning's government decided on 18 July to risk calling new *Reichstag* elections, providing the Nazis with the opportunity to present themselves as the only party able to save Germany in a time of crisis.

Goebbels had now been involved in running election campaigns for several years, and put all his accumulated experience to use in the *Reichstag* elections of September 1930. He still concentrated on public speaking, and on journalism. These activities, coupled with the preparation of posters and placards, took up the bulk of his time. He travelled only infrequently to Munich to coordinate the propaganda campaign nationwide. He was fairly impressed by his secretary, Heinrich Himmler, and enjoyed the opportunity to see Hitler, but he was sickened by the petty-bourgeois provincialism of the circle which surrounded him. He particularly loathed having to sit for hours every afternoon amongst the 'horrible philistines' in the Café Heck.[43] Away from Munich, as in previous campaigns, Goebbels threw himself into public speaking, but now he was buoyed up by the sense that the masses were at last coming around. In town after town he spoke to meetings which were completely sold out. The Party paid 500 marks for a special flight to take him to speak in distant Königsberg on 6 September. On 10 September Goebbels stage-managed a rally in the Berlin *Sportpalast* which was attended by over 100,000. Snatching sleep where and when he could, Goebbels addressed crowds across Germany, claiming a record when he addressed seven separate meetings in Berlin on 12 September. His early estimate that the Nazis might get 40 *Reichstag* seats began to appear cautious, and shortly before the poll he was estimating that they would get 250,000 votes in Berlin alone.[44]

The *Reichstag* was not sitting before the elections, and Goebbels had therefore temporarily lost his immunity from prosecution. Several court cases were brought against him, mainly on charges of libel or of inciting violence against the state authorities. In one case he was accused of libelling the former Prussian Interior Minister Grzesinski in *Der Angriff*, by suggesting that he was a Jew, but he managed to get the judgement against him postponed.[45] Goebbels oscillated between fear that he would be arrested and imprisoned, a yearning for martyrdom, and more prosaically, the rest that imprisonment might bring. He revelled in the publicity and notoriety court cases brought him, and escaped in every case either with an acquittal or a fine which he could easily meet. Two cases illuminate the relationship between Goebbels and the legal system particularly well. The first arose from an article in *Der Angriff* on 29 December 1929, entitled 'Is Hindenburg still alive', attacking the President for having signed the Young Plan. It was accompanied by a cartoon which depicted Hindenburg as a Teutonic god looking down with indifference on a German nation in bondage. Following this Goebbels was charged with libelling the *Reich* President, but the case was abandoned until May 1930, when Goebbels' immunity was lifted. On 31 May Goebbels was found guilty and fined 800 marks, although the prosecution had earlier asked for a sentence of nine months' imprisonment. Goebbels gave a speech in his defence lasting one and a half hours, in which he argued that he had not attacked Hindenburg as a Field Marshal or as an individual, but had criticized his authority as a politician. Goebbels' described the judgement of the court, which stated that he should not be imprisoned because he had acted from conviction, as a 'speech in defence' of him. *The Times* in London, reporting on the case, described how police outside the court could hardly keep a turbulent crowd under control. Goebbels, who thought he had been 'fabulously in form' described the whole event as a 'a day of celebration', and in one of his favourite phrases, as 'a victory right down the line'.[46]

In June 1930 the Supreme *Reich* Court in Leipzig instigated a charge of high treason against Goebbels. This was potentially far more serious than a libel case, but the prosecutor in Leipzig attempted unwisely to base the charge on Goebbels' reported statements to a Party meeting in Munich back in June 1927, and specifically on his alleged threat that if 120,000 Nazis were to march in Berlin, they would not leave the city as they found it. Goebbels was called in for examination on 31 July in Berlin, and noted that the judge was 'very respectful'. He thought that the authorities were 'completely crazy' to expect him to remember details of what he had said in 1927, and thus provide them with ammunition.[47] In August the judge in Leipzig looking at the case wrote to the Munich police to ask if there was a record of this alleged statement, but they replied that the record of the meeting was derived from a confidential source who could not be exposed. The police in Munich then looked for another witness, and examined, of all people, Hermann Esser, one of Hitler's closest associates in Munich. Given that Goebbels despised Esser, and had frequently been critical of him, it speaks for Esser's sense of Party loyalty that he told the police on 2 September 1930 that although he had indeed attended the meeting, he could not remember Goebbels' exact words. He denied that Goebbels had made the alleged statement, and asserted that he was willing to testify to this under oath. Four months later the court in Leipzig was still pursuing the matter with the Munich police, who repeated that they could not supply evidence which would stand up in court. By this time Goebbels' was once again immune from prosecution as a *Reichstag* deputy.[48]

Reading the documents left over from this failed endeavour, several questions arise. Why did the Supreme Court act so slowly? Why did it try to base its case against Goebbels on alleged statements from 1927 when he had since then orally and in print delivered many threats which were equally, if not more inflammatory? Why, when they needed a witness, did they choose a dedicated Nazi who was, to say the least, unlikely to provide incriminating evidence against Goebbels? Why was it considered more important to protect the anonymity of one police informer then to prosecute someone like Goebbels, who by this time presented a significant danger to the Republic? It is difficult to escape the conclusion that the legal authorities were both lacking in determination and in competence. There is also a wider context to consider. Numerous writers have noted how the whole judiciary in Germany was unsympathetic to the Republic, and actually felt a loyalty to the now-disappeared Empire. Individual judges were typically conservative nationalists far more concerned with the political threat posed by Communism than by the Nazis. Between 1919 and 1933 the courts of the Weimar Republic were notorious for their lenient treatment of political murderers, even acquitting some who confessed to their crimes. They were similarly lax with the thousands of cases of high treason which came before them.[49]

Only days before the elections, Goebbels faced a crisis in Berlin which scared him far more than the futile efforts of the law, the 'Stennes *Putsch*'. The SA in Berlin had grown into a turbulent organization, with thousands of unruly members led by ex-captain Walther Stennes. For months Goebbels and Stennes had argued about the status and function of the SA, and over its financing. Although Goebbels retained a certain reverence for men who had fought in the war, he was no soldier himself, and his frequent quarrels with Stennes led to dismissive remarks in his diary about the narrow-mindedness of the 'military men'. As the elections approached, Stennes wanted influence over the selection of candidates for the Party election list, a matter Goebbels considered should be reserved for the political leadership. Finally, the tension came to a head while

Goebbels was away from Berlin. On 27 August, Goebbels, then in Dresden, heard that some of Stennes' men were threatening to rebel, and to ransack the new Party office in Berlin. He appears to have been genuinely frightened by this, and for a few days the spectacle of disintegration confronted him. Desperately, he telephoned Munich for help, knowing that Hitler's intervention would be necessary to resolve the crisis. Goebbels had in many respects a strong relationship with ordinary SA men, and he depended on them utterly for personal protection, particularly in Berlin, where he was now an easily recognized figure, liable to be attacked at any time by Communists.

Hitler was not initially available, and when finally roused, he told Goebbels he could not come to Berlin. Goebbels had to return and confront the situation himself. He held long talks with Stennes, and believing that matters were at least temporarily settled, rushed off to Breslau for further speeches. Here he heard that a group of SA men had indeed wrecked the Party office in Berlin while he was away, injuring two SS men who tried to defend the premises. Now Hitler did agree to come to Berlin, and after a series of meetings, he and Goebbels were able to win over the disgruntled SA. Stennes agreed to respect Hitler's leadership, and the unruly men came to heel. A few days later, Goebbels, who had been going anxiously from one SA section to another in Berlin, had to address the group which had wrecked his offices, leaving pools of blood on the floor in his own room.[50]

Neither the Stennes *Putsch* nor the earlier departure of Otto Strasser damaged the wider Nazi cause, despite the efforts of the Communists to get supporters of both Strasser and Stennes to come over to their side.[51] The election results on 14 September 1930 changed the political landscape of Germany. The Nazi Party polled over 6 million votes, giving them 107 deputies in the *Reichstag*, the second largest group behind the Social Democrats. From being a fringe group, the Nazis became a significant factor in national politics. Their huge success attracted attention all over the world, and foreign journalists flocked to Germany to interview the Nazi leaders. It was, wrote Goebbels, the reward for four years of work.[52] 'The *Volk* arises!' was the triumphant headline in the *Völkischer Beobachter*.[53] Although jubilant, Goebbels was not carried away. Over the next few months Hitler had his first power-broking conversations with Heinrich Brüning, the Chancellor of the Republic, and through his new press secretary Ernst Hanfstaengl, interviews with the world's press. He recalled Ernst Röhm from Bolivia in November 1930 to lead the SA, and through him began to court the leaders of the small German army permitted by the Versailles Treaty, the *Reichswehr*. He extended his links with industrialists, and had his first meeting with the former President of the *Reichsbank*, Hjalmar Schacht. Hitler also took the opportunity as a witness in a case before the Supreme Court in Leipzig shortly after the elections to make long speeches in which he declared, under oath, his commitment to a path of legality. The case had been brought against three army officers who were Nazis, and were accused of preparing high treason. It was the perfect opportunity to soothe the fears of the military and political classes, but although Hitler declared his commitment to legality in order to gain power, he made no secret of his less peaceful intentions once that goal had been achieved. For the second time in his career, speeches given in court were publicized nationally and internationally, including his statement that 'If our movement is victorious in its legal struggle, then there will be a German State Court and November 1918 will find its atonement, and heads will roll.'[54]

For Goebbels, the elections of September 1930 also brought changes. He too moved into a far more public light. He also attended the court case in Leipzig, and made his own comment on the path of legality afterwards, in conversation with one of the accused officers: 'I think this oath is a stroke of genius. What will our brothers do about us after that? They have only to wait now until they are sent packing. Now we are strictly legal.'[55] On 5 January 1931 he took part in a meeting with Hitler, Göring, Schacht and the industrialist Fritz Thyssen. Schacht later recorded that Goebbels kept virtually silent, but he was certainly observing carefully, and made detailed notes in his diary. He was greatly impressed by Thyssen, but not by Schacht.[56] Although Wilhelm Frick was appointed 'fraction leader' of the 107 Nazi *Reichstag* deputies, Goebbels actually played a more important role.[57] When the *Reichstag* convened on 13 October, the Nazis made an ominous statement. Shortly after the session was opened, they all walked out of the debating chamber, leaving Goebbels alone to act as an observer. The others then returned, in brown-shirted uniforms, in defiance of the rule prohibiting the wearing of uniforms.[58] Outside, turbulent crowds shouted and sang; hundreds of windows of Jewish-owned shops were broken. In his diary Goebbels wrote: 'The revolution is on the march.'[59] He celebrated the 'One Hundred and Seven' in *Der Angriff*,[60] and over the next few months took every opportunity to obstruct the proceedings of the *Reichstag*. In February 1931 Goebbels gave a long speech there in which he publicly stated his view of legality. 'According to the constitution, we are only bound to the legality of the way, but not to the legality of the goal. We want to conquer power legally, but what we will start with that power, once we possess it, that is our affair.'[61]

Goebbels also spent time on the reorganization of his office, and in changing its staff. He was preoccupied with finance, and with finding the money for his campaigning. He worked hard to get *Der Angriff* published as a daily, and fretted constantly about the situation with the SA. He also began to conceptualize and work on the book later published as *The Struggle for Berlin*, which he intriguingly described as a 'novel'.[62] Unfortunately many historians have taken this romanticized narrative of the Nazi movement in Berlin as a historical record. Goebbels also gave many speeches to groups of Nazi functionaries. The Party had started to expand massively, with a wave of new entrants. All the Party's groupings were growing rapidly, and demanded larger organizational structures.

Goebbels was now acquiring, internationally, the reputation as a 'fiery orator',[63] uniquely able to raise a crowd into a frenzy, which he has had ever since. He spoke regularly to audiences of thousands, and had made the Berlin *Sportpalast* his favoured venue. One of many who heard Hitler and Goebbels for the first time at this point was Albert Speer, then a young architect, and he later recorded his memory of both events. Speer was greatly impressed by the sober speech Hitler delivered to students at Berlin University, and subsequently went with friends to

> a demonstration at the Sportpalast. Goebbels, the Gauleiter of Berlin, spoke. How different my impression was: much phrase-making, careful structure, and incisive formulations; a roaring crowd whom Goebbels whipped up to a wilder and wilder frenzies of enthusiasm and hatred; a witches' cauldron of excitement.

Although Speer claims to have been repelled by this spectacle, he joined the Party the next day.[64] Goebbels' diary account of the same meeting suggests that Speer may not have exaggerated. Goebbels wrote that he had spoken in a 'breathless silence' for over two hours, before ending his speech in 'storms of excitement'. He described how afterwards the crowd poured out into the Potsdamer Strasse, 'as if they were crazy, storming through the traffic. It has never been as wild as this before'.[65]

Goebbels was treading a fine line along the path of legality, reluctant to abandon the habits of confrontation he had acquired over the past few years. As he struggled to reform the SA in Berlin after the September crisis, he found himself often in sympathy with Stennes, and with other militants in the Party. He still celebrated bloody encounters in the street between Nazis and Communists, and sought to incite his followers. On 6 December 1930 he led the notorious disruption of the showing of the anti-war film *Im Westen nichts Neues* (*All Quiet on the Western Front*), an event followed by several days of violent demonstrations in central Berlin, before the film was withdrawn on 12 December. Describing the showing of the film as 'Jewish provocation', Goebbels triumphantly portrayed the Nazi protesters in *Der Angriff* as 'the bearers of state morality'.[66] He still travelled to Munich every few weeks to supervise the coordination of the national propaganda effort, but he loathed the atmosphere around Hitler and resisted the impulse to move there. In November 1930 he was given 15,000 marks by the Party treasurer, Xavier Schwartz, which he used to buy a handsome apartment in Steglitz, to the south of the city centre in Berlin.[67] On New Year's Day 1931 he moved in, and here he enjoyed entertaining, hosting gatherings of Nazi leaders, and of the high society they were now mixing with. Goebbels was attracting the attention of several young women, several of whom helped him to furnish his new home, complete with a 'glorious' grand piano.[68]

There was a far more important change in Goebbels' life after the September elections. On 7 November 1930 he wrote:

Yesterday: morning, midday, afternoon, meetings. Frau Hella Koch spoke about the National Socialist theatres. A beautiful, blonde, intelligent woman. Modern and aggressive. I liked her ...

At home: reading, dictation. Once again to the office. A beautiful woman by the name of Quandt is setting up a new private archive for me.

This is the first mention of Magda Quandt in his diary, and ironically, it is immediately followed by a longer comment on another worker of longer standing in his office:

Fr. Ilse Stahl helped me on into the evening on the corrections for the conversation with Piscator. And she – stays then until 6.00 this morning. A wonderful, good, beautiful, affectionate girl. And in that way quite innocent. I like her very much. And think about her all morning.[69]

Despite this interest in Hella Koch and in Ilse Stahl, over the next few weeks, Goebbels developed a relationship with Magda Quandt which was quite different from all those he had previously conducted with women. He wrote about her next on 14 November:

Yesterday afternoon the beautiful Frau Quandt was with me and helped to sort out the photos.[70]

As well as Ilse Stahl, several other women were helping Goebbels with personal matters at this time. There is a clear suggestion, in the bracketed numbers included in his diary, that his relations with some of these women were sexual. On 7 December he wrote:

Yesterday ... Spent the evening with Olga Förster. She is a sweet abandoned woman. And loves me madly. (1.2.)[71]

It appears that he had sex again – three times – with Förster, who was due to get married to the writer Arnolt Bronnen, as he wrote on 12 December:

Yesterday ... A pleasant evening with Olga F. She is very unhappy with Bronnen, but she is a rational and lovely girl. (3.4.5.)[72]

A few weeks later there is a series of entries referring to Magda Quandt. On 28 January 1931:

Frau Quandt came to prepare the archive with me at home. She is a very beautiful woman.

1 February:
Yesterday afternoon Frau Quandt was there at work [in my flat]. She is in fact a fabulous woman, and I really wish that she loved me.

15 February:
Yesterday ... Magda Quandt comes in the evening. And stays a very long time. And blossoms in an enchanting blonde sweetness. How you are my queen! (1) A beautiful, beautiful woman! I will love you very much.

19 February:
At home. Magda Quandt comes. To a perfect, beautiful evening. She is a glorious woman and gives me peace and completion. I am very grateful for that. Beautiful Magda![73]

Goebbels now invited Magda to Party events with him, and they travelled to Weimar on 21 February for a meeting. Goebbels' account of the visit is interspersed with comments about her:

Saturday ... Magda is blissful. Such a beautiful woman, worthy of love! ... Magda looks fabulous.
Sunday ... Until late at night I sit alone, together with Magda Quandt. She is a rapturously beautiful, lovely and good woman, and she loves me beyond measure ... Berlin! Magda is beautiful and dreamy. I love her.[74]

From early in the relationship, Goebbels and Magda quarrelled. On 26 February he wrote:

With Magda Qu. to eat and to the Car Exhibition. She wants to buy a new car but can't yet decide. At home we had the first argument over a thoughtless word from me. She writes me a note of departure and leaves crying. Always the old song! I see now how beautiful she is and how much I love her![75]

It appears they were quickly reconciled, and the relationship deepened through March 1931, with Goebbels several times marking sex with her in his diary.

Magda Quandt was a 28-year-old divorcee, formerly married to Günther Quandt, a businessman who had made millions of marks from selling material for army uniforms in the First World War.[76] They had a nine-year-old son, Harald, whom Goebbels met on 12 March. Goebbels wrote that Harald was 'Quite blond and somewhat cheeky. But I like that.'[77] Magda was living at this time with

Harald in an expensive flat in the Reichskanzlerplatz, in the heart of Berlin, on a generous allowance settled on her by Günther Quandt. She was by all accounts an intelligent and beautiful woman. She was also a musician. There has been endless speculation about why she fell in love with Goebbels, but there is no doubt that the two of them shared much more than a strong sexual attraction. Very quickly they developed a shared lifestyle. Magda had the charisma to make an impression wherever she went, and clearly enjoyed being part of Nazi Party activities, from seeing unemployed SA men to attending functions as a dignitary. All accounts of Goebbels in this period mention the presence of his beautiful consort. The society columnist Bella Fromm's comment on first meeting Magda is typical:

> Tonight at the ball, Magda was lovely. No jewels except the string of pearls around her neck. Her golden hair owes nothing to any drugstore or chemist. It, too, is real. Her big eyes, iridescent and ranging from dark blue to steel gray, radiate icy determination and inordinate ambition.[78]

Goebbels delighted in having an elegant, articulate woman alongside him, and, importantly, she was in complete accord with his political ideas.

When they did quarrel, it was about Magda's past. When she first met Goebbels, she was still involved with another lover, who became intensely jealous of Goebbels. Knowledge of this and other previous affairs cast what Goebbels called a 'shadow' over the relationship, and Magda was assertive on several critical occasions early in their time together. The first was in April 1931, when the tension between Hitler's public commitment to 'legality' and the violent, confrontational approach still pursued by Goebbels came to a head. Since September 1930, Goebbels had tried to restrain the frustration of the SA in Berlin, but the dispute had taken on new dimensions. Stennes resented bitterly the imposition of Ernst Röhm as commander of the SA in January 1931, not least because he thought Röhm a homosexual. Goebbels, who had highly reactionary views about sexuality, had also picked up the rumours about Röhm. On 27 February he wrote in his diary: 'Nauseating! Hitler also lets that go too easily. The Party should not be an Eldorado for homosexuality. I will fight against that with all my power.'[79] As Stennes' complaints became more voluble, Goebbels decided, nonetheless, as he had at Bamberg in 1926, to stay on Hitler's side. On 6 March he wrote: 'I will support Stennes in the justified demands of the SA. Against that, I will fight as sharply as possible against any *Putsch* against the Party or Hitler.'[80] As in September 1930, the crisis came when Goebbels was away from Berlin.

On 28 March 1931 Brüning issued an emergency decree limiting the public activities of political parties, and Hitler immediately ordered compliance with this in the *Völkischer Beobachter*. Stennes and a group of his supporters decided to protest, and while Goebbels was in Weimar with Hitler and other leaders, Stennes' men occupied the Party offices in Berlin on Good Friday. He was apparently joined there by the renegade Otto Strasser.[81] As soon as he heard of this rebellion Goebbels, who had privately written that compliance with this legality 'made him want to be sick',[82] decided to 'stand loyally with Hitler ... The movement is above everything. The SA must obey.'[83] The next few days were a time of intense crisis for Goebbels. With his own offices in Berlin occupied, he had to travel with Hitler to Munich, where he stayed for the next five days, while Hitler denounced Stennes and his supporters, and called for loyalty to the Party, and of course to himself. While in Munich, Goebbels heard that Göring, still in Berlin, had sought to take 'full power' in Goebbels' absence. 'I'll never forget that of Göring', he wrote bitterly.[84] Two factors were decisive in steadying Goebbels' nerves: first, Hitler constantly and publicly assured him of his support, and thus rejected Göring's suggestion that he assume control in Berlin while Goebbels was absent. Hitler renewed Goebbels' 'full powers' as *Gauleiter* of Berlin, giving him authority to purge the Berlin SA, and he published an appeal for loyalty in the *Völkischer Beobachter* on 4 April.[85] Second, Magda Quandt rushed to Munich to be with Goebbels, and her personal support at this time of crisis made a lasting impression upon him. He wrote: 'She stood loyally by my side in the difficult days. I will never forget that of her.'[86] On 7 April Magda had to leave, and later that night, Goebbels separately took the train back to Berlin.

He had developed a fever, and when he arrived in Berlin, he went straight to bed. Over the next few days, running a high temperature, and with an aching head, Goebbels had to try to pick up the pieces of his authority in Berlin. He was consumed by anxiety about Magda – despite her show of loyalty in Munich – and he telephoned her dozens of times, but could not make contact. Magda was in fact seeing her former lover at the Quandt family estate in Severin, in rural Mecklenburg. Goebbels heard nothing from her, and felt deserted; in his diary his feelings for her fluctuated between intense longing and bitter reproach. The feeling of isolation only compounded his deepening contempt for all around him. Finally, Magda telephoned on 12 April, and told him that she had finally parted with her lover, who had lost all reason and shot at her with a pistol. Goebbels and Magda met the next day, and although Magda explained all her difficulties with her family, and with her lover, Goebbels was still reproachful: 'I am somewhat unfair to her. But she ought to have come to me, when I was ill. She departs in tears. This evening we will see each other again.'

Before seeing Magda again, Goebbels had to go to his office in Hedemannstrasse. Even though it had been tidied up, and the SA men outside were 'standing straight', it was a sorrowful experience. Later he briefly saw Magda and they were partially reconciled. To end the day, he attended a Party meeting in central Berlin. Although he thought his popularity had, if anything, grown as a result of the Stennes revolt, it 'tasted stale'.[87] The next day Hans Schweitzer called on Goebbels, and they talked over the situation. Although few men had left the

Party with Stennes, and virtually all SA men and Party members were affirming their loyalty to Hitler, they were both deeply disillusioned. Goebbels wrote:

> We sit until midnight. He complains a lot about Munich. Wants more Prussian spirit. Munich is so lacking in vigour. We must learn from the Stennes affair. Become more Prussian, harder, more thrifty, more socialist. No compromises. Otherwise we will go under. Schweitzer is as ever true to the Party, but he also has many critical thoughts. And not without reason.[88]

This was for Goebbels a time of wider disillusionment with the Party. He had repeatedly pressed Hitler to get rid of homosexuality in the Party, but nothing was done. He had learnt in January 1931 that his new comrade Göring was a morphine addict, and soon took the view that he was unfit to represent the Party.[89] In Braunschweig for a speaking engagement, he met an old colleague from his 1925/26 days, Bernhard Rust, and wrote: 'Rust makes a notably bad impression. He looks drunk.'[90]

The relationship with Magda Quandt was a locus of escape for Goebbels. He was now 33 years old, and longed for the trappings of a more settled life. Over the next few weeks he and Magda made a commitment to a shared future. On 25 April, Goebbels wrote: 'I sit up late into the night with Magda. We forge plans for the future ... The good, beautiful woman!'[91] In May 1931, Goebbels went for the first time with Magda and Harald to stay in rural Severin. On this first visit, his enjoyment was tempered by consciousness of her former life. He wrote:

> Went out to the hide in the evening. Sat there with Magda and Harald. And watched rabbits and deer as they ate. An unending stillness descended. Darkness crept through the trees. Silence in the woods. How poor we city people have become! Here there is peace, outside only noise and shouting. That makes me sick.
> Later Magda hurt me very much with a thoughtless comment. What a pity that I didn't love this wonderful woman when she was a girl.[92]

Evidently they decided in Severin to get married, but to postpone this until the Party had taken power.[93] This aim seemed now not altogether unrealistic. For all the obvious failings of its leaders, and its lack of a detailed programme, the Nazi Party grew in strength and wealth in the summer and autumn of 1931, as the Brüning government appeared increasingly unable to manage the growing economic despair. After years of bachelor solitude, Goebbels spent more and more time with Magda, and her flat in the Reichskanzlerplatz became a meeting place for the Party leaders. Magda had met Hitler in Munich during the Stennes revolt, and the two of them evidently got on very well. Magda developed an enormous admiration for Hitler, and was prepared to play a mothering role with him, preparing him food and listening to his long monologues. Hitler, whose complex relationships with women remain obscure, was clearly attracted to Magda, and appears to have made advances to her. He obviously enjoyed her company, and particularly liked to relax in her well-appointed flat, listening to 'Putzi' Hanfstaengl playing the piano. There has been speculation that Magda used her relationship with Goebbels primarily as a way to get close to Hitler, but this is not convincing.[94] There was clearly a genuine, strong mutual attraction between Magda and Hitler. There is a cryptic account in Goebbels' diary of an episode between Magda and Hitler in September 1931, while he was away, speaking in the Ruhr:

> Magda explains: She had a conversation on Saturday with G. Quandt. Said to him that we wanted to get married. He was cast down. Magda has taken revenge for many sufferings which he has caused her. Then with the Chief. Also said the same to him. He was also cast down. He loves her. But maintains his loyalty to me. And Magda also. She is a fabulous woman. We had a little argument first, but then were completely in agreement. Hitler resigned. He is indeed very alone. Has no happiness with women. Because he is too soft-hearted to them. Women don't like that. They must feel a man over them. Now I am very happy. A blissful evening.[95]

What do we make of this extraordinary but cryptic passage? Kershaw does not mention it, and nor does Goebbels' biographer Reuth. From several earlier entries in Goebbels' diary it is clear that Hitler was very taken with Magda: he told Goebbels on 23 August that Magda was 'the most beautiful woman around'; and on 1 September he invited Magda to a meal while Goebbels was in Hamburg on Party business. Goebbels wrote: 'The rogue! I am really sad … A terrible night of agonizing jealousy!' The next morning Magda called him, and evidently set his mind at rest: 'Magda is on her way. The sweet thing!' Further to complicate matters, Magda's former husband Günther Quandt had also been seeing her, and evidently advised her not to pursue her relationship with Goebbels. On 12 September Goebbels wrote: 'Nauseating: Herr Günther Quandt has been to see the Chief. Naturally, he struck a pose and sought to impress. The Chief fell for it. Was enthusiastic about him. When I told Magda about it, she was white with worry and anger.' Later that evening, after a speech, Goebbels 'consoled' Magda on the telephone, before setting off for further speaking engagements in the Ruhr. After a meeting in Bochum, Goebbels telephoned Magda, who had just spoken again with Hitler. This conversation – and it is not clear what Magda said – left Goebbels in a state of 'desperate agitation'. Unfortunately, at this point, three lines have been cut out of Goebbels' diary and replaced with clear paper, leaving only this line: 'see above: very angry with Magda. I am cutting her off because she is unjust.'[96]

It is clear that Hitler made some kind of an approach to Magda in early September, although given everything else we know about him, it is unlikely that this was a formal proposal of marriage. There can be no doubt that Hitler and Magda did form a very strong bond, one which lasted until their deaths in 1945. It is also clear that Magda, after some hesitation, and possibly some encouragement of Hitler, turned Hitler down in favour of Goebbels, but that Hitler resigned himself to this, and even gave their prospective marriage his blessing. This is confirmed by Goebbels' next diary entry. On 16 September, he wrote that after a meeting of senior Party officials in Munich:

> Hitler asked me to come outside and is then really sympathetic to me. A friend and brother. An angel of happiness, he says. He loves Magda. But he does not begrudge me my happiness. 'An intelligent and beautiful woman. She will not hold you back, but support you.' He takes both my hands and tears come to his eyes. All best wishes! I am really grateful. He says many good things about me. My brave comrade and *Führer*! We will get married right away. He is somewhat resigned. Fortune has not smiled upon him. Poor, dear Hitler! I will stay eternally loyal to you! He also is seeking a good woman, whom he will later marry. I found Magda. Lucky devil. We will all three be good to one another. He will be our most loyal friend. Tears come to me. Live well, Hitler!

A few hours later, Goebbels returned to Berlin:

> Magda picks me up. I explain, and she cries with joy. And now a new life shall begin. Günther Quandt has also resigned himself. I want work and happiness. And to help my *Volk*. Thanks to Magda. Thanks to Hitler. Thanks to heaven. Be merciful to me, ye great gods![97]

A few days later, Hitler's niece Geli Raubal, with whom he had been conducting a very public relationship, was found dead in his flat in Munich. Hitler's intimate relationship with Geli Raubal and the circumstances of her death remain obscure,[98] but it is entirely possible that Hitler's infatuation with Magda might have been a contributory factor if she committed suicide. Magda's rejection clearly left Hitler in a highly emotional state, and surely had implications for his already troubled relationship with Geli Raubal. Goebbels and Magda certainly felt a sense of guilt, as well as of sorrow for Hitler. These contrary emotions dominated Goebbels' thoughts for days. When he next met Hitler, on 24 September, Goebbels thought Hitler looked 'thin and white as chalk'. Neither of them mentioned Geli.[99] Whatever Hitler's feelings about Geli's untimely death, or his part in this, he kept his pledge to Goebbels and

Magda.[100] On 6 October Goebbels visited his mother back in Rheydt and told her of his intention to marry Magda.[101]

There was a further twist before the marriage was finalized. On 25 October Goebbels wrote:

> Back home. Dead tired. Magda is sitting there, completely crushed. She has heard from her mother that she was not married to her father. Magda knew nothing of this. Now she is inconsolable. Personally she remains for me what she always was: the sweetest woman. Objectively, there is the possibility that the Jewish press will exploit this and thereby direct heavy attacks on the Party. Only Hitler can judge on that.

Clearly, Hitler, who (not for the last time) had to act as a counsellor for this couple, was untroubled by the revelation:

> The Chief is tenderly kind to her. He laughs about it with us. An unmarried woman with a child is to him preferable to a married woman without a child. Typical Hitler! ... She stays by me, now and for evermore. I will never leave her. I am marrying her, not the world.[102]

On 1 December Goebbels and Magda decided to hold the wedding quickly, in a quiet ceremony at Severin, even though Günther Quandt insisted that if Magda remarried, young Harald would have to live with him. The marriage would be consecrated in a small Protestant chapel, and everything would be 'as simple as possible'.[103] The wedding, which was held on 19 December 1931, was kept largely secret. Hitler, the elderly General Epp, and a few family guests attended, along with Harald in SA uniform. Goebbels wrote an idealized description:

> We both sign. Me first, then Magda, then Epp, then Hitler. And then Magda is my wife. I am quite blissful. Hitler takes me emotionally in his arms. Magda gives him a kiss. Tears are in his eyes. Happiness has now come to us.
> Outside the SA stands and calls *Heil*! Snow falls. It is all like a poem.[104]

6
'These Masses Are What Matter'

On 14 September 1930 our party numbered 293,000 members, and today, on 1 January 1932, it has already gone past 800,000. On 1 January 1931 there were about 100,000 men in our SA and SS organisations; today, on 1 January 1932, well over 300,000. The number of our supporters is right now more than 15 million! It is a procession of victory without parallel in the history of our *Volk* ... Comrades, we march into this year as fighters, in order to leave it as victors. Long live our glorious national socialist fighting movement! Long live our eternally beloved German *Volk*! Germany awakes!

Hitler's 'New Year Declaration' in the *Völkischer Beobachter*, 1 January 1932.[1]

The worsening economic depression, which led to over 6 million unemployed workers in Germany by the end of 1932, helped to create an atmosphere of social tension and political crisis, which was heightened by a succession of elections. As well as several regional elections, there were in quick succession two ballots for the presidency of the Weimar Republic in March and April 1932, and national elections for the *Reichstag* in July and November. Almost as important as the feverish campaigning which accompanied these elections were the constant negotiations between politicians, businessmen, generals, and bankers, all directed to the formation of a stable government. A succession of Chancellors, relying increasingly on the support of the President to rule by emergency decree, wrestled with the problems of growing political extremism on the right and the left. Their political intrigues were conducted in an increasingly confrontational atmosphere, where violence became horribly commonplace. Hundreds were killed in rioting and in political murders. Rumours of a Communist revolution, or of an SA 'march on Berlin', provoked anxious questions about the stance of the *Reichswehr* in the event of a complete constitutional breakdown.

Goebbels was not, for the most part, directly involved in these intrigues, which were largely conducted, on behalf of the Nazis, by Hitler's three other key subordinates, Göring, Röhm, and Gregor Strasser. During 1932, there was a significant shift in the physical centre of power in the Nazi Party, from Munich

124

to Berlin, as Hitler had to visit the capital much more frequently. He stayed, with his entourage, in the Kaiserhof Hotel, close to the city centre and to Magda Goebbels' flat in the Reichskanzlerplatz. Here Goebbels was able to exercise a critical influence, often late at night, when Hitler sought relaxation in the company of intimates. Goebbels maintained a consistent position through all the vicissitudes of 1932, advocating a policy of no compromise with other politicians or groups. His personal and political doubts about Göring, Röhm, and Strasser meant that this was an incredibly anxious time for him.

It was in the public sphere of campaigning that Goebbels played a critical role. The propaganda methods which he had been developing in Berlin for six years were now extended to cover all of Germany. Guidelines were issued from the 'Reich Propaganda Leadership' for all Party newspapers and speakers, to avoid any public inconsistencies. Der Angriff was now published daily in Berlin and much of northern Germany. Goebbels also edited a satirical illustrated magazine, Der Flammenwerfer (The Flamethrower), and devoted much of his attention to the production of posters, placards, and flyers. Key speeches, mainly by himself and Hitler, were quickly printed as small pamphlets, and for the first time in 1932 issued as records which could be sent to supporters through the post. Goebbels had by now developed a fascination for the possibilities offered by new technologies, and since the production of the first Party Rally film in 1927, he had been involved in the production of other short, silent films. The Völkischer Beobachter in July 1930 had listed five which were available:

1. Reich Party Rally 1927. Duration c. 30 minutes.
2. Reich Party Rally 1929. Duration c. 90 minutes.
3. Battle for Berlin. Duration c. 50 minutes.
4. 1. NS-Pictorial Report with scenes from the funeral of Horst Wessel and from the Relay Berlin-Nuremberg in 1929, from the communal elections in Berlin and pictures of our Reichstag deputies. Duration c.10 minutes.
5. 2. NS-Pictorial Report. Scenes from the SA-Ski Meeting in the Riesengebirge, of the SA-Motor-Storm and of the Hitler Meeting in the Sportpalast in Berlin. Duration c. 15 minutes.[2]

Goebbels was behind the production of several of these films, the third of which bears the same name as his regular column in Der Angriff. He had observed a special screening of the first three films held for Party members in Berlin in October 1929, but they had failed him as propaganda instruments for two reasons.[3] First, Goebbels was not a technician of film. He had no experience of operating cameras or cutting film, and therefore could only try to influence the shooting and editing from behind the scenes. The films themselves were of an experimental nature, had no soundtrack, and were as yet insufficiently developed in their narrative structure and artistic execution to be as powerful as later productions. Second, although, as *Reich* Propaganda Leader, Goebbels encouraged the use of these films, before 1933 the Party did not have the equipment to screen them in many places, and therefore few meetings were able to see these early ventures in cinematic propaganda. Those that did were very enthusiastic. More significantly, as the Party played an ever more important role in national politics, its activities were featured in the weekly newsreels produced by Germany's largest film company, UFA. On 4 March 1932, Goebbels saw and heard himself for the first time in a public cinema. 'Quite alien,' he wrote, 'otherwise fabulous.'[4]

Although Goebbels was still constantly troubled by financial concerns, his propaganda benefited during 1932 from huge injections of cash. Partly as a form of insurance, big business was now contributing substantial sums to Hitler, and much of this was diverted from the Party treasury in Munich to subsidize the production of propaganda materials. The precise sources and extent of Nazi Party funding remain obscure, but Goebbels was given large sums, and was able to produce literally millions of posters and flyers, as well as his newspapers. On 6 March he noted receipt of 200,000 marks for propaganda material.[5] He was able to indulge his passion for expensive cars, and cultivated a close relationship with some of the directors of Mercedes. As well as a Cabriolet for Magda (who shared his passion for cars), he bought several new vehicles for himself and his staff. Although he detested most businessmen and aristocrats, he did enjoy the company of artists, and he and Magda – now a respectably married couple – were delighted to host gatherings of musicians, actors, and painters.

Public speaking was still at the centre of all Goebbels' propaganda. Through the various election campaigns of 1932 he maintained an extraordinary schedule of speeches, travelling by car, train, and sometimes by aircraft to reach all parts of Germany, often speaking several times a day. Although he found this exhausting, he had come to depend on this activity. The emotion and adulation he could stir in a crowd, and in individuals he met before and after his speeches gave him new energy and motivation. As in earlier years, he revelled in the atmosphere of a hostile proletarian audience, and many observers – typically not well-disposed towards him – have testified to his courage in these situations, and to his ability to convert an initially antagonistic audience. There is no reason to doubt the broad accuracy of Goebbels' summary of a speech in the East Prussian port of Elbing in April 1932. He wrote: 'Spoke in a factory hall in front of 10,000 proletarians. Greeted with whistles, and departed amidst jubilation.'[6] He needed the reaction of an audience, and of hecklers to show to best advantage the aggressive sarcasm that was his trademark. His earliest recorded speeches, delivered without an audience, are strangely flat, and it took him some time to develop his technique for radio.[7]

Significantly, Goebbels was supported in 1932 as a public speaker by Hitler. In a disastrous coincidence, the seven-year term of the President of the Republic ended in 1932, and Goebbels decided in January that Hitler should announce his candidacy for the post. Although this meant standing in opposition to the elderly Field Marshal Hindenburg, it did offer the opportunity to present Hitler as a national leader. Characteristically, Hitler vacillated for several weeks, but once he had allowed Goebbels on 22 February to announce his candidacy to a huge audience in the *Sportpalast*, he cast off the lethargy of previous years, and threw himself into what Kershaw calls 'a remarkable electioneering performance, the like of which had never been seen before in Germany'.[8] As one campaign followed another through 1932, Hitler stepped up the tempo of his public speaking, by the end of the year almost matching Goebbels, delivering several speeches in a day. Famously, he took to flying from town to town in a chartered Lufthansa aircraft, allowing Goebbels to develop slogans like 'the *Führer* over Germany', and providing opportunities for a god-like descent from the clouds before speaking to huge waiting crowds. Between 3 and 10 April, Hitler gave 20 speeches; between 16 and 24 April, he gave 25.[9]

On 23 February 1932, the *Reichstag* convened to set the first ballot of the presidential election, and Goebbels was allowed to speak before a packed house. In his diary he wrote that this was 'great theatre'.[10] The written transcription of his speech allows us to analyse in some detail his style and method as a parliamentary speaker. He began, as he described it, 'academically', or as the correspondent for *The Times* put it, with 'unwonted quietness', pointing to the Nazi success in the 1930 elections as the 'most significant political development' in recent German political history. He used this, and the results of subsequent elections to portray the Nazi movement's rise as an awakening of the people, in opposition to the bankruptcy and illegitimacy of the Brüning government. Developing this theme he reviewed the period since 1918, calling it one of 'tribute and disarmament', of 'catastrophic' foreign policy, of domestic 'decay' and 'abdication'. He highlighted the increasing isolation of the government and its use of police powers to try to suppress the Nazi movement and its newspapers. As he proceeded Goebbels was frequently interrupted by both his own supporters, and by opponents, and the *Reichstag*'s President had to call for order as the atmosphere became increasingly unruly. Carefully avoiding personal attacks on Hindenburg, Goebbels lampooned the 'system' that he represented, and criticized the government's efforts to postpone the Presidential election. As the atmosphere degenerated, Goebbels mounted a vicious attack on 'the asphalt press', and, turning deliberately to the Social Democrats in the chamber, what he called 'the Party of deserters'. This provoked, as Goebbels had intended, shouts of retaliation and invective. Many deputies were infuriated and the SPD war veteran Kurt Schumacher called out that Goebbels had not served a day at the front; others less diplomatically called him a 'cowardly dog', and a 'shirker'. The President attempted to get Goebbels to withdraw his description of the SPD (*Sozialdemokratische Partei Deutschlands* (Social Democratic Party of Germany)) as a 'Party of deserters', but Goebbels fought on through a storm of jeers to hit out again at the 'Jewish asphalt press'.

Various SPD deputies now called out 'You bastard!' and 'Mongrel', while others sarcastically shouted 'front soldier Goebbels'. After some minutes of this, the President suspended the sitting. This of course was precisely what Goebbels had intended. Two days later, the sitting was resumed and Goebbels was allowed to finish his speech, which was again frequently interrupted. He ended with a prophecy that the Presidential election would be a day of reckoning.[11]

17. Hitler and Goebbels in the *Lustgarten*, Berlin, before the second presidential ballot in 1932. Although the arrangements appear improvised, Goebbels alleged in his diary that he and Hitler spoke here to a vast crowd: '*Lustgarten.* 200,000. I speak first. Then he speaks. Boundless enthusiasm.' (*TBJG*, 5 April 1932, TI, 2/II, p. 255.)

Intoxicated with their campaigning, and with speeches in front of huge audiences, Goebbels and Hitler imagined that they might win the presidential election outright, but the result on 13 March was a grave disappointment. Hindenburg polled 18 million votes, and Hitler 11 million. Calling together his minions in Munich, Hitler displayed resilience, and determined to fight on in a second ballot, which was necessary because Hindenburg had narrowly failed to get an outright majority. After a brief recess, the campaigning started again, the Nazis now also looking ahead to the regional elections in April which would involve a majority of the population. The second ballot of the presidential election on 10 April saw Hitler's vote rise to 13.4 million. Although Hindenburg was the clear winner with 19 million votes, Hitler declared that this was 'a new, great victory', giving his voters the right to think of themselves as 'flag bearers of national freedom and the national future'.[12] In the Prussian elections on 24 April the Nazis were returned as the largest single party with 38.3 per cent of the votes. Goebbels called this a 'phenomenal victory'.[13] The Nazi attitude towards parliamentary government in Prussia was displayed in the first plenary session of the *Landtag* on 25 May 1932, which turned into a brawl. The Nazi deputies 'punched the Communists and the other parties out of the chamber', and then sang the *Horst-Wessel-Lied*. Goebbels wrote: 'That was an exemplary warning. Creates respect.'[14]

Goebbels now led a strange life, poised between domestic respectability, public notoriety, and a gangster underworld. In January 1932 he had learnt that Magda was pregnant. In May he and Magda rented a lakeside villa at Caputh outside Berlin, and this became a place both of retreat and of political intrigue. Miraculously Goebbels still escaped imprisonment or serious injury, although his health was strained by his campaigning style. He had by this time often been fined by courts around Germany, but was able to pay these fines without great difficulty. The details of one case pursued against him in the winter of 1931 reveal how utterly farcical the attempt to constrain him legally had become. In October 1931 Goebbels was fined 1500 marks by the *Land* Court in Berlin and ordered also to pay 340 marks in costs. Although for many ordinary German citizens this would have represented a considerable sum, this was pretty insignificant for Goebbels. Nonetheless, over the next few months he worked hard to avoid even this mild punishment, and was aided by the ponderous working of the law. Goebbels' lawyer Otto Kamecke argued that Goebbels would have difficulty in meeting the fine, and, three weeks after the sentence, Goebbels was told that he could pay in three instalments over the next few months. Kamecke, acting on Goebbels' instructions, argued that his client could not manage this, and evidently the court then made further investigations into Goebbels' finances. Arguing that Goebbels had an income of 2,000 marks per month, and also disposed of a special fund to meet fines, the court informed Kamecke that 250 marks per month, beginning in February 1932, was the absolute minimum it could accept.[15]

Goebbels, now playing the humble supplicant, told Kamecke to inform the court that it was mistaken, that he had no special fund, and that he could only pay 100 marks monthly. Kamecke was told to assure the court that this sum at least would be paid punctually. Goebbels' stalling tactics had worked well, and well before the fine had been paid, Goebbels was able to benefit from a general amnesty passed in the summer of 1932. With what now appears as appalling weakness, the state prosecutor was still writing to Goebbels in September 1932, asking him to pay the costs, which were not subject to amnesty. One can only imagine the contempt with which Goebbels annotated this request in the margin, writing 'Pay 100 marks!'[16] Faced with such a lack of resolution on the part of the law, and aided by reasonably competent lawyers, it is small wonder that Goebbels came to think he was invulnerable.

Goebbels' involvement in another prominent case demonstrates how he even participated in the manipulation of justice. While Goebbels had been preoccupied with the triangular relationship between himself, Magda, and Hitler in September 1931, the Berlin SA had staged another violent demonstration against Jews in the Kurfürstendamm, attacking individual Jews on the street, and wrecking a café. A number of SA men were arrested and subsequently charged before a 'Speed Court' with a range of offences. These courts were intended to act quickly and firmly to deal with the growing number of politically motivated disturbances, and in this case handed out some lengthy prison sentences. The leader of the Berlin SA, Count Helldorff, who had overseen the disturbances, was also arrested and now faced a potentially serious punishment. Goebbels had not been in Berlin at the time of the disturbances, and was not directly implicated. He was though called to the *Reich* Chancellery to speak with Chancellor Brüning about the case. Brüning was anxious not to provoke the Nazis just before the planned visit of the French Prime Minister Pierre Laval and his Foreign Minister Aristide Briand to Berlin. In two separate meetings with Brüning, Goebbels complained bitterly about the sentences already passed on the SA rioters, and demanded that Helldorff be tried before a different judge. Evidently he agreed in return not to disturb the visit of the French dignitaries. Brüning intervened directly with the court to change the presiding judge, and to postpone Helldorff's case. In his own brief account he argued that this was done without 'injury to the court's constitution'.[17] Laval and Briand's visit passed off quietly, and Helldorff was eventually fined a paltry 100 marks in February 1932. Characteristically this display of flexibility on Brüning's part only provoked Goebbels' scorn.[18]

As a prominent politician Goebbels now socialized with leading figures in society, and wherever he travelled he was entertained by local dignitaries and representatives. He was finding that many of these were wholehearted Nazi supporters. A few days after the fight in the Prussian *Landtag*, Goebbels went to Horumersiel, on the flat north-western coast of Germany, where he met Hitler. They went on to Wilhelmshaven, the home of the then much-reduced German navy. There were two large ships there, the old battleship *Schlesien*, and the newer cruiser *Köln*. They were welcomed aboard the *Köln*, and given a guided tour of what Goebbels called 'A wonder work of technology'. He wrote:

The officers and crew are fabulous. Fully for us. They read only the *V.B.* and *Angriff*. Our presence aroused joy and enthusiasm amongst them. An officer comes from the *Schlesien* and, in the name of the Captain, invites me to dinner … Ate in the officers' mess with the lieutenants of the *Schlesien*. Fabulous, tall, blond guys. Real pictures of young men. And all for us. Poor system.[19]

A number of aristocrats and members of Germany's royal families were by this time also active with the Nazi Party, and one of them, Friedrich-Christian, Prince of Schaumburg-Lippe, was taken on as an adjutant by Goebbels. Schaumburg-Lippe was one of few aristocrats to enjoy Goebbels' confidence, and he lived after 1945 to write a memoir about his former boss. His description of his first encounter with Goebbels gives us a flavour of the campaigning in Berlin. He arrived at Goebbels' headquarters, 'the spiritual command post of the revolution', just as Goebbels was leaving for the funeral of a Hitler Youth killed by Communists, Herbert Norkus:

The light, somewhat washed-out trench coat suited him well, and made a modest, nimble, sporty impression, suited to the tempo of his life. He didn't like to wear anything that looked like a uniform. The clear grey felt hat with a thin black band was always immaculately clean, tilted forwards, the brim high at the back. Elegant, tailored. Emphasized the brown colour of his face. When – as most of the time – he was hurrying, he took little leaps. It is not true that he tried to conceal his malformed foot. He was, rather, proud that he still managed to be as nimble and quick as others, and displayed and talked about this. He also made a virtue from necessity with his physique: 'My foot is sometimes a hindrance, I am small and not strong, but nature is just, and she gave me in compensation a brain that few others have.'

Schaumburg-Lippe was rushed into the open-top Mercedes, where Goebbels, as ever, sat in the front. At high speed he was driven to the cemetery where a large, hostile crowd had gathered. Goebbels said as they arrived:

These masses are what matter, Schaumburg-Lippe, only these. If we win them over, they are Germany's future – if we don't win them over, Germany is lost!

It was apparently a grey, bitterly cold day, and Goebbels had to shout to make his speech at the graveside heard over the shouts of the Communists. Stones were thrown into the cemetery. In the privacy of his diary Goebbels recorded that there were 'many riff-raff' there, as were Magda and Harald.[20]

Heinrich Brüning's government finally collapsed in May 1932, and another *Reichstag* election was called for July. Goebbels conducted an exhausting campaign, which finished in a fist-fight with a Communist outside the polling station when he went to vote. Hitler spoke in 53 towns in his third 'Germany Flight'.[21] Goebbels and Hitler had now settled on an appeal beyond party, class, confession, or region, using the slogan 'Unity for the German *Volk* and the German *Reich*'.[22] On 9 July Goebbels addressed a vast crowd – he estimated 200,000 strong – in the open-air setting of Berlin's *Lustgarten*, and on 18 July his speech on 'National character as the foundation of national culture' was broadcast by all German radio stations.[23] The day before Goebbels noted that he 'had got hold of 55,000 marks for the Berlin *Gau*'.[24] This election campaign was marked by constant violence, most notably in Hamburg on 18 July, when 15 people were killed in fighting between Communists and Nazis. To many observers, Germany seemed on the brink of civil war. On 25 July Goebbels spoke at the funeral of another SA man killed in one of the numerous incidents which marked that summer. According to the police report he said: 'The SA is no longer inclined to accept further sacrifices without atonement. Eye for eye, tooth for tooth, that shall from henceforth be the motto of the SA.'[25] The results on 31 July gave the Nazis 230 seats in the *Reichstag*, making them the largest single party, but still with no clear majority. The Communists also made notable gains, leading Goebbels to conclude: 'Now we must come to power and root out Marxism. This way or that way! Something must happen. The time of opposition has ended.' In fact he and Hitler were

18. A characteristic Hans Schweitzer poster, 1932, which represents National Socialism as 'The organized will of the nation'. Schweitzer always signed his posters with the pseudonym 'Mjölnir', an ancient Norse symbol for Thor's hammer.

shaken. Goebbels wrote: 'This way we will not get an absolute majority. So we must take another way. We are facing difficult consequences.'[26]

Over the next fortnight, the Nazis debated their next move. The Party demanded that as the largest in the *Reichstag* its leader should be invited as Chancellor to form a government. Goebbels had to hang around in Munich while Hitler travelled to Berlin for talks with General Schleicher, Chancellor von Papen's Minister of Defence. On his return Hitler and Goebbels discussed on the Obersalzberg their hopes for what they already called the *Machtergreifung*, the 'seizure of power'. Hitler would become Chancellor, and Goebbels would be Minister for 'People's Education', a brief to include responsibility for 'schools, universities, film, radio, theatre, and propaganda'.[27] On 13 August, after further negotiations, Hitler met Schleicher and Papen in Berlin, only to be offered the post of Vice Chancellor. There was a feverish atmosphere in the city, and in the afternoon Hitler was summoned to see President Hindenburg himself. Huge crowds turned out to watch Hitler arrive at the Wilhelmstrasse, but when Hitler confirmed that he was unwilling to accept anything less than 'leadership of the state', his audience with the President was quickly terminated.[28] 'Therefore, opposition', commented Goebbels.[29] This bitter disappointment only strengthened his view that any coalition or compromise should be avoided. It provoked what even a later Nazi Party history described as 'a not insignificant crisis'.[30]

Much has been made of the idea that during 1932, Hitler and the Nazis played down their anti-Semitism to gain public support; many have claimed that it almost disappeared from their programme. Just as Goebbels stirred up the violent tendencies of many Nazi supporters with his constant agitation amongst the SA, he maintained an anti-Semitism that was so public as to challenge these complacent notions. In August 1932 the Papen government announced a clampdown on political violence, shortly before SA men in the Silesian village of Potempa stabbed a miner, Konrad Pietzuch, to death. This was one case among many at the time, but in an attempt to display exemplary firmness, the court dealing with the case sentenced the five killers to death. Goebbels immediately wrote a vitriolic attack on the court in *Der Angriff*, titled 'The Jews are guilty!' In the article he portrayed the convicted Nazis as 'German men, tested in war and peace', who carried 'honourable wounds' from the struggles to protect Silesia from 'Polish insurgents'. He then turned the article into one of his most vicious anti-Semitic polemics. The court which had sentenced the Nazi killers, and the 'Jewish newspapers' which commended the sentence were part of a 'system', linked with Communist murderers. Repeating the phrase 'The Jews are guilty!' Goebbels concluded:

We will arouse the *Volk*, so that it throws this alien tyranny from its shoulders! We will carry the fight through to the end, come what may! ... The genuinely guilty are still sitting securely behind the police cordons! The hour will come when state prosecutors will have other tasks to fulfil than that of protecting the traitors of the *Volk* from the fury of the *Volk*.

Never forget it, comrades! Say it to yourself a hundred times a day, until it haunts you in your deepest dreams: the Jews are guilty!'[31]

Hitler himself sent an open telegram of support for the killers, declaring that he was 'tied to you in unbounded loyalty'.[32] The shocking brutalization of young people in Germany was also noted by outsiders at this time. A Czech diplomat, Camill Hoffmann, wrote in his diary on a 'glorious summer day' in August 1932 that he observed three young cyclists singing 'When the hour of vengeance comes, we will be ready for any mass murder'.[33]

Goebbels was also about to become a father. Since learning that Magda was pregnant he had wished constantly for a boy. Just before the baby was born on 1 September he wrote: 'Early today it started with Magda. She is very brave. Straight to the clinic. I pray that all goes well and that it will be a boy. I am slightly afraid. But Destiny will be merciful to us.'[34] The next day he wrote:

Sadly only a girl. But I am happy right from my heart. She shall be called Helga. Everything went smoothly. At 14.20 she was there. Magda and child healthy.

God grant that this child shall only live and breathe in a free Germany. Hitler was excited when I gave him the news. He had always prophesied a girl. Because I had strongly expected a boy, I was disappointed about that.

It seems Goebbels' feelings were shared by others. He wrote that at the Kaiserhof Hotel later that day everyone was cheerful and excited, 'Only, always, a shame, not a boy!'[35] Fatherhood did not change the daily routine of Goebbels' life much. A well-off working man was not expected to share in the daily chores of child-rearing in Weimar Germany, and Magda was helped by a succession of maids. Goebbels' demanding schedule of work continued without any interruption.

The Nazis now had their eyes not just on power in Germany. In September 1932 Goebbels and Hitler travelled in quick succession to Vienna to fortify the Nazi Party there, and to make it absolutely plain that their vision of a future 'Third Reich' included a union with Austria. Goebbels was enthusiastically received by Nazi supporters in Vienna, and by Geli Raubal's mother. He spoke for two hours to a large crowd at a 'Union rally', and announced: 'we have made it clear to the world that over and above treaty borders there is one German people [*Deutschtum*], and that one can persecute and gag this German people as one will, but they will always find their way together on one road.' According to the triumphant report on the rally in *Der Angriff*, these words released 'in the masses', 'a cry for the *Reich*, for the great common Fatherland'.[36] After the rally, Goebbels went to a performance of Mozart's *The Magic Flute* at the Vienna Opera

House, and was entranced. He admired the singing of Elisabeth Schumann, of Helge Roswaenge, and Richard Mayr, writing: 'I have never heard Mozart like this before. Absolutely authentic in style.' He was hugely impressed by the building, and its acoustics, and reflected on how Hitler as a young man had listened to concerts from the gallery. Although Goebbels felt constrained by his personal loyalty to Hitler to display some affection for Austria, this was entirely insincere. Goebbels thought of himself as a north German, a Prussian, and in his view of race, people from further south were – with rare exceptions – of inferior quality and value. This is one of the reasons he was always uncomfortable in Munich, and he was even less well-disposed to the Austrians, whom he also considered to be too racially mixed. In his diary account of this visit to Vienna, he noted typically, of his visit to the 'Adolf Hitler House': 'All very neat. But Austrian.'[37]

Goebbels was in fact quite ill when he travelled to Austria, and his ill-health was, as so often in his life symptomatic of wider political difficulties. After years of success, the Nazi Party was facing a crisis, one which was all the more severe as it involved Goebbels' arch-enemy, Gregor Strasser. By the winter of 1932 there were signs that the economic situation in Germany, if not getting much better, was not getting worse. There were the first indications of recovery. Internationally there were improvements, not least the end of reparations payments in July 1932. The unity of the Nazi Party after September 1932 seemed at moments potentially very fragile. Elements at the bottom of the Party, notably the SA, were restless, and asked why the talk of revolution had not led to anything in practice. At the top, there were some inclined towards compromise, notably Gregor Strasser. The huge spending on election campaigning and on material rewards for Party leaders had left the coffers empty. In a surprising development the *Reichstag* was again dissolved in September 1932, when the new *Reichstag* President Göring famously ignored Chancellor Papen while conducting a vote of no confidence, and another election was called for November. The prospect of yet another campaign brought no rejoicing amongst the Nazis. Nonetheless, Hitler, for all his indecision in previous years, was still energetic and undertook a fourth 'Germany Flight', speaking in 49 towns between 4 and 11 November.[38]

Goebbels, by now thoroughly jaded, summoned up more energy and pushed his propaganda machine into action again, but to less avail. When the election returns were counted on 7 November 1932, the Nazi vote had dropped. With 196 deputies they were still the largest party in the *Reichstag*, but there was also the nagging possibility that they had reached a high-water mark, and were receding. Goebbels called it a 'nauseating thing to swallow'. More objectively he wrote: 'We have suffered a severe set-back.'[39] In the aftermath, the Party leadership experienced a grave crisis when rumours percolated through that Gregor Strasser was clinching a deal with General Schleicher which would give him the post of Vice Chancellor. This was a culmination of all Goebbels' fears, and he watched, horrified, as Hitler again hesitated. For years now Goebbels had been suspicious

19. Adolf Hitler in the early 1930s. This uncharacteristically boyish image was also used on Nazi election posters.

of Gregor Strasser, and he urged Hitler finally to break with him. At Goebbels' villa in Caputh Hitler paced up and down for hours before announcing that if the Party broke up, he would shoot himself.[40]

Although this sounds melodramatic, Goebbels certainly felt that the Party was staring into the abyss. He was not alone. Reporting on the public mood to the Foreign Ministry in Paris, the French Military Attaché in Berlin wrote that some envisaged the Nazi Party splitting into three groups, 'one loyal to Hitler, the second in Bolshevik form with Goebbels, and the third with syndicalist tendencies led by Gregor Strasser ... it is evident that Hitler has let his hour pass by'.[41] Goebbels had no intention of forming a splinter group, but his sense of crisis was undoubtedly strengthened by his perception that Gregor Strasser, against whom he had fought now since 1926, was about to lead the Party astray. If, as appeared to be the case, the Party had peaked electorally, Strasser's intended compromise was perhaps all that could be achieved. The knowledge that, all around them, commentators were arguing that the Nazis were now electorally spent only heightened Goebbels' fears. Finally, the crisis was defused when Strasser, after a last meeting with Hitler, resigned all his Party offices on 8 December. Strasser himself appears to have been completely unprepared for this dénouement. Former Chancellor Heinrich Brüning relates how he was told that Strasser 'had been thrown out of the Kaiserhof without a plan, and was left walking to and fro on the Wilhelmsplatz, talking to himself'.[42] The next day, Hitler spoke to a meeting of *Gauleiter* and *Reichstag* deputies in Berlin. Goebbels watched anxiously, but was delighted with what he heard:

> Fabulously certain. Annihilating towards Strasser and even more towards Feder. People were calling out in anger and pain. A really great success for Hitler. At the end a spontaneous commitment to loyalty. All give Hitler their hands. Strasser is isolated. Dead man!
>
> I have fought six years for that.

Goebbels sat up late communing with Hitler, and when he got home found that Magda was unwell.[43] In fact, Gregor Strasser's departure, like that of his brother in 1930, caused more agitation within the Party than without. Strasser did not campaign against the Nazis, but went on holiday. Hitler took over his post of Party Organization Leader, and was quickly assured that the overwhelming majority of Party members would stand by him. In any case, as Richard Evans points out, 'In no sense did Strasser represent an alternative vision of the future to Hitler's.'[44] Although Gregor Strasser did not after December 1932 pose a threat to Hitler and Goebbels, he was not forgiven or forgotten. As Christmas came near, there were one or two encouraging developments for Goebbels. He sold the rights for a photograph book about the Nazis in Berlin for 10,000 marks, and a few days later, on 20 December, he wrote in his diary: 'Frau v. Schroeder brings me 2,000 marks.'[45]

Domestic life had been difficult, as it is for most couples with a new-born baby. Goebbels recorded after his return from Vienna that he had quarrelled with Magda, and that she had justifiably reproached him for his impatience towards Helga.[46] One can imagine that he was not an easy person to live with at this time; even Magda and the baby saw little of him. Although her health had been poor, she still helped Goebbels with the mountains of work he had to complete before Christmas, arranging presents for SA men, attending Christmas parties, and entertaining gatherings at home. On Christmas Eve, Magda was again ill, and her doctor ordered that she be admitted to hospital. Although Goebbels tried to make a go of things, visiting the hospital, and seeing various acquaintances, he was profoundly lonely without Magda. His comment on Christmas was: 'Everything is so empty of joy.'[47] A few days later, reassured that Magda was relatively well, Goebbels went to Munich with Harald, but almost as soon as they arrived, they heard by telephone that Magda's condition had deteriorated. Goebbels had to endure a New Year's celebration with the Party leadership in Munich while he fretted about her. He wrote: 'O heaven, I pray of you, leave her with me. I am nothing any more without her.' The next day he travelled back to Berlin, writing: 'God keep this woman for me. I can not live without her.'[48] The next day he found her weak, but over the worst.

> To the clinic. Magda much better. The fever has abated. She is so happy that I am there. We talk much of our love, and how good we will be to one another, when she is healthy again.
>
> I have grown so with Magda, that I really can not exist without her.

It was several weeks before Magda was well enough to return home, and Goebbels had to carry on without her. He and Hitler had decided to put all their efforts into campaigning in the tiny state of Lippe, where elections were due on 15 January 1933. Preoccupied with this, Goebbels did not participate in the meeting held in Cologne on 4 January between Papen, Hitler, and the banker Kurt von Schroeder, at which the possibility of a Hitler Chancellorship in a minority government was first opened. Hitler kept Goebbels up to date with the developing negotiations while the campaign in Lippe unfolded. Magda's improving health and a favourable result in Lippe on 15 January seemed to justify his continued exertions. As Hitler continued the negotiations, Goebbels planned a final propaganda spectacle, a 'Festival of Remembrance for Horst Wessel', with an SA march in Berlin's Bülowplatz, outside the Communist Party Headquarters, and on to Wessel's grave. This was held, under the protection of armed police, on 22 January. Crowds of angry Communists were held back in the side streets. Goebbels' pleasure was only marred by difficulties with Horst Wessel's mother, who evidently, and understandably, wanted some influence in the commemoration of her son's death. Goebbels wrote: 'She is unbearable in her arrogance. Our dead belong to the nation.'[49]

Over the next few days Goebbels mixed a hectic round of Party activities with visits to Magda in hospital, and conversations with Hitler. In Rostock, meeting with Nazi students on 28 January, he heard that Chancellor Schleicher had resigned. He returned to Berlin, where Göring told him about the deal that Hitler had finally struck:

> Hitler Chancellor, Papen Vice, Frick *Reich* Interior, Göring Prussian Interior, Hugenberg crises etc. I go without at the moment, to lead an election struggle. The *Reichstag* will be dissolved. The last time. We will fiddle that.[50]

On 30 January these arrangements were confirmed to Goebbels at the Kaiserhof. 'There are tears in our eyes. We shake Hitler's hand. He has deserved this.

Great jubilation. Outside the people are rampaging.'[51] *Der Angriff* was the first newspaper to break the news that evening, with a banner headline: 'Hitler Reich Chancellor'.[52] Later that evening, after seeing Magda in hospital, Goebbels joined Hitler and new members of the government at the Wilhelmstrasse, where from the balcony they watched a torchlit march of Nazi formations and supporters. Shortly after 10.00 p.m. Goebbels spoke on live radio with the sound of rejoicing supporters in the background:

> I can only say a few words. We have been on our feet since five o' clock this morning and are dog-tired ... It is striking for me to see, in this city where we started six years ago with a handful of people, really to see in this city how a whole people has risen up, like the people marching past underneath us, workers and middle classes and farmers and students and soldiers – a great *Volksgemeinschaft* – in which one no longer asks, whether one is a bourgeois or a proletarian, a Catholic or a Protestant, in which one only asks: What are you, what are you part of, and do you declare your support for your country? ... We have begun to fight for work and bread, for freedom and honour, and we will lead this fight until the end.[53]

The euphoria of 30 January 1933 was genuine. This was a consummation of nine years of exhausting work. Bizarrely, over the next few days, Goebbels fell

20. Hitler and followers at the Kaiserhof Hotel on 30 January 1933 after hearing of his appointment as Chancellor. This was a day of high excitement, but the Nazi leaders have all adopted suitably grave faces for this photograph. Goebbels has characteristically made sure he is at the centre of events.

into a deep depression. While Hitler, Göring, and Frick attended Cabinet meetings and met their civil servants, Goebbels had to turn straight back to his normal routine of meetings with local Party officials and with the production team of *Der Angriff*, and to preparations for yet another election. Magda was allowed home from hospital only on 2 February, but she was still weak and emotionally fragile. Goebbels himself, as often after a period of prolonged work, developed a fever, and felt neglected. He heard rumours that he would be made 'Radio Commissar', and the 'nauseating' news that Bernhard Rust would be promoted over him to a new position of Culture Minister. Magda, who was nothing if not ambitious, 'cried all the time', and within a week of the Nazi 'seizure of power', Goebbels was lying ill in bed. 'Hitler scarcely helps me. I have lost heart. Reaction dictates. The Third Reich!'[54] For several days he did not even make an entry in his diary, and even when he was again up and about, he felt discouraged. On 15 February, although he was enthused by visiting an exhibition of new cars, he wrote: 'I am tired and despondent. I have no goal, and no longer any joy in my work.'[55]

Goebbels' disappointment was indeed understandable. In a celebratory booklet issued by a Nazi cultural organization profiling the 'Hitler Cabinet', there were eulogistic portraits of Hitler, Göring, Frick, and the non-Nazis in the Cabinet, like Vice Chancellor Papen, Economics Minister Alfred Hugenberg, and Franz Seldte, the *Stahlhelm* leader now appointed Minister of Labour. There was no mention of Goebbels. The notion that he might be superseded by a drunken mediocrity like Bernhard Rust, who had a minor position in the Cabinet with the title of '*Reich* Commissar for the Prussian Ministry of Culture', was obviously particularly galling to Goebbels, but also only a temporary arrangement.[56] One can only presume that Hitler, in the first instance, was entirely preoccupied with his new responsibilities, and was unaware of Goebbels' feelings during these weeks; and secondly that he had greater plans for him. In the existing federal structure of the Republic, there was not a *Reich* Ministry of Culture, or of Education. There was no single post which could fully make use of Goebbels' talents.

Characteristically, it was work which brought Goebbels around over the next few weeks. Hitler had been appointed Chancellor of a coalition government, and had much to do over the next few months to try to consolidate the Nazi hold on power. Even with a minority in the government, the Nazis were able to tighten their grip by changing leading policemen around Germany, and by banning opposition newspapers. Their own election propaganda was now on a different footing, as they had direct access to the radio, and on 21 February Goebbels noted receipt of no less than 3 million marks for the campaign.[57] Their preparations were given a feverish twist by a telephone call from Hanfstaengl in the evening of 27 February, telling Goebbels that the *Reichstag* building was on fire. Together with Hitler, he rushed to the building, where they found Göring and Papen already on the scene. Goebbels, like Hitler, assumed that the fire was the work of the Communists, the prelude to a wider uprising. It also provided the

21. The Cabinet of 30 January 1933 which Hitler headed as Chancellor. Goebbels was 'completely depressed' not to be included. (*TBJG*, 6 February 1933, TI, 2/III, p. 125.)

pretext for draconian measures against the Communists, and, just as in the past he had revelled in street fighting, Goebbels was intoxicated by the prospect of confrontation. He worked with Hitler through the night on leaders for *Der Angriff* and the *Völkischer Beobachter*, on the preparation of an emergency decree, and on issuing instructions for the arrest of leading Communist functionaries.[58]

This decree, suspending the civil liberties enshrined in the constitution of the Weimar Republic, has been described as 'the charter of the Third Reich'.[59] It inaugurated a reign of terror in Germany, giving free rein to the aggressive and sadistic instincts of the SA, so long kept in check. This was indeed the day of reckoning which had been threatened for so long. A recent estimate suggests that by April 1933, 50,000 alleged opponents of the Nazis had been arrested and held in so-called 'wild' concentration camps, as well as in the existing penal institutions across Germany.[60] Many were subjected to horrible brutality. Nor was this wave of repression carried out in secret. The arrest and detention of hundreds was front-page news. The evening edition of *Der Angriff* carried on its front page on 28 February news of the arrest of 130 Communists in Berlin and another 140 in Hanover.[61] The future novelist Heinrich Böll was a schoolboy in 1933, and he later described how, in Cologne, 'Social Democrats disappeared, Centre politicians, Communists too, and it was no secret that in the barracks around the military training area concentration camps were set up by the SA.'[62]

Goebbels was no stranger to violence at close quarters during this turbulent period. The British journalist Sefton Delmer had worked his way into Hitler's

22. Hermann Göring in 1933. When Goebbels was first introduced to Göring in 1927 he wrote: 'Captain Göring. A face like a big baby. Such a hero! I was at first indescribably disappointed. Afterwards he grew on me a lot. He makes intelligent, courageous comments.' (*TBJG*, 2 May 1927, TI, 1/II, p. 216.)

confidence in 1932, and sometimes travelled with him and his entourage. He later wrote this account of Goebbels 'entertaining' all of them while they were waiting for a flight at Tempelhof Airfield:

> Goebbels was recounting the 'gloriously funny saying' of one of 'his Stormtroop boys', which he had overheard when visiting a Stormtroop cellar the previous evening.
> 'There was the lad hard at work giving some fellow in the corner a "rub down"' cackled Goebbels. 'He had taken off his belt and was using it as a lash. And what do you think I heard him saying in between the blows? You'll never guess. It really is excruciatingly funny,' and Goebbels cackled some more. 'He was saying, "And now we shall teach you atheists to say your prayers. Jetzt werden wir euch Atheisten das Beten beibringen!"'

Goebbels kept repeating the phrase, rolling it around his tongue as though it was a savoury delicacy. What so delighted him – apart from the sadism – was the alliteration of the vowels in 'euch Atheisten' and the consonants in 'Beten beibringen'. A great man for a phrase was Goebbels.[63]

In the days after the *Reichstag* fire, Goebbels rejoiced in the atmosphere of frenzied rumour and alarm which was stoked up by his propaganda. He had already been planning the centrepiece of the election campaign, a 'Day of the Awakening Nation', which was to become the blueprint for many similar events in the future. Goebbels called for torchlit parades in every town and village, and for swastika flags to be hung from every window 'behind which German people live', so people could demonstrate their 'faith in the future of Germany', and their determination 'to live and to fight for Germany, come what may'.[64] To bring together the celebrations in different parts of the country Goebbels planned an extension of the political speech which he and Hitler had so successfully used over previous years, using the national broadcasting network to communicate this to a much larger audience. In his hands propaganda had become not merely an art form, but a surrogate religion, with its own liturgy, and with the Nazi belief in the 'German *Volk*' displacing the tenets of Christian faith.

For the 'Day of the Awakening Nation' on 5 March 1933, Goebbels planned a nationwide broadcast of Hitler's speech from the historic city of Königsberg, which he hoped would reach 40 million listeners. He had developed a technique he called 'reportage', in which he acted as a live commentator, describing the setting for a speech, complete with background sounds of cheering and tumult, and giving Hitler a fervent introduction. Thus he provided on live radio a vivid impression of the visual and aural spectacle of the whole ceremony. We can judge how this was added to in some places by a report on Hitler's Königsberg speech from a commentator who, unknown to Goebbels, had taken upon himself the responsibility of recording his methods. Victor Klemperer was a Jewish academic in Dresden, and from 1933 until 1945 he consciously set out to analyse what he called 'the language of the Third Reich'. In one of his first observations he described how the 'Day of German Awakening' was presented:

a huge animated crowd jostled in front of the illuminated hotel façade next to the main railway station in Dresden from which a loudspeaker relayed the speech, storm-troopers stood on the balconies with large flags bearing swastikas and a torch-light procession approached from the Bismarckplatz. I only caught scraps of the speech itself, in truth more sounds than sentences. But already at that point I had the same impression which was subsequently to be repeated again and again until the very end.[65]

If Klemperer – and presumably many others – heard only fragments of the speech, this mattered little. What was more important was the overall effect, the potentially intoxicating mixture of impressions. Klemperer described it as 'a total work of art simultaneously addressing itself to the ears and the eyes, the ears indeed twice over, since the roaring of the crowd, its applause and disapproval have at least as powerful an effect on the individual member of the audience as the speech itself'. After hearing a similarly presented speech a few months later, Klemperer noted the way that the Nazis had appropriated Christian rituals and symbolism: 'the dividing line separating it from ecclesiastical ceremony has been broken down, the antiquated costume has been shed, and the legend of Christ has been transported into the here and now'.[66] This was not coincidental. We have seen Goebbels' fascination with the Passion story, and others have noted how Hitler similarly saw himself as a Christ-like figure, shorn of the trappings of compassion and forgiveness. During 1933, as Goebbels stage-managed the Nazi progression from participation in a coalition government to dictatorship, he railed frequently against the churches. In September 1933, ecstatically describing the culminating ceremonies of the Nuremberg rally, he wrote: 'That is a church service. We don't need the priests for that any more.'[67] The film of the rally, directed by Leni Riefenstahl, was called *Victory of Faith*.

After the elections of March 1933, even though he had no outright majority, Hitler proceeded with the construction of his dictatorship, and with what he and Goebbels called *Gleichschaltung*, the 'coordination' of areas of German life. On 13 March Goebbels was confirmed as Minister for People's Enlightenment and Propaganda.[68] He was delighted, both to be one of the youngest ever ministers in the world, and to be at the head of an altogether new ministry. The word 'propaganda' has long had rather sinister connotations in the English language, with its suggestions of manipulation, and no one has done more than Goebbels to reinforce these, but we should bear in mind that for Goebbels 'propaganda' was not a dirty word, something he stressed in a speech to the directors of German radio stations on 25 March:

> I refute the notion that propaganda is something of inferior value, for we would not be here in ministerial seats if we had not become the great artists of propaganda. And we would not have lost the war if we had understood the art of propaganda somewhat better. *That* is the secret of propaganda: he, who the propaganda is to grasp, is to be completely saturated with the ideas of propaganda, without being aware of this. Obviously propaganda has a purpose, but that purpose must be so cleverly and virtuously concealed that he who is to be imbued with this purpose is unaware of it. I believe it to be obvious, and not to need emphasis, that in future the radio is no longer to be a playground for intellectual asphalt experiments, that Jewish-Marxist writers

should no longer be heard on the radio, to offload there the waste products of their sick minds.

During the speech he frequently struck the lectern to emphasize his points.[69] For this failed artist, would-be writer or theatre director, it was indeed an honour to be in charge of Germany's cultural life, with far-reaching influence over its mass media. Magda shared in his joy.

Goebbels' position as a minister also gave him a seat in the Cabinet, and through 1933 he used this as well as his private influence with Hitler to influence the wider policy of the new government. As before, Goebbels pressed constantly for the most radical approach. He styled the Nazi access to power a 'national revolution',[70] and in his speeches he celebrated this as a victory of youth over old age. Above all, he pressed for action against the Jews. There is no single document which tells us precisely what Hitler or Goebbels intended to do with the Jews of Germany if they achieved control of the German state. Neither man could anticipate the very changed circumstances they would find themselves in after 1939. The nearest to a programme the Nazis had was still the 'Twenty-five Points' of 1920; several of these 'points' referred to the Jews, but in vague terms. Point 4, for example, stated that 'Only members of the nation may be citizens of the State. Only those of German blood, whatever their creed, may be members of the nation. Accordingly no Jew may be a member of the nation.'[71] Goebbels had particular concerns about the exclusion of Jews from what he thought of as 'German' cultural life, thus from the arts and the mass media. There were examples of Jews who were beaten and killed in February and March 1933 in Germany by Nazi thugs, and there were others who committed suicide rather than face the prospect of life under the Nazis. There was an immediate exodus of many Jews who could afford to escape to another country, or who had personal connections which allowed this, but at this stage there was no realistic prospect that Germany might in the short term somehow get rid of its Jewish population altogether. Goebbels, who was now able publicly to encourage violence against and intimidation of German Jews, must bear a significant responsibility for creating and fostering an atmosphere in which Jews felt isolated and threatened, and in which many Germans thought it appropriate to sever their personal and economic ties with Jewish fellow-citizens, to dismiss them from employment, and in many cases to treat them with open hostility and violence. He undoubtedly hoped that the exclusion of Jews from the life of the 'nation' would in large measure be achieved by informal pressure from all levels of society.

Goebbels thus supported the intimidation of prominent Jewish musicians and conductors like Bruno Walter and Otto Klemperer (a cousin of the celebrated philologist and diarist), who left Germany after threats that concerts they directed would be disrupted, or the halls burnt down.[72] Even before Goebbels' appointment as Propaganda Minister, a 'Beethoven evening' on German radio by the Jewish pianist Artur Schnabel had been cancelled.[73] Schnabel was an Austrian citizen. Walter and Klemperer were men with an international reputation, who were able to leave Germany and continue their careers abroad, but this was not an option easily available to all who felt threatened. It is instructive to look at the fate of a less well-known German musician in this horrible situation. Ernst Hermann Meyer was a young musician who had recently received his doctorate from Heidelberg University, ironically studying under some of the same professors as had Goebbels himself. Meyer was both a Jew and a Communist, and had in the last years of the Weimar Republic worked for the Communist newspaper *Die Rote Fahne* (*The Red Flag*). He knew after 30 January 1933 that he was a marked man. In February, along with many others, Meyer was briefly arrested and detained after a police raid on the Karl-Liebknecht-Haus, the Communist Party Headquarters building in Berlin. After this, Meyer left Berlin on a bicycle, and travelled towards Heidelberg to escape. He felt safest during the next few weeks, he later testified, cycling in the countryside. Meyer and his comrades kept moving to avoid arrest, staying no more than a few days in any one place. His future would indeed have been uncertain had he not received an invitation to attend a musicological conference at Cambridge University. Meyer's younger brother Klaus told this author that one day in 1933, Ernst called, unannounced, at the family home in Berlin, to tell his parents he was leaving the country. He was, his brother said, 'literally shaking with fear'. Meyer made his way, via Paris, to England, where his brother Klaus later joined him.[74]

Goebbels led the public campaign against the Jews, and pressed for a nationwide boycott of all Jewish shops, which was staged on 1 April 1933, ostensibly as a protest against 'atrocity propaganda' abroad, especially in Britain and the USA. Describing British journalists as 'apes', Goebbels complained that they 'talk a lot of rubbish and think that they can sit in judgement on Germany'.[75] On 27 March he wrote: 'I am writing a call for a boycott against the German Jews. With that we will soon stop the hate abroad.'[76] On 29 March Hitler telephoned to sanction the publication of this declaration, and instructions were issued to branches of the Nazi Party nationwide on how to coordinate the action.[77] Goebbels noted that in the Cabinet 'All the others are afraid about the boycott.' It was agreed there that the boycott would last for a few days, and would then be called off, Goebbels thought temporarily, before being renewed. On 1 April Goebbels spoke to the press about the boycott in a 'breathless silence'. The next day he spoke at a huge meeting in the Berlin *Lustgarten*, after he and Hitler had met a gathering of film stars. The boycott was, he wrote, 'A great moral victory.'[78] In *Der Angriff*, Goebbels celebrated the Berlin public's 'violent participation' in the whole event, but many other observers, like the British Ambassador in Berlin, Horace Rumbold, noted the indifference or active disapproval of many people across Germany towards the boycott.[79]

The consensus among historians today is that the boycott did not get the widespread support the Nazis hoped for; Friedländer calls it a 'failure'. Given that the boycott was called off after one day, and not subsequently renewed, and that it did not stop the criticism of anti-Semitism in Germany from abroad, this is understandable, but there is a wider context to consider. The boycott did not provoke any kind of mass protest in Germany, and it did not dissuade the Nazis from further measures. Indeed, as Friedländer notes, frustrated by the level of public indifference to their anti-Semitism, the Nazis turned their energies to legislative measures against the Jews.[80] The public boycott of shops by consumers on 1 April was in any case only the most visible aspect of a larger ongoing campaign to sever economic connections with Jewish concerns in Germany, and this continued apace. In May 1933, for example, Germany's largest commercial enterprise, the Imperial Railway (*Deutsche Reichsbahn*) ordered its many divisions 'to suspend all contracts with Jewish firms and to avoid doing business with them in the future'.[81] Jochen Klepper, a devout Protestant writer and radio employee in Berlin, noted before 1 April that the public boycott only legalized what he called the existing 'silent boycott' of Jewish enterprises of all kinds. Recording in his diary on 5 April that the boycott had not been resumed, he asked what help that was when Jewish doctors, lawyers, and artists were still being excluded from their professions.[82] The French Ambassador, André François-Poncet, made a similar point in his report to the Foreign Ministry in Paris. He noted that the boycott of Jewish shops was only one form taken by the anti-Semitic struggle, and that it was 'the most dangerous for the German economy and for the prestige of the *Reich*'. It was only this form which had been abandoned after 1 April. 'In all other domains', François-Poncet wrote, the anti-Semitic struggle 'is pursued with an implacable method and a bitter hatred'.[83]

Goebbels, although disappointed with the public reaction to the boycott, was undeterred, and quickly followed this with his participation in the notorious burning of the books. This 'action against the un-German spirit' was actually organized by a nationalistic student group, which planned a nationwide campaign to gather books written by racial or political opponents, and to burn them publicly in university towns.[84] On the evening of 10 May 1933 lorry-loads of books, some 20,000 in all, were brought from various libraries around Berlin and consigned to a huge bonfire by students on the Opera Square in front of the University. Large crowds had gathered, despite steady rain, forewarned of the event. When the fire was started, according to *Der Angriff*, which reported on the event in the present tense favoured by Goebbels, 'Eager expectation lights up all eyes ... The burning glow is reflected in the countless windows of the adjoining state buildings, and over the flames a rain of sparks rises vertically into the sky.' Goebbels spoke to the crowd from a hastily erected rostrum. He began his short speech by announcing that 'the age of an overreaching Jewish intellectualism is now at an end'. He celebrated the way 'youth' was seizing the initiative, and declared: 'The old lies in the flames. The new will rise anew out of the flames of our own hearts!'[85] The next day Goebbels wrote: 'I was in the best form ... A glorious summer begins outside today.'[86]

This complacent satisfaction extended to Goebbels' perception of the press reaction to his behaviour. He noted that the coverage in Germany of the boycott on 1 April was 'fabulous',[87] without appearing to concede that much of the German press was already deferential to the point of sycophancy to the Nazi movement. He entirely misjudged the reaction abroad, which he simply could not understand. This incomprehension, which was also manifested as contempt, was evident in Goebbels' wider attitude towards foreign affairs. In 1933, he was twice involved in an entirely new role, as a state representative abroad. The first came in late May when he and Magda went as honorary guests with a German delegation to Fascist Italy. They were warmly welcomed, and treated with great hospitality. Goebbels, who had an exaggerated admiration for Mussolini, basked in the atmosphere of mutual admiration and wrote with great regard of the achievements of Italian Fascism. He was delighted by the enthusiasm shown for Magda, and rather flattered, when he met Mussolini, to be called 'Il dottore'.[88]

In September 1933 Goebbels travelled to Geneva briefly to represent Germany at the League of Nations' Disarmament Conference. He loathed the whole thing, which he described as a 'parliamentarianism of the nations'. The very process of diplomacy antagonized him, and he dismissed those conducting it on behalf of the other nations as fools. 'For us that is nothing', he wrote. Nor did he like Switzerland. The climate, he thought, was 'musty and mild. Unbearable for a north German.'[89] *The Times* in London was not convinced by Goebbels' sincerity, noting that he used many 'fine phrases' in trying to portray the benign character of the new regime in Germany, and its peaceful intentions.[90] Goebbels was happy to fly back to German soil, and delighted when Hitler withdrew from the Conference and the League of Nations altogether in October 1933. This he thought a great propaganda coup, and he rejoiced in the greater isolation it brought the Nazi government in Germany. It was too much effort for Goebbels to try to make sense of foreign countries or their representatives, and he retreated to the bubble of Nazi propaganda which he was constructing with Hitler, and now with the help of others like Albert Speer, Leni Riefenstahl, and, less willingly, the conductor Wilhelm Furtwängler.

Although Goebbels argued frequently with Magda, as indeed they had since the earliest days of their relationship, there were no disputes between them about the central tenets of Nazism, with one exception: Magda wished to be more involved in Party work than any woman was allowed. Already she was moving into the position of idealized '*Reich* mother' that she later so fully occupied. She even gave a radio speech on 'The German Mother' in May 1933, which Goebbels conceded was 'complete in form'.[91] Apart from this, Magda was confined to a representative role, appearing at official functions, and to an informal role, helping individual German women with private problems. She was aware that she was very much in the public eye, and took great care not to compromise her husband. In May 1933 for example, the Berlin journalist Bella Fromm wrote a short feature on Magda, but before publication she was advised in a letter from Magda's secretary that the 'Frau Reichsminister does not desire the fact to be made public that she is interested in Buddhism.'[92]

23. Goebbels in 1933 with his wife Magda, their first child Helga and, in the background, Harald Quandt, Magda's son from her first marriage. Only Harald survived the collapse of the 'Third Reich'.

In July Magda was again pregnant. Through these months, although he now spent much of his time with foreign pressmen, and with the mass media, Goebbels was still a Party activist, and this was the work he enjoyed most. For him, the 'socialism' in the Party's title was not mere rhetoric. Economic conditions were slowly improving in Germany in 1933, but from a very low base. There was grinding poverty in the big cites, and Goebbels worked hard to promote two characteristic Nazi social measures, the *Winterhilfe* (Winter Help), and the *Eintopfgericht* (a fortnightly 'one pot meal', instituted as a symbol of collective austerity). The latter was no great hardship for Goebbels, who did not care greatly for food or drink, and, more enthusiastically than most of the Nazi leaders, he relished his first 'one pot meal' on 1 October 1933. He wrote that it tasted 'glorious'.[93] Later that month, on his birthday, Goebbels diverted 80,000 marks from the *Gau* office to the 'Winter Help'. He went to Moabit, one of the poorest areas of Berlin, for a Party meeting. Schoolchildren sang folk songs for him, and he wrote that he was 'really happy in the love of all the people.' He was 36 years old, and he reflected later that night:

> Magda is my sweet wife and comrade. My colleagues and friends are loyal to me. Hitler is my leader and my friend. I have a great task, I am healthy, and furious for work [*arbeitswütig*].[94]

In November 1933 elections were held for the *Reichstag*, and added to these was a referendum on Hitler's decision to leave the League of Nations. Most foreign observers thought this whole process a farce: only the Nazi Party was allowed to stand for the *Reichstag*, and huge pressure was exerted on the population to vote 'Yes' in the referendum. Opening the campaign, Goebbels declared that in

24. Goebbels inaugurates the 'one pot meal' with Hitler, October 1933. This was an austerity measure all good Germans were encouraged to share once a fortnight. For Goebbels, who cared little for food or drink, this was a real pleasure. In his diary he wrote that this one pot meal tasted 'glorious'. (*TBJG*, 2 October 1933, TI, 2/III, p. 282.)

its foreign affairs Germany wanted above all an honourable reconciliation with France.[95] In the event some 90 per cent of the votes cast were in support of the Nazis. Goebbels, who had organized a sophisticated propaganda campaign, and given speeches in several major cities before the elections, was delighted: 'It is achieved', he wrote, 'the German *Volk* is united. Now we can stand up against the world.'[96] Even critics of the Nazis were amazed by what the new regime had accomplished since coming to power in January. The French Ambassador to Berlin wrote:

> The astonishing thing in this revolution is the speed with which it has been executed; it is also the ease with which it has been carried through, and the little resistance it has encountered.[97]

Victor Klemperer, who had voted 'No' in the referendum, and written 'No' on his *Reichstag* ballot paper, wrote: 'I was laid low ... I too am beginning to believe in the power and permanency of Hitler. It's dreadful.'[98]

For Goebbels, these were days of rare fulfilment. Ten years previously, he had sat alone in a cold bedroom in provincial Rheydt, dreaming of success as a playwright or author. Now he was married to a beautiful woman; he had a lovely daughter, and hoped for a son in the New Year. He was a man of property, and a published author. Above all he was a celebrated public figure, and everywhere he went in Germany he received the acclamation of ordinary people. 'I am completely happy among the *Volk*', he wrote on 18 November. A couple of days later he attended a celebration of German choral music at the State Opera in Berlin: 'Wonderful. Complete. Really great choral culture. And glorious music: Schubert, Beethoven. Dances and singing.'[99]

Nor did Goebbels forget his attachment to his supporters. Magda had also taken to heart her husband's concern for the families of the SA men, especially for 'those left behind by the fallen'. As Christmas approached, she and her secretary sent out invitations to a list of these women and their children, inviting them to a Christmas party. Magda's chauffeur-driven car would pick them up and return them to their homes in the poorer parts of Berlin afterwards.[100] On 17 December Goebbels spoke in 'biting cold' to a gathering of old fighters at the dedication of a memorial to SA man Kütemeyer by the Landwehr canal.[101] The party for those 'left behind' was held on 20 December, and he commented: 'Magda is really in her element.'[102] 25 December 1933 was, Goebbels wrote, 'my most beautiful Christmas'. He went to a street party in Moabit, where 1,400 children were given presents by the SA:

> A stirring festival. Stormy applause breaks out when I arrive. I speak briefly right from the heart. And it goes also to the heart. Many mothers cry when they step up with their children to the tables with the presents.[103]

7
'We Are Not Suited to Be Executioners'

Perhaps the closest of Hitler's associates is Dr Paul Goebbels, the Minister of Propaganda, ... That this pale-faced little man with the haggard cheeks and the clubfoot should have built up for himself so outstanding a position in the New Germany, which has been taught to make physical perfection its ideal, is a tribute to his genius and determination, while all who know him will bear testimony to the keenness of his mind.

G. Ward Price, Berlin correspondent for the Daily Mail.[1]

Goebbels will go down in history as Hitler's Propaganda Minister, and most of his working time after March 1933 was taken up with this role. With characteristic disdain, when he moved into a nineteenth-century building in the Wilhelmplatz to take up his appointment, he had the interior rearranged to suit his own tastes. Hindenburg, when formally confirming the young Goebbels as Propaganda Minister, urged him to exercise office in an 'above-party' manner,[2] but this was hopelessly naïve. In an interview in *Der Angriff* Goebbels declared bluntly that the main task of the new ministry was 'to shape public opinion'. More specifically he said that what he called 'People's Propaganda' was not a cliché, 'but rather an art, which demanded enormous tact and knowledge of the people's soul [*Volksseele*]'.[3] In office, Goebbels devoted all his energies to ceremonies designed to glorify the Nazi movement, and to making the arts and the media – as far as he could – support the Party. Goebbels delighted in the opportunity to deploy theatrical effects, music, and huge masses of people in Party rituals. In the first few months of his ministry, he developed the essential features of the huge Nazi rallies which shocked and fascinated the rest of the world, and which they now apprehended more fully, thanks to the use of radio and film.

The funeral still had pride of place in Goebbels' repertoire, and he now exploited the opportunity to present dead Nazis as martyrs for the nation as well as the movement. Within days of Hitler's appointment as Chancellor on 30 January 1933, Goebbels had staged the funeral of an SA man and a policeman killed that day as a 'state burial'.[4] The annual Party rally in Nuremberg was also now presented as a national occasion, rather than as a Nazi Party ceremony.

Albert Speer claims to have contributed the idea of using vast swastika flags as a backdrop, with searchlights pointing into the sky to form a 'cathedral of light', initially for the ceremonies on the Tempelhof field on 1 May 1933, which subsequently became standard fixtures at Nuremberg.[5] With this enhanced visual dimension to the spectacle Goebbels engaged Leni Riefenstahl to shoot a documentary film of the rally in September 1933, to be called *The Victory of Faith*, a title encapsulating Hitler and Goebbels' belief in the importance of 'the idea'. The film today appears clumsy, a trial run for the later *Triumph of the Will*, but Goebbels was enthusiastic when it was premiered in December 1933, calling it a 'picture-symphony'.[6]

Hitler and Goebbels invited the British, American, and French ambassadors to the Party rally, as well as other foreign guests, but they failed entirely to understand the perception of most foreigners that Nazism was crude, violent, and barbaric. Goebbels was intoxicated by the huge enthusiasm for his propaganda spectacles in Germany itself. He found himself at the centre of vast crowds, often hundreds of thousands strong, generating a mass hysteria which was new in European history. He thought that the Party rally in 1933 went 'like clockwork', and he waxed lyrical about the quasi-religious nature of the occasion.[7] He and Hitler had developed a narcissistic fascination with their propaganda, and they often relaxed together by watching their own speeches on film, or listening to sound recordings of themselves. As they made their first excursions into the polished world of international diplomacy, they felt that they were misunderstood, and they used their massive popularity inside Germany to justify their acts, and to justify the worst excesses of their supporters. At the Nuremberg Rally in September 1933 Goebbels reviewed the government's handling of the 'Jewish question', which he said had been at the heart of the 'national revolution'. He repeated Richard Wagner's description of 'the Jew' as 'the demon of decay', and proclaimed: 'In opposition to him stands the Aryan man as creative figure.' In case anyone still imagined that anti-Semitism was a marginal aspect of Nazism Goebbels stated that: 'The future of our *Volk* lies in the solution of this problem.' He argued that the April boycott of Jewish shops had been carried through without violence or bloodshed, and, in typically truculent fashion, declared that just as the Nazis had fought the internal opposition during the Weimar years, now they would stand up against international condemnation.[8]

Goebbels frequently took this line with foreign journalists and diplomats in 1933. Not least because of the enormous publicity Goebbels himself gave to them, his speeches were relayed to an outside world which rapidly took on a view of him as the most rabid and uncompromising of Hitler's lieutenants. The American Ambassador William Dodd wrote this description of Goebbels – whom he called 'Hitler's first lieutenant' – shortly after arriving in Germany in 1933:

He makes a point of stirring animosities and hatreds wherever there is opportunity, and he has combined all the newspapers, radio, publications and art activities of Germany into one vast propaganda machine ... He is far cleverer than Hitler, is much more belligerent, and, I am told, always refuses to have contacts with foreigners.[9]

Culture had been at the heart of the political view of Hitler and Goebbels, and they had both openly declared that in a national socialist dictatorship the arts would be expected to serve the *Volk*, after they had been rescued from the hands of the Jews. The burning of the books in May 1933 had far more than a symbolic impact. Accompanied as it was by widespread physical intimidation of Jewish intellectuals and artists, the clearest possible public message was sent out, that Jews were not to take further part in German cultural life. It followed the passing of the Law for the Restoration of the Professional Civil Service on 7 April, which demanded the immediate 'retirement' of 'Civil servants not of Aryan origin'. This law applied to a huge range of state and municipal employees, including musicians, and was followed by similar discriminatory measures applying to other occupational categories. Goebbels moved immediately in April to enforce the exclusion of Jews from positions in the mass media. He welcomed the challenge thrown down by the conductor of the Berlin Philharmonic Orchestra, Wilhelm Furtwängler, who requested in an open letter in the *Vossische Zeitung* on 11 April that Jews who were 'genuine artists ... like Walter, Klemperer, and Reinhardt' be allowed to perform in Germany. The only distinction which should be recognized, he argued, was between 'good and bad' artists.

Goebbels was a huge admirer of Furtwängler's conducting, as were many others around the world. As Propaganda Minister Goebbels frequently attended the opera and the concert hall, and he often commented in his diary, as he had done since 1923, on the performance of individual musicians. Becoming more finicky as he became accustomed to world-renowned performers in Berlin, he found provincial concerts, and even the performance of Party groups like the National Socialist Symphony Orchestra increasingly unbearable. Furtwängler was one musician he always singled out for glowing praise. Nonetheless, Goebbels relished the opportunity provided by Furtwängler's request to justify the exclusion of Jews from the arts. He replied in an open letter, which was published in all Germany's leading newspapers. 'There can be no art in the absolute sense, as it is understood by liberal democracy', he declared, and he thanked Furtwängler for the 'many hours of genuinely formative, great, and often overwhelming art' which he had given to 'his political friends and hundreds of thousands of good Germans'. Without actually referring to Jews as such, Goebbels used the coded language of the 'Third Reich' to justify the exclusion of 'rootless' and 'destructive' artists from public performance in Germany.[10]

The exchange of letters attracted huge interest around the world, and was misinterpreted by many as a genuine dialogue. In fact, Goebbels easily outmanoeuvred Furtwängler, who was himself a passionate German nationalist, and had already compromised hopelessly by seeking only exemptions to the more general exclusion of the Jews from wide areas of German life. He was trapped in understandings of 'German' nationalism and 'German music' which overlapped with Goebbels' own vision, and was mollified by Goebbels' temporary acceptance of the continued presence of Jewish musicians in the Berlin Philharmonic Orchestra. The orchestra was in any case on the verge of bankruptcy, and was shortly after this brought effectively under state ownership. Furtwängler continued to conduct the orchestra at prominent state occasions, while the exclusion of the Jews continued around him.[11] The Jewish musicians in the Berlin Philharmonic were excluded by 1935, and Furtwängler's Jewish secretary, Berta Geissmar, escaped to Britain.[12]

Goebbels was delighted with this success, and planned a central role for Furtwängler in his broader reorganization of the arts in Germany. Goebbels took from Fascist Italy the corporatist notion of the occupational chamber, and in July 1933 secured Hitler's agreement to the establishment of a '*Reich* Chamber of Culture', to be controlled from the Propaganda Ministry. Goebbels planned within this seven separate Chambers, of Music, Press, Film, Theatre, Radio, the Visual Arts, and Literature. His fondest hope was to secure the cooperation of leading artists in every field to serve as 'Presidents' and 'Vice Presidents', as well as in subordinate posts. In this he was extraordinarily successful, and the capitulation of famous artists to the Nazi regime was encapsulated in the *Reich* Music Chamber, which aroused more international interest than the others. The elderly composer Richard Strauss, the living embodiment of the German classical tradition, agreed to serve as President of the *Reich* Music Chamber, and Furtwängler took on the vice presidency. Both attended the festive opening of the *Reich* Chamber of Culture on 15 November 1933. They sat in the front row, along with Hitler and his Cabinet, while Goebbels, who was named as the President of the whole organization, delivered an introductory speech. This was preceded by a performance of Beethoven's *Egmont Overture*, and Strauss' *Festive Prelude*. Goebbels wrote that this was 'My dream fulfilled.'[13]

This ecstatic comment can be interpreted in several ways. At one level Goebbels was surely speaking of his long held ambition to be an artist. As a young man he had dreamed of working in the theatre, perhaps as a producer, or as a playwright. Now he had unparalleled influence over the artistic life of a nation. At another level, the *Reich* Chamber of Culture gave Goebbels authority in an area which he thought he had earlier secured Hitler's agreement to control, but which since January 1933 was disputed by other state and Party authorities. Despite the rather vague remit given to the Propaganda Ministry to oversee the arts, Goebbels had found himself fighting to delineate his powers against those of the Interior

Ministry run by Wilhelm Frick, the Prussian Ministry of Culture run by Bernhard Rust, and since July 1933 against those of the German Labour Front, run by Robert Ley. This body had supplanted Germany's trade unions and Ley had sought to bring the professional associations of German artists under his control. It was this specifically which had prompted Goebbels to request permission to organize a *Reich* Chamber of Culture. Outside these bodies, Alfred Rosenberg had since 1928 run the so-called 'Fighting League of German Culture', which had led the revolutionary agitation against what the Nazis called 'cultural Bolshevism' at street-level. Rosenberg's 'Fighting League', acting with the SA and local Party groups, had played an important part at local level in organizing the notorious demonstrations against Jewish conductors and musicians after January 1933.[14]

25. The 'Senate' of the *Reich* Chamber of Culture meeting in the 'Throne Room' of the Propaganda Ministry. Through this institution Goebbels hoped both to reinvigorate and to control 'German culture'.

Between November 1933 and April 1945, the *Reich* Chamber of Culture was the chief instrument through which Goebbels sought to control the arts in Germany. It rapidly grew into a huge organization, with over 2,000 employees of its own, and hundreds of thousands of members from every field of the arts, ranging from internationally known celebrities like Strauss and Furtwängler to technicians in the film industry and theatre costumiers. In ideological terms, Goebbels represented the Chamber of Culture as a new development in the relationship between culture and the state, which replaced the traditionally individual, atomized role of the creative artist, with one in which the artist was bound to and part of the larger *Volksgemeinschaft*. The *Volk*, Goebbels declared in his inaugural speech, was the 'source of his [the artist's] fertility'. More practically Goebbels was now able to redirect the localized, revolutionary agitation against 'cultural Bolshevism' into legislative channels.[15]

Through the Chamber of Culture Goebbels was able to exercise direct control over the arts in two ways: first, by sponsoring and encouraging certain kinds of artistic production and, second, by regulating membership of the separate chambers within the organization. The Law establishing the *Reich* Chamber of Culture also gave it wide-ranging powers of censorship, and the power to exclude artists from membership of an individual chamber. Those excluded were at the same time forbidden to work in any artistic capacity. Above all, this allowed Goebbels to pursue the exclusion of Jews from what he imagined as 'German culture', frequently applying more discriminatory criteria than were used in other occupational categories. It is no exaggeration to say that getting anyone suspected of Jewish ancestry or even with Jewish family connections out of the multifarious branches of the Chamber of Culture became an obsession for Goebbels. Inevitably it took time to set up the bureaucratic machinery of the Chamber of Culture, but from early in 1934 Goebbels started to exclude Jews from membership. From 1935 this was systematically applied.[16]

Given that so many musicians and other artists of international distinction had fled Germany since January 1933, it was enormously helpful to the Nazi regime to have the public support of celebrities like Strauss and Furtwängler. The other art in which Goebbels took particular interest was cinema. He had, since his early days in Berlin with Schweitzer, become increasingly fascinated by film and its growing possibilities. After 1933, there was more scope for the Nazis to produce films for the general public, and potentially, to realize Goebbels' vision of a 'National Socialist film', which could sublimate propaganda messages in the established model of the commercial feature film.

There was also potential for the clumsy representation of Nazi mythology, and Goebbels was wary of the highest ideals of 'the movement' being cheapened, or battened on by opportunists. This is undoubtedly why he acted first to censor, and then significantly to alter the film of *Horst Wessel* made in 1933 by a group including Franz Wenzler and 'Putzi' Hanfstaengl, now Hitler's foreign press chief. The film was based on a biography of Horst Wessel by Hanns Heinz Ewers, which ironically Goebbels had greatly admired when he read it in November 1932. As the film neared its premiere, scheduled to coincide with Wessel's birthday on 9 October 1933, Goebbels acted with characteristic intransigence. On the day of the anniversary, Goebbels banned any showing, and arranged for an 'interview' to be published in *Der Angriff* to justify the ban. In the interview Goebbels argued that any film made about 'the National Socialist idea' must be of 'absolutely first-class artistic quality'; and that a film about Horst Wessel was even more important than others made depicting the SA. His martyrdom must not be sentimentalized. In this case, argued Goebbels, the music for the film was splendid, but there was much about the film that contradicted the 'historical truth'. The figure of Horst Wessel as portrayed did not approach the character of the man in reality. Asked by his interviewer whether the ban was an attack on artistic freedom, Goebbels answered that it was the very opposite, and would be welcomed by all true artists because of its demand for the highest standards.[17] Hanfstaengl later wrote that the film was censored because 'It was too bourgeois in approach, emphasized Horst Wessel's Christian background too much, was not full of the National-Socialist revolutionary spirit, was trite – everything was wrong.'[18] At the time Goebbels was privately more succinct, and more brutal: 'Most bloody stupid dilettantism.'[19]

There has been much discussion of why *Horst Wessel* was censored, and David Welch has argued that it was primarily a move intended to assert Goebbels' control of the German film industry.[20] It is instructive to look at what Goebbels did on the same day as the film was censored, a move which was by no means guaranteed to bring him popularity with Party activists. His involvement with the Horst Wessel cult was more than an opportunistic gesture, as it is frequently portrayed. This is Goebbels' own record of what he was doing the day before the premiere:

> In the afternoon, Riefenstahl and Cemnitzer to coffee. We rummaged through *Der Angriff* from Horst Wessels' time. Blessed memories.
>
> Guest performance of Italian opera at the *Städtische* opera. 'Aida'. Really great. These glorious, wonderful, voices. That is the most beautiful in music that one can hear.
>
> Afterwards at home with us, Leni Ri. and Willi Fritsch. Chatted about film.
>
> Prohibition of the Horst Wessel film is arousing great interest. But I stand firm.[21]

And on the day of the anniversary:

> Yesterday: talked through my concerns with Funk. Magda and myself ill. Flu.
>
> Mister Ebbutt from *The Times*. I am building up a new reputation with the Berlin foreign correspondents. I think it will work. Things are bad in foreign affairs. We are quite isolated. Italy? Pah!
>
> With the Chief: prohibition of the *Wessel* film. Hanfstaengl is agitating. Won't offer me his hand. Chief is furious with him. I will not give up. I am

responsible for the remembrance of Wessel. Chief agrees. The press has its sensation.

To the Friedrichshain hospital. Spoke in pouring rain on Wessel's birthday. Dedicated his death room as a memorial chamber. Went alone to the grave. His mother insufferable.[22]

In the course of this speech in the hospital courtyard, Goebbels said: 'Today it is cheap and easy to step behind the dead and to misuse them for trivial effect.' He portrayed the followers of Horst Wessel as 'a sworn community' pledged to a memory which must not be 'falsified'.[23] Only after many cuts had been made, and the direct reference to events in Wessel's life had been removed, was the film reissued, under the name *Hans Westmar*, in December 1933. In its synthesis of a heroic personal narrative, the funeral ceremony, and stirring music, the cult of Horst Wessel embodied all the elements most central to Goebbels' propaganda, the cult of sacrifice, the overtones of religion, and the centrality of death. It was aesthetically located in wintry scenes, always most emotional for Goebbels. Although Goebbels resented the attempt of others to usurp (or, as with Wessel's mother, to share) his monopoly of the representation of this cult, he also found Wenzler and Hanfstaengl's representation unacceptably trivial.

By the spring of 1934, the Nazis had been in power for a year. Although Hitler had succeeded in establishing dictatorial executive powers, and in destroying many possible centres of opposition to his rule, the Party was approaching a fateful crisis. In contrast to the euphoria of 'national revolution' in the spring of 1933, a widespread feeling of discontent was abroad in Germany, not just amongst Jews and the many others who had direct cause to loath Nazism, but amongst Party members and other circles on the right. Goebbels even had to start a 'Campaign against Fault Finders and Grumblers'. Klemperer in Dresden read a report of Goebbels' speech inaugurating this in the *Sportpalast*, and summarized parts of it:

Gross rabble rousing and a 'last warning to the Jews'. Flagrant threat of a pogrom if the foreign boycott does not cease. Promise not to harm them 'if they remain in their homes' and do not claim to be of 'full or equal value'. Europe 1934, Germany! – there is desperation behind the speech, a last attempt at diversion. Work on the housing projects and the *Reich* motorways is apparently faltering already.[24]

Goebbels himself enjoyed this occasion, which he described as 'a fighting meeting like in the old times. Against bleaters and carpers.'[25]

As so often in Goebbels' life, a political crisis coincided with important developments in his private life. Since January 1933, Goebbels, like many senior Nazis, had become a wealthy man. His books, initially printed by the

Nazi publishing house in Munich, Franz Eher, now sold thousands of copies, generating large royalties, and he earned a considerable salary as a minister. The heroic narrative of his leadership in Berlin, with the title *Kampf um Berlin* (*The Struggle for Berlin*), first published in 1932, went through several reprints, and he sold the rights for this for 15,000 marks in April 1933.[26] His rewritten diary of events before the 'seizure of power', published in Germany as *Vom Kaiserhof zum Reichskanzlei* in 1934, and in English translation as *My Part in Germany's Fight* in 1935, sold even better.[27] He also published pamphlets and books containing selected speeches, and an exercise in photo-journalism, *Das erwachende Berlin* (*Berlin Awakening*). The collection of speeches entitled 'Revolution of the Germans' had sold over 10,000 copies by January 1934, earning Goebbels another 1,500 marks.[28] Sales of Goebbels' books were boosted by local Party branches and organizations which bought them to distribute as gifts to activists.

Goebbels bought a string of new cars for himself and Magda, and by early 1934 was learning to drive himself. According to Schaumburg-Lippe, Goebbels was a reckless driver with more confidence than competence, and it seems that he mainly, perhaps wisely, left this to others.[29] He and Magda now rented a lakeside house in Kladow on the Wannsee, where they frequently entertained artists, musicians, film stars and producers. In March 1934 Goebbels bought a motor boat, with the Nordic name of *Baldur*, and used this for excursions on the many waterways around Berlin and Potsdam. He had a definite vision of the role a minister's wife in the 'Third Reich' ought to play, and on the whole Magda conformed very well to this. She was nonetheless strong-willed, and at times they quarrelled angrily. There was 'a terrible row' when she received guests at a New Year's reception in 1934 dressed in a negligee.[30] Magda had been pregnant since July 1933, and there was a serious deterioration in marital relations. Their second daughter, Goebbels recorded, was born on 13 April 1934: 'It is a girl and is called Hilde. At first she brought disappointment, but then joy and happiness.'[31] Family life with young children was not easy for Goebbels. He complained a few weeks later that he felt himself 'unbearably unfree'.[32]

Goebbels had long been aware of the difficulties the Party had with the SA. This organization had grown enormously during 1933, providing opportunities and salaries for a handful of leaders, but leaving many of the rank and file disgruntled and underemployed. Many SA men had participated in lawless violence in the early months of the Nazi 'revolution', but by early 1934, Hitler had made efforts to restrain this. The improvised torture cellars and detention centres of the SA had given way to the beginnings of the concentration camp system, run by the SS.[33] Expectations that the SA would be turned into some kind of 'people's army' had been frustrated, and the *Reichswehr* had made clear to Hitler its opposition to any usurpation of its own role. Goebbels had a complex position in this growing confrontation. He had strongly identified with the SA, with its socialist aspirations, its activism, and its embodiment of the revolutionary ideal. He had, on the other hand, long been disgusted by the homosexuality of several SA leaders, and when the crisis came in late June 1934, this weighed heavily with him. It appears that he had no foreknowledge of Hitler's decision to act ruthlessly, and to carry out a bloody purge of opponents on the night of 30 June, but Goebbels had long ago cast his lot with Hitler. As the events which have become known as the 'Night of the Long Knives' unfolded, he had no hesitation in acting with him.

Through May 1934, Goebbels fretted about the SA, and about its leadership. He recorded on 14 May a private conversation with Hitler about Röhm's 'nauseating' homosexuality.[34] Over the next few weeks he noted his growing concern over the tension between Röhm and Hitler, and between the SA and the *Reichswehr*. In June Hitler sent the whole SA on leave for a month. From a completely separate quarter, a nucleus of opposition to Nazism had formed in the conservative, Catholic circles around the former Chancellor von Papen, still Vice Chancellor in Hitler's Cabinet. The tension in Germany was enormously heightened on 17 June when Papen delivered a speech at Marburg University, unambiguously calling for a return to some form of representative, pluralistic government, and criticizing 'pseudo-religious materialism'.[35] At the time Goebbels had just returned from another excursion into German foreign policy, a visit to Poland to consolidate the 'Non-Aggression Pact' signed in January 1934 between the two countries.

26. Goebbels with Marshal Pilsudski on a state visit to Poland, 14 June 1934. Although Goebbels in his diary described Pilsudski as 'half-Asiatic' and a 'despot', he thought he was a 'great man and a fanatical Pole ... At his wish we were photographed together.' (*TBJG*, 16 June 1934, TI, 3/I, p. 63.)

Goebbels moved immediately to prevent publication of Papen's speech, 'on Hitler's order',[36] but not before it had been printed in early editions of the *Frankfurter Zeitung*, and over the next few days Papen was on several occasions applauded in public. Rumours of an alternative government around Hindenburg and Papen gathered pace. It was in this fraught atmosphere that Goebbels argued bitterly with Magda. Before his trip to Warsaw he had written that 'crises' with her had become 'almost unbearable'. After his return they quarrelled more bitterly and he wrote on 22 June that he had learned 'a dreadful thing from Magda', and that there were 'terrible scenes'. It is not clear what Magda told him, but we may presume that it was to do with a former or current infidelity, sexual or emotional. After a busy day dealing with numerous agitated callers, including Papen, and a speech before a massive audience in Berlin, Goebbels wrote:

> Magda comes from Kladow. Tears, scenes, it is no longer to be borne. She is at bottom good. I also carry much guilt. Must atone for that. Today grey and rainy. We are, inside, separated.[37]

Goebbels had never before written about the problems in his relationship with Magda in such strong and unequivocal terms.

As Goebbels' marriage was shaken, the larger crisis in Germany was brewing. On 21 June Hitler had been summoned to see the President at his Prussian estate. There, he encountered Blomberg, the commander of the *Reichswehr*, who had just spoken with Hindenburg, and now threatened to impose martial law if Hitler failed to deal with the SA leadership.[38] Hitler worked himself into a fury in the last days of June, convincing himself that Röhm was plotting a *coup d'état*, together with Schleicher, the French Ambassador François-Poncet, and other dissidents. Crucially, Hitler secured the support of the SS and the *Reichswehr* for a 'secret and very important commission', that is to say a mass execution of Röhm, other SA leaders, and other opponents of the regime.[39] In the last days of June, groups of SS men in Berlin and in Munich were equipped with lorries and weapons by the *Reichswehr*. On 29 June Goebbels wrote:

> Today, morning: call from the *Führer*: fly to Godesberg straight away. So it's all starting. In God's name. Anything is better than this terrible waiting. I am ready.[40]

In Bad Godesberg, Hitler told Goebbels that Röhm was conspiring with Schleicher, François-Poncet, and Gregor Strasser. At 2.00 a.m., Hitler and Goebbels flew to Munich, where they drove straight to the Bavarian Interior Ministry, arriving at dawn. Goebbels described how Hitler tore the badges of rank from two local SA commanders before they drove off to Bad Wiessee, some 50 kilometres from Munich, where Röhm and other SA leaders were gathered, ostensibly for a conference. Goebbels described what then followed:

> Chronology: Arrest at Wiessee. Leadership very courageous. Chief brilliant. Heines tragic. With a pleasure boy. Röhm maintains his bearing. All without a hitch. Back to Munich …

Interior Ministry Munich. Alarming news. But all calm. *Führer* with Killinger. Goes smoothly. Speech in front of the SA leaders. New laws for the Party. Fabulous impression. Something to eat. Then a 'Call to the People'. Not a moment for sleep. From Berlin: Strasser dead, Schleicher dead, Bose dead, Clausener dead. Seven SA leaders in Munich shot.

Summing up, Goebbels wrote that there had been no problems, 'except that Frau Schleicher also fell. A shame, but nothing can be changed.'[41]

The 'Night of the Long Knives' was a significant moment for Goebbels, who was not merely involved in giving or communicating orders, but had been with Hitler when he confronted Röhm, Heines, and others who were later killed. After returning to Berlin, Hitler, 'somewhat pale from the responsibility and the bitterness', and Goebbels heard about continuing executions:

Göring reports: Executions nearly finished. A few more are necessary. That is difficult, but necessary. Ernst, Strasser, Sander, Detten +. One last haggling session, then it all is over. It is difficult, but is not however to be avoided. There must be peace for 10 years. The whole afternoon with the *Führer*. I can't leave him alone. He suffers greatly, but is hard. The death sentences are received with the greatest seriousness. All in all about 60.

Later that evening, Goebbels – and Magda – rejoined Hitler:

The *Führer* is very nice to Magda and I. Also Göring, who stays for the whole day. Constant new reports. Dietrich reports on executions. Quite pale. We are not suited to be executioners.[42]

This was a defining moment in the relationship between Goebbels and Hitler, when they took it upon themselves to be mass murderers, or as Goebbels reluctantly conceded, 'executioners'. In future years the temptation to resort to killing opponents was one to which they had ever more frequent recourse, and became totally habituated to. It is highly significant that Magda spent so much time with Hitler and Goebbels over these few days. She made no protest about the killings. She undoubtedly also assumed a degree of responsibility, and this weighed heavily upon her in the last days of her life.

Göring was the first to confront the outside world, giving a brief statement to the press at 3.00 p.m. on 1 July. Goebbels gave a longer account of events on the radio the same evening. Even at this stage, there was no effort to deny that a number of people, including SA and army officers, had been murdered in cold blood. Röhm, who had not yet been killed, was accused of plotting with Schleicher and the representative of a foreign power. Reuters in London reported that Schleicher and his wife were amongst those killed, allegedly for resisting arrest.[43] In a scathing leading article *The Times* in London described Goebbels' radio speech as a 'flamboyant broadcast account ... in keeping with the medievalism of the whole proceeding'.[44] In Germany there was a tense calm. Hindenburg sent Hitler a congratulatory telegram, saying 'you have rescued the German *Volk* from a serious threat',[45] and the *Reichswehr* did not protest about the shooting of Schleicher, or his wife. On 3 July Hitler reported on events to his Cabinet. Goebbels described how Papen attended, 'completely broken', and pleading for a dispensation. 'All his people have been shot', he wrote. 'Also Edgar Jung. He deserved it.'[46] Jung was a conservative politician who had prepared Papen's speech in Marburg.

Characteristically, Hitler delayed before making a public statement on the killings. By 7 July Goebbels was, equally characteristically, fretting about this: 'It is high time that the *Führer* spoke. That the list of people shot and the heap of available material is secured and published.'[47] As Hitler remained silent, Goebbels took the initiative, but in a curiously clumsy way. He determined to speak to the foreign press correspondents in Berlin, but instead of trying to explain the murders, he turned against his audience in a speech on 11 July, and heaped abuse on them. For all his professed intentions to develop better relations with foreign journalists, Goebbels treated them as he had treated 'the asphalt press' of the Weimar Republic, with contempt. The greater part of his speech consisted of a denunciation of the international press, supported by a sarcastic recitation of small errors in the reporting in different newspapers and on various radio stations, from Moscow to London. He did not discuss the actual events of the Röhm purge, but referred repeatedly to the orderly way in which German people were now going about their daily business. Working himself into a lather of indignation and scorn, he finished by responding to the foreign press, 'in the name of the German people', with the phrase *'Pfui-Teufel!'*, which he often used in his diary, and combines revulsion and disdain, translated best as 'Ugh!' or 'Yuck!' in English.[48] Later he played Hitler a recording of the speech, and was pleased with his enthusiastic reaction. Together they discussed what Hitler might say to the *Reichstag*.[49] Famously Hitler claimed there on 13 July that he had acted as 'the Supreme Justiciar of the German Volk', and had been compelled to dispense summary justice to prevent a revolution.[50] A retrospective law was passed to legitimize the murders. The German judiciary made no protest about this *post factum* use of the law to legalize murder.[51]

The killings of 30 June and succeeding days were also an important moment in the history of the Nazi movement. Before the people of Germany, and the outside world, the leaders of the Party were revealed as calculating killers. Estimates of the number murdered varied, and are still not clear. Hitler admitted to 77 who had been killed in his *Reichstag* speech; the official list drawn up by the Nazis of those executed had 82 names on it. Historians today suggest the total was twice that.[52] For Goebbels, who had idealized the SA, the sense of guilt was greater.

His adjutant Schaumburg-Lippe wrote later that he 'more than once' said to Goebbels '30 June 1934 was a day of treason against our revolution'. Goebbels did not answer, 'except with a facial expression which expressed agreement'.[53] Well before June 1934, Goebbels was a man used to violence at close quarters. For years he had carried a firearm, and may well have used it in anger. He had frequently been present at brawls, and had undoubtedly seen opponents beaten in SA offices and cellars. Now it was clear that even members of their own Party who threatened the authority of Hitler, Goebbels, Göring, and Himmler, were dispensable, and might expect the harshest treatment. For Goebbels there was a deep sense of loss that the old SA he had fought with was a thing of the past.

The Nuremberg Rally in September 1934 was an opportunity to showcase the Nazi Party after the purge. Thanks to Leni Riefenstahl's representation in *Triumph of the Will*, scenes from this rally have become the most familiar of all images from Hitler's Germany. Goebbels was pleased with the successful production of the film, but of the actual event he wrote: 'With the SA. A bunch of layabouts. No getting through. Some enthused, a few also embittered. The SA is not what it was.'[54] Although he still made a point of speaking to SA meetings, and of directing charity towards injured SA men and those 'left behind by the fallen', the revolutionary idealism of earlier days was gone forever. Goebbels frequently complained that his old colleague from Elberfeld, Viktor Lutze, who had accompanied Hitler and Goebbels in the arrest of SA leaders at Bad Wiessee, and subsequently replaced Röhm as SA leader, did not know how to inspire the SA or to give it new tasks, but in truth, it had no sufficient role after 1933. In March 1935 Hitler announced the introduction of compulsory military service in Germany, and he concentrated after this on building up the regular armed forces.

After the killings of June 1934, Hitler and Goebbels moved to consolidate further their grip on power in Germany. Papen, who had only narrowly escaped with his life, was sent to Vienna as Ambassador after the murder of the Chancellor, Dollfuss, by Austrian Nazis and the botched attempt to seize power there in July 1934. In August, Hindenburg died, and Goebbels, again aided by Speer, turned the funeral into a sombre celebration of Prussian militarism. Hindenburg was buried at the Tannenberg Memorial in East Prussia, and the fortress-like monument was draped in black cloth to receive the body.[55] A special train was laid on to carry foreign diplomats and dignitaries to the funeral. The office of President was combined with that of the Chancellor, obviating the need for any replacement, and the armed forces took a personal oath of loyalty to Hitler. Although the Nazi grip on power in Germany was now secure, and the public construction of the *Volksgemeinschaft* was able to proceed in the full glare of Goebbels' propaganda, it was to be many months before Goebbels shook off the gloom induced by private and public developments in 1934. Reviewing events early in 1935, Goebbels wrote: 'The old year? It has burdened us with a mountain of cares. Away with them! The new! Hopefully it will bring only success, and also victory through work and struggle.'[56]

This determined optimism was not helped by Goebbels' perception of failings in many of his Party comrades. The oldest, and in some ways the closest, of these was Hans Schweitzer, who, after his days of caricaturing opponents in *Der Angriff*, had found less to do since 1933, and typically complained about this when he now met Goebbels. In February 1935 Goebbels blamed marriage for ruining Schweitzer, using what had long been one of the ultimate terms of contempt in his vocabulary: 'That's what a philistine marriage can make of a man.'[57] At a higher level in the Party, Goebbels was most concerned by the course taken by his fellow executioner, Hermann Göring. Since the 'seizure of power' Göring had developed his passion for pomp and ceremony, and for ever more ludicrous uniforms, much to the horror of Goebbels, who genuinely preferred a more austere simplicity, and saw clearly the incompatibility of Göring's lavish lifestyle with the ideals of the movement. In April 1935 Göring married Emmy Sonnemann in a grotesquely luxurious ceremony, which provoked Goebbels: 'This troubles my conscience', he wrote. 'Have we the right to complain about the reds? I must only keep myself simple and not allow this pomp-hysteria to disturb me.'[58]

'Putzi' Hanfstaengl, who had entertained Hitler and Goebbels with his piano playing through the 'time of struggle', and foolishly imagined he could help to educate Hitler towards a broader view of foreign policy, had seriously antagonized Goebbels through his involvement with the abortive *Horst Wessel* film in 1933. By early 1935 Goebbels was describing him as a 'plagiarist', who was 'embarrassing'.[59] Hanfstaengl left Germany in early 1937. Goebbels was more concerned by the subtle rise to power within the Party of a new figure, Martin Bormann. In April 1935 he wrote, after a long conversation with him in Munich, 'He is a lively lad. But certainly very dangerous as an enemy.'[60] Goebbels constantly criticized other senior Nazis, like Streicher, Frick, Rust, and Ley. Above all he was continually irritated by Alfred Rosenberg, who had pretensions to be the philosopher of the Party, and its guardian of cultural integrity. More than anyone else, Rosenberg threatened constantly to trespass on affairs Goebbels considered his own domain: culture, the arts, and propaganda. The dislike was mutual. Rosenberg, who had been a comrade of Hitler in Munich since 1919, mistrusted Goebbels, and had been horrified by his open contempt for the foreign press after the killings of 30 June 1934. In his own diary, Rosenberg wrote that not since 1914 had a public speech damaged German interests so seriously. He complained bitterly to Hitler about the 'catastrophic impression' Goebbels' conduct had made abroad, and over the next few months both Rosenberg and Goebbels sought their leader's support in their growing rivalry.[61]

Although the establishment of the Propaganda Ministry and its *Reich* Chamber of Culture in 1933 appeared to have confirmed Goebbels' authority over the arts in Germany, Rosenberg had not taken this lying down. In January 1934 Hitler had conferred on him what Evans calls 'the grandiloquent but essentially empty title' of 'Representative of the *Führer* for the Overall Philosophical and Intellectual Training and Education of the National Socialist Party', and Rosenberg went on to create a multi-faceted and well-staffed organization of his own to meddle in cultural affairs.[62] This included separate 'offices' dealing with Schooling, Philosophical Information, Literature, Research, Pre-History, Art Cultivation, and Press.[63] Petropoulos calls it 'a shadow propaganda ministry'.[64] Rosenberg's organization put on art exhibitions, commissioned academics to publish books, and ran several of Germany's leading cultural journals, such as *Die Musik* (*Music*), and, from 1938, *Die Kunst im Dritten Reich* (*Art in the Third Reich*). It built up a so-called 'Cultural-Political Archive', a card index on all artists working in Germany. In 1935 Rosenberg sponsored the production of an 'aggressively anti-Christian' play in Low German dialect, featuring 650 actors, and intended for performance to audiences as large as 40,000 at a time.[65]

The rivalry between Goebbels and Rosenberg has typically been cast in terms of ideological differences, or as part of struggle for power. Typically Rosenberg is portrayed as dogmatic and driven by ideology, Goebbels as pragmatic and opportunistic. Some writers have focused on their respective attitudes to specific artistic movements, for example casting Rosenberg as totally hostile to modernism in any form, and Goebbels as more open, particularly to Expressionism in the visual arts. Others have seen a simple jockeying for power behind their specific differences over artistic matters. Although there is more than a grain of truth in some of these portrayals – Rosenberg was dogmatic; Goebbels as a young man had flirted with Expressionism – they are too reductive, and ignore the personal factors which underlay the relationship.[66] Goebbels had never been close to Rosenberg; although he contributed frequently to the *Völkischer Beobachter*, which Rosenberg nominally edited, this had not brought them into any kind of working partnership. Nor had they at any time socialized together, in the way that Goebbels had with Göring. Goebbels, who proudly identified himself as a Prussian, a north German, was scathing about Rosenberg's Estonian origins, and saw him as an outsider, frequently referring to him in his diary as 'the Balt'. Furthermore, Rosenberg was for Goebbels identified with Munich, and with the whole circle of hangers-on around Hitler which he detested. Before 1933, Rosenberg had rarely come to Berlin where Goebbels felt the real struggle for power took place. This was more than a geographical quibble. Goebbels, although proud of his intellectual and cultural credentials, saw himself as an activist. Rosenberg had never been one of the Party's street fighters, and although there were occasions when Goebbels admired him as a public speaker, his work for the Party was on the whole conducted from his desk. Rosenberg had never put in anything like the time and commitment Goebbels had on the speaking circuit. He was not to be found amongst the poor at a Christmas street party, or at Horst Wessel's grave in the February wind and rain. Nor could Rosenberg match Goebbels for sustained hard work. Goebbels despised his abilities as a practical politician.

Goebbels was also jealous of Rosenberg's relationship with Hitler, which predated his own by five years. Although Hitler was privately scathing about the nebulous 'philosophy' expressed in Rosenberg's book *The Myth of the Twentieth Century*, he retained a certain loyalty to him, expressed after 1933 in his willingness to allow Rosenberg to build up his own ludicrously inflated organization. Goebbels since 1925 had become closer to Hitler than any other senior Nazi, and was confident in this, but he knew that Rosenberg still had access to Hitler, and was constantly inflamed by what he saw as Rosenberg's stirring. Above all, Goebbels, who saw himself as a man of deeds as well as words, thought that he was better qualified, intellectually and practically, to shape the culture of the 'Third Reich'. His diary is constantly peppered with scathing asides about 'the Balt', his amateurish efforts, his 'half crazy' colleagues, and his intriguing. Goebbels' favourite way of describing Rosenberg and his activities involved the German noun *Stänkerer*, or the verb *stänkern*. The noun is insufficiently translated as a 'grouser', but the verb is better translated in this context as 'to kick up a stink'. In 1934, Goebbels wrote about Rosenberg on 50 separate occasions in his diary. Only once was he complimentary. All the other references are critical, and range from milder comments about 'annoyance' and 'concerns' through to statements like 'He really sours my life', on 11 December 1934. In more relaxed mood, Goebbels had noted a fortnight earlier that, according to Hitler, Rosenberg 'was like a woman who can cook, but instead of cooking plays the piano'.[67]

In addition to Rosenberg's meddling, Goebbels faced other difficulties in his efforts to shape the development of the arts, and these are exemplified in 1934 and 1935 by his relationship with the *Thingspiel* (which might be most accurately translated as a 'play in a place of judgement'). This was a theatrical form which combined music, speech, and movement in open-air settings intended to be reminiscent of the meeting places of ancient 'Germanic' tribes. Building partly on the 'proletarian festival plays' of the 1920s, and on older traditions of 'nature theatre' and of '*Volk* theatre', the *Thingspiel* emerged after 1933 as a kind of drama which offered a synthesis of German landscape, the *Volk* community, and the political messages of Nazism. It offered an alternative to the 'bourgeois' conventions of the classical theatre, located in the cities, embodying class distinctions and a separation between performers and audience.[68] By 1931 a '*Reich* League for the Encouragement of Open-air Theatre' had been formed, and in 1933 Goebbels gave it great encouragement. Around Germany, hundreds of new *Thing* sites were planned, often in places of great natural and symbolic beauty, like the Loreley rock overlooking the Rhine, or on the Annaberg, a mountain in Silesia which was the site of a famous *Freikorps* victory over the Poles in 1921. When placed in cities, the *Thing* sites were surrounded by trees, and often integrated with existing historic buildings. Some were colossal, like that for 120,000 people on the Annaberg.[69] They were typically modelled on Greek amphitheatres, but some went further in seeking to symbolize the new *Volksgemeinschaft*. The *Thing* site built on the Holy Mountain outside Heidelberg was designed in the form of a human torso, to represent the symbolic union between performers and audience. The actual plays performed in these sites involved hundreds or even thousands of performers, and sought to represent types rather than individuals, partly through the use of a *Sprechchor* or 'speaking choir', a device also employed to chant slogans at Party rallies. The costumes worn had sometimes to be exaggerated so they would be visible from a great distance. Gerwin Strobl has drawn attention to the portrayal in the *Thingspiel* of the resurrected soldiers of the Great War, writing: 'Faces whitened under their steel helmets, the fallen of the Great War marched in battalion strength across the arenas and open-air stages of the new Reich.' The *Volksgemeinschaft* was extended to include the heroic dead, and 'the

27. The *Thing* site on Heidelberg's Holy Mountain, which Goebbels opened on the summer solstice in 1935. This was an open-air theatre, conceived of as an organic whole shaped like a human torso, for the performance of plays in which spectators and performers became one. Goebbels was doubtful about these plays, but liked the amphitheatre. It was, he wrote: 'National Socialism in stone.' (*TBJG*, 24 June 1935, TI, 3/I, p. 252.)

Thingspiel appeared to give meaning at last to the German deaths in the Great War'.[70] The amphitheatre on the Annaberg was overlooked by a mausoleum for the *Freikorps* men who had died there in 1921.

Particularly in 1934, as new *Thing* sites were opened around Germany, the *Thingspiel* appeared genuinely popular, giving, as Strobl argues, expression to a yearning for national unity. By 1935, the movement was faltering. Goebbels was invited to the formal opening of the *Thing* site outside Heidelberg on midsummer night in 1935. He was lyrical in his enthusiasm for the amphitheatre: 'A miracle work. National Socialism in stone. That is my plan. In the evening there a festive opening and solstice festival. I give a short speech, in the best form.' He was less certain about the *Thingspiel* presented after his speech, Kurt Heynicke's *The Road to the Reich*:

> The *Thingspiel* which follows is still very problematic. But at least it is an effort. In general we will do well to strike the word 'cultish' from our linguistic usage. That kind of thing will come of itself, and organically. A mild June night above Heidelberg. Old, not always completely happy memories.[71]

The reasons for the subsequent demise of the *Thingspiel* appear to be largely prosaic. The emphasis on types, and the need for a simple, declamatory, vocal delivery seriously limited the dramatic possibilities of the *Thingspiel*, and too few plays were written for the new sites. Those that were produced were increasingly banal and predictable. An element of rank amateurism also threatened the regime's attempt to portray itself as the guardian of German high culture. Goebbels withdrew the Propaganda Ministry's support for the *Thingspiel* movement in the autumn of 1935, and used his speech to propaganda officials at Nuremberg in September that year to proclaim publicly his previously private doubts. First he mocked the movement's adherents:

> We do not have to stage a cult festival every time five national socialists are together ... I would like to therefore only to hope that we will keep words like 'cult' or '*Thing*' or 'mysticism' out of our linguistic usage for at least ten years.[72]

Otto Laubinger, the President of the *Reich* Theatre Chamber and a fervent supporter of the *Thingspiel*, died a few weeks later.

Goebbels appears to have been genuinely affected by Laubinger's unexpected death. At the higher levels of the Party, Goebbels was now an isolated figure, rightly feared and mistrusted by others. Critically, he had the confidence and friendship of Hitler, by this time well used to the bickering of his senior officials. In these early years of the Nazi regime, Hitler discussed all major issues, internal and external, with Goebbels. They frequently watched films together, and attended concerts and other cultural events. Hitler was a regular guest at the various Goebbels residences, and on boat trips. He enjoyed the company of Magda, and, according to Goebbels, of their children, sharing Goebbels' own favouritism for his eldest daughter Helga. In contrast to the period between 1929 and 1931, when he had been frequently frustrated with Hitler's indecision, Goebbels had now developed an unqualified admiration for Hitler's political skill and decision making, above all in foreign affairs. In recent years, historians have agreed that all the most significant decisions in Nazi Germany were taken by Hitler alone. Typically he appears to have consulted Goebbels after taking a decision, seeking from him confirmation of his earlier judgement. Goebbels, mesmerized by Hitler, was happy to play this role, and also took upon himself the responsibility to try to lighten the burden falling on Hitler. We can see this very clearly in the internal and external decisions of 1935 and 1936, which had such significance in the future.

In September 1935, while at the Nuremberg Rally, Hitler called upon civil servants from the Ministry of the Interior to draft new laws on German citizenship. Working in a nearby villa, the officials soon 'ran out of paper and requisitioned old menu cards' for their work.[73] On the evening of 15 September a special meeting of the *Reich* was convened in Nuremberg, and Hitler called upon it to pass the three laws thus produced, which were then read out by Göring. The *Reich* Flag Law proclaimed that black, red, and white would henceforth be the national colours, and that the swastika flag was the national flag. The *Reich* Citizenship Law declared that only 'Germans or those of kindred blood' would henceforth be citizens. Others – mainly Jews – would be 'subjects'. The Law for the Defence of Blood and Honour forbade marriage and sexual intercourse between Germans and Jews, and the employment of Jewish women below the age of 45 in 'German' houses. Jews were forbidden to display the national flag or the national colours. These laws, which were subsequently extended by numerous 'supplementary decrees', provided the legal basis for the future persecution of the German Jews, and there has been much discussion of whether they were a hastily improvised response to a snap decision of Hitler's, or whether they were part of a more considered programme.[74]

Goebbels first mentioned what he called the 'Jewish laws' in his diary on 13 September 1935: the previous day, he wrote, he had discussed the proposed new Flag Law. On 14 September, Frick Hess and Goebbels went through the new citizenship laws with Hitler. On 17 September Goebbels wrote: 'Jewry has been seriously cast down. We are the first for hundreds of years to have the courage to take the bull by the horns.'[75] In a speech to 'propaganda workers' the previous evening Goebbels had described the newly adopted laws as of 'fundamental and secular importance'.[76] These late discussions with Hitler, and the last-minute improvisation by officials from the Interior Ministry,[77] appear superficially to confirm the idea that these laws were hastily adopted, but in fact there were a whole series of previous measures and consultations which suggest the opposite. We should bear in mind also that both Hitler's 'Twenty-five Points' of 1920, and the abortive Strasser/Goebbels 'programme' of 1925 had called for definitions of German citizenship which excluded Jews. In his earliest publication, *Das kleine abc des Nationalsozialisten*, Goebbels had used the concept of 'German blood'.[78] Since 1933 Goebbels had gone further than other ministers in excluding Jews from the media and the arts, and in the months before September 1935 he was particularly exercised by what he called the 'Jewish question'.

In March 1935 he was complaining that there were still too many Jews in the theatre and the cinema.[79] In May, Goebbels supported the decision to exclude Jews from the new requirement for military service. This was, he wrote, a 'National Socialist law'.[80] A few days earlier, strolling with Magda in the Kurfürstendamm, Berlin's main shopping street, he had been outraged by the number of Jews still in evidence there. He was even more appalled in July by reports that there had been a 'Jewish demonstration' against an anti-Semitic film, and his diary entry on this suggests that Hitler was already considering further legislation against the Jews.[81] With rather more satisfaction Goebbels recorded on 19 July that there had been a 'riot' in the Kurfürstendamm, in which Jews had been 'beaten up'.[82] This was in fact only one of many anti-Jewish disturbances which had occurred across Germany since March 1935. Alongside attacks on Jewish people and property, in many German towns Jews had been excluded from swimming pools, cinemas, and other public places. Klemperer in Dresden heard that Goebbels had called on people to 'eradicate them like bedbugs and fleas!'[83] Although Goebbels welcomed the new citizenship laws in September, he did not for a moment think that this was the realization of the Nazi dream of a racially pure community. Over the next few months, as lawyers and politicians haggled over the precise definitions of 'half-Jews' and 'quarter-Jews', Goebbels invariably pressed for the adoption of the most radical course.

Hitler's position inside Germany as the campaign against the Jews was intensified was greatly strengthened by a string of foreign policy successes. In January 1935 a plebiscite in the Saar had returned an overwhelming majority in favour of returning the province (administered since 1919 by the League of Nations) to German sovereignty. During the campaign leading up to the plebiscite Goebbels had worried that the only thing which could lose the Nazis the vote was Rosenberg's anti-clericalism, hardly calculated to appeal to an overwhelmingly Roman Catholic population. After the vote, Hitler, deploying the tactics which were to bring him such success over the next few years, hastened publicly to declare his peaceful intentions towards France, and on 1 March he and Goebbels spoke at a festive rally in Saarbrücken, celebrating the 're-conquest of a province'. On a train journey through the Saar, where the crowds 'raved and cried', they listened to gramophone records of Wagner's *Parsifal* and *Tristan*.[84] Days later the existence of a new German air force was publicly acknowledged, and on 16

March Goebbels announced the reintroduction of conscription in Germany, providing the basis for an army of 36 divisions.[85] This repudiation of the Treaty of Versailles was followed by negotiations in London which led to the signing of an Anglo-German Naval Agreement in June 1935. 'The *Führer* really happy', wrote Goebbels: 'A great success for Ribbentrop and us all.' Following Hitler, he imagined that a rapprochement with Britain would allow Germany a free hand in Europe. He added: 'The goal comes closer. Friendship with England.'[86] Goebbels was impressed by these successes, and with the divided and hesitant international response to German rearmament. He had grown up with a burning sense of indignation and national inferiority, and although no soldier himself, he idealized the concept of military service. Viewing the increasingly fraught European landscape in April 1935, he wrote: 'our only salvation lies in strength ... Through crises and dangers lies the route to our freedom.'[87] Goebbels was also aware of the risks Hitler was taking, and his enthusiasm was occasionally tempered by a note of realism. After the Italians invaded Abyssinnia in October 1935, provoking a crisis in the League of Nations, Goebbels confided to his diary his fear that Mussolini would provoke 'a catastrophe'.[88]

This comment is highly significant. Although increasingly intoxicated by Hitler's apparent mastery of foreign policy, Goebbels was horrified by the prospect of war. He rejoiced in the return to German sovereignty of the 'people's comrades' in the Saar, and he shared Hitler's ambition to bring 'back to the Reich' Germans still living in Austria, in Poland, and in Czechoslovakia. He was absolutely committed to the construction of the *Volksgemeinschaft* and to what he saw as a renaissance of 'German culture'. He saw strong, modern, armed forces as integral components of both of these aims, and fully approved of military service for all young German men. He lauded the 'Great Power' status he felt had been regained by Hitler's leadership on rearmament. He did not, like Hitler, glory in the idea of war for its own sake, and he was terrified by the prospect of a premature confrontation with the victors of the First World War, which he felt would jeopardize everything the Nazis had thus far achieved.

Goebbels' apprehension grew through the winter months as Hitler contemplated the remilitarization of the Rhineland. Since 1919 Germany had been forbidden to station troops or to have any military installations on the east bank of the Rhine, and Hitler and Goebbels knew that violation of this provision of the Versailles Treaty (and of the Locarno Pact, which Germany had also signed in 1925) might provoke a military response from France and Britain. They sensed also the weakness of France and Britain, and felt that if only they could get the timing right, they could take advantage of this. Goebbels' diary illustrates the decision-making process. On Wednesday 19 February 1936 he met Hitler at midday:

He broods on. Should he remilitarize the Rhineland? A difficult question. What if Paris ratifies the pact with the Russians? The *Führer* stands ready to strike.

He thinks and broods, and suddenly he acts. He is splendid. The situation is ripe at the moment. France will do nothing. England, really, nothing at first. But we will wait and hold our peace. All preparations go forward in the deepest darkness.

That evening, the topic was avoided. Hitler came to Goebbels' house, as so often, to see a film, and talked about the old days until 3.00 a.m. Goebbels wrote: 'It is my duty to be as near to him as possible at the making of his most difficult decisions and to make his life lighter.'

Two days later, they were scheming again: 'With the *Führer* at midday. He meditates and broods. To act or not? He will act in the end.'[89] For all the confidence exuded here, Goebbels became more anxious over the next few days. He was called to Munich and spoke with Hitler there on 1 March: 'He is now firmly decided. His face radiates calm and resolution … History will be made again!' Goebbels had to go to Leipzig immediately after this. He was back in Berlin on 3 March, where Hitler called a meeting at the *Reich* Chancellery: '*Führer*, Göring, Blomberg, Fritsch, Raeder, Ribbentrop. The *Führer* speaks. Decision made: the

28. Hitler's announcement of the remilitarization of the Rhineland to the *Reichstag*, 8 March 1936. Goebbels is at the extreme left. He wrote of Hitler's speech: 'Brilliant exposition; thrilling verve; the conclusion brought tears to the eyes.' (*TBJG*, 8 March 1936, TI, 3/II, p. 35.)

29. 'Voting Sunday', 29 March 1936, at the conclusion of the referendum campaign on the remilitarization of the Rhineland. Goebbels described the scene in the Wilhelmplatz: 'All of Germany a sea of joy. Oh, this pleasure, to live, to work, to create.' (*TBJG*, 31 March 1936, TI, 3/II, p. 52.)

Reichstag on Sunday.' That night, Goebbels 'scarcely slept'.[90] On Friday 6 March Hitler outlined his plan for the remilitarization before his Cabinet, 'with deep seriousness, but also with firm resolution. The whole Cabinet stands with him. But now there is no way back.'[91] An American journalist in Berlin, William Shirer, was in the *Reichstag* on Sunday 8 March when Hitler announced that German troops were marching into the demilitarized zone:

> They spring, yelling and crying, to their feet. The audience in the galleries does the same, all except for a few diplomats and about fifty of us correspondents. Their hands are raised in slavish salute, their faces now contorted with hysteria, their mouths wide open, shouting, shouting, their eyes, burning with fanaticism, glued on the new god, the Messiah.[92]

Hitler and Goebbels had indeed predicted accurately. France and Britain protested, but did no more. With immense relief Goebbels wrote: 'With the

30. Women take part in a civil defence exercise in Berlin in 1936. Goebbels disagreed with Hitler about the wisdom of issuing 'people's gas masks' to the public, fearing that it would create a 'war psychosis'.

Führer. Brilliant voices from abroad. France wants to call the Council of the League. Indeed! Nothing will therefore happen. That is the main thing.' As a genuine 'son of the Rhineland' he was well cast as a leading actor in the theatrical reassertion of German sovereignty there. He spoke 'in the name of the *Führer*' on the radio, in response to a greeting from the cathedral square in Cologne, and he and Hitler reviewed a torchlit march past the Chancellery in Berlin. It was, he wrote, 'like earlier years'. He concluded a jubilant account in his diary with the words: 'the dead have not fallen in vain'.[93]

Over the next fortnight Goebbels developed this sense of 'earlier years' by treating Hitler's 'election campaign' for the *Reichstag* as if it were one from before 1933. He supervised a huge propaganda offensive, from the State in Berlin, and from the Party in Munich, and fronted this with as many speeches as he could manage. He replicated Hitler's strategy in 1932 by flying from one major German city to another, speaking to huge crowds every day. Although for the most part these were intoxicating celebrations, one of his first campaign speeches, in Kiel on 13 March, went badly. He was 'not in good form', and there was 'a terrible atmosphere'.[94] Public speaking had changed for Goebbels. The days when he had argued with hecklers, in front of brawling crowds, were gone, and his speeches now unfolded in an often celebratory, sometimes intoxicating atmosphere, but largely without confrontation. Goebbels concluded a gruelling fortnight of speaking by introducing Hitler before (he claimed) 120,000 Krupp workers in Essen, and attending a final ceremony in Cologne. Goebbels treated the election on 29 March, which recorded an overwhelming majority in favour of Hitler's foreign policy, as if it had been some kind of genuine contest, even though he had cynically intervened with the Interior Ministry to reject the idea that some votes might be considered 'invalid'.

There was coercion and manipulation of this 'election', but many foreign observers confirmed the wide extent of genuine popular support for the Nazis at this time. The *Volksgemeinschaft* Goebbels had dreamed off since the early 1920s was becoming a reality, even if it was increasingly confused in his own mind with the illusions he was creating. After the ceremony in Cologne, Goebbels and Hitler travelled by train through the darkened land. It was

the fulfilment of a propagandistic vision. Only we in the world could do that. Everybody really happy. In silence we travel through the Ruhr area. Lights, flames, beacons. Our Germany. We sit with the *Führer* in the darkened compartment and keep silent.[95]

8
An 'Indissoluble Community of Destiny'

> Today a new state is being established, the unique feature of which is that it sees its foundation not in Christianity and not in a concept of state; rather it places its primary emphasis on the self-contained *Volksgemeinschaft*.
>
> Hitler, speaking at the *Ordensburg* in Sonthofen, 23 November 1937.[1]

As a schoolboy, and then as a student during and after the First World War, Goebbels had grown up in a society where there was much talk of the *Volksgemeinschaft*, an idealized 'people's community' where a sense of shared belonging would transcend class and confessional differences. When he became a political activist in the 1920s, this was a central ideal of the Nazi Party, and after 1933 Goebbels had the opportunity to play a leading role in the construction of the *Volksgemeinschaft*. Although his formal office as Propaganda Minister might suggest that he was involved directly only with presentation and with the manipulation of opinion, he used his position to intervene much more widely in the formation of policy. He also used his unique status as Hitler's closest confidant to discuss the smallest details of domestic and foreign policy with him. Inevitably, as a minister and an internationally notorious public figure, his relationship with ordinary people had changed from that cultivated during the 'years of struggle'. He shared Hitler's increasing detachment, and together they developed illusions about their enemies and their supporters which often had little correspondence with reality.

Goebbels' role as the head of a growing family also cast him, Magda, and their children as exemplary representatives of the *Volksgemeinschaft*. In October 1935, weeks after the exclusion of Jews from German citizenship, Magda gave birth to a son, who was named Helmut. Needing a slightly larger car, she had recently taken delivery of Mercedes-Benz Type 290 Cabriolet Goebbels bought her, costing 7,400 marks. In contrast to the sombre black preferred for official vehicles in the 'Third Reich', this luxurious roadster was finished in blue, with beige leather seats.[2] In February 1937, after a difficult pregnancy, Magda gave birth to a third daughter, Holde. Magda had by this time taken on a semi-official role as representative mother in the 'Third Reich', and her secretary had to deal with letters to her from all over Germany, asking for help and intervention, typically in domestic matters such as housing and custody of children. Many were from mothers who described themselves as 'rich in children' like her. Before responding, Magda always contacted local Party officials for information on the political attitude, and conduct of these applicants. If the reply was positive, Magda often sent her correspondent a small amount of money – usually 50 marks – to accompany her best wishes. If the local Party's opinion was negative, a curt refusal was issued. Frequently Magda had to inform her correspondents that she was not able to intervene in court proceedings. Magda and her children were featured in news magazines and in newsreels, and fashion houses vied for her custom. When in early 1937 it was rumoured that Magda was buying from a Jewish supplier, she intervened to make it clear that she was not, writing to the German Labour Front: 'it is unpleasant, and for me unbearable, that I should be thought to allow myself to be dressed by a Jewish fashion house'.[3] Goebbels was hugely excited by Helmut's birth in 1935,[4] but took little interest in the baby boy after that. His oldest daughter Helga was by this time his firm favourite, and he was delighted that Hitler, still a frequent visitor to the family home, had similarly taken to her.

Most writers on Goebbels have repeated without any substantial evidence the notion that he was an insatiable womanizer, and that after 1933 he used his influence – particularly over aspiring cinema actresses – to demand sexual favours from women. Even recent historians write of his 'constant affairs, lies, and adulteries'[5] and describe him as keeping 'a string' of film 'starlets at his disposal'.[6] Some of the most lurid accounts of Goebbels' womanizing appeared in Leni Riefenstahl's autobiography, first published in 1987. The first is loosely placed 'a few days' before Christmas, 1932, just after Strasser's split from the Nazi Party. According to Riefenstahl, Goebbels was at this time telephoning her every day, sometimes several times. She recounts how one afternoon 'he stood at my door, unannounced'. Having reluctantly let him into her flat, Riefenstahl realized that he was now 'after me chiefly as a woman'. She writes that Goebbels asked her to admit that she loved Hitler, and when she denied this, she continues:

Now Goebbels lost control. 'You must be my mistress, I need you – without you my life is a torment! I've been in love with you for such a long time!' He actually knelt down in front of me and began to sob. It was sheer madness. I felt quite stunned at the sight of Goebbels on his knees, but then, when he grabbed my ankles, it was too much for me and I ordered him to leave my apartment immediately ... With hanging head and without glancing at me, he left.

Riefenstahl then alleges that Goebbels called on her again on Christmas Eve to give her a present, and to renew his protestations, but she again told him that his place was with his wife.[7] She then presents an even more implausible tale, which she locates in the late summer of 1933. Goebbels apparently called on her again, and because she did not wish to invite him inside, where she was entertaining friends, they took refuge from the rain in her car. To avoid being seen, Riefenstahl drove to Grunewald, a wooded area to the south-west of Berlin city centre. While she was driving, Goebbels took a gun 'from his raincoat pocket and thrust it into the glove compartment'. She continues:

> Suddenly Goebbels put his arm around my waist, the Mercedes jerked violently, the engine stalled, and to my horror I realized that it was leaning at a dangerous angle. We dared not stir lest the car overturn altogether. Goebbels, who remained astonishingly calm, cautiously removed his pistol from the glove compartment and thrust it into his raincoat pocket. Then he tried to open the car door and fortunately we managed to climb out unscathed. Because of the poor visibility I had driven into a mound of soft earth. The back part of the Mercedes was stuck in mud up to the left running board, while the front wheels dangled in the air. There was no way the two of us could pull the car out of the quagmire.

Goebbels then apparently told her that the two of them could not be seen together, advised her to catch a taxi home, and walked off into the darkness with his coat collar pulled up.[8] Shortly after this, Riefenstahl alleges that she was summoned to the Propaganda Ministry, and was asked by Goebbels to work on a film about the press, but when she rejected this idea,

> The expression on Goebbels' face changed. In a soft voice he said, 'I like the fact that you have a mind of your own. You're an unusual woman, and you know I desire you. I will never stop fighting for you.'
>
> Then he made the biggest mistake a man can make in such a situation. He grabbed my breast and tried to force himself upon me. I had to wrestle my way out of his arms and dashed to the door, with Goebbels pursuing me. Beside himself with rage, he held me against the wall and tried to kiss me. His eyes were wide open and his face completely distorted. I desperately resisted and, moving along the wall, I managed to push my back against a buzzer and press it. Goebbels immediately let go of me and he seemed to pull himself together even before the servant arrived.

Riefenstahl relates how she was subsequently invited to the *Reich* Chancellery. She devotes several pages of her memoir to Hitler's efforts to get her to film the Party Rally in September 1933, and to the intrigues between different senior

Nazis over this. After filming the rally, she claims that she was again summoned to the Propaganda Ministry, and specifically highlights the date of this meeting, on '13 October 1933, the day Dr Goebbels went to the Disarmament Conference in Geneva to announce Germany's withdrawal from the League of Nations'. Goebbels now alleged that she had criticized his staff – and implicitly himself – and told her to get out of his sight.[9]

A recent biographer of Riefenstahl, Audrey Salkeld, rehearses these incidents, but introduces a note of caution:

> Riefenstahl makes a point of highlighting her ability to recall conversations verbatim, with particular reference to Hitler and the important members of his entourage. Actually, she relates them as scenes from a silent movie – with over exaggerated actions to convey emotion and the dialogue between characters. People beat their chests and heads with fists, fling wide their arms, are shaken by sobs. It is not surprising that her memory codifies material in this way. This was the medium of her brilliance, after all ...

Salkeld also notes how the story of the incident in Grunewald reappears in the memoirs of Hans Ertl, embroidered with details of Goebbels and Riefenstahl enjoying lobster, caviare, and pheasant together in a quiet tavern before the car accident. Ertl, who was a lover of Riefenstahl's, places the story in the summer of 1935.[10]

What are we to make of Riefenstahl's account? It was written between 1982 and 1987, with the express purpose of refuting allegations that she was a Nazi propagandist. Although she claims to have used earlier notes from her interrogations after 1945 by American and French authorities, no documentary evidence is presented to support or to reference her account. The one specific date she mentions, 13 October 1933, is obviously incorrect. Goebbels had left the Disarmament Conference in Geneva on 29 September, and did not return. On 13 October Goebbels attended a Cabinet meeting in Berlin, and in the evening he saw a performance of *Tosca* at the Opera. He did not refer to Riefenstahl in his summary of the day's events.[11] Her representation of her relationship with Goebbels, both as a film-maker and 'as a woman', is difficult – if not impossible – to reconcile with the many references to her in Goebbels' diary. There is nothing there to substantiate her stories, or the even less plausible version from Hans Ertl. Even if we accept that Goebbels may not have wished to record amorous and sexual passion for Leni Riefenstahl in his diary, and certainly would not have revealed humiliating rejections, there are many references portraying a friendly and cooperative relationship which is totally at variance with Riefenstahl's narrative. There are also references to meetings with Riefenstahl in Berlin which she does not mention, or indeed when she claims to have been elsewhere. For example, Riefenstahl claims to have been away from Berlin, shooting a film in the Swiss Alps, for six months after Christmas 1932, and not to have heard about 'the book burnings in front of the university in May or about the start of the persecution of the Jews with the first boycott in all cities'.[12] Goebbels claims to have spent the afternoon of 16 May (less than a week after the book burning!) with Leni Riefenstahl, listening to her plans, and to have suggested to her that she make a 'Hitler film', an idea she was 'enthusiastic' about. He claims that she accompanied him and Magda to see *Madam Butterfly* in the evening, something one imagines she might have remembered. This lengthy encounter is not referred to in her autobiography.[13]

Although it is possible that Goebbels did make advances to Leni Riefenstahl, her stories appear on the most generous reading to be highly exaggerated, and, given the larger pattern of deception which characterizes her account of her relationship with Hitler and with Goebbels, they must be treated with great scepticism. Interestingly, the most plausible detail she includes is in the story of Goebbels visiting her on Christmas Eve 1932, when she mentions that Magda was in hospital. Goebbels' wife had indeed been admitted to hospital on 23 December, and Goebbels was obviously very lonely and depressed in her absence. Although he had Magda's son Harald and his own baby Helga with him at home, he did go out several times, and one wonders if he did call on Leni Riefenstahl. If he did, it appears that nothing sufficiently dramatic occurred to prevent the two of them continuing a friendly relationship through 1933.

Although Goebbels' philandering has been exaggerated, there is no doubt that he enjoyed the company of young and beautiful women, or that he judged women largely on their appearance. He undoubtedly flirted with many, and developed more serious but platonic relationships with several, like the actress Jenny Jugo, and with Magda's sister-in-law, Ello Quandt. His relationship with Magda continued as it had started, oscillating between devotion and estrangement. In addition to repeated pregnancies, Magda was frequently unwell, and took to spending long periods of convalescence in a sanatorium in Dresden. Goebbels' long and irregular hours of work, and his constant travelling often kept him away from the family home, and it is hardly surprising that he and Magda developed separate lives even as they came to personify the ideal 'child-rich' family of the *Volksgemeinschaft*. As in 1934, the most serious rifts between them coincided often with important developments in public affairs.

In 1930 the International Olympic Committee had met in Berlin, and subsequently accepted the offer made there to stage the Olympic Games of 1936 in Germany. Despite wide international discussion about the wisdom of this decision after the Nazi accession to power in 1933, it was upheld, allowing Hitler and Goebbels an unparalleled opportunity to present the acceptable face of the *Volksgemeinschaft* to the world. The Winter Olympics in Garmisch-Partenkirchen in February 1936 served as a dress rehearsal for the administrative and technical arrangements for the much larger Games staged in Berlin in August

1936. Predictably, the Nazis presented themselves as the natural heirs of the original Hellenic Games, and took every opportunity to celebrate the triumph of 'Aryan' German athletes. Scenes from Leni Riefenstahl's two films of the Games have been shown frequently, and Hitler's anger over the victories of the black American sprinter Jesse Owens has become a cliché in school textbooks.

31. The 'Entry of the Nations' at the Olympic Games in Berlin, 1936. Goebbels had no great interest in sport, and the Games coincided with an acute crisis in his marital life. He could not wait for the end of the whole rigmarole.

Goebbels was centrally involved in the presentation of the Olympics, and attended most of the publicity events around them, as well as the sporting competitions. He rejoiced in the success of German athletes, but it was not easy for him to maintain the attitude of relaxed enjoyment he had to portray for the cameras. The day before the opening ceremony on 1 August, he had met with Rosenberg, and for once recorded a positive conversation with him. After discussing cultural affairs, Rosenberg told Goebbels that Magda was having an affair with one of Hitler's advisers, Kurt Lüdecke. Goebbels immediately spoke to Magda about this, but wrote that 'the matter is not yet clear'.[14] The next morning Goebbels argued with her again, but she would not admit the truth of Rosenberg's charge. He tried to put this from his mind while he watched the international teams marching into the Olympic Stadium. Most, he noted, were demonstratively greeted, but the British only 'coolly'. He listened through an 'Olympic hymn' composed by Richard Strauss, and Handel's *Hallelujah* chorus, and described the ceremony as 'A victory for the German cause'. That evening, at home, Magda confirmed the allegations about her and Lüdecke. He wrote: 'A great breach of trust. It is all so awful. One only comes through life with compromises'.[15] Over the next few days he had publicly to participate in the whole Olympic spectacle, and was to an extent drawn into the sporting contest. He shared Hitler's disgust about the gold medals won by black Americans: 'That is a disgrace. White humanity ought to be ashamed of itself.' His heart was not in it though. After several days of the Games he wrote: 'I am so tired. And think all the time about Magda. Today work and sport. If only the Olympics would end!'[16]

At the height of the Rhineland crisis in March 1936 the Goebbels had, with the help of 100,000 marks from the Nazi Party publisher Max Amann and a gift of 70,000 marks from Hitler, bought a villa at Schwanenwerder, a peninsula on the opposite side of the Wannsee from their rented summer house at Kladow.[17] Goebbels' sense of separation from Magda was heightened in October by the gift to him from the City of Berlin of a secluded log cabin on another lake, the Bogensee, near Lanke, some 25 kilometres north of the city. He had another small house built in the woodlands there for guests, and this became his retreat from the world. Here he entertained artists and fellow party workers, and enjoyed solitude and silence. It was at this house on the Bogensee that Goebbels conducted his affair with the Czech actress Lida Baarova, whom he had first met in June, before the Olympics.[18] The story has often been told of how at the Nuremberg Rally in September 1936 Goebbels communicated secretly with Baarova, sitting in the front row of the audience, by wiping his lips with a handkerchief.[19] In his diary he wrote 'A miracle has happened.'[20] Schaumburg-Lippe later wrote that Baarova was the only woman other than his wife that Goebbels really loved.[21] Over the next two years Goebbels' relationship with Baarova became increasingly public, and a source of increasing conflict between him and Magda. Although at times they came close to a formal separation, until the summer of 1938 they did maintain a genuinely loving relationship, and Magda continued to bear his children.

The Nazi *Volksgemeinschaft* was defined by inclusion and exclusion, and Goebbels concerned himself with all aspects of this. He worked tirelessly to exclude Jews from the media and the arts, largely through the mechanism of the *Reich* Chamber of Culture. The wrangling within the Nazi Party and the Interior Ministry about the classification of 'half-Jews' and 'quarter-Jews' had ended in November 1935 with the publication of 'supplementary' clauses to the *Reich* Citizenship Law announced at Nuremberg in September, excluding 'half-Jews' from citizenship. Goebbels tired of the negotiations, and was impatient with quasi-scientific attempts at categorization. He insisted that 'quarter-Jews' be excluded from the *Reich* Chamber of Culture, and devoted great energies to this over the next few years. In February 1937 he wrote: '*Reich* Chamber of Culture now completely cleared out of Jews. A grandiose achievement, of which I am proud.'[22] Jochen Klepper recorded in his diary an excerpt from one of Goebbels'

32. Hitler Youth at the Nuremberg Rally in 1936. Goebbels wrote that this was 'a glorious festival. The style of the songs and the singing a bit insipid. But this enthusiasm! This life! Wonderful!' (*TBJG*, 13 September 1936, TI, 3/II, p. 181.)

33. By 1936 Himmler's SS was becoming a huge organization. The original caption to this review of the SS at the 1936 Nuremberg Rally declared that 'All follow one belief: eternal Germany.' Goebbels was enthusiastic, writing: 'The most beautiful! The SS. Discipline, clarity, dash. Himmler has his men up to the mark.' (*TBJG*, 13 September 1936, TI, 3/II, p. 181.)

speeches at this time, in which he declared that: 'the *Reich* Chamber of Culture is one of the few organizations outside the Party which has no Jews, no half-Jews, and no members related to Jews'. Klepper himself, although an 'Aryan' by law, had a Jewish wife. He was stripped of his membership of the *Reich* Chamber of Writers five weeks later.[23]

Even after this Goebbels constantly fretted about the participation in cultural life of people he suspected of partial Jewish ancestry, or who, like Klepper, had in his eyes betrayed the *Volk* by their association with Jews. In very rare cases he made exceptions. He wrote with a rare degree of indulgence at the conclusion of the Bayreuth Festival in July 1937 about Furtwängler's insistence on maintaining a number of 'half-Jews' in the Berlin Philharmonic. He was so impressed with Furtwängler's musicianship that he was also prepared to concede to him on other points, like the stupidity of making violinists do '*Reich* Labour Service', or the danger of young singers' voices being ruined in the Hitler Youth. He also agreed with Furtwängler that there ought to be more 'serious music' on the radio.[24]

Goebbels kept a close eye on other exclusions from the *Volksgemeinschaft*. In June 1935 Paragraph 175 of the *Reich* Criminal Code, which dealt with male homosexuality, was amended 'to regard as felonious almost any conceivable contact, however tenuous, between males'. Men could now be imprisoned for mutual masturbation or a kiss, if this was interpreted as 'criminally indecent'.[25] The SS journal *Das Schwarze Korps* (*The Black Corps*) had already called for the death penalty for homosexuals. Goebbels was particularly vexed by the presence – or imagined presence – of homosexuals in the German theatre. At Bayreuth in 1937 he and Hitler were guests of the Wagner family at the villa Wahnfried: 'Chatted about paragraph 175. The *Führer* quite intransigent about this. There can be no pardon there. Rightly so. We must also purify the theatre of that.'[26] Goebbels liaised closely with Himmler after 1934 as the latter built up the SS, and from June 1936 when Himmler was appointed head of all German police forces.[27] Hitler and Goebbels discussed their shared appreciation of Himmler's work a few weeks later.[28] They were equally supportive of the drive against 'asocials' which was mounted after February 1937, when Himmler announced that suspected 'habitual criminals' should be taken into 'protective custody' without prior legal proceedings.[29] Goebbels wrote that he would like to see 'asocials' put in 'forced labour camps' or sent 'soon' to a German colony.[30]

The Nazi concept of the 'asocial' was a broad and flexible one which catered for anyone thought unfit to be a member of the *Volksgemeinschaft*, even though they met its racial criteria. It might include criminals, alcoholics, those considered sexually deviant, or otherwise deemed mentally or physically unfit. One of the earliest pieces of Nazi legislation in 1933 was the law providing for the compulsory sterilization of those judged to have 'hereditarily determined' conditions. Goebbels had no scruples about this, fully supporting the theory that preventing these people from reproducing would improve the collective health of the *Volks*-

gemeinschaft. He followed closely the application of this law, and its extension in June 1935 to allow abortions on women considered fit for sterilization, up to six months' pregnant. Abortion was otherwise completely illegal.

The Nazi campaigns against the Jews, homosexuals, the 'hereditarily ill', and those stigmatized as 'asocial' were carried through with massive support from Goebbels' Propaganda Ministry, and the resources of a growing police apparatus. They were conducted against groups or individuals who were largely isolated and defenceless, and Goebbels and other Nazis could rejoice in a considerable measure of success. Hitler and Goebbels were preoccupied in the middle years of the 1930s with another group which was better able to defend itself, the priests. The Nazis had since 1934 ruled in Germany without any legal political resistance. Even the well-organized Communist and Social Democratic Parties had been driven underground or into exile. Thanks in large measure to Goebbels, the media and the arts were increasingly subservient, and used to promote Nazi ideals. Goebbels and Hitler were not able, despite all their efforts, to do away with the Protestant and Catholic Churches in Germany, or with their networks of power. They had some success with the divided Protestant Churches, one of which, the German Christians' Faith Movement, was a strong supporter of Nazism. This body lent itself to the creation of a new '*Reich* Church' in July 1933, and its leader, Ludwig Müller, was appointed '*Reich* Bishop' in September. Many Protestants were dismayed by this, and in May 1934 a so-called 'Confessing Church' was established under the leadership of Martin Niemöller, a former U-boat commander, and the theologian Dietrich Bonhöffer. Niemöller courageously declared that the Confessing Church was the legitimate Protestant Church of Germany, and it remained a thorn in the flesh of the Nazis over the next four years.[31]

Relationships with the Catholic Church were more difficult as it was an international organization with its seat of power outside Germany. Hitler concluded a Concordat with Pope Pius XI in July 1933 which guaranteed the freedom of the Catholic Church in Germany, but had since then introduced dozens of measures intended to weaken its authority, including the suppression of many Catholic newspapers. Loyalty to the Catholic Church, to its priests, and its symbols was deeply rooted in parts of Germany, and some Catholic bishops had the courage to speak out against the Nazis. While this undoubtedly irritated Hitler and Goebbels, it was not necessarily uppermost in their minds as, in 1935, they embarked on a course of direct confrontation with the Catholic Church. Together they became obsessed with the notion that the Catholic Church and its monastic houses were hotbeds of homosexuality and child abuse. Again and again when they met, their conversation turned to this subject. On 27 May 1936 Goebbels travelled with Hitler to Kiel to visit the growing navy. He wrote: 'Big morality trials against Catholic priests. All homosexuals. The *Führer* believes that this is a characteristic of the whole Catholic Church.'[32] A few weeks later they met again on a train, travelling on this occasion to Weimar, and the same topic came up: 'Hard judgement against the Catholic Church and its Orders with homosexuals. That must be burnt out.'[33] During 1935 and 1936 hundreds of priests, mainly but not exclusively Catholic, were charged in German courts with sexual and financial offences. Goebbels gave the widest publicity to these cases in the press and on the radio, and used this to present the churches in the worst possible light. Cartoons were published showing monks and nuns concealing money in their habits, and plotting with Jews and freemasons. The publicity from the court cases was used to justify withdrawal of licences from certain Orders to run schools, and to restrict the activity of Catholic charities, which were increasingly replaced by Goebbels' own Party-based charities, the National Socialist Welfare and Winter Help.

The campaign against Roman Catholicism focused several of Goebbels' political and personal prejudices. He saw loyalty to the Papacy as treason against the *Volk*; he detested the Christian message of forgiveness, which contrasted with his own ever more strident belief in harshness towards opponents; and his suspicion that all Catholic priests were homosexuals and pederasts derived from his deeply felt convictions about sexuality. It is tempting to speculate on the origins of Hitler and Goebbels' obsession with the notion of Catholic sexual immorality. Both had been brought up in Roman Catholic environments, but although Hitler had attended an abbey school where there might well have been rumours of sexual relationships between adults and boys, there is no evidence that Goebbels had been subject to any kind of sexual abuse, or that the abuse of others had been an issue which confronted him in childhood or adolescence. One cause of Goebbels' adult resentment was the involvement of priests in funerals. Frequently, in describing the funerals of Nazi heroes which he attended, and later stage-managed, Goebbels railed about the participation of priests. It is significant that in November 1935 he arranged the funeral of Otto Laubinger, the former President of the *Reich* Theatre Chamber, as 'a German funeral service, without priests and candles'. It was, he wrote, 'so deep and moving'.[34]

In 1937 the persecution of Catholic priests finally provoked a papal response. On 14 March, Pius XI delivered an encyclical, 'with burning anxiety' (*Mit brennender Sorge*) from the Vatican, 'on the situation of the Catholic Church in Germany'. Although much of the encyclical was phrased with diplomatic caution, it was unequivocal in its condemnation of the Nazis. In the first paragraph Pius referred to 'gradually increasing oppression'. He went on to deplore 'open violation of agreements', and 'intrigues which from the beginning had no other aim than a war of extermination'. In a clear assault on the Nazi Party, he declared:

> Whoever transposes Race or People, the State or Constitution, the executive or other fundamental elements of human society ... from the scale of earthly things and makes them the ultimate norm of all things, even of religious

values, and defies them with an idolatrous cult, perverts and falsifies the divinely created and appointed order of things.

'Only superficial minds', he continued, 'can fall into the error of speaking of a national God, a national religion.' The Pope might have been speaking directly of Goebbels when he added: 'Whoever does not wish to be a Christian ought at least to renounce the desire to enrich the vocabulary of his unbelief with the heritage of Christian ideas.'[35]

It took some days for this unusually acute attack on Goebbels to reach him. Sunday 21 March was a fairly typical day for him. He travelled between central Berlin and his retreat on the Bogensee, lunching with Hitler and Magda. He spent the afternoon alone, doing 'interesting work', on 'questions of music and film'. Later he went back into Berlin and spent the evening with Hitler and a few others. They watched a film starring the young Swedish actress Zarah Leander. Goebbels thought she was 'very overestimated', and the film prompted more thoughts on national identity. 'The film is the typical product of a small state. I wouldn't want to be a Swede. Only a member of a world power.' His equanimity was then disturbed by one of Himmler's men:

Unfortunately, Heydrich comes late in the evening with a pastoral letter from the Pope, which is directed most sharply against Germany, and accuses us of breaching the Concordat and other fine things. With a fresh arrogance, a provocative dark power.

Goebbels decided to shelter Hitler from this unpleasant news, rather than disturb his rest. He disagreed with Heydrich's advice to respond 'sharply', and thought it better – at least initially – to stay 'dead silent'. Goebbels went to bed 'furious and full of wrath'.[36]

Hitler, when he heard about the encyclical, also initially accepted this counsel, but Goebbels brooded on a more aggressive response. Over the next few weeks, further trials against priests were instituted, and Goebbels followed their progress closely. He kept his eyes open for potentially incriminating material, and was delighted when a priest was found who was willing to testify on oath against the Bishop of Trier. Goebbels made a sound recording of this testimony, and put it by for future use.[37] In mid-May he met with Hitler and they discussed the whole question:

He greets the radical turn in the trials of priests. Does not want the Party to be turned into a religion. Or to see himself elevated as a God. That is why he is in sharp disagreement with Himmler. We must bend the churches to us and make servants of them. Celibacy must also go. Church assets will be taken away, and no man will study theology before the age of 24. That way we will take the best of the next generation. The Orders must be dissolved, and churches taken away from educational provision. Only thus will they be diminished over several decades. Then they will eat out of our hands.[38]

On 25 May Goebbels discussed his forthcoming speech against the priests with Hitler, who gave him 'a few more tips'.[39] On 28 May he spoke for two hours to a huge audience in the *Deutschlandhalle* in Berlin. The speech was broadcast live and widely reported on abroad, and Goebbels was especially delighted when Hitler later told him that he had been so excited, listening on the radio, that he had been unable to sit down during the speech. Amongst other things, Goebbels said:

A vast number of Catholic clerics have been tried for sexual crimes ... It is not a matter of regrettable individual lapses, but of a general corruption of morals such as the world has never known ... No other class of society has ever come to shelter so much depravity ... In our civilized world no other class of society has contrived to practise immorality and indulge in filth on such a scale resembling that achieved by the German clergy in all its ranks ... There is no doubt that even the thousands of cases which have come to light represent but a small fraction of the total moral corruption.

Goebbels also delivered an open threat to any priests judged to be homosexual:

The Party has set a clear example. In 1934, more than sixty members who had indulged in this vice were shot, and the Party gave the greatest national publicity to its procedure.[40]

Clearly, there were some present with the courage to express their disagreement. Goebbels recorded in his diary that he was disturbed by hecklers, but that it was 'A real meeting, like in the old times.'[41]

If Goebbels spoke on this occasion with the subtlety of a Mafia boss, a few days later he showed his more academic pretensions in a very different speech. A bust of the composer Anton Bruckner had been made for the 'Valhalla' hall for the dead outside Regensburg, originally built on the banks of the Danube in 1842 as a 'Temple to German Honour'. Bruckner was the first 'great German' to be installed there since the Nazi accession to power, and Hitler and Goebbels lent their seal of approval to the ceremony on 6 June 1937. Bruckner was typically understood as an Austrian composer, underpinned by a profound Catholic spirituality, but Goebbels spoke next to the composer's likeness in stone, and challenged these ideas. Bruckner, he claimed was a 'great master of German composition', 'a fruitful synthesis of the symphonist and the choirmaster'. He could not merely be seen as a follower of Wagner:

Like every genius Bruckner has something thoroughly unique and individually developed. And to understand him one must go back to the roots of his existence, the foundational forces of his humanity, conditioned by blood and race.

Sentimental descriptions like 'God's music maker' or 'Our Dear Lady's Singer' must be retracted. Bruckner could not express himself fully as a church composer, Goebbels argued, but had 'long burst all confessional bonds' and was rooted in the 'heroic world feeling of German mankind'. Turning to Hitler, who was also present, and addressing him directly, Goebbels declared that Bruckner, as 'a son of Austrian soil' was called to symbolize the 'indissoluble community of destiny that embraces our whole German *Volk*'.[42] The famous 'sparrows' of the Regensburg cathedral choir sang at the ceremony.[43]

While Goebbels analysed Bruckner's evolution as a composer and dreamed of union with Austria, the trials against priests and members of monastic Orders proceeded. Despite enormous pressure, many of the courts still operated with a remarkable degree of fairness, and a surprising proportion of those accused were acquitted. According to figures given in November 1937 by the Nazi Minister for Ecclesiastical Affairs, 955 people had been convicted and 187 acquitted.[44] Goebbels, who followed many cases in individual detail, recording with horror the allegations made against the priests, was frustrated by this, and demanded that 'Special Courts' be used which could be relied upon to produce speedy convictions and harsh sentences.[45] Goebbels clothed this growing recourse to extra-legal remedies as part of his larger aversion to bureaucracy, and his admiration for action. Looking at this sad chapter in German history today, what is most striking is how little difference the campaign against the churches made, either to the willingness of many German Christians to continue supporting the Nazi Party, or to maintain their religious faith. Although individual trials continued, after 1937 the campaign against the churches was scaled down. In January 1938, Hitler told Goebbels that for the time being, he wanted no further 'great struggle against the churches'.[46]

Goebbels and Hitler made an exception to this rule in the case of the Protestant Martin Niemöller, who was brought to trial in February 1938. Despite the decision to tone down the campaign against the church, Goebbels paid particular personal attention to Niemöller's trial, even as, in foreign affairs, the Austrian crisis gathered pace. Back in July 1937, Goebbels had made a note in his diary when Niemöller was 'finally arrested', and while he was held in Moabit police station in solitary confinement, he and Hitler had decided that Niemöller would not be released 'until he was broken'.[47] Before the trial opened in February 1938, Goebbels summoned to his ministry lawyers from Saxony presenting the case and told them what he expected of the trial: 'As brief as possible, a hard punishment, no publicity.' Goebbels expected that proceedings would be concluded in three days, and that Niemöller would get 'no opportunity for agitation'.[48] Despite this, the trial lasted almost a month, and Niemöller was allowed to speak at length. For over three hours on the opening day he presented a 'thrilling' presentation of his career as a fiercely patriotic officer of the Imperial Navy, who had refused to surrender his U-boat to the British in November 1918, and subsequently fought as a *Freikorps* volunteer to 'cleanse Westphalia from the red mob'. Since 1924, he stated, he had always voted for the Nazis, and had become a priest 'to contribute to Germany's resurrection'. Two admirals and a general testified that it was inconceivable that he was a traitor to his Fatherland. Different reports agree that all present, including the judge and prosecution, were hugely impressed by his bearing. When charged by the prosecution that Jews attended his sermons, Niemöller replied that 'the Jews were alien and disagreeable to him'.[49] Although the German public was excluded from the trial, it was closely followed abroad.[50]

Goebbels intervened several times with officials from the Ministry of Justice to try to stop the publicity Niemöller was getting, and was furious about what he saw as a complete scandal. On 22 February Goebbels complained to Hitler: 'He is furious. Niemöller won't get free so easily.'[51] Goebbels was left fuming as the trial continued, and was outraged on 2 March when Niemöller was finally sentenced to seven months' imprisonment. Given that Niemöller had already been that long in custody, he ought to have been released, but Goebbels arranged that he would be taken immediately to 'protective custody' in a concentration camp: 'The foreign journalists are waiting for Niemöller outside the court, but he will be taken straight from a side door to Oranienburg. There he can serve God through work and inner searching. He will not be let loose any more on the *Volk*.' Goebbels and Hitler had already agreed that there could be no repeat of this 'scandal'. At least one good thing would come out of the trial, Goebbels wrote: 'the judiciary will be rigorously cleansed'.[52] The next day, Hitler and Goebbels spoke again: 'It is a proof that Niemöller is our enemy that the enemy press praises him ... In general, it is good that Niemöller is kept in a concentration camp. He will not come back out so soon. And so it will be with all enemies of the state. Whoever takes the good Hitler for a weakling will and must get to know the hard Hitler.'[53] A telegram signed by the Archbishop of Canterbury and leading churchmen from Sweden, Greece, France, and America was sent to Hitler protesting about Niemöller's continued detention, but to no avail.[54] Niemöller was still in Dachau when the Americans liberated the camp on 29 April 1945.

Why was Goebbels so obsessed with Martin Niemöller? It is well known that Niemöller had supported the Nazis before 1933, and had indeed met Hitler in 1934, before breaking with him and taking up a leading role in the 'Confessing Church', but this change of direction does not explain the depth of Goebbels' feelings. It may have been because Goebbels recognized in Niemöller somebody remarkably like himself. Niemöller was a passionate German nationalist, who after his distinguished wartime service, and involvement with the *Freikorps* movement, had trained for the priesthood. Coincidentally, he was from Elberfeld, and like Goebbels, he had moved from the Ruhr to Berlin. He was also a writer, and had published a bestselling autobiography, *From U-boat to Pulpit*, with a title strangely reminiscent of Goebbels' *From the Kaiserhof to the Reich Chancellery*.[55] By 1939 Niemöller's book had sold nearly 100,000 copies, bringing him national and international recognition. Above all, Niemöller was a powerful and effective public speaker, and he used the same passionate language of German nationalism as Goebbels, with urgent appeals to the *Volk*, and a proud contempt for all adversity. He shared other views with the Propaganda Minister, for example a belief that women should bring up children and support their men, and a deeply rooted anti-Semitism. Like Goebbels, he mocked his opponents, and like him, he published his sermons in cheaply priced editions. Through the mid-1930s a continuing series of Niemöller's 'Dahlem sermons' were published in Berlin, with an ever more outspoken rejection of the Nazi claim to supreme authority, and an assertion that Germans must confess their primary allegiance to Jesus Christ. In 1933 Niemöller had declared that a turning away from this would end the 'historical existence' of the *Volk*, and that this would be not a natural death, but 'suicide'.[56] Over the next four years his public criticisms of Nazi ungodliness became ever more contemptuous. This is an example of his rhetoric, from one of the last sermons he gave before his arrest:

> That the church announces the gospel to the German *Volk*, convinced that this and nothing else is its task, and that this and nothing else is what the German *Volk* needs – that is the decisive factor! ...
>
> We can in these stormy times do nothing other than to take God's word into the life of our *Volk*. We are guilty of that. We will do that as long as there is breath left in us.[57]

Niemöller's sermons were also published in Switzerland, and in translation in Britain and Holland. Goebbels undoubtedly saw in Niemöller – and this may have been an overestimation – someone with the potential to rival his own powers of influence.

On 29 October 1937, Goebbels was 40 years old. Magda and the children greeted him with gifts, and after that he had to endure celebrations at the Propaganda Ministry. There were 'mountains of presents, flowers, letters, telegrams'. Then Hitler visited with another gift, a painting by Keller.[58] Goebbels was not pleased to reach this landmark. On the day of his birthday he wrote: 'A terrible feeling. The best is now over.'[59] The advancing years and continuing hard work were beginning to take a toll on him. He was frequently working between 12 and 16 hours a day, dealing with a multiplicity of problems. He travelled constantly between his office in central Berlin, Schwanenwerder, where he saw Magda and

34. The 'May Field' in Berlin on 28 September 1937, at a meeting called to celebrate a state visit by Mussolini to Germany. Goebbels wrote: 'Words are not capable of describing the scene. Mussolini is deeply moved. I open the meeting. During his speech, Mussolini constantly nods in my direction.' (*TBJG*, 29 September 1937, TII, 4, p. 334.)

the children, and Lanke, where he stayed mainly alone, or with Lida Baarova. He suffered from headaches, and from problems with his teeth; he frequently had to visit the dentist. He was constantly tired, and took out his ill-feeling on colleagues in the Party, as well as on his imagined enemies, the Jews, the Bolsheviks, and the priests. He spent hours every day reading foreign press reports (in translation), and giving instructions to the German press, at home and abroad. He intervened in disputes outside his jurisdiction, and spent much time trying to regulate the different arts. He had become so involved with the cinema that he no longer merely previewed and demanded alterations to almost every film produced in Germany, but intervened to rewrite plots and to alter the dialogue in individual films.

Goebbels was, largely through his involvement with the press, taking an ever closer interest in foreign affairs. He summarized political affairs in many countries in his diary, and met with Hitler every few days to discuss developments. Since the remilitarization of the Rhineland in March 1936, Goebbels had become ever more slavishly devoted to Hitler's judgements on all things. He had come to see him as 'one of the most extraordinary men of the last thousand years', and was carried along by his vision of German expansion and conquest.[60] Hitler had decided that all Germans living outside the current borders of the *Reich* should be reunited, and that further land in Europe was needed for the *Volk*. He accepted that this would provoke war with France and Britain, but believed that Germany would be equipped to win such a war by 1943.

Goebbels was treated to a full exposé of Hitler's vision in private on 2 August 1937,[61] shortly before Hitler presented this to the leaders of his armed forces in November.[62] He was less ready than Hitler to countenance the reality of war, particularly if this came when Germany was still unready. He had watched with anxiety the growing tension over Abyssinia, the Civil War in Spain, and the increasingly strident German pressure on Austria, Czechoslovakia, and Poland over the question of German minorities there. In December 1936 he wrote: 'We must only take care ... that we are not involved unforeseen in a war. That would now be the most worrying thing that could happen.' A visit that day to the scene of an underground railway fire in the Potsdamer Platz in central Berlin prompted further reflection: 'A huge heap of ruins. One gets an impression from it of what a future fire, air, and gas war will look like. A gruesome vision!'[63] He was realistic enough to see that the popularity of Hitler and Nazism in Germany did not imply an equal enthusiasm for war with Britain, France, or the Soviet Union. Significantly one of the very few actual disagreements he had with Hitler at this time was over the issue of 'people's gasmasks' to the German public. When this idea was first mooted, Goebbels opposed it on the grounds that it would generate a 'terrible war psychosis'.[64] He maintained this position, but in December 1937 he noted: 'The *Führer* has decided for the introduction of the gasmasks. A shame! That will create so much bad blood.'[65]

This minor difference was quickly overtaken by larger events. Shortly before Christmas 1937 Goebbels wrote that Field Marshal Blomberg, since 1935 the Minister for War, had told him of his plan to marry 'a young girl from the *Volk*'. Although he recognized that this might create difficulties, Goebbels was delighted, and felt that Blomberg (who had enthusiastically supported Hitler since 1933) fully 'deserved' this new happiness.[66] The wedding took place in the War Ministry on 12 January 1938, with Hitler and Göring as witnesses, but within a fortnight it was revealed that Blomberg's young wife had previously been a registered prostitute. Goebbels, when he first heard of this on 25 January, tried to cheer Hitler up, but soon realized that this was potentially a huge scandal.[67] The next day he wrote that Blomberg would have to resign, and that 'for a man of honour, only the pistol remains'. Matters were made worse when, later on 26 January, Goebbels heard that Werner Fritsch, the Commander of the *Wehrmacht*, had been accused of homosexuality. These two scandals in an officer corps with a rigid code of honour prompted what Goebbels called the 'most severe crisis since 1934'.[68] For several days Goebbels was unable to sleep; Hitler was tense and strained, fearing that he was compromised by his appearance at Blomberg's wedding. Goebbels, who faced 'the most difficult problem' of 'what to say to the *Volk*', had an ambivalent attitude to both scandals. He was never convinced that the accusations against Fritsch were proven, and obviously had some sympathy with Blomberg. He was himself conducting an affair with a younger woman, and this undoubtedly influenced him. He reluctantly accepted in this situation that both men would have to resign, and advised Hitler to assume the leadership of the *Wehrmacht* himself.[69] After some hesitation, Hitler accepted this course of action.

Even this crisis was quickly superseded by developments abroad. On 12 February 1938 the Austrian Chancellor Schuschnigg was subjected to a prolonged and theatrical intimidation by Hitler on the Obersalzberg. In the weeks following this, Goebbels helped Hitler to increase the pressure on the Austrian government to include Nazis in the Cabinet, and to amnesty Nazis in Austrian jails. Behind the pressure lay the constant threat of an armed German invasion. In early March Schuschnigg yielded to this pressure, and was replaced by Artur Seyss-Inquart, who promptly agreed to draft a telegram asking for German support to maintain order in Austria.[70] Seizing the initiative, Hitler ordered the *Wehrmacht* into Austria on 12 March, and entered the country on the same day, crossing the border at Braunau, where he had been born. His drive from there to Linz and on to Vienna turned into a triumphal procession, and he was acclaimed by frenzied crowds. On 13 March Hitler signed a hastily written 'Law on the Reunion of Austria with the German Reich', and he subsequently announced that a plebiscite would be held on 10 April to seek the support of the German people for this.[71]

Goebbels did not travel to Vienna with Hitler, but remained in Berlin to coordinate the propaganda presentation of the 'reunion'. He had for several years been manipulating 'camouflaged propaganda' in Austria, and the orchestration of the campaign in Germany to present the Austrians as part of the larger German *Volk*. Before *Wehrmacht* units crossed the border, Goebbels discussed with Hitler plans to control printing in Austria and to jam Austrian radio broadcasts. As the crisis developed, he was in close communication with Hitler, often very late at night, and was thrilled by the sense of action. It was, he wrote, 'once again a great time'. On 12 March, as Hitler progressed through Austria, Goebbels read out his leader's proclamation, first to assembled foreign correspondents, then to German journalists, and finally on the radio, while crowds 'raved' outside in the Wilhelmplatz: Austria, he declared, was 'a part of the community of race and destiny common to all Germans'. In his diary he celebrated the news that many Jews were fleeing from Vienna.[72] Goebbels threw himself into plans for the immediate establishment of a propaganda office in Vienna, and to take over Austrian cultural life. On 20 March he and Hitler discussed plans to rebuild Vienna, to 'force the Jews and Czechs out ... and to make it a purely German city'.[73]

While he rejoiced publicly and privately over this 'great hour in history',[74] it also brought Goebbels renewed worries. He saw himself as a 'north German', a 'Prussian', and he believed that Bavarians and other Germans from further south were of lower racial value. We have seen his dislike of Munich and his contempt for the atmosphere there. He mistrusted Austrians even more, and loathed Vienna, which he regarded as a multi-racial sink. Bizarrely in this racialist view, Goebbels made an exception for the area of the Upper Danube – where Hitler's family had its roots. This he thought was an isolated pocket where the population had some of the qualities he essentialized in north Germans. Goebbels was particularly unhappy about the inclusion in a 'Greater Germany' of Austria's large Jewish minority. Before March 1938 the number of Jews in Germany had been dropping as many left and the birth rate of those remaining declined. Statistics compiled by the SS indicated that in addition to the remaining 370,000 Jews in Germany, the incorporation of Austria brought some 200,000 Jews into the *Reich*.[75] It inaugurated a notable intensification of the campaign against them. Austria was also an overwhelmingly Catholic country, and Goebbels was from the first utterly contemptuous of this. When the Archbishop of Vienna, Cardinal Innitzer, visited Hitler to tell him that he wanted Austrians 'actively to join in the German reconstruction work',[76] Goebbels reacted by describing him in his diary as 'a cowardly clerical hypocrite'.[77] Goebbels was happy to stay in Berlin during the *Anschluss*, but he did have to travel twice to Vienna for public appearances in the next few weeks. On arrival there for a 'Day of the Greater German *Reich*' at the conclusion of the voting campaign, he was pleased to see Vienna decked out with Nazi flags, but wrote: 'However, one can't start much with the people here. They are too easy-going [*gemütlich*].'[78]

From the balcony of Vienna's town hall on 9 April, Goebbels gave the command for a coordinated demonstration of German unity: 30,000 doves were released in Vienna, and all over Germany the traffic was stopped for two minutes. Locomotive and factory sirens were sounded, and squadrons of aircraft circled overhead. Hitler joined Goebbels on the balcony to 'indescribable storms of jubilation'. As soon as this ceremony was completed, Goebbels was scheming with Hitler – who had his own personal reasons for disliking the Austrian capital – to downplay the importance of Vienna, and to make sure that it had no further pretensions to be a capital city. He was flattered that the Viennese crowd outside called for him to appear again, chanting '*Lieber Führer, ach ich bitt', bring doch unseren Doktor mit!*', which might be translated as 'Dear *Führer*, I ask of you, bring out our doctor too!' After a rally that evening, Goebbels and Hitler left Vienna; on the train back to Berlin they discussed plans for getting all the Jews out of Germany, perhaps to Madagascar or a former penal colony. Hitler raved about the Austrian 'legitimists' whom Himmler was already arresting, and about the 'completely internationalized' Austrian nobility. Magda and the children greeted them with flowers on the station platform in Berlin, and together they went to the *Reich* Chancellery to hear the results of the plebiscite. There was an overwhelming vote in favour of union, and Goebbels claimed that it brought tears to his eyes to hear Hitler's response to this. He wrote: 'Leipzig voted very badly. Berlin particularly well. That pleases me most. And Vienna really strongly. I had not expected that.'[79]

The successful incorporation of Austria strengthened Goebbels' sycophantic admiration for Hitler, and his contempt for the opinions of others. When Hitler returned from Vienna, he and Goebbels studied a map and decided: 'at first comes Czechoslovakia. We will divide that with the Poles and Hungary. And indeed rigorously at the next opportunity. We want also to grab Memel, if Kovno comes into conflict with Warsaw ... After that, the Baltic, part of Alsace and Lorraine. France will sink ever more deeply into its crisis.'[80] In the same reckless spirit Goebbels discussed the 'Jewish question' with Helldorff, the Chief of Police in Berlin, in May 1938: 'We want to force the Jews out of the economy and out of cultural life, and in general out of public life. Somehow one really must make a start with this.'[81] A few days later Hitler agreed to Goebbels' plan, and orders were given to Helldorff.[82] From developments after this it appears that there were several components to Goebbels' 'plan'. Three hundred Jews were to be arrested and imprisoned; Jewish shops and businesses, particularly in the fashionable shopping streets of Berlin, were to be labelled, and their owners and patrons intimidated. This focused physical attack on individual Jews in Berlin was part of a larger programme now being embarked upon to strip Jews of their assets, and to bar them from employment and from public services. Beyond this it was intended to intimidate Jews into emigrating.

Initially, Goebbels' plan misfired. Helldorff had 300 Jews arrested, but most were almost immediately released.[83] After this Goebbels spoke personally to 300 assembled police officers in Berlin and told them to avoid any sentimentality: 'Not the law but harassment is our watchword. The Jews must get out of Berlin.' He added, 'The police will help me with that.'[84] On 19 June, Goebbels reported 'many arrests ... The police understood my instructions.'[85] Eye-witness accounts suggest that 'youngsters' from the Hitler Youth were amongst those who looted shops and harassed individual Jews in this 'action'.[86] Goebbels himself wrote that 'gypsies and other shady elements' had participated in the looting, and ordered that they be sent straight to concentration camps. Helldorff had directly contravened his orders, which were that 'the police act with an appearance of legality, the Party provides spectators'. Goebbels ordered that all illegal acts cease forthwith, but noted that 'this kind of people's justice [*Volksjustiz*] also has its own good points'.[87] After the 'action', Goebbels had further discussions: 'Helldorff wants to establish a ghetto in Berlin. The rich Jews should pay for it themselves. That is correct. I support him in that.'[88] It appears that Goebbels and Helldorff were restrained by Hitler, perhaps concerned at the effect such a move might have on international opinion.

The physical intimidation of Jews in Berlin was paralleled by a continuing ideological assault against their participation in the arts. Goebbels had given his sanction to a *Reich* Music Festival to be held in Düsseldorf in May 1938, and although much preoccupied with foreign affairs, he travelled there to deliver a keynote speech to 'all of Germany's creative musicians',[89] in which he declared:

> Jewry and German music are opposites, which following their nature, stand in the starkest contrast to one another. The fight against Jewry in German music, which Richard Wagner once took up completely on his own, is therefore today our great, never to be relinquished, historic task ... [90]

This festival, at which Richard Strauss conducted, was accompanied by an academic conference on the subject of 'Music and Race', and by the infamous exhibition on 'Degenerate Music', where visitors could listen to examples of 'Jewish music' and 'nigger jazz' on headphones, and see lurid images of Jewish and black musicians. Goebbels was in fact critical of the exhibition, but was enthused by the music festival. Shortly after this, on 25 July, before a performance of Wagner's *Tristan and Isolde* at Bayreuth, Goebbels and Hitler talked over the 'Jewish question'. Hitler approved the measures so far taken in Berlin. Goebbels summarized their discussion: 'The main thing is that the Jews are forced out. They must be out of Germany in ten years. But for the time being we want the rich ones here as a security.'[91]

For Goebbels, this evolution of Nazi domestic and foreign policy in the face of the 'defenceless trembling fear'[92] of the outside world was to be rudely shattered by developments in his private life. Since meeting Lida Baarova in July 1936, Goebbels had taken to seeing more of her, increasingly in public, and less of Magda. Since the establishment of his private house on the Bogensee, he had become only a visitor at the family home in Schwanenwerder; the demands of his work were such that he also had a flat fitted out for him in the Propaganda Ministry, and after April 1938 took to staying there overnight. Our knowledge of Goebbels' relationship with Lida Baarova is much hazier than of other aspects of his life, because, apart from occasional cryptic references, he did not write about her in his diary. When writing of Magda, although he frequently recorded meetings, excursions, and quarrels, he again used an allusive style, so that often he did not reveal specifically what they had quarrelled about. With a vivid and melodramatic style reminiscent of his diaries from the mid-1920s, he described in 1938 the intensity of his moods and experiences, but rarely the specific cause. Much of the writing about Goebbels' complex relationship with Lida and with Magda in 1938 derives from hearsay or from anecdotal evidence of dubious reliability.

What is clear is that matters came to a head on 15 August 1938, when Magda decided to seek Hitler's intervention in her marital affairs. Hitler still had a particular affection for her, and he took her side in the dispute, not only – as many have suggested – because he did not wish to see a further scandal in the private conduct of such a senior figure as his Propaganda Minister. He undoubtedly disapproved of the way that Goebbels was treating her, and he may have been unaware that Magda herself was not a model of marital fidelity. Goebbels was summoned in Berlin, and Hitler bluntly told him that his affair with Lida Baarova had to cease forthwith. Magda, now armed with a new confidence, was prepared to try to repair her marriage in accordance with Hitler's instructions, but was cold and unforgiving towards Goebbels. He was utterly cast down by this turn of events, even though he decided straight away to accept Hitler's advice and to renounce Lida Baarova. Typically, he resolved the conflict on the surface by recording how devotion to duty would now have to be his sole consolation.[93] Rumours of Goebbels' disgrace were clearly circulating in public. The British Ambassador in Berlin, Nevile Henderson, reported back to London on Goebbels' 'recent considerable loss of prestige'.[94]

Over the next eight weeks, although he somehow managed to get through his work, and even to deliver a number of speeches, at a time of great tension in foreign affairs, he saw little of Magda, or of Hitler, and in isolation Goebbels experienced an acute mental and physical crisis. He was insomniacal, and could sleep only with the help of narcotics; he lost interest in his work, and found it difficult to concentrate on reading or listening to music. The autumnal weather in north Germany, with its rain and fog, depressed him further. Occasional visits from the children lifted his spirits briefly, but reminded him also of the family life he had lost. In the first few weeks of this crisis, Goebbels managed to function remarkably effectively as Hitler racked up the pressure on the Czech government. He realized though that this was different from the remilitarization of the Rhineland, and from the 'union' with Austria. On 1 August Goebbels wrote of the Czech crisis, after watching a mass display of gymnastics in Breslau: 'We are dealing here not with a hostile government, but with a hostile people.'[95] This was a significant comment. Goebbels shared entirely with Hitler the desire to re-unite all Germans in a 'Greater Germany', but he had no desire to include what he saw as 'non-Germans' in this. Nor did he share the fascination Hitler, Himmler, and Rosenberg had for grandiose schemes of colonization in 'the East'. Furthermore, Goebbels was not a soldier, and did not wish Germany to be involved in another world war. He was prepared to countenance a limited war, perhaps against Czecho-slovakia or Poland, but had less confidence in Germany's ability to win a larger conflict. Although contemptuous of the French, Goebbels had kept an anxious eye on British rearmament, and, even though he did not know or understand Britain, he had realized that at some stage a conflict was very likely, and would not be straightforward. As the Czech crisis deepened, he wrote with a rare moment of clarity that the Americans would also fight on the British side.[96]

He was immensely relieved when, with the late intervention of Mussolini and his suggestion of a Four-Power Conference in Munich, Hitler compromised, and agreed with the British and French only to occupy the Sudetenland, rather than all of Bohemia, as he had earlier intended. Although publicly constrained to rejoice in this new triumph, Goebbels was privately overwhelmed by grief. On 2 September he had written that he could not speak with Magda any more, and resolved not even to telephone her again.[97] On 1 October, recording in his diary the outcome of the conversations between Hitler, Mussolini, Chamberlain, and Daladier in Munich (which he had not attended), he noted the relief all over Europe that war had been avoided, but added: 'Today was for me personally a tragic, painful day.'[98] Over the next few weeks, although he observed and commented on the occupation of the Sudetenland, he plummeted deeper into isolation, insomnia, and depression. He was now only able to communicate with Magda through intermediaries like his State Secretary Karl Hanke, and had for the first time since 1925 lost something of Hitler's confidence.[99]

Goebbels was not prepared to retire from public life, and after much private reflection decided to try to defend himself with both Hitler and Magda. In an unprecedented move, he asked first Göring, and then Helldorff to intercede directly with Hitler on his behalf. On 23 October, Goebbels went to Berchtesgaden to see Hitler after an interval of several weeks, and spoke at length with him. Magda was then called in and the pair was enjoined to a truce for the next three months. It says much for the relationships between the three of them that Hitler was willing to spend so long dealing with their private matters, and that both

Goebbels and Magda seem to have thought it quite appropriate that Hitler act as a final arbiter in these. After the meeting, although Goebbels and Magda were evidently still not reconciled, the children were brought along and the whole group posed for press photographers.[100] A week later Goebbels and Magda made a public appearance together at the theatre, and a similar façade was presented on Goebbels' birthday on 29 October. He suffered 'as if in bodily agony' as he attended various formal ceremonies, and listened to congratulations from family, colleagues, artists, municipal officials, and Party members. Significantly, Hitler was absent and sent only 'a short, frosty telegram'. Goebbels wrote: 'Can a man endure and suffer all that? I am at the end of my strength.'[101]

9

'This People's War Must Be Carried Through'

The news that England had declared war on 3rd September came like a bombshell to most people in Germany and Danzig. Everywhere there were bleak faces and a hushed atmosphere as in the presence of death ... I listened day and night to the gunfire on the frontier only a few miles away, every minute imagining it was drawing nearer.

Sybil Bannister, an Englishwoman living in Danzig in 1939.[1]

The year before Germany plunged Europe into war in September 1939 was an intensely paradoxical time for Goebbels. This was the last period in which his plans for the Nazi *Volksgemeinschaft* could be freely developed; above all, his ambitions for a reordered cultural life. He was able to extend his control over the media and the arts to the areas now incorporated into the Greater German *Reich*, and to reshape significant cultural events like the Salzburg Festival in August 1938 and 1939. This was a time in which his propaganda slogans, like *'Ein Volk, ein Reich, ein Führer'* (One People, one Empire, one Leader), and *'Heim ins Reich'* (Home to the *Reich*) seemed to represent popular sentiment in Germany, and to reflect changing political realities. When he spoke in public, as he still did frequently, he was greeted with wild enthusiasm. At the same time, Goebbels was an increasingly isolated and melancholy figure, and the celebratory bombast of his speeches corresponded less and less with his inner feelings.

Under great pressure from Hitler, Goebbels had agreed to a 'truce' in his marriage, and in January 1939 he signed a formal nuptial contract with Magda.[2] Whatever the extent of his past philandering, it was now precisely that. Magda was now emotionally distant from him, not least because she was herself conducting an affair with one of Goebbels' most trusted officials, his State Secretary Karl Hanke. Goebbels lived for the most part away from his five young children, and he saw them only infrequently. His private affairs were the subject of public gossip and much comment within the Nazi Party. His old enemy Rosenberg wrote in February 1939 after a conversation with Himmler that Goebbels was 'today the most hated man in Germany'. Rosenberg also recorded that Hanke had drawn up a list of the women Goebbels had allegedly demanded sexual favours from, and presented this to Hitler, severely damaging his standing with him.[3] An unsigned letter from a member of the public to Hitler's secretary in December 1938 also suggests that there were complaints coming in to the highest levels of the Party about Goebbels' behaviour.[4] Goebbels suffered from a range of largely psychosomatic illnesses, and struggled to keep a grip on his work. He was obsessed with his lack of sleep, and it did not help that in the frequent domestic and foreign crises which marked this period, he was forced to share Hitler's predilection for late-night work and conversation.

Christmas 1938 was a low point for Goebbels. He was unable to attend the customary celebrations amongst Party workers, SA men, and Berlin's poor, as he collapsed and had to be taken to hospital with severe kidney pains. Significantly, for two weeks he was unable even to motivate himself to write his diary, which undoubtedly served in this time as a therapeutic tool. Although he recovered from this physical problem, his comment on Hitler's famous speech to the *Reichstag* on 30 January 1939 was typical of this period of his life in its juxtaposition of enthusiasm for political developments and deep inner depression. Hitler used the commemoration of six years of Nazi rule to deliver a wide-ranging statement on foreign and domestic policy, and made a 'prophecy' that if there was a European war, it would bring with it 'the extermination of the Jewish race in Europe'.[5] Goebbels had worked carefully with Hitler on the preparation of the speech, and described it as a 'real masterpiece'. Afterwards he watched the now traditional torchlit march of Party formations from the *Reich* Chancellery with Hitler, and wrote: 'I think back to the time six years ago. It was good then. Everything now is awful and terrible.'[6]

During the spring and summer of 1939 there was some improvement in Goebbels' private situation, largely as he devoted himself to work; he saw more of Hitler, who – preoccupied with foreign affairs – needed his Propaganda Minister as never before. He and Magda were still alienated from one another though, and Goebbels was repeatedly cast into gloom by arguments with her. Only weeks before the outbreak of war, while attending the Salzburg Festival, Goebbels heard from Magda the full extent of her infidelity with Hanke, and was plunged into despair. Together the couple went on to attend the Bayreuth Festival, where Magda hovered on the edge of a public breakdown. 'When will we find a way out of all this tragedy?' wrote Goebbels.[7] In fact, after the initial shock, the revelation of Magda's affair with Hanke restored some equilibrium to this troubled relationship, casting Goebbels as the injured party, and allowing him to take a forgiving stance which was clearly more comfortable than the position he had previously occupied. Hanke was sent from the Propaganda Ministry to serve in the *Wehrmacht*.

Undoubtedly Goebbels' private unhappiness during this crucial year helped to harden his heart towards his enemies, and to make him more reckless in his approach to both foreign and domestic affairs. Although he struggled to maintain interest in the minutiae of work in the Propaganda Ministry, a series of critical developments provided an outlet for his energies. On 8 November 1938, shortly after the annexation of the Sudetenland, Goebbels was in Munich for the Party's commemoration of its 'martyrs' of the 1923 *Putsch*, and it was here that he first heard the news that a German diplomat in Paris, Ernst vom Rath, had been shot by 'a Polish Jew', Herschel Grynszpan. Goebbels immediately saw the opportunity here for a retaliatory attack on the whole Jewish community in Germany, commenting: 'If for once the anger of the *Volk* could be unleashed!'[8] The next evening Goebbels conferred privately with Hitler at a reception for the Party leadership:

> I lay the whole matter out before the *Führer*. He agrees: Let the demonstrations proceed. The police to hold back. The Jews shall for once get a feeling of the *Volk*'s anger. That is correct. I immediately give corresponding instructions to the police and Party. Then I speak briefly before the Party leadership. Stormy applause. All rush straight to the telephones. Now the *Volk* will act.[9]

When Goebbels returned to his hotel, the sky over Munich was 'blood red' with the flames from burning synagogues. Through the night, reports came in from around Germany of the attacks on Jews and their property. By 11 November Goebbels was back in Berlin to oversee the situation there, and the 'action' had been called off, something Goebbels felt the Jews ought to be grateful to him for.[10] By that time more than 1,000 synagogues in Germany had been burnt; 100 Jews had been killed, with many more injured, and some 30,000 arrested and taken to concentration camps.[11]

In the German and foreign press on 12 November and over the following days, Goebbels represented the pogrom as a justified act of retaliation by a community which itself had been attacked. A Chargé d'Affaires at the British Embassy in Berlin, George Ogilvie-Forbes, reported that Goebbels 'in his public utterances, condoned what had been done'.[12] Following Goebbels' interpretation, the Jews themselves were ordered to clear up the mess created, and no insurance would be paid to them for damage sustained. A fine of 1 billion marks was levied on the Jewish community. Over the next few weeks, a series of new legislative measures was introduced, preventing Jews from attending concerts, plays or cinemas, and closing down Jewish newspapers. All Jewish business enterprises were to close by 1 January 1939, and any Jewish children still in German schools were excluded. Jews were forbidden to drive cars, and had to hand in their driver's licences.[13] Ogilvie-Forbes was one observer who grasped the full import of these measures. He wrote to the British Foreign Minister:

I can find no words strong enough in condemnation of the disgusting treatment of so many innocent people and the civilized world is faced with the appalling sight of 500,000 people about to rot away in starvation.[14]

The outlines of the pogrom of 9/10 November 1938 have become so well-known that it is easy to overlook the horrible impact it had on the Jews of Germany. Many who had become sadly accustomed to legislative discrimination were for the first time exposed to direct physical assault. There is a tone of real fear in the diaries of some of the most sensitive observers, like Victor Klemperer, as they grasped for the first time the very real danger they now faced, after 'the catastrophe'.[15] The pogrom was followed by a renewed wave of Jewish emigration from Germany. What did Goebbels hope to gain from the pogrom, which he has so rightly been identified with?[16] There is no doubt that he was unhappy with the pre-existing situation, which still allowed a significant number of Jews to live alongside the 'Germans', and still to share many everyday activities in the public sphere. Goebbels used the pogrom to prepare the way for a much more extensive separation of the Jews from the German population. He also wanted simply to instil fear in the Jews. Friedländer expresses this well: 'In essence the life of the Jews of Germany was to be made so unpleasant that they would make every effort to leave by whatever means.'[17] Although stressing after 11 November that Germany would respond to the shooting of Rath by legal means, Goebbels was happy to encourage the resort to mob violence, or what he called 'the *Volk*'s anger', much as he had encouraged illegal violence in Berlin before 1933. Notably, in interviews with foreign press correspondents after the pogrom, Goebbels insisted that the attacks on Jews and their property had not been organized, but were spontaneous.[18] In a speech on 13 November, Goebbels also hinted that there was more to come, declaring in language which has since become notorious, that 'the Jewish question will finally be solved'.[19]

Goebbels never expressed human sympathy for the Jews who suffered so grievously as a result of his actions. He was clearly a man capable of finer feelings: he displayed a tender concern for his children, and his empathy with 'martyrs' like Horst Wessel was genuine. His reactions to literature, music, and to nature show that he was a man of some sensitivity. Although unscrupulous and cynical he was not altogether lacking in a sense of conscience. His racially centred view of the world put the Jews beyond any of this; he considered them, as a whole, and without exception, so fiendish and diabolical that they merited absolutely no empathy. Rather as Himmler later enjoined his SS executioners to dignity and correct conduct, Goebbels was only troubled by the thought of 'unpleasant excesses' against the Jews, which, he noted, had occurred in Bremen during the pogrom he had licensed on 9 November 1938.[20] Earlier that year, after the 'action' that he and Helldorff had mounted in Berlin, Goebbels had expressed his disapproval of 'disgusting things' which had happened to Jews arrested and detained in Sachsenhausen.[21] This derived from his preoccupation with 'order', and from concern that Germans were lowering themselves, and not from sympathy with the Jews themselves. Nor did Goebbels confront the blatantly obvious fact that his speeches and proclamations encouraged profound insensitivity, cruelty, and sadism, and helped to create a situation in which 'excesses' were likely to occur.

He gave an example of this moral blindness in a speech in Reichenberg, the newly appointed 'capital' of the annexed Sudetenland, only ten days after *Kristallnacht* (the 'Night of Broken Glass'). Before a large and enthusiastic crowd, Goebbels referred to the horrified reaction of the outside world towards the violence perpetrated against Jews in Germany. He generated laughter with this observation: 'The world will gradually calm down about the Jewish question. I believe so, I hope so. I hope so above all in the interests of the Jews who still remain in Germany.'[22] In the weeks after the November pogrom, Goebbels was briefly roused from depression, consistently taking the most radical course in the discussions among leading Nazis about the intensification of anti-Jewish measures. Goebbels' involvement in the November pogrom, and his incitement of the SA to violence against the Jews, is typically ascribed to opportunism.[23] Most writers suggest that he saw the assassination of Rath in Paris as an excuse to curry favour with Hitler by encouraging a retaliatory pogrom against the Jews, but this overlooks his deep-seated hostility to the Jews, and his real frustration with their continued presence in Germany. It also overlooks the 'actions' he had directed with Helldorff in Berlin only a few months previously. Goebbels had long wanted to see measures taken to force the Jews out of Germany altogether.

Goebbels was more decisively lifted from his depression by the quickening tempo of German expansion in the spring of 1939. From the time of the Munich settlement, Goebbels had been clear in his own mind that the annexation of the Sudetenland was merely temporary, and that what remained of the 'cadaver state' of Czechoslovakia would have to disappear. He was recovering from another bout of intense kidney pains, when on 10 March internal tensions between Czechs and Slovaks provided the pretext the Nazis had been waiting for. Hitler summoned Goebbels, Ribbentrop, and Keitel, and informed them that on 15 March, German troops would invade Czechoslavakia. In his report of a later meeting that day Goebbels made no effort to hide the conspiratorial behaviour which now underpinned German foreign policy: 'In the late afternoon with the *Führer* again. We sketch out an announcement that the Tiso government had again appealed to the German Government in a note before its arrest. We can submit later the precise content according to need. The *Führer* rightly says that history cannot be made with lawyers.' Goebbels suggested that Hitler show his face at the theatre that evening, and the two of them went afterwards to the artists' club in Berlin that Goebbels had established. 'It is very nice and happy there, and we have an alibi. There is conversation on many things. I feel myself once again quite well.'[24]

He was elated by the capitulation of the Czechs, Hitler's entry into Prague on 15 March, the proclamation that the provinces of Bohemia and Moravia were now a German 'Protectorate', and the impotent reaction of Britain and France. He wrote: 'In the evening the *Führer* arrives in Prague and takes a flat in the Hradchin. That sounds like a fairy tale, and it is indeed the truth, complete, full, gladsome truth. What a great time we live in! And what bliss to work in it!'[25] Goebbels' conviction that the indignation expressed in Paris and London was 'only theatre'[26] was strengthened by the Lithuanian concession of the town of Memel to Germany only days after the invasion of Czechoslovakia. 'Pitiful democracy,' he wrote, 'your name is cowardice!'[27] Goebbels was unimpressed by the British Prime Minister Neville Chamberlain's speech in Birmingham on 17 March in which he reacted with measured but unambiguous terms to the invasion of Bohemia, and warned Hitler that 'no greater mistake could be made' than to imagine that Britain would not resist an attempt 'to dominate the world by force'. Commenting in his diary on this speech, Goebbels wrote 'this good old man [this phrase was written sarcastically, and unusually, in English] is getting fresh, as only the English can be'. Publicly he mocked the spectacle of 'England as the somewhat aged moral aunt of Europe, sitting on the plush sofa of its Empire'.[28] By the time that Chamberlain announced to the House of Commons on 31 March that Britain would go to the aid of Poland if that country were attacked, Goebbels had left Germany for a holiday in the Mediterranean. When he read about Chamberlain's guarantee to Poland some days later, he was again dismissive.[29]

By then Goebbels was relaxing in the Italian-controlled island of Rhodes, musing about past cultures and the mixing of different peoples he saw there. He thought most of the decent architecture on Rhodes was the product of Italian Fascism, and was horrified when he toured the Jewish quarter of the city of Rhodes in a horse-drawn wagon. He described it as 'poor and stinking with refuse and filth'. He thought the Turkish quarter 'not much better', but he comforted himself with the thought that there were always 'master races' which had to put these others to use.[30] Goebbels even made a quick excursion by aeroplane to Cairo, where he visited the pyramids and the Sphinx. He was hugely impressed, observing that 'here the reality surpasses the imagination'.[31] Back in Rhodes he heard that the Poles had concluded a reciprocal agreement with Britain, but noted only that the Poles would 'perhaps have to pay heavily' for this.[32]

Over the next few months, Hitler assumed that the British, and the French, who had also offered a guarantee to Poland, were bluffing. Anxiously reading public opinion reports through the summer months, Goebbels reassured himself that the mood in Germany was resolute, if not enthusiastic for war. As Hitler's attention turned to the 'free city' of Danzig, and to Poland, he and Goebbels persuaded themselves that once again the timing was everything. If only they struck at the right moment, Britain would stand aside. Danzig, an ancient Hanseatic city with an overwhelmingly German population, had been declared a 'free city' after the First World War, and was supervised by a League of Nations High Commissioner. Critically, the city was included in the Polish customs area, giving the Poles rights to use the city's harbour and waterways. The Poles were also placed in charge of the city's post and telephone services; after 1920 they were allowed a military base on the Westerplatte peninsula, which overlooked the entrance to the harbour. There was an active Nazi movement in Danzig, led since 1930 by Albert Forster, and Hitler was now demanding that the city and its surrounding enclave be returned to German sovereignty.[33] The Poles, rightly fearing that this was not the last demand Hitler would make affecting their sovereignty, were determined not to yield. On 17 June, Goebbels flew to Danzig to deliver what the British Consul-General called 'a bellicose speech'.[34] Goebbels declared, before (he recorded) a 'sea of people' outside the opera house:

> I come from the *Reich* to bring you the greetings of the *Führer* and of the German *Volk*. I stand here on the soil of a German town, before me are tens of thousands of German people, and all around there are innumerable signs of German culture, German customs, German style, and German architecture.

Later in his speech, Goebbels repeated Hitler's recent words to the *Reichstag*: 'Danzig is a German town and it wants to be part of Germany.'[35] Over the next few weeks the British government was informed by its Consul-General of various German military preparations in Danzig and East Prussia, and on 10 July, Neville Chamberlain announced in the House of Commons that Britain would regard any German attempt to change the status of Danzig as a matter 'affecting Polish national existence and independence'. He reminded the House of the guarantee already made to Poland, and stated that 'we are firmly resolved to carry out this undertaking'. Goebbels bizarrely thought this was 'not quite so curt' as previous announcements, and hoped that London and Paris would still 'give way if we build a golden bridge to them'.[36]

Berlin was gripped by an oppressive heat in the last days of August as German troops massed along the Polish frontier, and Goebbels supervised arrangements to put his ministry on a wartime footing. He had for some time been apprised of Hitler's intention to seek a non-aggression Pact with Stalin, and was – on the surface at least – delighted with the announcement of this on 24 August 1939.[37] He was genuinely dismayed the next day by the news that Italy was not prepared to go to war alongside Germany. Goebbels had for years been a huge admirer of Mussolini, and of what he perceived as the achievements of Italian Fascism. Now he was forced to confess to himself that he had always feared that the Italians

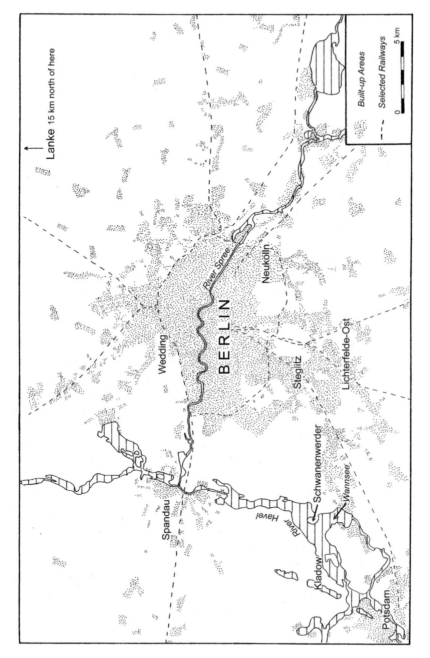

35. Map of Berlin and the surrounding area, 1939.

would let them down. Nonetheless, Goebbels was fatally committed to Hitler's aggressive plans, and was still convinced that he would find 'a way out of this devilish situation'.[38]

It is impossible to know with any certainty what Goebbels thought about the risk of war with Britain and France. He did not complacently assume, as did Hitler and Ribbentrop, that Britain and France might again stand aside if Germany attacked Poland and reclaimed Danzig. Goebbels thought this was possible but did not rely on it; he also sensed that war with Britain might be a protracted affair. He was by this time though so intoxicated by Hitler's foreign policy successes and his apparently infallible sense of timing that he failed to restrain him. His sense of personal dependence on and submission to Hitler may also have prevented him from fully speaking his mind. Intriguingly, the British Ambassador in Paris reported to London on 24 August a conversation with his American counterpart, who told him that Goebbels had 'recently advised Hitler against war as long as Mr. Roosevelt was President, owing to the likelihood of the latter dragging in the United States on the side of Great Britain and France, but this advice apparently fell on deaf ears'.[39] There was a real difference between the attitude of Hitler, as recorded by the British journalist Leonard Mosley in July 1939, and Goebbels. 'There will be no war', Hitler told Mosley: 'There was no war over the Sudetenland, nor over Czechoslovakia. There will be no war over Danzig.' When Mosley disagreed, Hitler repeated: 'There was no war over Sudetenland! There will be none over Poland! The conditions are exactly the same and your actions will be the same.'[40] Goebbels never expressed this conviction in his diary. When, despite Mussolini's lack of nerve, Hitler continued with his plan to attack Poland, Goebbels concealed from his diary any real misgivings he might have had, and resorted to the euphemistic language already being developed to camouflage the most sinister plans of the Nazis. On 31 August Hitler told him that the order for the attack on Poland at 5.00 a.m. next day had been issued. Goebbels wrote:

> Göring is still sceptical. The *Führer* also does not believe that England will attack. Nobody can determine that at the moment. The SS gets special orders for the night.

It is not clear what Goebbels meant here by 'special orders'. He may have been referring to the plans to arrest and murder members of the Polish intelligentsia and priesthood in the wake of a German advance, but it is much more likely that he was referring specifically to the plan to use murdered concentration camp inmates to simulate a Polish attack on the German radio transmitter at Gleiwitz on the morning of 1 September. Later in the same diary entry he wrote, as if recording a factual occurrence, 'Polish attack on the Gleiwitz transmitter. We will make the most of that.'[41] After getting up early the next day, Goebbels attended the 'historic sitting' of the *Reichstag* on 1 September, where Hitler declared that since 5.45 a.m. that morning, German forces had been 'returning fire' on Poles.[42]

For several hours German troops had in fact been advancing into Polish territory. A group of Polish customs officials and railway workers near Danzig had already been executed, and Polish buildings in the city had been occupied. The Polish garrison on the Westerplatte was under bombardment.[43] There followed an anxious two days in Berlin while Goebbels followed the reports from Poland, and awaited the British and French response. It has been suggested that Goebbels, like many others around Hitler, was shocked and dismayed when Britain and then France declared war on Germany on 3 September, but Goebbels was notably objective in his private response to this, writing only: 'Will London actually go the whole way?' Presumably he still thought an all-out confrontation might be avoided. He was more concerned by the news later that day that Churchill had been brought into Chamberlain's Cabinet. This provoked him to dissent from Hitler's view that the war in the West would be only 'a potato war'. Nonetheless, he wrote, 'we will fight and work one way or another until victory'.[44]

Although war has been seen as the fullest expression of Nazism,[45] it was not altogether comfortable for Goebbels. He delighted in the extraordinary German military successes that characterized the first nine months of the war, and in the part he played in supporting them. He saw himself – in a phrase he frequently used in his diary – as 'always a civilian', and had no particular interest or expertise in purely military matters. He made no attempt to interfere in military strategy. He did not like wearing uniform, and maintained his scorn for the narrow-mindedness of the military caste. Inevitably, the coming of war meant a change in his role, and in his relationship with Hitler, who had symbolically donned a field-grey uniform on 1 September, and soon left for the front. Since 1925 Goebbels had championed an all-or-nothing approach to politics, declaring that his commitment to Nazism was 'to death', and he fully espoused Hitler's crude Darwinism which saw war as a necessary condition of life. He and Hitler were also fully committed to the idea that German defeat in the First World War had not been a consequence of military failure, but was brought about by superior Allied propaganda and the insidious influence of enemies within. They therefore saw propaganda, and the maintenance of public opinion in Germany not as tangential matters, but just as important as the military conduct of the war.

Goebbels, who had always made a virtue of work, applied himself with renewed devotion to the propaganda war, determined that this time, the *Volk* would not let down the military. He immediately secured Hitler's approval for a law making listening to foreign radio broadcasts an offence punishable by death.[46] He himself followed the reporting of the war by overseas newspapers and radio stations as closely as he could, and either reacted to or tried to pre-empt the propaganda from other countries, above all Britain and the USA. He instituted a daily 11.00

a.m. 'ministerial conference' in the Propaganda Ministry for departmental heads of Radio, Film, and Press, as well as representatives of other ministries, and the *Wehrmacht*. Here Goebbels would issue his daily reading of the international and internal situation, and seek to dictate the broad lines of propaganda in all its manifestations.[47] He fought tenaciously to preserve his sphere of influence in this changed situation, concerned particularly by the new importance conferred on Ribbentrop by Hitler, temporarily impressed by his handling of the negotiations with the Soviet Union. Even as the first sweeping successes in Poland were being reported, and as Goebbels embarked on the first of what he saw as personal duels with Churchill – over the sinking of the passenger liner *Athenia* – he had to bother Hitler with one of the demarcation disputes endemic to Nazism.[48] On 7 September he was flown out in a bomber to Hitler's field headquarters in an armoured train; before discussing Goebbels' propaganda work they discussed his relationship with Ribbentrop. It was, wrote Goebbels, 'a disgrace that one has to do this in the middle of a war'. The next day Hitler dictated a new 'decree', which outlined a 'middle way' between his two lieutenants.[49] In a typically confused arrangement, this gave Ribbentrop responsibility for the 'general policy' in 'the domain of foreign policy propaganda'.[50] Goebbels had to tolerate the presence in his ministry of a number of Ribbentrop's men, and his contempt for the Foreign Office only grew as the war went on.

Significantly, Goebbels did not deliver any speeches of his own during the Polish campaign, something noticed by Klemperer in Dresden, who asked himself, 'Where is Goebbels?'[51] Presumably Hitler, who postponed a planned radio speech by Goebbels on 17 September,[52] feared that Goebbels might impede the conclusion of a favourable peace with the British and French after the Polish campaign by an over-inflammatory speech. It was not until late October that Goebbels delivered one of his own speeches on the radio, which centred on an intemperate attack on Churchill. In the meantime Goebbels concealed his frustrations by concentrating on other forms of propaganda. As well as the foreign media, he anxiously scrutinized the public opinion reports from around the German *Reich* compiled every week after the start of the war by the security police (SD). He interrogated anyone he met who had been to the front, or to any part of Germany, about the mood there. He rapidly regained ground lost to Ribbentrop and the military men with the huge success of his war newsreels, and to a lesser extent, of his broadcasting.

For years Goebbels had taken a particular interest in newsreel, and had been more enthusiastic about its development as a propaganda tool than that of other cinematic genres. The *Blitzkrieg* in Poland provided him with the opportunity to take war newsreels to a new stage. His Propaganda Companies, advancing with the frontline units of the *Wehrmacht*, provided action footage of unprecedented immediacy; he – aided by technicians and film directors like Fritz Hippler – edited this and added a spoken commentary and music. The resulting films of German tanks advancing past burning buildings, of dive-bombers pulverizing Warsaw, and of columns of marching troops, were hugely popular with most of the German public. Film attendance went up dramatically, and an impression of German invincibility was strongly conveyed abroad. Goebbels also extended his programme of foreign-language broadcasting. He had before the war started 'secret transmissions' to the Soviet Union, and sponsored a huge expansion of Germany's broadcasting capacity. He now pursued this more vigorously, and existing transmitters had to relinquish German-language programmes for broadcasts in 19 other languages,[53] like those notoriously delivered by William Joyce – Lord Haw-Haw – in English.

If Goebbels' propaganda was enormously successful in conveying an impression of menace and of military invincibility, it was markedly less successful in winning support for Nazism, or in gaining trust in its sincerity. Goebbels had a notoriously flexible attitude to any concept of 'truth' in his propaganda, and believed that the end justified any means. In January 1940 he summarized his credo in his diary, reporting a conversation with a key aide, Hans Fritzsche: 'He does not correctly understand the value of repetition in propaganda. One must eternally say the same in eternally changing forms. The *Volk* is at bottom very conservative. It must be completely imbued with our points of view by constant repetition.'[54]

The rapid success of German arms in Poland, and the extraordinary quiescence of the British and French led Goebbels to hope that peace might swiftly follow. He was not alone. Foreign correspondents and diplomats had all remarked on the obvious apprehension of the German public when Poland was invaded (the British Ambassador, Nevile Henderson, described the mood in Berlin as one of 'utter gloom and depression'[55]), and on 6 October Hitler made a 'peace speech' to the *Reichstag*, offering to take part in an international conference, which would have to accept the partition of Poland by Germany and the Soviet Union as irrevocable. Days later, rumours spread through Germany that the British government had resigned, George VI had abdicated, and there was to be an armistice. The SD reported that there were stoppages at work as people downed tools to find out more, and that there were excited gatherings in streets. The news ran through Berlin, and was formally announced to students at the University. Troops arriving on a train were joyously told that 'the war was over'.[56] Goebbels himself saw 'people on the street embracing one another', and immediately spoke on the radio to refute the rumour, something which he admitted caused 'great disappointment'.[57]

After the hectic excitement of September 1939, Goebbels had now to endure the suspense of the 'phoney war'. He consoled himself after the peace rumours of 10 October with the thought that, like Brüning and Schleicher before them, Chamberlain and Daladier would be overcome. 'If we don't mess things up ourselves, we must win. And we will.'[58] He concealed his disappointment over what he saw as British intransigence with an increasingly reckless philosophy.

He and Hitler agreed in a conversation in January 1940 that people were most courageous when they had burnt their bridges behind them, and that this should always be done 'when one stood before really difficult decisions'. Hitler apparently exemplified this with reference to wide-ranging historical examples – notably that of Frederick the Great – but also with reference to the Polish campaign, and the 'present situation', leading Goebbels to assert: 'We simply must not lose the war.'[59] Even at this early stage of the war, Goebbels seems to have realized that Hitler had over-reached himself, and his underlying sense of doubt is only underscored by his repeated protestations.

In these private conversations Goebbels and Hitler also developed their racial convictions, and their ambitions for the growing German *Reich*. Since March 1939, they controlled not only a population of some 90 million 'Germans', but an increasing number of other peoples. The war did nothing to diminish the crude stereotyping which underlay Goebbels' view of these different 'races', or to soften his extraordinarily brutal attitudes towards them. As the Polish campaign was drawing to a close on 29 September, Hitler told Goebbels of his plan to divide Poland into three strips: one in the west to be 'Germanized', a second to contain 'the good Polish element', and a third, east of the River Vistula, into which they would 'force the bad Polish element and the Jews, also those from the *Reich*'.[60] A week later, they spoke again about Poland, Hitler relating experiences from the campaign. The Poles carried 'the dangers of the steppes right up to the frontiers of Europe'; as for the Jews, they were 'not even humans any more'. They had 'to be made harmless'.[61] Even before this, Goebbels had started work on what he called a 'ghetto film' with Fritz Hippler, an anti-Semitic production using footage of Polish Jews. It would make 'the most cutting anti-Semitic propaganda that could be imagined'.[62] Although Goebbels initially hoped this film would be ready for showing in three or four weeks, it took much longer, and working on it became an obsession for him. Hippler and his production team travelled to Łódź and Warsaw, forcing Jews to slaughter animals and to read from the Torah for the cameras, and filming the most graphic examples of poverty and ugliness they could find.[63] Over the next year he and Goebbels worked this material into the film entitled *Der ewige Jude* (*The Eternal Jew*). The scenes of ritual slaughter had a particular fascination for Goebbels, and after first seeing them he wrote: 'This Jewry must be exterminated.' Earlier that day he had discussed the film with Hitler, who was 'very interested'.[64] This was the first time that Goebbels had used this kind of language in speaking of the Jews. It marks a radical intensification of his views. A fortnight later, Goebbels showed the same scenes to Hitler and his entourage.[65]

Always keen to see things for himself, Goebbels flew to Poland on 31 October for a brief tour of Łódź and Warsaw. He was horrified by what he saw of Łódź, and its Jewish quarter: 'It is indescribable. These are not people any more, these are animals. And that is therefore not a humanitarian, but a clinical task.' He was not much more impressed by the 'Polish streets': 'That is already Asia'. He spoke with his staff in the city, and they agreed that they would have to proceed 'radically against the Poles'. As for Warsaw: 'That is hell. A city demolished ... People creep through the streets like insects.' He was glad to get away.[66] What Goebbels meant by proceeding 'radically' can be judged from a comment he had made in his diary several days previously, when he noted with regard to reports from the city of Posen that 'there is not much left of the intelligentsia'.[67] With horrifying rapidity, Goebbels joined with Hitler and Himmler in their plans for huge population movements as part of a racial restructuring of Eastern Europe. He spoke of these displacements – most of them involuntary – with shocking bluntness. Goebbels did though place limits on the territory he thought fit for incorporation into the *Reich*. He was horrified by the idea of turning Łódź, which lay in the area now styled as the 'Wartheland', into a German city, noting: 'We could so well have used this city as a dumping ground [*Abladeplatz*].'[68]

Goebbels displayed a similarly unenthusiastic attitude to the Czechs in the 'Protectorate' of Bohemia and Moravia. Although, after hearing Hitler praise the quality of Czech munitions captured in Poland, Goebbels was prepared to concede that they had some technical aptitude, he still believed that they were an inferior race which had to be repressed. He was incensed by the obvious support displayed in the 'Protectorate' for France and Britain in the opening weeks of the war, and after student demonstrations in Prague, he was pleased by the closing of the universities for three years, and by the arrival of SS troops from Graz to restore order, writing: 'The war against enemies of the state must be carried out with force, not with formalities.'[69]

With this crude belief in the virtue of force, and that any sympathy in dealing with occupied populations was misplaced, Goebbels failed to understand why feeling outside Germany towards Nazism in 1939 and 1940 was so hostile. He concentrated during the 'phoney war' on attacking the 'plutocrats' ranged against Germany, a formula adopted after the Pact with Moscow, and on maintaining support for Hitler. Once it became clear that Britain and France would not negotiate on Hitler's terms, Goebbels was allowed to resume public speaking, and this brought him, as it always had done, real pleasure. In December 1939 he travelled to Danzig, Posen, Bromberg, and Thorn, all now reinstated as German towns, rejoicing in the German architecture he saw there. He made a distinction between these towns, which he thought of as essentially 'German', and Łódź, which he did not, even when its name was changed to 'Litzmannstadt', in honour of a First World War German general. Goebbels then journeyed to Aachen and Trier, near the Western Front, and spoke to troops there. Back in Berlin he spoke to leaders of the League of German Girls. In the New Year, Goebbels travelled in the 'Siberian cold' to Posen, where he spoke to '20,000 Germans'. This rally was staged for 'Germans [*Volksdeutsche*] from the Wartheland and from the Baltic and from Volhynia', these latter groups ethnic Germans now being repatriated from outside Germany under the terms of the Pact with Stalin in 1939. Goebbels enjoyed this greatly, writing that it was 'a real fighting meeting like old times'.[70] A 20-minute recording of the end of this speech has survived, allowing us to see the rhetorical strategies Goebbels was employing at this still uncertain stage of the war. Most of his audience had not previously been German citizens, and he spoke at length about the *Volk* of which they were now a part. He told his listeners that 'this people's war [*Volkskrieg*] must be carried through', and that if they did not prevail, their right to existence as a *Volk* would be lost. Trust in the *Führer* would see them through. In his peroration, Goebbels called on his audience to 'look on the *Führer* with belief, and in good and bad times call to him: You order, and we will follow!'[71] Back in Berlin, Goebbels resumed his tradition of an annual pilgrimage to the grave of Horst Wessel in February 1940, where he spoke briefly to a gathering of Party veterans.[72]

These were difficult months in Germany. The winter of 1939–40 was unusually severe, and frozen rivers and canals disrupted the normal distribution of coal. There was a prolonged shortage in Berlin, forcing the closure of many public buildings, and Goebbels fretted about the effects this had on morale. Frustrated by the lack of military activity, Goebbels struggled to maintain a realistic appraisal of developments. His propaganda was able successfully to present genuine German successes, like the sinking of the battleship *Royal Oak* in Scapa Flow in October 1939 by a German submarine, but he miscalculated when reporting the naval encounter off the River Plate in December. The battle between the pocket battleship *Graf Spee* and three smaller British cruisers was initially presented in Germany as a victory, but Goebbels was forced into an embarrassing retreat when the *Graf Spee* was subsequently scuttled. He gave instructions that only the barest details of this should be released to the press.[73] Goebbels seemed even further from reality, when he reported on a German air attack on the British naval base at Scapa Flow in March 1940. He appears here to have been led by his hatred for Churchill, writing in his diary: 'He has suffered the greatest defeat of this war at Scapa Flow.'[74] In fact the German attack had only damaged one British vessel, and Churchill was pleased by the pretext this gave the British for attacking Germany with bombs rather than propaganda leaflets.[75] There was a prolonged propaganda duel over the subsequent retaliatory British raid on the island of Sylt. Conducting this in Berlin, Goebbels wrote: 'There I am in my element.'[76]

He was presented with much more dramatic material in April 1940, when the 'phoney war' was ended by Hitler's surprise attack on Denmark and Norway. This was followed in May by the attack on the Low Countries and on France. In the space of a few weeks the political and military situation in Europe was completely transformed by the unprecedented success of German arms. From all sides the role played by Goebbels' propaganda in this was acknowledged. He was widely credited with having undermined French self-belief, and with having helped to intimidate smaller countries like Holland and Belgium which offered little resistance to the onslaught of the *Luftwaffe* and the *Wehrmacht*. In Germany cinema audiences flocked to see the dramatic newsreels produced every week. At the height of the French campaign, Goebbels wrote that the weekly newsreels 'with their realistic scenes of war aroused not relief, but only anger and satisfaction'.[77] Reports from the SD spoke of the universal 'amazement' German audiences had for the technical quality of the newsreels, and the rapidity with which scenes from the front line were available for public consumption.[78]

Goebbels was also planning a return to the field of journalism. As Germany expanded he had seized the opportunity to establish German-language newspapers in occupied areas, and had devoted particular attention to setting up a new weekly newspaper which might appeal to audiences both in Germany and abroad, and to which he could contribute regularly. This was *Das Reich* (*The Empire*), a broadsheet which was published first on 26 May 1940 and then appeared every Sunday until the last days of the war in 1945. Goebbels contributed a leading article, published on the front page, to every issue, commenting typically on the conduct of the war, and on internal German affairs, but also expounding his views on culture, the arts, and history more generally. Initially, *Das Reich* had a circulation of 100,000 copies, but this soon rose to 1.4 million, as the supply of paper was channelled to publications favoured by the Nazi Party.[79] There was an insatiable demand for news and information in wartime Germany, and even opponents of the Nazis, like Victor Klemperer, were anxious readers of *Das Reich*.

Goebbels shared with most of the German population the sense of relief and exultation at the French collapse which came to a head on 22 June 1940, when a ceasefire was signed between France and Germany at Compiègne in the same railway carriage used for the signing of the Armistice in November 1918. While Goebbels' cameramen filmed the ceremony in Compiègne for cinema audiences, Goebbels himself was at Schwanenwerder, waiting anxiously for news. Hitler telephoned him to report on the successful conclusion of the German-French negotiations, and Goebbels wrote: 'Everything is perfect ... Great, glorious, Germany!'[80] There was an anxious wait of 48 hours before the formal end of fighting between the French and the Italians, who had joined in, on the German side, at the last moment. In the last hours, Goebbels gathered with 'a small circle of fellow-workers', Magda, and her sister-in-law Ello, by the lakeside at Lanke on a 'silvery clear night'.[81] According to Schaumburg-Lippe, who was among those present, when the ceasefire was announced on the radio, Goebbels did something very unusual, and ordered champagne. Apparently finding it difficult to speak, he said, 'Gentlemen, it is pretty much certain that the war is over.'[82]

Over the next few days, Goebbels also shared the widespread hope that Britain would not fight on. On 7 July he arranged a huge ceremonial welcome for Hitler's return from the front to Berlin, and as soon as they could get away from the crowds, the two men spoke about 'the situation'. Hitler was evidently undecided on how best to proceed against the British: 'He still does not know above all whether he should again appeal to England.'[83] Hitler went on to the Obersalzberg to contemplate this further, and Goebbels was informed a few days later of the plan to mount a campaign against Britain, 'the main burden of which will be carried by the Luftwaffe. We will hit suddenly and hard. The English Lords [*Die Herren Engländer*] can not hold out long against that.'[84] Goebbels was longing for peace, and for the possibilities that a Nazi domination of mainland Europe held out. After a long and beautiful summer day spent out at Lanke he wrote with longing: 'What will we first be able to get started on when there is peace'.[85] There is no doubt that in the summer of 1940 Goebbels – unlike Hitler – was hoping for an early end to the war.

Hitler had decided to appeal to Britain before an aerial onslaught, and he convened the *Reichstag* for 19 July 1940 to summarize his reasons for going to war, and to declare that he could see 'no compelling reason which could force the continuation of the war'.[86] Revealingly, in his summary of the speech, Goebbels wrote: 'Appeal to London with strong dramatic accents. But no closer precision on war aims. But psychologically of immense effectiveness. Appeal to reason. We didn't want this war.' Pessimistically he concluded his diary account of that day: 'A great hour is past. Now the speech goes out to the whole world through our transmitters. It is London's turn to speak. I don't believe in peace. First war!'[87] Famously, the BBC German Service broadcast an immediate rejection of any offer of peace, and Churchill gave no reaction at all to Hitler's speech, commenting only to colleagues that he was not on speaking terms with Hitler.[88] Goebbels wrote: 'Yesterday: first English reaction: completely negative. The sharpest, quite cynical rejection. No official voice, although one sees Churchill's guiding hand. Also a very frosty reaction from the USA.'[89]

It is no exaggeration to say that over the next six months, Goebbels was entirely preoccupied with the war against Britain. At first he entertained the notion that Churchill had only limited public support in Britain, but gradually realized that this was not the case. He thought Churchill was a liar and was genuinely outraged by the propaganda against Germany which emanated from Britain. Goebbels had already conceded that Churchill had certain qualities, and his hatred of him was increasingly tempered by a grudging respect. Back in April 1940, commenting on one of Churchill's speeches, he had written: 'Churchill has a good style. A man with great gifts, but without character and stature.'[90] Goebbels had little close contact with the aerial campaign against Britain, or the preparations for invasion, and he became increasingly frustrated with the poor level of intelligence reaching Germany from Britain. He was desperately frustrated by the delay before the *Luftwaffe* started to attack targets in Britain in August 1940, and constantly used the weather to explain the *Luftwaffe*'s failure to gain aerial supremacy over southern Britain. On 23 August Goebbels used his ministerial conference to tell subordinates that they must prepare the public for the possibility that the war would carry on over the winter.[91] He was delighted by the shift from bombing airfields and military targets to direct attacks on London's civilian population in September 1940, and like British strategists later, he assumed initially that aerial attacks on civilians would force the enemy out of the war. Hitler told him as early as 23 September 1940 that an invasion of Britain was impossible,[92] but still Goebbels repeatedly expressed the idea that Britain would not be able to hold out, that a few weeks of good weather, and a few more aerial attacks would finish the war. He reported constantly on rumours of panic, defeatism, and social dissent from Britain. As the *Luftwaffe* turned to night bombing, he kept a daily record of the tonnage of ordnance unloaded on British cities, rejoicing in the damage done to each. As late as 18 November, as he contemplated how the German people might be prepared for a second war winter, he wrote that with a couple of weeks' good weather, 'the case of England could be eventually liquidated'.[93] He finished a volume of his diary in a hotel in Munich on 20 November in some frustration, writing: 'When will the Churchill creature finally capitulate?'[94]

Other factors were contributing to what Goebbels conceded was a 'small spiritual crisis' in mid-October 1940, one he clearly shared with many others in Germany.[95] The war had come home directly to Germany, and to Berlin specifically in August 1940, with the first British bombing raids. Most histories of British bombing in the Second World War emphasize the difficulties and the relative weakness of the early attacks made on German cities. Few aircraft were involved and only small bomb-loads could be carried to a city as distant as Berlin in 1940.[96] Even locating a blacked-out city on a dark night in cloudy weather was difficult. It is all the more striking then to see the effect the British attacks had in Berlin, where, although an air-raid alarm had been sounded on the second day of war, with the exception of a solitary French visitor, no enemy aircraft had been seen before August 1940. Goebbels heard the first British bombers which arrived on the evening on 25 August. From outside the city he watched the 'majestic display' of the flak, and noted that he got only a few hours of sleep.[97] When a British bomber was shot down near Lanke in October, Goebbels went to see the wreckage: 'A heap of iron and steel, amongst it the charred parts of three bodies. A ghastly sight. But always better the English than us.'[98]

Goebbels was also compelled, like the rest of Berlin's population, to spend many hours in air-raid shelters as a result of these early raids. His evening conversations with Hitler, and their shared viewing of films was on occasion interrupted. On 20 December the two of them had to take refuge underground, and while they waited for the all-clear, they discussed a range of topics, including a plea for clemency from Martin Niemöller. Neither was inclined to be merciful, according to Goebbels' summary of the conversation: 'Out of the question. He can eat well, and get fat, so that nobody can any longer confuse him with a martyr. But he will not be let loose upon humanity again. He should have thought about that earlier.'[99] Although the bombing raids of the RAF caused relatively few casualties

36. Goebbels paid close attention to the 'Blitz' on Britain in the winter of 1940/41. Of this attack on Sheffield on 12 December 1940 he wrote: 'Sheffield hit with 500,000 kg. Our airmen report that it was worse than Coventry.' (*TBJG*, 14 December 1940, TI, 9, p. 51.)

in Germany that winter, and did little material damage, they had an enormous psychological effect in many German cities, something noted by William Shirer, admittedly a biased observer. He wrote that 'morale tumbled noticeably in Berlin when the British visited us almost every evening'.[100] Millions of people were kept awake for night after night, and as early as September 1940 Goebbels had to discuss with Hitler plans to evacuate children from Berlin.[101] Shrapnel from the flak barrages put up against the British aircraft was a hazard, and Goebbels complained that unexploded German ordnance was a greater problem than the actual bombs dropped.[102] By October a programme of construction of air-raid shelters in German cities had begun. Little did Goebbels or the German public know of the terrible future that lay ahead of them.

37. The composer Richard Wagner was a huge influence on Hitler and, to a lesser extent, on Goebbels. Both men discussed Arno Breker's bust of the composer in 1940, and admired the way it presented Wagner not as an individual, but as the representative of a racial type. Goebbels wrote that Hitler 'praises Breker's bust of Wagner. It is the art of sculpture to present the typical and the permanent, and not just photography or mere fantasy.' (*TBJG*, 6 April 1940, TI, 8, p. 37.)

Goebbels' fifth daughter Heide was born on 29 October 1940, his 43rd birthday. His relationship with Magda had improved noticeably since the outbreak of war, helped no doubt by the absence of Karl Hanke and Lida Baarova. Goebbels actually saw little of his family after the outbreak of war, as he was almost constantly at work. Magda was also away much of the time, ill or convalescing in Dresden. They were still ambitiously planning new houses, and Goebbels finally moved into one on Hermann-Göring-Strasse in central Berlin on the day Heide was born. The details of the interior fittings and furnishings for this house were finalized during the heady days of the French campaign, and reflect the huge ambitions of that time. Although there were difficulties with the procurement of certain materials, notably metals listed as important to the war effort, Goebbels and his wife spent much time, energy, and money on meticulous consideration of light fittings, carpets, and statuary for the new house and the adjacent Propaganda

Ministry. Separate lists of brown, grey and white uniform clothing required for Goebbels were drawn up, as well as casual outfits, including 27 suits and 89 ties. Leading artists and sculptors, including Professors Klimsch, Kampf, Wackerle, Gradl, Schmidt-Ehmen and Arno Breker were commissioned to provide suitable statues for house and garden.[103]

Other Nazi leaders were developing private ideas and projects under the cover of war. Rosenberg – for all Goebbels' earlier efforts to clip his wings – was developing grandiose plans for a university or *Hohe Schule*, and as part of this, an 'Institute for the Study of the Jewish Question'.[104] In July 1940 he established a group of academics charged with safekeeping 'material for political research', that is to say, looting cultural artefacts from occupied countries.[105] Göring was similarly expanding his private art collection, and Hitler was thinking of a future religion based on vegetarianism which could supplant Christianity. He was also planning to build a naval base larger than Singapore at Drontheim in Norway, and an *Autobahn* to link this with Graz at the opposite end of the German *Reich*. Goebbels shared in the discussions about these projects, and participated actively in several of them. He was instrumental in drawing up lists of art works to be confiscated in France and Belgium. He listened with apparent fascination to Hitler's ideas about smoking and diet, although as a heavy smoker and a carnivore Goebbels was unable to practise the high ideals preached by the *Führer*. Goebbels was also privy to a more sinister development, the mass murder of the mentally ill. On 1 May 1940 he had recorded a conversation with Hitler and Philipp Bouhler, the head of Hitler's private Chancellery:

> Bouhler reports on the liquidation proceedings with the insane, which are so necessary and will now be carried through. Still secret. This is causing many difficulties.[106]

Goebbels made no further comment at this point, and it is not clear what he meant by 'difficulties'. At this point the 'euthanasia' programme authorized by Hitler in October 1939 was getting into its stride, and an effective procedure had been developed to kill mentally ill patients with carbon monoxide gas in selected institutions, and to pretend to their relatives that they had succumbed to 'natural causes'. Given Goebbels' acceptance of the killings as 'necessary', it is most likely that he was referring to 'difficulties' with public opinion in Germany. He reported a further conversation on this topic in January 1941:

> Discussed the question of the silent liquidation of the mentally ill with Bouhler. 40,000 have gone, 60,000 still must go. That is a hard, but also a necessary work. And it must be done now. Bouhler is the right man for it.[107]

From this cryptic summary, and from his description of the killing now not as 'secret', but as 'silent', it appears that Goebbels was aware of the growing unease and many complaints about the 'euthanasia' programme from different sections of the population. The diplomat Ulrich von Hassell was one who had recorded disquiet with the 'systematic, but uncontrolled killing of the so-called "incurably mentally ill"' in his diary in November 1940, and in January 1941 he wrote about the 'criminal thoughtlessness' with which this was being done. He recorded how parents of a mentally ill daughter had removed her from care after being told that she had to be transferred to 'another institution'. They had subsequently received a notice regretting that she had passed away, even though she was at home with them.[108] The Protestant writer and diarist Jochen Klepper recorded as early as May 1940 an accurate summary of the procedure being used for the 'euthanasia' programme which he had heard from the leader of a 'large Christian institution'. In August 1940 he wrote that he had spoken to 'a leading man from the Inner Mission' (a large Protestant missionary foundation) who had attended a conference in Hanover, where the 'extermination' of those considered 'unworthy of life', such as 'criminals, cripples, and the insane' had been discussed. He wrote that '15,000 have already been killed'. Klepper, who was an 'Aryan' living with a Jewish wife and stepdaughter in ever more difficult circumstances, was fully aware of the moral enormity of the step that had been taken, commenting: 'The glimmering flame is extinguished, the damaged reed is broken.'[109]

Rumours had reached beyond Germany, and on 29 April 1941 Goebbels felt compelled to refer in his daily ministerial conference to British reports that the programme of forced sterilization and killing of the hereditarily and mentally ill in Germany was to be extended after the war to wounded soldiers. The press was instructed that 'the theme of euthanasia should not in any circumstance be touched upon', and that it should concentrate on stressing the care given to war wounded.[110] Goebbels clearly felt impelled to do something more proactive to combat public unease, and within a fortnight of his second conversation with Bouhler, he was at work on a 'film on euthanasia' with the director Wolfgang Liebeneiner, and giving guidelines for its production.[111] This was the film later released as *Ich klage an* (*I Accuse*), which used established modes like the courtroom drama and love story to present a subtle pro-euthanasia message. It was, according to Michael Burleigh, 'powerfully lit, with smooth and graceful camera-work'. The film was eventually seen by more than 15 million viewers in wartime Germany and was, on the whole, well-received.[112] The whole approach taken to *I Accuse*, and its avoidance of obviously strident propaganda, suggests that Goebbels was quick to learn from the experience of his earlier anti-Jewish films.

By February 1941, the anti-Jewish films Goebbels had embarked on at the start of the war were being shown to huge audiences around Germany, and elsewhere in Europe. The 'documentary' scenes filmed in Poland in 1939 had finally, after much reworking, been presented as *Der ewige Jude* (*The Eternal Jew*) in

November 1940. Before this, several feature films with anti-Semitic messages had played to large audiences, most notably *Jud Süß*, a historical portrayal of Jewish villainy which had been enormously successful with not only the German public. Goebbels reported delightedly how it had provoked anti-Semitic disturbances in Hungary.[113] The SD reported that in many places around Germany the film had provoked 'open demonstrations against the Jews'. The SD also reported that the public reaction to *The Eternal Jew* had been far more ambivalent, and that many had simply stayed away from it – at a time when cinema attendances were at an unprecedented peak.[114] This was despite Goebbels' earlier recognition that the film was too horrible, and the resultant preparation of two separate editions, a complete one for Party activists, and a version with some of the worst slaughterhouse scenes edited out for the general public.[115] Klemperer in Dresden recorded that *The Eternal Jew* was withdrawn after 'less than a week'.[116] Goebbels did not refer to the reception of the film in his diary; it was presumably a great disappointment to him. This silence stands in marked contrast to his frequent references to the making of the film.

Despite the unpopularity of *The Eternal Jew*, Goebbels was still determined to get all Jews out of Berlin. On 6 September 1940, his aide Hans Hinkel had reported to the ministerial conference on plans to transport most of Berlin's remaining 71,800 Jews 'to the East' in the next four weeks.[117] On 17 September Hinkel briefed the conference on the larger plan to deport some 3.5 million Jews from Germany and German-occupied territories to the French colony of Madagascar.[118] This unrealistic project came to nothing, but in March 1941 Goebbels again discussed the whole issue with Hitler and Hans Frank, the Governor of the occupied area of Poland called (since July 1940) the 'General Government'. Hearing that Jews were now being deported from Vienna to the General Government, Goebbels wrote: 'And now Berlin will come in line.'[119] Although the Jews in the General Government were not yet being systematically exterminated, Goebbels was aware that many were being killed there during forced deportations. He wrote the next day, on a visit to Posen, that 'a lot has been liquidated here, above all Jewish misbehaviour'.[120] Two days later he wrote that he was forbidding 'our people to watch executions of Jews'.[121]

There should be no doubt whatsoever that Goebbels knew in great detail about, and fully complied with the implementation of the mass killing of the mentally ill in Germany, and with the developing persecution of the Jews. For a brief period in the middle of 1941, his main attention was though diverted elsewhere. After a lunch with Hitler on 28 March 1941, Goebbels wrote in an analysis of the military situation: 'on 4 April the long prepared operation against Greece should start'. After exploring this he wrote: 'The great operation then comes later: against R. It will be most carefully camouflaged, only the fewest know about it.' Recognizing that there was a 'Napoleon parallel' here, Goebbels added 'Psychologically, the whole thing does present some difficulties.'[122]

10
'A Life and Death Struggle'

This nation is about to take a great and salutary reducing course which will free it of its ugliness, and teach it, at a cost of what may well be immense suffering, to believe in other gods than the unholy Trinity of Krupp, Röchling, and cheap radio.

> Friedrich Reck-Malleczewen, on hearing Goebbels' radio proclamation that Germany had invaded the Soviet Union.[1]

We do not know exactly when Goebbels first learned of Hitler's intention to attack the Soviet Union. Since 1936 a clear pattern had emerged, in which Hitler made important foreign policy decisions, then communicated them to Goebbels and told him to take appropriate propaganda measures. Although Goebbels did privately record disagreements with Hitler over minor matters, such as the issue of gasmasks to the public before the war, or in early 1941 about the compulsory employment of German women,[2] he did not express dissent over fundamentals of foreign policy. Thus in August 1939, he did not record any reservations about the Pact concluded with Moscow, or about the subsequent decision to attack Poland and to risk war with Britain and France. Over the next 18 months, Goebbels did frequently record his discomfort with the Soviet alliance, but accepted it as a pragmatic necessity, further proof of Hitler's grand vision. Goebbels was scathing about Ribbentrop's flirtation with the Soviets, and with the notion that this was anything other than a temporary and unholy alliance. When Ribbentrop returned from Moscow in October 1939, proclaiming that amongst the Bolsheviks he had felt as if amongst old Nazi Party comrades, Goebbels was for once united with Rosenberg in his contempt.[3] He shared the unease of most Germans over the Soviet attack on perceived racial comrades in Finland in 1939, and over the Soviet occupation of the Baltic States in 1940. With more pragmatic concern he noted the Soviet encroachments into Romania in June 1940, which brought them close to the main German source of crude oil from the refineries in Ploesti.[4]

Goebbels had indeed moved a long way from his heroic vision of the Russian people in the early 1920s. One wonders if he ever thought back to the way he had toured Germany in 1925, celebrating the Russian peasantry as 'full of faith, religiosity, fanaticism, and mysticism', and proclaiming that 'if Russia awakes, then the world will see a wonder'.[5] After his move to Berlin in 1926 he never deviated from his portrayal of Bolshevism as a Jewish creed intending to enslave Europe, to destroy its culture, and to perpetrate the most monstrous cruelties. This view was only fortified by his observation of the Spanish Civil War, of the show trials in Moscow in 1937, and by Soviet conduct after the signing of the Pact with Germany in August 1939. By November 1940, when Stalin's Foreign Minister Molotov visited Berlin, Goebbels' view of Soviet Bolshevism was entirely negative. He wrote a revealing account of his impressions after a 'breakfast' with Molotov and the Soviet delegation:

> Molotov makes an intelligent, mischievous impression ... Molotov's entourage is more than mediocre. Not a single figure of stature. As if they wanted completely to confirm our theoretical insights into the workings of Bolshevik mass ideology. One cannot have a rational word with any of them. On their faces fear of one another and inferiority complexes are written. Even a harmless conversation is as good as closed off. The GPU [the Soviet secret police] is watching. It is terrible. In this world life is no longer worth living. The dealings with Moscow must in the future be determined by considerations of pure expediency. The closer we are politically, the more alien we become in spirit and in world-view.[6]

We know that Hitler had since July 1940 been contemplating an attack on the Soviet Union, and that military preparations for this were initiated then. Molotov's visit in November 1940 helped to confirm his decision to attack in 1941.[7] On 18 December 1940 Hitler issued his 'Directive No. 21' to the armed forces, directing them 'to crush Soviet Russia in a rapid campaign'.[8] By this time there were rumours of a future war with the Soviet Union all over Germany, and Goebbels of course knew about these. If he was not privy to Hitler's detailed plans before March 1941 he certainly knew of his ultimate intention to confront the Soviet Union, recording this in his diary in August 1940.[9] Nonetheless, through the winter of 1940–41 Goebbels focused his attention on the war against Britain.

If Hitler's decision to extend the war to the Soviet Union appears almost incomprehensible today, there was a rationale which Goebbels fully accepted at the time, and which was embodied in Directive No. 21. Hitler intended the attack on the Soviet Union as a swift preventive war, after which Germany could secure *Lebensraum* – or living space – in the East. This, as Adam Tooze has persuasively argued, would then provide the economic foundation for a successful war against Britain and its American backers.[10] On 7 May 1941 Goebbels wrote of a campaign against the Soviet Union: 'If the blow succeeds, and it will succeed, then we are for the first time secure. With what plausible goal will England then fight?'[11] Hitler and Goebbels' view of war with the Soviet Union was also governed by a shared miscalculation. They seriously underestimated the potential of the Red Army. As early as September 1939, Goebbels had noted reports on the poor equipment and performance of the Red Army in eastern Poland, and he developed this theme repeatedly during the winter of 1940. Newsreels of the Soviet attack on Finland fortified his racial prejudice: he judged that the Russian peasants were not able to operate modern armaments, and that Stalin had erred fatally in purging the 'Germanic' officer corps of the Red Army.[12] In June 1941 he conferred with Hitler, who explained the military plans for the forthcoming campaign in greater detail. Hitler estimated that it would take four months to bring this to a successful conclusion, but Goebbels judged that 'much less' time was needed, writing: 'Bolshevism will collapse like a house of cards.' Goebbels also accepted Hitler's notion that once the Red Army had been destroyed it would only be necessary to occupy European Russia and police it with a relatively small force, adding: 'the example of Napoleon will not be repeated'. Goebbels knew also that Hitler did not intend a straightforward military confrontation with the Soviet Union, merely to gain territory, but that this was an ideological and racial war, with exterminatory consequences:

> The Bolshevik poison must get out of Europe … In Russia, Tsarism will not be reinstated, but genuine socialism will be carried through in opposition to Jewish Bolshevism. To experience this will bring deep satisfaction to every old Nazi. The accord with Russia was really a blot on our escutcheon. That will now be washed away. That which we have fought against for our whole lives will also now be exterminated. I say that to the *Führer* and he agrees with me completely.[13]

What did Goebbels mean here by 'That which we have fought against for our whole lives'? In the context of the passage above, this could only mean the Jews, and there is a clear suggestion here that Goebbels was leading Hitler in demanding that they 'be exterminated' once the campaign in the Soviet Union was underway.

Hitler and Goebbels' evaluation of Soviet potential was accompanied by a similar underestimation of America. Goebbels was fully aware of the debate there between Roosevelt, his advisers, and the isolationists represented by the aviator Charles Lindbergh, and knew that Germany was moving towards war with America. On 8 May 1941 he discussed this possibility with Hitler, and they agreed, astonishingly, that America could not overtake Germany in weapons production.[14] A fatal complacency was developing. A parallel over-estimation of German military potential was strengthened by the successful campaign against Yugoslavia, Greece, and Crete which preceded the attack on the Soviet Union. Hitler had already sent German troops to secure the supply of oil from Romania, and the failure of the Italian attack on Albania and Greece in October 1940 confirmed his determination to strengthen his position in south-eastern Europe, not least to deny the British, who landed in Greece in March 1941, a foothold there. In a brief and destructive campaign, the Yugoslavian and Greek armies were overwhelmed in April, and the British were forced, again, to evacuate their forces from the European mainland. In May German paratroopers played a vital part in conquering the island of Crete, and serious losses were inflicted on the British Navy by the *Luftwaffe*. Once again Goebbels excelled in the production of newsreels depicting the seemingly invincible progress of German arms, and the discomfiture of his opponents.

Closer to home, Goebbels was temporarily shocked by the decision of Rudolf Hess in May 1941 to fly to Britain in a bizarre personal effort to secure peace. Goebbels had not held a particularly high estimation of Hess, but equally had not previously criticized him in the way that he had other senior Nazis, like Rosenberg, or Ribbentrop. He had never doubted Hess' loyalty, and was genuinely dumbfounded by his flight to Scotland. Within days of Hess' disappearance he was reflecting, with horror that 'a fool like this' was Hitler's successor.[15] Bizarrely, in a characteristic shift between shrewd realism and flight into fantasy, Goebbels never extended this critique to Hitler himself: he appears not to have questioned how Hitler could tolerate men with such glaring flaws in his close circle. Instead, Goebbels blamed Hess for his meddling with occultism, and his wife and adjutants for encouraging him. Goebbels himself had dabbled with astrology and with the writings of Nostradamus in the early months of the war,[16] and it may have been with some embarrassment that he now learnt more of Hess' preoccupation with similar ideas. On 13 June 1941, days before the still secret attack on the Soviet Union, Goebbels noted that 'all astrologers, magnetopaths, anthroposophists, etc.' had been arrested. 'Strangely enough,' he wrote, 'not one clairvoyant had predicted that he would be arrested.'[17]

Goebbels was initially terrified by the potential fall-out from Hess' flight to Scotland, but in fact little came of it. For several days Goebbels' ministerial conference was dominated by long statements on Hess. On 14 May Goebbels stressed that Hess had taken leave of his senses, and had been motivated by a desire to make peace. Hess, he declared, was absolutely convinced in the certainty of a German victory, and wished to avoid further unnecessary bloodshed.[18] The next day, Goebbels, in a long statement, developed what was to become one of his favourite rhetorical strategies, likening the difficulties with Hess to the crisis in the Party in November 1932: just as the Party had triumphed then, it would overcome the problems now.[19] To Goebbels' surprise and relief, the British simply imprisoned Hess and scorned any idea of negotiation. A more persistent if still manageable problem was the continued British bombing of German cities and industrial targets. In March 1941 Goebbels' children were moved temporarily to the safety of Bischofswiesen, near Berchtesgaden, and then in May to more permanent quarters in Aussee, near Salzburg, beyond the reach of British bombers. Goebbels recorded that on the same day as the children reached Aussee, some 100 people in Hamburg were killed in a British attack.[20] A few weeks before, the State Opera in Berlin, where Goebbels had spent 'so many beautiful hours', was completely burnt out after being hit by a bomb.[21] Goebbels was particularly concerned by the British tactic of repeated attacks on individual cities, such as those on Kiel in April 1941, when no fewer than 900 sorties were flown against the city.[22] Goebbels reported that as a result, every evening 'thousands moved into the surrounding woods', and he had to permit the evacuation of women and children from the city.[23] A few weeks earlier, he had taken the precaution of depositing all his handwritten diaries, 'twenty thick volumes', in the underground vaults of the *Reichsbank*. For once he predicted accurately when he wrote that future generations would take some interest in them.[24]

As preparations continued for the attack on the Soviet Union, Goebbels lived in a state of suspense. Anxiously he scanned the world's media for any sense that the Soviets were aware of the impending onslaught, and he played a full part in circulating misinformation in Germany. He observed, and helped to foment the wild rumours that proliferated in June 1941, on 'a huge scale, from peace to war, from which anyone can choose what he wants', and tried to displace his anxiety with intensive work. In the last hours before the German onslaught on 22 June 1941, he was still experimenting with different fanfares to introduce the radio bulletins announcing future successes in the Soviet Union. He and Hitler agreed on one based on Liszt's 'Hungarian Rhapsody', and another using a motif from the *Horst-Wessel-Lied*. They parted at 3.30 a.m., and Goebbels went back to the Propaganda Ministry on the Wilhelmplatz. Unable to sleep, he wrote that 'the breath of history is audible'. As dawn was breaking the new fanfare was broadcast, and Goebbels read out on the radio Hitler's proclamation announcing the start of 'Operation Barbarossa'. German troops, according to Hitler, were invading the Soviet Union to protect 'European culture and civilization', which were threatened by a 'conspiracy of Jewish-Anglo-Saxon warmongers and the equally Jewish rulers in the Bolshevik headquarters in Moscow'.[25] This was, for Goebbels, a 'moment of celebration'. Afterwards he returned to Schwanenwerder, where the birds were singing, feeling immensely relieved. He wrote: 'I feel myself entirely free.'[26]

The war with the Soviet Union brought about a significant change in Goebbels' life. Although Germany had already been at war for almost two years, its major land campaigns had been decided in days, or at most in weeks. None had experienced any major difficulties. The war at sea and in the air had been conducted for the most part far from Germany itself, and Goebbels had underestimated the significance of the failure of the aerial campaigns against Britain in 1940 and 1941. Only relatively small forces had been committed to support the Italians in

North Africa, and under the dynamic leadership of Rommel, these appeared to be making great progress. As after 22 June 1941 German armies advanced into eastern Poland, the former Baltic States, and the huge open spaces of Belorussia and Ukraine, it soon became evident that they were involved in a conflict of a different kind. Initially, there were huge successes, and Hitler's plans to destroy the Red Army in 'battles of annihilation' appeared close to fulfilment. Huge victories, with unprecedented numbers of captured prisoners and equipment, were trumpeted on German radio in twelve 'special announcements' on 29 June. The SD reported on 3 July that there were 'widespread rumours' amongst the public that German troops were already close to Moscow; and on 7 July that a 'victorious forward march' was 'simply expected by a population used to military victories'.[27] The next day, Goebbels flew out to see Hitler at his new field headquarters near Rastenburg in East Prussia, the complex of bunkers in the Masurian forest known as the 'Wolf's Lair'.

This was the first of many visits to the bizarre and artificial environment where Hitler, with an ever-growing retinue, and in ever-larger bunkers, spent most of the next three years.[28] Although impressed by the peace and quiet there, Goebbels noted straight away that the whole area was infested with swarms of mosquitoes. In contrast to other senior Nazis, like Göring, Ribbentrop, Todt, and later Speer, Goebbels did not carve out a niche for himself at Rastenburg with a bunker of his own; he never stayed there longer than was necessary to conduct his immediate business with Hitler. On his first visit, he noted with some scepticism that Otto Dietrich, Hitler's press chief, had built 'an apparently extensive press apparatus in a huge bunker' at the Wolf's Lair. Most of Goebbels' time was taken up in discussion with Hitler, who was 'surprisingly positive' about the military situation. There was a general conviction in Rastenburg that the war was already won. Sharing in this enthusiasm, Goebbels noted that Napoleon had invaded Russia – also on 22 June – with infantry, whereas they were using 'motorized tanks', which would make it far easier to overcome the huge spaces there.[29]

Over the next few weeks, nagging doubts set in. As early as 26 July, Goebbels noted his concern over the activities of partisans in the huge spaces behind the German armoured spearheads; his former police chief in Berlin, Helldorff, returned from the Eastern Front a few days later, and told him that the *Wehrmacht* was fighting a war of a different kind there. The same day the High Command of the *Wehrmacht* (OKW) admitted that it had underestimated the fighting quality of the Soviet soldiers.[30] In August, as the German advance continued, Goebbels conceded that their foreknowledge of Soviet armaments had not been good. 'Above all,' he wrote, 'we knew next to nothing about the availability of heavy tanks.'[31] His growing anxiety was not helped by news from Münster, in Westphalia, which had been subjected to four successive attacks by British bombers. On 3 August 1941 Münster's Roman Catholic Bishop Galen preached a sermon in which he denounced the killing of the mentally ill, and raised the disturbing possibility that 'wounded soldiers, if they were no longer useful for practical work, would be murdered by us'. Noting that this would doubtless be used by enemy propagandists, Goebbels wrote that Galen's sermon was 'a stab in the back of the fighting front'.[32] It was in fact the third highly critical sermon given in quick succession by Galen, a paradoxical figure, who, while criticizing aspects of Nazi policy, was a strong nationalist and opponent of Bolshevism.[33]

On 18 August Goebbels travelled to see Hitler in Rastenburg after an interval of six weeks. He found him looking 'somewhat strained and sickly', not surprising given that Hitler had hardly been outside his bunker since Goebbels' last visit. In a long discussion Goebbels and Hitler reviewed the whole situation. Tellingly, Hitler acknowledged that he had severely underestimated the military strength of the Soviets, above all their tanks and aircraft, and that as a result they were now 'dealing with a serious crisis'. Nonetheless he presented an optimistic prognosis: the *Wehrmacht* would surround Kiev and Leningrad, and their populations would be allowed to starve. Moscow would be taken before the onset of the winter, and the remaining Soviet resistance in the Urals could be dealt with later, using aircraft if necessary. Hitler still felt that Stalin might seek to conclude a separate peace with Germany on favourable terms. He expressed his view that Japan would soon attack the Soviet Union, and the hope that Churchill might resign or be replaced. Bolstered by this, Goebbels urged Hitler to speak again to the German public, and was given permission to organize a meeting in the *Sportpalast*. The two men spent a long time on their favourite topics: the Catholic Church, the Jews, and homosexuality. They agreed that it was best to defer dealing with Bishop Galen until an outburst of popular sentiment would allow them to put him before a people's court which would sentence him to 'a severe punishment'.[34]

On the other hand, they felt the time was ripe for further measures against the Jews. Since April 1941 Goebbels had been advocating that German Jews should have to wear a distinguishing sign in public,[35] an idea which had been aired by Heydrich after the November 1938 pogrom. Only days before the 18 August visit to Rastenburg, Goebbels had convened a meeting at the Propaganda Ministry in Berlin to thrash out a proposal for him to take to Hitler, and from the notes made at this meeting by the representative from the Interior Ministry who attended, it is clear that most of those present understood that making the Jews wear a distinguishing sign was also a prelude to other measures. Goebbels was not at the meeting, but was represented by his State Secretary Leopold Gutterer, who opened proceedings by explaining that Goebbels had received many complaints from front soldiers and officers about the visible presence of Jews in Berlin, and that the Propaganda Ministry was therefore convinced that 'immediate measures' were necessary. Running through a list of possible measures, which included evicting Berlin's Jews from their flats to make these available for 'Aryans', and putting the Jews in barracks, Gutterer noted that only 19,000 of Berlin's 70,000 Jews were in productive employment. The Propaganda Ministry was in favour of 'combing out' from the unemployed those capable of work. The rest should be 'carted off to Russia'; Gutterer said that 'it would be best anyway to kill these'. He concluded by stating that making the Jews wear a sign was a necessary precondition for the successful implementation of all these measures.[36]

From Goebbels' account of the conversations he had with Hitler in Rastenburg on 18 August, it is clear that he put all these ideas to him. Hitler agreed that all Jews in Germany should have to wear a distinguishing sign in public, and that Berlin's Jews would be deported 'to the East as soon as the transportation possibilities arose'. There they would be 'put to work in a harsher climate'. Later in the conversation, Hitler stated that his prophecy about the annihilation of the Jews was now being borne out, and Goebbels wrote: 'I will not rest and not halt, until we have also with respect to Jewry exacted the ultimate consequences.' One has the unmistakable impression that although the two men had the same murderous intentions, Goebbels was pushing Hitler further than he was prepared to go *at this point* in dealing with the 'Jewish question', in particular with the Jews of Berlin. Before the two men parted they reminisced about old times, and agreed that, just as before, they could find a way out of the present crisis. Goebbels retired to the 'guest bunker' at two in the morning, with the feeling that everything 'had been solved, or at the least clarified'.[37]

This qualification was significant. Although Goebbels returned to Berlin fortified and optimistic, he no longer believed in an imminent victory in the East, or in a quick end to the war. Even when in the second phase of Operation Barbarossa in September 1941 huge encirclements led to further victories, Goebbels now accepted that the 'Bolsheviks' presented a far more formidable opposition than he had earlier realized. The change is reflected in the way he kept his diary. Since lodging his handwritten earlier volumes with the *Reichsbank* he had taken to dictating his diary to a stenographer, and from 10 July 1941 he preceded each day's entry with a résumé of the 'military situation' which he received from the High Command of the Armed Forces. He had determined that his diary would serve as a document of record, and thus paid great attention to faithfully noting all military and political developments he thought significant. Goebbels was already aware that his diary constituted a remarkable historical document, and entertained fond hopes of reworking it at some future stage for further publication, devoting hours to each day's entry. Already he was making plans to put the handwritten and dictated entries on microfilm.[38]

Goebbels now saw little of Magda, and virtually nothing of his children, even after they returned to Schwanenwerder in late August. His diary reflected his growing isolation, and his belief that personal frivolities were now out of place. Although each day's entry was much longer, less space was devoted to reflections on people around him, on the landscapes he saw, and on the music and literature he was involved with. Instead, each entry took on the character of a military communiqué, followed by a précis of the propaganda situation.

It was as if Goebbels was fighting a parallel war, one he took as seriously as the actual fighting on the different, distant fronts. He followed every nuance in the presentation of the war news from London, Moscow, Washington, and Tokyo, as well as in the rest of Europe, and in Germany itself. Still conducting his ministerial conference every morning at 11.00 a.m., he tried to pre-empt, to parry, or to counter every twist and turn in the representation of military and political developments. Through the summer and autumn of 1941 he noted with dismay the growing number of acts of resistance in the occupied territories, and fretted about what he perceived as the weak and inconsistent response to them. Invariably he recommended a harsh policy of collective punishment to deter resistance, summing up his attitude in September, with reference to developments in Norway: 'Executions are indeed a very convincing argument.'[39] He was very concerned by the developing resistance in Serbia, which soon demanded the employment of whole military units, and failed entirely to see that this policy of violent repression might lead to an escalating cycle of conflict. By October he was noting in his résumé of the 'military situation', as if it were a matter of course, that '1,700 men and 10 women were shot in Serbia', and that 'two villages were burnt down and 202 people shot in Greece'.[40]

He paid equal attention to public opinion in Germany, particularly as the Russian winter came closer. Popular notions of Goebbels as an irrepressible liar and cynic have led to many misconceptions about his wartime propaganda. He was indeed untroubled by conscious deceit, but his propaganda was far more thoughtful and sophisticated than is often imagined. In wartime he consistently argued that the German people should be told as much as was possible without compromising military security, and above all, that false expectation should not be aroused by thoughtless predictions of victory. He was deeply troubled when on 9 October, following the huge successes at Vyasma, Otto Dietrich announced to the German press in Berlin that 'the campaign in the East has been decided'. This aroused wild hopes all over Germany that the Soviet Union had capitulated. Franco sent Hitler a telegram from Spain congratulating him on the 'final and conclusive success of the glorious German army against the enemy of civilization'.[41] In Romania, the newspapers carried headlines like 'The decision has been reached', and 'The Russian campaign is over'.[42] Goebbels' reaction was less complacent, noting: 'I hope to God that military operations develop in such a way that we suffer no psychological setback.' Noting that Hitler was also 'completely optimistic', Goebbels went on to admit that the last three months had strained his nerves more than any other time in his life.[43] This was not to be his last disagreement with Dietrich.

Worried by the 'illusionist' hopes engendered by Dietrich's announcement, Goebbels also fretted about the provision of food and clothing at home, particularly as the growing diversion of rolling stock to provision the armies in the Soviet Union left the German potato crop in the countryside at risk of frost damage. He was concerned by beer and tobacco shortages, and spent an inordinate amount of time worrying about how best to ration these commodities. By November 1941 he was forced to refer these issues to Hitler, who recommended weakening the beer, but not making this public. Goebbels noted that, as a 'non-beer drinker', Hitler was mistaken here, and that it would be better to tell the truth. When Hitler suggested similarly that the quality of cigarettes be lowered so more could be produced, Goebbels had to tell him that the cigarettes available were already so awful that this was not advisable.[44] Goebbels was a heavy smoker, and already had reservations about the anti-smoking policies of certain branches of the Party and state. He was convinced that during wartime it was more important to make tobacco freely available to the German public, and to soldiers at the front. He was painfully aware that tobacco consumption had risen since the start of the war, but that since May 1941 production had fallen significantly. By the autumn of 1941 a quarter of overall production was going directly to the armed forces, and long queues outside tobacconists were to be seen all over Germany.[45] Hitler had agreed with Goebbels that issues that were not of immediate importance for the conduct of the war, like the anti-smoking campaign, and more importantly, the earlier campaign against the churches, should be postponed. Even though Goebbels frequently expressed his anger with Bishop Galen in private, he accepted that the time was not ripe for further confrontations with Catholicism.

There was one apparent exception to this policy. Goebbels had returned from his meeting with Hitler in August armed with full authority to intensify the campaign against the Jews. Undoubtedly the acquiescence in, or indifference of the German people to the persecution of the Jews encouraged Hitler and Goebbels in their belief that this was the time to realize their anti-Semitic dreams. As soon as he got back from Rastenburg on 19 August, Goebbels ordered his State Secretary Gutterer to implement the decision to make Jews wear a sign 'as a preparation for all further measures'.[46] On 5 September 1941 all German Jews over six years old were required to wear a yellow star on their clothing if they went out in public, and, shortly after this across the *Reich* a systematic programme of deportations 'to the East' was started. The SD reported that the enforced wearing of the yellow star had been 'welcomed by the overwhelming part of the population and received with satisfaction'.[47] There is considerable anecdotal evidence that many Germans were deeply shocked by the imposition of the yellow star, but the deportations of Jews from German cities which followed this were not hindered by significant protests or adverse popular reaction.[48]

Few areas of modern history have been so intensively researched and debated as the 'fateful months' in the autumn of 1941 in which Hitler made the decision to proceed with the mass murder of all the Jews of Europe. There is now a consensus amongst serious historians that, whereas in late August, Hitler was still delaying the deportation of Jews from Berlin and Germany 'to the East', he had by 17 September changed his mind and ordered an immediate programme of deportations. The deportations from Germany began in October 1941, and at the same time all Jewish emigration from Europe was forbidden. The first experiments with the use of different poisonous gases to kill large groups of Jews were initiated, and the construction of extermination camps was begun at Chełmno in the Wartheland, and at Bełżec in the 'General Government'. These appallingly sinister developments have been linked with the favourable turn in German military fortunes in Russia in September and early October, and with pressures on Hitler from other officials around Germany and occupied Europe.[49]

Goebbels was undoubtedly one of the most influential – if not the most influential – of these officials. As *Gauleiter* of Berlin he exercised particular pressure on Hitler to deport the Jews of the German capital city. In frequent, regular, and long conversations with Hitler he had discussed the extermination of 'that which we have fought against for our whole lives' before the attack on the Soviet Union, even though it was not then clear exactly when or how this would be done. On 18 August Hitler had assured Goebbels that his prophecy that the Jews would be exterminated was being borne out, and Goebbels had urged him to see this through. On 23 September Goebbels again visited the Wolf's Lair, along with Himmler and Heydrich, and discussed in detail the intensifying persecution. News of huge victories from the front had just arrived. Goebbels discussed the deportation of the Berlin Jews with Heydrich before meeting privately with Hitler, and made this record: 'The *Führer* is of the opinion that the Jews must be brought out of all of Germany step by step. The first cities which should be made free of Jews are Berlin, Vienna, and Prague. Berlin will be first in line, and I have the hope that it will even be possible for us to transport a significant part of Berlin's Jews to the East in the course of this year.'[50]

Goebbels knew in considerable detail about the larger context in which the deportation of German Jews took place. On 11 August 1941 he noted that in the Baltic States there had been 'mass' killings of the Jews in the streets. On 5 September he reported that 'in large areas, above all in Bessarabia', there were shootings of Jews. On 19 October he recorded that there had been 'enormous shootings of Jews in Ukraine'.[51] Goebbels heard these reports from people returning from the Eastern Front, but in early November he visited the ghetto in Vilna, where, he wrote, thousands of Jews had already been shot. Those remaining, he concluded, must be 'rooted out'.[52] He knew that the Jews of Germany being deported to ghettoes in 'the East' faced almost certain death from starvation, disease, or deliberate murder. The first train carrying Jews from Berlin left for Łódź on 18 October 1941, and was followed by others on 24 October, 27 October, and 1 November. Six further 'transports' took Berlin Jews to Minsk, Kaunas, and Riga before the end of January 1942. The Jews arriving in Riga on 30 November were shot immediately, as were some of those arriving in Kaunas.[53]

Goebbels, as he had with the boycott of Jewish shops in April 1933 and with the pogrom of November 1938, wanted to involve the whole German population

38. From May 1940 a leader written by Goebbels appeared every week on the right-hand side of the front page of the mass-circulation Sunday newspaper *Das Reich*. In this notorious leader, 'The Jews are guilty!', Goebbels announced plainly that Hitler's earlier 'prophecy' that the war would result in the 'extermination of the Jewish people in Europe' was being fulfilled.

in these measures. In an extraordinarily frank statement, he wrote a front-page article for *Das Reich* on 16 November 1941, returning to the title 'The Jews are guilty!' which he had first used in 1932. After reminding readers of Hitler's 1939 prophecy that if there was war the Jews of Europe would be exterminated, Goebbels stated: 'We are experiencing precisely the execution of this prophecy, and thus a destiny is being fulfilled for Jewry which is indeed hard, but more than deserved.' Lest any of his readers misunderstand him, Goebbels reiterated: 'In the initiation of this war, world Jewry has completely misjudged the forces it has available, and it is now suffering a gradual process of extermination which it had intended for us.'[54] *Das Reich* had at this time a circulation of nearly 1 million copies; the article was also read out on national radio the following Friday evening. The day after the publication of this article, Goebbels again discussed the deportation of the Jews from the *Reich* with Heydrich.

Goebbels was clearly convinced that anti-Jewish policy needed to be communicated to the public in uncompromising, if cryptic terms. On 1 December 1941 he spoke to representatives of the German intelligentsia at a solemn assembly of the German Academy in Berlin. Diplomats, journalists, civil servants, officers, artists, scientists, and other 'very select' members of 'public circles' were present, and Goebbels decided to make what he called 'an absolutely factual presentation of the situation, in order at the least to make these circles more firmly tied to the state, and to give them greater belief in the war than was previously the case'. The German Academy's published account of this 'factual presentation' included this statement:

> Dr Goebbels particularly stressed the fact that the final solution of the Jewish question would constitute a decisive factor.[55]

One wonders, given Goebbels' previous public pronunciations, and the prevalence of rumours in Germany about mass killings in the East, what the learned members of the audience thought Goebbels was talking about, or whether they subsequently asked one another precisely what he had meant by the 'final solution of the Jewish question'.

After 1945, many Germans claimed that they had not known of the mass murder of the Jews, and some historians investigating this have paid little attention to Goebbels' very public statements about this.[56] It is instructive to look at the contemporary record of some who were most closely affected by the identification and deportation of the Jews in Germany and around Europe. In Romania, the Jewish writer Mihail Sebastian had recorded in September 1941 how he felt 'poisoned' by having to wear a 'six-pointed star' in public, and made a special note in November of Goebbels' article 'The Jews are guilty!' Sebastian linked these developments clearly with the recent 'deportation and killings'.[57] Jochen Klepper in Berlin, desperately concerned about the threat hanging over his Jewish wife and stepdaughter, similarly read what he called 'Goebbels' gruesome article', and on 20 November had a conversation with an officer from his former army unit. This officer told Klepper that 'after the big Goebbels article in *Das Reich* one could indeed expect nothing other than the extermination of the Jews'. Klepper's former comrade pointed to the way that Goebbels in the article had identified even old Jewish women and Jewish babies as carriers of guilt for the death of every German soldier as an indication of how literally this should be understood. A few days earlier, speculating on the fate of those now being deported, Klepper wrote that they could expect forced labour, starvation, and freezing cold, and that many would be shot. Like many others around Germany, Klepper and his family were contemplating suicide as a preferable alternative to this.[58]

If Goebbels recognized the significance of these issues for public opinion, he was also fully aware of the deep yearning of the German people for peace, and their hope that the war would be ended before Christmas. He saw clearly the danger of arousing unreal expectations with premature announcements of victory, and argued that it was best to keep as close to the truth as possible, pressing Hitler, for example, to announce German casualty figures in the Soviet Union to the public. Reading the SD opinion reports, he perceived a tendency for Germans to oscillate between wild optimism and groundless pessimism, and saw it as his task to try to moderate between these extremes. He was desperately aware of the oncoming Russian winter, and could see that the *Wehrmacht* was slowing down in front of Moscow. On 28 October, the first snow had fallen in Berlin, as Goebbels visited the grave of Horst Wessel with a group of old Berlin Party men, provoking him to think what the soldiers on the Eastern Front had to endure.[59] He had a salutary experience when he was invited to the front line in November: his aircraft was unable to land in Smolensk because of fog, and he found himself grounded in Vilna for two days by the weather. He was horrified by the vast extent of the Russian plain and the difficulties facing any kind of transport in the winter. Visiting the ghetto in Vilna during his enforced stay only confirmed his vision of Jewish primitiveness, and he felt sorry for the German troops out there. He was glad finally to escape from 'this godforsaken hole' and get back to Berlin, which he found covered in snow.[60]

Although now clear in his own mind that the war would not be won before the winter, Goebbels was still unaware of the impending catastrophe. Even though he spoke with a staff officer from General Guderian's army on 14 November, he did not note in his 'military situation' reports the arrival of fresh Soviet troops from Siberia opposite Guderian's forces near Moscow on 17 November, or that, faced with these reinforcements and T-34 tanks, some of Guderian's men had retreated in 'a panic'.[61] As, after this, German forces crept forward in the snow, still urged on by Hitler, Goebbels found it impossible to concentrate on everyday affairs. On 4 December he had to travel to Vienna for the 150th anniversary of Mozart's death, and was racked by the tension between the festivities and alarming reports from the front. In his speech at the State Opera, Goebbels declared that Mozart's music was one of the things which 'our soldiers were defending from the wild onslaught of eastern barbarism'.[62] He had to undergo a 'spiritual martyrdom', conversing all evening with Richard Strauss' 'awful' wife,[63] at the very moment when the Soviets turned to the offensive on the central front outside Moscow.

The next afternoon, still unaware of the extent of the crisis, Goebbels heard the Mozart *Requiem* for the first time, listening to Furtwängler rehearsing the Vienna Philharmonic and the Opera Choir. It was, he wrote: 'A unique musical experience. The effect is immense.' He nonetheless forbade a broadcast of the performance: 'Right now we need funeral music which is heroic, but not Christian or certainly not Catholic.'[64] Over the next few weeks Goebbels learnt more of the precarious situation outside Moscow, where a rout of Napoleonic proportions was only narrowly averted. He had to manage the presentation of the crisis to the public, including the news of Hitler's assumption of direct command of the *Wehrmacht*, and the dismissal of its most senior figures on the Eastern Front. We know now that this was a decisive moment in the Second World War, when the possibility of an outright military victory slipped forever beyond Hitler's grasp, but it was strangely overshadowed for almost everyone at any distance from the actual fighting by the Japanese attack on Pearl Harbor on 7 December.

The months before Pearl Harbor had been incredibly difficult for Goebbels. He had indeed been staring into the abyss, conscious that failure to break the Soviet Union would ultimately be fatal for the 'Third Reich'. He had been anxious the previous autumn when Britain refused to give way, but at that time it was not really conceivable that Britain alone could present much of a threat to Germany. Now the spectre of a two-front war loomed large, and Goebbels faced the difficulty of presenting this to the German people. He was horribly aware that the whole notion of a short 'preventive war' against the Soviet Union had disappeared, and was slowly being replaced, at best, with a longer war of attrition, and at worst, with the prospect of military defeat. It is striking how Goebbels worried, particularly in the early years of the war, about the morale of the German people if they were faced with a long war. Each year he fretted about the difficulties posed by another 'war winter', an idea which took on new psychological dimensions with the German army bogged down in Russia. Behind all these worries was the recognition that everything he had worked for, and achieved, was now threatened. Goebbels knew that if Germany lost the war there would be no comfortable retirement for someone like him; he and Hitler had long since steeped themselves in blood.

It was thus a huge relief to hear that the Japanese had attacked the American fleet at Pearl Harbor. Goebbels described the outbreak of war between Japan and America as 'an extraordinarily favourable change for us', and used the dramatic developments in the Pacific to bury the bad news that all offensive operations in the East had been cancelled.[65] Expecting that Japan would also declare war on the Soviet Union, Goebbels and Hitler thought nothing of declaring war on the USA in anticipation. Hitler returned to Berlin to announce this to the *Reichstag* on 11 December. If the SD opinion surveys are to be believed, this further extension of the war was also received favourably by the German public. 'Solely in peasant circles' was concern expressed about the further extension of the conflict. The rest of the population apparently believed – as Goebbels certainly did – that for all practical purposes the two countries were already at war.[66] Goebbels also believed, correctly, that America posed no immediate military threat to Germany, but mistakenly underestimated the potential of the American armaments industry. Over the next few weeks, as the Soviets pressed their attacks outside Moscow, Goebbels allowed his amazement at the success of what he called 'the Prussians of the Orient' in the Pacific,[67] and his pleasure in the setbacks of Britain and the USA to compensate for his increasing knowledge of the gravity of the situation of the *Wehrmacht* in the Soviet Union.

Over the next few months Goebbels spoke at regular intervals with Hitler, and heard him address select groups like the Party *Gauleiter*. On every occasion he was swayed by Hitler's oratory, and accepted apparently without question his vision of the future: Germany would regroup in the spring, and a renewed offensive would finish off the Soviet Union. The expanses of the East would be colonized by Germanic settlers, and the line of the Urals would be defended in an endless war which would not threaten Germany, but provide a useful training ground for young men. We can only speculate on what Goebbels really thought of this idea – so different from that of the short, preventive war he and Hitler had planned only a few months previously. It clearly appealed to Hitler's military mind, and to his philosophy of 'struggle', but Goebbels still allowed himself privately, with increasing rarity, to dream of 'peace'. He was too far committed now to Hitler to question his vision. The 'New Order' in Europe, Hitler assured Goebbels, was too strong to be seriously threatened by the British or the Americans, weakened by Japanese successes in the Pacific. In his diary, Goebbels lamented the collapse of the 'white empires' in the Far East, but felt it was nothing less than the corrupt plutocracies had invited.

Imagining themselves secure from outside attacks, Hitler and Goebbels determined to continue the extermination of the Jews of Europe. On 13 December 1941, Goebbels reported Hitler's unambiguous declaration to the assembled *Gauleiter* at a meeting in Berlin:

With regard to the Jewish question, the *Führer* is resolved to make a clean sweep. He prophesied to the Jews that if they once again brought about a world war, they would thereby experience their extermination. That was no phrase. The world war is there, the extermination of the Jews must be the necessary consequence ... If the German people have now sacrificed a further 160,000 dead in the campaign in the East, so the originators of this bloody conflict must pay for it with their lives.[68]

Speaking to a meeting of armaments workers, nurses, and wounded soldiers in the *Sportpalast* on 30 January 1942, Hitler was equally clear, declaring that 'the outcome of the war will be the extermination of the Jews'.[69] On 20 January 1942, a meeting originally scheduled for 9 December 1941 was convened by Heydrich at a villa on the Wannsee, and here the process euphemized as the 'Final Solution' was mapped out. Goebbels again used this term when he reported reading a 'memorandum' on the meeting.[70] On 27 March he dictated in his diary a passage which has often been quoted:

> Starting with Lublin, the Jews are now being deported from the General Government to the East. The procedure used is quite barbaric and is not to be described in any further detail. Not much remains of the Jews themselves any more.

With discernible horror, Goebbels continued:

> The prophecy which the *Führer* pronounced on them if they brought about a new world war is beginning to be realized here in the most terrible way.

After reflecting how the war had opened up a 'whole range of possibilities which were not open to us in peacetime', Goebbels continued:

> The ghettos of the General Government which are now being freed up will now be filled with Jews deported from the *Reich*, and, after a certain time, the same process will take place again.[71]

Goebbels was clearly referring here to 'Operation Reinhard', the extermination of the Polish Jews. The reticence in his diary on this occasion is in marked contrast to his previous frankness in referring to 'mass shootings', and there is no doubt that he was referring here quite specifically to the gassing of the Jews, which had begun only a few days earlier in the Bełżec extermination camp near Lublin.[72] Given the secrecy around 'Operation Reinhard', Goebbels was presumably told about this by Himmler, Heydrich, or Hitler. In numerous public announcements in 1942, Nazi leaders and Nazi publications continued to announce the 'extermination of the Jews', but not the detailed manner in which this was being implemented.

Goebbels regularly discussed with Hitler and with others the murder of Jews from all over Europe. He noted in May 1942 his horror about the influence of Jews in France, and his relief that they 'must pay for their crimes'.[73] He was obsessed by the continued presence of some 40,000 Jews in Berlin, and frustrated that he could not get them deported as many of them were now working in the armaments industry. Despite the fact that most of those remaining were elderly people he was convinced that they were a source of potential and actual resistance to the Nazi regime and its prosecution of the war. When an anti-Soviet exhibition in Berlin was damaged by an arson attack, he seized upon the arrest of a number of Jews as proof of this: 'One sees in this connection how correct our Jewish policy is, and how necessary it appears to pursue the old course as radically as possible.' The 40,000 Jews left in Berlin were, he continued, 'in reality serious criminals let free, who have nothing more to lose'. They should be either 'concentrated or evacuated as quickly as possible. The best thing would obviously be liquidation.'[74]

Winston Churchill, reviewing the now global war situation before the House of Commons shortly after the Japanese attack on Pearl Harbor, had referred to the 'sombre panorama of the world',[75] but he did not know in anything like the detail Goebbels did of some of the most terrible cruelties being perpetrated under the fog of war in Europe. With his access to German and foreign news media, and to the highest levels of all Nazi agencies, Goebbels was fully aware of the developing toll the war was taking on soldiers and civilians across the continent. Unlike Hitler, who did not visit bombed cities, or the wounded in hospitals, let alone see the victims of his ideology in concentration camps, Goebbels liked to see things with his own eyes. From early in the campaign against the Soviet Union he had recorded his knowledge that most of the Soviet prisoners of war would be left to starve, as would the populations of major cities in the Soviet Union. In the harsh winter of 1941–42 he noted the belated decision to try to save as many Soviet POWs as possible as a source of labour, but recognized also that this change of course came when most – he estimated 900,000 – had already died, or would soon die from starvation.[76] Back in August 1941, Goebbels had spent several hours visiting a 'camp' for Soviet POWs near Riesa in Saxony, and recorded his impressions:

> The prisoner of war camp presents a gruesome spectacle. Some of the Bolsheviks have to sleep on the bare earth. It is pouring with rain. Some of them have no roof over their heads; insofar as they have, these are sheds with no sides. In short, the picture is not at all good. The types are not all as bad as I had imagined. One finds amongst the Bolsheviks many fresh, good-natured peasant lads.[77]

How is Goebbels' acceptance of Nazi cruelty and barbarism to be understood? How was this product of a pious Catholic family and a humanist education reconciled to so much cruelty? Several factors should be considered. First, Goebbels measured the suffering of all other peoples against that of Germans on the Eastern Front, and under attack from British bombers. He regularly recorded precise casualty figures, and knew by early 1942 that there had been over 1 million Germans killed and wounded on the Eastern Front. He spoke with officers and soldiers who had been at the front, and he received many letters – often anonymously written – which told him of the terrible conditions there. On Christmas Eve 1941 he visited wounded soldiers at a Berlin hospital.[78] He was shocked in January 1942 at Hitler's headquarters in Rastenburg to hear that frostbitten German soldiers had to be transported back from the front in open freight wagons.[79] Every day he recorded the numbers of dead and wounded – at this stage still relatively small – in British bombing attacks. He organized and attended the state funerals of colleagues like Ernst Udet and Fritz Todt.[80] He had by this time convinced himself that Germany was fighting a defensive war, one forced upon it by the Jews, by the British, the Americans, and the Bolsheviks.

Goebbels had also, at least since June 1934, accepted that there was no way back from the course of violence he had advocated and pursued. Hitler, speaking to his *Gauleiter* in December 1941, had stressed that they had to win the war 'because otherwise we as individuals and as a nation would be liquidated'. Significantly, Goebbels himself repeated more or less the same formula in a New Year article published only weeks later on 4 January 1942: 'We know that we are fighting for our national life, and in most cases also for our individual lives.'[81] Goebbels, trapped by knowledge of crimes already committed, and of others in commission, saw no alternative in 1942 but to prosecute the war ever more brutally. He fretted not only about perceived enemies like the Jews, but also about those Germans whose commitment to the war effort was less than complete. He was outraged by the behaviour of wealthy women who had apparently nothing better to do than sit in cafés smoking when there was a tobacco shortage, and took up seats on the trains going on holiday, when soldiers returning from the front had to stand in the corridors. He did not extend this criticism to Magda, who was a heavy smoker, and spent much time 'convalescing' at a spa in Dresden.

He was similarly aware of the developing problem of resistance in the extensive occupied territories, but failed to link this with the self-defeating policy of ever harsher repression which he advocated. He anxiously noted the growing number of attacks on German officers and soldiers all over Europe, and the huge problem of 'partisan bands' operating behind the lines in the East. He was outraged and saddened by the assassination of Heydrich in Prague in May 1942, blaming it on the Jews and the British secret service. Goebbels had collaborated closely with Heydrich in the implementation of the 'Final Solution', and valued his dedication and competence, seeing his brutal rule in the 'Protectorate' as exemplary. Goebbels ordered the arrest and execution of many Jews in Berlin after the attack on Heydrich, writing: 'the more of this filth that can be disposed of, the better for the security of the *Reich*'.[82] He agreed fully with Hitler's decision 'to make an example' of Lidice as a reprisal: 'the male population of this village will be shot, the women taken to concentration camps and the children to educational institutions, and the village then burnt and levelled to the ground'. He accepted that the British would make propaganda capital from this, but still felt it was necessary 'for the life interest of the German *Reich* and the German *Volk*'.[83] Speaking with Hitler when he came to Berlin for Heydrich's funeral, Goebbels agreed that they were in 'a life and death struggle ... We have nothing to lose'. Hitler also expressed his sorrow that virtually the only time the Party leadership now gathered together was for state funerals.[84]

The winter crisis took a severe toll on Goebbels' morale and physical health. The cold weather extended into March 1942, and across Germany there were severe shortages of food, coal, and tobacco. All contemporary observers commented on the poor quality of everyday items like clothing, and even paper. Even though Goebbels wanted to share Hitler's belief that the planned summer offensive would finish off 'the Bolsheviks', he was obsessed, like Hitler, with worries about the next winter. On 19 April he gave a speech in the Philharmonic Hall in Berlin to a large meeting gathered to celebrate Hitler's 53rd birthday – Hitler himself stayed in Rastenburg – and he spoke at length about the hardships of the previous winter, and how Hitler alone had carried the weight of the nation's destiny on his shoulders. The Italian Foreign Minister Ciano heard a broadcast of this 'strange speech', and recorded that Goebbels 'reaffirmed his faith in final victory in rather gloomy terms'. Hitler did come to Berlin briefly to speak to the *Reichstag* on 26 April, and Ciano noted how he dwelt on his preparations 'to face another winter'.[85] Evidently many German listeners to the speech were also struck by this, as was Goebbels himself.[86]

Through the early months of 1942 Goebbels waited anxiously for better weather, and for the resumption of offensive operations. Although he did have constant concerns, the gradual improvement of the military situation on the Eastern Front, and the succession of extraordinary Japanese victories in the Far East gave him grounds for optimism. He was worried by the British aerial attacks on Lübeck and Rostock in March, and by the first 'thousand bomber raid' on Cologne on 31 May, but he judged, correctly, that the British were not able to sustain attacks on this scale. He followed the news reports of the distant naval battles in the Coral Sea and near Midway Island in June, but did not appreciate their significance. As the days lengthened he was heartened by Rommel's dramatic victories in North Africa, by the capture of Sevastopol in the Crimea, and by the successes of German U-boats. These he trumpeted in a series of 'special announcements' on the radio. He thought the British Empire was on the verge of collapse, and in June he rejoiced in reports of panic in Alexandria as Rommel's forces came close to the city.[87]

Goebbels and Hitler even found time to discuss cultural developments in Germany. Goebbels was delighted by the box-office success of the films he was sponsoring, like *Der große König*, a re-creation of the life of Frederick the Great, and by the number of books being produced in Germany. Hitler reported in June 1942 his assessment of new magnetic tape recordings Goebbels had sent him of Germany's leading orchestras. They agreed that the Berlin Philharmonic was better than Vienna Philharmonic, judging that this was because the Berlin string players were younger.[88] 'Never', Goebbels dictated a few days later, had 'German cultural life bloomed as now in the third year of the war'. This, he was sure, was 'one of the most pleasing signs of the inner stance of the German nation'.[89] On 23 June Goebbels had a long and relaxing conversation with Hitler, Bormann and Ley: 'What glorious weather! We sit in the garden the whole afternoon, and one has the impression of the most profound peace. The *Führer* is in a wonderful mood, and, God be thanked, he is at the moment in the best physical health.' Later that evening, Goebbels took a moment's rest alone 'on the terrace, in the moonlight'. He reflected: 'How wonderful it would be, if the war would end! But that is for the time being only a pious wish. It will not be fulfilled by yearning, but only through work and struggle.'[90] Goebbels presided over the opening of the German Art Exhibition on 4 July, and took the opportunity in Munich to see the grandiose plans being developed for the rebuilding of several German cities. He also visited a Nazi Party school in nearby Feldafing, and decided that he would like to send his son Helmut there when he was old enough.[91]

Another reason for Goebbels' good mood in these summer days was the success of the renewed German offensive in the southern Soviet Union. In July and August 1942 huge German forces advanced, much of the time against little opposition, towards the oil fields of the Caucasus. Goebbels rejoiced in the news of territorial gains, and in depicting victories in the weekly newsreels. The announcement that mountain troops had hoisted the *Reich* war flag on the summit of Mount Elbrus, the highest peak in the Caucasus, was a propaganda coup which helped to raise public expectations that the end of the war was in sight.[92] Hitler had divided ambitions, and hoped to secure not only the oil wells of the Caucasus, but to reach the Volga considerably further to the north, and to prevent its use for river traffic. Goebbels too had succumbed to what Alan Clark described as 'the strange magnetism' of the industrial city named after Stalin on the Volga.[93] On 8 August 1942 Goebbels dictated: 'The battle for Stalingrad has begun.'[94]

From the first, Goebbels understood the significance of Stalingrad, and knew that the Soviets would defend it as far as possible. He was convinced that its capture and destruction would deal more than a merely symbolic blow to the Soviet Union's hopes of continuing the war. As the 6th Army fought through Stalingrad's industrial landscape, and more and more of the German offensive effort was drawn into the struggle there, Goebbels came to see this as more than a battle for one city. It was a continuation and a culmination of the struggle which he had led in Berlin before 1933: 'the conflicts between SA and Red Front, which started back then in the dark streets of the metropolis, have now taken on world wide forms'.[95] As the battle for Stalingrad dragged into the autumn, Goebbels worried about the over-optimism of the German public. On 23 August he instructed the German press that 'the city of Stalingrad was not to be mentioned' before 'decisive events' there had been reported by the Army High Command; in mid-September he forbade the printing of any predictions of an early capture of the city.[96] Although Goebbels had no pretensions as a military strategist, he privately noted in September the vulnerability of the exposed Don front north of Stalingrad, held largely by Romanian troops.[97] Although certain that Stalingrad would eventually be captured, he had also realized by this time that the war would not be ended before the winter. On 20 September his leader in *Das Reich* was entitled 'The steep climb', and in it he warned his readers that it was not possible to give a definitive answer to the question of how long the war would continue. Attempting to take a longer view of the course of the war and its future development, Goebbels argued that time was on Germany's side, and wrote: 'What should lead us to view the situation more favourably than it is? It gives us already every chance of victory. It will demand from us still many sacrifices and exertions.'[98]

Goebbels' fragile optimism was put to the test in November, when news gradually filtered through to him of the extent of the British victory at El Alamein in North Africa. Goebbels had an exaggeratedly high opinion of Rommel: he thought him a great strategist, and a genuine Nazi, with a talent for leadership and improvisation. While Rommel was back in Berlin in September 1942, he had stayed for several days at Goebbels' house, and the two men had got on very well. Goebbels had his own liaison man attached to the *Afrikakorps*, and he knew in some detail of the material deficiencies which had halted Rommel's advance into Egypt in August. He nonetheless imagined that Rommel was capable of almost superhuman feats, and was shocked when he heard news reports from Cairo on 5 November that the Axis forces in Egypt were in headlong retreat.[99] On 8 November, Goebbels was in Munich for the Party's annual commemoration of the 'martyrs' of November 1923 when he heard news of Anglo-American landings in French North Africa, news which spread like wildfire in Germany, despite the ban on listening to foreign radio.[100] Hitler arrived later that day, and over the next fortnight he and Goebbels devoted most of their attention to shoring up the rapidly collapsing situation in North Africa. German forces moved rapidly to occupy Vichy France, and to secure a bridgehead in Tunisia.

By the time Goebbels went on a previously planned visit to the Rhineland on 17 November, he felt that the worst danger had been averted. That afternoon he gave a speech in Elberfeld before a turbulent and enthusiastic audience. It was, he told them, 'a profound joy for him to be able to speak again for the first time in ten years in this city'. Speaking apparently without notes, Goebbels excitedly declared that this was 'a people's war, a holy war', for clearly defined goals, the agricultural and mineral resources of Ukraine and the Caucasus. There could be no 'lazy compromise': this was 'a confrontation between two world principles, which cannot live alongside one another, and therefore one must triumph and exterminate the other'. Goebbels portrayed recent developments in North Africa as temporary setbacks, and likened the current situation to that before the Nazi seizure of power: The 'Jewish newspapers in Berlin on 29 January 1933' had called Hitler 'a great man of yesterday', but '24 hours later the Jews were sitting in night trains to Berne and Basel'. Now, the Jews were threatening 'to deport German children or to enforce a super-Versailles upon us'. In a clear reference to the ongoing deportations he stated: 'I believe that the Jews who earlier threatened us with this have for the most part meanwhile themselves suffered this fate.' He ended by quoting Nietzsche: 'Praise be to that which makes us hard!'[101]

After the speech, Goebbels made the short journey to Rheydt, where he stayed in the local Party headquarters, in a renovated castle. The next afternoon he attended a special performance in Rheydt of the Berlin Schiller Theatre, and dreamt of establishing a theatre school in his home town. He was pleased that his speech in Elberfeld was receiving considerable attention abroad, dictating that 'It came at a point when clear words were necessary.' The next day, Goebbels made this note in his military situation report:

Yesterday: ... stronger enemy attacks were turned back by the Romanians on the Don front. Stronger attacks have also followed early today after stronger artillery preparation. One presumes that this is the start of a long-awaited offensive; this presumption is not however yet confirmed.[102]

11
'We Have Done the Right Thing'

Recent weeks have brought the most severe crisis of this war experienced thus far, really the first genuine crisis, unfortunately not only a crisis for the leadership and the system, but also for Germany. It is symbolized by the name of Stalingrad.

From the diary of Ulrich von Hassell, 14 February 1943.[1]

Three days after the attack on the Romanian positions on the Don, Soviet forces completed the encirclement of nearly 250,000 German soldiers in Stalingrad. All efforts at relief failed, and the last remnants of this force surrendered on 2 February 1943. In the meantime the whole German position in the Caucasus collapsed, and the armies which had advanced into the mountains and towards the oil fields there were forced into a desperate retreat, abandoning huge quantities of material. This was a military defeat unprecedented in German history. At the same time Rommel's *Afrikakorps* was compelled to abandon Tripoli and to take up defensive positions in Tunisia. On 27 January the first American daylight bombing raid was made on Germany, and night after night German cities were targeted by British bombers. These military disasters were accompanied by significant diplomatic moves. On 17 December 1942 a Joint Allied Declaration was released in London, Washington, and Moscow. The British Foreign Secretary Anthony Eden read the text to the House of Commons, including this statement:

The German authorities ... are now carrying into effect Hitler's oft repeated intention to exterminate the Jewish people in Europe. From all the occupied countries Jews are being transported, in conditions of appalling horror and brutality, to Eastern Europe ... The above-mentioned Governments and the French National Committee condemn in the strongest possible terms this bestial policy of cold-blooded extermination.

Significantly for Goebbels, Eden continued:

They reaffirm their solemn resolution to ensure that those responsible for these crimes shall not escape retribution, and to press on with the necessary practical measures to this end.[2]

In January 1943 Churchill and Roosevelt met in Casablanca and announced their intention to compel Germany to an unconditional surrender.[3]

Goebbels was at the centre of the unfolding crisis in Germany. Although he tried to conceal news of the encirclement at Stalingrad from the German people, he was as ever well-informed of developments there, and knew from the start of 1943 that the army trapped there was lost. He understood the difficulties involved in trying to supply the force in Tunisia, and heard rational voices calling for a total withdrawal from North Africa. Reports from the occupied territories and from neutral countries spoke of a rising tide of anti-German feeling. He recognized the gravity of the changed military situation, and the difficulties of representing this to an increasingly weary and sceptical German population. He responded with characteristic energy, and placed his hopes in a demand for 'total war'. Not until 16 January did the German army's regular communiqué allude to the encirclement of the force in Stalingrad; and it was only on 27 January that Goebbels gave instructions to the German press on how to prepare the public for the news that the fight there was coming to an end.[4] On 30 January 1943, he had the difficult job of facing the German public on the ten-year anniversary of the *Machtergreifung*, the Nazi 'seizure of power'. Hitler, characteristically, refused to come to Berlin, and instead drafted a 'proclamation' which he asked Goebbels to read out at a mass meeting in the *Sportpalast*. The meeting was postponed for an hour at the last moment to minimize the possibility of disruption by British aircraft, but Goebbels rose to the occasion, delivering a rousing speech before reading Hitler's more tedious proclamation. It was clearly an emotional occasion, and all present obviously recognized that Germany stood at a momentous point in its history. Himmler, Rosenberg, and Ley were among other senior figures present. Goebbels' speech was frequently interrupted by supportive calls from his audience, and he found himself in the middle of 'an ocean of enthusiasm'. It recalled, he thought, 'the best times from the *Kampfzeit*'. During the delivery of Hitler's proclamation, the air-raid sirens sounded, and anti-aircraft guns could be clearly heard outside, but Goebbels steeled himself to continue as if nothing had happened. 'Nobody', he recorded, 'got up from his place or showed the slightest sign of unease or nervousness.' That evening, Hitler telephoned from Rastenburg to congratulate Goebbels, and also spent some time talking to Magda.[5]

Over the next few days, the news of the surrender of all remaining pockets of German resistance in Stalingrad, together with their commanding officer, von Paulus, and 24 of his generals, filtered through. Goebbels shared Hitler's dismay that Paulus had chosen to surrender rather than to commit suicide, but now had to present this unprecedented catastrophe to the German public. Goebbels, no stranger to the funeral ceremony, had decided that a 'national-political lesson' had to be learnt from Stalingrad; the 'special announcement' on the radio would be 'very realistic, very sober, and completely without pathos'; all light music would be suspended for three days. 'The *Volk*', Goebbels dictated, 'wants not light entertainment, but seriousness and objectivity.' All theatres, cinemas, and dance halls were also closed for the three days of national mourning. At 4.00 p.m. on 3 February, the 'special announcement' was broadcast. A communiqué from the *Wehrmacht* announced: 'The fight in Stalingrad has ended.'[6] Even Goebbels' critics conceded that he rose to this occasion. Mihail Sebastian in Bucharest recorded that 'the whole press has a solemn, majestic tone, as in a funeral hymn. A kind of tragic grandeur, probably by directive, conceals the questions and doubts concerning political and military affairs.'[7]

Well before the final capitulation in Stalingrad, Goebbels had decided that only an acceptance of what he called 'total war' could now deliver a German victory; the alternative was the extermination of the German people. He determined to use the crisis as an opportunity to get Hitler's support for this vision, convinced that he had broad public support. Goebbels has also been portrayed at this time as a 'conspirator', seeking to challenge the leadership structures around Hitler, and to use the crisis to enhance his personal authority and to bring more rationality and focus to Germany's war effort. The architect of this idea is Albert Speer, who was Goebbels' closest ally in the drive for 'total war'. In his post-war memoirs Speer wrote:

> All of Goebbels' speeches sounded the note of stereotyped fanaticism, but it would be quite wrong to think of him as a hot-blooded man seething with temperament. Goebbels was a hard worker and something of a martinet about the way his ideas were carried out. But he never let the minutiae make him lose sight of the whole situation. He had the gift of abstracting problems from their surrounding circumstances so that, as it seemed to me then, he could arrive at objective judgements. I was impressed by his cynicism, but also by the logical arrangement of his ideas, which revealed his university training … In December 1942 the disastrous course of affairs prompted him to invite three of his colleagues to call on him more often: Walther Funk, Robert Ley, and myself.

In a subsequent passage Speer added: 'I was fascinated by his dazzling friendliness and perfect manners, as well as by his cool logic.'[8] In later interviews, Speer claims that Goebbels said to him in February 1943: 'What we have is not a leadership but a *leader* crisis.'[9] The narrative first put forward by Speer, and developed by others since, portrays Goebbels at this time as the clear headed realist who wanted to revitalize Hitler's leadership by setting up a committee, nominally headed by Göring, but including himself, Speer and Ley, which could wrest affairs from Hitler's sole grasp, and from the supine hands of the sycophants around him, notably Bormann, Lammers, and Keitel.[10] There is some truth in this, but other aspects need to be challenged.

39. After the defeat at Stalingrad, Albert Speer and Robert Ley became Goebbels' closest supporters in the campaign for 'total war'. Here Speer and Ley appear alongside Goebbels at a meeting of Knight's Cross holders in Berlin in 1943.

First, although frustrated by aspects of Hitler's conduct, Goebbels had no thought of challenging him, or of replacing him by any individual or committee. He had long privately criticized Hitler's isolation at his headquarters, and his unwillingness to speak to the German people, or even to be represented in the newsreels. He deplored his absence from Berlin, and what he described as the consequent lack of a 'central political leadership' there.[11] He was aware that Hitler devoted almost all of his time to military rather than civilian matters; and he was incensed by the overlapping bureaucracies which had proliferated in wartime Germany. He believed that Hitler had been misled by his military advisers. He did not see, as some of the rebels in the officer corps now did, that the problem lay with Hitler himself. Goebbels did not criticize Hitler's strategic ideas on the conduct of the war, and he shared his obsessive and totally muddled view that Germany was fighting a Jewish world conspiracy, which manipulated the different political systems in Britain, America, and the Soviet Union, and still presented a threat in Berlin itself.

Second, although it suited Speer to claim that Goebbels was logical and clear-headed, this will not stand up to analysis. Goebbels was in a highly emotional state by this time. His portrayal of the pitiful German soldiers trapped underground in Stalingrad as heroic idealists standing against the Bolshevik hordes who threatened to debauch from the steppes and to destroy European culture was more than a propaganda pose. Goebbels genuinely felt for the plight of these men, just as he had for their forbears, the SA men who had died in clashes with Communists before 1933. Nor did Goebbels have any rational alternative to Hitler's plan to continue the war until victory or extermination. His plan for 'total war', which, alongside nebulous *völkisch* ideas, did have practical ingredients like the extension of work for German women, the enlistment of men from civilian occupations, and the closing of bars, restaurants, and other civilian establishments considered superfluous to the war effort, was not new. Goebbels had been using the phrase 'total war' since 1939, and had long advocated a much more radical mobilization of German potential. His vision of 'total war' drew heavily on the book with this title published in 1935 by Ludendorff, which had presented a vision of war based on the 'spiritual unity of the *Volk*'. This unity, Ludendorff argued, was based on 'racial heritage and faith'.[12] It is widely recognized now that Goebbels' call for 'total war' in 1943 was largely unrealized, and that its significance was more psychological than practical. Indeed, every way Goebbels turned, he was frustrated: Hitler himself insisted that all theatres, opera houses, and cultural institutions stay open; Göring demanded that his own favourite restaurant, Horchers, be spared; every institution, like the huge German railway system, argued that it could not spare more men for the armed forces; even the *Gauleiter*, whom Goebbels idealized as Germany's best leaders, continued to go their separate ways, frequently continuing with individual building projects, cultural plans, or merely a dissipated lifestyle in direct contravention of Hitler and Goebbels' wishes.

Would it have made any great difference if Goebbels' vision of 'a radicalization and totalization of our war leadership' had been more fully implemented? He now recognized that there had been a fundamental underestimation of Soviet potential, and admitted frequently in his diary that their reserves of manpower and machines appeared inexhaustible. He admired the British for what he perceived as their innate tenacity, but still did not appreciate the destructive power of the bomber force being developed under the command of Arthur Harris. He was utterly scornful of the Americans, now coming into direct contact with German land forces for the first time in Tunisia. He accepted reports that the American units in Tunisia were made up mainly of criminals and jailbirds, who 'shied away from fighting and feared death'. He commented: 'So the British also have their Italians.'[13] As yet Goebbels had no realistic appreciation of American military potential. He veered between his long-held view that propaganda and the spoken word were the most powerful weapons, and a realistic appreciation that, in the mid-twentieth century, wars were determined by soldiers, weapons, and raw materials. When he did take this more realistic view, he turned increasingly to a belief in the potential of new weapons, like the Tiger tank now being produced, or, more improbably, the He.177 bomber.[14]

When he surveyed the psychological dimensions of the war, Goebbels veered similarly between realism and fantasy. He had long been aware of the disastrous consequences of German racial hubris in the occupied territories of the Soviet Union, where Rosenberg's leadership had resulted in economic collapse and the total alienation of the population. Goebbels saw clearly that more needed to be offered to these wretched people than an existence at subsistence level, subject to arbitrary violence and deportation. Similarly, Goebbels' propaganda devoted much time to publicizing the 'New Order' in Europe, but the images of contented and healthy workers in Nazi films and magazines could never compensate for the realities of forced labour, economic misery, and political subjugation. Goebbels never really confronted these problems, but as in Germany itself, resorted in practice only to an extension of terror. In February 1943, he developed plans for the SA in Berlin to act as an emergency force to put down any rebellion by the hundreds of thousands of foreign workers now quartered there.[15]

Finally, for those inclined to imagine Goebbels as having 'the clearest head and the cleverest mind'[16] in the Nazi leadership in early 1943, it is worthwhile to consider his understanding of what the war was about. Goebbels firmly believed that the war had been forced upon Germany by an international 'Jewish-Bolshevik-plutocratic' conspiracy. Just as in the 1920s he had detected Jewish influence behind any book or piece of music he disliked, now he saw the hand of the Jews at work in London, Washington, and Moscow. When the British House of Commons stood for a minute's silence in December 1942, after hearing the Joint Allied Declaration, to mark their respect for the persecuted Jews of Europe, Goebbels' response was: 'This Parliament is in reality a kind of Jewish stock-exchange. The English are really the Jews amongst the Aryans. The perfumed English Foreign Minister also cuts a good figure amongst these synagogue people. His whole education and also his whole appearance can be described as thoroughly Jewish.'[17] On the rare occasions Goebbels met with Hitler at Rastenburg during the winter crisis, they always found time to consider the particular threat posed by the pathetic and cowed remnant of Berlin's Jewish community. Part of Goebbels' vision of 'total war' was the continued deportation of these to the death camps in Poland.[18] Nor was this paranoid vision of Jewish conspiracy something private. In Goebbels' famous 'total war' speech at the *Sportpalast* on 18 February 1943, he turned – as ever – to this problem in a passage overlooked by most commentators: 'Jewry shows itself here once again as the incarnation of evil, the plastic demon of decay, and the carrier of an international, culture-destroying chaos ... Germany at any rate has no intention to submit to the Jewish threat, but rather that of counteracting it punctually, and when necessary with the most complete and radical extermination – elimination of Jewry.' It is not clear whether Goebbels' hesitation, and correction here, from the German *Ausrottung* (extermination) to *Ausschaltung* (elimination) was premeditated or spontaneous. His comments were greeted with applause, wild calls, and laughter.

Goebbels was particularly pleased that as well as Magda, his two oldest daughters Helga and Hilde were present at the meeting: 'I am happy that our children are already introduced to politics at such an early age.'[19]

Goebbels had devoted great care to the preparation of this most famous of all his speeches. Every detail, including words, gestures, timing, and the intended reaction of his audience was pre-meditated. The film of the occasion deliberately included the sober faces of wounded soldiers and ordinary workers as well as of key Nazi figures like Albert Speer and Robert Ley who were present. What the Nazis called 'speaking choirs' provided well-timed chants of slogans like 'German men, to the rifle, German women, to work!', and '*Führer* command, and we will follow!' The radio broadcast was prolonged for twenty minutes after the speech to project the agitated response of the listeners. The centre point of the speech was formed by ten questions which Goebbels put to his audience, all of which were answered by fervent cries of 'Yes!' These included the famous question 'Do you want total war?'[20] After the event, Goebbels entertained a group of Party workers at his house, and shocked Speer by his calm analysis of how effective his speech had been.[21] Nonetheless, listening to the sound recording today, there can be no doubt that the emotion Goebbels generated and manipulated was real; even 60 years later an extraordinary tension can be felt as he puts his questions to a seething and turbulent audience. He was justly pleased with the response.[22]

Although most historians have overlooked the anti-Semitic content of the 'total war' speech, others did not. Goebbels had ordered his propaganda departments around Germany to report back urgently to him on reaction to the speech, and in the preliminary response which reached him the next day, his 'handling of the Jewish question' was singled out for praise. From Bochum in the Ruhr it was reported that one district leadership of the Party had responded by demanding the 'immediate deportation' of Jews.[23] They were not disappointed. On 27 February an operation to deport Jews still employed in German industry began. Saul Friedländer notes that 'within a few days some 7,000 Jews were deported from the capital, and 10,948 from all over the Reich'.[24] The accelerated pace of persecution was clearly visible. One Berlin diarist wrote on 6 March: 'In these weeks many Jews have been evicted.'[25]

As Goebbels struggled to rebuild German morale at home, there was a gradual stabilization, and in March 1943, a remarkable recovery for German forces on the Eastern Front. Quite coincidentally Goebbels also received at this time what was potentially one of the most important propaganda opportunities of the war, the news in early April that German forces, alerted by locals, had uncovered the bodies of thousands of Polish officers in mass graves in the Katyn Forest, near Smolensk. Forensic evidence and witness testimony quickly established that the Poles had been murdered by Soviet police, all in the same manner, in April and May 1940. Since the surrender in Stalingrad Goebbels had been holding up before the eyes of the world the prospect of a future Europe overcome by 'Bolshevik hordes', in which intellectuals and dissidents would be ruthlessly liquidated. He had also noted the growing tension between the Soviets and the Polish government in exile in London. Now he was presented with the most graphic evidence of Soviet mass murder of another nation's elite. He quickly secured Hitler's consent to the fullest possible exploitation of the Katyn massacre, and arranged for groups of Polish and foreign journalists to be taken to the site.[26] Although the International Red Cross declined Goebbels' invitation to take part in a full forensic examination, the Germans did succeed in getting a genuinely international group of doctors and criminologists to visit the Katyn Forest and to conduct extensive exhumations. This group's report was published in Germany, and detailed summaries of its work, together with many photographs, were published all over Europe.[27] Several weekly German newsreels gave extended reports on the exhumations. Through April and May 1943, Goebbels' daily ministerial conferences were dominated by anti-Bolshevik diatribes fuelled by details from the Katyn massacre.

Le document de Katyn

40. A mass grave of Polish officers shot by the Soviet secret police in 1940 in the Katyn Forest, discovered by the Germans in April 1943. With widely-published photographs like this, Goebbels sought to persuade Europeans of the terrible fate that awaited them if Germany should lose the war.

Goebbels had high hopes that the genuinely shocking details of the Katyn massacre would create a serious rift between the Allies, and also strengthen anti-Bolshevik feeling across Europe. The fate of the Polish officers at Katyn, tied and gagged before being finished off with one or more bullets in the back of the neck, was – he argued – exactly what awaited the middle classes and the intellectuals in Germany if the Soviets prevailed in the East. On 27 April he wrote that there had been 'an absolutely sensational development' when the Soviets severed diplomatic relations with the Polish government in exile, and noted also the discovery of more mass graves near Odessa, containing 'some 6,000 bodies – victims of the GPU'.[28] As so often, though, he had miscalculated in thinking that the Katyn revelations would lead to a more serious crisis in relationships between the Allies, and several factors contributed to this.

There was, understandably, an issue with Germany's own credibility, which Goebbels recognized. In his ministerial conference on 25 April he warned German editors and journalists to play down the news of the mass graves near Odessa, clearly concerned lest they turn out in fact to be the victims of German or Romanian killers.[29] In his diary he noted that the Romanians had got 'cold feet' about this, and were unwilling to see the whole issue of mass killings near Odessa given publicity.[30] Furthermore, Goebbels recognized that lurid details of Soviet massacres were profoundly worrying to the many German families with relatives now in Soviet captivity. Confusing the whole issue, Hitler saw the Katyn massacres as evidence of Jewish rather than Soviet conduct, and Goebbels agreed. In his ministerial conference on 16 April he said 'We face here a system which is directing a racial war of the first order with the most brutal disregard.'[31] The Katyn massacre was – to Goebbels – the most striking evidence to support the thesis he had been advancing for years, that the Jews would exterminate their enemies if the Germans did not first succeed in exterminating them. He again put this belief before the German public in unambiguous terms in a leading article in *Das Reich* on 9 May, arguing that if Germany lost the war, 'countless millions of people in our own and other European countries ... would be delivered without defense to the hatred and will for extermination of this devilish race'. Again he reminded his readers of Hitler's prophecy of 1939, writing:

> The fulfilment of the *Führer's* prophecy, about which world Jewry laughed in 1939 when he made it, stands at the end of our course of action. Even in Germany, the Jews laughed when we stood up for the first time against them. Among them laughter is now a thing of the past. They chose to wage war against us. But Jewry now understands that the war has become a war against them.[32]

Above all, Goebbels underestimated the determination of the British and the Americans to maintain good relations with the Soviet Union. In a manner which is still disturbing today, the British and American governments accepted the Soviet denial of guilt for the Katyn massacre, and accepted that the Germans were the killers.

Although for several weeks Goebbels tried also to use Katyn to divert attention from the course of military events, he was rapidly overtaken by events. During April the Axis position in Tunisia collapsed, and as ever Hitler forbade an orderly withdrawal. Goebbels took comfort from the knowledge that many of the soldiers lost in North Africa were taken prisoner rather than killed, but he acknowledged that this was a serious setback:

> One sometimes has the feeling that we are lacking the necessary initiative in our conduct of the war. The enemy has had the upper hand almost everywhere in the last five months. He beats us in the air war, he has inflicted serious wounds on us in the East, he beats us in North Africa, and the U-boat campaign is also not leading to the results which we really had expected. It is high time that we – and this indeed is to be expected – came to a tangible outcome in the East. With that, the whole situation would naturally be brightened for us.[33]

It is striking that Goebbels started this brief summary with reference to the air war. Through the spring and the summer of 1943, RAF's Bomber Command directed a relentless series of attacks against German cities, mainly, but not exclusively those in the Ruhr. Arthur Harris now had a force of 851 heavy bombers at his disposal[34] and interpreted the 'Directive' given to him by the Combined Chiefs of Staff after Casablanca as a green light for his policy of 'area bombing'.[35] Numerous contingent factors, above all weather conditions, could still greatly diminish the impact of individual attacks, but repeatedly during this period, Harris' force succeeded in causing concentrated material destruction and great loss of life in individual German cities. Goebbels actually reacted with a certain satisfaction when Berlin was bombed for the first time in many months on 16 January 1943, not least because this attack caused few casualties and little material damage. He was pleased that the population of the capital city would once again have to experience the war directly.[36]

He was less amused when the city's defences were overwhelmed in the first really serious attack on 1 March 1943, which left over 600 dead; after this he never felt secure about staging public ceremonies, like 'Heroes Day' on 21 March, Hitler's birthday on 20 April, and the national celebration of 1 May in the capital, fearing that they invited aerial attack. When Hitler made a now rare public appearance in Berlin for 'Heroes Day', Goebbels recorded that he spoke for 'somewhat over ten minutes', and this was preceded by the performance of only the first movement of Bruckner's 7th Symphony.[37] When the speech was subsequently broadcast, there was a widespread view in Germany that Hitler had read this unusually short speech as quickly as possible lest he was interrupted by an attack.[38]

Many of the RAF's heaviest attacks at this time were on the Ruhr, on cities which Goebbels knew well. On 9 April 1943 he visited Essen after an attack which caused huge damage and left many of the city's streets impassable: 'I suffer almost physically from this sight, as I know the city of Essen so well from my youth, and I can compare what is was like then with what it is today.'[39] Shortly after this, Goebbels suffered a personal blow when his old comrade from the Rhineland, Viktor Lutze, was killed in an accidental car crash. Lutze, who had been given the thankless task of leading the SA after July 1934, had not earned praise from Goebbels for the way he had gone about this. Over the years Goebbels had frequently complained in his diary about Lutze, but he appears to have been genuinely moved by the loss of an old friend. Schaumburg-Lippe wrote that this was the only time he saw Goebbels cry.[40] Goebbels wrote, after visiting Lutze's wife Paula, and his son, who had been driving the car at the time of the accident, that Lutze was 'the one amongst the well-known Nazis whom I have known for longest'. Goebbels then went to the hospital in Potsdam to see Lutze's body, and, unconsciously replicating his adolescent poem, described how he stood, 'deeply moved', before the coffin of 'one of my best and most loyal friends'.[41]

Meanwhile the war continued with unrelenting fury. On 14 May Goebbels recorded 'an extraordinarily heavy attack on Duisburg'; a few days later he recorded 'thousands of victims' and unprecedented damage to war production as a result of the successful British raid on several dams in the Ruhr. Bizarrely, Goebbels thought that the plan for the 'dambusters' raid had been suggested to the British by émigré Jews: 'One therefore sees here how dangerous the Jews are and how we have done the right thing to bring them into more secure custody.' On 25 May he grimly noted that Dortmund had been subjected to 'apparently the heaviest attack yet directed against a German city', which had caused '600 large fires, 1300 medium, and some 4000 small fires'. This attack alone left between 80,000 and 100,000 people homeless.[42] Goebbels had a shrewd appreciation of the consequences of the air war, in some ways better than that of Arthur Harris, who was pleased with the 'succession of catastrophes' which was now being visited on Germany.[43] Goebbels was realizing that industry recovered surprisingly quickly from aerial bombardment. In fact, under Speer's direction, German arms production was increasing dramatically. Goebbels recognized that the dislocation to civilian life, and the damage to morale, was far more dangerous, but he was impressed by the resilience shown by the population in German cities. A report to Goebbels on the effects of the 'dambusters' raid, while stressing the enormous damage to industry and agriculture, concluded with these optimistic words: 'The meadows are greening again, fields are in large measure newly cultivated, houses and industrial works repaired or reconstructed.'[44] Tellingly, Goebbels noted after the attack on Dortmund in May:

You must conquer a country if you want to take possession of it; unless a people loses its morale and delivers itself willingly under extreme pressure into the enemy's hand. That is what we did in 1918; it will not be repeated in 1943.[45]

On 25 June the RAF dropped nearly 2,000 tons of bombs on Elberfeld, laying waste to 870 acres of the city centre, and leaving another 100,000 people homeless; Goebbels wrote that this made him suffer 'in his most inner soul'.[46] The culmination of this phase of the British offensive came on the night of 27/28 July 1943, when over 700 bombers attacked Hamburg. The British Official History cites the report of Hamburg's Police President, Major-General Kehrl:

Before half an hour had passed, the districts upon which the weight of the attack fell, and which formed part of the crowded dock and port area, where narrow streets and courts abounded, were transformed into a lake of fire covering an area of twenty-two square kilometres. The effect of this was to heat the air to a temperature which at times was estimated to approach 1,000 degrees centigrade. A vast suction was in this way created so that the air 'stormed through the streets with immense force, bearing upon it sparks, timber and roof beams and thus spreading the fire further and further till it became a typhoon such as had never before been witnessed, and against which all human resistance was powerless'. Trees three feet thick were broken off or uprooted, human beings were thrown to the ground or flung alive into the flames by winds which exceeded 150 miles an hour. The panic-stricken citizens knew not where to turn. Flames drove them from the shelters, but high explosive bombs sent them scurrying back again. Once inside, they were suffocated by carbon-monoxide poisoning and their bodies reduced to ashes as though they had been placed in a crematorium, which was indeed what each shelter proved to be.[47]

When Goebbels heard the first reports of the catastrophe from his old friend Karl Kaufmann, now *Gauleiter* of Hamburg, he could only assume that Kaufmann had lost his nerve and was exaggerating.[48] From Hamburg a mass of traumatized survivors spread out, carrying with them stories of charred bodies lying in the streets, and speaking of 100,000 dead.[49] Friedrich Reck-Malleczewen recorded how a group of 40 or 50 refugees from Hamburg reached a railway station hundreds of miles away, in Bavaria; fighting for space on a train one of their suitcases broke open on the station platform, spilling out 'the baked corpse of a child, shrunk to the proportions of a mummy'.[50] Even before he visited the stricken city, and saw for himself the hundreds of acres of burnt-out ruins, Goebbels was aware that morale in Germany was at a low: 'Doubt, scepticism, indeed despair is to be found everywhere.'[51]

Hamburg was not an isolated disaster. On 10 July allied forces had landed in Sicily, opening a new front, provoking the collapse of Mussolini's government, and his arrest. By early August it was also apparent that Hitler's offensive at Kursk had failed, and for the first time his armies in the East were forced onto the defensive during the summer months. Under enormous Soviet pressure they were forced into further retreats, particularly in Ukraine. Hitler, remote in his field headquarters, refused to speak to his people. Public opinion reports after Mussolini's arrest reaching Goebbels quoted as 'typical' statements from the public such as: 'That is the end. All the sacrifices in the war thus far have been in vain'; and: 'After Stalingrad, one blow after another. I no longer believe that we will win the war.'[52] On 30/31 August, over 600 British bombers attacked Rheydt, totally destroying the city centre, including both of Goebbels' former schools, and tearing up the graveyard in which his father lay. His parents' house, 'as if by a miracle', was saved. Goebbels wrote that a speech from Hitler was desperately needed, and again commented that amongst the broad masses there was 'scepticism, not to say hopelessness'.[53] A few days later the Americans and the British landed in mainland Italy, and on 8 September the new Italian government surrendered unconditionally to the Allies.

Goebbels recognized the extent of the crisis. In conversation with his own aides, and in his diary, he acknowledged that Germany could not, in the long run, win a war on two fronts. He put this to Hitler in Rastenburg on 9 September, asking him whether he thought negotiations with Stalin were possible. This was Goebbels' preferred option, but Hitler argued that the British were more likely to be open to diplomacy, once they had seized Sicily, Sardinia, and Corsica. At least on this occasion Goebbels managed to get Hitler to record a speech which he subsequently broadcast.[54] Six weeks later, as the situation on the Eastern Front deteriorated, Goebbels was back in Rastenburg, and again raised with Hitler what he called 'the cardinal question: how do we get out of a two-front war, and is it better to come to an eventual arrangement with England or with the Soviets?' If there was a degree of realism underlying these discussions, it disappeared when the two men went into further detail. They discussed how various territories they still controlled, in Eastern Europe, in the Balkans, and in Scandinavia, might be used as bargaining counters with one side or another. Goebbels on this occasion argued that the British might be willing to come to an arrangement in the West, allowing Germany to secure its necessary living space in the East.[55] He clung to the mistaken idea that, faced with a choice in Europe, the British would prefer to see a National Socialist, rather than a Communist hegemony.

At the same time as Hitler and Goebbels were conducting their own semi-delusional conversations in East Prussia, the Foreign Ministers of Britain, America, and the Soviet Union were meeting in Moscow, and the communiqué issued on 1 November at the conclusion of their talks highlighted the gap between Goebbels' wishful thinking and the real intentions of the Allies. The Moscow Declaration renewed the joint commitment to compel Germany to an unconditional surrender; it added an intention 'to restore the independence of

41. Wilhelm Furtwängler was Goebbels' favourite conductor. Although Furtwängler disagreed with the exclusion of Jewish musicians from German cultural life, he was prepared to appear at numerous Nazi ceremonies; here he conducts the Vienna Philharmonic in an armaments factory during the drive for 'total war' in 1943.

Austria' and to punish 'those German officers and men and members of the Nazi Party who have had any connection with atrocities and executions in countries overrun by German forces'.[56] Any notion Goebbels had that there was scope for negotiation with the Allies, separately or collectively, was entirely misplaced, and Hitler probably saw this more clearly. In any case, both men still clung to the idea that military developments might still turn to their advantage. Hitler was placing great store in the new 'vengeance weapons' being developed, flying bombs and rockets, and Goebbels had been convinced that they would wreak such havoc in London, even eventually in New York, that the British would come to their senses and desist from their attacks on German cities.[57] The German occupation of Italy in September, the freeing of Mussolini from captivity, and the temporary successes against the Allied beachhead at Salerno all served to bolster the illusion that Germany was still capable of military successes and had some room for manoeuvre.

Goebbels also made great efforts to preserve an outward appearance of calm and resolution. We have an intimate, if uncritical record of him in the last years of the war from the pen of a new press aide, Wilfred von Oven, who joined Goebbels' staff in July 1943. Oven was hugely impressed by Goebbels' fastidious care with his personal appearance, his meticulous attention to punctuality, his

42. Goebbels was a huge admirer of the Norwegian writer Knut Hamsun, who is shown here at the Congress of National Associations of Journalists held by the Nazis in Vienna, 22–25 June 1943. Shortly before this, Hamsun had visited Goebbels at home in Berlin, and Goebbels wrote: 'The wisdom of age is written in his face ... His belief in the German victory is completely unshakeable.' (*TBJG*, 19 May 1943, TII, 8, p. 327.)

constant energy, and his mastery of every detail of his work. He described how Goebbels maintained his daily routine, even when travelling: his own private train was equipped with every facility for him and his staff, and could be linked up to the telephone network at every station so that Goebbels could keep up to date with the news. Goebbels' different residences, in Berlin, Schwanenwerder, and in Lanke, were similarly equipped so that he could be accompanied by a small retinue and could work where he chose. Goebbels had now moved his own family to Lanke, which was judged least at risk from stray bombs intended for Berlin, and where a large underground bunker had been constructed. His own children now attended local schools, and he gathered here several other family members like his mother and sister.

Goebbels' relations with Magda had improved, and she continued to play the public role demanded of her, to the extent of doing some factory work as a contribution to the 'total war' effort. Magda was a dedicated Nazi, and shared Goebbels' public faith in final victory; privately she must, like him, have worried about the direction of events, and the consequences this would have for the whole family. Apparently Goebbels himself first admitted to Oven on 27 August 1943 the possibility that the war might be lost, and explained to him the logical consequence of this: 'I would happily throw away a life under the authority of our enemies. Either we will master this crisis – and I will employ all my powers to that end – or I will once again bow deeply to the English spirit and put a bullet through my head.'[58] Although Goebbels now had less time to attend to cultural affairs, he still found some consolation in the arts. In May 1943 he had even managed to meet one of his most revered cultural figures, the 84-year-old Norwegian author Knut Hamsun. Goebbels had first read Hamsun in his childhood, and in the 1930s he had often revisited his works. Hamsun professed his 'unshakeable' faith in a German victory, but conversation was difficult because he was very deaf. Nonetheless, Goebbels declared this 'one of the most valuable encounters of my life', and noted that Magda was also 'deeply struck' by the meeting.[59]

German propaganda subsequently gave prominence to the decision of Hamsun's son Arhild to serve with the SS,[60] and Goebbels found that he and Magda were not alone in their admiration for the elderly Norwegian. After years of studied reticence, Goebbels had at last admitted to the existence of 'Fräulein Eva Braun'. He referred to her for the first time in his diary on 25 June 1943; apparently she was also a fan of Hamsun's.[61] It is difficult to explain Goebbels' reluctance to discuss Eva Braun in his diaries, not least because he frequently – and increasingly as the war went on – expressed his concerns there about Hitler's apparent isolation and loneliness. By 1943, when Goebbels first mentioned Eva Braun in his diary, she had been involved in a close relationship with Hitler for many years; even after this first reference, Goebbels only mentioned her again infrequently, and never at any length. He wrote more about Hitler's dog Blondi, and how much the dog meant to Hitler. We can rule out prudery or straight-forward jealousy. The brief references to Eva Braun in Goebbels' diary contain no hint of disapproval, personal dislike, or jealousy. We know that when Field Marshal Blomberg married a much younger woman from a lower social class in February 1938, Goebbels had only approval for a relationship which scandalized many others. When it was revealed that Blomberg's new wife had previously been a prostitute, Goebbels appears to have been concerned only by the way this was viewed by the public.

Equally, we can rule out the possibility that Goebbels knew little about the relationship between Hitler and Eva Braun. Although she was studiously kept from the public eye, and hidden away from many visitors to Hitler's court, Goebbels did not suggest in his first references to her that he had only just been introduced; given his long and close relationship with Hitler this would be quite improbable. Goebbels may well have wished to respect Hitler's own desire that his relationship with Eva Braun should remain entirely private. When Goebbels next referred to her, in August 1943, he recorded that she was 'an intelligent girl, who meant a great deal to the *Führer*'.[62] It is also possible that Goebbels thought that Eva Braun provided little more than a diversion for Hitler. He always wrote about her in an approving, but patronizing tone, and may well have felt that she had no importance beyond helping Hitler to relax when he was not making important decisions. There is a marked contrast between Goebbels' tone towards Eva Braun – a 'girl' – and the way he wrote about Magda.

During 1943 Goebbels still found time for film and music. Shortly before meeting Hamsun, Goebbels discussed with Veit Harlan and Karl Liebeneiner plans for a film intended as an example to German cities under aerial attack. The film would depict the courageous resistance of the Prussian town of Kolberg to the Napoleonic armies, and would hopefully be premiered at Christmas.[63] Even as one German city after another was pulverized by the RAF, Goebbels found some consolation in music. On 2 June, shortly after Wuppertal had been badly hit, Goebbels entertained the Swiss poet Margaret Knittel and some musicians at Lanke:

> In the evening Alfieri, Professor Raucheisen, the tenor Anders from the State Opera and a few other singers come, and perform some beautiful music. Knittel's daughter plays Bach and Beethoven, Professor Raucheisen plays Chopin, and Schubert, Schumann, and Wolf *Lieder* are sung. I am happy to be able to indulge a little in music. One does this so infrequently today that an exception like this brings a deep inner bliss.[64]

A few days later Goebbels travelled out, with leading munitions producers, to Hillersleben to see a display of new weapons hosted by Speer. Goebbels was impressed not only by the weapons, but by the attitude of the industrialists

Two pictures of the reception given by Reich Minister Dr Goebbels and his wife to a delegation of the S. S. tank grenadier divisions which played an outstanding part in the recapture of Kharkov and of an afternoon in the Minister's family circle. With a wealth of details the soldiers, who are holders of all including the highest decorations, present a living picture of the spirit of the troops and the character of the fighting in the fourth year of the war

Reich Minister Dr Goebbels has once more assembled round him holders of the Knight's Cross who have come from the centres of fighting at the front

Eye-witness reports

Front soldiers visit Reich Minister Dr Goebbels

General Field Marshal Rommel photographed with the children of the Reich Minister on the occasion of a visit to Dr Goebbels

43. A spread of propaganda pictures showing soldiers visiting the Goebbels family in mid-1943. In the first, SS soldiers involved in the recapture of Kharkov are shown relaxing with Magda and four of her daughters, including Heide, the youngest; at the bottom left, Field Marshal Rommel is walking with the four eldest daughters. In the two middle pictures Goebbels is shown talking with holders of the Knight's Cross.

there, whom he described as 'cold and energetic fanatics'. He noted also that many of them harboured artistic pretensions, and that 'characteristically, the day ends with a piano performance by Professor Kempff; he plays Beethoven and Chopin'.[65]

Goebbels' morale was also bolstered by the new role he created for himself in 1943 as 'defender of Berlin' and coordinator of the response to the British aerial offensive. He had always been at his most energetic under pressure, and he now found his moment, as Hitler retreated from the public gaze, and as other senior Nazis like Göring, Ribbentrop, and Rosenberg took refuge in sybaritic living, or in pursuance of private schemes. After Hamburg, Goebbels was convinced that the British would attempt to deliver a similarly heavy attack on Berlin, and he threw himself in an effort to prevent a repetition of the catastrophe in Germany's capital. He immediately insisted on the evacuation of nearly a million women and children from Berlin, even though this was enormously unpopular.[66] He used the local Party apparatus and a leafleting campaign to ensure that measures were in hand to prevent – as far as possible – the spread of major fires. In his own ministry, Goebbels organized a 'defence company' armed with machine guns, which would secure the building in the event of unrest. By this time Berlin was surrounded by successive rings of searchlights and anti-aircraft guns, making it the most heavily defended of German cities. A deep bunker under the Wilhelmplatz served as Goebbels' headquarters during a raid, and from here he tried to coordinate the response of fire and rescue services, emerging as soon as he judged safe to get in person to the most critically affected areas.

In the nights after the Hamburg attack Goebbels anxiously awaited the news that a large British force was approaching Berlin. Arthur Harris had in fact decided to try to inflict a series of attacks on Berlin, but was waiting for favourable weather before launching his onslaught. The first attack came on 24 August: some 600 British bombers flew over Berlin on a clear night, and were engaged by over 200 German aircraft. Goebbels was impressed by the cooperation between searchlights and night fighters, and watched five bombers being shot down after being coned by searchlights.[67] As soon as the all-clear sounded Goebbels moved to coordinate the response, above all to prevent the development of huge combined fires. More than 800 civilians were killed, and thousands of buildings were damaged or destroyed. The British returned on 1 September and on 3 September, but these attacks were less damaging. Then for a period of seven weeks, Harris directed his bombers to other targets, notably Hanover and Kassel. Goebbels travelled to both these cities, both to supervise the response to the raids, and also to deliver morale-building speeches. Just as in the *Kampfzeit*, his public speaking again served to energize both himself and his audiences. During this period, he spoke frequently, to selected groups of Party workers and members of the armed forces, to large public meetings, and to groups of people who clustered around him in the streets. He discovered that, just as in Britain in 1940 and 1941, the experience of being bombed from the air sometimes brought people together and seemed to bolster the morale of survivors, united in common suffering.

Goebbels spoke to Party workers in Kassel on 5 November, shortly after more than 5,000 people had been killed there in a firestorm. He told them that the sacrifice of their city and their houses would turn out to be worthwhile, and that they would see the ruins as 'the pledge and guarantee of victory'. Privately he was furious that the local *Gauleiter*, Karl Weinrich, had failed to prepare adequately for attack, and to organize the response with sufficient energy. Weinrich was

44. The morning after a British bombing raid on a Rhineland city in August 1943. Goebbels was terrified by the intensification of the British offensive and its effect on the public mood, writing: 'It is mainly due to the British aerial terror that in wide circles of the German public there is scepticism about victory.' (*TBJG*, 1 September 1943, TII, 9, p. 399.)

dismissed from his post. Travelling on to Hanover, which had suffered four concentrated raids, Goebbels was much more impressed by the energy and application of *Gauleiter* Lauterbacher. Thousands of people crowded outside the town hall to hear Goebbels speak, and he was frequently interrupted by applause – as, for example, when he declared that 'We believe that this war, with all its suffering, is still better than a peace imposed upon us by enemies.'[68]

Back in Berlin, Goebbels concentrated on the many problems arising from earlier attacks, notably providing for the many thousands of people now homeless. Every evening he scanned the reports of the weather over England, and followed the news of incoming flights from the West. On 22 November he was in Steglitz, an already damaged area in south Berlin, to speak to local Party members. Twenty minutes into his speech, the air-raid sirens wailed, and after a further ten minutes, the whole meeting had to take refuge in the air-raid shelter.[69] Berlin was about to undergo its 'greatest bombing ordeal in the war',[70] a series of three concentrated raids which left thousands dead, hundreds of thousands homeless, and inflicted huge damage on government buildings and industrial plants. In the first attack, the inner city was badly hit, and Goebbels' own house in Hermann-Göring-Strasse was partially burnt out. In the second, the government quarter was particularly badly affected: the Propaganda Ministry was set on fire in two places, and the Kaiserhof Hotel, where the Party leadership had congregated before the 'seizure of power' was completely destroyed. In the third, the Alkett and Borsig plants, which between them produced a significant proportion of Germany's self-propelled guns and artillery pieces, were badly damaged. Repeated hits on the zoo left over 700 animals dead, and there were rumours that escaped lions were prowling around the Kaiser Wilhelm Memorial Church in the city centre. Meat from buffaloes, antelopes, and crocodiles was available to some of the city's inhabitants afterwards; bear meat was apparently particularly prized.[71]

Goebbels was intoxicated by the whole experience. As the bunker under the Wilhelmplatz shuddered under the impact of huge bombs, he felt that 'we really are living in the middle of the war'. Although he was horrified and saddened by the extent of the fires in Berlin, he was hugely impressed by the resilience and morale of the population. When his car was held up by wreckage as he tried to supervise the emergency services, people came up, 'clapped him on the shoulder' and wished him well. After the third raid, he visited the ruins of working-class Wedding, and had to give an impromptu speech standing on a crate. Women embraced him. Still dictating his diary entries every day, Goebbels confessed that it was 'a real joy, to throw oneself into the sea of troubles and, swimming, to reach the saving bank'.[72]

Although Goebbels was understandably preoccupied by the aerial attack on Germany, and with coordinating the response to this, he was also aware of a serious threat developing on the Eastern Front, where through the autumn and winter months, the Red Army maintained a relentless pressure, above all in Ukraine. The increasingly demoralized German forces were pushed back, and had to relinquish territory which they had occupied for two years. In early November Kiev was liberated, and shortly after this Soviet forces reached the Black Sea coast, isolating the Germans and Romanians left in the Crimea. In January 1944 a strong Soviet offensive – the first of what Stalin called the 'ten crushing blows' of that year – was mounted near Leningrad, forcing the Germans to retreat from positions they had held since 1941. The emphasis was switched back to the south in the spring, when the Germans were driven back to the Romanian frontier; in April and May 1944 the Crimea was liberated. Goebbels followed these developments day by day, noting the ever greater material and numerical strength of the Red Army. He was incensed by what he saw as the weak-willed leadership of the *Wehrmacht*, and from numerous eye-witnesses he learnt of the increasing demoralization of the German frontline troops.

Goebbels was now fully aware of the growing material supremacy of the Allies on all fronts. He was increasingly sceptical of those who maintained that Stalin had thrown his last reserves into the struggle, and he knew that the Americans and British were building up a huge force in preparation for an invasion somewhere in north-western Europe. He could see and hear for himself the huge aerial fleets which now roamed over Germany. In March 1944 he watched from Lanke as the first American bombers attacked Berlin in daylight, and every day he recorded a growing number of attacks, now from aircraft based in Italy as well as in Britain. Although he rejoiced in the occasional successes of German defences, he was deeply frustrated by what he saw as the inadequate leadership of the *Luftwaffe*. In April 1944 he recorded that his desk was covered with so many reports of air raids that he scarcely had time to read them all.[73]

After ten years in which the role of Propaganda Minister had largely been a happy one for Goebbels, this had become an impossible task. In retrospect, the 'total war' speech of February 1943 can be seen as the last occasion on which Goebbels successfully used his tried and tested propaganda techniques to achieve any great success. After the disasters which followed this, although Goebbels continued his work with his typical energy and determination, he was swimming against strong currents. He still controlled a network of propaganda departments across Germany and occupied Europe, and these fought to implement his directives in an increasingly hostile environment. In the occupied territories, this was a hopeless cause. Years of German control had brought – for the majority of the occupied populations – political subjugation, the deportation of young people for forced labour, the savage exploitation of economic resources, and dismal poverty. The supposed benefits of belonging to the German 'New Order' palled beside these everyday horrors. By early 1944 the prospect of Allied liberation was near at hand for many of these people.

We can gain an insight into the poverty of Goebbels' propaganda at this late stage of the war by looking at an isolated 'action' in an area typically overlooked, the Grand Duchy of Luxembourg. This small, independent state with its population of just over 300,000 had after occupation in May 1940 been incorporated into the 'Greater German *Reich*', and in 1942 been made part of the *Gau Moselland*, run from Koblenz. Under the direction of *Gauleiter* Gustav Simon, a brutal and uncompromising programme of 'Germanization' had been conducted to extirpate any traces of French or indigenous culture. The Jews of Luxembourg had been deported, and a number of German settlers were brought in from outside. In early 1944, conscious of deteriorating morale, the *Gau* propaganda office conducted a 'New Year action', and reported on this to Goebbels. Alongside the usual techniques of holding meetings, showing films, and presenting Nazi speeches, the office staged an 'internal Party action of public confession' designed to restore sagging confidence. A six-point programme was promulgated for all members of the Party and the 'German people's Movement' in Luxembourg. This demanded that 'always and everywhere' Party badges were to be worn; and that 'always and everywhere the German greeting of "*Heil* Hitler", correctly pronounced, was to be used'. Party members were 'in every personal and private conversation to express confidence and faith in victory'. All were required during March to write at least one letter to someone they knew 'at the front'. Every individual had 'personally to combat rumour-mongering and uncalled-for political jokes in comradely circles'. Finally the propaganda office reminded all Party members that: 'Against genuinely ill-willed defeatists, the fist, as the most tried and tested method, was immediately to be used.'[74]

Whatever the outcome of local initiatives like this – and one doubts that many hearts and minds were now to be won with these 'tried and tested' methods – they were not going to change the course of the war. Goebbels was now pinning his faith in the prospect of casting the British and American invaders – when they arrived – back into the sea. This alone, he hoped, would force them to negotiate. As an eerie calm descended on the Eastern Front, and much of the American and British aerial offensive was turned against targets in France and the Low countries, Goebbels anxiously scanned the news reports for clues about when and where the Allies might land. He spent Easter 1944 with his family in Lanke, but Oven records how he was unable to concentrate on family activities, as he was preoccupied with the idea that conditions were favourable for a landing in France.[75] He tried to soothe his nerves with music, taking pleasure in the 'evenings of German music' broadcast every Sunday. On 'Heroes Day', 12 March, this was a 'beautiful Bach concert'. On Easter Sunday he enjoyed a Mozart concert – 'a glorious pleasure' – and the following week he listened to a programme of Handel, although he felt this was 'somewhat too baroque'.[76] He rejoiced in the progress of 'one of his own favourite children', the *Reich* Bruckner Orchestra in Linz.[77] With Hitler's approval this orchestra had been established in 1943 partly to build up Linz as a cultural centre in opposition to Vienna, and specifically to create a first-class orchestra for radio broadcasting.[78] None of this could really distract Goebbels from the war. He recorded, perhaps unconsciously repeating his earlier threat that thoughts of the Jews would haunt the Germans even in their dreams, that now the fear that another German city would be attacked 'accompanied him in his sleep'.[79]

For the last four years, Goebbels had been living 'in the stretch and sag' of his nerves,[80] and he was clearly now haunted by fear of the future. He must have realized, at some level of his conscious as well as unconscious being, that the war was lost, and that Germany could not prevail against the Allied coalition. Strangely, he had lost his earlier fear that morale on the home front would collapse, and he had seen that the German population was astonishingly resilient under sustained attack. The systematic pillaging of occupied Europe and the dispossession of its Jewish communities had helped to maintain a relatively high standard of living in Germany itself. Houses, flats, furniture, and clothes stolen from Jews were directly used to alleviate the worst distress of many of those made homeless by British and American bombing. Nonetheless the aerial war was the one that Goebbels was closest to, and most directly involved in. He could see that for all huge resources invested in anti-aircraft guns, night fighters, searchlights, and early warning systems, the German defences against British night bombing and American daylight attacks were being overwhelmed. The front line in the Soviet Union was still a long way from the German frontier, and this seems to have cushioned Goebbels from a clearer realization of the immense danger facing the German armed forces there. The front line in Italy had been stabilized, and this made it possible for Goebbels still to cling to the idea that the German army was superior to any land force the British and Americans could mobilize.

Goebbels had no doubts about his own future in the event of an Allied victory. He had paid close attention both to formal declarations by the Allies that they would hold Nazi leaders responsible for atrocities committed during the war, and to journalistic utterances in Allied countries which demanded more summary retribution. For years his declared philosophy had been one of risk-taking, and of burning bridges behind him. Magda undoubtedly knew about many of the crimes committed by the Nazis, perhaps in less detail than her husband, and also felt a sense of responsibility. Goebbels had in the past been very critical of senior Nazis who had not taken their own lives when dishonoured, or facing capture by the Allies, and was absolutely clear in his own mind that suicide was the only course of action he could take if Germany was defeated. From the evidence of others, it appears that he was already contemplating taking the lives of his own children in this event.[81] This readiness to face his own death made it easier for Goebbels to maintain – in public – his unwavering faith in a German victory.

Haunted by doubts and anxieties, Goebbels still maintained his childlike veneration for Hitler, but even this faith was now called into question. Through the spring and summer of 1944, Hitler spent much of his time away from the fronts, on the Obersalzberg, and Goebbels was summoned to see him there every few weeks. On every occasion he was impressed by Hitler's 'sovereign calm', and his apparently untroubled optimism. He was though unable to agree with all his views, and privately he expressed growing frustration. In February he dictated: 'The *Führer* has thus far not honoured any city in the air war with a visit. That cannot be sustained in the long term.'[82] In March 1944, Hitler explained to Goebbels how the increasing numbers of Panther and Tiger tanks would restore German military supremacy. Goebbels noted: 'I would like to see this prognosis of the *Führer* borne out. One has been so often disappointed recently, that one feels a degree of scepticism arising within oneself.' Together, he and Hitler railed against their own 'nauseating' generals, and concluded that Stalin had been right to shoot his own in good time. They were similarly united on the 'Jewish question', agreeing that this was the one area where they had pursued a genuinely radical policy. As a result, Goebbels dictated, 'the Jews can no longer cause us any damage'.[83] Goebbels was so concerned by what he perceived as the defeatist attitude of the generals that he staged a bizarre charade to demonstrate their loyalty to Hitler. He secretly wrote a 'statement' of 'unconditional loyalty', and persuaded Hitler's adjutant General Schmundt to fly around Europe getting signatures from all the Field Marshals to the document. This accomplished, the declaration was formally presented by Gerd von Rundstedt – as if it came from the Field Marshals – to Hitler on 19 March.[84] When Hitler told him about this little ceremony, Goebbels noted: 'I am very pleased that I am the author of this declaration, without the *Führer* knowing it.'[85] One wonders whether Hitler did know or not, and also what Goebbels thought was achieved by this exercise. A few days before this Goebbels had noted alarming signs of Hitler's physical deterioration, how his hand shook when he signed a document, and how he could only go up and down steep stairs very slowly.[86]

Hitler was still placing increasing hope in other new weapons, and this was a constant theme of his talks with Goebbels. In May 1944 Goebbels heard a detailed report from the Armaments Ministry which explained why the A-4 rockets (later called the V2) would not be ready for two or three months yet. This was so different from what Hitler had told him that he could only conclude that Hitler had been 'wrongly informed'.[87] Goebbels knew already that the failure to realize the many threats of 'retaliation' against the British issued since the summer of 1943 had seriously damaged the credibility of the Nazi leadership in the eyes of the German public. In fact the A-4 rocket programme was still beset with developmental problems, and the rockets would not be ready for another four months.[88] The sense of unreality deepened when Goebbels travelled again to the Obersalzberg to visit Hitler on 5 June 1944. He found a whole group of people here, coming to terms with, amongst other developments, the loss of Rome to the British and Americans. Amongst other wide ranging plans, Hitler explained to Goebbels his belief that 'England was lost' and that he had therefore decided to deal it a 'death blow'. Goebbels, who was himself inclined to clutch at any news which suggested cracks in British morale, commented: 'How he will do that in detail, is not clear to me at present.' As ever, the two men reviewed the conduct of other senior Nazis, and Goebbels bitterly criticized Ribbentrop for his failure to develop a constructive foreign policy. Hitler, who still thought highly of Ribbentrop, said that he had thought about replacing him with Alfred Rosenberg. Goebbels, who had imagined that he was the only possible successor to Ribbentrop's post, recorded that he was 'appalled' by this, and clearly implied that he was also deeply affronted by Hitler's insensitivity to his own views.

After this, Goebbels had a long discussion with Speer, who also had a house on the Obersalzberg. Speer developed his theory that the Americans and the British would try to destroy the bridges over the Rhine to trap German forces in France, and then mount an invasion from somewhere near Hamburg on the north German coast. Late that night Goebbels sat by the fireside with Hitler, and as ever, they rehearsed anecdotes from the *Kampfzeit*. The dawn was breaking when Goebbels arrived back at his hotel in Berchtesgaden, to find reports which confirmed that the Allies had landed in France. 'Thus,' he wrote, 'the deciding day of the war has broken.'[89]

12

'How Distant and Alien this Beautiful World Appears'

The strongest moral factor in this coming victory is the *Führer* himself! [Calls of 'Bravo' and '*Heil*', applause.] It is now for twenty years that I have stood at his side. I have shared joy and suffering with him, victory and defeat and crisis. I can only say: in these twenty years we have experienced more anxious than happy days and gone through more crises than we have celebrated victories. But we have still overcome every crisis! As insoluble as they sometimes seem, they have in the end been resolved. And the sky might be dark as it often is; suddenly, unexpectedly, in some place, small blue or white spots reveal themselves. And in a short time [an aeroplane flies over the meeting] the whole panorama of the heavens is clear again, and the sun shines on our heads once again. So it will be today.

Goebbels, speaking in Nuremberg, 4 June 1944.[1]

Goebbels welcomed the invasion of Normandy. He saw it as an opportunity to inflict a decisive defeat on the Western Allies, and open the way towards an end to Germany's war on two fronts. He still had huge faith in Rommel, who was commanding the forces around the Allied beachhead, and hoped that within two or three days he would deploy sufficient armoured reserves to drive the Allies back into the sea. He was rapidly disappointed. The overwhelming Allied air supremacy made it almost impossible for Rommel to move his reserves, or to attack effectively with those he could get in place. Goebbels was similarly disappointed with the long-postponed use of the 'vengeance weapons'. The flying bombs (soon called the V1, at Goebbels' suggestion) were launched against London on 15 June, and over the next few weeks a sustained offensive was maintained against the British capital. Goebbels had built up great expectations in the German press about the impact the 'vengeance weapons' might have, and he was hugely frustrated by the British tactic of keeping silent about their effects. Lacking any detailed intelligence, Goebbels was only able to speculate, largely on the basis of rumours, about this, and he quickly realized that, whatever damage

276

the V1s were causing in London, they were not bringing the British to their knees. As early as 18 June he moved to tone down the 'sometimes grotesque' exaggeration about them in the German press. At the same time he admitted that there could be no German counter-offensive in Normandy because of Allied air superiority.[2]

These concerns were soon overwhelmed by Goebbels' gradual realization of the danger posed by the renewed Soviet offensive in the centre of the Eastern Front. Although the start of this long-planned offensive was timed for the anniversary of Operation Barbarossa on 22 June, it took several days to develop in full strength, and for the scale of its success to become apparent in Berlin. On 26 June Goebbels dictated that 'as if from a clear sky comes the news that the Bolsheviks have achieved a breakthrough in great style'.[3] In fact the situation was far worse than he realized. The German Army Group Centre was totally overwhelmed; whole units surrendered with their commanders; towns bombastically imagined as 'fortresses' were abandoned, and the apparatus of German occupation collapsed. All who could fled, using any means of transport available, carrying what booty they could, but abandoning huge quantities of equipment and supplies. For the next six weeks Soviet armoured units and motorized infantry advanced swiftly across Belorussia, and into what had been eastern Poland. By mid-July refugees were streaming into East Prussia, and Soviet forces were close to the Baltic coast, threatening to cut off Army Group North. It was, according to a recent historian, 'the most crushing single defeat in the history of the German Army'.[4]

Goebbels now realized the gravity of the situation; this was, he dictated: 'the end-phase of our historic fight for the *Reich*'.[5] But he sensed drift and defeatism at all levels of the German leadership. For the first time in his diary in early July he had used the phrase 'if I were the *Führer*',[6] with all its implied criticism of Hitler. He was scathing about Göring and the total failure of the *Luftwaffe*; and he was disgusted by the willingness of generals and senior officers to lay down their arms. Nothing incensed him more than those captured officers who had joined the Soviet-sponsored 'Free Germany National Committee', and now broadcast on Soviet radio, appealing to German soldiers to give up the unequal struggle.[7] On 20 July, Goebbels was in the Propaganda Ministry with Speer and Funk, when at lunchtime he received a telephone call telling him that there had been an unsuccessful attempt to kill Hitler in Rastenburg.

Goebbels did not dictate an entry for 20 July, or the following day in his diary, but we do have accounts from both Speer and Oven, who were with him on that critical day, and in a broadcast speech on 26 July Goebbels gave his own résumé of events.[8] Although Kershaw suggests that Goebbels initially procrastinated, wanting 'to hedge his bets',[9] he acted with characteristic energy and resolution once he knew that the attempted assassination was part of a larger plot to replace the Nazi government. Goebbels' reaction appears all the more important when it is contrasted with the indecision of the conspirators gathered nearby in Bendlerstrasse, who failed to arrest Goebbels, or to cut off his telephone. Goebbels was able to convince Major Remer, the commander of the guard battalion sent by the plotters to seal off the government quarter (including the Propaganda Ministry), that Hitler was alive; he put him on the telephone to Hitler, and then delivered a brief but effective speech to Remer's men in the garden outside his flat. Goebbels had already broadcast to the nation to announce brief details of the attempted assassination, but above all to reassure the public that Hitler was alive and had already resumed his work.[10] The conspirators were arrested, and several were shot that evening. Through the night Goebbels coordinated the suppression of the plot in Berlin, and it was indeed with some justification that at 4.00 a.m. he emerged from his office, smiling and energized, to announce to his officials: 'Gentlemen, the *Putsch* is over.'[11] One detail overlooked in most accounts of 20 July is that Goebbels had only four weeks earlier met Remer when he was appointed to his post in Berlin, and established a strong personal contact with him.[12] This undoubtedly helped to win Remer over to his side on 20 July. If the main reason the plot failed was because Hitler survived the bomb blast, the second most important factor was the plotters' failure to arrest Goebbels. It has been argued that the plot had little realistic chance of success even if Hitler had been killed, because either Himmler or Göring might have intervened to crush the plot in Berlin. This though is speculation.[13] Goebbels actually did intervene.

On 22 July, confident that the plot was over, and pleased with his own role in its suppression, Goebbels travelled to Rastenburg. He was determined to use the opportunity to push his agenda for 'total war' with Hitler, but before speaking to him, he met with others, like Lammers, Bormann, and Keitel, who had previously obstructed him. They now readily agreed to support his plans, as did Hitler himself. He issued a decree appointing Goebbels 'Plenipotentiary for Total War', and agreed in principle to a raft of measures to 'comb out' men for the armed forces, and to curb production of unnecessary luxuries.[14] Goebbels was moved to see Hitler still alive, and quickly accepted the notion that his survival was proof of some kind of divine intervention. Hitler appeared to him now as 'a man who worked under God's hand';[15] here was the confirmation that Hitler was the man to lead the German people out of the crisis. This interpretation of the plot had been developed by Hitler when he finally broadcast to the public late on night on 20 July, and Goebbels developed it in his radio speech on 26 July. He and Hitler also saw the plot, particularly as it was further investigated, as vindication of their mistrust of the officer corps, the aristocracy, and of the non-party bourgeoisie. From this point onwards, they turned ever more to the Party and the SS as the only dependable elements in their collapsing world.

In the short term, the 20 July plot gave Goebbels new hope. When he returned to Berlin on 24 July, he met ordinary soldiers who 'all enthusiastically and for the first time' greeted him with the Hitler salute, now imposed on the armed forces in place of the traditional military salute. Reading public opinion reports, he dictated: 'One has the impression that we had won a great victory.' On 4 August he travelled to Posen to address the *Gauleiter*, whom he had always considered Germany's elite leadership corps, and decided that this gathering of old fighters was 'the best I have yet experienced'.[16] Magda had by this time returned from Dresden, after a successful operation on a trapped nerve, and this was a further comfort. As further revelations of the extent of the conspiracy were forced out of the surviving plotters, Goebbels was shocked, particularly to hear that his old Berlin comrade Count Helldorff, and his great hero Rommel, were implicated. He did not allow his personal sympathies to mitigate his harsh judgement on them, noting without objection Hitler's order that Helldorff should watch three of his fellow-conspirators being hanged before his own execution. Ted Harrison, who has researched Helldorff's role in the plot, notes that 'personal loyalty was the unwritten law of National Socialism', and relates how one of Helldorff's sons tried to see Goebbels, hoping he might intercede on his father's behalf, unaware that he had already been executed. Goebbels refused to receive him, and did not let him know that his father's sentence had already been carried out.[17] Goebbels took some comfort from the knowledge that the Propaganda Ministry was the only government department which had not harboured any conspirators.

He worked with renewed determination to implement his vision of 'total war', looking to provide hundreds of thousands of new soldiers, and even securing Hitler's agreement to the closure of all theatres, and most of Germany's orchestras. As with all attempts to curb bureaucracy, Goebbels had to create new agencies to coordinate the 'combing out' of men from civilian occupations, in this case a 'Planning Committee', and an 'Executive Committee'. He assured all civil authorities in the *Reich* that these bodies would employ no more than 20 people, and demanded that they should look not just to release a few people from their organizations, but to make significant structural changes. To set a good example, Goebbels announced that he was cutting 75 per cent of the provincial posts in the Propaganda Ministry, and upwards of 30 per cent from his central administration.[18] In fact Goebbels, like others, provided exemptions from military service for people in his own sphere of activity. In late August he issued a list of several hundred 'divinely favoured' artists exempted from military service. He also preserved several leading orchestras, mainly to provide music on the radio.

All this activity provided an outlet for Goebbels' energy, but he was painfully aware that the war was being determined on the fighting fronts. On 18 August advance Soviet forces crossed the German frontier at Schirwindt in East Prussia, but were forced to pull back. *Gauleiter* Koch had been improvising a system of defences, mobilizing civilians, concentration camp prisoners, and fleeing remnants of Army Group Centre, and in the last days of August the Soviet tide came slowly to a halt.[19] In the West though, the Americans had broken through even as Hitler and Goebbels congratulated themselves on his survival from the bomb plot, and in August the German position in Normandy collapsed totally.

As in the East, there was a disorganized retreat as frontline units, rear-echelon troops, and collaborators fled for their lives, in this case greatly hampered by the prior destruction of the transport network. In a few short weeks, virtually all of France and Belgium was liberated, and in mid-September the first American units crossed the German frontier near Aachen. By this time, Romania, Bulgaria, and Finland had also come to terms with the Soviets, forcing a complete withdrawal of German forces from the Balkans. Bringing matters closer to home, a random bomb from a British Mosquito landed in the garden of Goebbels' house – ironically where he had harangued Remer's men only weeks earlier – stripping the roof off the building, destroying several of the beautiful old trees, and forcing Goebbels to live out in Lanke for several weeks until a few rooms could again be made habitable. Only days earlier, Goebbels had heard that Magda's son Harald was missing in action in Italy. He decided to conceal this from Magda until he could find out more about his fate.[20]

The collapse of the German position, above all in the West, provoked a crisis of confidence. The combination of prolonged aerial assault and of rumours of the disorganized flight from France resulted in a mood of widespread resignation and hopelessness in western parts of Germany, and Goebbels was frustrated by Hitler's reluctance to appear before, or even to broadcast to the German people. On 12 September Goebbels confessed privately that this was 'an extraordinary shame'. He was profoundly suspicious of Hitler's entourage, and reflected sadly that 'the *Führer* seems to be alone now'. In talks with the other Nazis who were coming to prominence after 20 July, Goebbels put the blame on Ribbentrop. On 18 September he confided to his diary that: 'If I were leading German foreign policy, it would have to be possible to come to a settlement of the conflict with one side or another'; nor was this merely his own wishful thinking. He heard from Hitler's headquarters that Himmler, Bormann, and Guderian all wanted to see Ribbentrop dismissed and Goebbels appointed in his place.[21] Goebbels agonized for days about how best to put this to Hitler, and finally decided to write directly to him. He spent hours composing a long memorandum, and took the unusual step of dictating a verbatim copy in his diary. Kershaw states that this was because 'Goebbels was evidently so pleased with it', but it is more likely that Goebbels wanted to put what he thought was an important document on the record.[22] He wrote:

My *Führer*
The development of the war in recent months, which has brought the enemy to the borders of the *Reich*, and even beyond them, in the East and the West, leads me to present my thoughts on our war politics to you in the following exposition.

Although he took care to flatter Hitler with glowing compliments, Goebbels was blunt:

> We stand in a two front war in its sharpest form, something which we wanted to avoid in all circumstances at the start of the war. We have never in our history won a war on two fronts, and today also it would not be possible for us to win militarily, given the numerical relations of strength.

Goebbels developed the parallel he had often used before with Hitler, and with the German public, comparing the current military situation with the political crisis which had confronted the Nazi Party in November 1932, when it faced enemies inside and outside its own ranks. He continued:

> The question arises here, whether either side has any inclination to enter into negotiations with us, and if so, which one.

Goebbels then argued that with Japanese diplomatic support, it might be possible to negotiate with the Soviet Union; the Americans and the British would not then be able to prolong the war.

> What we might attain would not be the victory we dreamed of in 1941, but it would still be the greatest victory in German history.

Turning to the conduct of these negotiations, Goebbels was again blunt:

> I do not consider our Foreign Minister to be capable of initiating such a development.

Goebbels stated that he wrote in these terms because he 'felt it his duty as a National Socialist'. He did not explicitly suggest himself as the candidate to replace Ribbentrop, but clearly implied that he was the man with the necessary vision. Goebbels finished the letter with a declaration of loyalty, despatched it by courier to Rastenburg, and waited anxiously for Hitler's reaction.[23] On 25 September he heard that Hitler had read it, without comment, in the presence of his adjutant Julius Schaub, and put it in his briefcase with his reading for the night. Goebbels recorded that Hitler wanted him to come to Rastenburg, presuming that this would be to discuss the letter.[24]

In fact, Hitler never discussed this letter with Goebbels. He took to his bed, and the projected visit was cancelled. Hitler's illness was probably more than psychosomatic, or a way of avoiding Goebbels and others who were confronting him with difficult demands. He was still suffering from the effects of the bomb blast of 20 July. It was several weeks before Goebbels travelled to Rastenburg again, and when he did, Hitler concentrated on his plans for an offensive in the West.[25] Goebbels' hope of negotiating with the Soviet Union was by this time as misplaced as the hope of the 20 July conspirators that they might negotiate with Britain and America if Hitler could be disposed of. In any case, Hitler did not accept Goebbels' view that the war could not be won militarily, and had no intention of negotiating with either side. If Goebbels was realistic in his acceptance that a military victory was no longer possible, and in his assessment of Ribbentrop as a hopeless failure, he overlooked one critical point: there was no possibility in September 1944 that the Soviet Union, Britain, or America, would negotiate with Goebbels as German Foreign Minister. Apart from Hitler himself, and possibly Himmler, there was no one in the Nazi leadership more mistrusted and loathed outside Germany than Goebbels.

If Goebbels was hurt or disappointed by Hitler's refusal to engage with his ideas, he did not show it. In any case, he was again overtaken by events. In the last weeks of September and in early October, there was a consolidation of the German position, brought about by Allied exhaustion, and problems of supply. Even while Goebbels awaited Hitler's reaction to his letter, the ambitious Allied attempt to force a crossing of the Rhine using paratroopers at Arnhem was repulsed, and a new defensive line was stabilized in the West. The Soviets, who had similarly over-extended supply lines after their huge advances in July and August, made efforts to break into East Prussia, but were checked. Goebbels was convinced that his efforts as Total War Plenipotentiary, which had freed some 500,000 men for the fighting fronts, and his unceasing propaganda efforts were largely responsible for the Allied setbacks. He portrayed the British and Americans, who eventually captured the ruins of Aachen in early October, as intent on enslaving the German people, and reducing them to medieval serfdom. He welcomed the news of the Morgenthau plan, which entailed the punishment of German war criminals and the destruction of German industry, when this emerged after the Quebec conference, and served as a useful confirmation of the line he had previously promoted. He seized upon the collective rape of German women by Red Army soldiers after an incursion into the village of Nemmersdorf in East Prussia in October 1944, and sent newsreel teams to photograph the evidence of Soviet brutality there.

Goebbels also placed great hope in the formation of the *Volkssturm* (People's Storm) in September 1944. This was a militia of men, too old or too young to have been already considered for military service, armed with whatever weapons could be scraped together in a given locality, and sent to the front lines with a minimum of training. Hitler's decree announcing the formation of the *Volkssturm* argued that it was a necessary response to the 'known total will to extermination of our Jewish-international enemies'.[26] There is agreement today that *Volkssturm* units were militarily of negligible value, and that the high casualties they suffered were almost entirely futile. Goebbels saw the *Volkssturm* as an embodiment of

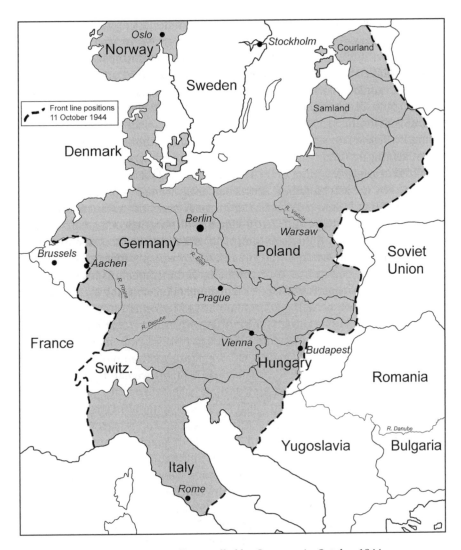

45. Map showing the territory still controlled by Germany in October 1944.

the revolutionary tradition he had idealized in the 1920s, and in the last months of the war, it still seemed to offer a concrete expression of his ideals of 'will' and 'sacrifice'. He was by this time so disillusioned with the regular army that he preferred the idea of these new recruits being assembled in separate units rather than sent as reinforcements to existing formations. When the levy was first discussed in early September 1944, Goebbels felt that Himmler was the 'only' candidate to lead the new force. A few weeks later he fantasized that he himself would assemble a force of 150,000 volunteers in Berlin.[27] Several times he was to record in his diary instances where regular army soldiers retreated past *Volkssturm* units as they moved up to engage the enemy, but this has the smack of the wishful thinking that was increasingly clouding his whole view of the war.

On 12 November, the *Volkssturm* was formally sworn in all over Germany; Goebbels recorded that 100,000 men took the oath of loyalty 'to the *Führer*, to the freedom of the *Reich*, and to social future of our *Volk*' in Berlin alone. On a misty morning, columns of *Volkssturm* recruits marched in from different directions to the Wilhelmplatz; as they converged there, singing the old Nazi song 'We Are Marching through Great Berlin', Goebbels appeared on the balcony of the Propaganda Ministry. He gave a brief speech after the taking of the oath, and was impressed by the demeanour of the men, some of whom 'were already armed'. The Japanese Ambassador to Berlin, Oshima, was present and was – according to Goebbels – 'deeply impressed' by the ceremony. Oven, who was also listening, thought that one could 'only laugh or cry' about Goebbels' declaration that *Volkssturm* regiments would be thrown into any gaps which appeared in the front lines. That afternoon in Lanke, Goebbels listened to a broadcast of the first act of Wagner's *Valkyrie* performed by the Dresden State Opera. It was, he thought, 'a masterful achievement'.[28]

Some of the records relating to the *Volkssturm* battalion formed from workers at the Propaganda Ministry workforce have survived, and it is instructive to look at what they reveal. One company was formed from radio employees. The oldest amongst them was 59 and the youngest was 30; most were in their forties, the same age as Goebbels. They were armed with a collection of rifles, machine guns, sub-machine guns, and the hand-held anti-tank weapon called the *Panzerfaust*.[29] The men were given a programme of meetings for training during November and December, to include a film on how to fight Soviet tanks. The company commander was ordered to pay particular attention to the 'political activization' of the men, and they were also ordered to learn the words of particular songs.[30] Some of the documents suggest that the men had only a limited fighting capacity. The company commander was told in December that of his 200 men, only 104 actually had weapons, that there was no ammunition for the pistols and sub-machine guns, and that many weapons had parts missing.[31] The idea that these men could offer any serious resistance to an army using tanks and heavy artillery appears patently absurd today, and one wonders how many of these men survived the subsequent fighting in Berlin.

As Germany entered the sixth winter of the war, Goebbels tried to preserve a semblance of normality in German life. With the exception of a small area around Aachen in the west, the territory of the *Reich* was still in German hands; Norway, Denmark, Croatia, Slovakia, and parts of Holland, Italy, Poland, and of Hungary, were still under German control. Arms production was running at an extraordinarily high level; new weapons were being developed. Cultural life still continued: Goebbels was supervising the production of Veit Harlan's film *Kolberg*, and he found time to discuss with Furtwängler the problems arising from the use of recorded music for radio broadcasts. Out at Lanke all was peaceful, and family life continued; everyone there was cheered by the news in mid-November that Harald was alive in British captivity. Goebbels even found time for 'a very serious talk with our Helga', now aged 13; he was concerned because she was 'lazy at school and is otherwise letting herself go'.[32]

One wonders how far Helga was affected by the increasingly schizophrenic mood prevailing at Lanke. By all accounts, Magda was increasingly depressed as she, like Goebbels, contemplated a desperate future. Publicly, Magda was still doing her bit for the war effort, for example contributing 100 marks, as she had done in previous years, to a fund for the production of a Braille calendar for soldiers who had lost their sight. In early November she had 3,000 cigarettes sent to wounded men from the Berlin Order Police. But things were falling apart. The calendar for the blind could not be produced in 1944 because of air-raid damage, and the plan for a replacement in 1945 was hindered, ironically because the Propaganda Ministry would not grant an allocation of paper for it. As for her gift, Magda received an anonymous letter from one of the wounded soldiers complaining that the cigarettes intended for them had been appropriated by the two officers appointed to distribute them.[33]

Similarly, although her husband daily detected growing rifts between the Allies, and marvelled at the heroic resistance of the German soldiers who were realizing his new slogan 'Every house a fortress', he was all too aware of the real problems ahead, and was clearly contemplating suicide. Significantly, when the commander of the 'fortress' of Brest surrendered, Goebbels noted grimly that 'there are very few men to whom immortality is preferable to their own life'.[34] After listening to a Beethoven concert on the radio in October he wrote: 'How distant and alien indeed this beautiful world appears. Inwardly I have already fully taken leave of it.'[35] Significantly it was in November 1944 that Goebbels gave instructions for his accumulated diaries to be copied, using the technology of microfilming recently developed by – bizarrely – one Dr Joseph Goebel. A special room in Goebbels' flat in Hermann-Göring-Strasse was dedicated to this task, with a specially ordered camera, and two secretarial assistants supervised by Goebbels' private stenographer Richard Otte.[36] Above all Goebbels was oppressed by the growing weight of the aerial offensive; in early November he noted in his diary that people, particularly in western Germany, wanted peace at any price, and that even in the Party there was resignation. Goebbels saw very little of Hitler in the autumn of 1944, and on 1 December he noted that even though neutral reporters were speaking of 'a miracle' of resistance, inside Germany there was 'a crisis of trust in the Party leadership, even in the *Führer* himself'. There were wild rumours about Hitler, even that he was dead.[37]

Hitler had in fact returned to Berlin, his headquarters in Rastenburg now dangerously close to the Soviet front line. On 1 December Goebbels was summoned to the *Reich* Chancellery, where he found his leader 'more boisterous and optimistic' than he had seen him for a long time. Hitler expounded to Goebbels his plans for an imminent offensive in the Ardennes which would divide the Allies from one another, starting with the Canadians. Later that evening Goebbels was called back and the two men talked until 5.30 a.m. Hitler explained how his offensive would reach Antwerp in ten days, and cut off the whole northern section of the Allied front: 'There would be a Cannae of unimaginable scale.' Once the Channel coast had been regained there would be a renewed onslaught on London with flying bombs and rockets. The plan, thought Goebbels, 'is conceived with a simplicity of genius and offers possibilities for a total extermination of the enemy forces'. Working themselves into a frenzy of enthusiasm, the two men walked up and down the room, finally exchanging 'old memories', and they were happy that 'at bottom, they had not changed'.[38] A few days later Hitler even accepted Magda's invitation to tea at Lanke. Goebbels was delighted to see him, after an interval of four years, relaxing and chatting with his own family. Together they bemoaned the Allied air raids, and Hitler 'emphasized that he had done everything to avoid this kind of warfare'. Goebbels was so carried away by his admiration that he continued: 'That corresponds entirely with the facts. He has tried by every means possible to allow the war to play out in humane forms.'[39]

The Ardennes offensive started in the early hours of 16 December, and achieved a considerable measure of surprise. For a brief period Goebbels was able to rejoice in the illusion of success: 'The map now shows significant blue arrows, markings which we have not seen for a long time.'[40] Although sceptics like Guderian claim to have seen within days that the offensive had failed,[41] Goebbels clung right into the New Year to the notion that it had at least thrown the Americans and the British completely off balance, and restored the initiative in the West to the Germans. The Christmas and New Year festivities were inevitably sombre, but there was a note of renewed optimism. Magda dispensed cards and gifts as she had done before; sending, for example, 100 marks – as she had done every Christmas since 1933 – to the mother of Hans Hoffmann, a Hitler Youth killed in street fighting back in 1931. She added: 'the hope that the coming year might bring us the victorious peace which has been earned with such difficulty and honour'.[42]

To see in the New Year Goebbels staged what was to be his last great set-piece of propaganda. He persuaded Hitler, after a long silence, to broadcast to the German people, and framed this carefully in a larger radio programme. Shortly before midnight on New Year's Eve, the actor Heinrich George read out Clausewitz's 'Political Testament'. After the ringing of bells at 12.00, and the playing of the Badenweiler March, Hitler himself spoke. Goebbels then delivered his own now traditional New Year's speech. The Propaganda Ministry in Berlin had ordered its offices all around the beleaguered *Reich* to report back immediately on the reaction to the whole broadcast amongst the people, with separate comments on Hitler's and Goebbels' speeches, and a collection of reports was on Goebbels' desk the next evening. Given that these reports were compiled by Party activists, and intended for the Propaganda Minister, they must be interpreted with care, but several things are clear. First, there was a huge audience for the broadcast, which was anxiously heard by millions of listeners. Second, widespread gratitude and relief that Hitler himself had once again spoken was reported. Many listeners were moved by the presentation of the speech within the larger broadcast. The report from Posen struck a heroic note:

> The day and evening of 31 December were filled with expectation of the speech, and when shortly after midnight the Badenweiler March rang out, the whole *Volk* felt itself almost bodily connected with its *Führer*, on whose shoulders in the newly beginning year the fate of the *Reich* and the whole continent lies.[43]

It was similarly enthusiastic about Goebbels' speech, and he marked the following passage with his pencil:

> The speech of the *Reich* Minister was generally described as a masterpiece, which surpassed all ministerial speeches of recent times, including that at Christmas, in expressive force, linguistic richness, and warmth. He had once again spoken to the hearts of the *Volk*, as indeed only the doctor knows how to do.[44]

There was much more in this sycophantic vein. From Cologne, one of the most heavily bombed German cities, it was reported that Goebbels' speech had been generally understood as 'Manly words spoken at the right time.' His portrayal of Germany as the cultural centre of the world, and his 'practical examples' of what lay in store for Germany if the Allies triumphed, that is to say domination by 'drunken niggers' and 'garrulous Anglo-American agitators', had been particularly well-received.[45] Apparently around Schwerin in northern Germany, women were 'particularly grateful' for Goebbels' speech. Enthusiasm was likewise reported from bomb-damaged Bremen and Wilhelmshaven.[46]

In amongst the flattery and Nazi hyperbole there were though indications that all was not well. In several places, like Oslo, listeners could not hear the speeches because of air-raid alarms. Tellingly, from Salzburg, a city almost untouched by the war, it was reported that listeners were disappointed by the lack of concrete examples in Hitler's speech of new weapons or offensives which might turn the tide of war. From Klagenfurt, much closer to the front, similar complaints were linked to the criticism that the population there felt itself completely undefended against aerial attack.[47] Even from Posen, that apparent bastion of loyalism, it was reported that a minority had expected from Hitler 'a sensational relevant announcement', and 'were disappointed by the general character of the speech'. As if to apologize for this lapse in devotion, Goebbels' official in Posen added that it had actually been very difficult to follow the speech because of poor reception.[48]

Goebbels teetered similarly between optimism and gloom. He recorded that he expected Hitler's speech to create an 'extraordinary effect among the German *Volk*, and however also in neutral and even in hostile foreign countries'. He also dictated this comment: 'At the end of the year, one's thoughts wander again to the past year. It was the most terrible in my whole life. What we have had to bear this year in cares and burdens now stands as a most horrible memory. I hope that destiny will spare us having to undergo another year like it.'[49]

Any final illusions were shattered in mid-January, when after several months of calm, the Soviets attacked from their bridgeheads across the river Vistula, heading directly for the eastern frontiers of Germany. Goebbels had long anticipated the offensive, but amazingly, had thought that the German forces there could hold the line established in August 1944. In fact these forces, denied the reinforcements and new weapons which Hitler had built up for his cherished Ardennes offensive, were in no position to withstand the Soviets' carefully prepared offensive. Starting on 12 January 1945, and building momentum, the Soviets brushed aside German defences in Poland, and took advantage of the icy ground and frozen rivers to advance with astonishing rapidity towards Berlin. Millions of terrified German civilians fled towards the west, using any means of transport available. Those left behind were subjected to appalling brutalities; many killed themselves rather than face the Red Army.

Once again, Goebbels in Berlin was slow to realize the scale of the catastrophe. Not until 16 January did he accept that the Soviets had broken through completely; on 21 January he recorded that 2–3 million civilians were fleeing, having now realized that large areas of Prussian heartland were already lost. This advance into Germany brought about a change in the nature of the war from Goebbels' perspective. The regular armed forces had again failed, and he turned now to his old comrades, the *Gauleiter*, hoping that they would lead the resistance and make arrangements for civilians in areas threatened by the Soviets. His old belief in 'will' and 'sacrifice' came to the fore, and he agreed totally with Hitler's notion that every German town should be defended as a 'fortress' until the last man and the last bullet. Typically, this has been written off by historians as totally illusory and pointless, but we should bear in mind that as the Soviets advanced, unlike previous offensives, they had to encircle many German towns where improvised groups of *Wehrmacht* and SS, anti-aircraft crews and *Volkssturm* units conducted a fierce defence, lasting in some cases for months. No large German city in the East surrendered without a fight in January or February 1945. Goebbels in these critical days was constantly on the telephone to the *Gauleiter* in the 'fortresses', exhorting them to take whatever measures were necessary to keep fighting. He was contemptuous of Arthur Greiser, *Gauleiter* of the Wartheland, who with most of his staff abandoned Posen several days before the Soviets arrived, leaving a subordinate to conduct a bitter resistance for several weeks. In contrast, he had only the highest praise for his old colleague Karl Hanke, who prepared Breslau for a siege lasting months with rousing speeches, preceded by the public execution of the mayor for 'defeatism'.[50]

On 22 January Goebbels met Hitler, now returned from his temporary headquarters in the West. Before they discussed the situation they watched the latest newsreels, which concentrated on the launch of V2s against Britain. Having recently read a report which alleged that most of London had been evacuated, and that 'whole areas of the city were deserted',[51] Goebbels was no doubt cheered by this. He agreed with Hitler's plan to transfer the best remaining forces available from the Ardennes, not to the collapsing fronts in Prussia and Silesia, but for a new offensive to secure the Hungarian oilfields. Goebbels also agreed with Hitler's bizarre decision to appoint Himmler to command an imaginary 'Army Group Vistula' on the central front in the East, with the job of stemming the Soviet advance. Both had no doubt that an old Party fighter was better equipped for this than a regular army general. Goebbels even wanted Himmler to be given overall command of the armed forces.[52] On 24 January they met again, and discussed the huge refugee columns that were struggling through the frozen landscape ahead of the Soviet advance. Goebbels' summary of this conversation sounds callous: 'We are doing what we can, the rest is destiny.'[53]

We know from many sources that Hitler was as indifferent to the fate of these wretched civilians as he was to those under aerial bombardment in the West. Goebbels was genuinely shocked by the spectacle of German suffering, and had in fact been working tirelessly to try to provide some help for the refugees. On 27 January Goebbels spoke with Göring, who disagreed with Hitler's idea of an offensive in Hungary, and pleaded with Goebbels to get Hitler to negotiate with the British, using Göring's Swedish contacts. Although Goebbels thought that Göring was 'almost defeatist', he did pursue this idea with Hitler, but to no avail. Shortly after this conversation with Hitler, Goebbels was visited by Magda and the three older children. They had seen refugees from the East at nearby Wandlitz, and were understandably upset. That night, Goebbels recorded cryptically: 'Until long past midnight I have further long conversations with Magda. One can imagine what worries we are all troubled with.'[54] We can only speculate about this conversation, but it would be reasonable to assume that they discussed what to do with their children if the war was lost. According to General Guderian, Goebbels had told him as early as July 1943 that he thought 'of the Russians reaching Berlin and us having to poison our wives and children so that they should not fall into the hands of that atrocious enemy'.[55]

These were desperate times. The military communiqués were unable to keep pace with the Soviet advance, and there were rumours that the Soviets were increasingly close to Berlin. Goebbels' adjutant recorded that on 29 January Magda came to his room in an agitated state to ask whether, as her husband had said, the Soviets were only 100 kilometres from Berlin. When Oven said that this was indeed possible, she wept 'without restraint'. According to him, Magda had not yet decided what to do with the children.[56] The people of Berlin were stunned to hear on 31 January that Soviet tanks had crossed the river Oder at Kienitz, and were only two hours' drive from the city centre. No significant German forces stood between them and the capital. Berlin was undefended, with no fortifications; many of its anti-aircraft guns and *Volkssturm* units had already been sent to the front. Rumours spread that Soviet tanks had been seen in the outskirts of the city.

Goebbels was undoubtedly as shocked, and scared, as others in Berlin were. He immediately set about coordinating some kind of defence, summoning various officers and colleagues, and giving them precise tasks. He requisitioned a consignment of 25,000 *Panzerfäuste* from Leipzig, and discovered that there were about 150 tanks and armoured vehicles – in various states – in different places in Berlin. He dragged Speer, who was ill with flu, out of bed and told him to get whatever arms were in factories and awaiting transport in Berlin to the units hastily being assembled. Stocks of petrol and food were gathered. The first anti-tank barriers were thrown up in the city streets. The extent of Goebbels' fear can be judged from his decision that afternoon to send his ministerial car to fetch Magda, the children, and other family members from Lanke and bring them in to the half-wrecked house on Hermann-Göring-Strasse. Goebbels was utterly determined to conduct a heroic resistance in the capital, and indeed no other course of action would have been at all consistent with everything he had said since the start of his political career. How could he praise SA men killed in street fighting, or exhort his *Gauleiter* and Party workers to fight to the death in Königsberg, Danzig, and Breslau, if he was not prepared to stand and fight in the *Reich* capital itself? That evening Goebbels spoke with Hitler in the *Reich* Chancellery. Again he pressed him to seek a negotiated settlement. He told Hitler that he would not leave Berlin while a single house was left to defend, that Magda would also stay, and had refused to send the children away. The implication was clear. They would all die there if necessary. Hitler said that he thought Magda was wrong, but added that Eva Braun had made a similar decision.[57]

The Soviets did not advance into Berlin, and again paused to consolidate their position. After the panic of 31 January, Berlin was granted an uneasy interlude of some ten weeks in which a semblance of normal life was reasserted. Before any complacency could develop, there was a huge aerial attack by American bombers on 3 February which caused extensive damage and left fires burning for days. Water, gas, and electricity could not be restored to large parts of the city, and government business was conducted in buildings with no glass in the windows. Speaking with Hitler on 5 February, Goebbels agreed that they would never capitulate. He dictated: 'I no longer have, inwardly, any personal connections with what is called private life.'[58] According to Oven, Goebbels again told Magda to take the children to the West, saying 'You will be safe there. The British will do nothing to you', but she refused. Goebbels told Oven that Magda had poison for the children, but would not use it until the last moment. Separately he told him that the Nazis would be branded for all time as monsters and criminals, and that he was not prepared to have himself, his wife, or any of his children live to see 'our debacle'.[59] On 11 February Goebbels recorded privately his concern for his family and children: 'One can imagine what huge psychological burdens are bound up with them for Magda and myself.' Nonetheless, on 4 March he again told Hitler that Magda and the children would stay with him in Berlin 'in all circumstances'.[60]

Between January and April 1945 Goebbels continued his outward life much as he had for the last few years. He still recorded the Armed Forces communiqué in his diary, although this was frequently outdated by rapid advances on one front or another. He detailed the growing breakdown of the German armed forces, the collapse of civilian morale, and most hurtfully for him, the disintegration of the Party. He too was losing hope. When he heard that Himmler had declared in a flyer that God would not desert 'his brave German people', he commented: 'At any rate, in my view, this Lord God is indeed a little hard-hearted.' When he heard that the Allied leaders at Yalta had pledged themselves to the abolition of the German General Staff, he grimly noted that if this were their only demand, he would happily agree with them.[61] Goebbels was in fact slightly misinformed: Himmler's leaflet assured the German people that 'the Lord God' would give them victory.[62] Goebbels clung with diminishing hope to the possibility of a schism amongst the Allies, and railed about the dire fate awaiting a Europe divided between 'Bolsheviks' and 'plutocrats'. Although he still proclaimed in public his unshakeable faith in Hitler, and in victory, he had realized that Hitler would not dismiss Göring or Ribbentrop, and that his view of the military situation was over-optimistic. He recorded scornfully that Rosenberg still refused to disband his Ministry for the Occupied East, wanting to style this now as a 'Ministry for the East'. Rosenberg might as well, he thought, set up a 'Ministry for the West', or 'for the South'.[63] Perhaps most galling for Goebbels, as the *Reich* was pulverized from the air, and occupied from East and West, was Hitler's refusal to speak to the public. Goebbels still believed in the power of oratory which – he thought – had won the day for him and Hitler before 1933, and, he argued, for Churchill in 1940 and Stalin in 1941.

Hitler had in fact made his last broadcast speech on 30 January, the anniversary of his accession to power, and was not moved by Goebbels' entreaties. Goebbels himself broadcast to what was left of the nation on the evening of 28 February.

He still spoke with all the passion he had earlier deployed, but the poverty of his argument was shown by his statement that political leaders had 'to look not just at facts, but at possibilities and chances'. Again he railed at 'international Jewry', and he undoubtedly struck a chord with some listeners when he spoke furiously about the 'enemy air terror' and 'indescribable Bolshevik atrocities'. Goebbels declared that 'We will more happily die than capitulate', and chillingly he stated his contempt for the idea of living under a 'cowardly subjection'. He stated that he would not value his own life, or that of his own children in such a circumstance. He would 'willingly and with joy throw away such a life'. His willingness to die had less resonance with most of his listeners; by this time it was becoming clear all over Germany that many people were keener to surrender than to die. Goebbels' adjutant was shocked by what he called a 'speech of the grave'.[64] He was not the only one. Victor Klemperer, who had miraculously survived the terrible British attack on Dresden on 13/14 February, heard parts of the speech, and wrote:

> Goebbels spoke differently from usual. He largely dispensed with rhetorical tone and structure and instead let the individual words fall very slowly with a strong, even emphasis, like hammer blows, with a pause between every blow. And the content was utter despair.[65]

In the West the Americans and the British were being greeted with white flags, and the last opinion reports reaching Goebbels made it plain that people no longer had any belief in the possibility of victory. Hitler, although unwilling to speak, had issued a proclamation on 24 February in which he prophesied victory, but the last surviving opinion report to the Propaganda Ministry suggested that this had been met with complete scepticism. It quoted as representative comments such as 'the *Führer* has already eternally prophesied victory', and 'always the same old record again'.[66]

On 8 March 1945 Goebbels had a last taste of the 'good old days' whose memories had sustained him since 1933. He drove out of Berlin to visit the front line in Silesia, where troops commanded by General Schörner had recaptured the town of Lauban. It was a clear frosty day, and gunfire from the front could be heard. In the marketplace in Lauban, surrounded by burnt out Soviet tanks, Schörner and Goebbels gave speeches. Goebbels admired Schörner enormously, not least because of his draconian policy of hanging deserters and leaving their bodies on display. Goebbels travelled on to Görlitz, where he spoke in the 'overflowing town hall to soldiers and *Volkssturm* men', before sitting down to a meal with some of them. 'Once again', he dictated afterwards, 'I observe that firm faith in victory and in the *Führer* is prevalent among these men ... These are fine moments which have a directly healing effect.' A film crew accompanied Goebbels and scenes from the visit were shown in one of his last newsreels.

Goebbels was shown in Lauban talking with a 16-year-old Hitler Youth who had been awarded the Iron Cross. In the film of him addressing the crowd in Görlitz, the camera lingered on the face of a nun wearing a habit, as Goebbels spoke of the 'slaughtered children and dishonoured women' left behind by the Soviets.[67]

In these last weeks, the remains of Goebbels' propaganda apparatus were still at work, but there is an air of unreality about some of the last surviving documents from the half-ruined Propaganda Ministry. This organization, which had amazed the world with it stage management of huge party rallies and theatrical state funerals, was reduced now to pitiful improvisations. In mid-March 1945 it was considering the idea that 'the best and cheapest way to provide the enemy with our propaganda material' was simply to leave this 'material' in areas about to be abandoned, in the East and the West.[68] Advice was still despatched to regional propaganda offices. The office in Linz sent in examples of two flyers it had prepared for the *Wehrmacht*, and was requested at the end of March to make them – and future 'propaganda materials' – more concise, and to print the text in larger type.[69] The *Reich* Chamber of Culture was still operating from its Berlin head office in Schlüterstrasse, and attempting to regulate what was left of German cultural life. The conductor Eugen Jochum – one of the 'divinely favoured' artists spared from military service – had been demanding that he be paid 2,000 marks per engagement, the same as other star conductors like Clemens Krauss, Hans Knappertsbusch, and Karl Böhm. This request was not made for personal reasons, he explained, but in order that his orchestra, the Hamburg Philharmonic, should be seen to be on the same level as those in Munich and Vienna. By April 1945, the sum being discussed for Jochum had almost doubled. The Chamber of Culture wrote finally to Jochum to confirm that he would be paid 4,000 marks per engagement on 17 April 1945, by which time Vienna was in the hands of the Red Army. British and American units were fast approaching Hamburg and Munich, where ironically, both would attempt to get Jochum to conduct for them.[70]

Goebbels did still engage with details of policy. In a last effort to coordinate manpower, he issued an order to all civilian refugees and soldiers separated from their units to register with the police or the army in the areas they had fled to. This applied particularly to all males aged between 15 and 60.[71] After the devastating aerial attack on Dresden in February Goebbels demanded that Germany should renounce the Geneva Convention, and execute equal numbers of British and American POWs in retaliation for the attack.[72] Goebbels had other reasons for this suggestion than vengeance. He wanted to provoke the Americans and the British into behaving more badly as they occupied Germany, so that the population would fear and resist them, as they did the Soviets. But Hitler rejected this, as he did so many of Goebbels' proposals in the last months of the war. There was a distinct shift in Goebbels' attitude to Hitler in March and April 1945, as he came to realize that Hitler would never make fundamental changes, notably in the leadership, and that as a result there was no hope for a negotiated settlement, or for any change in the military situation. Everyone Goebbels spoke with confirmed his utter contempt for Göring and Ribbentrop, and begged him to intervene with Hitler to dismiss them. On 11 March Hitler and Goebbels even turned on their old comrade Himmler, who according to Hitler had 'in direct disobedience' not carried out his orders to concentrate his Army Group Vistula against the Soviets in Pomerania. Goebbels, who only weeks previously had been thinking that Himmler should be given overall command of the armed forces, now added that he did not think it had been wise to entrust him with the command of an army group. On 15 March Hitler told Goebbels that he had given Himmler 'an extraordinarily energetic reprimand', and compared his failures to those of the officers who had let the Americans capture intact one of the Rhine bridges at Remagen. Four of these men had already been tried and shot.[73]

Goebbels may have felt a sense of *Schadenfreude* at the fall from grace of so many of his former comrades, and, in contrast, his continued favour with Hitler, but inwardly he was in despair. He spoke with Hitler almost every evening now, and he constantly badgered him to get rid of Göring and Ribbentrop. After one of these conversations on 21 March which, like many at this time, was held in an air-raid shelter while British Mosquitos dropped bombs overhead, Goebbels returned to his house:

> When I arrive home, the whole house is in darkness. A lighting cable has again been broken. A gloomy and somewhat melancholy evening. Magda has gone to Dresden to visit Frau von Arendt. One can get quite depressed in hours like these, above all when I put this question to myself: what should I do, to get that which I know to be right to be actually carried through? I feel in myself a great moral and national responsibility to the German *Volk*, in that I am one of few who even now have the ear of the *Führer*. A possibility like this must be used in all ways. But I really can not do more than I am doing.
>
> I have again today put really open opinions to the *Führer*, in a way that I otherwise have seldom in my life spoken to him. But, as I have said, a success is not to be seen at the moment.[74]

The next day Goebbels dictated:

> From the letters to me also a deep apathy and resignation is expressed. Here too everywhere the word is quite openly about the crisis of leadership. Göring, Ley, and Ribbentrop enjoy the outspoken disapproval of all letter writers. Sadly, the *Führer* is also increasingly named in critical comments … I believe also, that my own work today is no longer absolutely effective. It appears to me disastrous that now the criticism does not stop at the person of the *Führer*, or

the national socialist idea and the national socialist movement. Many Party comrades are also beginning to waver.[75]

Even as Goebbels dictated his diary entry, British, Canadian, and American forces were fanning out of their bridgeheads on the East bank of the Rhine, to the north and south of the Ruhr valley, and towards Berlin. Reading through letters from the public which reached him in the next few days, Goebbels noted that many correspondents now posed the question of 'how they might in the best and most honourable way leave this awful life'.[76]

The *Reich* was collapsing: in the West, the Ruhr was encircled; in the East, the defenders of Königsberg surrendered on 10 April. On the previous day, Magda sent a letter to the defenders of besieged Breslau, still holding out under the leadership of her former lover, Karl Hanke. Her words suggest that she knew the end was near. She praised the latest 'wonderful broadcast' from the city, which she described as 'the last gift to me from Breslau'.[77] Goebbels was particularly dismayed by what he perceived as the cowardly failure to defend Vienna, which was taken by the Soviets after a struggle of only a few days. After years of restraint, he was able to reveal his true feelings about the Viennese in one of the last surviving entries in his diary: 'They are a disgusting rabble, made up of a mixture of Poles, Czechs, Jews, and Germans.'[78] Goebbels had taken great care to have all his diaries, handwritten and dictated, microfilmed onto glass plates, but no entries after 10 April have survived. The glass plates were carefully packed in aluminium cases and buried near Potsdam. The original handwritten notebooks and the typewritten entries since 1941 were similarly packed and taken to the *Reich* Chancellery.[79] On 16 April, the final Soviet assault on Berlin began, and within a few days, the last defences in front of the city were prised open. Goebbels had dreamed of a heroic resistance, conducted from one of the huge flak towers in the city centre, fondly imagining that the city could hold out for weeks or even months, but in the event, there were hardly any tanks, guns, or soldiers left.

On the evening of 18 April, Goebbels, with the help of his adjutant Oven, spent several hours burning his personal papers and photographs. Apparently he paused before a photograph of Lida Baarova was consigned to the flames, and said, 'Look at that. That is a perfectly beautiful woman.'[80] The next evening, Goebbels delivered his last broadcast speech, on the eve of Hitler's 56th birthday. He conceded that this was 'perhaps the last time' on which he would carry out this traditional function, and devoted most of the speech to praising Hitler and his achievements, contrasting these with the terrible fate now descending upon Europe: 'The most brilliant culture that the earth has ever seen is sinking in ruins and leaving behind only a memory of the greatness of an age which these satanic powers are destroying.' In a flight of fantasy, Goebbels declared that 'Order, peace, and prosperity' had always been Hitler's goals. He continued:

If the enemy powers have their way, mankind will sink in a sea of blood and tears ... If we carry through our purpose, then the work of social reconstruction begun in Germany in 1933 and so suddenly interrupted in 1939 will be taken up again and resumed with greater strength. Other peoples will join in this – not compelled by us, but from their own free will – because there is no other way out of the world crisis.

Goebbels finished on a defiant note:

Our misfortune has aged us, but not made us characterless. Germany is still and for ever the land of loyalty. In danger it will celebrate its greatest triumph. Never will history be able to say of this time that a people deserted its leader, or a leader his people. That is victory. That which we have so often in happiness asked of the *Führer* on this evening, is today in sorrow and in danger for all of us a much deeper and more inward request of him. He shall remain for us, what he is and always was for us, our Hitler.[81]

On 20 April, as Soviet spearheads advanced closer towards Berlin, Hitler's birthday was celebrated at the *Reich* Chancellery. His senior aides, including Goebbels, assembled for the last time to offer their greetings, and photographs were taken of him reviewing SS men and Hitler Youths in the open air. Several people around Hitler urged him to take the last chance to leave Berlin, but he declared his intention to stay there. For all the rhetoric of loyalty in Goebbels' final broadcast, this was the moment at which several of Hitler's closest aides, including Göring, Himmler, Speer, Dönitz, and Ribbentrop, chose to leave Berlin and to try to save their own skins.

The next day at 11.00 a.m., Goebbels held his last ministerial conference in the film room of the Propaganda Ministry, and shortly afterwards, the first Russian shells started to fall in the government quarter. That evening, Oven records that he had a long conversation with Magda Goebbels, who was 'calm and decided. Her decision to kill the children stands. She did not cry any more.'[82] If Magda was calm, Hitler was not. On 22 April, as the shelling above intensified, he discovered that his plans for a counter-attack on the Russians had not materialized, and finally the façade of self-assurance cracked. Trevor-Roper described the scene:

Hitler flew into a rage. He shrieked that he had been deserted; he railed at the Army; he denounced all traitors; he spoke of universal treason, failure, corruption, and lies; and then, exhausted, he declared that the end had come. At last, and for the first time, he despaired of his mission. All was over; the Third Reich was a failure, and its author had nothing left to do but to die.[83]

Ironically, as Hitler despaired, Goebbels' final written exhortation to the German public was reaching some of his ordinary citizens. The last issue of *Das Reich* was published on Sunday 22 April, carrying, as it has since its inception in 1940, a leading article by '*Reich* Minister Dr Goebbels' on its front page. Next to a picture of Hitler receiving birthday greetings from Himmler and Keitel, Goebbels' leader was entitled 'Resistance at any price'. He declared:

> The war has entered a stage in which only the full deployment of the nation and of every individual can bring deliverance. The defence of the freedom of our *Volk* is no longer just a matter for the armed forces at the front, it must also be taken on with an unparalleled fanaticism by every man and woman and boy and girl in the civilian population.

Reverting to the revolutionary language of his earlier years, Goebbels continued:

> Our whole leadership of war must be revolutionized. The rules of war of earlier centuries are obsolete and have become completely useless for our

46. Goebbels' last words to the German people: 'Resistance at any price', in *Das Reich*, 22 April, 1945. The newspaper was printed, but very few copies could be distributed and it is rare today, hence the poor-quality reproduction.

purposes. Our age is that of the people's war. And as the continued existence of whole peoples is threatened, so whole peoples must rise up in defence of their threatened further existence ... Not much more in this war is to be achieved with chivalry alone.

He concluded, appropriately, by turning again to the theme of sacrifice which had run through his political speaking and writing since 1923:

In 1918 we gave up the victory at the last minute through our own weaknesses. That will not happen in 1945. We all have to take care of that. This is the precondition of our final success. That may sound fantastic today, but it is so! The hour of ultimate victory awaits us. It will be bought with tears and blood, but it will also justify all the sacrifices we have made.[84]

This talk of 'people's war', and fighting was now completely redundant, but the rhetoric of sacrifice was not. According to the account later put together by Soviet intelligence, after the dramatic conference on 22 April, Goebbels was summoned by telephone to the bunker under the *Reich* Chancellery. Hitler spoke privately with him for some minutes in his study, and when Goebbels emerged he was 'pounced upon by Bormann, Keitel, Dönitz, and Jodl'. Goebbels 'informed them that Hitler believed the position to be hopeless, and had concluded that the war was lost ... Goebbels added that he was horrified because on the telephone Hitler had requested him in a quavering voice to come over to him in the bunker immediately with his wife and children, because everything had come to an end.'[85]

After a further telephone conversation with Hitler at 6.00 p.m. on that Sunday, Goebbels decided to move, with Magda and the children, into the bunker under the *Reich* Chancellery. Two cars were called, and carried the minister and his family, with a few possessions, the short distance from the Propaganda Ministry to their final home underground. This was not merely a symbolic entombment; Goebbels and Magda knew that they would not emerge alive, and did not intend that their children would either. Although Goebbels did not have time to give his faithful adjutant a final farewell, Magda shook Oven's hand, and said: 'We are going to the *Reich* Chancellery. We must all poison ourselves.'[86]

The 'last days' in Hitler's bunker have been recounted by survivors, by historians, and by film-makers. They were exhaustively researched by Allied intelligence services. From eye-witness accounts, and from surviving documents produced in the bunker, we can reconstruct something of the final days of Goebbels' life. He evidently took part in the discussions and conferences which were still held, and played a central part in all details of the final drama. Speer records that he was 'exaltedly heroic', and this impression is confirmed by the surviving documents produced in the bunker. Goebbels was undoubtedly dismayed, if not surprised by the news that first Göring, and then Himmler, betrayed Hitler by attempting to usurp his authority and start negotiations with the Allies. Magda, for all her apparent earlier calmness, was – according to Speer – in a state of 'total collapse',[87] and spent much of the last few days lying in her room. The test pilot Hanna Reitsch, who arrived in the bunker on 26 April, later provided a contradictory account, stating that during her three days in the bunker, on every occasion she met her, she found Magda Goebbels 'composed in an exemplary manner'.[88] The Goebbels' children were apparently happy and brought a much-needed sense of humanity into their grim new surroundings. Hitler's secretary Traudl Junge wrote:

> The five little girls and the boy were happy and cheerful. They were pleased to be staying with 'Uncle Hitler', and soon filled the bunker with their games. They were charming, well brought-up, natural-mannered children. They knew nothing of the fate awaiting them, and the adults did all they could to keep them unaware of it. I took them over to the storeroom where Hitler's birthday presents were kept. There were children's toys and clothes among them, and the children chose what they liked.[89]

Traudl Junge agrees with Speer that Magda was in a terrible state, but suggests that Goebbels himself was struggling to maintain his bearing. She also contradicted her earlier statement by suggesting that not all the children were so guileless:

> In the evening she [Hanna Reitsch] put the children to bed. Their mother hardly had the strength to face her children with composure now. Every meeting with them made her feel so terrible that she burst into tears afterwards. She and her husband were nothing but shadows, already doomed to die.
>
> When I passed the door of the children's room I heard their six clear childish voices singing. I went in. They were sitting in three bunk beds, with their hands over their ears so as not to spoil the three-part round they were singing. Then they wished each other good night cheerfully, and finally fell asleep. Only, the oldest, Helga, sometimes had a sad, knowing expression in her big brown eyes. She was the quietest, and sometimes I think, with horror, that in her heart that child saw through the pretence of the grown ups.
>
> I left the children's room wondering how anyone could allow these innocent creatures to die for him. Frau Goebbels talked to me about it. There were no differences of class or rank any more, we were all bound together by fate. Frau Goebbels was in greater torment than any of us. She was facing six deaths, while the rest of us only had to face one. 'I would rather have my children die than live in disgrace, jeered at. Our children have no place in Germany as it will be after the war.'[90]

According to Anja Klabunde, Helga 'was aware that they had all been consigned to death, and she repeatedly begged to be allowed to leave the bunker, saying she didn't want to die'.[91] Hanna Reitsch confirmed that she taught the children part-songs and told them stories, but did not refer to Helga's fears.[92]

Goebbels himself continued his heroic exhortations from the bunker, issuing 'declarations' for what was left of the German press on 22 and 23 April. In the first he confirmed that 'I and my colleagues are obviously staying in Berlin; my wife and children are also here, and stay here.' In the second he restated an oft-used propaganda theme, arguing that more than Hitler's and his own life were at stake: 'We are facing a decision of the greatest importance, not only for us, but for all of Europe.'[93] In fact, Goebbels and Hitler had lost forever their power to influence the rest of the world, although they clung to its outward appearance, conducting meetings, making decisions, and dictating documents. On 28 April, Goebbels wrote a letter to Magda's son Harald, with a determinedly heroic ring, suggesting that he may have intended it also for a wider audience. 'My dear Harald', he wrote:

> We are now confined to the *Führer's* bunker in the *Reich* Chancellery and are fighting for our lives and our honour. God alone knows what the outcome of this battle will be. I know, however, that we shall only come out of it, dead or alive, with honour and glory. I hardly think that we shall see one another again. Probably therefore, these are the last lines you will ever receive from me. I expect from you that, should you survive this war, you will do nothing but honour your mother and me. It is not essential that we remain alive in order to continue to influence our people. You may well be the only one able to continue our family tradition ... You may be proud of having such a mother as yours. Yesterday the *Führer* gave her the Golden Party Badge which he has worn on his tunic for years and she deserved it ... Farewell my dear Harald. Whether we shall ever see each other again is in the lap of the gods. If we do not, may you always be proud of having belonged to a family which, even in misfortune, remained loyal to the very end to the *Führer* and his pure sacred cause.[94]

On 29 April, Hitler asked Goebbels to find an official who could conduct his marriage to Eva Braun. Goebbels called upon Walter Wagner, a Berlin official, who turned up in his *Volkssturm* uniform, and held a brief ceremony in the bunker's conference room. Goebbels was the first witness on the marriage certificate.[95] Afterwards there was a little party, at which apparently the Goebbels' wedding back in 1931 was fondly remembered. The end was drawing near though, and Hitler withdrew from the party to dictate his political and private testaments to Traudl Junge. In his 'Political Testament' he named Goebbels as the *Reich* Chancellor after his own death, and perhaps surprisingly named Dönitz as

'*Reich* President'. Goebbels was the first of four witnesses to sign the document. The 'Private Testament' was a shorter document in which Hitler declared his wish that his and Eva Braun's bodies should be burned immediately after his death. He named Martin Bormann as the executor of his Testament, strangely describing him as 'his most loyal Party comrade'.[96] Goebbels, who also witnessed this document, must have read this, and we can only speculate on what his reaction to this ingratitude was.

Hitler then apparently ordered Goebbels to leave Berlin, and to join Dönitz in northern Germany. Traudl Junge recorded:

> Suddenly Goebbels bursts in. I look at his agitated face, which is as white as chalk. Tears are running down his cheeks ... His usually clear voice is stifled by tears and shaking. 'The Führer wants me to leave Berlin, Frau Junge. I am to take up a leading post in the new government. But I can't leave Berlin, I cannot leave the Führer's side! I am Gauleiter of Berlin, and my place is here. If the Führer is dead my life is pointless.'[97]

Goebbels then dictated a short 'Appendix' to Hitler's Private Testament, in which he explained further why he could not accept Hitler's order:

> For the first time in my life, I must categorically refuse to obey an order of the *Führer*. My wife and children stand by this refusal. First, we would never find it in our hearts, from human considerations, and from considerations of personal loyalty, to leave the *Führer* alone in his hour of greatest need; second, I would for the rest of my life be known as a dishonourable apostate and a common blackguard who had lost all self-esteem and also the respect of his *Volk*. I believe that thereby I perform a better service to the future of the German *Volk*, for which in the coming difficult times examples will be more important than men. For these reasons, I express with my wife our unalterable decision not to leave the *Reich* capital and rather to end a life which no longer has any value for me, at the side of the *Führer*, if I cannot spend it in service to the *Führer* and by his side.[98]

Three copies of Hitler's Testaments, one with Goebbels' Appendix attached, were then despatched from the bunker. The next day, 30 April, in mid-afternoon, Hitler and Eva Braun took their leave from all those left in the bunker. Accounts of Hitler's final moments differ. According to Otto Günsche, one of Hitler's aides, who was outside their room, Magda Goebbels came rushing down the corridor, and burst into Hitler's room. She was curtly ordered out, and fled, sobbing. A shot was heard from their room, and Goebbels and Artur Axmann (the leader of the Hitler Youth) entered the room to find both Hitler and Eva Braun lying dead. They stayed there for some minutes in silence before the bodies were carried upstairs to the Chancellery garden by two adjutants. According to the Soviet report based on earlier post-war interrogations of Günsche and Linge, Hitler took his leave from Magda Goebbels in her room, after finally rejecting an appeal from Goebbels to leave Berlin. Linge and Bormann were the first to enter Hitler's room to find him, and Eva Braun, dead there.[99] All are agreed that the bodies of Hitler and his wife were put in a shell crater, and doused in petrol before being set alight. Goebbels, together with Bormann and others of Hitler's personal staff, gave a final salute from the shelter of an entrance to the bunker while the bodies burned. The Soviet report alleges that the watchers were forced to close the door to the bunker and retreat inside by the force of the flames as soon as the petrol ignited.[100] It was a squalid and ignoble end to a life of violence. We can only wonder what Goebbels thought of this wretched, improvised cremation, which was in such marked contrast to the grandiose funeral ceremonies he had supervised since the 1920s.

There followed a confused period of 24 hours or so, in which Goebbels and Magda desperately tried to decide what to do. It would have been strange if they had not wavered in their decision to kill themselves and the children. According to Heinz Linge, Goebbels spoke to him the morning after Hitler's suicide, and said:

> I have had a horrible night. I have also decided to bring my life to an end; but it is a very difficult moment. I have been arguing with myself for ages, but I lack the courage.[101]

Others in the bunker, including Bormann, were determined to try to escape. In the afternoon of 1 May Goebbels despatched a telegram to Dönitz, announcing Hitler's death, and informing him of his new position. Goebbels had also decided to do what he had urged upon Hitler for months, to negotiate with the Soviets. During the night of 30 April/1 May, Goebbels managed to send General Krebs, who had been Hitler's last Chief of the General Staff, to the headquarters of General Chuikov, commander of the Soviet 8th Guards Army, with instructions to negotiate a surrender in Berlin, and a safe conduct out of the bunker for all those still there. Chuikov left a detailed account of his negotiations with Krebs – a Russian-speaker – in his later memoir, and from this we can try to deduce Goebbels' intentions. Krebs arrived at Chuikov's command post at 3.50 a.m. on 1 May, and stayed for some twelve hours. He carried with him several documents, including a message from Goebbels:

> In accordance with the testament of the departed *Führer*, we empower General Krebs as follows:
> We inform the leader of the Soviet people that today, at 15 hours 30 minutes, the *Führer* voluntarily quitted this life. On the basis of his legal right, the

Führer in the testament he left behind him transmitted all power to Doenitz, to myself and Bormann. I am empowered by Bormann to establish contact with the leader of the Soviet people. This contact is essential for peace talks between the powers which have born the heaviest losses. Goebbels.

One wonders why Goebbels felt he had to say that he was 'empowered by Bormann', as in the subsequent negotiations, Krebs repeatedly made it clear that Goebbels was now 'in Hitler's place'. Goebbels – through Krebs – asked the Soviets to allow the new German government to meet, in order to come to a favourable peace agreement between the two countries, but this was simply asking too much. The Soviets had no need to grant any favours to any government in what was left of Germany, and Chuikov – on the instructions of his superiors – demanded nothing less than unconditional surrender. Krebs finally left Chuikov's post to return to the bunker to confer with Goebbels at around midday on 1 May.[102] Was Goebbels still hoping that he might have a future as the leader of a German government negotiating with the Soviets, or was he determined to kill himself and his family, even if the Soviets agreed to negotiate? We will never know.

He knew after Krebs' return that there would be no negotiations. If he, or Magda, had wavered in their determination to kill themselves, they now decided that the time had come. The last moments of their lives have been described by Rochus Misch, a telephone operator in the bunker:

It was only just after 5 p.m. when Frau Goebbels walked past me followed by the children. They were all wearing white nightgowns. She took them next door; an orderly arrived carrying a tray with six cups and a jug of chocolate. Later somebody said it was laced with sleeping pills. I saw her hug some, stroke others as they drank it. I don't think they knew about their Uncle Adolf's death; they laughed and chatted as always. A little later they passed me on their way upstairs. Heidi turned around. I waved to her, she waved back with one hand, and then, suddenly, letting go of her mother's hand, she turned all the way around and, bursting into that happy clear laugh of hers, she scraped one forefinger along another and chanted the little rhyme she always sang when she saw me: 'Misch, Misch, you are a fish.' Her mother put her arm around her and pulled her gently up the steps, but she went on chanting it.

Magda Goebbels then took Dr Stumpfegger to the children's room, and reappeared 'about an hour later':

She was crying. She sat down at the long table in the conference room and played solitaire. Goebbels came and went, but I didn't see them talk.[103]

The children were evidently killed with cyanide capsules after first being dosed with morphine. It appears that Helga may have struggled. Shortly after this, Goebbels and Magda went up to the Chancellery garden. They bit on cyanide capsules, and Goebbels may also have shot himself. Their adjutant, Schwägermann, made an effort to burn the bodies, but there was insufficient petrol available, and possibly it was too dangerous out in the open air to do this properly. The next day, Soviet troops entered the now deserted bunker, where they found the bodies of a number of officers (including Krebs), and of six children. The partially burned bodies of Goebbels and his wife were in the same room, on the floor. Major Boris Polevoi was one of the first to enter the room. 'Both bodies had been burned', he said, 'and only Josef Goebbels' face was recognizable.'[104]

Epilogue

> When I told a few people today about Hitler's death, they all said to me something like: 'Indeed? Finally! Sadly too late.' Then they went about their daily business ... To the people here it is all the same whether Hitler, the once so divinely worshipped *Führer*, is still alive or whether he is already dead. He has played out his role.
>
> Ursula von Kardorff, in her diary, 2 May 1945.[1]

Goebbels has not had a good press. His hope in the last days of the 'Third Reich', to set an example which would impress future generations, has not thus far been fulfilled. Only a few far-right fanatics have been anything other than horrified by the killing of his six children in the bunker, an action for which he must share responsibility with Magda. He has no grave or memorial stone. In the silent forests around what is now Kętrzyn in northern Poland, dense layers of moss and lichen thrive on the ruined bunkers where Hitler and Goebbels agreed to murder the Jews of Europe. The Nazi Party which had provided a surrogate religion for Goebbels was 'completely and finally abolished' by the Allied Control Council in September 1945;[2] the government he had worked for with such energy, including his Propaganda Ministry, had already been disbanded in the ruins of a divided Berlin. Today parts of the building survive, but its underground bunker is covered by some of the 2,711 concrete stellae which form a huge public memorial to the murdered Jews of Europe. The *Reich* Chamber of Culture – Goebbels' 'dream' – was one of over 60 Nazi organizations also abolished by the Allied Control Council in 1945;[3] its headquarters building in Berlin is now a hotel. The central control of the arts and media in Germany which Goebbels had supervised has been replaced by deliberately regionalized and pluralistic structures, and there is still no Ministry of Culture or any equivalent in the Federal German Republic. Goebbels certainly did more than any other individual to make 'propaganda' a dirty word, forever associated with control, manipulation, and deceit. He is irrevocably associated with the mass hysteria of the 'Third Reich' and its most horrible acts. For all the noisy activities of neo-Nazis in Germany itself and in other parts of the world today, the *völkisch* National Socialism which Goebbels propagated with such extraordinary energy has never been resurrected as a serious political ideology. The terraced house in which Goebbels spent most of the first

25 years of his life in Rheydt still stands, but is completely anonymous. One wonders how many of the ethnically diverse people who now walk and drive past it know anything of its historical significance.

During his lifetime, Goebbels was not a man to whom others were indifferent. Amongst fellow Nazis, he aroused adulation and affection. Particularly during the intense bombing of Germany in the last three years of the war, he was genuinely popular with large swathes of the public. Others loathed and detested him, not only his political opponents, or those who suffered in one way or another from his actions. Throughout his working life, Goebbels was the target for sustained vilification, often from those who knew him at close quarters, and several of the central themes developed by observers between 1925 and 1945 have been taken up – more or less critically – by historians since then.

One of the earliest surviving assessments of Goebbels set the tone. At the meeting in September 1925, where the Working Community of the north and west German *Gaue* of the Nazi Party was established by Gregor Strasser and Goebbels, was an activist from the Göttingen branch of the Party, Hermann Fobke. He sent a report on proceedings to the Party Headquarters in Munich, in which he described Strasser's young assistant from Elberfeld as

> sharply intellectual, demanding in-depth character study, in that he does not, on first appearance, seem unconditionally trustworthy.[4]

As we have seen, from the time of his first involvement with the Nazi Party in the Rhineland-Ruhr, Goebbels made enemies, even of colleagues with whom he was to have a long association. Max Amann, the Party publisher who secured lucrative deals with Goebbels for his various writings between 1925 and 1945, was quoted in a British anti-Nazi publication of 1934, describing Goebbels as

> the Mephistopheles of the Party, a disagreeable man with the dark look of a Bolshevik, one whom the Lord God has marked with a cloven hoof.[5]

Otto Strasser was one who had good reason to detest Goebbels, or 'the little cripple', as he called him. Only by fleeing Germany before 1933 did he escape with his life. In his 1940 memoir he wrote that 'Goebbels was ambitious, an opportunist, and a liar'.[6] 'Putzi' Hanfstaengl was another Nazi who fell out with Goebbels and had to leave Germany in fear of his life. He was particularly harsh, describing Goebbels as 'this mocking, jealous, vicious, satanically-gifted, dwarf'. Goebbels was, according to Hanfstaengl, 'not only schizophrenic but schizopedic'.[7] It is hardly surprising that anti-Nazis like Carl von Ossietzky echoed these descriptions which mixed character assessment with references to Goebbels' physical appearance, and to his disability. In the critical journal

Weltbühne Ossietsky, referring to Goebbels' successful campaign against the film *All Quiet on the Western Front* in 1930 called him 'a club-footed psychopath'.[8] The society columnist Bella Fromm was in the public gallery of the *Reichstag* on 10 February 1931 and watched 'the raging dwarf' (as she called him) deliver a vitriolic attack on Chancellor Brüning. She wrote:

> He is a Nazi Party Deputy, and very greedy for power. 'The Doctor,' as they call him, almost a dwarf, hobbled to the speaker's desk. But before he did so, the Communists had indulged in a veritable flood of invective. Apparently that was just what he needed to start him right. You have to be impressed by the way he uses the German language, whether you like him or not. A kind of combination of Mephisto and Savonarola, sinister and frantic, intriguing and fanatically obsessed. He uses his hands violently enough for Yvonne to remark, 'Funny way of speaking for a full-blooded Aryan.' But his voice is soft enough, and he knows how to make the most effective use of it.[9]

Louis Lochner was an American journalist who first saw and heard Goebbels in 1932, and remarked upon the same characteristics:

> His voice, of a deeply resonant quality, seemed to quiver with emotion. His gestures seemed passionate. His general attitude seemed to be that of a man so wrapped up in his fanaticism that time meant nothing so long as he had a message to deliver.
>
> I noticed something else, however: his fascinatingly delicate hands moved in powerful gestures without the slightest trembling and belied the quiver in his voice. His gestures, although seemingly spontaneous, indicated careful planning, for he always threw himself into position for a particular gesture before beginning to execute it ...
>
> In short, here was a showman who knew exactly what he was doing ...
>
> With Goebbels I had the feeling that he would have defended Communism, monarchy, or even democracy with the same pathos and emotion, yes, even the same fanaticism, had his idol, Hitler, chosen to sponsor any of these.[10]

Lochner's words were matched by the more concise descriptions of two British diplomats. The Ambassador to Berlin in 1933, Horace Rumbold, reporting on the formation of the Propaganda Ministry there, wrote that the new Propaganda Minister was 'an ingenious and unscrupulous demagogue'.[11] Five years later, with more passion, George Ogilvie-Forbes, writing after the pogrom of November 1938, described Goebbels as 'that vile and dissolute demagogue'.[12]

Even Nazis who liked and admired Goebbels saw something demonic in his character. Reinhard Spitzy was an aide to Foreign Minister Ribbentrop, and knew of the contempt which Goebbels had for both Ribbentrop and the institution he headed. He nonetheless wrote:

> I admired Goebbels, who was the most intelligent of the whole circle. He was a genial but nevertheless diabolical person.[13]

People outside the Nazi Party, both Germans and non-Germans – recognized this combination of intelligence and extremism. Victor Klemperer provides a balanced assessment which is representative of many. He wrote in his diary on 30 July 1936 simply that Goebbels was 'the most poisonous and mendacious of all Nazis'.[14]

Historians, biographers, and journalists writing after 1945 have recycled several of these themes. William Shirer, whose 1959 history of Nazism is still in print, described Goebbels as:

> This swarthy, dwarfish young man, with a crippled foot, a nimble mind and a complicated and neurotic personality.[15]

Few writers on Goebbels have been able to resist the temptation to use clichés like the 'poison dwarf' when describing him, or to avoid describing him as 'limping' or 'hobbling' when talking of his movements. Audrey Salkeld calls him 'the bantam Doctor', and providing a variation on the theme, Fred Prieberg speaks of 'the undersized Minister'.[16] Most have conceded his mental agility, but almost all have picked up the idea that he was a liar, an opportunist, and an actor, motivated only by greed for power, money, and sex. Some have realized that his devotion to Hitler was a driving force in his adult life, but have still suggested that he was completely cynical and flexible in his willingness to do anything which he thought would earn Hitler's favour. His ability as a propagandist – to which we shall return – has often been linked to this notion of him as an actor, carrying the implication that the messages of his propaganda were chosen to exploit anything he thought might temporarily be valuable. Curt Riess, Goebbels' first English-language biographer, exemplified several of these trends. In the preface to his 1949 biography of Goebbels, he wrote:

> This alone would be a fascinating phenomenon to contemplate: a Propaganda Chief who despised most of the things he propagandized and who made no bones about his contempt – and who still did a brilliant job. A cripple as the principal exponent of the Master Race theory![17]

Thirty years later, a more distinguished historian, Hugh Trevor-Roper, rehearsed the same ideas in his introduction to an English-language translation of the 'final entries' in Goebbels' diary:

he was a man of postures, not ideas or beliefs. However, he had another characteristic, which would serve him well: opportunism. With his complete freedom from conviction, and his remarkable mental agility, he was able to anticipate events and change course with great dexterity and to justify the changes by nimble arguments.

Warming to his theme, Trevor-Roper continued:

In fact, of course, Goebbels was not a cultivated man. He had no aesthetic interests. He burned the German classics and destroyed 'decadent' art. He closed the Berlin theatres during the war. He was indifferent to the State Opera. He never went to concerts. His tastes were as banal and trivial as those of Hitler himself.[18]

This is still the most widely-read edition of any of Goebbels' diaries in the English-speaking world. Trevor-Roper's ideas that Goebbels had no convictions, that he 'never went to concerts' and that 'he was indifferent to the State Opera' are so far from the truth that we can only take them as expressions of personal hostility rather than as empirical historical observations. Since then, the publication of the full Goebbels' diary has provided historians with a better base from which to challenge these frequently recycled opinions. Nonetheless, they persist. In a recent and very lengthy book on the history of Berlin (in which Goebbels plays, from 1926 to 1945, a significant part), we read:

As with his attacks on the Communists, Goebbels did not take the racial theories or the anti-Semitism of the party seriously ... His motives were purely self-serving.[19]

This view of Goebbels has also gained credence from the misuse of his own fictional writings. Helmut Heiber, who has done so much excellent work editing Goebbels' speeches, published in 1962 a biography in which he cited a now famous line from Goebbels' novel *Michael*, and argued that it was intended as an autobiographical description:

'It is not so much of importance, *what* we believe in, only *that* we believe.' That is Goebbels *par excellence*, this sentence is a key to his life.[20]

Other writers have picked up on this phrase, and not even acknowledged that it is taken from a novel. Thus Klaus Fischer, in a widely acclaimed 'new history' of Nazi Germany published in 1995, wrote:

Having rejected his Catholic faith, which alarmed his devout parents, he [Goebbels] desperately looked for a new one – for 'it is almost immaterial,' he confessed, 'what we believe in, so long as we believe in something.' When at length, he found his new faith, it was really in a man, Adolf Hitler, rather than a doctrine; but the merchandizing of this personal faith now became his sacred mission in life.[21]

Neither Heiber nor Fischer knew that Goebbels had in fact written this sentence in his diary in 1923, but in a context which they totally misunderstood. Only in the last few years, as more and more of Goebbels' diary has become available, have a few writers questioned these deeply entrenched ideas. As late as 1995, Joachim Fest was still arguing that a 'habitual need for compensation' was the 'general key to Goebbels' character', and that a 'never-overcome feeling of inferiority' was a driving force in his behaviour. In what Fest called the 'bundle of motives' which led Goebbels to join the Nazi movement in 1924, he included 'class-specific resentments', also 'opportunism', 'ambition', and 'a yearning for belonging'. He still argued that Goebbels was one of many who might, but for 'biographical coincidences' have found an ideological home on the left or the right, or indeed have changed from one side to another.[22] Claus-Ekkehard Bärsch, relying heavily on a Freudian model of the 'disturbed narcissistic personality', has presented a detailed investigation of the emerging beliefs of 'the young Goebbels' which analyses particularly his appropriation of religious language and ideas, and gets away from more facile notions of 'opportunism'. Although Bärsch did not have access to the critical first nine months of Goebbels' diaries, he did recognize the early emergence of a totally destructive anti-Semitism in him, linked to a desire for 'redemption'.[23] This has been further investigated by Christian Barth in his work on 'Goebbels and the Jews'. Barth recognized that Goebbels' anti-Semitism was not a tactical manoeuvre, and that his involvement in critical stages of the Holocaust was not motivated by shallow opportunism, but his focus on this one aspect of Goebbels' personality necessarily results in only a partial view of the man.[24] Jeffrey Herf has also recognized that Goebbels was no opportunist, noting in his analysis of Goebbels' wartime propaganda 'the continuity and consistency of his own fanaticism'. Referring to Goebbels' huge literary output from 1923 to 1945, he highlights 'the unshakable character of his "delirious discourse"'.[25]

More controversially Richard Steigmann-Gall has also picked up on Goebbels' use of religious imagery, and on his fascination with the figure of Christ. Using highly selective quotations from parts of Goebbels' diary and from the published edition of his novel *Michael*, he argues that Goebbels' view of religion was 'more than a simple deism divorced of Christian content'. Again recognizing that Goebbels was 'a committed and consistent ideologue', he argues that Goebbels had a 'low regard for the churches and high regard for Christianity'. Steigmann-Gall does not present a detailed analysis of Goebbels' understanding of religion, and totally misunderstands some of the statements by Goebbels which he quotes. Although he initially recognizes that Goebbels was 'nominally Catholic', later in his book he merely presents him as 'Catholic', and speaks without further evidence of 'his religious convictions'.[26] I think that this is completely to misunderstand Goebbels. He was fascinated with Christ as a historical and dramatic figure, and he used a whole range of concepts and terms drawn from Christianity, but he stripped these of their distinctively Christian content, and recast them in the quasi-religious mysticism of *völkisch* ideology.

It is high time that the different, enduring misunderstandings of Goebbels are challenged. First, let us admit that Goebbels was an actor. It is not possible that someone who delivered thousands of public speeches, as many as 189 in one year, and sometimes gave several on a single day, could always speak with a uniform degree of sincerity or conviction; there were of course times when he was tired, jaded, or otherwise preoccupied, when he had to pretend to certain emotions in front of an audience. But this does not mean that the central ideas which he explored in 20 years of public speaking were entirely insincere, or assumed. Similarly, it is clear that Goebbels was concerned with the impression he made on contemporaries, and might make on posterity. He was fastidious in his personal appearance, to the point of vanity. He was acutely conscious of the image he projected in any given situation, and knew perfectly well that he would be the subject of historical analysis after 1945. His actions were affected by this perception. This again does not mean that he did not believe what he was saying, or that he was a mere chameleon.

Second, of course Goebbels was, when it suited him, a liar. From his earliest days as a writer, as a young man in the 1920s, he set out to falsify the record he presented of his own life, to create a mythology. A number of his deliberate distortions have been accepted, and alarmingly, are still accepted by writers, when the evidence to challenge them is straightforwardly available. One is a notion he introduced through his apparently autobiographical novel *Michael*, which he reworked extensively before its publication by the Nazi Party in 1929. In the *revised* edition of this work, Goebbels gave the impression that as a young man in Munich in 1922, he had seen a charismatic nationalist leader speaking, and had been moved to join his organization, the Nazi Party.[27] Curt Riess embroidered this account in his 1949 biography, concluding the story thus:

> That is why Goebbels stepped up to a table near the exit and obeyed the sign reading: 'Application for membership to the National Socialist German Workers Party may be signed here.' He filled out a blank and was given the membership number of 8762.
>
> A moment later he left the building just in time to see Hitler enter a car and drive away.[28]

Early historians of Nazism, like Shirer, who repeated this story, albeit without Riess' journalistic exaggerations, may be forgiven. It is troubling though, to see the same story presented in the early twenty-first century. Anja Klabunde writes of Goebbels in 1922:

> Shortly after his arrival in the city Joseph Goebbels attended a meeting called by one of the many nationalist parties. Huge posters around the Bavarian capital had attracted his attention ... Goebbels had heard of the speaker whose name was announced, Adolf Hitler, and his rhetorical gifts, and now he was curious to listen to his speech making.

She then quotes Goebbels' own description of this alleged meeting – from his novel – before citing Curt Riess' account above of Goebbels filling out his application for Nazi Party membership.[29]

Goebbels himself would doubtless have been hugely amused to think his fabrications would still be so uncritically accepted decades after his death, but it is instructive to look in more detail at how he reworked the story of his first encounter with Hitler. It is absolutely clear from Goebbels' diary that he did not meet Hitler in the flesh until 12 July 1925, in Weimar. The first mention of Hitler in his diary, as recorded in Chapter 2 here, was on 13 March 1924. Goebbels may have heard of Hitler before then, but he certainly had not thought him worthy of mention in his diary. This put Goebbels at a certain disadvantage compared to some of Hitler's associates, like Rosenberg, who had worked with him from as early as 1920. Goebbels, from his later manipulations, clearly felt this, and sought to suggest that he had in fact identified Hitler as the hope for Germany's future back in 1922. He had to face the question why, as a student in Munich in the winter of 1919–20 (he was not in Munich in 1922!), he had not joined the Nazi Party, or taken any notice of Hitler.

As early as the summer of 1924 – before he met Hitler – Goebbels sought to anticipate this. He then wrote, privately, his *Erinnerungsblätter* (*Pages of Reminiscence*) as a memoir of his childhood, adolescence, and early adulthood, leading up to the time when he formally began to keep his diary. He used for this document the terse, concise style he had already adopted for his diary, with many short sentences, and an implied, if not always stated use of the present tense. Goebbels even called this memoir a 'diary', although it was not. Re-creating his experience of the summer of 1923, when he was working in Cologne at the Dresdner Bank, Goebbels wrote:

> The opera. Klemperer as conductor. The Jewish question in art. Gundolf. Spiritual clarification. Bavaria. Hitler.[30]

This passage implies that Goebbels was at this time, in July and August 1923, preoccupied with musical and artistic affairs, with Jewish involvement in the arts, and that he experienced some kind of new understanding of this. It then suggests that he noticed developments in Bavaria, and in particular, noticed Hitler. This may not be a fabrication. It is entirely possible that Goebbels had noticed Hitler in 1923, but we are left with the incontrovertible fact that he did not think Hitler worthy of mention in the first six months of his actual diary, not even in connection with the failed *Putsch* in Munich of 9 November 1923. By inserting the single word 'Hitler' in the passage quoted above in his *Erinnerungsblätter*, Goebbels sought to redress this. We can find another example of Goebbels' concern with his relatively late involvement with the Nazi Party much later in his career in 1940, when he gave a speech in the newly annexed city of Posen.

Goebbels visited Posen, formerly – and once again today – Poznań in Poland, in January 1940, during the winter of the 'phoney war', to speak to a special meeting for newly arrived 'German' settlers from the Baltic and the Volhynia. Posen had been made the capital of the newly established *Gau* called the 'Wartheland', annexed from Poland after the brief campaign in September 1939, and was already a target for 'Germanization'. Thousands of Jews and Poles were being deported or executed, and their land and property was being given to these settlers. This was the front line of Hitler's racial restructuring in the East, a programme which Goebbels fully supported. The Nazi press reported that there were 15,000 present in Goebbels' audience in January 1940, and it is not clear whether or not Goebbels knew how many of these were newly arrived settlers. He seems to have thought that most of the audience had previously been Polish citizens. He could reasonably assume that few of them knew in great detail about his own early political history when he referred to the past:

> I believe that we National Socialists of the first hour, we have experienced a whole series of historic experiences in the past 15, 20 years. They have shot past our eyes with such lightning speed, that we can hardly order them correctly. In how many critical situations have we, and we who stand by the *Führer*, seen our movement and our *Führer* himself? How often has one of us said, yes, it's all up now. How often have we thought: now there is no way out! How many of us for example thought after 9 November 1923: yes, now everything is lost. And in spite of that, there was a way out.[31]

This reference to the way that the Nazis had surmounted seemingly insuperable obstacles in the past was a favourite rhetorical strategy of Goebbels, and one he used increasingly as the war went on, but what is of interest here is his portrayal of himself as a 'National Socialist of the first hour'. With his reference – and his correction – to 'the past 15, 20 years', he could avoid the charge that he was directly lying. He had at this point been a Party member for 15 years only. He was not in fact a 'National Socialist of the first hour', nor had he taken any part in the events of 9 November 1923, as he clearly implied here. One wonders whether he would have made such a suggestion in front of an audience in what had been Germany before September 1939.

Goebbels was also capable of barefaced lies when he referred to events outside his own life, both in his diary, and in his public propaganda. Several examples have been cited in this book, as for example his diary comment on 1 September 1939 about a 'Polish attack' on the German radio station in Gleiwitz.[32] Goebbels obviously knew that this 'attack' had been faked as one of a series of pretexts for the German invasion.[33] Another example is his statement to the audience at the Nuremberg rally in 1933, and subsequently published, that 'not a hair had been disturbed' on any Jew's head during the boycott of Jewish shops on 1 April 1933. In fact, as Robert Gellately notes, 'violence was used on a wide scale, several Jews were murdered, and some fought back'.[34] Goebbels, who had incited his followers to violence against Jews since his arrival in Berlin in 1926, knew perfectly well that all administrative measures taken against the Jews in the weeks after 30 January 1933 were carried out against a background of widespread physical intimidation and brutality. Goebbels, who often repeated favourite phrases, used exactly the same formula, even more implausibly, when he spoke to foreign press correspondents in Berlin after the pogrom on 9 November 1938. Louis Lochner was one who heard him declare that 'all the accounts that have come to your ears about alleged looting and destruction of Jewish property are a stinking lie. Not a hair of a Jew was disturbed.' This formula was repeated in newspapers, even though many Jews had been killed, and as many as 20,000 forcibly arrested.[35]

Indeed, Goebbels became so used to misrepresentation that we are left wondering how aware he was of how ludicrous some of his statements were. Trevor-Roper argued that 'To the end, he [Goebbels] could distinguish the objective truth from his own propaganda',[36] but this is difficult to sustain. What, for example, do we make of the assertion in Goebbels' diary on 4 December 1944, with reference to the British air raids, that Hitler had 'done everything to avoid this kind of warfare'? Goebbels continued: 'That corresponds entirely with the facts. He has tried by every means possible to allow the war to play out in humane forms.'[37] Goebbels knew perfectly well about the German bombing of Warsaw in September 1939; he visited the ruined city and recorded this in his diary: 'Warsaw: that is hell. A demolished city. Our bombs and shells have done a thorough job.'[38] He knew similarly about the aerial attack on Rotterdam in April 1940, and through the winter of 1940–41 he celebrated daily the attacks on British cities. As for allowing the war 'to play out in humane forms', Goebbels knew in horrible detail about, for example, the starvation of Soviet POWs in 1941, and the brutal German reprisals against civilians all over occupied Europe. As we have seen, he supported Hitler's harsh collective punishments at every opportunity. It seems that when he was thinking or writing about Hitler, Goebbels' ability to distinguish between what Trevor-Roper called 'objective truth' and his own propaganda frequently deserted him.

The fact that Goebbels frequently lied in his public speeches and in his private record of events does not mean that he always lied, or that he was entirely incapable of distinguishing between fantasy and reality. During the war he argued constantly for a propaganda based on accuracy and realism, and was far more aware than many of his colleagues and rivals of the dangers posed by exaggeration and concealment. He was profoundly scornful of the propaganda from countries like Britain and the Soviet Union which foolishly exaggerated their own successes and played down the military difficulties they were facing. Goebbels' skill as a propagandist has of course been conceded, and indeed overestimated by many. In the years after 1945, it was straightforward, and for many people convenient to argue that it was Goebbels' propaganda, and his unprecedented manipulation of the mass media which had paved the way for Hitler's success, ensured the support of the German people for Nazism between 1933 and 1939, and kept them fighting for Hitler until the bitter end. Curt Riess again exemplified this, writing:

He [Goebbels] was ordered to keep up public morale, and he did. The struggle in Germany lasted until there was not a square foot left on which the fighting could have been carried on. In a manner of speaking, Goebbels was perhaps the only general of World War II who was not in the end defeated.[39]

Riess was writing shortly after the Nuremberg Trial, in which surviving 'major Nazi criminals' were charged with crimes against humanity before an International Military Tribunal. Goebbels, who had killed himself partly to make sure that he did not have to face any such proceeding, was frequently mentioned during the trial. Several of the defendants, anxious to play down their own parts in the 'Third Reich', were prepared to try to shift responsibility onto others, and the absent propagandist was a convenient scapegoat. Hermann Göring, in interviews during the trial with American psychologist Leon Goldensohn, was outspoken in his criticism of Goebbels, whom he described as 'that clubfooted fanatic', a 'thief' and an 'opportunist', alleging that he was 'the strongest representative of anti-Semitism', and that he 'influenced Hitler to become anti-Semitic more than Hitler had been before'.[40] Albert Speer shifted the emphasis onto propaganda in his final speech to the Tribunal:

Hitler's dictatorship differed in one fundamental point from all its predecessors in history. His was the first dictatorship in the present period of modern technical development, a dictatorship which made complete use of all technical means in a perfect manner for the domination of its own nation.

Through technical devices such as radio and loudspeakers 80 million people were deprived of independent thought. It was thereby possible to subject them to the will of one man.[41]

Speer, who after 1945 tried to play down his very close and harmonious cooperation with Goebbels, particularly in the drive for 'total war' in 1943 and 1944, had his own reasons for putting forward this notion of the supremacy of propaganda, but the American prosecution had suggested much the same thing at the beginning of the whole trial process:

By means of this vast network of propaganda machinery, the Nazi conspirators had full control over the expression and dissemination of all thought, cultural activities, and dissemination of news within the *Reich*. Nothing was or could be published in Germany that did not have the approval, express or implied, of the Party and State.[42]

This was in itself a repetition of the Propaganda Ministry's own bombastic claims. A wartime article which appeared in the glossy magazine *Signal*, aimed at audiences all over Europe, had made this alarming statement:

During the course of the years, the Ministry of Propaganda has become a gigantic institute in the form of political control extending to all spheres of public life and, fortunately for the person concerned, also of private life.[43]

Other defendants at Nuremberg, who had worked closely with Goebbels, supported these ideas, but again minimized their own involvement. Walther Funk, who was State Secretary in the Propaganda Ministry between 1933 and 1938, and subsequently President of the *Reichsbank*, was one of the few senior Nazis who escaped criticism from Goebbels. Indeed, Goebbels frequently praised Funk, particularly in the 1930s, as an exceptionally diligent and competent colleague. At Nuremberg, Funk said:

The entire cultural life of the nation was permeated with this propaganda in a measure appropriate to the overwhelming, fundamental significance which was rightly attached to propaganda in the National Socialist State.

Funk nonetheless denied that he had any part in 'the political direction of the Propaganda Ministry – or in the actual work of propaganda', implying that this was totally in Goebbels' hands.[44] Hans Fritzsche, Goebbels' chief radio commentator from 1937, and from 1942 director of the radio section of the Propaganda Ministry, was also on trial at Nuremberg. He maintained, stretching credibility, that he had not known about the mass murder of the Jews, or of the poor conditions in which slave labourers were forced to work in Germany. His own work at the Propaganda Ministry had been intended only 'to win the voluntary co-operation, especially of the occupied territories, for the fight of the *Reich*'. Propaganda policy, he alleged, was determined entirely by Dietrich, in charge of the press, Amann in charge of publishing, and Goebbels, in charge of the Propaganda Ministry. Fritzsche also declared:

> it is a mistake to believe that in the Propaganda Ministry thousands of little lies were hatched out. In details we worked quite cleanly and honestly, technically even perfectly. If we had lied on a thousand small things, the enemy would have been able to deal with us more easily than was the case.[45]

Fritzsche was acquitted of all charges at Nuremberg, and in a subsequent 'de-nazification' proceeding before a German tribunal, he again sought to present himself as having been 'abused' by Goebbels.[46]

This view of Goebbels the master propagandist, the Mephistophelean manipulator of the mind of a nation, has been perpetuated in dozens of histories, and has penetrated deeply into popular understanding of the 'Third Reich'. It has been closely linked to the whole phenomenon of 'the Hitler myth', the allegedly uncritical adulation of Hitler which was the foundation of the sustained support of the German people for the Nazi regime. Thus, for Viktor Reimann, writing one of the better biographies of Goebbels in 1971, Goebbels was 'the man who created Hitler'. Ralf-Georg Reuth, writing 20 years later, had access to many more primary sources, but still replicated this notion in his conclusion:

> It had been Goebbels's fateful achievement to transform Hitler into the 'Führer'. He had early on proclaimed Hitler the 'savior', the 'new Messiah,' first to a small following, then to hundreds of thousands, and finally, with the help of a comprehensive propaganda apparatus, to an entire receptive nation.[47]

This must be challenged. Goebbels clearly did not create Hitler, or the extraordinary charisma which he possessed. Nor did he supply him with any of his central ideas. By the time the two men first met, Hitler had been active as leader of the Nazi Party for nearly six years. The Party programme had been in place for five and a half. The Party's central tenets, hatred of the Jews, repudiation of the Treaty of Versailles, an expansionist foreign policy and the creation of a racially oriented *Volksgemeinschaft*, were firmly established. We have seen how Goebbels, after joining the Party, failed to alter Hitler's basic foreign policy orientation in favour of Italy and Britain and against the Soviet Union, or to persuade him to accept a more radical approach to the issue of private property. Hitler's exceptional ability as a public speaker, and his equal powers of persuasion in private conversation were similarly not created by Goebbels. It was indeed precisely those qualities which attracted Goebbels to Hitler, as they had already attracted many other followers. Conversely, it would be equally foolish to claim, as did Konrad Heiden, that Goebbels merely copied Hitler in his own public speaking,[48] as he similarly developed his career as a Nazi demagogue in isolation for a full year before he ever heard Hitler address an audience.

This is not to deny that Goebbels played a significant role in further developing Hitler's popularity, his electoral appeal, and the mythology with which he surrounded himself. Nor is it to suggest that Hitler and Goebbels did not learn from one another after 1926, when they were in increasingly close contact, and collaborated in developing the electoral appeal of the Nazi Party. There is not though any discernible major shift in the style of either man as a public speaker after they became familiar with one another's style. Writing about Hitler, J. P. Stern went further, noting 'how little difference there is between [Hitler's speeches] delivered before February 1933, for the purpose of securing votes in supposedly democratic election campaigns, and those spoken after Hitler's assumption of power and designed to secure popular support for his policies'.[49]

Indeed perceptive observers have noted the differences in the style of public speaking used by these two great persuaders, as well as the many similarities. Several have remarked upon the very different speaking voices they possessed, Hitler's 'raucous voice', which 'grated disgustingly and frequently broke as he talked himself into a high pitch of frenzied exaltation',[50] and Goebbels' more sonorous baritone, as well as on their different use of language. What of their use of technology? Both initially developed their public speaking at a time, and in contexts where they could rely on no technical aids. Both learnt their trade – separately – without the help of public address systems. As we have seen, it was years before the Nazi Party had access to the newly emerging technologies of radio and film with soundtrack. Both Hitler and Goebbels appear to have been equally alive to the possibilities offered by these, and although Goebbels, as *Reich* Propaganda Leader from 1930, and Propaganda Minister from 1933, had the more direct relationship with the practical use of these technologies, Hitler had earlier worked closely with him on the Party's first use of film, and was quick to seize the opportunities offered by broadcasting. If we analyse more closely the cinematic techniques developed by the Nazis to enhance their propaganda, and to portray Hitler as a quasi-godlike figure, it is clear that responsibility for individual techniques and striking visual innovations lies more with collaborators like Leni Riefenstahl and Albert Speer than with Goebbels, whose role was that of a facilitator. If we turn to a prosaic, but effective propaganda technique like the use of aircraft in the election campaigns of 1932, it is not clear whether this originated with Hitler or Goebbels, or was indeed first suggested by someone else.[51]

Goebbels then did not create Hitler, or the 'Hitler myth'. This is not to underestimate his importance in helping to build support for Hitler and the Nazi

Party, particularly after 1925. We can isolate four areas in which Goebbels played a critical role. First, between 1924 and 1927, Goebbels was of huge importance in developing a power base for Nazism in the Ruhr, and in heightening its profile outside Munich and Bavaria, at a time when Hitler was banned from public speaking in most parts of Germany. This is when Goebbels first displayed his extraordinary capacity for sustained work, and his ability to thrive in conditions of adversity. Second is Goebbels' own much mythologized role as *Gauleiter* of Berlin between November 1926 and January 1933. Here, in addition to his well-known achievement of building support for Nazism in a city previously renowned as a left-wing citadel, we should highlight his role in developing a more popular Nazi journalism and a distinctive visual propaganda. Third is the period between 1933 and 1939, when according to some, Goebbels found himself without a role. Hans-Otto Meissner wrote:

> He found himself in the position of the publicity agent who has to boost goods which have already been sold. For ten long years Goebbels had menacingly attacked the government and the State. Now he himself was a member of the government, and the N.S.D.A.P. was the power in the State, with Adolf Hitler at the helm. [...] the victory of the N.S.D.A.P. condemned Goebbels largely to administrative duties, at best as overlord of the press, films, radio, literature, and so on.[52]

Overlooking the inaccuracy of the 'ten long years' in this statement, Goebbels certainly made a good fist of these 'administrative duties'. Between 1933 and 1939 Hitler's regime became one of the most popular in Europe, pursuing a run of unbroken foreign policy successes on the back of a remarkable economic recovery at home, accompanied by wide-ranging measures of social reconstruction. These popular developments were accompanied by the isolation and persecution of several groups identified as racially separate, like the Jews, or as a danger to the *Volk*, such as priests, homosexuals, the mentally and physically disabled, and others stigmatized as 'asocial'. Goebbels played a critical part in the development, implementation, and presentation of all these policies. His propaganda was important in preparing the ground for the successful plebiscite in the Saar, the remilitarization of the Rhineland, and particularly for the *Anschluss* with Austria. It was equally important in helping to secure widespread support for the marginalization of the Jews and others not considered fit for inclusion in the *Volksgemeinschaft*, and in trumpeting the success of the social reconstruction that was so closely linked with these persecutions. The social cohesion maintained in wartime Germany would have been impossible without these years of earlier consolidation.

Fourth, there is Goebbels' role as a wartime propagandist to consider. This was again a time in which – potentially – he might have been marginalized, as guns, tanks, ships and aircraft took over the role previously played by words. We have seen how Hitler moved into the isolation of his military headquarters, what Goebbels called 'this eternal bunker-life', and gradually became more and more distant from the German people; this was paralleled to an extent by the retreat into private indulgence of Göring, and the death or disappearance of other senior figures like Hess. Goebbels, with a few other senior Nazis like Ley, refused to move into a bunker – until the final days – and actually increased his contact with the ordinary public, particularly when the British and American bombing of Germany intensified in 1943. At the most difficult moments, such as in February 1943 in the aftermath of Stalingrad, or in cities which had just suffered an ordeal by fire, Goebbels was ready to face the German people, and to exhort them to continue an increasingly unequal struggle. There is no doubt that his propaganda affected many Germans, like the 14-year-old schoolgirl who wrote in her diary in August 1944:

> Things are getting ever worse ... Dr Goebbels has now released a call for 'Total war'. We, and our schools, will also now be deployed for work of any kind. That would also be right, because we must win!!! Better now to employ any means, than to end up in Siberia.

A young woman working in a bank wrote in similar vein in her diary:

> The 'total war' demands strong measures. Everything, which is not uncondi-tionally needed for the war must go. Many businesses will be closed. Paper, coal, electricity, and everything must be saved. Dr Goebbels, in his great speech, has called upon all women to offer themselves for war work.[53]

Nor were these diarists the only ones, consciously or unconsciously, to echo Goebbels' own phrases. Klemperer cited in his diary numerous examples of ordinary Germans who parroted slogans or ideas directly from Goebbels' propaganda, right into the final weeks of the war. Nothing is more striking in the history of the Second World War in Europe than the continued resistance of the German people for years after any rational calculation would have indicated that they were fighting a losing battle, and Goebbels undoubtedly played a part in this.

Any assessment of Goebbels as propagandist must now though be accompanied by a revised understanding of the nature and influence of propaganda in the 'Third Reich'. Two central parts of what might be called the post-Nuremberg understanding of propaganda in Nazi Germany are now questioned by serious scholars. The first is the notion that, between 1933 and 1945, 'nothing was or could be published in Germany that did not have the approval, express or implied, of the Party and state'; the second is the idea that this propaganda was all-pervasive, and that virtually a whole population fell under its spell. Both ideas have been, and still are endlessly rehearsed, but will not stand up to serious analysis.

The idea that nothing that the Propaganda Ministry disapproved of could be published, or by implication discussed in public, can be disproved by looking at a number of examples which particularly troubled Goebbels. We have seen how, in the 1930s, he was constantly angered by the preaching of Martin Niemöller. Not only did Niemöller regularly address public audiences between 1933 and July 1937, but his sermons were published, in repeated editions, in Germany, at the same time. His biography, which contributed significantly to his high public profile, and to the esteem in which he was held, was published in Germany until 1941, and sold many thousands of copies. There were numerous other Protestant and Catholic publications which Goebbels would have liked to get rid of, but was unable to. Another priest who enraged Goebbels after Niemöller had been locked up was the Catholic Bishop Galen. His anti-'euthanasia' speech in Münster in August 1941 was probably the most damaging public criticism made of Nazi policies in Germany between 1933 and 1945. Galen was not prevented from delivering the sermon, nor was he punished for it. It was, as Goebbels feared, widely discussed in Germany, and used for Allied propaganda; thousands of copies of the speech were subsequently dropped over Germany by RAF bombers. It was fortunate for Hitler and Goebbels that neither Galen nor the other clerics who courageously denounced the euthanasia programme spoke up with similar vigour in support of the Jews of Germany.

Finally, there are many examples of material published and distributed in the 'Third Reich' from within the Nazi Party which Goebbels objected to, like the statement by Otto Dietrich in September 1941 that the war in the Soviet Union had been decided. Right up to the final weeks of the war, Goebbels was frustrated by the work of some of his own colleagues, and by his inability to control them. An example is the articles published by his long-standing colleague Robert Ley in his capacity as leader of the 'German Labour Front' in – of all publications – Goebbels' old newspaper *Der Angriff*. In March 1945 Ley published several articles which celebrated in a nihilist spirit the destruction of Germany's cultural heritage by Allied air raids, much to Goebbels' annoyance. On 10 March 1945 Goebbels dictated that this was 'no longer bearable'. Notwithstanding this, a fortnight later Ley pronounced in *Der Angriff* that the developments in the west of Germany could be seen as a 'health cure'; by 29 March Goebbels was recording that further articles by Ley 'on the front and the air war' were worded with such 'lax cynicism that they made one shiver'; on 31 March Goebbels complained directly to Hitler, telling him that Ley's articles had 'a catastrophic effect on public opinion', but Hitler, 'smiling', confessed that he had not read the offending articles. On 8 April, as well as complaining about another article by Ley, Goebbels recorded his disgust with an article in the SS magazine *Das*

Schwarze Korps.[54] In truth, the publishing industry in Germany was by 1933 so large and so diverse, that all the strenuous and multifarious Nazi efforts to centralize and control the country's print media were not able to establish the monolithic and uniform control imagined by the prosecutors at Nuremberg, or by careless historians since then.

Secondly, the idea that a whole nation was brainwashed with Nazi propaganda, and uncritically followed the dictates of the Nazi Party, has for some time now been discarded by more subtle and realistic historians. David Bankier, writing in 1992, focused on that most critical area of Goebbels' attempted manipulation, his anti-Semitic propaganda, and wrote in conclusion:

> The party's aestheticization of politics, its dynamism, rituals and cult of symbols all certainly attracted the population. Nevertheless, in the short run these external trappings failed to captivate the public. Instead, Nazi politics, became ritualized, the populace politically satiated. Though the party assumed that incessant rallies, bombardment with loudspeakers and shrill propaganda could radically change the public's basic opinions, traditional mental patterns persisted beneath the outwards signs of conformity. Large sections of the population continued to adhere to independent positions despite the party propaganda, the terror and repression.[55]

Since the 1990s a broad consensus has emerged that Nazi propaganda, unsurprisingly, was most successful when it built on perceived realities, and that it became increasingly unsuccessful when it departed from these. It was thus hugely successful in the peacetime years between 1933 and 1939, when it trumpeted the decline in unemployment, the programmes of social reconstruction, and the foreign policy successes of the Nazi regime. The anti-Semitic measures taken by the Nazis at this time, to exclude Jews from German cultural and professional life, to restrict their economic influence, and to alter their status as citizens, were also widely welcomed. Goebbels' propaganda was not able to induce great popular support for the war against Poland in 1939, which was greeted with widespread anxiety, but it was most successful in 1940 and 1941 when it celebrated the unparalleled success of German arms in Scandinavia, Western Europe, and the Balkans. The extraordinarily dramatic newsreels which portrayed the campaigns in France and the Low Countries were not falsified, nor were they overstated. The enthusiastic response of most of the German population to these unprecedented military successes was mixed with relief derived from the hope that the attrition of the First World War would not be repeated. The intensified anti-Semitic propaganda between 1939 and 1941 highlights clearly the difficulty Goebbels faced with the presentation of more difficult issues.

David Bankier noted how Goebbels' most virulent anti-Semitic propaganda struck a chord with those Germans who already saw the Jews as the source of all their misfortunes. The gruesome scenes of Jewish poverty and distress, mixed with film of rats in sewers, which Goebbels and his collaborators presented in *The Eternal Jew*, served to reinforce the convictions of those, who like Goebbels himself, were convinced that Jews were always filthy, destructive, and dangerous; clearly the same cinematic sequences disgusted many others whose understanding of the Jews was not so overwhelmingly negative. There was a similarly divided reaction to the forced wearing of the yellow star which Goebbels helped to bring about for German Jews in September 1941. Goebbels, who had long argued for some public marking of the Jews, felt that it would be a useful propaganda measure, helping to show 'Aryan' Germans how many Jews there were in their midst, and to tell if, for example, Jews were spreading defeatist rumours. From the wealth of evidence now available, it is clear that anti-Semites like him welcomed the measure, but that many Germans were horrified by what they perceived as a reversion to medieval barbarism. It does not appear that as a propaganda measure, the introduction of the yellow star helped to make the German population significantly more anti-Semitic than it already was.

From around October 1941 Goebbels had to present an increasingly difficult military situation to the German public, as it became clear that the Soviet Union would not be defeated before the winter of that year. From then on, and particularly from the start of 1943, he had somehow to present a series of increasingly catastrophic defeats, counterbalanced by only occasional and relatively minor successes. As the British and American bombing grew in intensity, the war was not something which could be kept at any kind of comfortable distance from many Germans at home. Bankier writes that 'the public withdrew from propaganda because it offered no reliable information on these developments or their significance. Until then many had believed that Germany would achieve peace on favourable terms, but now no rhetorical pyrotechnics could dissipate the gloom of a hard reality.'[56] Indeed, one of Goebbels' key strategies after 1942 was to exaggerate the potential consequences of German defeat, hoping thereby to convince the public that there was no alternative but to continue the increasingly unequal struggle. The success of Goebbels' propaganda during the years of opposition before 1933, the years of peace between 1933 and 1939, the first years of war, and its failure thereafter can not be attributed merely to the artistry and intelligence which went into its production, or the quantities in which it was produced.

In a recent and penetrating analysis Peter Fritzsche has argued that broad swathes of the German public before 1945, while never accepting some of the most extreme implications of Nazi ideology, such as the mass murder of the Jews, did internalize a set of narratives which strengthened their reception of Nazi policies in the years of peace between 1933 and 1939, and bound them fatally to the regime's actions until the last days of the war in 1945. These narratives included a reading of recent German history in which an initially united *Volks-*

gemeinschaft in the First World War had been undermined by a 'stab in the back', and an un-German political democracy had been thrust upon the country by outsiders, resulting in 'complete moral and political chaos, the end of collective national life'. This perception helped to prepare the widespread acceptance of political repression and racial discrimination after January 1933, and genuine support for the ideals of the *Volksgemeinschaft* trumpeted by the Nazis. Using diaries written by Germans of differing political persuasions and social status, Fritzsche has analysed the emergence of a common narrative in which the war against Poland in 1939 was seen as a justified reassertion of German sovereignty and cultural superiority. After the invasion of the Soviet Union in 1941, more and more Germans were tied to the regime by awareness of and complicity in crimes against the Jews and other civilians. After 1941, although victory appeared ever more distant, and – after Stalingrad – unattainable, this terrible knowledge, and an inability to conceive of anything other than a National Socialist future for Germany ensured that an increasingly weary population still fought on with enormous energy.[57]

It is striking how closely the narratives documented and explored by Fritzsche mirror those developed by Goebbels in the private space of his own writings as a young man, and subsequently propagated by him in the public sphere as a Nazi activist and a government minister. From this perspective, one would have to conclude that his vision not only of the racially pure *Volksgemeinschaft*, but also of a justified war for national survival after 1939, evoked a deep response in much of the German population. Goebbels' conviction that the German people would fight with more commitment if their bridges were broken behind them after 1940 appears also to have been vindicated, and his deliberate attempt to tie them to the war effort by involving them in knowledge – however imprecise – of the mass murder of the Jews can only be seen as a success. We have to look more closely at the relationship between propaganda and reality, and to understand Goebbels properly, we must look at his own relationship with the central ideas he propagated.

There are four central ideas which dominated Goebbels' adult life, and his propaganda, and it is completely mistaken to think that he only adopted them for tactical reasons. The first was a passionate German nationalism, identified closely with Goebbels' understanding of German culture, and developed during the First World War, when the Goebbels family shared many of the hardships common to others at the time. The second was a hatred of the Jews, identified as the enemies of Germany and German culture. We cannot say with precision when Goebbels developed this hatred, or why, but it was clearly central to his view of the world as a young adult, in the immediate post-war years, well before he encountered Hitler. His subsequent career as a Nazi politician, and his move to Berlin served only to strengthen Goebbels' anti-Semitism, as did all his experience as Propaganda Minister of the 'Third Reich'. The third was Goebbels' belief in 'socialism', which he seems to have derived initially from his friendship with Richard Flisges between 1919 and 1923, and again to have developed strongly during his early years as a Nazi politician. Finally, there was his veneration for Hitler, which was so great, and so uncritical, that it was far greater than the actual person it was focused on. This sense is bolstered particularly by the opening and closing stages of Goebbels' relationship with Hitler. Between March 1924 and July 1925 Goebbels developed a boundless admiration for a man he had never even seen, based solely on his reported speeches, and on what others said or wrote about him. This hero-worship, which already had quasi-religious dimensions, appears to have fulfilled a deep and hitherto unfulfilled need for Goebbels, and this is reinforced if we look at the closing stages of the relationship in 1945. In the last months of the war it was perfectly clear to Goebbels that Hitler had actually failed as a leader, and that his failings were directly linked with Germany's impending defeat. In his diary Goebbels was open in his criticism of Hitler's unwillingness to replace key figures around him like Göring and Ribbentrop, whose obvious incompetence had – in Goebbels' view – contributed significantly to Germany's hopeless military and diplomatic situation. Goebbels also in the last weeks distanced himself from a number of Hitler's less important decisions, such as his petulant demand that Sepp Dietrich's SS men have their badges torn from them after the failed final offensive in Hungary in March 1945. We can only speculate as to whether, deep inside, Goebbels was critical of more fundamental decisions taken by Hitler, such as the invasion of Poland in 1939, which clearly risked war with Britain and France, or more importantly, the decision to invade Russia. When he first learnt of this, Goebbels must surely have thought back to his reading of Dostoyevsky and his admiration for the Russian people, but he never alluded to doubts in his diary, or in any public pronouncement.

In the final weeks of the war, it is clear that although Goebbels still went through the routine of conferences and the outward show of decision making with Hitler, he had lost faith with precisely Hitler's capacity for decision making and for political judgement which he had earlier prized so highly. Goebbels' continued public praise for Hitler, and his private decision to kill himself and his children in the bunker with him can be understood largely as a commitment to an idealized image, to the Christ-like figure that he had imagined in 1924 before he actually met Hitler, an image greater, more perfect, and less flawed than any real human being could be. Indeed it is clear from Goebbels' earliest writings about Hitler, that he saw in him the incarnation of a previously imagined '*Führer*'. This is a critical point which has been recognized and analysed in greater detail by Claus-Ekkehard Bärsch, who notes that a yearning for 'the *Führer*' – and he specifically distinguishes this from the more prosaic English-language concept of 'a leader' – was prevalent in Germany before 1914. Goebbels wrote in 1926, with clear reference to his own first engagement with Hitler: 'Before the court in Munich, you grew in front of us into the complete form of the *Führer*.'[58]

Goebbels' extraordinary success as a public speaker, journalist, and propagandist must be related to the conviction with which he held these four ideas, to the resonance they had with a wider public, and to the success with which he and the movement he represented implemented them, as well as to more straight-forward factors like his energy, his intelligence, and his ability to exploit new technologies.

Goebbels' passionate German nationalism can be clearly located in the context of the late Wilhelmine Empire, the First World War, and the 'bitter, evil time' which followed it. The bombastic fragility of Goebbels' nationalism, and its assertive sense of victimhood after 1919 were widely shared. Not surprisingly, Goebbels dwelt in his speeches and writings less on the alleged physical superiority of the Germanic people – we have seen that privately he was sceptical about this – and more on his passionate conviction of their cultural superiority. His engagement with literature, music, and theatre was genuine, and his constant reference in public to the canonized heroes of an imagined 'German' cultural tradition always evoked a powerful response amongst people long used to thinking of themselves as a *Kulturnation*, or 'cultural nation', a 'land of poets and thinkers'. Goebbels' presentation of himself as a man of letters, and of wider culture, struck a deep chord with his audiences. His identification of the Nazi movement with well-known symbols of 'German culture', literary, musical, architectural, and visual, was well received not only amongst the better-off and better-educated public. Frequently he tied these elements together to evoke a mystical sense of shared ownership and community. Speaking at the opening of the *Reich* Theatre Festival in Heidelberg in 1936, Goebbels declared, typically: 'In Heidelberg the triad of genuine German landscape, living history, and rich German art is ideally realized.'[59] The presentation of Nazism as a movement which had liberated 'German culture', returned it to its rightful owners, and helped to distribute its greatest treasures more widely amongst the *Volk* was a powerful propaganda tool precisely because it was matched by deeds. For hundreds of thousands of people working in different branches of the music industry, in cinema, theatre and the visual arts, the 'Third Reich' offered greatly enhanced financial and career opportunities until the final year of the war, not least because those identified as Jews were rigorously excluded after 1933. Similarly, Goebbels rejoiced, with most other Germans, in the great foreign policy successes achieved between 1939 and 1941, which appeared to restore a justified sense of pride in Germany and an understanding of its rightful place in the world.

Goebbels' hatred of the Jews is more difficult to explain today, and it was more difficult for him to stir this feeling up amongst German audiences. From his first involvement with politics in 1924 until the last days in 1945 this hatred was a consistent theme in Goebbels' private and public life. Unlike Hitler, who carefully modulated his anti-Semitism in public with an awareness of both domestic and international opinion, Goebbels constantly spoke and wrote about his hatred, in terms which were so extreme as to be almost incredible today. He appeared at and associated himself with the most radical public measures taken against the Jews, like the boycott of Jewish shops in April 1933, the burning of the books in May 1933, the pogrom of November 1938, and the introduction of the yellow star and the deportation of German Jews 'to the East' in November 1941. As we have seen, he celebrated in print and in speeches the 'fulfilment' of Hitler's 'prophecy' in 1939 that the Jews would be 'exterminated' or 'eradicated'. He typically used this unambiguous language rather than the euphemism 'final solution' preferred by others. This phrase appears only very rarely in his diaries or speeches. Whereas Hitler frequently gave speeches in which he did not refer to the Jews, and was indeed for long periods silent about this, Goebbels almost invariably brought the subject up when he spoke in public.

Where did this hatred come from? We have seen how Goebbels, in a prolonged identity crisis or 'second birth' between 1917 and 1924, came to see 'international Jewry' as the source of all his own and Germany's problems, above all in the area that he himself most strongly identified with, the field of culture and the arts. This book is not a psychoanalytical study, and this author is not qualified to speculate on how far Goebbels' hatred derived from earlier periods of his life, particularly his childhood *before* the failed operation on his foot in 1907. The idealized portrayal he consistently gave of his mother, particularly after his father's death in 1929, is so patently exaggerated as to suggest a far more complicated and fraught relationship with her. Although Goebbels later similarly presented a ludicrously idealized image of his father, we know from his diary and from surviving letters between them that this was far from an easy relationship.[60] It may be that Goebbels projected an early acquired sense of his own worthlessness onto his imagined enemies as he grew through a troubled adolescence. There is undoubtedly a psychotic quality in the most virulent expressions of his hatred, some of which I have quoted in this book.

Ron Rosenbaum, in his analysis of the origins of 'Hitler's evil', was struck by Lucy Dawidowicz's attention to Hitler's frequently repeated assertions that the Jews would no longer be laughing as his programme of extermination unfolded after 1939. Rosenbaum explored this further to support his conclusion that Hitler was not in the least hesitant, unsure, or apologetic about the mass murder of the Jews, and he noted also how Hitler and Goebbels frequently laughed together about the discomfiture of their opponents.[61] He did not remark on how Goebbels, recording his conversations with Hitler, invariably repeated the idea that the Jews would no longer have anything to laugh about. This was undoubtedly a shared conceit, and I think that Rosenbaum's conclusions about Hitler can be extended to Goebbels. In everything Goebbels wrote and said about the Jews, there was never the least sense of misgiving, of uncertainty, or of remorse. When he cryptically alluded to the gassing of the Jews in Poland in 1942, there was a sense of horror in his diary entry, but this was about the means employed – which he conceded were 'quite barbaric' – but not about the ends intended.[62]

We have insufficient evidence to quantify how far Goebbels' anti-Semitic propaganda influenced the wider German population. From individual accounts, it is clear that many were repelled by it, and equally, that many responded positively to it. Goebbels may have failed (as some historians have argued) to convince many Germans that it was necessary to kill the Jews, but there can be no doubt that with his constant repetition of central ideas, already well established in public discourse, he helped to make them more receptive to an escalating programme of exclusion which ended in the death of millions. How many Germans after 1945 have written or said that they knew nothing of the killing of the Jews, and would not have supported this, but that they did think the Jews had too great an influence in the arts, in journalism, in finance, and that measures to curtail this were justified? Let us give the last word on this vexed topic to that most perceptive of contemporary observers, Victor Klemperer. Having survived the British bombing of his home town of Dresden (which, coincidentally saved him from deportation), Klemperer, now pretending to be an 'Aryan', spoke one evening in March 1945 with a young woman. She was beginning to have many doubts about the course of the war, and about the Nazi regime. But, she said, 'it's only the Jews I hate, I think I've been influenced a bit in that'.[63]

The pioneering historian of the Holocaust, Raul Hilberg, assessed Goebbels' role in this in 1985. Analysing the situation after the pogrom of November 1938, he wrote:

> From now on we shall have little to say about Goebbels. While he made a few attempts at a comeback, his role in the destruction of the Jews was never again of paramount importance. As Gauleiter of Berlin, he was to have some say in the deportation of Jews from the capital; as Propaganda Minister and chief of the party's Propaganda Office, he remained the principal dispenser of words, but even this function he had to share with others.[64]

In one sense, Hilberg was correct. Goebbels was not directly involved in the administration of the *Einsatzgruppen* which shot hundreds of thousands of Jews in Poland and the Soviet Union, or in the running of the ghettos and camps in which millions of Jews from all over Europe perished after July 1941. He was though of central importance in the destruction of the Jews, not merely in his role as Propaganda Minister, but as Hitler's closest colleague and confidant. Every time these two men met for more than a few minutes – with only rare exceptions – they discussed what they called the 'Jewish question'. We will never know exactly who took the initiative in these conversations, which of the two first suggested ideas, and which then played the role of supporter. We do know that Goebbels consistently advocated radical policies. Before 1939 he hoped to see a ghetto established in Berlin, but this was never realized. He pressed Hitler to make the German Jews wear a distinguishing sign for some time before this policy was adopted in September 1941. From the start of the war in 1939 Goebbels argued privately that the Jews would have to be exterminated, and from November 1941 he took this argument into the public sphere, using the mass media of newspapers and radio. Shortly before the invasion of the Soviet Union in June 1941, Goebbels recorded a conversation with Hitler in which he appears to have urged Hitler to take the opportunity to exterminate 'that which we have fought against for our whole lives'.[65]

In the last weeks of the war, when Goebbels and Hitler reviewed the deteriorating situation, they consoled one another with the thought that they had at least dealt with the Jews. Equally striking is Goebbels' close association with the most critical developments in the escalating mass murder of the Jews. Within weeks of the German invasion of Poland he was in Łódź, touring the area which would soon be established as the ghetto, the destination for so many subsequently deported German Jews, and many more Polish Jews. In the late summer and autumn of 1941, Goebbels was closely and accurately informed about the mass shootings of Jews in occupied areas of the former Soviet Union. Only days after the gas chambers started operating at Bełżec in March 1942, Goebbels knew in detail about what was going on there. His veiled description of this in his diary is, significantly, the only time he appears to have been shocked by the nature of the cruelties he was helping to perpetrate. Less than a month after the start of the deportation of the Jews from the Warsaw ghetto to their deaths in Treblinka in July 1942, Goebbels was in Warsaw to hear a report on this from the SS commander in charge of proceedings. He wrote: 'This is apparently proceeding splendidly. Here the Jewish question is being handled in the right way, without sentimentality and without too many considerations. Only in this way can the Jewish question be solved.'[66] In March 1944, as Hitler and Goebbels contemplated a seizure of power in Hungary, the Jews there were uppermost in both their minds. Goebbels noted in his diary: 'Hungary has 700,000 Jews. We will take care that they don't slip through our fingers.'[67] Hundreds of thousands of Hungarian Jews were murdered in the months after Goebbels made this comment. In March 1945, as the Allies penetrated into Germany itself, Goebbels wrote: 'These Jews must be killed off like rats, when one has the power to do this. In Germany, thank God, we have already honestly taken care of this. I hope that the world will take an example from this.'[68] The last deportations of Jews from Berlin took place in March 1945, and from Vienna in April, days before the arrival of the Red Army.[69] Most other senior Nazis tried, with more or less credibility, to distance themselves both from the decision making behind these crimes and their actual implementation. Goebbels was at the heart of the process, and must bear a heavy responsibility.

There has long been confusion and misunderstanding about Goebbels' commitment to 'socialism', a word which was part of the Nazi Party's official title. Much of the confusion stems from the idea that early in his political career, Goebbels flirted with Bolshevism, or from the idea that he had no fixed beliefs. We should be clear that Goebbels, from the start of his practical involvement with politics in 1924, adhered to a consistent vision of 'socialism', one which resonated profoundly with many of his fellow citizens. He rejected completely the internationalism of Marxism, and its economic determinism, but he had a strong vision of a 'socialist' or a 'social' society, one of course restricted to those 'of German blood'. Having been brought up in conditions of real austerity, and experienced many financial humiliations as a young man, he had a genuine devotion to an ideal of communitarian solidarity, and sought actively to realize this as a Party activist before 1933, during the years of peace, and then in the increasingly difficult circumstances of the war. This was the foundation of the genuine popularity which Goebbels enjoyed amongst many of the population until the final days of the regime. It was a critical area where Goebbels' propaganda appeared to chime with perceived realities.

More importantly, the commitment to 'socialism' was a vital foundation of the genuine popularity of the Nazi regime between 1933 and 1939, and during the war. Götz Aly has recently recognized this in his book *Hitler's Beneficiaries*, which explores how during the war, the territories of occupied Europe, and above all the Jewish populations of these areas, and of Germany itself, were systematically exploited to maintain and even to improve living standards in Germany until the last months of the war.[70] Goebbels again played a direct part in this, using his favoured Nazi charities like the National Socialist People's Welfare, and the Winter Help schemes as a conduit to channel the clothes and possessions of Jews to 'Aryans' in Germany, and as the war progressed, particularly to alleviate the sufferings of those bombed out in Allied raids. The directness of this relationship may be glimpsed in one of the dozens of letters written to Magda Goebbels by members of the public, in January 1942. The letter, written four days after the Wannsee conference, was from a woman who was unhappy with her current accommodation. Politely she asked Magda whether she might be able to help her exchange her flat for a larger one, perhaps one previously occupied by Jews.[71] From its inception in 1933 Goebbels followed closely the fortunes of the Winter Help scheme; he spoke every year at the public meeting where its achievements were trumpeted, and was enthusiastic about the material benefits it brought to the neediest members of the *Volksgemeinschaft*. Goebbels may not have known specifically about the complaint made by the Winter Help in Posen in January 1943, that many of the clothes it had been provided with by the ghetto administration in Łódź were unsuitable because they were dirty, with blood stains, and yellow stars still attached, but he knew, like the authors of the complaint, that these clothes were taken from murdered Jews.[72] During the war, as the strains on the German people grew, Goebbels frequently noted what he perceived as the differing levels of cohesion between the 'social' organization of the German *Volksgemeinschaft* and that of enemy countries like Britain, or allied countries like Hungary. He was in no doubt that the 'social' organization of Nazi Germany contributed enormously to its capacity to continue the war.

The fourth of Goebbels' guiding beliefs, his faith in Hitler, was also widely replicated amongst the German people. It is tempting to see in Hitler a replacement for the father Goebbels had so sorely disappointed, and with whom he was unable to communicate, but this is too facile. There were times when Hitler played out a father role to Goebbels, but he was less than ten years older than Goebbels, and more often they met and communicated as colleagues and friends, albeit in a relationship that was always unequal. When it came to Magda's affections, they clearly competed, particularly in 1931 when they both first got to know her. Goebbels wrote then, in a moment of triumph (having secured Magda's consent to marriage):

Poor, dear Hitler! I will stay eternally loyal to you! He also is seeking a good woman, whom he will later marry. I found Magda. Lucky devil. We will all three be good to one another.[73]

Although this might be dismissed as sentimental hyperbole, there is evidence that the three of them did place great store by the contract they entered into here. They stood by one another and assumed a mutual responsibility after the killing of their enemies in the 'Night of the Long Knives' in 1934, and during the Goebbels' prolonged marital crisis in 1938 and 1939. The decision of Joseph and Magda Goebbels, made both as individuals and as a couple, to take their children into the bunker with Hitler in the last days of the war, and to take all their lives there, was not an isolated or surprising act, but one which was fully consistent with their behaviour of the previous 14 years, and which acknowledged their shared responsibility with Hitler for the actions taken during those years.

It was also fully consistent, in Joseph Goebbels' case, with his whole adult life. The threads of 'destiny' and 'sacrifice' had been with him since his adolescence, even before the First World War. As a boy of 15 he had written poetry addressed to his 'dead friend', and mused upon leaving the world, 'with all its joys'. Before he met Hitler or joined the Nazi Party he had mythologized the death of Richard Flisges, and greeted him 'in the Empire of the dead'. His first article in the Nazi Party newspaper was titled 'Idea and Sacrifice', and in July 1926, speaking in Munich, he described participation in the Nazi Party as 'a fight for life and death'. He had written in 1926, in typically biblical language, a passage addressed to 'Dear, honoured Adolf Hitler':

The ring around you stands united, sees in you the bearer of the idea which through thought and form binds us until the inexpressible end: the Legion of the Future, which is determined through doubt and agony to travel the terrible path to the end. Then a day may come, when everything collapses. We will not collapse. Then an hour may come, where the mob celebrates around you and shouts and calls 'crucify him!' We shall stand like iron and call and sing 'Hosannah!' Then the Phalanx of the Last, who themselves do not fear death, shall stand around you.[74]

His cult of 'the unknown SA man', and his elevation of the funerals of 'martyrs' like Horst Wessel to central rituals of the Party were not mere propaganda stunts. When his first daughter was born in 1932 Goebbels wrote: 'God grant that this child shall only live and breathe in a free Germany.'[75] His idea of a 'free' Germany is not one which all agreed with, then or since, but this was not empty rhetoric.

Goebbels was able, in a way that few can, to play out his personal life drama in the larger arena of history. Through his association with Hitler and with the Nazi Party he was able to project his unresolved personal conflicts onto the broader stage of first German, and then international politics. It is part of the larger tragedy of the first half of the twentieth century that such an obviously unbalanced, but talented individual was able to see his individual problems reflected in the wider constellation of politics and international relations, and was given the opportunities and the power to try to resolve them in the public sphere, with fatal consequences not only for himself and his immediate family, but for so many others.

Notes

Introduction

1. See Wilfried Bade, *Joseph Goebbels* (Lübeck: Charles Coleman, 1933); Max Jungnickel, *Goebbels* (Leipzig: Kittler, 1933); Rudolf Semmler, *Goebbels: The Man Next to Hitler* (London: Westhouse, 1947); Boris Borresholm and Karena Nichoff (eds), *Dr. Goebbels. Nach Aufzeichnungen aus seiner Umgebung* (Berlin: Journal, 1949); Stephan Werner, *Joseph Goebbels. Dämon einer Diktatur* (Stuttgart: Union deutsche Verlagsgesellschaft, 1949); Prinz Friedrich Christian zu Schaumburg-Lippe, *Dr. G. Ein Porträt des Propagandaministers* (Wiesbaden: Limes Verlag, 1963); and Wilfred von Oven, *Finale Furioso. Mit Goebbels bis zum Ende* ([1949/50] Tübingen: Grabert Verlag, 1974).
2. Curt Riess, *Joseph Goebbels* (London: Hollis and Carter, 1949); Roger Manvell and Heinrich Fraenkel, *Doctor Goebbels: His Life and Death* (London: Heinemann, 1960).
3. Helmut Heiber, *Joseph Goebbels* (Berlin: Colloquium Verlag, 1962); see also Helmut Heiber (ed.), *Goebbels-Reden, Band 1: 1932–1939* (Düsseldorf: Droste Verlag, 1971); and *Goebbels-Reden, Band 2: 1939–1945* (Düsseldorf: Droste Verlag, 1972).
4. Viktor Reimann, *The Man who Created Hitler: Joseph Goebbels* (trans. Wendt, London: William Kimber, 1977).
5. See, for examples in otherwise thoroughly referenced scholarly studies, p. 147 in Henning Eichberg, 'The Nazi *Thingspiel*: Theater for the Masses in Fascism and Proletarian Culture', *New German Critique*, 11 (Spring 1977), pp. 133–50; or p. 184 in Reinhard Bollmus, 'Alfred Rosenberg: National Socialism's "Chief Ideologue"?', in Ronald Smelser and Rainer Zitelmann (eds), *The Nazi Elite* (London: Macmillan, 1993), pp. 183–93; or, more recently, the unreferenced quotation on p. 544 of Adam Tooze, *The Wages of Destruction: The Making and Breaking of the Nazi Economy* (London: Penguin, 2007). These may all of course be individual oversights, but there is a pattern which is alarmingly magnified in more popular histories.
6. Louis Lochner (ed.), *The Goebbels Diaries* (London: Hamish Hamilton, 1948); Helmut Heiber (ed.), *The Early Goebbels Diaries: The Journal of Joseph Goebbels from 1925–1926* (trans. Watson, London: Weidenfeld and Nicolson, 1962); H. R. Trevor-Roper (ed.), *The Goebbels Diaries: The Last Days* (trans. Barry, London: Book Club Associates, 1978).
7. Elke Fröhlich (ed.), *Die Tagebücher von Joseph Goebbels. Sämtliche Fragmente* (Munich: Saur, 1987); Ralf Georg Reuth (ed.), *Joseph Goebbels. Tagebücher 1924–1945* (Munich: Piper, 1992).
8. Elke Fröhlich (ed.), *Die Tagebücher von Joseph Goebbels: Teil I, Aufzeichnungen 1923–1941* (Munich: Saur, 1998–2006), 14 volumes; Elke Fröhlich (ed.), *Die Tagebücher von Joseph Goebbels: Teil II, Diktate 1941–1945* (Munich: Saur, 1993–98), 15 volumes (hereafter *TBJG*, TI, or *TBJG*, TII).
9. Ralf Georg Reuth, *Goebbels* (trans. Winston, London: Harcourt Brace, 1993). The brief sketch by Elke Fröhlich, 'Joseph Goebbels: The Propagandist', in Ronald Smelser and Rainer Zitelmann (eds), *The Nazi Elite* (London: Macmillan, 1993), pp. 48–61, which was originally published in German in 1987, is littered with inaccuracies. See also Joachim Fest, 'Joseph Goebbels: Eine Porträtskizze', *Vierteljahrshefte für Zeitgeschichte*,

43:4 (1995), pp. 565–80; Thomas Altstedt, *Joseph Goebbels. Eine Biographie in Bildern* (Berg: Druffel, 1999); Christian Barth, *Goebbels und die Juden* (Paderborn: Schöningh, 2003); Claus-Ekkehard Bärsch, *Der junge Goebbels. Erlösung und Vernichtung* (Munich: Fink, 2004).

10. On Goebbels' journalism see Carin Kessemier, *Der Leitartikler Goebbels in den NS-Organen 'Der Angriff' und 'Das Reich'* (Munich: Fahle, 1967); and Russell Lemmons, *Goebbels and Der Angriff* (Lexington: University Press of Kentucky, 1994).

11. For his earliest political publications, see Joseph Goebbels, *Das kleine abc des National-sozialisten* (Elberfeld: Verlag der Nationalsozialistischen Briefe, no date given [1925]); Joseph Goebbels, *Die zweite Revolution. Briefe an Zeitgenossen* (Zwickau: Streiter-Verlag, 1926); and Joseph Goebbels, *Wege ins Dritte Reich* (Munich: Eher Verlag, 1927). For early collections of his speeches, see Joseph Goebbels, *Revolution der Deutschen. 14 Jahre Nationalsozialismus* (Oldenburg: Stalling, 1933); Joseph Goebbels, *'Goebbels spricht'. Reden aus Kampf und Sieg* (Oldenburg: Stalling, 1933); Joseph Goebbels, *Signale der neuen Zeit; 25 ausgewählte Reden* (Munich: Franz Eher, 1934); and from the wartime years, Joseph Goebbels, *Die Zeit ohne Beispiel. Reden und Aufsätze aus den Jahren 1939/40/41* (Munich: Franz Eher, 1941); Joseph Goebbels, *Das eherne Herz. Reden und Aufsätze aus den Jahren 1941/42* (Munich: Franz Eher, 1943); Joseph Goebbels, *Dreißig Kriegsartikel für das deutsche Volk* (Munich: Franz Eher, 1943); and Joseph Goebbels, *Der steile Aufstieg. Reden und Aufsätze aus den Jahren 1942/43* (Munich: Franz Eher, 1943). For collections of his early journalism see Joseph Goebbels, *Der Angriff* (Munich: Franz Eher, 1936); and Joseph Goebbels, *Wetterleuchten: Zweiter Band 'Der Angriff'* (Munich: Franz Eher, 1939). See the bibliography for a fuller list of Goebbels' publications.

12. On Goebbels' earliest writings see Kai Michel, *Vom Poeten zum Demagogen: Die schrift-stellerischen Versuche Joseph Goebbels'* (Vienna: Böhlau, 1999); Lovis Maxim Wambach, *'Es ist gleichgültig, woran wir glauben, nur dass wir glauben.' Bemerkungen zu Joseph Goebbels Drama 'Judas Iscariot' und zu seinen 'Michael-Romanen'* (Bremen: Raphael-Lemkin-Institut für Xenophobie- und Genozidforschung, 1996); and David Barnett, 'Joseph Goebbels: Expressionist Dramatist as Nazi Minister of Culture', *New Theatre Quarterly*, 17:2 (May 2001), pp. 161–9.

13. See Bärsch, *Der junge Goebbels*, pp. 12, and 147.

14. Joseph Goebbels, *Vom Kaiserhof zur Reichskanzlei. Eine historische Darstellung in Tage-buchblättern* (Munich: Franz Eher, 1934); and Joseph Goebbels, *Kampf um Berlin. Der Anfang* (Munich: Franz Eher, 1932).

15. *Trial of the Major War Criminals before the International Military Tribunal, Nuremberg, 14 November 1945 – 1 October 1946* (Nuremberg: International Military Tribunal, 1947), Vol. 5, p. 442.

16. *TBJG*, 15 September 1942, TII, 5, p. 504. At this time Goebbels dictated every day a record of the *previous* day's events.

17. See my comments on this in Chapter 11; also Glenn Cuomo, 'The Diaries of Joseph Goebbels as a Source for the Understanding of National Socialist Cultural Politics', in Glenn Cuomo (ed.), *National Socialist Cultural Policy* (New York: St. Martin's Press, 1995), pp. 197–245, p. 203.

18. Ian Kershaw, *Hitler 1889–1936: Hubris* (London: Allen Lane, 1998), xiii.

19. See Hendrik Eberle and Matthias Uhl (eds), *The Hitler Book: The Secret Dossier Prepared for Stalin* (London: John Murray, 2006), pp. 191 and 208.

20. There are large historiographies of propaganda in the 'Third Reich', and separately of different branches of the arts and media. See, with particular reference to Goebbels, Ernest Bramsted, *Goebbels and National Socialist Propaganda 1924–1945* (London:

Cresset Press, 1965); and Felix Möller, *The Film Minister: Goebbels and the Cinema in the Third Reich* (Stuttgart: Axel Menges, 2000).

Chapter 1

1. Hermann Hesse, *Der Steppenwolf* (Frankfurt-am-Main: Suhrkamp, 1977), p. 31.
2. Manvell and Fraenkel, *Doctor Goebbels*, p. 2.
3. Much of the evidence for the earliest biographies of Goebbels, particularly for his childhood and adolescence, was gathered in interviews held after 1945 by Curt Riess, and by Heinrich Fraenkel, notably from Goebbels' mother, Maria Katharina, and his sister, Maria Kimmich (see Riess, *Joseph Goebbels*, p. 3; and Manvell and Fraenkel, *Doctor Goebbels*, p. 299). All existing biographies of Goebbels also illustrate his childhood with his own anecdotes, recorded by his associates in the Propaganda Ministry decades later, above all by von Oven, *Finale Furioso*, and Semmler, *Goebbels*. These anecdotes must be treated with caution, particularly given Goebbels' known tendency to rewrite his own history.
4. Bundesarchiv Koblenz (hereafter BAK) N1118/70, 'Erinnerungsblätter'. This document is an autobiographical memoir describing Goebbels' life up to October 1923, when he began consistently to keep a diary. It was written in the summer of 1924, and again must be treated with caution, not least because by this time Goebbels had become politically active, and wanted to project this retrospectively onto his young adulthood. Because the 'Erinnerungsblätter' was printed with parts of the genuine diary in 1987, it is misleadingly referred to as a 'diary' in a number of academic studies from the 1990s. Readers should be aware that the genuine diary commences no earlier than 17 October 1923.
5. Rheydt was in Prussia, although the predominantly Roman Catholic population of this area formed a religious minority within this largely Protestant state. Goebbels always identified himself as 'Prussian'.
6. Oven, *Finale Furioso*, pp. 280–4.
7. See the reports from the *Gymnasium zu Rheydt* in BAK N1118/113.
8. BAK N1118/131, 'Der tote Freund'. For an analysis of Goebbels' adolescent poems see Michel, *Vom Poeten zum Demagogen*.
9. Versions of this anecdote are rehearsed in Riess, *Joseph Goebbels*, p. 13; Manvell and Fraenkel, *Doctor Goebbels*, p. 5; Heiber, *Joseph Goebbels*, pp. 16–17; and Reimann, *The Man who Created Hitler*, p. 15. None of these authors provides a specific reference.
10. Cited in Manvell and Fraenkel, *Doctor Goebbels*, p. 12.
11. Cited in Reuth, *Goebbels*, pp. 17–18.
12. *TBJG*, 18 June 1934, TI, 3/I, p. 65.
13. Cited in Manvell and Fraenkel, *Doctor Goebbels*, p. 13.
14. BAK N1118/70, 'Erinnerungsblätter'.
15. BAK N1118/113, Friedrich Goebbels to Joseph Goebbels, 21 December 1918.
16. Erik Erikson, *Young Man Luther: A Study in Psychoanalysis and History* (London: Faber and Faber, 1959), p. 12.
17. See, for one typical description of Flisges, Borresholm and Nichoff, *Dr. Goebbels. Nach Aufzeichnungen aus seiner Umgebung*, pp. 54–6.
18. See Reuth, *Goebbels*, p. 23; and Barnett, 'Joseph Goebbels: Expressionist Dramatist as Nazi Minister of Culture', pp. 163–4.
19. BAK N1118/113, Friedrich Goebbels to Joseph Goebbels, 9 November 1919.

20. Readers should be aware that the title of 'Doctor' was awarded at this time in Germany after completion of a dissertation which might take one year's study, rather than the three years or longer required in a British or American university today.

21. BAK N1118/70, 'Erinnerungsblätter'.

22. See the letter from Goebbels to Anka Stalherm, 14 April 1920, cited in Barth, *Goebbels und die Juden*, p. 266.

23. BAK N1118/110, Möcklinghoff to Goebbels, 6 March 1921.

24. BAK N1118/70, 'Erinnerungsblätter'.

25. *TBJG*, 8 March 1928, TI, 1/II, p. 337.

26. See Detlev Peukert, *The Weimar Republic: The Crisis of Classical Modernity* (London: Penguin, 1991), p. 18.

27. See Michel, *Vom Poeten zum Demagogen*, p. 67, and pp. 91–4.

28. BAK N1118/70, 'Erinnerungsblätter'.

29. BAK N1118/70, 'Erinnerungsblätter'.

30. *TBJG*, 17 October 1923, TI, 1/I, p. 29.

31. Elke Fröhlich, 'Joseph Goebbels und sein Tagebuch: Zu den handschriftlichen Aufzeichnungen bis 1941', *Vierteljahrshefte für Zeitgeschichte*, 35:4 (1987), pp. 489–522. See in particular pp. 494–5.

32. Public radio broadcasting in Germany started from Berlin in October 1923, and only spread gradually to more distant parts of the country.

33. *TBJG*, 17 October 1923, TI, 1/I, p. 30.

34. *TBJG*, 17 October 1923, TI, 1/I, p. 31.

35. See Benedict Anderson, *Imagined Communities: Reflections on the Origin and Spread of Nationalism* (London: Verso, 1983); and George Mosse, *Germans and Jews: The Right, the Left, and the Search for a 'Third Force' in Pre-Nazi Germany* (London: Orbach and Chambers, 1971), p. 8.

36. Kurt Sontheimer, 'Antidemokratisches Denken in der Weimarer Republik', *Vierteljahrshefte für Zeitgeschichte*, 5:1 (1957), pp. 42–62, p. 57.

37. See James Edmonds, *The Occupation of the Rhineland, 1918–1929* (London: HMSO, 1987), pp. 247–55.

38. Wasserman was then living in Austria; *Christian Wahnschaffe* was published in 1919.

39. *TBJG*, 22 October 1923, TI, 1/I, p. 35.

40. *TBJG*, 23 October 1923, TI, 1/I, p. 36. On the unsuccessful French effort to promote a separatist Rhenish movement, see Edmonds, *The Occupation of the Rhineland*, pp. 255–8. A vivid sense of the disturbances around Germany in 1923 may be gained from *Victor Serge: Witness to the German Revolution* (London: Redwords, 2000); unfortunately Serge did not refer specifically to the disturbances in Mönchen-Gladbach and Rheydt which Goebbels observed.

41. *TBJG*, 10 November 1923, TI, 1/I, pp. 48–9. Hindemith and Strauss were both composers with whom Goebbels would later have close dealings. Hermann Wetzler (1870–1943), virtually unknown today, was also a composer of songs and vocal music.

42. For an introduction to Hermann Hesse's writings, see Theodore Ziolkowski (ed.), *Hesse: A Collection of Critical Essays* (Englewood Cliffs, New Jersey: Prentice-Hall, 1973). Hesse, who had lived in Switzerland since 1912, was profoundly out of sympathy with the *völkisch*, militarist, and national socialist currents which developed in Germany after 1918. He had earlier become hugely unpopular with many because of his opposition to the First World War.

43. See, for Spengler's influence on the young Goebbels, Michel, *Vom Poeten zum Demagogen*, pp. 101–4.
44. 'The Rich against Culture', in *Victor Serge: Witness to the German Revolution*, pp. 204–14, pp. 204–5.
45. Cited in Stephen McClatchie, 'Hans Pfitzner's *Palestrina* and the Impotence of Early Lateness', www.utpjournals.com/product/utq/674/674_mcclatchie.htm, accessed 18 August 2008.
46. 'The Rich against Culture', p. 210.
47. Fritz Stern, *The Politics of Cultural Despair: A Study in the Rise of the Germanic Ideology* (Berkeley, Los Angeles, and London: University of California Press, 1961).
48. See Peter Gay, *Weimar Culture: The Outsider as Insider* (Harmondsworth: Penguin, 1974), pp. 73–106.
49. Kurt Sontheimer, *Antidemokratisches Denken in der Weimarer Republik: Die politischen Ideen des deutschen Nationalismus zwischen 1918 und 1933* (Munich: Deutscher Taschenbuch Verlag, 1978). See, for a selection of relevant writings, Anton Kaes, Martin Jay, and Edward Dimendberg (eds), *The Weimar Republic Sourcebook* (Berkeley and London: University of California Press, 1995), pp. 355–87.
50. Klaus Theweleit, *Male Fantasies I. Women, Floods, Bodies, History* (Cambridge: Polity Press, 1987); and *Male Fantasies II. Male Bodies: Psychoanalyzing the White Terror* (Cambridge: Polity Press, 1989).
51. Hans Mayer, 'Hermann Hesse and the "Age of the Feuilleton"', in Ziolkowski, *Hesse: A Collection of Critical Essays*, pp. 76–93, p. 87, and p. 88.
52. Hermann Hesse, *Peter Camenzind* (London: Peter Owen, 1961), pp. 26, 27 and 35.
53. See Barbara Ehrenreich's 'Foreword' to Theweleit, *Male Fantasies I*, pp. xiii–xiv.
54. *TBJG*, 17 October 1923, TI, 1/I, p. 30.
55. Jeffrey Herf, *Reactionary Modernism: Technology, Culture, and Politics in Weimar and the Third Reich* (Cambridge: Cambridge University Press, 1984).
56. On the relationship with 'Expressionism', or modernism, in Goebbels' early plays, see Barnett, 'Joseph Goebbels: Expressionist Dramatist as Nazi Minister of Culture'. Barnett unfortunately did not have access to the critical first nine months of Goebbels' diary, from October 1923 to June 1924. Barnett also assumes that Goebbels' attitude towards modernism was the same in all art forms. He does not consider music, and does not therefore entertain the idea that while Goebbels may have been receptive to modernist ideas in drama, he was not equally receptive to modernist ideas in music.
57. Theweleit states: 'Culture distinguishes what is German from the remaining mass of the world'. *Male Fantasies II*, p. 43.
58. Sontheimer, *Antidemokratisches Denken in der Weimarer Republik*, p. 244.
59. Oswald Spengler, *The Decline of the West* (London: George Allen and Unwin, [1928]), Vol. 2, *Perspectives of World History*, p. 415.
60. Hesse, *Peter Camenzind*, pp. 72–3.
61. *TBJG*, 27 October 1923, TI, 1/I, p. 40.
62. See, for example, Heiber, *Joseph Goebbels*, p. 25. It is important to recognize that Heiber was quoting this line not from Goebbels' diary (which was not then available to him), but from its later repetition in his novel *Michael*. This of course affected his understanding of the context in which the quotation arose. See my discussion of this in the Epilogue.
63. *TBJG*, 2 November 1923, TI, 1/I, p. 46.
64. *TBJG*, 12 December 1923, TI, 1/I, p. 58.
65. *TBJG*, 23 November 1923, TI, 1/I, p. 53.

66. *TBJG*, 13 December 1923, TI, 1/I, pp. 59–60. One can only presume that it was possible to attend these events for a nominal sum, or indeed without payment.

67. *TBJG*, 27 October 1923, TI, 1/I, p. 40.

68. *TBJG*, 14 November 1923, TI, 1/I, p. 51.

69. *TBJG*, 12 December 1923, TI, 1/I, p. 58.

70. *TBJG*, 23 December 1923, TI, 1/I, p. 63.

71. BAK N1118/113, Joseph Goebbels, 'Schöpferische Kräfte. Richard Flisges, dem toten Freunde', *Rheydter Zeitung*, 22 December 1923

72. *TBJG*, 29 December 1923, TI, 1/I, p. 65.

73. *TBJG*, 31 December 1923, TI, 1/I, pp. 67–8.

74. *TBJG*, 25 January 1924, TI, 1/I, p. 80.

75. *TBJG*, 31 January 1924, TI, 1/I, p. 84.

76. *TBJG*, 16 February 1924, TI, 1/I, p. 97. Schreker was an Austrian composer of Jewish descent, with an eclectic and experimental style. He was appointed Director of the High School for Music in Berlin in 1920. Schreker was, after Richard Strauss, the second most frequently performed living opera composer in the early Weimar Republic.

77. *TBJG*, 18 February 1924, TI, 1/I, p. 98.

78. See *TBJG*, TI, 1/I, entries from 25 February 1924 to 11 March 1924, pp. 101–6. Goebbels was not able to get *Michael Voorman* into print before 1929, when it was produced by the Nazi Party publishing house in Munich, the Franz Eher Verlag, under the title *Michael. Ein deutsches Schicksal in Tagebuchblättern* (*Michael: A German Destiny in Pages from a Diary*). Before this Goebbels spent considerable time in 1928 reworking *Michael Voorman*, longer indeed than he spent writing it in 1924 (see *TBJG*, TI, 1/III, entries from 1 June 1928 to 19 September 1928, pp. 29–85). Because all versions of *Michael Voorman* are written in a very similar style to Goebbels' genuine diary – the published version actually replicates whole passages from the diary verbatim – writers on Goebbels have tended to quote from them, or to paraphrase whole passages *as if they were* from Goebbels' own diary, or a contemporary record of his thoughts. Thus Reuth relies heavily on the 1919 manuscript, and to a lesser extent on those of 1924 and 1929 in his narrative of Goebbels' early adulthood. Curt Riess took from the rewritten 1929 edition of *Michael* the narrative he then represents of Goebbels in Munich in 1922, seeing a charismatic politician (for whom read Hitler) speak, and subsequently joining the Nazi Party in a state of inspiration (see Riess, *Joseph Goebbels*, pp. 23–5). Shirer, like many others, has rehearsed this fictional narrative as fact (see William Shirer, *The Rise and Fall of the Third Reich* (London: Book Club Associates, 1973), p. 127). Theweleit uses selected passages from the 1929 edition of *Michael* to support his larger analysis of 'fascist males'. His comments are always interesting, but his psychoanalytical reading and symbolic interpretation of these decontextualized passages is highly speculative. More recently, the published edition of *Michael*, now readily available in print and on the internet, has been interpreted as an 'expression' of Goebbels' fundamentally Christian view of religion (see Richard Steigmann-Gall, *The Holy Reich: Nazi Conceptions of Christianity, 1919–1945* (Cambridge: Cambridge University Press, 2004); and the critique by Irving Hexham, 'Inventing "Paganists": A Close Reading of Richard Steigmann-Gall's *The Holy Reich*', *Journal of Contemporary History*, 42:1 (2007), pp. 59–78). Difficulties clearly arise when fictional accounts are used as historical sources, and these difficulties are compounded by Goebbels' tendency – well-established by 1919 – to mythologize his own life. For a detailed analysis of the 1919, 1924, and 1929 versions of *Michael*, see Michel, *Vom Poeten*

zum Demagogen. Michel did not have access to Goebbels' diary from October 1923 to June 1924, and therefore places the writing of the 1924 manuscript in 1923.
79. *TBJG*, 10 March 1924, TI, 1/I, p. 105.

Chapter 2

1. Cited in Ernst Deuerlein (ed.), *Der Aufstieg der NSDAP in Augenzeugenberichten* (Munich: Deutscher Taschenbuch Verlag, 1974), p. 214.
2. *TBJG*, 13 March 1924, TI, 1/I, p. 106.
3. *TBJG*, 15 March 1924, TI, 1/I, p. 107.
4. *TBJG*, 17 March 1924, TI, 1/I, p. 108.
5. *TBJG*, 20 March 1924, TI, 1/I, pp. 108–9.
6. *TBJG*, 22 March 1924, TI, 1/I, p. 110.
7. See Kershaw, *Hitler 1889–1936*, pp. 213–19.
8. *TBJG*, 5 April 1924, TI, 1/I, p. 118.
9. On the *Völkischer Beobachter* in the early years of the Nazi movement, see Detlef Mühlberger, *Hitler's Voice: The Völkischer Beobachter 1920–1933* (Oxford: Peter Lang, 2004), 2 volumes.
10. Wiegershaus served as a deputy in the Prussian *Landtag* (or regional Parliament) between 1925 and 1928 before retiring. He died in 1934. Jeffrey Herf notes that: 'From 1918 to 1933 the German Right comprised over 550 political clubs and 530 journals.' *Reactionary Modernism*, p. 25. On the fragmentation of the Nazi Party and the German right in 1924, see Dietrich Orlow, *The History of the Nazi Party* (Newton Abbot: David & Charles, 1971), Vol. 1, 1919–33, pp. 46–51. On the *Deutsch-völkisch* groups and their relationship with Nazism, see Sontheimer, *Antidemokratisches Denken in der Weimarer Republik*, pp. 130–41.
11. *TBJG*, 31 March 1924, TI, 1/I, p. 116.
12. *TBJG*, 5 April 1924, TI, 1/I, p. 119.
13. *TBJG*, 8 April 1924, TI, 1/I, p. 119.
14. Norman Cohn, *Warrant for Genocide: The Myth of the Jewish World Conspiracy and the Protocols of the Elders of Zion* (London: Serif, 1996), p. 27, and pp. 138–63. The 'Protocols' had by 1924 been conclusively exposed as a forgery in Britain and in America. On Ford's *The International Jew*, see Cohn, *Warrant for Genocide*, pp. 174–80.
15. *TBJG*, 10 April 1924, TI, 1/I, pp. 120–1.
16. *TBJG*, 31 March 1924, TI, 1/I, pp. 116–17.
17. *TBJG*, 3 April 1924, TI, 1/I, p. 117.
18. *TBJG*, 5 April 1924, TI, 1/I, p. 118.
19. *TBJG*, 16 April 1924, TI, 1/I, pp. 124–5.
20. See BAK N1118/112, Esenwein to Goebbels, 21 April 1924.
21. *TBJG*, 29 March 1924, TI, 1/I, pp. 114–15.
22. It is significant also that Bach's portrayal of Judas Iscariot – the subject of Goebbels' first play in 1918 – in the *St Matthew Passion* is deeply sympathetic.
23. *TBJG*, 12 April 1924, TI, 1/I, p. 122.
24. *TBJG*, 5 May 1924, TI, 1/I, p. 131.
25. *TBJG*, 6 June 1924, TI, 1/I, p. 145.
26. *TBJG*, 3 May 1924, TI, 1/I, pp. 129–30.
27. BAK N1118/112, Esenwein to Goebbels, 1 July 1924.
28. *TBJG*, 25 July 1924, TI, 1/I, p. 179.

29. See *TBJG*, 31 July 1924, TI, 1/I, p. 186.
30. *TBJG*, 15 August 1924, TI, 1/I, pp. 197–8.
31. See, for example, Kershaw's comments in *Hitler 1889–1936*, p. 233; also Orlow, *The History of the Nazi Party*, Vol. 1, p. 50. Shirer, *The Rise and Fall of the Third Reich*, is one widely-read example which overlooks the Weimar meeting altogether.
32. The SA or *Sturmabteilung* (Storm, or Assault Detachment) was the paramilitary wing of the Nazi Party. It took its name from the 'Storm Detachments' used by the German army in 1918 to spearhead infantry attacks.
33. *TBJG*, 19 August 1924, TI, 1/I, pp. 198–202. On Fritsch, who must be considered one of the most influential anti-Semites in Germany before 1933, see Günter Hartung, 'Pre-Planners of the Holocaust: The Case of Theodor Fritsch', in John Milfull (ed.), *Why Germany? National Socialist Anti-Semitism and the European Context* (Providence and Oxford: Berg, 1993), pp. 29–40. Erich Ludendorff had ended the First World War in effective charge of the German war effort. He emerged from retirement to take part in the Nazi *Putsch* of 1923 but was acquitted at the subsequent trial. He then stood for election to the *Reichstag* as a representative of the German-*völkisch* Freedom Party. Albrecht von Graefe was a Pomeranian aristocrat. Feder, an economist who had a considerable influence on Hitler, was marginalized in the Nazi Party after 1930, although he was given a string of largely honorary posts. He died in 1941.
34. *TBJG*, 20 August 1924, TI, 1/I, pp. 202–6.
35. See Sontheimer, *Antidemokratisches Denken in der Weimarer Republik*, pp. 267–70.
36. This suggests that the group earlier founded by Goebbels and Prang had collapsed.
37. *TBJG*, 22 August 1924, TI, 1/I, pp. 208–9. On the importance of the speech in Fascism, see Theweleit, *Male Fantasies II*, pp. 118–29, which refers particularly to the representation of a speech in the 1929 edition of Goebbels' *Michael*.
38. See Wilfried Böhnke, *Die NSDAP im Ruhrgebiet 1920–1933* (Bonn: Verlag Neue Gesellschaft, 1974).
39. *TBJG*, 5 September 1924, TI, 1/I, p. 218.
40. *TBJG*, 30 August 1924, TI, 1/I, p. 214.
41. *TBJG*, 4 September 1924, TI, 1/I, p. 217.
42. For an introduction to Strasser, see Udo Kissenkoetter, 'Gregor Strasser: Nazi Party Organizer or Weimar Politician?' in Ronald Smelser and Rainer Zitelmann (eds), *The Nazi Elite* (London: Macmillan, 1993), pp. 224–34.
43. *TBJG*, 15 September 1924, TI, 1/I, pp. 222–3.
44. *TBJG*, 17 and 18 September 1924, TI, 1/I, pp. 224–5.
45. *TBJG*, 19 September 1924, TI, 1/I, p. 225.
46. *TBJG*, 27 September 1924, TI, 1/I, pp. 230–1.
47. *TBJG*, 29 September, TI, 1/I, p. 231.
48. *TBJG*, 24 September 1924, TI, 1/I, p. 228.
49. One is reminded here of Peter Gay's comment on how young *völkisch* enthusiasts in the early Weimar Republic sought 'to make adolescence itself into an ideology'. See his *Weimar Culture*, p. 83.
50. *TBJG*, 7 October 1924, TI, 1/I, p. 235.
51. *TBJG*, 25 October 1924, TI, 1/I, p. 240.
52. See for example Reimann, *The Man who Created Hitler*, pp. 67–9, and Reuth, *Goebbels*, p. 75.
53. *TBJG*, 4 November 1924, TI, 1/I, p. 243. Reinhold Wulle was leader of the *völkisch* and Nazi 'fraction' (or group) in the *Reichstag* in 1924. Between 1925 and 1928 he served as a deputy in the Prussian *Landtag*. He was a prolific writer, and was briefly

imprisoned in Sachsenhausen concentration camp between 1940 and 1942 for his continuing involvement with nationalist politics outside the NSDAP. He died in 1950. Ernst Graf zu Reventlow, who had been one of the first publicists of the 'Protocols of the Elders of Zion' in Germany, joined the NSDAP in 1927, but was mistrusted by Hitler and never held a government office after 1933. He died in 1943. Wilhelm Kube joined the NSDAP with Reventlow and went on to a prominent career in the SS. He was General Commissar for occupied 'White Russia' from 1941 until his assassination by partisans in Minsk in 1943.

54. See Kyra Inachin, '"Märtyrer mit einem kleinen Häuflein Getreuer": Der erste Gauleiter der NSDAP in Pommern', *Vierteljahrshefte für Zeitgeschichte*, 49:1 (2001), pp. 31–51. Vahlen was *Gauleiter* of Pomerania until his dismissal by Hitler in 1927. He apparently died in prison in Prague in 1945.

55. *TBJG*, 22 November 1924, TI, 1/I, p. 246.

56. Inachin, '"Märtyrer mit einem kleinen Häuflein Getreuer"', pp. 36–9.

57. *TBJG*, 22 November 1924, TI, 1/I, p. 246.

58. *TBJG*, 22 November 1924, TI, 1/I, p. 247.

59. *TBJG*, 27 November 1924, TI, 1/I, p. 247.

60. Victor Klemperer, *I Shall Bear Witness: The Diaries of Victor Klemperer 1933–41* (London: Book Club Associates, 1998), 30 July 1936, p. 172.

61. We must therefore now disregard statements like this: 'The younger man copied the older in manner, speech, ideas, even hobbies', and 'True that Goebbels coldly copied his Führer, learning his tricks of public speaking'. See Konrad Heiden, *Der Fuehrer: Hitler's Rise to Power* (Boston: Houghton and Mifflin, 1944), pp. 289, and p. 290.

62. Albert Krebs, *Tendenzen und Gestalten der NSDAP* (Stuttgart: Deutsche Verlags-Anstalt, 1959), p. 158. Krebs was expelled from the Nazi Party in May 1932.

63. See, amongst others, Reinhard Kühnl, *Die nationalsozialistische Linke 1925–1930* (Meisenheim: Hain, 1966); and Jeremy Noakes, 'Conflict and Development in the NSDAP 1924–1927', *Journal of Contemporary History*, 1:4 (1966), pp. 3–36.

64. Ripke was dismissed from the *Gau* leadership of North Rhineland in July 1925 after being accused of embezzling Party funds. He was expelled from the NSDAP in 1932. Karl Kaufmann was appointed *Gauleiter* of Hamburg in 1928 and remained in this position until 1945 when he helped to arrange the surrender of the city to the British. He was briefly interned, and was active in neo-Nazi politics after his release.

65. *TBJG*, 19 December 1924, TI, 1/I, p. 252. Gensicke's name in this first entry was incorrectly spelt.

66. *TBJG*, 9 February 1925, TI, 1/I, p. 268.

67. *TBJG*, 23 December 1924, TI, 1/I, p. 253.

68. *TBJG*, entries for 21, 23, and 26 February, TI, 1/I, pp. 272–4; see also Albrecht Tyrell, *Führer befiehl … Selbstzeugnisse aus der 'Kampfzeit' der NSDAP* (Düsseldorf: Droste Verlag, 1969), p. 376.

69. See, above all, Reinhard Kühnl, 'Zur Programmatik der nationalsozialistischen Linken: Das Strasser-Programm von 1925/26', *Vierteljahrshefte für Zeitgeschichte*, 14:3 (1966), pp. 317–33.

70. See, for example, Reimann, *The Man who Created Hitler*, pp. 34–41, where Goebbels is described as a 'National Bolshevik'. Reimann is at least sceptical about the story that Goebbels even went so far as to demand the expulsion of 'the petit-bourgeois Adolf Hitler from the NSDAP', which has reappeared in many later histories of Nazism. The original source of this completely implausible anecdote is Otto Strasser, *Hitler and I* (London: Jonathan Cape, 1940), p. 97. There is no meaningful sense in which

Goebbels was ever a 'National Bolshevik'. For an analysis of some who were, see Sontheimer, *Antidemokratisches Denken in der Weimarer Republik*, pp. 127–30.

71. *TBJG*, 27 March 1925, TI, 1/I, pp. 286–7; Karl Erb was a self-taught tenor, who had a 'unique voice', and 'was considered as the greatest Evangelist of his day in J.S. Bach's *St Matthew Passion*'. See www.bach-cantatas.com/Bio/Erb-Karl.htm, accessed 19 March 2009.

72. *TBJG*, 27 April 1925, TI, 1/I, p. 297.

73. *TBJG*, 8 June 1925, TI, 1/I, p. 312.

74. Theweleit's comments on 'the site of war' are, as ever, interesting. See *Male Fantasies II*, pp. 191–7.

75. Bundesarchiv, Außenstelle Berlin (hereafter BArch), (ehem. BDC) NS 26/2512, 'Göbbels, Dr. phil. Josef, Paul' [no date]. This document is a lengthy summary of many previous police and court reports from around Germany, apparently compiled in 1932.

76. 'Nationalsozialismus am Rhein und an der Ruhr', *Völkischer Beobachter*, 24 May 1925.

77. *TBJG*, 22 May 1925, TI, 1/I, p. 305.

78. 'Idee und Opfer', *Völkischer Beobachter*, 14/15 June 1925.

79. *TBJG*, 23 June 1925, TI, 1/I, p. 318.

80. *TBJG*, 14 July 1925, TI, 1/I, pp. 326–7. Weimar was in Thuringia, one of the few German states where Hitler was still allowed to speak in public. Dinter left the Nazi Party in 1928 after disagreeing with the Party line on religion.

81. Spengler, *The Decline of the West*, Vol. 2, *Perspectives of World History*, p. 443. See also Sontheimer, *Antidemokratisches Denken in der Weimarer Republik*, pp. 214–19.

82. Gay, *Weimar Culture*, p. 146.

83. Cited in Theweleit, *Male Fantasies II*, p. 94.

84. *TBJG*, 7 August 1925, TI, 1/I, p. 338.

85. *TBJG*, 24 August 1925, TI, 1/I, pp. 345–6.

86. *TBJG*, 28 September 1925, TI, 1/I, p. 358.

87. *TBJG*, 24 October 1925, TI, 1/I, p. 370.

88. *TBJG*, 26 October 1925, TI, 1/I, p. 371.

Chapter 3

1. Cited in Tyrell, *Führer befiehl*, p. 118.

2. *TBJG*, 11 September 1925, TI, 1/I, p. 352.

3. See Alan Bullock, *Hitler: A Study in Tyranny* (London: Odhams Press, 1952), p. 121; and Heiden, *Der Fuehrer: Hitler's Rise to Power*, p. 286. The account given by Otto Strasser in *Hitler and I*, pp. 90–104, must be treated with great caution.

4. See the 'Statuten der Arbeitsgemeinschaft der Nord- und Westdeutschen Gaue der N.S.D.A.P.', cited in Tyrell, *Führer befiehl*, pp. 113–14; and the letter from the 'Kanzlei von Adolf Hitler', 11 December 1925, cited in the same volume, pp. 116–17. See also Kühnl, 'Zur Programmatik der nationalsozialistischen Linken'.

5. BArch (ehem. BDC) NS 26/2512, 'Göbbels, Dr. phil. Josef, Paul' [no date].

6. *TBJG*, 30 September 1925, TI, 1/I, p. 359. Given that Vahlen had jeopardized his university career by making intemperate nationalist speeches, Goebbels' comment on him seems harsh. See Inachin, '"Märtyrer mit einem kleinen Häuflein Getreuer"', pp. 36ff. Elbrechter and Haase disappeared into obscurity; Pfeffer went on to lead the SA between 1926 and 1930 before being replaced by Ernst Röhm. After a career in the

police and as an occupation official Pfeffer was active in post-1945 politics in the state of Hesse; Lohse went on to be Reich Commissar in the occupied Baltic and White Russian territories in 1941, and was sentenced to ten years' imprisonment in 1948; Robert Ley was head of the German Workers' Front after 1933, and committed suicide in Nuremberg in October 1945 after being indicted as a 'major war criminal'.

7. *TBJG*, 26 October 1925, TI, 1/I, p. 371.

8. *TBJG*, 14 October 1925, TI, 1/I, p. 365.

9. *TBJG*, 2 November 1925, TI, 1/I, p. 374.

10. *TBJG*, 6 November 1925, TI, 1/I, pp. 374–5. Rust, a former schoolteacher and army officer, was appointed as Minister for Science, Teaching, and People's Education by Hitler in 1933; he committed suicide in May 1945.

11. See Alan Bullock's comments in his preface to Heiber, *The Early Goebbels Diaries: The Journal of Joseph Goebbels from 1925–1926*, p. 12.

12. *TBJG*, 14 November 1925, TI, 1/I, pp. 377–8.

13. *TBJG*, 23 November 1925, TI, 1/I, pp. 378–9. Mutschmann remained as *Gauleiter* of Saxony until 1945 when he was arrested by the Soviets. He died in Moscow in 1947.

14. Frick went on to serve as Minister of the Interior in the 'Third Reich', and was executed in October 1946 after being convicted by the International Military Tribunal at Nuremberg. Schlange was active in the Nazi Party in Brandenburg until 1933, when he disappeared into obscurity.

15. *TBJG*, 28 November 1925, TI, 1/I, pp. 380–1. Clara Zetkin was then in her late sixties; she continued to serve as a *Reichstag* deputy until her death shortly after Hitler's accession to power in 1933.

16. *TBJG*, 5 December 1925, TI, 1/II, pp. 29–30. Hildebrandt remained *Gauleiter* of Mecklenburg until 1945. He was sentenced to death by an American military court in 1947 and executed in 1948.

17. *TBJG*, 15 December 1925, TI, 1/II, p. 33.

18. *TBJG*, 16 December 1925, TI, 1/II, p. 34.

19. *TBJG*, 21 December 1925, TI, 1/II, p. 36.

20. *TBJG*, 29 December 1925, TI, 1/II, pp. 38–9.

21. *TBJG*, 2 January 1926, TI, 1/II, p. 40.

22. *TBJG*, 4 January 1926, TI, 1/II, p. 41.

23. *TBJG*, 11 January 1926, TI, 1/II, p. 44.

24. *TBJG*, 13 and 20 January 1926, TI, 1/II, p. 45, and p. 47. Jünger's book was, by common consent, the most influential German memoir of the First World War. English-language readers should see the recent translation, *Storm of Steel* (London: Penguin, 2004). Goebbels was subsequently disillusioned by Jünger, who in his view failed to match his literary achievement with social commitment. See *TBJG*, 30 June 1926, and 17 February 1927, TI, 1/II, pp. 101 and 185.

25. The passage from Bruck is cited in Kaes *et al.*, *The Weimar Republic Sourcebook*, p. 333; see also *TBJG*, 18 December 1925, TI, 1/II, p. 35. Curiously, Goebbels did not note Bruck's fascination with Dostoyevsky, or that Bruck had edited the German-language translations of Dostoyevsky's novels.

26. On Bruck, see Stern, *The Politics of Cultural Despair*; also Sontheimer, *Antidemokratisches Denken in der Weimarer Republik*, pp. 237–41.

27. *TBJG*, 20 January 1926, TI, 1/II, p. 47.

28. *TBJG*, 25 January 1926, TI, 1/II, pp. 48–9; also Kühnl, 'Zur Programmatik der national-sozialistischen Linken: Das Strasser-Programm von 1925/26', p. 321. Otto Strasser's account of this meeting in *Hitler and I*, p. 97, must be treated with scepticism.

29. For Hitler's 'Twenty-five Points', see Jeremy Noakes and Geoffrey Pridham (eds), *Nazism 1919–1945: A Documentary Reader* (Exeter: Exeter University Press, 1994), Vol. 1, *The Rise to Power, 1919–1934*, pp. 14–16. The original poster from February 1920 displaying the 'Twenty-five Points' is reproduced in Fritz Maier-Hartmann, *Dokumente der Zeitgeschichte* (Munich: Eher Verlag, 1938), Band I, p. 105.

30. *TBJG*, 6 February 1926, TI, 1/II, p. 52.

31. Krebs, *Tendenzen und Gestalten der NSDAP*, pp. 160–1.

32. Cited in Theodore Abel (ed.), *Why Hitler Came into Power* (Cambridge, Massachusetts: Harvard University Press, 1986), p. 212; see also p. 119, and p. 132. Unfortunately this account is not precisely dated or located, so it is difficult to see what Goebbels thought of the same meeting.

33. Joseph Goebbels, 'Nationalsozialismus oder Bolschewismus', *Nationalsozialistische Briefe*, 25 October 1925, cited in Barbara Miller Lane and Leila Rupp (eds), *Nazi Ideology before 1933: A Documentation* (Manchester: Manchester University Press, 1978), pp. 74–8.

34. Joseph Goebbels, *Lenin oder Hitler?* (Zwickau: Streiter-Verlag, 1926), p. 4.

35. 'National und international?' in Goebbels, *Die zweite Revolution*, pp. 40–3, p. 42.

36. 'Die Radikalisierung des Sozialismus', in Goebbels, *Die zweite Revolution*, pp. 51–5, p. 53.

37. 'Klassenkampf und Volksgemeinschaft', in Goebbels, *Die zweite Revolution*, pp. 13–17, p. 15.

38. Goebbels, 'National und international?' p. 40.

39. Goebbels, 'Die Radikalisierung des Sozialismus', p. 55, and p. 54.

40. Joseph Goebbels, *Das kleine abc des Nationalsozialisten* (Elberfeld: Verlag der National-sozialistischen Briefe, [1927]). See also the manuscript copy of *Das kleine abc des Nationalsozialisten* in BArch (ehem. BDC) NS 26/2512.

41. The programme was never published. A 'draft' is reproduced in Kühnl, 'Zur Programmatik der nationalsozialistischen Linken: Das Strasser-Programm von 1925/26', pp. 324–33. Extensive extracts are translated and cited in Lane and Rupp, *Nazi Ideology before 1933*, pp. 83–7.

42. See the letter from Strasser to Goebbels, 8 January 1926, cited in Tyrell, *Führer befiehl*, p. 123.

43. Konrad Heiden (in *Der Fuehrer*, p. 288) described Goebbels at the meeting thus: 'Suddenly Goebbels stood up and stammered with emotion: yes, he saw that had been wrong. The Führer in his address had disclosed fundamentally new paths. He must be followed; this was no Damascus.' No reference is provided. This account may be derived from Otto Strasser, who wrote: '"Herr Hitler is right", he [Goebbels] declared (the word Führer had not yet been introduced into the Nazi vocabulary). "His arguments are so convincing that there is no disgrace in admitting our mistakes and rejoining him."' See *Hitler and I*, p. 100. We have seen that Goebbels was using the word '*Führer*' in 1924.

44. *TBJG*, 15 February 1926, TI, 1/II, p. 55. Hermann Esser was a founding member of the Nazi Party, the first editor of the *Völkischer Beobachter*, and from 1923 until 1926 the Party's Propaganda Leader. After this his influence waned, and after 1933 he held a series of relatively insignificant offices dealing with tourism. He was sentenced to five years' imprisonment in 1950 by a German denazification tribunal.

45. 'Die Bamberger Tagung', *Völkischer Beobachter*, 25 February 1926.

46. *TBJG*, 22 February 1926, TI, 1/II, p. 57.

47. Kühnl, 'Zur Programmatik der nationalsozialistischen Linken: Das Strasser-Programm von 1925/26', p. 323.

48. *TBJG*, 6 March 1926, TI, 1/II, p. 60.
49. *TBJG*, 12 March 1926, TI, 1/II, pp. 62–3.
50. *TBJG*, 13 March 1926, TI, 1/II, pp. 63–4.
51. *TBJG*, 21 March 1926, TI, 1/II, pp. 64–5.
52. *TBJG*, 27 March 1926, TI, 1/II, pp. 66–7.
53. See Tyrell, *Führer befiehl*, p. 376.
54. *TBJG*, 29 March 1926, TI, 1/II, p. 68.
55. *TBJG*, 31 March 1926, TI, 1/II, p. 69.
56. *TBJG*, 13 April 1926, TI, 1/II, pp. 71–2; see also *Völkischer Beobachter*, 8 April 1926.
57. Alfred Rosenberg was an Estonian-born student of architecture, who had teamed up with Hitler after coming to Munich in 1919. He imagined himself as the Nazi Party's philosopher and cultural theorist, and was a virulent anti-Semite. Rudolf Hess was born in Egypt, and joined the Nazi Party in Munich in 1920. He was sentenced to imprisonment for his part in the 1923 *Putsch* and used the time he spent there with Hitler to gain the latter's confidence, working as his secretary. Rosenberg and Hess were tried as 'major war criminals' by the International Military Tribunal at Nuremberg. Rosenberg was executed in 1946, and Hess sentenced to life imprisonment. He died in Spandau prison in 1987.
58. BArch (ehem. BDC) NS 26/2512, 'Göbbels, Dr. phil. Josef, Paul' [no date].
59. *TBJG*, 13 April 1926, TI, 1/II, pp. 73–4. Heinrich Himmler took part in the 1923 *Putsch* in Munich, and pursued his career in politics as a Nazi activist and speaker in Bavaria during 1924. He was rewarded in 1925 with the post of deputy *Gauleiter* of Upper Bavaria-Swabia. See Heinz Höhne, *The Order of the Death's Head: The Story of Hitler's SS* (London: Penguin, 2000), pp. 29–44.
60. *TBJG*, 19 April 1926, TI, 1/II, pp. 75–7.
61. Joseph Goebbels, 'Der Generalstab', *Wege ins Dritte Reich* (Munich: Eher Verlag, 1927), pp. 7–9.
62. Cited in Borresholm and Nichoff, *Dr. Goebbels. Nach Aufzeichnungen aus seiner Umgebung*, p. 17. See also Reimann, *The Man who Created Hitler*, p. 57.
63. *TBJG*, 8 May 1926, TI, 1/II, pp. 82–4.
64. *TBJG*, 15 May 1926, TI, 1/II, p. 86.
65. *TBJG*, 24 May 1926, TI, 1/II, pp. 88–9.
66. 'Abrechnung Hitlers mit dem gegenwärtigen "Deutschland"', *Völkischer Beobachter*, 26 May 1926.
67. *TBJG*, 12 June 1926, TI, 1/II, p. 95.
68. 'Rückblick und Ausblick', *Völkischer Beobachter*, 3 July 1926.
69. The photograph is reproduced in Frederic Grunfeld (ed.), *The Hitler File: A Social History of Germany and the Nazis, 1918–45* (London: Book Club Associates, 1974), pp. 124–5.
70. *TBJG*, 6 July 1926, TI, 1/II, pp. 102–4.
71. On Hitler's involvement with Berchtesgaden, see Volker Dahm, Albert Feiber, Hartmut Mehringer, and Horst Möller (eds), *Die tödliche Utopie. Bilder, Texte, Dokumente, Daten zum Dritten Reich* (Munich: Verlag Dokumentation Obersalzberg im Institut für Zeitgeschichte, 2008), pp. 60–3.
72. See *TBJG*, entries from 12 July 1926 to 1 August 1926, TI, 1/II, pp. 105–17.
73. *TBJG*, 18 October 1926, TI, 1/II, p. 141.
74. *TBJG*, 10 June 1926, TI, 1/II, p. 94.
75. BArch NS 26/2512, 'Göbbels, Dr. phil. Josef, Paul' [no date].
76. *TBJG*, 27 and 28 August 1926, TI, 1/II, pp. 126–7.

77. Cited in Borresholm and Nichoff, *Dr. Goebbels. Nach Aufzeichnungen aus seiner Umgebung*, p. 65.
78. Victor Klemperer, *The Language of the Third Reich. LTI – Lingua Tertii Imperii: A Philologist's Notebook* (London: Continuum, 2002), p. 241.
79. Neither Schlange nor Schmiedicke went on to further positions of note in the Nazi Party, but Daluege did. He became leader of the SS (*Schutzstaffel* (Protective Echelon)) in Berlin in 1928, and Chief of the Order Police in 1936. In 1942 he was appointed *Reich* Protector of Bohemia and Moravia. In 1945 he was captured by the British and extradited to Czechoslovakia, where he was executed in October 1946 for his responsibility for the massacre at the village of Lidice.
80. See *TBJG*, entries for 13, 14 and 16 August 1926, TI, 1/II, pp. 120–2.
81. *TBJG*, 3 September 1926, TI, 1/II, pp. 128–9.
82. *TBJG*, 11 September 1926, TI, 1/II, p. 131.
83. *TBJG*, 17 September 1926, TI, 1/II, pp. 132–3.
84. *TBJG*, 23 September 1926, TI, 1/II, p. 134.
85. *TBJG*, 27 September 1926, TI, 1/II, p. 136.
86. *TBJG*, 28 September 1926, TI, 1/II, p. 137.
87. *TBJG*, 4 October 1926, TI, 1/II, p. 138.
88. *TBJG*, 16 October 1926, TI, 1/II, p. 139. Berlin lies in the province of Brandenburg, formerly an electorate in the Holy Roman Empire, before becoming a central part of the kingdom of Prussia. 'Mark', a word similar to the English 'March', is a word still used to describe this area. The Nazis particularly liked its echo of a heroic Prussian history.
89. Schmiedicke to Goebbels, 16 October 1926, cited in Heiber, *The Early Goebbels Diaries*, pp. 127–8.
90. *TBJG*, 18 October 1926, TI, 1/II, p. 141.
91. *TBJG*, 30 October 1926, TI, 1/II, pp. 143–4.
92. *TBJG*, 6 November 1926, TI, 1/II, p. 145.
93. *TBJG*, 8 November 1926, TI, 1/II, p. 146.

Chapter 4

1. Julius Lippert, *Im Strom der Zeit. Erlebnisse und Eindrücke* (Berlin: Dietrich Reimer, 1942), p. 113.
2. *TBJG*, 11 November 1926, TI, 1/II, p. 147.
3. *TBJG*, 12 November 1926, TI, 1/II, p. 148.
4. 9 November was the anniversary of the Munich *Putsch*. Goebbels' backdating of the circular to this day shows his intention of creating a mythology around his leadership in Berlin.
5. 'Circular No. 1 of the *Gau* Headquarters Berlin-Brandenburg of the NSDAP', 9 November 1926, cited in Heiber, *The Early Goebbels Diaries*, pp. 129–31.
6. See *TBJG*, 13 August 1926, TI, 1/II, p. 121.
7. In September 1926, Gregor Strasser had been appointed to direct the Nazi Party's propaganda; his deputy then was Heinrich Himmler.
8. 'Neue Methoden der Propaganda', Goebbels, *Wege ins Dritte Reich*, pp. 15–25, p. 18.
9. Joseph Goebbels, *Kampf um Berlin. Der Anfang* (Munich: Franz Eher, 1932), p. 18.
10. See for example the passage with Hitler's thoughts on the flag he designed for the Party, cited in Brandon Taylor and Wilfried van der Will (eds), *The Nazification of Art:*

Art, Design, Music, Architecture and Film in the Third Reich (Winchester: Winchester School of Art Press, 1990), p. 4.

11. See www.calvin.edu/academic/cas/gpa/posters/hitlerbanned1.jp, accessed 15 May 2008; also Maier-Hartmann, *Dokumente der Zeitgeschichte*, Band I, p. 237.

12. *TBJG*, 15 November 1926, TI, 1/II, p. 149.

13. For a broader account of Schweitzer and his work, see Peter Paret, *German Encounters with Modernism, 1840–1945* (Cambridge: Cambridge University Press, 2001), pp. 202–28.

14. See Sabine Behrenbeck, *Der Kult um die toten Helden: Nationalsozialistische Mythen, Riten und Symbole 1923 bis 1945* (Greifswald: SH-Verlag, 1996).

15. Goebbels, 'Schöpferische Kräfte. Richard Flisges, dem toten Freunde!' See also Joseph Goebbels, *Michael. Ein deutsches Schicksal in Tagebuchblättern* (Munich: Franz Eher, 1942), pp. 157–8.

16. *TBJG*, 30 December 1925, TI, 1/II, p. 39.

17. *TBJG*, 7 December 1925, TI, 1/II, pp. 30–1.

18. *TBJG*, 28 November 1926, TI, 1/II, p. 153.

19. *TBJG*, 8 January 1927, TI, 1/II, p. 169. One wonders whether this unnamed Party member was Edmund Brand, a Nazi from Unna who had taken part in the Munich *Putsch* in 1923, and was subsequently involved in two separate attacks on Communists involving firearms in Bernau, near Berlin, in 1930. See the documents relating to these incidents in BArch R 55/21719.

20. See the 'Situation reports' reprinted in Martin Broszat, 'Die Anfänge der Berliner NSDAP', *Vierteljahrshefte für Zeitgeschichte*, 8:1 (1960), pp. 85–118.

21. *TBJG*, 21 November 1926, TI, 1/II, p. 152. It was not until January 1928 that Hitler agreed to the affiliation of the German Women's Order with the Nazi Party. On Zander, see also Michael Kater, 'Frauen in der NS-Bewegung', *Vierteljahrshefte für Zeitgeschichte*, 31:2 (1983), pp. 202–41.

22. *TBJG*, 3 December 1926, TI, 1/II, p. 156.

23. *TBJG*, 8 December 1926, TI, 1/II, p. 158.

24. *TBJG*, 18 December 1926, TI, 1/II, pp. 161–2.

25. *TBJG*, 30 December 1926, TI, 1/II, p. 163.

26. *TBJG*, 26 January 1927, TI, 1/II, p. 176.

27. *TBJG*, 1 February 1927, TI, 1/II, pp. 177–8.

28. *TBJG*, 12 February, TI, 1/II, p. 182.

29. See Christian Striefler, *Kampf um die Macht. Kommunisten und Nationalsozialisten am Ende der Weimarer Republik* (Berlin: Propyläen, 1993), pp. 323–5, which is based on the account given in Borresholm and Nichoff, *Dr. Goebbels. Nach Aufzeichnungen aus seiner Umgebung*, pp. 50–3; this in turn is based entirely on accounts originally written by Goebbels himself in the years after the event; for example, in Joseph Goebbels, *Kampf um Berlin*, pp. 63–75.

30. *TBJG*, 16 February 1927, TI, 1/II, p. 184.

31. Report from the *Berliner Polizeipräsidium*, cited in Deuerlein, *Der Aufstieg der NSDAP*, p. 276.

32. *TBJG*, 21 March 1927, TI, 1/II, p. 199.

33. 'Spezialbericht über die Vorgänge auf dem Bahnhof Berlin-Lichterfelde-Ost am 20. März 1927', cited in Broszat, 'Die Anfänge der Berliner NSDAP', pp. 115–18.

34. BArch (ehem. BDC) NS 26/2512, 'Göbbels, Dr. phil. Josef, Paul' [no date]; see also *TBJG*, 11 May 1927, TI, 1/II, p. 220.

35. *TBJG*, 2 May 1927, TI, 1/II, p. 216.

36. *TBJG*, 13 May 1927, TI, 1/II, p. 221.

37. *TBJG*, 12 May 1927, TI, 1/II, p. 221.
38. See for example the article in the *Deutsche Allgemeine Zeitung*, 6 May 1927, reproduced in Nichoff and Borresholm, *Dr. Goebbels. Nach Aufzeichnungen aus seiner Umgebung*, pp. 69–70.
39. *TBJG*, 17 December 1926, TI, 1/II, p. 161.
40. Joseph Goebbels, 'Der unbekannte S.A. Mann', *Wege ins Dritte Reich*, pp. 60–4, p. 62.
41. *TBJG*, 13 January 1927, TI, 1/II, p. 171. Riefenstahl recalls that she danced on the stage to the music of Schubert's Unfinished Symphony before the film's premiere. See her *The Sieve of Time: The Memoirs of Leni Riefenstahl* (London: Quartet Books, 1992), p. 59.
42. *TBJG*, 25 March 1927, TI, 1/II, p. 201. For a succinct analysis of *Metropolis* see Gay, *Weimar Culture*, pp. 148–9.
43. See *TBJG*, entries for 8, 9, and 11 April 1927, TI, 1/II, pp. 207–8.
44. See 'Das neue Kampflied', in Goebbels, *Wege ins Dritte Reich*, pp. 29–32. See also Michael Meyer, 'The SA Song Literature: A Singing Ideological Posture', *Journal of Popular Culture*, 11:3 (1977), pp. 568–80; on Gansser, see pp. 573–4.
45. Herf, Jeffrey, *Reactionary Modernism*, p. 1.
46. *TBJG*, 17 December 1926, TI, 1/II, p. 161.
47. *TBJG*, 17 February 1927, TI, 1/II, p. 185.
48. *TBJG*, 19 February 1927, TI, 1/II, p. 187.
49. *TBJG*, 8 April 1927, TI, 1/II, p. 207. Despite this feud, Goebbels was to have dealings with Koch until the end of his life. Koch was appointed *Gauleiter* of East Prussia in 1928, where he gained a reputation for brutality and self-indulgence.
50. *TBJG*, 27 April 1927, TI, 1/II, p. 213.
51. See the 'Summary' of the meeting on 10 June 1927, sent to Rudolf Hess, 16 June 1927, cited in Heiber, *The Early Goebbels Diaries*, pp. 135–9.
52. *TBJG*, 1 June 1927, TI, 1/II, pp. 227–8.
53. See Gregor Strasser's letter to Hitler, and the 'Report', 21 June 1927, cited in Heiber, *The Early Goebbels Diaries*, pp. 139–44, and pp. 145–7.
54. 'Berlin Stahlhelm Manifesto', in Kaes *et al.*, *The Weimar Republic Sourcebook*, pp. 339–40.
55. BArch (ehem. BDC) NS 26/2512, 'Zentralsprechabend der N.S.D.A.P. München ... im Mathäser-Festsaal', 20 June 1927. On the *Stahlhelm* see Richard J. Evans, *The Coming of the Third Reich* (London: Allen Lane, 2003), pp. 71–2.
56. For an interesting, if highly partial account of working with Goebbels on *Der Angriff*, see Lipperts' memoir, *Im Strom der Zeit*, pp. 113ff.
57. *TBJG*, 4 July 1927, TI, 1/II, pp. 240–1.
58. *TBJG*, 17 July 1927, TI, 1/II, pp. 244–5.
59. *TBJG*, 23 July 1927, TI, 1/II, p. 248.
60. 'Warum Angriff?' *Der Angriff*, 4 July 1927.
61. 'Prozesse', *Der Angriff*, 11 July 1927.
62. See for example 'Warum sind wir Judengegner?' *Der Angriff*, 30 July 1928; 'Deutsche, kauft nur bei Juden!' *Der Angriff*, 10 December 1928; and 'Der Jude', *Der Angriff*, 21 January 1929.
63. 'Ein jüdischvölkischer Messerheld', *Der Angriff*, 19 September 1927.
64. 'Isidor' was seen in Germany at this time as a stereotypically Jewish first name. See, for an analysis of its symbolism, Michel, *Vom Poeten zum Demagogen*, pp. 130–2.

65. See, for example, 'Isidor', *Der Angriff*, 15 August 1927. For one analysis of *Der Angriff*, see Lemmons, *Goebbels and Der Angriff*; also Carin Kessemier, *Der Leitartikler Goebbels*.

66. Joseph Goebbels (ed.), *Das Buch Isidor. Ein Zeitbild voll Lachen und Hass* (Munich: Franz Eher, 1928); Joseph Goebbels (ed.), *Knorke. Ein neues Buch Isidor für Zeitgenossen* (Munich: Franz Eher, 1931).

67. Both cited in Abel, *Why Hitler Came Into Power*, p. 116.

68. See *TBJG*, entries for 18 and 19 July 1927, TI, 1/II, pp. 245–6. The poster is reproduced in Maier-Hartmann, *Dokumente der Zeitgeschichte*, Band I, p. 263.

69. *TBJG*, 1 August 1927, TI, 1/II, pp. 250–1.

70. Report on the Third Party Rally of the NSDAP from the *Reichskommisar für die Überwachung der öffentlichen Ordnung*, cited in Deuerlein, *Der Aufstieg der NSDAP*, pp. 279–85.

71. 'Das Heilige Tuch', *Der Angriff*, 29 August 1927.

72. *TBJG*, 10 September 1927, TI, 1/II, p. 267.

73. *TBJG*, 27 November 1927, TI, 1/II, p. 295.

74. 'Die "gespaltene" N.S.D.A.P.', *Völkischer Beobachter*, 21 December 1927.

75. *TBJG*, 20 December 1927, TI, 1/II, p. 304.

76. *TBJG*, 23 June 1927, TI, 1/II, p. 236.

77. *TBJG*, 24 November 1927, TI, 1/II, p. 294.

78. *TBJG*, 30 October 1927, TI, 1/II, p. 285.

79. *TBJG*, 4 November 1927, TI, 1/II, p. 287. Viktor Lutze was another ex-officer with early Nazi Party membership who rose through the ranks of the SA to command the organization after the murder of Ernst Röhm in 1934.

80. *TBJG*, 24 February 1928, TI, 1/II, p. 331.

81. *TBJG*, 26 February 1928, TI, 1/II, p. 331.

82. See Maier-Hartmann, *Dokumente der Zeitgeschichte*, Band 1, p. 272; also *TBJG*, 28 February 1928, TI, 1/II, p. 333.

83. See the report in the *Völkischer Beobachter*, 30 November 1927.

84. *TBJG*, 7 March 1928, TI, 1/II, pp. 336–7.

85. *TBJG*, 10 April 1928, TI, 1/II, pp. 351–2.

86. 'Wir fordern:', *Der Angriff*, 23 April 1928.

87. *TBJG*, 28 April 1928, TI, 1/II, p. 362.

88. *TBJG*, 3 May 1928, TI, 1/II, pp. 363–4.

89. Kershaw, *Hitler 1889–1936*, p. 303.

90. *TBJG*, 21 May 1928, TI, 1/II, pp. 372–3.

91. *TBJG*, 22 May 1928, TI, 1/II, p. 373.

Chapter 5

1. Christopher Isherwood, *Goodbye to Berlin* (London: Triad/Granada, 1977), p. 142.

2. *TBJG*, 13 June 1928, TI, 1/III, pp. 35–6.

3. 'Was wollen wir im Reichstag?' *Der Angriff*, 30 April 1928; and 'IdI', *Der Angriff*, 28 May 1928.

4. *TBJG*, 10 July 1928, TI, 1/III, pp. 50–1.

5. *TBJG*, 20 November 1928, TI, 1/III, p. 127. Gustav Stresemann died unexpectedly after a stroke in October 1929. Goebbels loathed his policy of seeking reconciliation with France and Britain.

6. 'Abschluss der nationalsozialistischen Führertagung', *Völkischer Beobachter*, 3 September 1928.
7. 'Reich Delegates Conference of the German Women's Order', *Völkischer Beobachter*, 25 October 1927, cited in Mühlberger, *Hitler's Voice: The Völkischer Beobachter 1920–1933*, Vol. 1, pp. 336–7.
8. *TBJG*, 29 March 1929, TI, 1/III, p. 214.
9. *TBJG*, 19 October 1927, 1/II, p. 280.
10. Claudia Koonz, *Mothers in the Fatherland: Women, the Family, and Nazi Politics* (London: Jonathan Cape, 1987), p. 73.
11. *TBJG*, 7 March 1929, TI, 1/III, p. 198.
12. See 'Unsere Pflicht', and 'Blond oder Dunkel?' in *Heim und Welt: Blätter für die deutsche Frau*, 1 (1929), issued with *Der Angriff*, 7 January 1929.
13. See *TBJG*, 1 April 1929, TI, 1/III, pp. 215–18.
14. *TBJG*, 26 July 1929, TI, 1/III, p. 289.
15. '20 000 Versammlungen im Jahre 1928', *Völkischer Beobachter*, 26 January 1929.
16. *TBJG*, 2 March 1929, TI, 1/III, p. 195.
17. *TBJG*, 26 March 1929, TI, 1/III, p. 212.
18. *TBJG*, 11 September 1929, TI, 1/III, p. 324.
19. On the May 1929 disturbances, see Striefler, *Kampf um die Macht*, pp. 205–6.
20. Maier-Hartmann, *Dokumente der Zeitgeschichte*, Band 1, pp. 303–4; *TBJG*, 23 September 1929, TI, 1/III, pp. 334–5.
21. Orlow, *The History of the Nazi Party*, Vol. 1, 1919–33, p. 179.
22. *TBJG*, 8 December 1929, TI, 2/I, pp. 38–9.
23. See *TBJG*, 1 March 1929, TI, 1/III, pp. 194–5.
24. See *TBJG*, 29 May 1929, TI, 1/III, pp. 256–7.
25. See *TBJG*, 29 December 1929, TI, 2/I, p. 51.
26. Since 1930 there has been controversy over whether Wessel's killing was politically motivated or occasioned by more prosaic and squalid motives. See, for a recent appraisal, Evans, *The Coming of the Third Reich*, pp. 266–8.
27. See Behrenbeck, *Der Kult um die toten Helden*, pp. 134–48.
28. 'Bis zur Neige', *Der Angriff*, 6 March 1930.
29. *TBJG*, 7 September 1929, TI, 1/III, p. 321.
30. See, for example, 'Unvergängliche Worte', *Der Angriff*, 10 November 1929; and 'Die Fahne hoch!' *Der Angriff*, 27 February 1930.
31. See Tyrell, *Führer befiehl*, pp. 296–7.
32. See 'Mitteilung', 1 February 1930, issued with *Der Angriff*, 6 February 1930, which informed readers of the plan to start a daily newspaper in Berlin, with Hitler's approval, which would take the place of *Der Angriff* and the *Völkischer Beobachter*. It added that nobody would be so stupid 'as to receive this plan unfavourably'.
33. See *TBJG*, 2 March 1930, TI, 2/I, p. 100.
34. *TBJG*, 16 March 1930 and 28 March 1930, TI, 2/I, p. 111, and p. 119.
35. *TBJG*, 28 April 1930, TI, 2/I, pp. 143–5.
36. *TBJG*, 2 May 1930, TI, 2/I, p. 148.
37. See the letter from Hitler to Goebbels, 30 June 1930, cited in Kühnl, *Die national-sozialistische Linke*, p. 374.
38. Otto Strasser's account of his break with the Party, in which Goebbels is presented as the arch-villain, should be treated with circumspection. See Strasser, *Hitler and I*, pp. 105–27.
39. *TBJG*, 22 April, 18 April, and 20 April 1930, TI, 2/I, pp. 139, 135, and 137.
40. *TBJG*, 1 May 1930, TI, 2/I, p. 146.

41. *TBJG*, 18 May 1930, TI, 2/I, p. 158.
42. Orlow, *The History of the Nazi Party*, Vol. 1, 1919–33, p. 182.
43. See *TBJG*, 12 May 1930, TI, 2/I, pp. 153–4; and 20 July 1930, TI, 2/I, p. 202.
44. *TBJG*, 12 September 1930, TI, 2/I, p. 237.
45. See the documents relating to this case in BAK N1118/143.
46. See 'Lebt Hindenburg noch?' *Der Angriff*, 29 December 1929; *TBJG*, 1 June 1930, T1, 2/I, p. 168; and 'Libel on President Hindenburg: German Fascist Fined', *The Times*, 2 June 1930, p. 13.
47. *TBJG*, 1 August 1930, TI, 2/I, p. 209.
48. BArch (ehem. BDC) NS 26/2512, 'Der Untersuchungsrichter des Reichsgerichts an die Polizeidirektion in München', 13 August 1930; 'Polizeidirektion in München an den Untersuchungsrichter des Reichsgerichts', 21 August 1930; 'Zeugenvernehmung i. S. Dr. Joseph Goebbels', 2 September 1930; and 'Der Untersuchungsrichter des Reichsgerichts an die Polizeidirektion in München', 19 January 1931.
49. See, for a valuable summary of this problem, Evans, *The Coming of the Third Reich*, pp. 134–8; also Gotthard Jasper, 'Justiz und Politik in der Weimarer Republik', *Vierteljahrshefte für Zeitgeschichte*, 30:2 (1982), pp. 167–205.
50. See *TBJG*, 30 August, 1 September and 3 September 1930, TI, 2/I, pp. 228–32.
51. See Striefler, *Kampf um die Macht*, p. 72, and p. 125.
52. *TBJG*, 15 September 1930, TI, 2/I, p. 239.
53. '106 Nationalsozialisten im neuen Reichstag', *Völkischer Beobachter*, 16 September 1930.
54. Cited in Kershaw, *Hitler 1889–1936*, pp. 337–8.
55. Cited in Deuerlein, *Der Aufstieg der NSDAP*, p. 337.
56. Hjalmar Schacht, *My First Seventy-six Years* (London: Allan Wingate, 1955), p. 279; *TBJG*, 6 January 1931, TI, 2/I, p. 319.
57. Wilhelm Frick had as a police official in Munich supported the Nazi Party in its early years, and was briefly imprisoned after the failed *Putsch* of November 1923. He had been one of the Party's *Reichstag* deputies since 1924. After 1945 he was one of the surviving 'major war criminals' convicted by the International Military Tribunal in Nuremberg. Frick was executed in 1946.
58. See Grunfeld, *The Hitler File*, p. 137.
59. *TBJG*, 14 October 1930, TI, 2/I, p. 260.
60. 'Einhundertsieben', *Der Angriff*, 21 September 1930.
61. From Goebbels' speech to the *Reichstag* on 5 February 1931, cited in Deuerlein, *Der Aufstieg der NSDAP*, p. 347.
62. *TBJG*, 19 November 1930, TI, 2/I, p. 285.
63. 'The Rise of the Nazis', *The Times*, 18 September 1930, p. 11.
64. Albert Speer, *Inside the Third Reich* (New York: Avon, 1971), pp. 43–6.
65. *TBJG*, 31 January 1931, TI, 2/I, p. 336.
66. 'In die Knie gezwungen', *Der Angriff*, 12 December 1930.
67. *TBJG*, 12 November 1930, TI, 2/I, p. 280.
68. *TBJG*, 19 December 1930, TI, 2/I, p. 307.
69. *TBJG*, 7 November 1930, TI, 2/I, p. 277.
70. *TBJG*, 14 November 1930, TI, 2/I, p. 281.
71. *TBJG*, 7 December 1930, TI, 2/I, p. 299.
72. *TBJG*, 12 December 1930, TI, 2/I, p. 302.
73. *TBJG*, 28 January, 1 February, 15 February, and 19 February 1931, TI, 2/I, pp. 334, 336, 346, and 348.
74. *TBJG*, 23 February 1931, TI, 2/I, pp. 350–1.

75. *TBJG*, 26 February 1931, TI, 2/I, p. 352.
76. The two most recent biographies of Magda Quandt are both heavily reliant on post-war accounts from people who knew her; both contain information about Joseph Goebbels, but much of this is anecdotal and inaccurate. See Hans-Otto Meissner, *Magda Goebbels: A Biography* (London: Sidgwick and Jackson, 1980); and Anja Klabunde, *Magda Goebbels* (London: Time Warner, 2003).
77. *TBJG*, 12 March 1931, TI, 2/I, p. 362.
78. Bella Fromm, *Blood and Banquets: A Berlin Social Diary* (New York: Carol, 1990), 16 December 1932, p. 66.
79. *TBJG*, 27 February 1931, TI, 2/I, p. 354.
80. *TBJG*, 6 March 1931, TI, 2/I, p. 358.
81. See Strasser, *Hitler and I*, p. 137. Otto Strasser also argues that 'the revolt was planned in agreement with Goebbels', but this appears completely unlikely. Stennes may have seriously overestimated the support Goebbels had earlier given him for some of his views.
82. *TBJG*, 29 March 1931, TI, 2/I, p. 374.
83. *TBJG*, 2 April 1931, TI, 2/I, p. 377.
84. *TBJG*, 4 April 1931, TI, 2/I, p. 378.
85. See Maier-Hartmann, *Dokumente der Zeitgeschichte*, Band 1, pp. 349–50; Deuerlein, *Der Aufstieg der NSDAP*, pp. 349–50; Kershaw, *Hitler 1889–1936*, pp. 349–50.
86. *TBJG*, 9 April 1931, TI, 2/I, p. 380.
87. *TBJG*, 14 April 1931, TI, 2/I, pp. 384–5. Stennes became a military adviser to the Chiang Kai Shek government in China in 1933. He died in 1989.
88. *TBJG*, 15 April 1931, TI, 2/I, pp. 383–4. Otto Strasser's claim that Stennes 'and thousands of resolute men passed that day into the Black Front' (*Hitler and I*, p. 139) appears exaggerated.
89. *TBJG*, 4 January, and 21 February 1931, TI, 2/I, p. 316, and p. 350.
90. *TBJG*, 15 May 1931, TI, 2/I, p. 406.
91. *TBJG*, 25 April 1931, TI, 2/I, p. 393.
92. *TBJG*, 26 May 1931, TI, 2/I, p. 413.
93. *TBJG*, 31 May 1931, TI, 2/I, p. 416.
94. See Klabunde, *Magda Goebbels*, pp. 138–46. This account unfortunately contains many errors, for example in stating that Magda first met Hitler in September 1931. It is clear from Goebbels' diary that she had met him in Munich on 3 April 1931.
95. *TBJG*, 14 September 1931, TI, 2/II, p. 98.
96. *TBJG*, 24 August, 4 September, 12 September, and 14 September 1931, TI, 2/II, pp. 84, 90, and 97.
97. *TBJG*, 16 September 1931, TI, 2/II, p. 100.
98. See Kershaw, *Hitler 1889–1936*, pp. 351–5.
99. *TBJG*, 25 September 1931, TI, 2/II, p. 107.
100. Some writers, like Anja Klabunde, and earlier Viktor Reimann, have attempted to unravel the triangular relationship between Goebbels, Hitler, and Magda Quandt, using notes written after 1945 by Otto Wagener, who was in 1931 Head of the Economics Office in the NSDAP leadership, and in close contact with Hitler. Unfortunately Wagener's account is so confused chronologically – it is based on the idea that Magda met Hitler for the first time *after* Geli Raubal's death – as to be completely unhelpful. See Klabunde, *Magda Goebbels*, pp. 138–43, and Reimann, *The Man who Created Hitler*, pp. 123–6. I am grateful to Paul Foster for his thoughts on the interpretation of the entries in Goebbels' diary which detail the relationship between himself, Magda, and Hitler.

101. *TBJG*, 7 October 1931, TI, 2/II, p. 118.
102. *TBJG*, 25 October 1931, TI, 2/II, p. 133.
103. *TBJG*, 1 December 1931, TI, 2/II, p. 161.
104. *TBJG*, 20 December 1931, TI, 2/II, p. 176. Franz von Epp was a highly decorated officer and *Freikorps* leader who had lent his support to the Nazis during the 1920s.

Chapter 6

1. Cited in Maier-Hartmann, *Dokumente der Zeitgeschichte*, Band 1, p. 369.
2. 'NS-Films', *Völkischer Beobachter*, 20–21 July 1930, cited in Mühlberger, *Hitler's Voice: The Völkischer Beobachter*, Vol. 2, pp. 366–7.
3. See 'N.S.-Filmbühne', *Der Angriff*, 3 October 1929; and *TBJG*, 24 October 1929, TI, 1/III, p. 357.
4. *TBJG*, 5 March 1932, TI, 2/II, p. 233. UFA stood for the Universum Film AG. This was Germany's most influential film company before 1933, owned since 1927 by Alfred Hugenberg.
5. *TBJG*, 6 March 1932, TI, 2/II, p. 235.
6. *TBJG*, 13 April 1932, TI, 2/II, p. 260.
7. See, for example, 'Appell an die Nation', transcribed from a recording in Heiber, *Goebbels-Reden*, Band 1: 1932–1939, pp. 1–3. I would agree with the editor's footnote which dates this recording to 1930.
8. Kershaw, *Hitler 1889–1936*, p. 363.
9. See Deuerlein, *Der Aufstieg der NSDAP*, pp. 384–5.
10. *TBJG*, 24 February 1932, TI, 2/II, p. 226.
11. See Heiber, *Goebbels-Reden*, Band 1, pp. 4–21 for the speech on 23 February 1932, and pp. 22–42 for that on 25 February 1932; and 'Stormy Scene in Reichstag', *The Times*, 24 February 1932, p. 11. See also the description of Goebbels' speech on 23 February cited in Johann Wilhelm Brügel and Norbert Frei, 'Berliner Tagebuch 1932–1934: Aufzeichnungen des tschechoslowakischen Diplomaten Camill Hoffmann', *Vierteljahrshefte für Zeitgeschichte*, 36:1 (1988), pp. 131–83, p. 142.
12. 'Aufruf', 10 April 1932, cited in Maier-Hartmann, *Dokumente der Zeitgeschichte*, Band 1, pp. 382–3.
13. *TBJG*, 25 April 1932, TI, 2/II, p. 267.
14. *TBJG*, 28 May 1932, TI, 2/II, pp. 289–90.
15. BArch R 55/21250, 'Die Geschäftsstelle der Staatsanwaltschaft bei dem Landgericht I, Berlin-Moabit, Kostenrechnung', 24 October 1931; 'Der Generalstaatsanwalt bei dem Landgericht I an den Schriftleiter Herrn Dr. Goebbels', 14 November 1931; 'Der Generalstaatsanwalt bei dem Landgericht I an Herrn Rechtsanwalt Otto Kamecke', 28 January 1932.
16. BArch R 55/21250, Kamecke to Goebbels, 3 February 1932; 'Privatsekretariat Dr. Goebbels an Herrn Rechtsanwalt Otto Kamecke', 5 February 1932; Kamecke to Goebbels, 4 March 1932; 'Gerichtstafel Berlin-Moabit an Herrn Dr. Goebbels', 23 July 1932; and 'Der Generalstaatsanwalt bei dem Landgericht I an den Schriftleiter Herrn Dr. Goebbels', 3 September 1932.
17. Heinrich Brüning, *Memoiren 1918–1934* (Stuttgart: Deutsche Verlags-Anstalt, 1970), p. 411.
18. See Ted Harrison, '"Alter Kämpfer" im Widerstand: Graf Helldorff, die NS-Bewegung und die Opposition gegen Hitler', *Vierteljahrshefte für Zeitgeschichte*, 45:3 (1997),

pp. 385–423, pp. 391–2; also *TBJG*, 25 September and 27 September 1931, TI, 2/II, pp. 107–8 and 109–10.

19. *TBJG*, 29 May 1932, TI, 2/II, p. 291.
20. Schaumburg-Lippe, *Dr. G.*, pp. 14–17; *TBJG*, 30 January 1932, TI, 2/II, p. 207.
21. Deuerlein, *Der Aufstieg der NSDAP*, p. 394.
22. *TBJG*, 29 June 1932, TI, 2/II, p. 311.
23. See the transcriptions of both speeches in Heiber, *Goebbels-Reden*, Band 1, pp. 43–50 and 51–5.
24. *TBJG*, 17 July 1932, TI, 2/II, p. 322.
25. Cited in Striefler, *Der Kampf um die Macht*, p. 370.
26. *TBJG*, 1 August 1932, TI, 2/II, p. 330.
27. *TBJG*, 7 August and 9 August 1932, TI, 2/II, pp. 334–5.
28. Kershaw, *Hitler 1889–1936*, p. 373.
29. *TBJG*, 14 August 1932, TI, 2/II, p. 340.
30. Maier-Hartmann, *Dokumente der Zeitgeschichte*, Band 1, p. 398.
31. 'Die Juden sind schuld!' *Der Angriff*, 24 August 1932, Joseph Goebbels, *Wetterleuchten: Zweiter Band 'Der Angriff'* (Munich: Franz Eher, 1939), pp. 323–5, p. 325.
32. Cited in Deuerlein, *Der Aufstieg der NSDAP*, p. 401.
33. See the entry for 13 August 1932 in Brügel and Frei, 'Berliner Tagebuch 1932–1934', p. 151.
34. *TBJG*, 1 September 1932, TI, 2/II, p. 354.
35. *TBJG*, 1 and 2 September 1932, TI, 2/II, pp. 354–5.
36. 'Dr. Goebbels in Wien! Oesterreich huldigt dem Gauführer Berlins. Eine gewaltige Anschluß-Kundgebung', *Der Angriff*, 19 September 1932.
37. *TBJG*, 19 September 1932, TI, 2/II, pp. 367–8.
38. Deuerlein, *Der Aufstieg der NSDAP*, pp. 402–3.
39. *TBJG*, 7 November 1932, TI, 2/III, p. 52.
40. *TBJG*, 9 December 1932, TI, 2/III, p. 78. See, for one account which blamed the divisions in the Nazi Party largely on Goebbels, 'Nazi Party Split', *The Times*, 12 December 1932, p. 11.
41. De la Forest-Divonne to Paul-Boncour, 27 September 1932, *Documents Diplomatiques Français 1932–1939, 1re Série (1932–1935)*, Tome I (19 Juillet–14 Novembre) (Paris: Imprimerie Nationale, 1964), pp. 393–4.
42. Brüning, *Memoiren 1918–1934*, p. 634.
43. *TBJG*, 10 December 1932, TI, 2/III, p. 79.
44. Evans, *The Coming of the Third Reich*, p. 303.
45. *TBJG*, 20 December 1932, TI, 2/III, p. 86. The book was later published as Joseph Goebbels, *Das erwachende Berlin* (Munich: Franz Eher, 1934).
46. *TBJG*, 19 September 1932, TI, 2/II, p. 366.
47. *TBJG*, 25 December 1932, TI, 2/III, p. 90.
48. *TBJG*, 2 January 1933, TI, 2/III, p. 96.
49. *TBJG*, 23 January 1933, TI, 2/III, p. 113.
50. *TBJG*, 30 January 1933, TI, 2/III, p. 119.
51. *TBJG*, 31 January 1933, TI, 2/III, p. 120.
52. Lippert, *Im Strom der Zeit*, pp. 191–4; also 'Reichskanzler Hitler!' *Der Angriff*, 30 January 1933.
53. Cited in Heiber, *Goebbels-Reden*, Band 1, pp. 62–3. It is striking how Goebbels, in this broadcast, highlighted the efforts of the Nazi Party in Berlin under his leadership, rather than its longer history in Munich.
54. *TBJG*, 6 February 1933, TI, 2/III, p. 125.

55. *TBJG*, 15 February 1933, TI, 2/III, p. 129.
56. See Hans Hinkel and Wulf Bley, *Kabinett Hitler!* (Berlin: Verlag Deutsche Kultur-Wacht, 1933).
57. *TBJG*, 21 February 1933, TI, 2/III, p. 133.
58. 'Der Reichstag brennt!' *Der Angriff*, 28 February 1928; *TBJG*, 28 February 1933, TI, 2/III, p. 137.
59. Kershaw, *Hitler 1889–1936*, p. 459.
60. Dahm *et al.*, *Die tödliche Utopie*, p. 305.
61. '130 Bolschewisten verhaftet', and '140 Kommunistenverhaftungen in Hannover', *Der Angriff*, 28 February 1928.
62. See Heinrich Böll, 'Was soll aus dem Jungen bloß werden?' in Marcel Reich-Ranicki (ed.), *Meine Schulzeit im Dritten Reich: Erinnerungen deutscher Schriftsteller* (Cologne: Kiepenheuer & Witsch, 1988), pp. 15–32, p. 22.
63. Sefton Delmer, *Trail Sinister: An Autobiography* (London: Secker and Warburg, 1961), Vol. 1, p. 183.
64. 'Der Tag der erwachenden Nation', *Der Angriff*, 25 February 1933.
65. Klemperer, *The Language of the Third Reich*, p. 54.
66. Klemperer, *The Language of the Third Reich*, pp. 52, and 39.
67. *TBJG*, 4 September 1933, TI, 2/III, p. 260.
68. 'Der Reichspräsident ernennt Dr. Goebbels zum Reichspropagandminister', *Der Angriff*, 13 March 1933.
69. 'Die zukünftige Arbeit und Gestaltung des deutschen Rundfunks', cited in Heiber, *Goebbels-Reden*, Band 1, pp. 82–107, p. 95.
70. See 'Die nationale Revolution', *Der Angriff*, 11 March 1933.
71. Cited in Noakes and Pridham, *Nazism 1919–1945*, Vol. 1, p. 14.
72. Josef Wulf (ed.), *Musik im Dritten Reich. Eine Dokumentation* (Gütersloh: Mohn Verlag, 1963), pp. 23–5. Wulf provides many other examples of Jewish musicians persecuted by the Nazis in 1933. See also Evans, *The Coming of the Third Reich*, pp. 392–5.
73. Jochen Klepper, *Unter dem Schatten Deiner Flügel: Aus den Tagebüchern der Jahre 1932–1942* (Stuttgart: Deutsche Verlags-Anstalt, 1956), entry for 8 March 1933, p. 41.
74. Klaus Meyer, interview with the author, 19 October 2001; see also Ernst Hermann Meyer, *Kontraste, Konflikte: Erinnerungen, Gespräche, Kommentare* (Berlin: Verlag Neue Musik, 1979), p. 110, and pp. 126–30.
75. *TBJG*, 25 March 1933, TI, 2/III, p. 154.
76. *TBJG*, 27 March 1933, TI, 2/III, p. 156.
77. See 'Aufruf an alle Parteiorganisationen der NSDAP', and 'Anordnung' in *Der Angriff*, 29 March 1933.
78. *TBJG*, 1 April and 2 April 1933, TI, 2/III, pp. 159–61.
79. 'Sturmzeichen!' *Der Angriff*, 1 April 1933; see also Rumbold to Simon, 1 April 1933, in *Documents on British Foreign Policy 1919–1939, Second Series*, Vol. V, 1933 (London: HMSO, 1956), p. 16.
80. Saul Friedländer, *Nazi Germany and the Jews: The Years of Persecution 1933–39* (London: Weidenfeld and Nicolson, 2003), pp. 20–4, and pp. 26ff.
81. Alfred Mierzejewski, *Hitler's Trains: The German National Railway and the Third Reich* (Stroud: Tempus, 2005), p. 21.
82. Klepper, *Unter dem Schatten Deiner Flügel*, 27 March 1933, and 5 April 1933, pp. 45 and 48.

83. François-Poncet to Paul-Boncour, 5 April 1933, *Documents Diplomatiques Français 1932–1939, 1re Série (1932–1935)*, Tome III (17 Mars–15 Juillet 1933) (Paris: Imprimerie Nationale, 1967), pp. 158–9.

84. See Christoph Schmidt, *Nationalsozialistische Kulturpolitik im Gau Westfalen-Nord: Regionale Strukturen und lokale Milieus (1933–1945)* (Paderborn: Schöningh, 2006), pp. 340–1.

85. 'Reichsminister Dr. Goebbels spricht auf dem Opernplatz', *Der Angriff*, 11 May 1933; the speech is transcribed in Heiber, *Goebbels-Reden*, Band I, pp. 108–12. There were similar book-burnings in other university towns across Germany. See Evans, *The Coming of the Third Reich*, pp. 427–31.

86. *TBJG*, 11 May 1933, TI, 2/III, p. 184.

87. *TBJG*, 2 April 1933, TI, 2/III, p. 161.

88. *TBJG*, 4 June 1933, TI, 2/III, pp. 194–200.

89. *TBJG*, 25 September and 27 September 1933, TI, 2/III, pp. 276–7.

90. 'Disarmament', *The Times*, 29 September 1933, p. 12.

91. *TBJG*, 15 May 1933, TI, 2/III, p. 186.

92. Fromm, *Blood and Banquets: A Berlin Social Diary*, 13 May 1933, p. 112.

93. *TBJG*, 2 October 1933, TI, 2/III, p. 282.

94. *TBJG*, 29 October 1933, TI, 2/III, p. 302.

95. 'Equality Demand: Dr. Goebbels on Jingoes', *The Times*, 23 October 1933, p. 14.

96. *TBJG*, 13 November 1933, TI, 2/III, p. 313.

97. André François-Poncet, *Souvenirs d'une Ambassade à Berlin* (Paris: Flammarion, 1946), p. 156.

98. Victor Klemperer, *I Shall Bear Witness: The Diaries of Victor Klemperer 1933–41* (London: BCA, 1998), entry for 14 November 1933, pp. 39–40.

99. *TBJG*, 18 November, and 19 November 1933, TI, 2/III, pp. 318, and 319.

100. See the invitations in BAK, N1118/148.

101. *TBJG*, 17 December 1933, TI, 2/III, p. 339.

102. *TBJG*, 20 December 1933, TI, 2/III, p. 341.

103. *TBJG*, 25 December 1933, TI, 2/III, p. 344.

Chapter 7

1. G. Ward Price, *I Know these Dictators* (London: Harrap, 1937), p. 139.

2. *TBJG*, 15 March 1933, TI, 2/III, p. 147.

3. 'Ein Interview mit Reichsminister Pg. Dr. Goebbels', *Der Angriff*, 1. Beilage, 15 March 1933.

4. *TBJG*, 6 February 1933, TI, 2/III, p. 125.

5. Speer, *Inside the Third Reich*, pp. 57–8.

6. *TBJG*, 2 December 1933, TI, 2/III, p. 328.

7. *TBJG*, 4 September 1933, TI, 2/III, p. 260.

8. Joseph Goebbels, *Rassenfrage und Weltpropaganda* (Langensalza: Beyer and Mann, 1934), p. 9, and p. 17.

9. William Dodd and Martha Dodd, *Ambassador Dodd's Diary, 1933–1938* (London: Victor Gollancz, 1941), p. 102.

10. See Furtwängler's letter, and Goebbels' response in Wulf, *Musik im Dritten Reich*, pp. 81–3.

11. Furtwängler has been represented as an astute opponent of the Nazis with a longer-term plan to combat the exclusion of Jews from German music. See Fred Prieberg, *Trial*

of Strength: Wilhelm Furtwängler in the Third Reich (Boston: Northeastern University Press, 1994).

12. See her memoir, *The Baton and the Jackboot: Recollections of Musical Life* (London: Hamilton, 1944); and Pamela Potter, 'The Nazi "Seizure" of the Berlin Philharmonic or the Decline of a Bourgeois Musical Institution', in Cuomo, *National Socialist Cultural Policy*, pp. 39–66.

13. *TBJG*, 16 November 1933, TI, 2/III, p. 316; 'Nazi Kultur', *The Times*, 16 November 1933, p. 13.

14. For a recent account of this 'messy nightmare' in the control of the theatre in Germany, see Gerwin Strobl, *The Swastika and the Stage: German Theatre and Society, 1933–1945* (New York: Cambridge University Press, 2007), pp. 153–73. Strobl stresses also the considerable authority of the *Gauleiter* in local cultural affairs.

15. See, for an excellent analysis, Volker Dahm, 'Anfänge und Ideologie der Reichskulturkammer: Die "Berufsgemeinschaft" als Instrument kulturpolitischer Steuerung und sozialer Reglementierung', *Vierteljahrshefte für Zeitgeschichte*, 34:1 (1986), pp. 53–84. Goebbels' speech, in which he listed all the key appointments in the individual chambers, is transcribed in Heiber, *Goebbels-Reden*, Band 1, pp. 131–41.

16. See, for a contemporary account, Robert Brady, *The Spirit and Structure of German Fascism* (London: Victor Gollancz, 1937), pp. 78–118; for a good recent overview, see Alan Steinweis, *Art, Ideology, & Economics in Nazi Germany: The Reich Chambers of Music, Theater, and the Visual Arts* (Chapel Hill and London: University of North Carolina Press, 1993); on the complexities and compromises involved in excluding Jews from one branch of the arts, see Strobl, *The Swastika and the Stage*, pp. 116–27.

17. 'Dr. Goebbels über die Gründe seiner Maßnahmen', *Der Angriff*, 10 October 1933.

18. Ernst Hanfstaengl, *Hitler: The Missing Years* (London: Eyre and Spottiswoode, 1957), p. 233.

19. *TBJG*, 7 October 1933, TI, 2/III, p. 286.

20. David Welch, *Propaganda and the German Cinema 1933–1945* (London and New York: Tauris, 2001), pp. 62–3.

21. *TBJG*, 9 October 1933, TI, 2/III, p. 287. Willi Fritsch was a leading actor in German silent films.

22. *TBJG*, 10 October 1933, TI, 2/III, p. 288.

23. 'Der Geburtstag des Nationalhelden Horst Wessel', *Der Angriff*, 10 October 1933; the speech is also transcribed in Heiber, *Goebbels-Reden*, Band 1, pp. 128–30.

24. Klemperer, *I Shall Bear Witness*, entry for 13 May 1934, p. 62.

25. *TBJG*, 13 May 1934, TI, 3/I, p. 48.

26. *TBJG*, 11 April 1933, TI, 2/III, p. 166.

27. Goebbels, *Vom Kaiserhof zur Reichskanzlei*; Joseph Goebbels, *My Part in Germany's Fight* (London: Paternoster, 1935).

28. BArch R 55/21250, 'Buchabrechnung für Herrn Reichsminister Dr. Goebbels', 12 January 1934. The book was published in German as Joseph Goebbels, *Revolution der Deutschen. 14 Jahre Nationalsozialismus* (Oldenburg: Stalling, 1933).

29. Schaumburg-Lippe, *Dr. G.*, pp. 166–7.

30. *TBJG*, 2 January 1934, TI, 2/III, p. 350.

31. *TBJG*, 14 April 1934, TI, 3/I, p. 33.

32. *TBJG*, 19 May 1934, TI, 3/I, p. 50.

33. On the evolution of the concentration camp system, see Wolfgang Sofsky, *The Order of Terror: The Concentration Camp* (Princeton: Princeton University Press, 1997), pp. 28–32.

34. *TBJG*, 15 May 1934, TI, 3/I, p. 49.

35. 'A Nazi Storm: Herr von Papen's Warnings', *The Times*, 19 June 1934, p. 14.
36. *TBJG*, 18 June 1934, TI, 3/I, p. 65.
37. *TBJG*, 22 June 1934, TI, 3/I, p. 67.
38. Werner von Blomberg was also Minister for the Army in Hitler's Cabinet. He cooperated enthusiastically with the Nazis between 1933 and 1938. Blomberg died in American captivity in 1946.
39. Kershaw, *Hitler 1889–1936*, p. 512.
40. *TBJG*, 29 June 1934, TI, 3/I, p. 71.
41. *TBJG*, 1 July 1934, TI, 3/I, p. 72. Edmund Heines was a notoriously brutal SA officer, who had previously served as a *Reichstag* deputy, and as Police President in Breslau; Manfred von Killinger was a long-standing Party member who went on to serve in Bucharest with responsibility for Jewish affairs from 1941 to 1944 before committing suicide when the Red Army arrived there. Herbert von Bose was Head of the Press Division in Papen's office; Erich Klausener was the leader of the 'Catholic Action' group, and an official in the Transport Ministry. Goebbels – as in this instance – frequently spelt proper nouns beginning with a 'K' with a more archaic 'C'.
42. *TBJG*, 4 July 1934, TI, 3/I, p. 73. Goebbels' account of proceedings on 30 June and on 1 July 1934 is substantially accurate; the conspiracy between Schleicher, François-Poncet, and Strasser was imagined. Karl Ernst was an early Party member who had made his way up the ranks of the SA partly through a homosexual relationship with Röhm; he had been a *Reichstag* deputy since 1932. Georg von Detten was head of the Political Office of the SA. Otto Dietrich, who reported on the executions, was in 1934 the Vice President of the *Reich* Press Chamber, although Goebbels had a low opinion of him. Dietrich wrote two books about his time in the Nazi movement, including the incredibly bland *12 Jahre mit Hitler* (Munich: Isar Verlag, 1955), which was published posthumously in 1952. See pp. 41–2 for his account of what he called the 'Röhm revolt'.
43. See 'Drunter und drüber im "Neuen Deutschland"', an undated newssheet in the Bundesarchiv Koblenz, ZSg 2/226(2).
44. 'Medieval Methods', *The Times*, 3 July 1934, p. 15.
45. Max Domarus, *Hitler: Speeches and Proclamations 1932–1945* (London: Tauris, 1992), Vol. 1, p. 480.
46. *TBJG*, 4 July 1934, TI, 3/I, pp. 73–4.
47. *TBJG*, 7 July 1934, TI, 3/I, p. 76.
48. The speech, which lasted nearly 30 minutes, was broadcast three times in quick succession on all German stations, and on 12 July in English, French, Spanish, and Portuguese over most of the world on shortwave. See Heiber, *Goebbels-Reden*, Band 1, pp. 156–65. Sweden and Denmark refused to relay the speech. See 'Dr. Goebbels's Broadcast', *The Times*, 12 July 1934, p. 13.
49. *TBJG*, 11 July 1934, TI, 3/I, p. 78.
50. Domarus, *Hitler: Speeches and Proclamations*, Vol. 1, p. 498.
51. See Hannsjoachim Koch, *In the Name of the Volk: Political Justice in Hitler's Germany* (London: I. B. Tauris, 1989), p. 40.
52. See Dahm *et al.*, *Die tödliche Utopie*, pp. 324–5; and Kershaw, *Hitler 1889–1936*, p. 517. For an excellent recent summary of the 'Night of the Long Knives', see Richard J. Evans, *The Third Reich in Power, 1933–1939* (London: Penguin, 2006), pp. 27–41.
53. Schaumburg-Lippe, *Dr. G*, p. 92.
54. *TBJG*, 10 September 1934, TI, 3/I, p. 104. See Evans, *The Third Reich in Power*, p. 40 for details of SA misconduct at the rally.
55. See Speer, *Inside the Third Reich*, pp. 90–1.

56. *TBJG*, 2 January 1935, TI, 3/I, p. 162.
57. *TBJG*, 26 February 1935, TI, 3/I, p. 190. Schweitzer's brutal artistic style was better suited to the 'time of struggle' than to express the triumphalism of the Nazis in power. Although he held a succession of posts within the Propaganda Ministry, and was in 1937 appointed a '*Reich* Cultural Senator', he never recovered the influence he had before 1933. Schweitzer continued to work as an illustrator after 1945, using the name 'Herbert Sickinger'. See Jonathan Petropoulos, *The Faustian Bargain: The Art World in Nazi Germany* (London: Allen Lane, 2000), pp. 159–63.
58. *TBJG*, 3 April 1935, TI, 3/I, p. 211.
59. *TBJG*, 10 March 1935, TI, 3/I, p. 197.
60. *TBJG*, 5 April 1935, TI, 3/I, p. 212.
61. See the entries for 13 July and 2 August 1934 in Hans-Günther Seraphim (ed.), *Das politische Tagebuch Alfred Rosenbergs 1934/35 und 1939/40* (Munich: Deutscher Taschenbuch Verlag, 1964), pp. 51–3. Characteristically, Rosenberg appears not to have realized that it was the actual killings which concerned international observers most, and not the way Goebbels presented them to the outside world.
62. Evans, *The Third Reich in Power*, p. 139.
63. See Max Weinreich, *Hitler's Professors: The Part Played by Scholarship in Germany's Crimes against the Jewish People* (New Haven and London: Yale University Press, 1999), pp. 22–7.
64. Petropoulos, *The Faustian Bargain*, p. 118.
65. See Strobl, *The Swastika and the Stage*, pp. 134–5.
66. See the sketch by Reinhard Bollmus, 'Alfred Rosenberg: National Socialism's "Chief Ideologue"?' in Smelser and Zitelmann, *The Nazi Elite*, pp. 183–93.
67. *TBJG*, 11 December 1934 and 26 November 1934, TI, 3/I, p. 152, and p. 144.
68. See Henning Eichberg, 'The Nazi *Thingspiel*'.
69. James Bjork and Robert Gerwarth, 'The Annaberg as a German-Polish *Lieu de Mémoire*', *German History*, 25:3 (2007), pp. 372–400.
70. See the discussion in Strobl, *The Swastika and the Stage*, pp. 51–88. The quotations above are from p. 61, and p. 64.
71. *TBJG*, 24 June 1935, TI, 3/I, p. 252.
72. Heiber, *Goebbels-Reden*, Band 1, p. 242.
73. Raul Hilberg, *The Destruction of the European Jews* (New York: Holmes and Meier, 1985), Vol. I, p. 70.
74. See Friedländer, *Nazi Germany and the Jews: The Years of Persecution*, pp. 137–44.
75. *TBJG*, 13 September, 15 September, and 17 September 1935, TI, 3/I, pp. 292–4.
76. Cited in Heiber, *Goebbels-Reden*, Band 1, p. 230.
77. See the first-hand account of one of these officials in Walter Strauss, 'Das Reichsministerium des Innern und die Judengesetzgebung: Aufzeichnungen von Dr. Bernhard Lösener', *Vierteljahrshefte für Zeitgeschichte*, 9:3 (1961), pp. 262–313.
78. Goebbels, *Das kleine abc des Nationalsozialisten*, p. 3.
79. *TBJG*, 28 March 1935, TI, 3/I, p. 207.
80. *TBJG*, 23 May 1935, TI, 3/I, p. 236.
81. *TBJG*, 15 July 1935, TI, 3/I, p. 262.
82. *TBJG*, 19 July 1935, TI, 3/I, p. 263.
83. Entry for 21 July 1935, Klemperer, *I Shall Bear Witness*, p. 122.
84. *TBJG*, 2 March 1935, TI, 3/I, pp. 192–3.
85. Domarus, *Hitler: Speeches and Proclamations*, Vol. II, p. 656.
86. *TBJG*, 19 June 1935, TI, 3/I, p. 249.
87. *TBJG*, 17 April 1935, TI, 3/I, p. 219.

88. *TBJG*, 9 December 1935, TI, 3/I, p. 343.
89. *TBJG*, 21 February 1936, TI, 3/I, p. 383.
90. *TBJG*, 4 March 1936, TI, 3/II, pp. 31–2.
91. *TBJG*, 8 March 1936, TI, 3/II, p. 35.
92. William Shirer, *Berlin Diary 1934–1941* (London: Sphere, 1970), pp. 49–50.
93. *TBJG*, 8 March 1936, TI, 3/II, p. 36.
94. *TBJG*, 15 March 1936, TI, 3/II, p. 41.
95. *TBJG*, 29 March 1936, TI, 3/II, p. 51.

Chapter 8

1. Cited in Domarus, *Hitler: Speeches and Proclamations*, Vol. II, p. 979. The *Ordensburgen* were training academies for young Nazi Party members, intended to groom a new elite.
2. BArch R 55/21250, Daimler-Benz Aktiengesellschaft an Herrn Ministerialrat Hanke, 4 July 1935.
3. BAK N1118/148, Magda Goebbels to Graf, DAF, 29 April 1937.
4. See *TBJG*, 3 October 1935, TI, 3/I, p. 304.
5. Klabunde, *Magda Goebbels*, p. 236.
6. Alexandra Richie, *Faust's Metropolis: A History of Berlin* (New York: Carroll and Graf, 1998), p. 444.
7. Riefenstahl, *The Sieve of Time*, pp. 132–3.
8. Riefenstahl, *The Sieve of Time*, pp. 138–40.
9. Riefenstahl, *The Sieve of Time*, pp. 141–7.
10. Audrey Salkeld, *A Portrait of Leni Riefenstahl* (London: Pimlico, 1997), p. 105, and pp. 116–20.
11. See *TBJG*, 14 October 1933, TI, 2/III, p. 291.
12. Riefenstahl, *The Sieve of Time*, pp. 134–5.
13. *TBJG*, 17 May 1933, TI, 2/III, p. 188.
14. *TBJG*, 1 August 1936, TI, 3/II, p. 145.
15. *TBJG*, 2 August 1936, TI, 3/II, pp. 146–7.
16. *TBJG*, 5 August 1936, TI, 3/II, p. 149.
17. Oven, *Finale Furioso*, p. 47.
18. Goebbels' diary first mentions Baarova on 3 June 1936, not on 10 June as Reuth asserts. See *TBJG*, 3 June 1936, TI, 3/II, p. 97; and Reuth, *Goebbels*, p. 216, and n.151, p. 405.
19. See Reimann, *The Man who Created Hitler*, p. 229.
20. *TBJG*, 11 September 1936, TI, 3/II, p. 180. This and other comments suggest that Goebbels was prepared to confide *something* about extra-marital affairs to his diary.
21. Schaumburg-Lippe, *Dr. G.*, p. 148.
22. *TBJG*, 3 February 1937, TI, 3/II, p. 357.
23. Klepper, *Unter dem Schatten Deiner Flügel*, 22 February 1937 and 27 March 1937, p. 426, and p. 434.
24. *TBJG*, 29 July 1937, TI, 4, p. 238.
25. Richard Plant, *The Pink Triangle: The Nazi War against Homosexuals* (Edinburgh: Mainstream, 1987), p. 212. The amended text of Paragraph 175 is reproduced here in translation on p. 206.
26. *TBJG*, 27 July 1937, TI, 4, p. 235.

27. Prior to this control of Germany's political police forces had been divided between Prussia (controlled by Göring), and all other *Länder* (controlled by Himmler). See Dahm *et al.*, *Die tödliche Utopie*, pp. 329–34; also *TBJG*, 19 June 1936, TI, 3/II, p. 110.
28. *TBJG*, 4 July 1936, TI, 3/II, p. 123.
29. Michael Burleigh and Wolfgang Wipperman, *The Racial State: Germany 1933–1945* (Cambridge: Cambridge University Press, 1991), p. 173.
30. *TBJG*, 22 February 1937, TI, 3/II, p. 387.
31. For an introduction to the complex relationship between the Nazis and the Christian Churches see Michael Burleigh, *The Third Reich: A New History* (London: Macmillan, 2000), pp. 252–66, and pp. 717–28.
32. *TBJG*, 29 May 1936, TI, 3/II, p. 93.
33. *TBJG*, 4 July 1936, TI, 3/II, p. 123.
34. *TBJG*, 1 November 1935, TI, 3/I, p. 320.
35. The encyclical is reproduced in *The Persecution of the Catholic Church in the Third Reich: Facts and Documents* (London: Burns Oates and Washbourne, 1942), Appendix II, pp. 523–37. The quotations here are from pp. 523, 525, and 530.
36. *TBJG*, 21 March 1937, TI, 4, p. 62. Reinhard Heydrich was a former naval officer who had been appointed by Himmler in 1932 to head the security service of the SS (the SD). By 1936 he was also head of the secret state police (the *Gestapo*), and of the criminal police (the *Kripo*). Heydrich was one of few fellow Nazis Goebbels genuinely respected. Zarah Leander, ironically, went on to star in one of the most popular wartime German films, *Die Große Liebe* (1942).
37. *TBJG*, 30 April 1937, TI, 4, p. 117.
38. *TBJG*, 12 May 1937, TI, 4, p. 135.
39. *TBJG*, 26 May 1937, TI, 4, p. 151.
40. Goebbels speaking on 28 May 1937, cited in *The Persecution of the Catholic Church*, p. 305, and p. 314.
41. *TBJG*, 29 May 1937, TI, 4, p. 157.
42. Goebbels speaking on 6 June 1937, cited in Heiber, *Goebbels-Reden*, Band 1, pp. 281–6; see also Wulf, *Musik im Dritten Reich*, pp. 145–6, and the photograph facing p. 224. At a huge rally shortly after this ceremony, Hitler first used the term '*Gottgläubigkeit*' (corresponding closely to the Pope's idea of a 'national God') to describe his own religious faith. See Domarus, *Hitler: Speeches and Proclamations*, Vol. II, p. 903.
43. *TBJG*, 7 June 1937, TI, 4, p. 172.
44. See *The Persecution of the Catholic Church*, p. 305.
45. 'Special Courts', in which an accelerated legal process was used to deal with political offences, without recourse to appeal, had been established by the Nazis in March 1933. In 1938 their remit was extended, and they were enabled to pass death sentences. See Dahm *et al.*, *Die tödliche Utopie*, p. 360.
46. *TBJG*, 15 January 1938, TI, 5, p. 98.
47. *TBJG*, 22 December 1937, TI, 5, p. 65.
48. *TBJG*, 5 February 1938, TI, 5, pp. 136–7.
49. Hans Buchheim, 'Ein NS-Funktionär zum Niemöller-Prozess', *Vierteljahrshefte für Zeitgeschichte*, 4:3 (1956), pp. 307–15, pp. 312–13.
50. See 'Dr. Niemöller on Trial', *The Times*, 8 February 1938, p. 14.
51. *TBJG*, 23 February 1938, TI, 5, p. 172.
52. *TBJG*, 3 March 1938, TI, 5, p. 185.
53. *TBJG*, 4 March 1938, TI, 5, p. 187.
54. 'The Detention of Dr. Niemöller', *The Times*, 10 March 1938, p. 14.

55. Martin Niemöller, *Vom U-Boot zur Kanzel* (Berlin: Martin Warner, 1934). Intriguingly, this is one of the central autobiographies used by Theweleit in his analysis of the 'Fascist male'. See Theweleit, *Male Fantasies I*, pp. 5–8, and p. 22.
56. Martin Niemöller, ... *daß wir an Ihm bleiben! Sechzehn Dahlemer Predigten* (Berlin: Martin Warner, 1935), p. 17.
57. Martin Niemöller and Otto Dibelius, *Wir rufen Deutschland zu Gott* (Berlin: Martin Warner, 1937), pp. 110–11.
58. *TBJG*, 30 October 1937, TI, 4, p. 383.
59. *TBJG*, 29 October 1937, TI, 4, p. 382.
60. Schaumburg-Lippe, *Dr. G.*, p. 125.
61. *TBJG*, 3 August 1937, TI, 4, p. 247.
62. See Domarus, *Hitler: Speeches and Proclamations*, Vol. II, pp. 959–72.
63. *TBJG*, 29 December 1936, TI, 3/II, p. 307.
64. *TBJG*, 26 January 1937, TI, 3/II, p. 344.
65. *TBJG*, 7 December 1937, TI, 5, p. 38.
66. *TBJG*, 15 December 1937, TI, 5, p. 54.
67. *TBJG*, 26 January 1938, TI, 5, p. 115.
68. *TBJG*, 27 January 1938, TI, 5, pp. 117–18.
69. *TBJG*, 28 January 1938, TI, 5, p. 119.
70. After the *Anschluss* with Austria, Seyss-Inquart went on to serve briefly as an SS police officer in Cracow before being appointed *Reich* Commissar for occupied Holland in May 1940. He was sentenced to death by the International Military Tribunal at Nuremberg in 1946 and executed.
71. Domarus, *Hitler: Speeches and Proclamations*, Vol. II, pp. 1052–3.
72. *TBJG*, 13 March 1938, TI, 5, pp. 205–6. Hitler's proclamation is cited in Domarus, *Hitler: Speeches and Proclamations*, Vol. II, pp. 1046–9.
73. *TBJG*, 20 March 1938, TI, 5, p. 221.
74. *TBJG*, 16 March 1938, TI, 5, p. 211.
75. Heinz Boberach (ed.), *Meldungen aus dem Reich. Die geheimen Lageberichte des Sicherheitsdienstes der SS 1938–1945* (Herrsching: Manfred Pawlak, 1984), Band 2, p. 21.
76. Cited in Domarus, *Hitler: Speeches and Proclamations*, Vol. II, p. 1059.
77. *TBJG*, 17 March 1938, TI, 5, p. 213.
78. *TBJG*, 9 April 1938, TI, 5, p. 251.
79. *TBJG*, 10 April and 11 April 1938, TI, 5, pp. 252–7; see also Klemperer, *I Shall Bear Witness*, p. 243.
80. *TBJG*, 20 March 1938, TI, 5, p. 222.
81. *TBJG*, 25 May 1938, TI, 5, p. 317.
82. *TBJG*, 30 May and 31 May 1938, TI, 5, p. 325, and p. 326.
83. *TBJG*, 2 June 1938, TI, 5, p. 329.
84. *TBJG*, 11 June 1938, TI, 5, p. 340.
85. *TBJG*, 19 June 1938, TI, 5, p. 351.
86. See the entry for 28 June 1938 in Fromm, *Blood and Banquets*, p. 274.
87. *TBJG*, 22 June 1938, TI, 5, p. 355.
88. *TBJG*, 2 July 1938, TI, 5, p. 366.
89. *TBJG*, 29 May 1938, TI, 5, p. 323.
90. Parts of the speech were printed in *Amtliche Mitteilungen der Reichsmusikkammer*, 1 June 1938. See the facsimile of the front page of this edition in Albrecht Dümling and Peter Girth (eds), *Entartete Musik. Zur Düsseldorfer Ausstellung von 1938. Eine kommentierte Rekonstruktion* (Düsseldorf: no publisher given, 1988), p. 123. See also Wulf, *Musik im Dritten Reich*, pp. 414–23.

91. *TBJG*, 25 July 1938, TI, 5, p. 393.
92. Entry for 20 March 1938, Klemperer, *I Shall Bear Witness*, p. 241.
93. *TBJG*, 16 August 1938, TI, 6, pp. 44–5.
94. Henderson to Halifax, 17 August 1938, *Documents on British Foreign Policy 1919–1939, Third Series*, Vol. II, 1938 (London: HMSO, 1949), p. 103.
95. *TBJG*, 1 August 1938, TI, 6, p. 29.
96. *TBJG*, 17 September 1938, TI, 6, p. 95.
97. *TBJG*, 2 September 1938, TI, 6, p. 68.
98. *TBJG*, 2 October 1938, TI, 6, pp. 122–4.
99. Karl Hanke had been appointed as one of Goebbels' personal assistants in the Propaganda Ministry in 1933, and had risen since then to the rank of State Secretary.
100. *TBJG*, 22 October and 24 October 1938, TI, 6, pp. 156–7.
101. *TBJG*, 30 October 1938, TI, 6, pp. 165–6.

Chapter 9

1. Sybil Bannister, *I lived under Hitler: An Englishwoman's Story* (London: Rockliff, 1957), p. 79.
2. *TBJG*, 23 January 1939, TI, 6, p. 236.
3. Seraphim, *Das politische Tagebuch Alfred Rosenbergs*, pp. 80–1.
4. BArch (ehem. BDC), Parteikorrespondenz, D83, Goebbels, Joseph, 29 October 1897, 'Persönlich, an den Stellvertreter des Führers', 9 December 1938.
5. Domarus, *Hitler: Speeches and Proclamations*, Vol. 3, p. 1449.
6. *TBJG*, 31 January 1939, TI, 6, p. 245.
7. *TBJG*, 27 July 1939, TI, 7, p. 51.
8. *TBJG*, 9 November 1938, TI, 6, p. 178.
9. *TBJG*, 10 November 1938, TI, 6, p. 180.
10. *TBJG*, 12 November 1938, TI, 6, p. 183.
11. For a balanced account of the November pogrom see Lucy Dawidowicz, *The War against the Jews 1933–1945* (London: Penguin, 1990), pp. 135ff.
12. Ogilvie-Forbes to Halifax, 16 November 1938, *Documents on British Foreign Policy 1919–1939, Third Series*, Vol. III, 1938–39 (London: HMSO, 1950), p. 277.
13. See Friedländer, *Nazi Germany and the Jews: The Years of Persecution*, pp. 280–8.
14. Ogilvie-Forbes to Halifax, 13 November 1938, *Documents on British Foreign Policy 1919–1939, Third Series*, Vol. III, pp. 270–1.
15. See Klemperer, *I Shall Bear Witness*, pp. 259–73; and Klepper, *Unter dem Schatten Deiner Flügel*, pp. 676ff.
16. It is not accurate to call this 'the Goebbels pogrom', as do Hilberg and Dawidowicz. The pogrom undoubtedly had, and needed, Hitler's sanction. I would argue also that there was less dissent over the pogrom between Goebbels and other senior Nazis like Göring, Funk, and Himmler than Hilberg portrays in his account. See Hilberg, *The Destruction of the European Jews*, Vol. 1, pp. 39–43; and note Goebbels' comment on the important meeting on 12 November that 'I am working splendidly together with Göring.' *TBJG*, 13 November 1938, TI, 6, p. 185.
17. Friedländer, *Nazi Germany and the Jews: The Years of Persecution*, p. 287.
18. See 'German Jews Rounded Up', *The Times*, 12 November 1938, p. 12.
19. Cited in Klepper, *Unter dem Schatten Deiner Flügel*, 14 November 1938, pp. 677–8; see also 'More Arrests', *The Times*, 14 November 1938, p. 12.
20. *TBJG*, 11 November 1938, TI, 6, p. 182.

21. *TBJG*, 8 July 1938, TI, 5, p. 372. See also p. 369.
22. Goebbels, speaking in Reichenberg, 19 November 1938, cited in Heiber, *Goebbels-Reden*, Band 1, p. 328.
23. See, for a representative example, Richard Breitman, *Himmler and the Final Solution: The Architect of Genocide* (London: Pimlico, 2004), p. 52.
24. *TBJG*, 11 March 1939, TI, 6, pp. 279–80.
25. *TBJG*, 16 March 1938, TI, 6, p. 288.
26. *TBJG*, 20 March 1939, TI, 6, p. 293.
27. *TBJG*, 28 March 1939, TI, 6, p. 302.
28. *TBJG*, 19 March 1939, TI, 6, p. 291; 'Die Moral der Reichen', in Goebbels, *Die Zeit ohne Beispiel*, pp. 84–9, p. 89. Goebbels, like most contemporary Germans, referred typically to 'Britain' and 'the British' as 'England' and 'the English'.
29. *TBJG*, 4 April 1939, TI, 6, p. 309. Chamberlain's speech in Birmingham, and his Statement to the House of Commons are reprinted in *Documents Concerning German-Polish Relations and the Outbreak of Hostilities between Great Britain and Germany on September 3, 1939* (London: HMSO, 1939), pp. 5–10, and p. 36.
30. *TBJG*, 3 April 1939, TI, 6, p. 308.
31. *TBJG*, 8 April 1939, TI, 6, p. 311.
32. *TBJG*, 10 April 1939, TI, 6, p. 313.
33. See Herbert Levine, *Hitler's Free City: A History of the Nazi Party in Danzig, 1925–39* (Chicago and London: University of Chicago Press, 1973).
34. Shepherd to Halifax, 19 June 1939, *Documents on British Foreign Policy 1919–1939, Third Series*, Vol. VI, 1939 (London: HMSO, 1953), p. 108.
35. *TBJG*, 18 June 1939, TI, 6, p. 383; 'Danzig vor der Entscheidung', Goebbels, *Die Zeit ohne Beispiel*, pp. 177–80, 177, and 179.
36. Statement by the Prime Minister in the House of Commons, 10 July 1939, *Documents Concerning German-Polish Relations*, pp. 74–6, p. 76; *TBJG*, TI, 7, 12 July 1939, p. 40.
37. *TBJG*, 24 August 1939, TI, 7, p. 75.
38. *TBJG*, 26 August 1939, TI, 7, p. 78.
39. Phipps to Halifax, 24 August 1939, *Documents on British Foreign Policy 1919–1939, Third Series*, Vol. VII, 1939 (London: HMSO, 1954), p. 203.
40. Cited in James Owen and Guy Walters (eds), *Voices of War: The Second World War Told by Those Who Fought It* (London: Penguin, 2005), p. 1. Here I differ in emphasis with Adam Tooze, who argues that Hitler 'knew that an attack on Poland would most likely provoke a declaration of war by Britain and France'. See Tooze, *The Wages of Destruction*, p. 321.
41. *TBJG*, 1 September 1939, TI, 7, p. 87.
42. Domarus, *Hitler: Speeches and Proclamations 1932–1945*, Vol. 3, p. 1754.
43. See Janina Grabowska-Chałka, *Stutthof Guide: Historical Information* (Gdańsk: Stutthof Museum, 2004), p. 17.
44. *TBJG*, 4 September 1939, TI, 7, pp. 91–2. The idea that Goebbels, after hearing of the British declaration, was 'downcast and pensive, looking literally like the proverbial drenched poodle', derives from the account by Paul Schmidt, a Foreign Office interpreter, but the reliability of this account has been challenged. See Reuth, *Goebbels*, p. 256; and Ian Kershaw, *Hitler 1936–1945: Nemesis* (London: Allen Lane, 2000), p. 223, and n. 305 on p. 906.
45. See Richard Bessel, *Nazism and War* (London: Phoenix, 2005), p. 1.
46. *TBJG*, 2 September 1939, TI, 7, p. 88.

47. A more or less complete stenographic record of the 'ministerial conferences' from October 1939 until May 1941, and increasingly sparse groups of conference records up to April 1943 have been preserved, and are in BArch, R 55/20001. Excerpts have been published in Willi Boelcke (ed.), *Wollt Ihr den totalen Krieg? Die geheimen Goebbels-Konferenzen 1939–43* (Herrsching: Manfred Pawlak, 1989).

48. The *Athenia* was sunk by a German U-boat on 3 September 1939, with the loss of 98 passengers and 19 crew members. The sinking was given great publicity in the English-speaking world, but Goebbels claimed that Churchill had engineered the sinking to provoke outrage in neutral countries.

49. *TBJG*, 9 September 1939, TI, 7, p. 98.

50. Domarus, *Hitler: Speeches and Proclamations*, Vol. 3, p. 1794.

51. Klemperer, *I Shall Bear Witness*, entry for 10 September 1939, p. 298.

52. *TBJG*, 18 September 1939, TI, 7, p. 110.

53. See 'Bericht zur innenpolitischen Lage (Nr. 6)', 20 October 1939, Boberach, *Meldungen aus dem Reich*, Band 2, p. 374.

54. *TBJG*, 3 January 1940, TI, 7, p. 255.

55. Nevile Henderson, *Failure of a Mission: Berlin 1937–1939* (London: Hodder and Stoughton, 1940), p. 288.

56. 'Bericht zur innenpolitischen Lage (Nr. 2)', 11 October 1939, Boberach, *Meldungen aus dem Reich*, Band 2, p. 339.

57. *TBJG*, 11 October 1939, TI, 7, p. 148.

58. *TBJG*, 13 October 1939, TI, 7, p. 151.

59. *TBJG*, 16 January 1940, TI, 7, p. 273.

60. *TBJG*, 30 September 1939, TI, 7, p. 130.

61. *TBJG*, 7 October 1939, TI, 7, p. 141.

62. *TBJG*, 5 October 1939, TI, 7, p. 138.

63. See Friedländer, *Nazi Germany and the Jews: The Years of Extermination*, p. 21.

64. *TBJG*, 17 October 1939, TI, 7, p. 157.

65. *TBJG*, 29 October 1939, TI, 7, p. 173.

66. *TBJG*, 2 November 1939, TI, 7, pp. 177–8.

67. *TBJG*, 25 October 1939. According to a recent study, most 'prominent Poles' had fled from Posen; 25 of those remaining were arrested as hostages. Across Poland SS units had instructions to arrest, and if necessary to murder members of the intelligentsia. See Alexander Rossino, *Hitler Strikes Poland: Blitzkrieg, Ideology, and Atrocity* (Lawrence: University Press of Kansas, 2003), pp. 15–16, and 132.

68. *TBJG*, 17 November 1939, TI, 7, p. 199.

69. *TBJG*, 18 November 1939, TI, 7, p. 200.

70. *TBJG*, 20 January 1940, TI, 7, p. 278.

71. Cited in Heiber, *Goebbels-Reden*, Band 2, pp. 7–14.

72. *TBJG*, 24 February 1940, TI, 7, p. 322.

73. BArch R 55/20001a, '11h – Konferenz vom 18. Dezember 1939'; Shirer, *Berlin Diary*, pp. 204–5.

74. *TBJG*, 20 March 1940, TI, 7, p. 358.

75. See Martin Gilbert, *Finest Hour: Winston S. Churchill 1939–1941* (London: BCA, 1983), p. 192.

76. *TBJG*, 24 March 1940, TI, 7, p. 364.

77. *TBJG*, 1 June 1940, TI, 8, p. 148.

78. 'Meldungen aus dem Reich (Nr. 91)', 27 May 1940, in Boberach, *Meldungen aus dem Reich*, pp. 1179–80.

79. *Das Reich. Register zur Mikrofilm-Ausgabe* (Bonn: Gesellschaft für die Fotographische Reproduktion der Presse, no date given [1971]), Vol. 1, preface; *TBJG*, 2 June 1940, TI, 8, p. 150.
80. *TBJG*, 23 June 1940, TI, 8, p. 189.
81. *TBJG*, 25 June 1940, TI, 8, p. 193.
82. Schaumburg-Lippe, *Dr. G.*, p. 237.
83. *TBJG*, 7 July 1940, TI, 8, p. 210.
84. *TBJG*, 10 July 1940, TI, 8, p. 215.
85. *TBJG*, 12 July 1940, TI, 8, p. 218.
86. Cited in Domarus, *Hitler: Speeches and Proclamations*, Vol. 3, p. 2062.
87. *TBJG*, 20 June 1940, TI, 8, p. 230.
88. See John Colville, *The Fringes of Power: 10 Downing Street Diaries 1939–1955* (New York and London: Norton, 1985), p. 200. Churchill gives more detail of his reaction to Hitler's speech in his *The Second World War* (London: Cassell, 1949), Vol. II, *Their Finest Hour*, pp. 229–30.
89. *TBJG*, 21 July 1940, TI, 8, p. 230.
90. *TBJG*, 1 April 1940, TI, 8, p. 29.
91. BArch R 55/20001d, '½11h – Konferenz vom 23. August 1940'.
92. *TBJG*, 24 September 1940, TI, 8, p. 342.
93. *TBJG*, 18 November 1940, TI, 8, p. 425.
94. *TBJG*, 20 November 1940, TI, 8, p. 428.
95. *TBJG*, 15 October 1940, TI, 8, p. 378; see also 'Meldungen aus dem Reich (Nr. 133)', 17 October 1940, Boberach, *Meldungen aus dem Reich*, Band 5, p. 1677, which reported that few 'people's comrades' now believed that the war would be ended soon.
96. See Denis Richards and Hilary Saunders, *Royal Air Force 1939–1945* (London: HMSO, 1974), Vol. 1, pp. 230–2.
97. *TBJG*, 26 August 1940, TI, 8, p. 291.
98. *TBJG*, 4 October 1940, TI, 8, p. 360.
99. *TBJG*, 22 December 1940, TI, 9, p. 63.
100. Entry for 18 September 1940, Shirer, *Berlin Diary*, p. 397.
101. See *TBJG*, 1 October 1940, TI, 8, pp. 354–5.
102. See *TBJG*, 17 October 1940, TI, 8, p. 381.
103. BArch R 55/23474, 'Aufträge zur künstlerischen Ausstattung des Hauses Hermann Göring Str. 20 und des Ministeriums, 4. Mai 1940'. Fritz Klimsch had earlier provided sculptures for the 1936 Olympiad; Arthur Kampf held a leading position at the Berlin Academy of the Arts; Arno Breker was by 1940 Hitler's favourite sculptor, and provided monumental statues for many state buildings. See Petropoulos, *The Faustian Bargain*, for further details on these artists.
104. See Weinreich, *Hitler's Professors*, pp. 95–106.
105. See Willem de Vries, *Sonderstab Musik: Music Confiscations by the Einsatzstab Reichsleiter Rosenberg under the Nazi Occupation of Western Europe* (Amsterdam: Amsterdam University Press, 1996), pp. 23–5.
106. *TBJG*, 1 May 1940, TI, 8, p. 87.
107. *TBJG*, 31 January 1941, TI, 9, p. 119. Philipp Bouhler was one of the earliest members of the Nazi Party; he was given responsibility for carrying through the 'euthanasia' programme in September 1939. Bouhler committed suicide after being captured by the Americans in 1945.
108. Ulrich von Hassell, *Vom andern Deutschland. Aus den nachgelassenen Tagebüchern 1938–1944 von Ulrich von Hassell* (Vienna: Humboldt, 1948), 23 November 1940, and 19 January 1941, p. 140, and p. 145.

109. Klepper, *Unter dem Schatten Deiner Flügel*, 2 May 1940, and 30 August 1940, p. 876, and p. 917.
110. BArch R 55/20001g, '11h – Konferenz vom 29. April 1941'.
111. *TBJG*, 14 February 1941, TI, 9, p. 142.
112. See Michael Burleigh, *Death and Deliverance: 'Euthanasia' in Germany 1900–1945* (Cambridge: Cambridge University Press, 1994), pp. 209–19.
113. *TBJG*, 8 March 1941, TI, 9, p. 176. On *Jud Süß* and *Ich klage an*, see also Erwin Leiser, *'Deutschland erwache!' Propaganda im Film des Dritten Reiches* (Hamburg: Rowohlt, 1978), pp. 130–46.
114. 'Meldungen aus dem Reich (Nr. 145)', 28 November 1940; and 'Meldungen aus dem Reich (Nr. 155)', 20 January 1941, Boberach, *Meldungen aus dem Reich*, Band 6, p. 1812, and pp. 1917–19.
115. BArch R 55/20001d, '¾11h – Konferenz vom 12. September 1940'.
116. Klemperer, *I Shall Bear Witness*, 10 December 1940, p. 348.
117. BArch R 55/20001d, '¾11h – Konferenz vom 6. September 1940'. Hans Hinkel had worked before 1933 as a journalist for the *Völkischer Beobachter*, and since 1936 as the 'business manager' of the *Reich* Chamber of Culture. Hinkel was interrogated by the Americans and the Poles after being captured in 1945; he died in 1960.
118. BArch R 55/20001d, '11h – Konferenz vom 17. September 1940'. On the 'Madagascar plan', see Christopher Browning, *The Origins of the Final Solution: The Evolution of Nazi Jewish Policy, September 1939 – March 1942* (London: Heinemann, 2004).
119. *TBJG*, 18 March 1941, TI, 9, p. 193.
120. *TBJG*, 19 March 1941, TI, 9, p. 195.
121. *TBJG*, 21 March 1941, TI, 9, p. 197.
122. *TBJG*, 29 March 1941, TI, 9, p. 211.

Chapter 10

1. Friedrich Reck-Malleczewen, *Diary of a Man in Despair* (London: Duckworth, 2001), p. 139. Krupp and Röchling were prominent German industrialists.
2. See *TBJG*, 13 May and 23 May 1941, TI, 9, p. 308, and p. 330.
3. See Seraphim, *Das politische Tagebuch Alfred Rosenbergs*, 5 October 1939, p. 100; and *TBJG*, 5 October 1939, TI, 7, pp. 137–8.
4. *TBJG*, 29 June 1940, TI, 8, p. 197.
5. Goebbels, *Lenin oder Hitler?* p. 15, and p. 31.
6. *TBJG*, 14 November 1940, TI, 8, pp. 417–18.
7. See Kershaw, *Hitler. 1936–1945*, pp. 304–7, and pp. 331–5.
8. H. R. Trevor-Roper (ed.), *Hitler's War Directives 1939–1945* (London: Pan, 1966), pp. 93–8.
9. *TBJG*, 9 August 1940, TI, 8, p. 262.
10. See Tooze, *Wages of Destruction*, pp. 665–6.
11. *TBJG*, 7 May 1941, TI, 9, p. 295.
12. See *TBJG*, 11 November 1939, 14 November 1939, and 15 March 1940, TI, 7, pp. 190–1, 194, and 350 for examples.
13. *TBJG*, 16 June 1941, TI, 9, pp. 377–9.
14. *TBJG*, 9 May 1941, TI, 9, p. 301. Tooze does not report this conversation, which contradicts his view of Hitler's realistic assessment of the potential of American armaments production.
15. *TBJG*, 14 May 1941, TI, 9, p. 311.

16. See *TBJG*, 23 November 1939, TI, 7, p. 207.
17. *TBJG*, 13 June 1941, TI, 9, p. 370.
18. BArch R 55/20001g, '11h – Konferenz vom 14. April 1941'. This document is incorrectly dated, and clearly refers to the conference of 14 May 1941.
19. BArch R 55/20001g, '11h – Konferenz vom 15. Mai 1941'.
20. *TBJG*, 9 May and 10 May 1941, TI, 9, p. 302.
21. *TBJG*, 11 April 1941, TI, 9, p. 242.
22. Richards and Saunders, *Royal Air Force 1939–1945*, Vol. 1, p. 237.
23. *TBJG*, 17 April 1941, TI, 9, pp. 252–3.
24. *TBJG*, 30 March 1941, TI, 9, p. 212.
25. See Max Domarus, *Hitler: Reden und Proklamationen 1932–1945* (Wiesbaden: Löwit, 1973), Band II, Untergang, Zweiter Halbband 1941–1945, pp. 1726–32.
26. *TBJG*, 22 June 1941, TI, 9, pp. 396–7.
27. See 'Meldungen aus dem Reich (Nr. 199)', 3 July 1941; and 'Meldungen aus dem Reich (Nr. 200)', 7 July 1941, Boberach, *Meldungen aus dem Reich*, Band 7, p. 2470, and p. 2486.
28. See Jerzy Szynkowski and Georg Wünsche, *Das Führerhauptquartier (FHQu) Wolfsschanze* (Kętrzyn: Kengraf, 2005).
29. *TBJG*, 9 July 1941, TII, 1, pp. 30–8.
30. *TBJG*, 26 July 1941, and 31 July 1941, TII, 1, p. 126 and p. 151.
31. *TBJG*, 12 August 1941, TII, 1, p. 219.
32. *TBJG*, 14 August 1941, TII, 1, p. 232.
33. On Galen see Terence Prittie, 'The Opposition of the Church of Rome', Hans-Adolf Jacobsen (ed.), *July 20, 1944: The German Opposition to Hitler as Viewed by Foreign Historians* (Bonn: Press and Information Department of the Federal Government, 1969), pp. 79–104, in particular pp. 89–96.
34. *TBJG*, 19 August 1941, TII, 1, pp. 258–66.
35. See BArch R 55/20001g, '11h – Konferenz vom 21. April 1941'; and *TBJG*, 22 April 1941, TI, 9, p. 264.
36. Strauss, 'Das Reichsministerium des Innern und die Judengesetzgebung', pp. 302–3. Gutterer was one of few close associates Goebbels regarded highly.
37. *TBJG*, 19 August 1941, TII, 1, pp. 265–6, 269, 272.
38. For a description of how Goebbels kept his diary in the final war years, see Oven, *Finale Furioso*, pp. 66–7.
39. *TBJG*, 20 September 1941, TII, 1, p. 459.
40. *TBJG*, 21 October 1941, TII, 2, p. 148.
41. Domarus, *Hitler: Reden und Proklamationen 1932–1945*, Band II, Zweiter Halbband, pp. 1767–8.
42. Mihail Sebastian, *Journal 1935–1944* (London: Pimlico, 2003), 10 October 1941, p. 425.
43. *TBJG*, 10 October 1941, TII, 2, pp. 87–8.
44. *TBJG*, 27 November and 30 November 1941, TII, 2, p. 374, and p. 397.
45. For a fuller discussion of the anti-smoking campaign, and of wartime regulation of tobacco consumption, see Christoph Maria Merki, 'Die nationalsozialistische Tabakpolitik', *Vierteljahrshefte für Zeitgeschichte*, 46:1 (1998), pp. 19–42.
46. See the letter from Lösener to Frick, 20 August 1941, cited in Strauss, 'Das Reichsministerium des Innern und die Judengesetzgebung', p. 305; and *TBJG*, 20 August 1941, TII, 1, p. 278.
47. 'Meldungen aus dem Reich (Nr. 227)', 9 October 1941, Boberach, *Meldungen aus dem Reich*, Band 8, p. 2849.

48. See David Bankier, *The Germans and the Final Solution: Public Opinion under Nazism* (Oxford: Blackwell, 1996), pp. 119–29.

49. See Peter Witte, 'Two Decisions Concerning the "Final Solution to the Jewish Question": Deportations to Lodz and Mass Murder in Chelmno', *Holocaust and Genocide Studies*, 9:3 (1995), pp. 318–45; and, for a recent overview, Browning, *The Origins of the Final Solution*, in particular pp. 323–6.

50. *TBJG*, 24 September 1941, TII, 1, pp. 479–85.

51. *TBJG*, 11 August and 5 September 1941, TII, 1, p. 213, and p. 361; and 19 October 1941, TII, 2, p. 142.

52. *TBJG*, 2 November 1941, TII, 2, pp. 221–2.

53. See Browning, *The Origins of the Final Solution*, pp. 375–7, and p. 305.

54. 'Die Juden sind schuld!' *Das Reich*, 16 November 1941; see also *TBJG*, 4 November 1941, TII, 2, p. 231.

55. Cited in Weinreich, *Hitler's Professors*, p. 157; see also *TBJG*, 2 December 1941, TII, 2, p. 416.

56. Goebbels' article in *Das Reich* is bizarrely neglected in Eric Johnson and Karl-Heinz Reuband, *What We Knew: Terror, Mass Murder and Everyday Life in Nazi Germany* (London: John Murray, 2005); David Bankier's earlier study *The Germans and the Final Solution: Public Opinion under Nazism* (Oxford: Blackwell, 1996) discusses a passage relating to the yellow star from Goebbels' article, but does not even mention its declaration that the Jews were being exterminated. From Bankier's footnotes it would appear that he did not use the whole article, but a reference to it in a contemporary British document (see pp. 127–8). An exception to this neglect is Jeffrey Herf, 'The "Jewish War": Goebbels and the Antisemitic Campaigns of the Nazi Propaganda Ministry', *Holocaust and Genocide Studies*, 19:1 (Spring 2005), pp. 51–80. Saul Friedländer, in *Nazi Germany and the Jews: The Years of Extermination 1939–1945* (London: HarperCollins, 2007), puts Goebbels' article in a wider context of other public announcements of the extermination of the Jews. On Goebbels' speech to the German Academy he says: 'Whether the ominous diatribe referred to an ongoing and systematic extermination of all the Jews of Europe is not clear, however' (p. 276).

57. Sebastian, *Journal 1935–1944*, 5 September 1941, p. 405; 14 November 1941, p. 442; and 12 November 1941, p. 441.

58. Klepper, *Unter dem Schatten Deiner Flügel*, 14 November 1941, p. 981; 20 November 1941, p. 987; and 17 November 1941, p. 984.

59. *TBJG*, 29 October 1941, TII, 2, p. 202.

60. *TBJG*, 2 November, 3 November, and 4 November 1941, TII, 2, pp. 220–7.

61. Heinz Guderian, *Panzer Leader* (London: Futura, 1974), p. 248.

62. See 'Im Herzen des Volkes', 4 December 1941, in Goebbels, *Das eherne Herz*, pp. 105–10, p. 107.

63. *TBJG*, 5 December 1941, TII, 2, pp. 434–7.

64. *TBJG*, 6 December 1941, TII, 2, p. 441.

65. *TBJG*, 9 December 1941, TII, 2, pp. 455–9.

66. 'Meldungen aus dem Reich (Nr. 246)', 15 December 1941, Boberach, *Meldungen aus dem Reich*, Band 8, p. 3089.

67. *TBJG*, 10 December 1941, TII, 2, p. 465.

68. *TBJG*, 13 December 1941, TII, 2, pp. 498–9.

69. Domarus, *Hitler: Reden und Proklamationen 1932–1945*, Band II, Zweiter Halbband, p. 1829.

70. *TBJG*, 7 March 1942, TII, 3, pp. 431–2. See Mark Roseman, *The Villa, the Lake, the Meeting: Wannsee and the Final Solution* (London: Allen Lane, 2002).
71. *TBJG*, 27 March 1942, TII, 3, p. 561.
72. See Yitzhak Arad, *Belzec, Sobibor, Treblinka: The Operation Reinhard Death Camps* (Bloomington: Indiana University Press, 1987), pp. 68ff.
73. *TBJG*, 22 May 1942, TII, 4, p. 334.
74. *TBJG*, 24 May 1942, TII, 4, p. 350.
75. Cited in Gilbert, *Finest Hour*, p. 1274.
76. *TBJG*, 12 December 1941, TII, 2, p. 484.
77. *TBJG*, 27 August 1941, TII, 1, p. 315.
78. *TBJG*, 25 December 1941, TII, 2, p. 580.
79. *TBJG*, 20 January 1942, TII, 3, p. 143.
80. See the documents relating to these state funerals in BArch R 55/1329.
81. *TBJG*, 13 December 1941, TII, 2, p. 499; 'Das neue Jahr', 4 January 1942, in Goebbels, *Das eherne Herz*, pp. 162–8, p. 162.
82. *TBJG*, 2 June 1942, TII, 4, p. 432.
83. *TBJG*, 12 June 1942, TII, 4, p. 506. It appears that one of the 'educational institutions' some of the children from Lidice were sent to was the death camp at Chełmno in the 'Wartheland'. See Łucja Pawlicka-Nowak (ed.), *Chełmno Witnesses Speak* (Łódź: Konin District Museum, 2004), p. 15.
84. *TBJG*, 10 June 1942, TII, 4, p. 486.
85. Malcolm Muggeridge (ed.), *Ciano's Diary, 1939–1943* (London: Heinemann, 1947), 20 April and 27 April 1942, p. 458, and p. 460. Goebbels' speech on 19 April is reproduced in *Das Eherne Herz*, pp. 286–94; Hitler's speech of 26 April is reproduced in Domarus, *Hitler: Reden und Proklamationen 1932–1945*, Band II, Zweiter Halbband, pp. 1865–77.
86. See Kershaw, *Hitler 1936–1945*, p. 512.
87. *TBJG*, 30 June 1942, TII, 4, p. 644.
88. *TBJG*, 30 May 1942, TII, 4, p.408.
89. *TBJG*, 12 June 1942, TII, 4, p. 507.
90. *TBJG*, 24 June 1942, TII, 4, pp. 610–11.
91. *TBJG*, 6 July 1942, TII, 5, p. 66.
92. 'Meldungen aus dem Reich (Nr. 312)', 27 August 1942, Boberach, *Meldungen aus dem Reich*, Band 11, p. 4135.
93. Alan Clark, *Barbarossa: The Russian-German Conflict 1941–1945* (Harmondsworth: Penguin, 1966), p. 250.
94. *TBJG*, 8 August 1942, TII, 5, p. 271.
95. *TBJG*, 13 September 1942, TII, 5, p. 489.
96. See Boelcke, *Wollt Ihr den totalen Krieg?* p. 275, and p. 279.
97. *TBJG*, 10 September 1942, TII, 5, p. 467.
98. 'Der steile Aufstieg', in Goebbels, *Das Eherne Herz*, pp. 466–72, p. 472.
99. *TBJG*, 6 November 1942, TII, 6, p. 245.
100. See Reck-Malleczewen, *Diary of a Man in Despair*, p. 186; and *TBJG*, 9 November 1942, TII, 6, p. 254.
101. Heiber, *Goebbels-Reden*, Band 2, pp. 125–57; *TBJG*, 18 November 1942, TII, 6, p. 308.
102. *TBJG*, 19 November and 20 November 1942, TII, 6, pp. 314–15.

Chapter 11

1. Hassell, *Vom andern Deutschland*, p. 237.
2. Cited in *History of the United Nations War Crimes Commission and the Development of the Laws of War* (London: HMSO, 1948), p. 106.
3. See Walter Langsam (ed.), *Historic Documents of World War II* (Princeton: Van Nostrand, 1958), pp. 86–8.
4. See Boelcke, *Wollt Ihr den totalen Krieg?* p. 322, and p. 328.
5. *TBJG*, 31 January 1943, TII, 7, pp. 229–30; see Domarus, *Hitler: Reden und Proklamationen*, Band II, Zweiter Halbband, pp. 1976–80 for Hitler's 'proclamation'; and Heiber, *Goebbels-Reden*, Band 2, pp. 158–71 for Goebbels' speech.
6. *TBJG*, 3 February and 4 February 1943, TII, 7, pp. 248–54, and p. 255; Domarus, *Hitler: Reden und Proklamationen*, Band II, Zweiter Halbband, p. 1985.
7. Sebastian, *Journal 1935–1944*, 4 February 1943, p. 543.
8. Speer, *Inside the Third Reich*, p. 334, and p. 350. Speer had been appointed Armaments Minister after the death of Fritz Todt in February 1942.
9. Cited in Gitta Sereny, *Albert Speer: His Battle with Truth* (London: Macmillan, 1995), p. 372.
10. These three men, living alongside Hitler at the Wolf's Lair, had become gatekeepers largely controlling access to Hitler, and serving as conduits for his ideas to other parts of the state apparatus. Bormann was by early 1943 Director of the Party Chancellery; Hans Lammers was Head of the *Reich* Chancellery; Wilhelm Keitel was Head of the High Command of the *Wehrmacht*. For all the grandeur of these titles, none of these men was notable for producing ideas or taking the initiative in decision making. Bormann died in 1945; Lammers was sentenced to 20 years' imprisonment but released in 1951; Keitel was executed in 1946 after being tried as a 'major war criminal' before the International Military Tribunal at Nuremberg.
11. *TBJG*, 19 February 1943, TII, 7, p. 374.
12. On Ludendorff's book, see Günter Moltmann, 'Goebbels' Rede zum totalen Krieg am 18. Februar 1943', *Vierteljahrshefte für Zeitgechichte*, 12:1 (1960), pp. 13–43, pp. 17–18. For an early use of the phrase 'total war' by Goebbels see his speech on 22 December 1939, cited in Goebbels, *Die Zeit ohne Beispiel*, pp. 224–8, p. 225.
13. *TBJG*, 20 February 1943, TII, 7, p. 377.
14. *TBJG*, 2 February 1943, TII, 7, p. 243.
15. *TBJG*, 13 February 1943, TII, 7, p. 335.
16. Albert Speer, cited in Sereny, *Albert Speer*, p. 371.
17. *TBJG*, 19 December 1942, TII, 6, p. 472.
18. See *TBJG*, 23 January and 18 February 1943, TII, 7, p. 177, and p. 369.
19. *TBJG*, 20 February 1943, TII, 7, p. 374.
20. The 'total war' speech is transcribed in Heiber, *Goebbels-Reden*, Band 2, pp. 172–208; the anti-Semitic quotation above is on pp. 182–3.
21. *TBJG*, 19 February 1943, TII, 7, pp. 373–5; Speer, *Inside the Third Reich*, pp. 337–8.
22. For brief excerpts of the sound recording, listen to the CD which accompanies Jürgen Schebera (ed.), *Stimmen des Jahrhunderts: Politiker aus Deutschland 1914–1990* (Berlin: Collection BuchPlus, 1992). One historian who has recognized the significance of Goebbels' anti-Semitic comments in the 'total war' speech is Jeffrey Herf. See 'The "Jewish War"', p. 69.
23. BArch R 55/612, 'Rede des Herrn Ministers', 19 February 1943.

24. Friedländer, *Nazi Germany and the Jews: The Years of Extermination*, pp. 424–5. Friedländer also notes the centrality of anti-Semitism in the 'total war' speech; see pp. 472–4.

25. 'Aus den Tagebüchern eines Schneiders', 6 March 1943, in Ingrid Hammer and Susanne zur Neiden (eds), *'Sehr selten habe ich geweint.' Briefe und Tagebücher aus dem Zweiten Weltkrieg von Menschen aus Berlin* (Zurich: Schweizer Verlagshaus, 1992), p. 334.

26. *TBJG*, 9 April and 14 April 1943, TII, 8, pp. 77 and 104.

27. See for example 'Un Document Officiel sur Katyn', *Signal*, 12/1943, pp. 15–19.

28. *TBJG*, 27 April 1943, TII, 8, p. 171. It appears that Goebbels was referring here to mass graves near Tatarka of GPU victims from Bessarabia, which were investigated by Romanian forensic specialists during the spring and summer of 1943.

29. BAK N1118/138, 'Weisungen des Herrn Ministers am 25. April 1943'.

30. *TBJG*, 2 May 1943, TII, 8, p. 197.

31. BAK N1118/138, 'Konferenz vom 16. April 1943'.

32. Cited in Herf, 'The "Jewish War"', p. 70.

33. *TBJG*, 14 May 1943, TII, 8, p. 297.

34. Richards and Saunders, *Royal Air Force 1939–1945*, Vol. 2, p. 280.

35. The 'Casablanca Directive' is reproduced in Charles Webster and Noble Frankland, *The Strategic Air Offensive against Germany 1939–1945* (London: HMSO, 1961), Vol. IV, Annexes and Appendices, pp. 153–4.

36. *TBJG*, 17 January 1943, TII, 7, p. 132.

37. *TBJG*, 22 March 1943, TII, 7, pp. 614–15; Domarus, *Hitler: Reden und Proklamationen*, Band II, Zweiter Halbband, pp. 1999–2002.

38. 'Meldungen aus dem Reich (Nr. 369)', 22 March 1943, Boberach, *Meldungen aus dem Reich*, Band 13, pp. 4981–2.

39. *TBJG*, 10 April 1943, TII, 8, p. 86.

40. Schaumburg-Lippe, *Dr. G.*, p. 101.

41. *TBJG*, 3 May 1943, TII, 8, p. 202.

42. *TBJG*, 14 May, 18 May, 19 May, and 25 May 1943, TII, 8, pp. 293, 316, 322, and 358.

43. Arthur Harris, *Bomber Offensive* (London: Collins, 1947), p. 148.

44. BArch R 55/20738, 'Die Katastrophe an der Möhnetalsperre und Ruhr (Bericht 2)', 27 August 1943.

45. *TBJG*, 27 May 1943, TII, 8, p. 373.

46. Max Hastings, *Bomber Command* (London: Pan, 1981), Appendix E, p. 448; *TBJG*, 26 June and 27 June 1943, TII, 8, p. 542, and p. 550.

47. Richards and Saunders, *Royal Air Force 1939–1945*, Vol. 3, p. 9.

48. *TBJG*, 29 July 1943, TII, 9, p. 190.

49. 'SD-Berichte zu Inlandsfragen vom 2. August 1943', Boberach, *Meldungen aus dem Reich*, Band 14, p. 5562.

50. Reck-Malleczewen, *Diary of a Man in Despair*, p. 209.

51. *TBJG*, 7 August 1943, TII, 9, p. 234.

52. 'SD-Berichte zu Inlandsfragen vom 29. Juli 1943', Boberach, *Meldungen aus dem Reich*, Band 14, p. 5542.

53. *TBJG*, 1 September 1943, TII, 9, pp. 398–9.

54. *TBJG*, 10 September 1943, TII, 9, pp. 464–5. The speech is cited in Domarus, *Hitler: Reden und Proklamationen*, Band II, Zweiter Halbband, pp. 2035–9.

55. *TBJG*, 27 October 1943, TII, 10, pp. 183–4.

56. Cited in Langsam, *Historic Documents of World War II*, pp. 89–96.

57. On Hitler and the rocket programme see Michael Neufeld, *The Rocket and the Reich: Peenemünde and the Coming of the Ballistic Missile Era* (New York: Free Press, 1995).
58. Oven, *Finale Furioso*, pp. 113–15.
59. *TBJG*, 19 May 1943, TII, 8, pp. 326–8.
60. See 'Un combatant contre le Bolchevisme', *Signal*, 23/1943, p. 2.
61. *TBJG*, 25 June 1943, TII, 8, p. 537–8.
62. *TBJG*, 10 August 1943, TII, 9, p. 267.
63. *TBJG*, 7 May 1943, TII, 8, p. 221. See also Welch, *Propaganda and the German Cinema*, pp. 189–97.
64. *TBJG*, 3 June 1943, TII, 8, p. 414.
65. *TBJG*, 8 June 1943, TII, 8, p. 443. Kempff is widely considered one of the great pianists of the twentieth century; his association with the Nazi regime is less frequently highlighted.
66. Jörg Friedrich argues in *Der Brand: Deutschland im Bombenkrieg 1940–1945* (Munich: Propyläen, 2002), p. 457, that the evacuation of children from the cities was 'the most unpopular measure of the whole Third Reich'.
67. *TBJG*, 24 August 1943, TII, 9, p. 353.
68. See Heiber, *Goebbels-Reden*, Band 2, pp. 259–85 for the speech in Kassel, and pp. 286–304 for that in Hanover; also *TBJG*, 6 November 1943, TII, 10, pp. 238–9. After the war, Weinrich was interned until 1950; Lauterbacher had a chequered career, escaping to Argentina in 1950, and returning to Munich in 1956.
69. *TBJG*, 23 November 1943, TII, 10, pp. 338–9.
70. Martin Middlebrook, *The Berlin Raids: RAF Bomber Command Winter 1943–44* (London: Cassell, 2001), p. 148.
71. See the accounts by employees at the zoo in Hans Dieter Schäfer (ed.), *Berlin im Zweiten Weltkrieg: Der Untergang der Reichshauptstadt in Augenzeugenberichten* (Munich: Piper, 1985), pp. 159–62, and pp. 162–6. The Kaiser Wilhelm Memorial Church is still a ruin today, a memorial to the bombing.
72. *TBJG*, 24 November, 27 November, 29 November, and 26 November 1943, TII, 10, pp. 346, 369, 382, and 361.
73. *TBJG*, 27 April 1944, TII, 12, p. 195.
74. BArch R 55/610, 'Reichspropagandaamt Moselland an den Herrn Reichsminister für Volksaufklärung und Propaganda', 28 April 1944.
75. Oven, *Finale Furioso*, pp. 272–5.
76. *TBJG*, 13 March 1944, TII, 11, p. 462; 10 April, and 17 April 1944, TII, 12, p. 81, and p. 120.
77. *TBJG*, 18 May 1944, TII, 12, p. 314.
78. See Erik Levi, *Music in the Third Reich* (Basingstoke: Macmillan, 1994), pp. 212–14.
79. *TBJG*, 25 May 1944, TII, 12, p. 357.
80. Goebbels did not know this phrase, which is from T. E. Lawrence, *The Seven Pillars of Wisdom* (London: Book Club Associates, 1976), p. 8, but he would have recognized the sentiment: he had read Lawrence's abridged earlier version *Revolt in the Desert* (in translation) back in 1934, and thought it 'wild, exciting, and thrilling'. *TBJG*, 27 December 1934, TI, 3/I, p. 159.
81. See, for example, Guderian, *Panzer Leader*, p. 325.
82. *TBJG*, 23 February 1944, TII, 11, p. 332.
83. *TBJG*, 4 March 1944, TII, 11, pp. 400–3.
84. Rundstedt was one of Germany's most senior soldiers. He had played a leading role in the Battle of France in 1940, and commanded 'Army Group South' in the first months of the German invasion of the Soviet Union. In March 1944 Rundstedt

was Commander-in-Chief of all German forces in Western Europe. He is frequently portrayed as the archetypal apolitical soldier. His early biographer Guenther Blumentritt characteristically omits to mention this declaration of loyalty to Hitler. See his *Von Rundstedt: The Soldier and the Man* (London: Odhams, 1952).

85. *TBJG*, 18 April 1944, TII, 12, p. 128; see also Domarus, *Hitler: Reden und Proklamationen*, Band II Zweiter Halbband, p. 2094.
86. *TBJG*, 4 March 1944, TII, 11, p. 408.
87. *TBJG*, 3 May 1944, TII, 12, p. 227.
88. See Neufeld, *The Rocket and the Reich*, pp. 220–5.
89. *TBJG*, 6 June 1944, TII, 12, pp. 405–15.

Chapter 12

1. Heiber, *Goebbels-Reden*, Band 2, p. 340.
2. *TBJG*, 18 June 1944, TII, 12, pp. 490–2.
3. *TBJG*, 26 June 1944, TII, 12, p. 551.
4. Evan Mawdsley, *Thunder in the East: The Nazi-Soviet War 1941–1945* (London: Hodder Arnold, 2005), p. 308.
5. *TBJG*, 13 July 1944, TII, 13, p. 105.
6. *TBJG*, 2 July 1944, TII, 13, p. 41.
7. The 'Free Germany National Committee' (NKFD) was formed in the Soviet Union in July 1943 from German POWs and Communist émigrés. The Soviets allowed it to publish a newspaper and to broadcast from Moscow, urging German soldiers to abandon the war. In November 1945 the NKFD was dissolved, but former members were active in the German Democratic Republic, and the memory of the NKFD became an important part of that state's 'anti-Fascist' mythology. See Willy Wolff, *Auf der richtigen Seite: Zum Wirken der Frontorganisation des Nationalkomitees 'Freies Deutschland'* (Berlin: Militärverlag der Deutschen Demokratischen Republik, 1985).
8. See Speer, *Inside the Third Reich*, pp. 486–96; Oven, *Finale Furioso*, pp. 415–30; and Heiber, *Goebbels-Reden*, Band 2, pp. 342–59.
9. Kershaw, *Hitler. 1936–1945*, p. 679.
10. Domarus, *Hitler: Reden und Proklamationen*, Band II, Zweiter Halbband, p. 2127.
11. Oven, *Finale Furioso*, p. 427.
12. *TBJG*, 20 June 1944, TII, 11, p. 503.
13. See Peter Hoffmann, 'Warum mißlang das Attentat vom 20. Juli 1944?' *Vierteljahrshefte für Zeitgeschichte*, 32:3 (1984), pp. 441–62, pp. 461–2.
14. See Domarus, *Hitler: Reden und Proklamationen*, Band II, Zweiter Halbband, p. 2132.
15. *TBJG*, 23 July 1944, TII, 13, pp. 134–48.
16. *TBJG*, 25 July, 26 July; and 4 August 1944, TII, 13, pp. 165, 173, and 223.
17. *TBJG*, 16 August 1944, TII, 13, p. 245. Harrison, '"Alter Kämpfer" im Widerstand', p. 422.
18. BArch (ehem. BDC) Parteikorrespondenz, D 83, Goebbels, Joseph, 29.10.1897, 'Vermerk über die Besprechung beim Chef der Reichskanzlei am 31.7.44', 2 August 1944.
19. Koch was the 'prole' who had made insinuations about Goebbels' disability for the Strasser brothers in 1927, and had gone on to a notoriously brutal career as *Reich* Commissar in the Ukraine. He was arrested by the British in 1949, and extradited

to Poland, where he was sentenced to death in 1959. The sentence was commuted on grounds of ill-health, and Koch died in prison in Poland in 1986.

20. *TBJG*, 13 September and 10 September 1944, TII, 13, p. 472, and p. 452.
21. *TBJG*, 12 September and 18 September 1944, TII, 13, p. 463, and pp. 510–11.
22. Kershaw, *Hitler 1936–1945*, pp. 729–30. Oven records that Goebbels told him, 'with glowing eyes' that the letter would 'go down in history'. See *Finale Furioso*, p. 480.
23. *TBJG*, 21 September 1944, TII, 13, pp. 536–42.
24. *TBJG*, 25 September 1944, TII, 13, p. 562.
25. See *TBJG*, 12 October and 24 October 1944, TII, 14, pp. 83–4, and p. 98.
26. Domarus, *Hitler: Reden und Proklamationen*, Band II, Zweiter Halbband, pp. 2153–4.
27. *TBJG*, 12 September and 21 September 1944, TII, 13, p. 464, and p. 535.
28. BArch R 55/1287, 'Zeitfolge Wilhelmplatz', Anlage 3; *TBJG*, 13 November 1944, TII, 14, pp. 208–9; Oven, *Finale Furioso*, pp. 511–12.
29. BArch R 55/1287, 'Deutscher Volkssturm Bataillon Propagandaministerium, IV Kompanie'.
30. BArch R 55/1287, 'Ausbildungsplan', 11 December 1944; 'Kompaniebefehl Nr. 2', 15 November 1944; 'An Bataillon Wilhelmplatz I, SS-Brigadeführer [sic] Dr. Naumann', 21 November 1944.
31. BArch R 55/1287, 'An den Kompanieführer Herrn Dr. Schrade', 9 December 1944.
32. *TBJG*, 20 November 1944, TII, 14, p. 244.
33. On the calendar, see the correspondence between Magda Goebbels and Wegelj-von Behen; on the cigarettes, see her letter to General Wünnenberg, 3 November 1944, and the undated anonymous letter to her, in BAK N1118/148.
34. *TBJG*, 23 September 1944, TII, 13, p. 545.
35. *TBJG*, 9 October 1944, TII, 14, p. 64.
36. See Fröhlich, 'Joseph Goebbels und sein Tagebuch', pp. 498–9.
37. See BArch R 55/612, 'R. P. A. Königsberg meldet:', 1 January 1945.
38. *TBJG*, 2 December 1944, TII, 14, pp. 318–34.
39. *TBJG*, 4 December 1944, TII, 14, pp. 349–50.
40. *TBJG*, 19 December 1944, TII, 14, p. 445.
41. Guderian, *Panzer Leader*, p. 381.
42. BAK N118/148, Magda Goebbels to Theresa Hoffmann, 15 December 1944.
43. BArch R 55/612, 'posen meldung nr. 22001 an propamin abt. pro', 1 January 1945.
44. BArch R 55/612, 'posen meldung nr. 22002 an propmin abt. pro', 1 January 1945.
45. BArch R 55/612, 'R. P. A. Köln meldet:', 1 January 1945.
46. BArch R 55/612, 'schw. an propamin', 1 January 1945; 'R. P. A. Oldenburg meldet:' 1 January 1945.
47. BArch R 55/612, 'rk oslo an das promi', 1 January 1945; 'Bericht über die Führerrede des RPA Salzburg', 1 January 1945; 'rpa klagenfurt an pro. min', 1 January 1945.
48. BArch R 55/612, 'posen meldung nr. 22001 an propamin abt. pro', 1 January 1945.
49. *TBJG*, 1 January 1945, TII, 15, p. 34, and p. 33.
50. Hanke escaped from Breslau at the end of the siege, but was killed by Czech partisans in June 1945; Greiser was later returned to Posen (now renamed Poznań) where he was hanged in July 1946.
51. BArch R 55/24818, 'VI-PROMI SS-Stubaf. Ulenberg. Betr: Lagebericht aus dem unter Fernbeschuß der V-1 und V-2 liegenden London', 11 December 1944.
52. *TBJG*, 23 January 1945, TII, 15, pp. 192–5.
53. *TBJG*, 25 January 1945, TII, 15, p. 219.

54. *TBJG*, 28 January 1945, TII, 15, pp. 251–7.
55. Guderian, *Panzer Leader*, p. 325.
56. Oven, *Finale Furioso*, p. 559.
57. *TBJG*, 1 February 1945, TII, 15, pp. 288–98.
58. *TBJG*, 6 February 1945, TII, 15, p. 323.
59. Oven, *Finale Furioso*, pp. 572–3.
60. *TBJG*, 11 February and 5 March 1945, TII, 15, p. 359, and p. 425.
61. *TBJG*, 10 February and 13 February 1945, TII, 15, p. 349, and p. 381.
62. BArch R 55/610, 'An die deutsche Bevölkerung!'
63. *TBJG*, 16 March 1945, TII, 15, p. 520.
64. Heiber, *Goebbels-Reden*, Band 2, pp. 429–46; Oven, *Finale Furioso*, p. 598.
65. Klemperer, *To the Bitter End*, p. 409.
66. See Domarus, *Hitler: Reden und Proklamationen*, Band II, Zweiter Halbband, p. 2206 for the prophesy; and 'Bericht an das Reichsministerium für Volksaufklärung und Propaganda vom 28. März 1945', Boberach, *Meldungen aus dem Reich*, Band 17, pp. 6732–44.
67. *TBJG*, 9 March 1945, TII, 15, pp. 457–62; David Welch, 'Goebbels, Götterdämmerung, and the Deutsche Wochenschauen', K.R. M. Short and Stephan Dolezel (eds), *Hitler's Fall: The Newsreel Witness* (London: Croom Helm, 1988), pp. 80–99.
68. BArch R 55/619, 'An die Hauptreferate Pro. Pol. Pro. G. Betrifft: Propagandistische Beeinflussung des Gegners bei Absetzungsbewegungen', 16 March 1945.
69. BArch R 55/610, 'An das Reichspropagandaamt Oberdonau in Linz. Betrifft: Flugblätter für die Wehrmacht', 28 March 1945.
70. See the correspondence on this is BArch (ehem. BDC) RKK 2300/0085/16.
71. BArch R 55/619, 'Meldepflicht für Evakuierte und Flüchtlinge', 23 March 1945.
72. See Frederick Taylor, *Dresden, Tuesday 13 February 1945* (London: Bloomsbury, 2004), p. 372.
73. *TBJG*, 12 March and 16 March 1945, TII, 15, p. 480, and p. 521.
74. *TBJG*, 22 March 1945, TII, 15, pp. 573–4.
75. *TBJG*, 24 March 1945, TII, 15, p. 586.
76. *TBJG*, 1 April 1945, TII, 15, p. 659.
77. BAK N1118/148, Magda Goebbels to Zeller, 9 April 1945.
78. *TBJG*, 9 April 1945, TII, 15, p. 692.
79. For accounts of the post-war history of the various copies of Goebbels' diaries, see Fröhlich, 'Joseph Goebbels und sein Tagebuch', and Astrid Eckert and Stefan Martens, 'Glasplatten im märkischen Sand: Zur Überlieferungsgeschichte der Tageseinträge und Diktate von Joseph Goebbels', *Vierteljahrshefte für Zeitgeschichte*, 52:3 (2004), pp. 479–526.
80. Oven, *Finale Furioso*, p. 646.
81. Heiber, *Goebbels-Reden*, Band 2, pp. 447–55.
82. Oven, *Finale Furioso*, pp. 651–2.
83. H. R. Trevor-Roper, *The Last Days of Hitler* (London: Pan, 1952), p. 124.
84. 'Widerstand um jeden Preis', *Das Reich*, 22 April 1945.
85. Cited in Eberle and Uhl, *The Hitler Book*, p. 230.
86. Oven, *Finale Furioso*, p. 654.
87. Speer, *Inside the Third Reich*, p. 611.
88. Hanna Reitsch, *Flugkapitän Hanna Reitsch. Fliegen – mein Leben* (Munich: Lehmanns Verlag, 1976), p. 359.
89. Traudl Junge, *Until the Final Hour: Hitler's Last Secretary* (London: Phoenix, 2005), pp. 168–9.
90. Junge, *Until the Final Hour*, pp. 174–5.

91. Klabunde, *Magda Goebbels*, p. 318.
92. See Reitsch, *Flugkapitän Hanna Reitsch*, pp. 353–9. Reitsch left the bunker in the early hours of 29 April with Ritter von Greim, who had accompanied her on her visit, and had been appointed by Hitler to replace Göring as Commander of the *Luftwaffe*. She survived to continue her flying career after 1945; Greim committed suicide in May 1945.
93. Domarus, *Hitler: Reden und Proklamationen*, Band II, Zweiter Halbband, p. 2228.
94. Goebbels to Harald Quandt, 28 April 1945, cited in H. R. Trevor-Roper (ed.), *The Goebbels Diaries: The Last Days* (London: Book Club Associates, 1978), pp. 329–30.
95. Domarus, *Hitler: Reden und Proklamationen*, Band II, Zweiter Halbband, p. 2234, n. 193.
96. Domarus, *Hitler: Reden und Proklamationen*, Band II, Zweiter Halbband, pp. 2236–41.
97. Junge, *Until the Final Hour*, p. 184.
98. Domarus, *Hitler: Reden und Proklamationen*, Band II, Zweiter Halbband, p. 2241, n. 213. Trevor-Roper cites a slightly longer version; see *The Last Days of Hitler*, pp. 186–7.
99. See Sereny, *Albert Speer*, p. 539; and Eberle and Uhl, *The Hitler Book*, pp. 270–1.
100. Eberle and Uhl, *The Hitler Book*, p. 272.
101. Cited in Eberle and Uhl, *The Hitler Book*, p. 274.
102. See Vasili Chuikov, *The Fall of Berlin* (New York: Ballantyne, 1969), pp. 219–55.
103. Sereny, *Albert Speer*, pp. 540–1. Stumpfegger was a doctor of medicine who had previously been Himmler's personal physician, and had been involved in experiments on humans at Ravensbrück concentration camp; since October 1944 he had been Hitler's personal doctor. He died in attempting to escape from the bunker on 2 May 1945.
104. Cornelius Ryan, *The Last Battle* (London: New English Library, 1967), pp. 375–6. The identification of the bodies of Goebbels, his wife Magda, and their six children was confirmed by an autopsy on 8 May 1945. The autopsy found cyanide poisoning to be the cause of death. See Eberle and Uhl, *The Hitler Book*, p. 282.

Epilogue

1. Cited in Christoph Studt (ed.), *Das Dritte Reich: Ein Lesebuch zur deutschen Geschichte 1933–1945* (Munich: Beck, 1995), p. 300.
2. 'Proclamation No. 2', *Official Gazette of the Control Council for Germany*, No. 1, 29 October 1945, pp. 8–19, p. 17. On 'denazification' more broadly, see Toby Thacker, *The End of the Third Reich: Defeat, Denazification, and Nuremberg, January 1944–November 1946* (Stroud: Tempus, 2006).
3. 'Law No. 2', *Official Gazette of the Control Council for Germany*, No. 1, 29 October 1945, pp. 19–21.
4. Cited in Werner Jochmann, *Nationalsozialismus und Revolution: Ursprung und Geschichte der NSDAP in Hamburg, 1922–1933. Dokumente* (Frankfurt-am-Main: Europäische Verlag, 1963), p. 209.
5. *Heil! A Picture Book Compiled from Authentic Material* (London: John Lane, 1934), p. 50.
6. Otto Strasser, *Hitler and I* (London: Jonathan Cape, 1940), p. 100, and p. 95.
7. Hanfstaengl, *Hitler: The Missing Years*, p. 224.
8. Cited in Gay, *Weimar Culture*, p. 144.
9. Fromm, *Blood and Banquets*, pp. 30–1.
10. Lochner, *The Goebbels Diaries*, pp. xxiv–xxv.

11. Rumbold to Simon, 14 March 1933, *Documents on British Foreign Policy 1919–1939, Second Series,* Vol. IV, 1932–33 (London: HMSO, 1950), p. 453.
12. Ogilvie-Forbes to Halifax, 3 January 1939, *Documents on British Foreign Policy 1919–1939, Third Series,* Vol. III, 1938–39, pp. 561–4, p. 563.
13. Reinhard Spitzy, *How We Squandered the Reich* (Norwich: Russell, 1997), p. 86.
14. Klemperer, *I Shall Bear Witness,* p. 172.
15. Shirer, *The Rise and Fall of the Third Reich,* p. 123.
16. Salkeld, *A Portrait of Leni Riefenstahl,* p. 105; Prieberg, *Trial of Strength,* p. 293.
17. Riess, *Joseph Goebbels,* p. 2.
18. Trevor-Roper, *The Goebbels Diaries: The Last Days,* p. xvii, and p. xx.
19. Richie, *Faust's Metropolis,* p. 388.
20. Heiber, *Joseph Goebbels,* p. 25.
21. Klaus Fischer, *Nazi Germany: A New History* (London: Constable, 1996), p. 201. The quotation Heiber referred to can be found in Joseph Goebbels, *Michael. Ein deutsches Schicksal in Tagebuchblättern,* p. 31.
22. See Fest, 'Joseph Goebbels: Eine Porträtskizze', pp. 566–72.
23. Bärsch, *Der junge Goebbels.*
24. Barth, *Goebbels und die Juden.*
25. See Herf, 'The "Jewish War"', p. 60.
26. Steigmann-Gall, *The Holy Reich,* pp. 21, 20, 252, 53, 84, and 124. One of the difficulties with Steigmann-Gall's analysis of Goebbels is that vague references to him are sprinkled throughout the book. For the most sustained analysis see pp. 20–2. See also Hexham, 'Inventing "Paganists"'.
27. See Michel, *Vom Poeten zum Demagogen,* pp. 127–30.
28. Riess, *Joseph Goebbels,* p. 25.
29. Klabunde, *Magda Goebbels,* pp. 61–3.
30. BAK N1118/70, 'Erinnerungsblätter'. Friedrich Gundolf was a Jewish literary historian under whom Goebbels studied in Heidelberg.
31. See Heiber, *Goebbels-Reden,* Band 2, pp. 7–14, pp. 11–12.
32. *TBJG,* 1 September 1939, TI, 7, p. 88.
33. See, for a recent account of the incident, Evans, *The Third Reich in Power,* pp. 699–700.
34. See Robert Gellately, *Backing Hitler: Consent and Coercion in Nazi Germany* (Oxford and New York: Oxford University Press, 2002), p. 27.
35. Lochner, *The Goebbels Diaries,* p. xxv; Gellately, *Backing Hitler,* pp. 127–8.
36. Trevor-Roper, *The Goebbels Diaries: The Last Days,* p. xvii.
37. *TBJG,* 4 December 1944, TII, 14, pp. 349–50.
38. *TBJG,* 2 November 1939, TI, 7, p. 178.
39. Riess, *Joseph Goebbels,* p. 2.
40. Robert Gellately (ed.), *The Nuremberg Interviews: An American Psychiatrist's Conversations with the Defendants and Witnesses* (London: Pimlico, 2006), pp. 114–18.
41. *Trial of the Major War Criminals,* Vol. 22, p. 404. Adam Tooze is blunt about this, writing that Speer 'saved his neck at Nuremberg'; he describes Speer's comments about technology as 'a bizarre burst of cod philosophy'. Tooze, *Wages of Destruction,* p. 552.
42. *Trial of the Major War Criminals,* Vol. 2, p. 211.
43. See 'Wilhelmplatz 8/9: At the Headquarters of Reich Minister Dr. Goebbels', in S. L. Mayer (ed.), *The Best of Signal: Hitler's Wartime Picture Magazine* (Greenwich, Connecticut: Bison, 1984). Unfortunately, this book, which reproduces many articles from the English-language edition of *Signal,* is not paginated, and the articles are not dated. This particular article appears to be from late 1941 or early 1942.

44. *Trial of the Major War Criminals*, Vol. 13, p. 93, and p. 95.

45. See Fritzsche's testimony in *Trial of the Major War Criminals*, Vol. 17, pp. 149–78.

46. See Ernst Klee, *Das Personenlexikon zum Dritten Reich* (Frankfurt-am-Main: Fischer, 2003), p. 169.

47. Reuth, *Goebbels*, p. 361.

48. Heiden, *Der Fuehrer*, p. 289, and p. 290.

49. J. P. Stern, *Hitler: The Führer and the People* (London: Collins, 1975), p. 36.

50. Lochner, *The Goebbels Diaries*, p. xxv.

51. Dietrich Orlow states that it was 'apparently Hitler's own idea'. See *The History of the Nazi Party*, Vol. 1, 1919–1933, p. 249, n.46.

52. Meissner, *Magda Goebbels*, p. 118.

53. Both diaries are cited in Susanne zur Nieden, 'Chronistinnen des Krieges. Frauen-tagebücher im Zweiten Weltkrieg', Hans-Erich Volkmann (ed.), *Ende des Dritten Reiches – Ende des Zweiten Weltkrieges. Eine perspektive Rückschau* (Munich: Piper, 1995), pp. 835–60, p. 845.

54. *TBJG*, 10 March, 28 March, 29 March, 31 March, and 8 April 1945, TII, 15, pp. 468, 612, 630, 646, and 681.

55. Bankier, *The Germans and the Final Solution*, p. 153.

56. Bankier, *The Germans and the Final Solution*, p. 145.

57. Peter Fritzsche, *Life and Death in the Third Reich* (Cambridge, Massachusetts: Belknap Press of Harvard University Press, 2008). The quotation is from p. 267.

58. Goebbels, 'Die Führerfrage', *Die zweite Revolution*, pp. 5–8, p. 7. See also Bärsch, *Der junge Goebbels*, pp. 73–4.

59. *Das Deutschland Adolf Hitlers: Die ersten vier Jahre des Dritten Reiches* (Munich: Franz Eher, 1937), p. 57.

60. In this context, Peter Gay's discussion of 'The Revolt of the Son', in *Weimar Culture*, pp. 107–24, may be read with profit, even though it does not refer specifically to Goebbels.

61. Ron Rosenbaum, *Explaining Hitler: The Search for the Origins of his Evil* (London: Papermac, 1999), pp. 385–9.

62. *TBJG*, 27 March 1942, TII, 3, p. 561.

63. Klemperer, *To the Bitter End*, 21 March 1945, p. 417.

64. Hilberg, *The Destruction of the European Jews*, Vol. 1, p. 41.

65. *TBJG*, 16 June 1941, TI, 9, pp. 377–9.

66. *TBJG*, 21 August 1942, TII, 5, p. 378.

67. *TBJG*, 13 March 1944, TII, 11, p. 462.

68. *TBJG*, 14 March 1945, TII, 15, p. 498.

69. See Martin Gilbert, *The Holocaust: The Jewish Tragedy* (London: Fontana, 1987), p. 793, and pp. 805–6.

70. Götz Aly, *Hitler's Beneficiaries: How the Nazis Bought the German People* (London: Verso, 2007). The book's original title in German, *Hitlers Volksstaat* (*Hitler's People's State*), is a more accurate summary of its central thrust.

71. BAK N1118/148, Irmgard Welde to Magda Goebbels, 24 January 1942.

72. The letter, dated 9 January 1943, is cited in Central Commission for the Investigation of German Crimes in Poland (ed.), *German Crimes in Poland* (1946–1947), available at www.nizkor.org/hweb/camps/chelmno/report.html, accessed on 27 July 2008.

73. *TBJG*, 16 September 1931, TI, 2/II, p. 100.

74. Goebbels, 'Der Generalstab', *Wege ins Dritte Reich*, pp. 7–9, p. 9; this short article appeared first in the *Nationalsozialistische Briefe*, 15 May 1926.

75. *TBJG*, 2 September 1932, TI, 2/II, p. 354.

Bibliography

Unpublished Sources

As recounted in Chapter 12, Goebbels took care to destroy most of his personal papers in Berlin in April 1945, shortly before his death. Surviving documents relating to his life are scattered in a number of archives around the world, but the fullest single collection is held at the Bundesarchiv Koblenz, in the Nachlass Joseph Goebbels, Bestand N 1118. This includes a number of letters from and to Goebbels from his father, Richard Flisges, Anke Stalherm, Else Janke, and Olgi Esenwein, school reports, manuscripts of his youthful poems and other writings, and the *Erinnerungsblätter*, an autobiographical account of his life up to October 1923. The holdings in Koblenz also include a number of Propaganda Ministry documents from 1943; papers from a court case against Goebbels in 1931 in Berlin, and a number of papers from between 1939 and 1945. Recently, several files with correspondence to and from Magda Goebbels have been added to this collection. The following publication gives an overview of the whole:

Gregor Pickro (ed.), *Nachlass Joseph Goebbels (1897–1945), Bestand N1118. Vorläufiges Verzeichnis* (Koblenz: Bundesarchiv Koblenz, 2007).

By far the largest and most important elements of this collection are the microfilms of Goebbels' diary from 1923 to 1945, which have now been edited and published, in the following two series:

Fröhlich, Elke (ed.), *Die Tagebücher von Joseph Goebbels: Teil I, Aufzeichnungen 1923–1941* (Munich: Saur, 1998–2006), 14 volumes.
Fröhlich, Elke (ed.), *Die Tagebücher von Joseph Goebbels: Teil II, Diktate 1941–1945* (Munich: Saur, 1993–1998), 15 volumes.

These 29 volumes constitute an almost unbroken record of Goebbels' adult life. In his earliest years as a diarist, Goebbels did not write every day, but often summarized his memories of the previous few days in one entry. As he grew older, his entries became longer and more thorough, and there were few days on which he did not write – or after July 1941 dictate – a long entry. There are sections of the diary, notably around November 1942, which the editors have had great difficulty reconstructing because of damage to the glass plates on which they were microfilmed, and particularly in the last few months of Goebbels' life, there are sections missing.

The Bundesarchiv, Außenstelle Berlin, has many files with potential relevance to Goebbels in its Abteilung R, Deutsches Reich 1495–1945. I have used documents from the following record groups:

R 55 Reichsministerium für Volksaufklärung und Propaganda

2 Ministeramt
3 Staatssekretäre
7 Abteilung Propaganda

18 Abteilung Reichsverteidigung
19 Abteilung für die besetzten Ostgebiete

In the collection of the former Berlin Document Center, now in the Bundesarchiv, Außenstelle Berlin, there are very few documents directly relating to Goebbels. These are in:

NS 26 Hauptarchiv der NSDAP
D 51 Oberstes Parteigericht
D 83 Parteikorrespondenz

I have also used these documents from the personnel files of the Reichskulturkammer:

Jochum, Eugen, RKK 2300/0085/16.

Newspapers and Magazines

Das Reich
Der Angriff
Der unbekannte S. A. Mann
Heim und Welt: Blätter für die deutsche Frau
Signal
The Times
Völkischer Beobachter

Published Documents

Boberach, Heinz (ed.), *Meldungen aus dem Reich. Die geheimen Lageberichte des Sicherheitsdienstes der SS 1938–1945* (Herrsching: Manfred Pawlak, 1984), 17 volumes
Boelcke, Willi (ed.), *Wollt Ihr den totalen Krieg? Die geheimen Goebbels-Konferenzen 1939–43* ([1967] Herrsching: Manfred Pawlak, 1989)
Broszat, Martin, 'Die Anfänge der Berliner NSDAP', *Vierteljahrshefte für Zeitgeschichte*, 8:1 (1960), pp. 85–118.
Buchheim, Hans, 'Ein NS-Funktionär zum Niemöller-Prozess', *Vierteljahrshefte für Zeitgeschichte*, 4:3 (1956), pp. 307–15.
Dahm, Volker, Feiber, Albert, Mehringer, Hartmut, and Möller, Horst (eds), *Die tödliche Utopie. Bilder, Texte, Dokumente, Daten zum Dritten Reich* (Munich: Verlag Dokumentation Obersalzberg im Institut für Zeitgeschichte, 2008)
Das Deutschland Adolf Hitlers: Die ersten vier Jahre des Dritten Reiches (Munich: Franz Eher, 1937)
Documents Concerning German-Polish Relations and the Outbreak of Hostilities between Great Britain and Germany on September 3, 1939 (London: HMSO, 1939)
Documents Diplomatiques Français 1932–1939, 1re Série (1932–1935) (Paris: Imprimerie Nationale, 1964–1984)
Documents on British Foreign Policy 1919–1939, Second Series (London: HMSO, 1946–1984)
Documents on British Foreign Policy 1919–1939, Third Series (London: HMSO, 1949–1961)
Dümling, Albrecht, and Girth, Peter (eds), *Entartete Musik. Zur Düsseldorfer Ausstellung von 1938. Eine kommentierte Rekonstruktion* (Düsseldorf: no publisher given, 1988)

Gellately, Robert (ed.), *The Nuremberg Interviews: An American Psychiatrist's Conversations with the Defendants and Witnesses* (London: Pimlico, 2006)

History of the United Nations War Crimes Commission and the Development of the Laws of War (London: HMSO, 1948)

Jochmann, Werner, *Nationalsozialismus und Revolution: Ursprung und Geschichte der NSDAP in Hamburg, 1922–1933. Dokumente* (Frankfurt-am-Main: Europäische Verlag, 1963)

Kaes, Anton, Jay, Martin, and Dimendberg, Edward (eds), *The Weimar Republic Sourcebook* (Berkeley and London: University of California Press, 1995)

Kühnl, Reinhard, 'Zur Programmatik der nationalsozialistischen Linken: Das Strasser-Programm von 1925/26', *Vierteljahrshefte für Zeitgeschichte*, 14:3 (1966), pp. 317–33.

Lane, Barbara Miller, and Rupp, Leila (eds), *Nazi Ideology before 1933: A Documentation* (Manchester: Manchester University Press, 1978)

Langsam, Walter (ed.), *Historic Documents of World War II* (Princeton: Van Nostrand, 1958)

Noakes, Jeremy, and Pridham, Geoffrey (eds), *Nazism 1919–1945: A Documentary Reader* (revised edition, Exeter: Exeter University Press, 1994), 4 volumes

Official Gazette of the Control Council for Germany, No. 1, 29 October 1945

The Persecution of the Catholic Church in the Third Reich: Facts and Documents (London: Burns Oates and Washbourne, 1942)

Schebera, Jürgen (ed.), *Stimmen des Jahrhunderts: Politiker aus Deutschland 1914–1990* (Berlin: Collection BuchPlus, 1992)

Strauss, Walter, 'Das Reichsministerium des Innern und die Judengesetzgebung: Aufzeichnungen von Dr. Bernhard Lösener', *Vierteljahrshefte für Zeitgeschichte*, 9:3 (1961), pp. 262–313.

Trevor-Roper, H. R. (ed.), *Hitler's War Directives 1939–1945* ([1964] London: Pan, 1966)

Trial of the Major War Criminals before the International Military Tribunal, Nuremberg, 14 November 1945 – 1 October 1946 (Nuremberg: International Military Tribunal, 1947), 22 volumes

Webster, Charles, and Frankland, Noble, *The Strategic Air Offensive against Germany 1939–1945* (London: HMSO, 1961), Vol. IV, Annexes and Appendices

Wulf, Josef (ed.), *Musik im Dritten Reich. Eine Dokumentation* (Gütersloh: Mohn Verlag, 1963)

Speeches, Letters, Diaries, and Other pre-1945 Literature

Abel, Theodore (ed.), *Why Hitler Came into Power* ([1938] Cambridge, Massachusetts: Harvard University Press, 1986)

Bade, Wilfried, *Joseph Goebbels* (Lübeck: Charles Coleman, 1933)

Baynes, Norman (ed.), *The Speeches of Adolf Hitler, April 1922–August 1939* (London: Oxford University Press, 1942)

Brady, Robert, *The Spirit and Structure of German Fascism* (London: Victor Gollancz, 1937)

Brügel, Johann Wilhelm, and Frei, Norbert, 'Berliner Tagebuch 1932–1934: Aufzeichnungen des tschechoslowakischen Diplomaten Camill Hoffmann', *Vierteljahrshefte für Zeitgeschichte*, 36:1 (1988), pp. 131–83.

Brüning, Heinrich, *Memoiren 1918–1934* (Stuttgart: Deutsche Verlags-Anstalt, 1970)

Colville, John, *The Fringes of Power: 10 Downing Street Diaries 1939–1955* (New York and London: Norton, 1985)

Deuerlein, Ernst (ed.), *Der Aufstieg der NSDAP in Augenzeugenberichten* (Munich: Deutscher Taschenbuch Verlag, 1974)

Dodd, William, and Dodd, Martha, *Ambassador Dodd's Diary, 1933–1938* (London: Victor Gollancz, 1941)

Domarus, Max, *Hitler: Reden und Proklamationen 1932–1945* (Wiesbaden: Löwit, 1973), Band II, Untergang, Zweiter Halbband 1941–1945

Domarus, Max, *Hitler: Speeches and Proclamations 1932–1945. The Chronicle of a Dictatorship* (trans. Wilcox and Gilbert, London: Tauris, 1992), 4 volumes

Fromm, Bella, *Blood and Banquets: A Berlin Social Diary* ([1943] New York: Carol, 1990)

Geissmar, Berta, *The Baton and the Jackboot: Recollections of Musical Life* (London: Hamilton, 1944)

Goebbels, Joseph, *Das kleine abc des Nationalsozialisten* (Elberfeld: Verlag der Nationalsozialistischen Briefe, no date given)

Goebbels, Joseph, *Die zweite Revolution. Briefe an Zeitgenossen* (Zwickau: Streiter-Verlag, 1926)

Goebbels, Joseph, *Lenin oder Hitler?* (Zwickau: Streiter-Verlag, 1926)

Goebbels, Joseph, *Wege ins Dritte Reich* (Munich: Eher Verlag, 1927)

Goebbels, Joseph (ed.), *Das Buch Isidor. Ein Zeitbild voll Lachen und Hass* (Munich: Franz Eher, 1928)

Goebbels, Joseph, *Michael. Ein deutsches Schicksal in Tagebuchblättern* ([1929] 17th edition, Munich: Franz Eher, 1942)

Goebbels, Joseph (ed.), *Knorke. Ein neues Buch Isidor für Zeitgenossen* (Munich: Franz Eher, 1931)

Goebbels, Joseph, *Kampf um Berlin. Der Anfang* (Munich: Franz Eher, 1932)

Goebbels, Joseph, *Revolution der Deutschen. 14 Jahre Nationalsozialismus* (Oldenburg: Stalling, 1933)

Goebbels, Joseph, *'Goebbels spricht'. Reden aus Kampf und Sieg* (Oldenburg: Stalling, 1933)

Goebbels, Joseph, *Signale der neuen Zeit. 25 ausgewählte Reden* (Munich: Franz Eher, 1934)

Goebbels, Joseph, *Das erwachende Berlin* (Munich: Franz Eher, 1934)

Goebbels, Joseph, *Rassenfrage und Weltpropaganda* (Langensalza: Beyer and Mann, 1934)

Goebbels, Joseph, *Vom Kaiserhof zur Reichskanzlei. Eine historische Darstellung in Tagebuchblättern* (Munich: Franz Eher, 1934)

Goebbels, Joseph, *My Part in Germany's Fight* (trans. Fiedler, London: Paternoster, 1935)

Goebbels, Joseph, *Wesen und Gestalt des Nationalsozialismus* (Berlin: Junker and Dünnhaupt, 1935)

Goebbels, Joseph, *Der Angriff* (Munich: Franz Eher, 1936)

Goebbels, Joseph, *Wetterleuchten. Zweiter Band 'Der Angriff'* (Munich: Franz Eher, 1939)

Goebbels, Joseph, *Die Zeit ohne Beispiel. Reden und Aufsätze aus den Jahren 1939/40/41* (Munich: Franz Eher, 1941)

Goebbels, Joseph, *Das eherne Herz. Reden und Aufsätze aus den Jahren 1941/42* (Munich: Franz Eher, 1943)

Goebbels, Joseph, *Dreißig Kriegsartikel für das deutsche Volk* (Munich: Franz Eher, 1943)

Goebbels, Joseph, *Der steile Aufstieg. Reden und Aufsätze aus den Jahren 1942/43* (Munich: Franz Eher, 1943)

Hammer, Ingrid, and zur Neiden, Susanne (eds), *'Sehr selten habe ich geweint.' Briefe und Tagebücher aus dem Zweiten Weltkrieg von Menschen aus Berlin* (Zurich: Schweizer Verlagshaus, 1992)

von Hassell, Ulrich, *Vom andern Deutschland. Aus den nachgelassenen Tagebüchern 1938–1944 von Ulrich von Hassell* (Vienna: Humboldt, 1948)

Heiber, Helmut (ed.), *The Early Goebbels Diaries: The Journal of Joseph Goebbels from 1925–1926* (trans. Watson, London: Weidenfeld and Nicolson, 1962)

Heiber, Helmut (ed.), *Goebbels-Reden, Band 1: 1932–1939* (Düsseldorf: Droste Verlag, 1971)

Heiber, Helmut (ed.), *Goebbels-Reden, Band 2: 1939–1945* (Düsseldorf: Droste Verlag, 1972)

Heiden, Konrad, *Der Fuehrer: Hitler's Rise to Power* (trans. Manheim, Boston: Houghton and Mifflin, 1944)

Heil! A Picture Book Compiled from Authentic Material (London: John Lane, 1934)

Henderson, Nevile, *Failure of a Mission: Berlin 1937–1939* (London: Hodder and Stoughton, 1940)

Hesse, Hermann, *Peter Camenzind* ([1904] trans. Strachan, London: Peter Owen, 1961)

Hesse, Hermann, *Der Steppenwolf* ([1927] Frankfurt-am-Main: Suhrkamp, 1977)

Hinkel, Hans and Bley, Wulf, *Kabinett Hitler!* (Berlin: Verlag Deutsche Kultur-Wacht, 1933)

Jünger, Ernst, *Storm of Steel* ([1920] trans. Hofmann, London: Penguin, 2004)

Jungnickel, Max, *Goebbels* (Leipzig: Kittler, 1933)

Klemperer, Victor, *I Shall Bear Witness: The Diaries of Victor Klemperer 1933–41* (trans. Chalmers, London: Book Club Associates, 1998)

Klemperer, Victor, *To the Bitter End: The Diaries of Victor Klemperer 1942–45* (trans. Chalmers, London: Book Club Associates, 1998)

Klemperer, Victor, *The Language of the Third Reich. LTI – Lingua Tertii Imperii: A Philologist's Notebook* (trans. Brady, London: Continuum, 2002)

Klepper, Jochen, *Unter dem Schatten Deiner Flügel: Aus den Tagebüchern der Jahre 1932–1942* (Stuttgart: Deutsche Verlags-Anstalt, 1956)

Lippert, Julius, *Im Strom der Zeit. Erlebnisse und Eindrücke* (Berlin: Dietrich Reimer, 1942)

Lochner, Louis (ed.) *The Goebbels Diaries* (London: Hamish Hamilton, 1948)

Maier-Hartmann, Fritz, *Dokumente der Zeitgeschichte* (Munich: Franz Eher Verlag, 1938)

Maier-Hartmann, Fritz, *Dokumente des Dritten Reiches* (Munich: Franz Eher Verlag, 1939)

Mayer, S. L. (ed.), *The Best of Signal: Hitler's Wartime Picture Magazine* (Greenwich, Connecticut: Bison, 1984)

Mühlberger, Detlef, *Hitler's Voice: The Völkischer Beobachter 1920–1933* (Oxford: Peter Lang, 2004), 2 volumes

Muggeridge, Malcolm (ed.), *Ciano's Diary, 1939–1943* (London: Heinemann, 1947)

Natorp, Paul, 'Hoffnungen und Gefahren unserer Jugendbewegung', Kindt, Werner (ed.), *Grundschriften der Deutschen Jugendbewegung* (Düsseldorf and Cologne: Eugen Diederich, 1963), pp. 129–47.

Niemöller, Martin, *Vom U-Boot zur Kanzel* (Berlin: Martin Warner, 1934)

Niemöller, Martin, *.... daß wir an Ihm bleiben! Sechzehn Dahlemer Predigten* (Berlin: Martin Warner, 1935)

Niemöller, Martin, *Alles und in allen Christus! Fünfzehn Dahlemer Predigten* (Berlin: Martin Warner, 1935)

Niemöller, Martin and Dibelius, Otto, *Wir rufen Deutschland zu Gott* (Berlin: Martin Warner, 1937)

Reck-Malleczewen, Friedrich, *Diary of a Man in Despair* (trans. Rubens, London: Duckworth, 2001)

Reich-Ranicki, Marcel (ed.), *Meine Schulzeit im Dritten Reich: Erinnerungen deutscher Schriftsteller* (Cologne: Kiepenheuer & Witsch, 1988)

Schäfer, Hans Dieter, *Berlin im Zweiten Weltkrieg: Der Untergang der Reichshauptstadt in Augenzeugenberichten* (Munich: Piper, 1985)

Sebastian, Mihail, *Journal 1935–1944* ([1996] trans. Camiller, London: Pimlico, 2003)

Seraphim, Hans-Günther (ed.), *Das politische Tagebuch Alfred Rosenbergs 1934/35 und 1939/40* (Munich: Deutscher Taschenbuch Verlag, 1964)

Shirer, William, *Berlin Diary 1934–1941* ([1941] London: Sphere, 1970)

Smith, Howard, *Last Train from Berlin* ([1942] London: Phoenix press, 2000)

Spengler, Oswald, *The Decline of the West* (trans. Atkinson, London: George Allen and Unwin, [1928]), 2 volumes

Strasser, Otto, *Hitler and I* (trans. David and Mosbacher, London: Jonathan Cape, 1940)

Trevor-Roper, H. R. (ed.), *The Goebbels Diaries: The Last Days* (trans. Barry, London: Book Club Associates, 1978)

Tyrell, Albrecht, *Führer befiehl ... Selbstzeugnisse aus der 'Kampfzeit' der NSDAP* (Düsseldorf: Droste Verlag, 1969)

Victor Serge: Witness to the German Revolution (trans. Birchall, London: Redwords, 2000)

Ward Price, G., *I Know these Dictators* (London: Harrap, 1937)

Post-1945 Memoirs

Bannister, Sybil, *I lived under Hitler: An Englishwoman's Story* (London: Rockliff, 1957)

Borresholm, Boris and Nichoff, Karena (eds), *Dr. Goebbels. Nach Aufzeichnungen aus seiner Umgebung* (Berlin: Journal, 1949)

Chuikov, Vasili, *The Fall of Berlin* ([1965] trans. Kisch, New York: Ballantyne, 1969)

Churchill, Winston, *The Second World War* (London: Cassell, 1949), 6 volumes

Delmer, Sefton, *Trail Sinister: An Autobiography* (London: Secker and Warburg, 1961)

Dietrich, Otto, *12 Jahre mit Hitler* (Munich: Isar Verlag, 1955)

Eberle, Hendrik, and Uhl, Matthias (eds), *The Hitler Book: The Secret Dossier Prepared for Stalin* (trans. MacDonogh, London: John Murray, 2006)

François-Poncet, André, *Souvenirs d'une Ambassade à Berlin* (Paris: Flammarion, 1946)

Guderian, Heinz, *Panzer Leader* ([1951] trans. Fitzgibbon, London: Futura, 1974)

Hanfstaengl, Ernst, *Hitler: The Missing Years* (London: Eyre and Spottiswoode, 1957)

Harris, Arthur, *Bomber Offensive* (London: Collins, 1947)

Junge, Traudl (with Müller, Melissa), *Until the Final hour: Hitler's Last Secretary* ([2002] trans. Bell, London: Phoenix, 2005)

Krebs, Albert, *Tendenzen und Gestalten der NSDAP* (Stuttgart: Deutsche Verlags-Anstalt, 1959)

Meyer, Ernst Hermann, *Kontraste, Konflikte: Erinnerungen, Gespräche, Kommentare* (Berlin: Verlag Neue Musik, 1979)

von Oven, Wilfred, *Finale Furioso. Mit Goebbels bis zum Ende* (Tübingen: Grabert Verlag, 1974)

Pawlicka-Nowak, Łucja (ed.), *Chełmno Witnesses Speak* (trans. Golden and Kamiński, Łódź: Konin District Museum, 2004)

Reitsch, Hanna, *Flugkapitän Hanna Reitsch. Fliegen – mein Leben* (4th edition, Munich: Lehmanns Verlag, 1976)

Riefenstahl, Leni, *The Sieve of Time: The Memoirs of Leni Riefenstahl* (London: Quartet Books, 1992)

Schacht, Hjalmar, *My First Seventy-six Years: The Autobiography of Hjalmar Schacht* (trans. Pike, London: Allan Wingate, 1955)

zu Schaumburg-Lippe, Prinz Friedrich Christian, *Dr. G. Ein Porträt des Propagandaministers* (Wiesbaden: Limes Verlag, 1963)

Speer, Albert, *Inside the Third Reich* ([1969] trans. Winston and Winston, New York: Avon, 1971)

Spitzy, Reinhard, *How We Squandered the Reich* (trans. Waddington, Norwich: Russell, 1997)

Studt, Christoph (ed.), *Das Dritte Reich: Ein Lesebuch zur deutschen Geschichte 1933–1945* (Munich: Beck, 1995)

Secondary Literature

Altstedt, Thomas, *Joseph Goebbels. Eine Biographie in Bildern* (Berg: Druffel, 1999)

Aly, Götz, *Hitler's Beneficiaries: How the Nazis Bought the German People* (trans. Chase, London: Verso, 2007)

Anderson, Benedict, *Imagined Communities: Reflections on the Origin and Spread of Nationalism* (London: Verso, 1983)

Arad, Yitzhak, *Belzec, Sobibor, Treblinka: The Operation Reinhard Death Camps* (Bloomington: Indiana University Press, 1987)

Bärsch, Claus-Ekkehard, *Der junge Goebbels. Erlösung und Vernichtung* (Munich: Fink, 2004)

Bankier, David, *The Germans and the Final Solution: Public Opinion under Nazism* (Oxford: Blackwell, 1996)

Barnett, David, 'Joseph Goebbels: Expressionist Dramatist as Nazi Minister of Culture', *New Theatre Quarterly*, 17:2 (May 2001), pp. 161–9.

Barth, Christian, *Goebbels und die Juden* (Paderborn: Schöningh, 2003)

Behrenbeck, Sabine, *Der Kult um die toten Helden: Nationalsozialistische Mythen, Riten und Symbole 1923 bis 1945* (Greifswald: SH-Verlag, 1996)

Bergmeier, Horst and Lotz, Rainer, *Hitler's Airwaves: The Inside Story of Nazi Radio Broadcasting and Propaganda Swing* (New Haven and London: Yale University Press, 1997)

Bessel, Richard, *Nazism and War* (London: Phoenix, 2005)

Bjork, James, and Gerwarth, Robert, 'The Annaberg as a German-Polish *Lieu de Mémoire*', *German History*, 25:3 (2007), pp. 372–400.

Blumentritt, Guenther, *Von Rundstedt: The Soldier and the Man* (trans. Reavely, London: Odhams, 1952)

Böhnke, Wilfried, *Die NSDAP im Ruhrgebiet 1920–1933* (Bonn: Verlag Neue Gesellschaft, 1974)

Bollmus, Reinhard, 'Alfred Rosenberg: National Socialism's "Chief Ideologue"?' Smelser, Ronald, and Zitelmann, Rainer (eds), *The Nazi Elite* (London: Macmillan, 1993), pp. 183–93.

Bramsted, Ernest, *Goebbels and National Socialist Propaganda 1924–1945* (London: Cresset Press, 1965)

Breitman, Richard, *Himmler and the Final Solution: The Architect of Genocide* (London: Pimlico, 2004)

Browning, Christopher, *The Origins of the Final Solution: The Evolution of Nazi Jewish Policy, September 1939 – March 1942* (London: Heinemann, 2004)

Bullock, Alan, *Hitler: A Study in Tyranny* (London: Odhams Press, 1952)

Burleigh, Michael and Wipperman, Wolfgang, *The Racial State: Germany 1933–1945* (Cambridge: Cambridge University Press, 1991)

Burleigh, Michael, *Death and Deliverance: 'Euthanasia' in Germany 1900–1945* (Cambridge: Cambridge University Press, 1994)

Burleigh, Michael, *The Third Reich: A New History* (London: Macmillan, 2000)

Clark, Alan, *Barbarossa: The Russian-German Conflict 1941–1945* (Harmondsworth: Penguin, 1966)

Cohn, Norman, *Warrant for Genocide: The Myth of the Jewish World Conspiracy and the Protocols of the Elders of Zion* ([1967] London: Serif, 1996)

Cuomo, Glenn, (ed.), *National Socialist Cultural Policy* (New York: St. Martin's Press, 1995)

Cuomo, Glenn, 'The Diaries of Joseph Goebbels as a Source for the Understanding of National Socialist Cultural Politics', Cuomo, Glenn (ed.), *National Socialist Cultural Policy* (New York: St. Martin's Press, 1995), pp. 197–245.

Dahm, Volker, 'Anfänge und Ideologie der Reichskulturkammer: Die "Berufsgemeinschaft" als Instrument kulturpolitischer Steuerung und sozialer Reglementierung', *Vierteljahrshefte für Zeitgeschichte*, 34:1 (1986), pp. 53–84.

Das Reich. Register zur Mikrofilm-Ausgabe (Bonn: Gesellschaft für die Fotographische Reproduktion der Presse, no date given [1971])

Dawidowicz, Lucy, *The War against the Jews 1933–1945* ([1975] London: Penguin, 1990)

Eckert, Astrid, and Martens, Stefan, 'Glasplatten im märkischen Sand: Zur Überlieferungsgeschichte der Tageseinträge und Diktate von Joseph Goebbels', *Vierteljahrshefte für Zeitgeschichte*, 52:3 (2004), pp. 479–526.

Edmonds, James, *The Occupation of the Rhineland, 1918–1929* ([1947] London: HMSO, 1987)

Eichberg, Henning, 'The Nazi *Thingspiel*: Theater for the Masses in Fascism and Proletarian Culture', *New German Critique*, 11 (Spring 1977), pp. 133–50.

Erikson, Erik, *Young Man Luther: A Study in Psychoanalysis and History* (London: Faber and Faber, 1959)

Evans, Richard J., *The Coming of the Third Reich* (London: Allen Lane, 2003)

Evans, Richard J., *The Third Reich in Power, 1933–1939* (London: Penguin, 2006)

Evans, Richard J., *The Third Reich at War, 1939–1945* (London: Allen Lane, 2008)

Fest, Joachim, 'Joseph Goebbels: Eine Porträtskizze', *Vierteljahrshefte für Zeitgeschichte*, 43:4 (1995), pp. 565–80.

Fischer, Klaus, *Nazi Germany: A New History* (London: Constable, 1996)

Friedländer, Saul, *Nazi Germany and the Jews: The Years of Persecution 1933–39* (London: Weidenfeld and Nicolson, 2003)

Friedländer, Saul, *Nazi Germany and the Jews: The Years of Extermination 1939–1945* (London: HarperCollins, 2007)

Friedrich, Jörg, *Der Brand: Deutschland im Bombenkrieg 1940–1945* (Munich: Propyläen, 2002)

Fritzsche, Peter, *Life and Death in the Third Reich* (Cambridge, Massachusetts: Belknap Press of Harvard University Press, 2008)

Fröhlich, Elke, 'Joseph Goebbels und sein Tagebuch: Zu den handschriftlichen Aufzeichnungen bis 1941', *Vierteljahrshefte für Zeitgeschichte*, 35:4 (1987), pp. 489–522.

Gay, Peter, *Weimar Culture: The Outsider as Insider* (Harmondsworth: Penguin, 1974)

Gellately, Robert, *Backing Hitler: Consent and Coercion in Nazi Germany* (Oxford and New York: Oxford University Press, 2002)

Gilbert, Martin, *Finest Hour: Winston S. Churchill 1939–1941* (London: Book Club Associates, 1983)

Gilbert, Martin, *The Holocaust: The Jewish Tragedy* (London: Fontana, 1987)

Grabowska-Chałka, Janina, *Stutthof Guide: Historical Information* (trans. Gałązka, Gdańsk: Stutthof Museum, 2004)

Grunfeld, Frederic (ed.), *The Hitler File: A Social History of Germany and the Nazis, 1918–45* (London: Book Club Associates, 1974)

Harrison, Ted, '"Alter Kämpfer" im Widerstand: Graf Helldorff, die NS-Bewegung und die Opposition gegen Hitler', *Vierteljahrshefte für Zeitgeschichte*, 45:3 (1997), pp. 385–423.

Hartung, Günter, 'Pre-Planners of the Holocaust: The Case of Theodor Fritsch', Milfull, John (ed.), *Why Germany? National Socialist Anti-Semitism and the European Context* (Providence and Oxford: Berg, 1993), pp. 29–40.

Hastings, Max, *Bomber Command* (London: Pan, 1981)

Heiber, Helmut, *Joseph Goebbels* (Berlin: Colloquium Verlag, 1962)

Herf, Jeffrey, *Reactionary Modernism: Technology, Culture, and Politics in Weimar and the Third Reich* (Cambridge: Cambridge University Press, 1984)

Herf, Jeffrey, 'The "Jewish War": Goebbels and the Antisemitic Campaigns of the Nazi Propaganda Ministry', *Holocaust and Genocide Studies*, 19:1 (Spring 2005), pp. 51–80.

Hexham, Irving, 'Inventing "Paganists": A Close Reading of Richard Steigmann-Gall's *The Holy Reich*', *Journal of Contemporary History*, 42:1 (2007), pp. 59–78.

Hilberg, Raul, *The Destruction of the European Jews* (New York: Holmes and Meier, 1985), 3 volumes

Hillenbrand, F. K. M., *Underground Humour in Nazi Germany* (London and New York: Routledge, 1995)

Höhne, Heinz, *The Order of the Death's Head: The Story of Hitler's SS* ([1969] trans. Barry, London: Penguin, 2000)

Hoffmann, Peter, 'Warum mißlang das Attentat vom 20. Juli 1944?' *Vierteljahrshefte für Zeitgeschichte*, 32:3 (1984), pp. 441–62.

Horn, Wolfgang, *Der Marsch zur Machtergreifung. Die NSDAP bis 1933* (Königstein: Athenäum Verlag, 1980)

Inachin, Kyra, '"Märtyrer mit einem kleinen Häuflein Getreuer": Der erste Gauleiter der NSDAP in Pommern', *Vierteljahrshefte für Zeitgeschichte*, 49:1 (2001), pp. 31–51.

Jacobsen, Hans-Adolf (ed.), *July 20, 1944: The German Opposition to Hitler as Viewed by Foreign Historians* (Bonn: Press and Information Department of the Federal Government, 1969)

Jasper, Gotthard, 'Justiz und Politik in der Weimarer Republik', *Vierteljahrshefte für Zeitgeschichte*, 30:2 (1982), pp. 167–205.

Johnson, Eric and Reuband, Karl-Heinz, *What We Knew: Terror, Mass Murder and Everyday Life in Nazi Germany* (London: John Murray, 2005)

Kater, Michael, 'Frauen in der NS-Bewegung', *Vierteljahrshefte für Zeitgeschichte*, 31:2 (1983), pp. 202–41.

Kershaw, Ian, *Hitler 1889–1936: Hubris* (London: Allen Lane, 1998)

Kershaw, Ian, *Hitler 1936–1945: Nemesis* (London: Allen Lane, 2000)

Kessemier, Carin, *Der Leitartikler Goebbels in den NS-Organen 'Der Angriff' und 'Das Reich'* (Munich: Fahle, 1967)

Kissenkoetter, Udo, 'Gregor Strasser: Nazi Party Organizer or Weimar Politician?' Smelser, Ronald, and Zitelmann, Rainer (eds), *The Nazi Elite* (London: Macmillan, 1993), pp. 224–44.

Klabunde, Anja, *Magda Goebbels* (trans. Whiteside, London: Time Warner, 2003)

Klee, Ernst, *Das Personenlexikon zum Dritten Reich* (Frankfurt-am-Main: Fischer, 2003)

Koch, Hannsjoachim, *In the Name of the Volk: Political Justice in Hitler's Germany* (London: I. B. Tauris, 1989)

Koonz, Claudia, *Mothers in the Fatherland: Women, the Family, and Nazi Politics* (London: Jonathan Cape, 1987)

Kühnl, Reinhard, *Die nationalsozialistische Linke 1925–1930* (Meisenheim: Hain, 1966)

Leiser, Erwin, *'Deutschland erwache!' Propaganda im Film des Dritten Reiches* (Hamburg: Rowohlt, 1978)

Lemmons, Russell, *Goebbels and Der Angriff* (Lexington: University Press of Kentucky, 1994)

Levi, Erik, *Music in the Third Reich* (Basingstoke: Macmillan, 1994)

Levine, Herbert, *Hitler's Free City: A History of the Nazi Party in Danzig 1925–39* (Chicago and London: University of Chicago Press, 1973)

McClatchie, Stephen, 'Hans Pfitzner's *Palestrina* and the Impotence of Early Lateness', www. utpjournals.com/product/utq/674/674_mcclatchie.htm, accessed 18 August 2008.

Mandell, Richard, *The Nazi Olympics* (London: Souvenir Press, 1972)

Manvell, Roger and Fraenkel, Heinrich, *Doctor Goebbels: His Life and Death* (London: Heinemann, 1960)

Mawdsley, Evan, *Thunder in the East: The Nazi-Soviet War 1941–1945* (London: Hodder Arnold, 2005)

Mayer, Hans, 'Hermann Hesse and the "Age of the Feuilleton"', Ziolkowski, Theodore (ed.), *Hesse: A Collection of Critical Essays* (Englewood Cliffs, New Jersey: Prentice-Hall, 1973), pp. 76–93.

Mazower, Mark, *Hitler's Empire: Nazi Rule in Occupied Europe* (London: Allen Lane, 2008)

Meissner, Hans-Otto, *Magda Goebbels: A Biography* (trans. Keeble, London: Sidgwick and Jackson, 1980)

Merki, Christoph Maria, 'Die nationalsozialistische Tabakpolitik', *Vierteljahrshefte für Zeitgeschichte*, 46:1 (1998), pp. 19–42.

Meyer, Michael, 'The SA Song Literature: A Singing Ideological Posture', *Journal of Popular Culture*, 11:3 (1977), pp. 568–80.

Michel, Kai, *Vom Poeten zum Demagogen: Die schriftstellerischen Versuche Joseph Goebbels'* (Vienna: Böhlau, 1999)

Middlebrook, Martin, *The Berlin Raids: RAF Bomber Command Winter 1943–44* (London: Cassell, 2001)

Mierzejewski, Alfred, *Hitler's Trains: The German National Railway and the Third Reich* (Stroud: Tempus, 2005)

Möller, Felix, *The Film Minister: Goebbels and the Cinema in the 'Third Reich'* (Stuttgart: Axel Menges, 2000)

Moltmann, Günter, 'Goebbels' Rede zum totalen Krieg am 18. Februar 1943', *Vierteljahrshefte für Zeitgeschichte*, 12:1 (1960), pp. 13–43.

Mosse, George, *Germans and Jews: The Right, the Left, and the Search for a 'Third Force' in pre-Nazi Germany* (London: Orbach and Chambers, 1971)

Mühlberger, Detlef, *Hitler's Followers: Studies in the sociology of the Nazi movement* (London and New York: Routledge, 1991)

Neufeld, Michael, *The Rocket and the Reich: Peenemünde and the Coming of the Ballistic Missile Era* (New York: Free Press, 1995)

Noakes, Jeremy, 'Conflict and Development in the NSDAP 1924–1927', *Journal of Contemporary History*, 1:4 (1966), pp. 3–36.

Orlow, Dietrich, *The History of the Nazi Party* (Newton Abbot: David & Charles, 1971), 2 volumes

Paret, Peter, *German Encounters with Modernism, 1840–1945* (Cambridge: Cambridge University Press, 2001)

Petropoulos, Jonathan, *The Faustian Bargain: The Art World in Nazi Germany* (London: Allen Lane, 2000)

Peukert, Detlev, *The Weimar Republic: The Crisis of Classical Modernity* (trans. Deveson, London: Penguin, 1991)

Plant, Richard, *The Pink Triangle: The Nazi War against Homosexuals* (Edinburgh: Mainstream, 1987)

Potter, Pamela, 'The Nazi "Seizure" of the Berlin Philharmonic or the Decline of a Bourgeois Musical Institution', Cuomo, Glenn (ed.), *National Socialist Cultural Policy* (New York: St. Martin's Press, 1995), pp. 39–66.

Prieberg, Fred, *Trial of Strength: Wilhelm Furtwängler in the Third Reich* (trans. Dolan, Boston: Northeastern University Press, 1994)

Reimann, Viktor, *The Man who Created Hitler: Joseph Goebbels* (trans. Wendt, London: William Kimber, 1977)

Reuth, Ralf Georg, *Goebbels* (trans. Winston, London: Harcourt Brace, 1993)

Richards, Denis and Saunders, Hilary, *Royal Air Force 1939–1945* ([1953] London: HMSO, 1974), 3 volumes

Richie, Alexandra, *Faust's Metropolis: A History of Berlin* (New York: Carroll and Graf, 1998)

Riess, Curt, *Joseph Goebbels* (London: Hollis and Carter, 1949)

Roseman, Mark, *The Villa, the Lake, the Meeting: Wannsee and the Final Solution* (London: Allen Lane, 2002)

Rosenbaum, Ron, *Explaining Hitler: The Search for the Origins of his Evil* (London: Papermac, 1999)

Rossino, Alexander, *Hitler Strikes Poland: Blitzkrieg, Ideology, and Atrocity* (Lawrence: University Press of Kansas, 2003)

Ryan, Cornelius, *The Last Battle* ([1966] London: New English Library, 1967)

Salkeld, Audrey, *A Portrait of Leni Riefenstahl* (London: Pimlico, 1997)

Schmidt, Christoph, *Nationalsozialistische Kulturpolitik im Gau Westfalen-Nord: Regionale Strukturen und lokale Milieus (1933–1945)* (Paderborn: Schöningh, 2006)

Sereny, Gitta, *Albert Speer: His Battle with Truth* (London: Macmillan, 1995)

Shirer, William, *The Rise and Fall of the Third Reich: A History of Nazi Germany* ([1962] London: Book Club Associates, 1973)

Short, K. R. M., and Dolezel, Stephan (eds), *Hitler's Fall: The Newsreel Witness* (London: Croom Helm, 1988)

Smelser, Ronald, *Robert Ley: Hitler's Labor Front Leader* (Oxford: Berg, 1988)

Smelser, Ronald, and Zitelmann, Rainer (eds), *The Nazi Elite* (London: Macmillan, 1993)

Sofsky, Wolfgang, *The Order of Terror: The Concentration Camp* (trans. Templer, Princeton: Princeton University Press, 1997)

Sontheimer, Kurt, 'Antidemokratisches Denken in der Weimarer Republik', *Vierteljahrshefte für Zeitgeschichte*, 5:1 (1957), pp. 42–62.

Sontheimer, Kurt, *Antidemokratisches Denken in der Weimarer Republik: Die politischen Ideen des deutschen Nationalismus zwischen 1918 und 1933* (Munich: Deutscher Taschenbuch Verlag, 1978)

Steigmann-Gall, Richard, *The Holy Reich: Nazi Conceptions of Christianity, 1919–1945* (Cambridge: Cambridge University Press, 2004)

Steinweis, Alan, *Art, Ideology, & Economics in Nazi Germany: The Reich Chambers of Music, Theater, and the Visual Arts* (Chapel Hill and London: University of North Carolina Press, 1993)

Stern, Fritz, *The Politics of Cultural Despair: A Study in the Rise of the Germanic Ideology* (Berkeley, Los Angeles, and London: University of California Press, 1961)

Stern, J. P., *Hitler: The Führer and the People* (London: Collins, 1975)

Striefler, Christian, *Kampf um die Macht. Kommunisten und Nationalsozialisten am Ende der Weimarer Republik* (Berlin: Propyläen, 1993)

Strobl, Gerwin, *The Swastika and the Stage: German Theatre and Society, 1933–1945* (New York: Cambridge University Press, 2007)

Szynkowski, Jerzy, and Wünsche, Georg, *Das Führerhauptquartier (FHQu) Wolfsschanze* (Kętrzyn: Kengraf, 2005)

Taylor, Brandon, and van der Will, Wilfried (eds), *The Nazification of Art: Art, Design, Music, Architecture and Film in the Third Reich* (Winchester: Winchester School of Art Press, 1990)

Taylor, Frederick, *Dresden, Tuesday 13 February 1945* (London: Bloomsbury, 2004)

Thacker, Toby, *The End of the Third Reich: Defeat, Denazification, and Nuremberg, January 1944–November 1946* (Stroud: Tempus, 2006)

Theweleit, Klaus, *Male Fantasies I. Women, Floods, Bodies, History* (trans. Conway, Cambridge: Polity Press, 1987)

Theweleit, Klaus, *Male Fantasies II. Male Bodies: Psychoanalyzing the White Terror* (trans. Turner and Carter, Cambridge: Polity Press, 1989)

Tooze, Adam, *The Wages of Destruction: The Making and Breaking of the Nazi Economy* (London: Penguin, 2007)

Trevor-Roper, H. R., *The Last Days of Hitler* (London: Pan, 1952)

Volkmann, Hans-Erich (ed.), *Ende des Dritten Reiches – Ende des Zweiten Weltkrieges. Eine perspektive Rückschau* (Munich: Piper, 1995)

de Vries, Willem, *Sonderstab Musik: Music Confiscations by the Einsatzstab Reichsleiter Rosenberg under the Nazi Occupation of Western Europe* (Amsterdam: Amsterdam University Press, 1996)

Wambach, Lovis Maxim, *'Es ist gleichgültig, woran wir glauben, nur dass wir glauben.' Bemerkungen zu Joseph Goebbels Drama 'Judas Iscariot' und zu seinen 'Michael-Romanen'* (Bremen: Raphael-Lemkin-Institut für Xenophobie- und Genozidforschung, 1996)

Weinreich, Max, *Hitler's Professors: The Part Played by Scholarship in Germany's Crimes against the Jewish People* ([1946] New Haven and London: Yale University Press, 1999)

Welch, David, *Propaganda and the German Cinema 1933–1945* (London and New York: Tauris, 2001)

Werner, Stephan, *Joseph Goebbels. Dämon einer Diktatur* (Stuttgart: Union deutsche Verlagsgesellschaft, 1949)

Winzer, Otto, *Zwölf Jahre Kampf gegen Faschismus und Krieg* (Berlin: Dietz, 1955)

Witte, Peter, 'Two Decisions Concerning the "Final Solution to the Jewish Question": Deportations to Lodz and Mass Murder in Chelmno', *Holocaust and Genocide Studies*, 9:3 (1995), pp. 318–45.

Wolff, Willy, *Auf der richtigen Seite: Zum Wirken der Frontorganisation des Nationalkomitees 'Freies Deutschland'* (Berlin: Militärverlag der Deutschen Demokratischen Republik, 1985)

Zimmerman, Clemens, 'From Propaganda to Modernization: Media Policy and Media Audiences under National Socialism', *German History*, 24:3 (2006), pp. 431–54.

Index

NB: Page references to illustrations are in bold type